# The American
# Immigration Collection

# The Background
## of
# Swedish Immigration

1840-1930

FLORENCE EDITH JANSON

*Arno* Press and *The New York Times*

NEW YORK 1970

Reprint Edition 1970 by Arno Press Inc.


Reprinted from a copy in
The Kansas State University Library


LC# 79-129403

ISBN 0-405-00556-3


The American Immigration Collection—Series II

ISBN for complete set 0-405-00543-1


Manufactured in the United States of America

# THE BACKGROUND OF SWEDISH
# IMMIGRATION

1840–1930

THE UNIVERSITY OF CHICAGO PRESS
CHICAGO, ILLINOIS

—

THE BAKER & TAYLOR COMPANY
NEW YORK

THE CAMBRIDGE UNIVERSITY PRESS
LONDON

THE MARUZEN-KABUSHIKI-KAISHA
TOKYO, OSAKA, KYOTO, FUKUOKA, SENDAI

THE COMMERCIAL PRESS, LIMITED
SHANGHAI

THE UNIVERSITY OF CHICAGO
SOCIAL SERVICE MONOGRAPHS
*Published in conjunction with the Social Service Review*
————————*Edited by*————————
THE FACULTY *of the* GRADUATE SCHOOL
OF SOCIAL SERVICE ADMINISTRATION

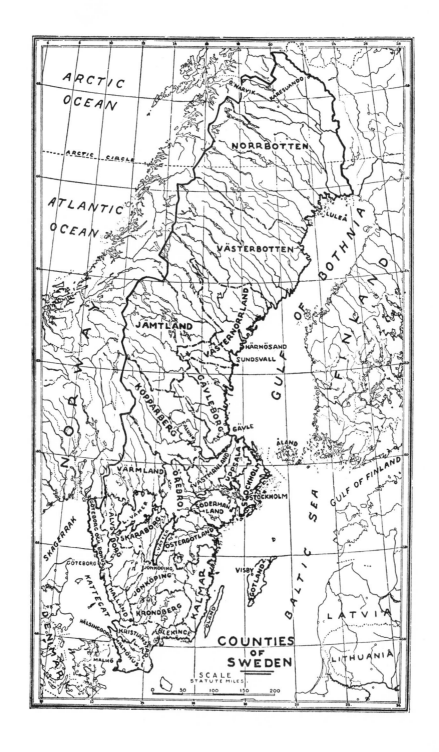

ARCTIC
OCEAN

ARCTIC  CIRCLE

ATLANTIC
OCEAN

NARVIK  KARESUANDO

NORRBOTTEN

LULEÅ

VÄSTERBOTTEN

GULF OF BOTHNIA

JÄMTLAND

VÄSTERNORRLAND

HÄRNÖSAND

SUNDSVALL

KOPPARBERG

GÄVLEBORG

GÄVLE

ÅLAND

VARMLAND

ÖREBRO

VÄSTMANLAND

UPSALA

STOCKHOLM

STOCKHOLM

GULF OF FINLAND

FINLAND

SKAGERRAK

GÖTEBORG OCH BOHUS

L. VÄNER

ÄLVSBORG

SKARABORG

L. VÄTTE

SÖDERMAN-
LAND

ÖSTERGÖTLAND

BALTIC  SEA

GÖTEBORG

JÖNKÖPING

JÖNKÖPING

VISBY

GOTLAND

LATVIA

KATTEGAT

KRONOBERG

KALMAR

ÖLAND

LITHUANIA

HÄLSINGBORG

KRISTIAN

HALLAND

BLEKINGE

MALMÖ

DENMARK

COUNTIES
OF
SWEDEN

SCALE
STATUTE MILES.
0    50    100    150    200

*Social Service Monographs, Number Fifteen*

# THE BACKGROUND
# OF
# SWEDISH IMMIGRATION
## 1840–1930

*By*

FLORENCE EDITH JANSON, Ph.D.

*Professor of Government in Rockford College*

THE UNIVERSITY OF CHICAGO PRESS
CHICAGO, ILLINOIS

COMPOSED AND PRINTED BY THE UNIVERSITY OF CHICAGO PRESS
CHICAGO, ILLINOIS, U.S.A.

TO
THE CHILDREN OF SWEDISH IMMIGRANTS
IN THE UNITED STATES
THIS VOLUME IS DEDICATED

# PREFACE

This book began as a study of the economic causes of Swedish immigration to the United States during the last century. With the discovery that the recent migration westward from Sweden received its particular impetus in 1840 and has continued unabated until the present time, it became evident that the causes have changed from time to time. A historical account of the movement from decade to decade seemed a feasible approach.

Most Americans appreciate the economic possibilities available to foreigners seeking our shores. We are aware of the social, religious, and political opportunities offered in a democratic country. But few, even the children of those immigrants who have come from the countries of the old world, know much, if anything, about the conditions that have stimulated the immense exodus across the Atlantic of the past century. There is a feeling that Europe offers little or no opportunity for economic prosperity or social satisfaction.

To discuss without bias, and with objective understanding, the causes of emigration from Sweden, it is necessary to know something about the economic, social, religious, and political conditions in that country. And so I have attempted to explain the background of this migration.

What were the factors that determined the first emigrants to leave Sweden for the United States? What changes in the causes of emigration and in the character of the emigrant have taken place during the ninety years of exodus? What differences were there within Sweden itself that made certain regions sources of dissatisfaction and exodus, and others, places of contentment?

I belong to the second generation of Swedes in America who knew so pathetically little about the country of their forefathers. My experiences of childhood have been among the Swedish immigrants, and upon my successive visits to Sweden to study conditions there, I have had an entrée into the homes of both the rural and urban population. It has been possible for me to make numerous case studies, which, supplemented with the case studies printed in the excellent *Report on Emigration* made by the Swedish government in 1907, have been used as illustrative material. My travels through Sweden have been invaluable for the interpretation of various parts of the country, and the rigors of a third-class passage on an emigrant boat in the summer of 1926 have helped me to understand the problems of those seeking opportunity in a new country.

My study began as a Doctor's thesis under Professor William E. Lingelbach of the History Department of the University of Pennsylvania. Through the financial aid of the Social Science Research Council, I was enabled to spend additional time in Sweden, both in travel and research. I wish to acknowledge the helpful assistance in Sweden of Rector Ludwig Stavenow of the University of Uppsala, Lector Oscar Olsson of the Swedish Riksdag, Dr. Adrian Molin, executive secretary of the A. B. Egna Hem, Sigfrid Hansson, editor of *Tiden*, and C. C. Schmidt, amanuensis in the Department of Labor.

Grateful acknowledgment is due to Professor William E. Lingelbach for his helpful guidance and advice in the preparation of this study, and for his valuable criticism of the manuscript. To Professor Edith Abbott, Dean of the Graduate School of Social Service Administration, of the University of Chicago, the author wishes to acknowledge her indebtedness for personal interest and encouragement. Financial aid was granted by the Committee of Scientific Aspects of Human Migration of the Social Science Research Council when Dean Abbott was chairman. As editor of the *Social Service Monographs*, she has accepted this book for publication. The author further acknowledges the useful criticisms on portions of the manuscript made by Professor A. J. Uppvall, of the University of Pennsylvania. Mr. Harold G. Arbo has given valuable assistance in the construction of maps and charts.

FLORENCE E. JANSON

ROCKFORD COLLEGE
APRIL, 1931

# TABLE OF CONTENTS

# CHAPTER I

## INTRODUCTION

Sweden, a country of six million inhabitants, has lost one million through emigration since 1850, one from every seven of her population. Most of these emigrants have found their way to the United States, where they and their children have played an important part in the development of the Middle West and the Pacific Coast. Some have remained in Massachusetts, western New York, and central Pennsylvania, while others have settled in northern Texas.

Emigration has been an immemorial characteristic of the Scandinavian countries. The old Vikings first raided and then settled in the British Isles beside their cousins, the Anglo-Saxons. In France where they were at first a scourge, they made Normandy more French than France. The first organized government in Russia was established by Viking invaders and settlers, the Duchies of Novgorod and Kiev. There were settlements in Greenland and Iceland, while Vinland is mentioned in the old sagas of the Icelanders. These restless peoples of the North found service in the armies of Constantinople, and Norman crusaders even organized the kingdom of the Two Sicilies.

Later, in the twelfth century when Sweden added the Duchy of Finland to her possessions, Swedish emigrants established colonies across the Bay of Bothnia. This exchange of population between the two countries went on for many centuries until Finland was conquered by Russia in 1809. In the sixteenth and seventeenth centuries, when the Baltic had become practically a Swedish lake, colonies of Swedes settled in Esthonia, Pomerania, and Stralsund. It was during this period of political ascendency that the Swedish colony on the banks of the Delaware River in North America was planted. The old Swede churches at Wilmington, and in and around Philadelphia, still bear witness to this colonial settlement, although it was soon lost by the Swedes, first to the Dutch and then to the English.

Times of economic distress were equally as fruitful in stimulating exodus as colonial and imperial ambitions. And so the stream became larger than ever after the disastrous wars of Charles XII, which reduced Sweden to a second-rate power, and raised on the horizon a powerful and dangerous neighbor, Russia. The growth of the cities of Copenhagen and St. Petersburg may be attributed to some extent to the exodus of the agrarian labor from Sweden. The migration threatened to drain Sweden of its agricultural labor supply in the eighteenth century. The complaints of the peasant proprietor in the middle of the century resulted in an attempt to stem the flow

TABLE I

| Years | Surplus of Births | Increase of Population | Loss through Emigration |
|-------|-------------------|------------------------|-------------------------|
| 1749–1800...... | 667,760 | 591,611 | 76,149 |
| 1801–1850...... | 1,161,840 | 1,135,238 | 26,602 |
| 1851–1900...... | 2,497,181 | 1,653,900 | 843,281 |
| 1901–1925...... | 1,233,835 | 937,927 | 295,908 |
| 1851–1925...... | 3,731,016 | 2,591,827 | 1,139,189 |

of emigrating people by the passage of laws prohibiting emigration of rural labor.[1]

Statistics of emigration from Sweden are available since 1749 when a bureau of government statistics was established, the first in Europe. From 1749 to 1930, a period of 180 years, Sweden's population had increased from 1,755,692 inhabitants to 6,120,080, while during the same period the country had lost 1,147,133 people through emigration.[2] It had more than trebled in population but had lost almost one-fifth of its population through exodus. This increase and loss of population has been historically distributed as shown in Table I.[3]

The 100 years prior to 1850 were rather insignificant in the amount of emigration as compared with the subsequent 125. The

[1] "Utvandringslagstiftning," *Emigrationsutredningens bilaga I* (Stockholm, 1908), pp. 3 ff.

[2] Gustav Sundbärg, "Den svenska och europeiska folköknings och omflyttningsstatistiken," *Emigrationsutredningens bilaga IV* (Stockholm, 1910), p. 46; Statistiska centralbyrån, *Statistisk årsbok för Sverige, 1930* (Stockholm, 1930), p. 3, Table 3.

[3] *Ibid.*, pp. 47 ff., Table 35, p. 72, Table 60.

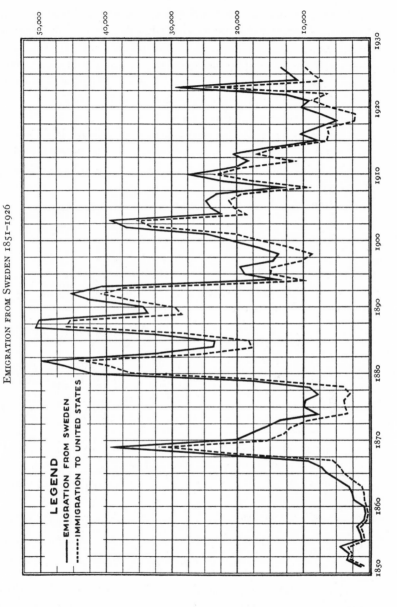

CHART I

EMIGRATION FROM SWEDEN 1851-1926

first period of this exodus from 1751 to 1815 was primarily an exchange of peoples between Sweden and her Grand Duchy of Finland.
There were some 91,320 persons who left Sweden, an average of
about 1,405 per year. Of these emigrants, the overwhelming majority were men, in all 88,858, while only 2,462 were women, chiefly the
wives of Swedish government officials in Finland. There was a corresponding immigration into Sweden of servant girls seeking employment in Stockholm from the Åland Islands and the Swedish portions
of Finland.[1] Some migration of seamen occurred. They settled in
foreign lands, while merchants established business abroad and an
occasional student-adventurer failed to return to his native land.
Emigration on a large scale similar to the modern exodus did not
exist, with the exception of that overflow at the boundaries of
the kingdom into neighboring countries which took place during
periods of crop failures. The disastrous Russian war of 1809, in
which Sweden lost Finland, marks the close of this first period of
emigration, although 1815 has been used in the statistical account.

Even though to us the exodus from 1751 to 1815 seems small as
compared with today, it brought great anxiety to a country whose
population was much less than at present. As early as 1726 and 1727
the cities of Southern Sweden complained of the scarcity of labor to
the Swedish Parliament (Riksdag) and were cautioned against giving passports over Öresund to Denmark.[2] The complaint of the
peasants in their House of Peasants in the Riksdag in 1734 resulted
in the emigration restriction law of August 21, 1739. This law provided that passports had to be attested by the parish pastor or the
government official on the farm of the peasant, if the farm laborer
desired to leave the country. In the cities, it was attested by a magis-
trate. The emigrant was required to return within two or three
years or lose his inheritance and citizenship. Anyone leaving without a passport and not returning within a year, not only lost his
inheritance, but was liable to punishment upon return. A series of
restrictive laws were passed. Although always difficult to enforce,
they were undoubtedly factors in the discouragement of emigration,
until their final repeal in 1860.

[1] Sundbärg, "Utvandringsstatistik," *op. cit.*, pp. 47–48
[2] "Utvandringslagstiftning," *op. cit.*, p. 3.

It was the peasant who felt most keenly the scarcity of labor caused by this exodus, for the large estates of nobles and gentry had a permanent labor-supply in the crofter, a tenant who paid for his land in days of labor. The nobles had a monopoly of this form of labor through a law passed in the sixteenth century. The law of Gustavus Vasa not only prohibited the erection of crofts on the peasant's lands but also limited the number of grown sons and daughters who might remain in the home to aid the father. It was this class that was migrating to neighboring countries where economic conditions offered greater opportunities and where pride suffered less than in the native land. The petition of the House of Peasants in 1746–47 again stated that "laborers along the frontiers of the country, who are raised there and are given their nourishment until they are able to do useful work, go to sea and serve foreign nations."[1] A complaint from the army of the same period regretted that "in Finland, in Bohuslän (on the west coast), and in other frontier provinces, many of the working classes, both men and women, some with and others without passports, leave the kingdom, making it difficult to procure necessary agricultural labor in these regions, and even to secure enough men for recruits."[2]

A committee on commerce and economy was selected by the Riksdag to study the question and recommend a remedy. The result of this investigation was a more stringent emigration law. A bond of 100 riksdalar, about $100, was now required for every servant, crofter, or day laborer, who desired to emigrate, as a surety for his return. The government officials were to hold all property or any inheritance of the absent person and, if he did not return, it was to be confiscated and the proceeds divided between the parish church and charity. There were fines for any sea captain taking a person without passport on board his ship. The governors of the provinces had the power to regulate the number of servants who might leave the province or the kingdom. It was their duty to find employment for agricultural laborers in the province. It was the business of the tax commissioners[3] to inform the governor of the number of people emigrating from, and immigrating into, the province. If a servant attempted to leave his employer without explaining where he was

[1] *Ibid.*, p. 4.  [2] *Ibid.*  [3] *Mantalskomissionerna.*

going, it was the duty of the employer to retain his trunk. A law of 1748 and several that followed in the nineteenth century dealt with deserting seamen.

The restrictive laws, a part of the mercantile policy of the age, continued to express the attitude of the government toward emigration. A law of February 18, 1768, placed prohibitions on five classes of citizens. It forbade soldiers and sailors to leave. The other classes, miners, artisans, and servants, members of the upper class and peasants might depart if they could furnish two sureties or deposit a sum of money as bond for their return.[1] The Ordinance of 1781, concerning skilled journeymen, laborers, and servants, stated that "they seldom have any other excuse for leaving the fatherland than unnecessary curiosity and an erroneous and exaggerated idea of foreign prosperity, and it will henceforth as hitherto be forbidden them to leave the kingdom."[2] If it were necessary for a few to leave in order to get further knowledge and skill in their trade, they had to receive permission from the governor and the court of chancery. By a law of 1785, the property of emigrants, who had failed to return, was forfeited by the decision of the chancery court. These laws were evidently difficult to enforce since prohibitions and restrictions continued to be passed. Again in the ordinance of December 27, 1811, it is stated, "although it is necessary for the successful cultivation of grain and the development of commerce that artisans seek to gain more skill in their trades in foreign lands, yet it cannot be for the welfare of the country to lose necessary agricultural laborers."[3]

But a more effective discouragement of emigration from Sweden than the restrictive laws was the loss of Finland in the Russian war of 1809. During the decade from 1815 to 1825 following the Napoleonic wars, there was a surplus of immigration into Sweden, mostly from Finland. The crop failures throughout Sweden in the later thirties again stimulated an exodus, but mostly to Norway, and it was not until in the forties that the stream of emigration began to flow toward the New World. From 1816 to 1850 exodus was rather insignificant for it totaled, in thirty-five years, only to the amount

---

[1] "Utvandringslagstiftning," *op. cit.*, pp. 7–8.

[2] Translated, *ibid.*     [3] Translated, *ibid.*, p. 9.

which reached the United States in one year, under the restrictions of the quota law of 1924.[1]

Since 1850, Sweden has entered into what might be considered the present epoch of emigration. It has been for some portions of the kingdom almost a devastating loss of population. As a whole, one out of every seven has left his native country in the last seventy-five years, and most of the migrating horde has found its way to the United States.

This migration is not characteristic of Sweden alone, but is a part of the history of Europe. In the first half of the nineteenth century, Europe lost four millions of its inhabitants, mostly to the western hemisphere, although there was some migration into Siberia. In the last half of the century, the European loss was twenty-four millions,[2] while, during the first quarter of the twentieth century, seventeen million Europeans migrated to the United States alone.[3] There were six years in this latter period in which more than a million aliens a year entered the United States, 1905–7, 1910, 1913, and 1914. The World War reduced the figures of American immigration, until in 1918 only 110,000 came to the United States. With the resumption of peace the figures rose rapidly to 805,000 in 1921 and threatened the United States with an inundation of aliens from Europe, so that she found it necessary to pass the quota laws restricting the number of foreigners that may be admitted in any given year.

The quota law of 1921 was based on the census of 1910 and permitted the admission of 3 per cent of the nationals present in the United States at that census date. It applied to Europeans, for Asiatics had been excluded in the eighties. Americans were not limited in any manner. The immigration of 1922 sank to 309,000, but economic conditions became very acute in Europe in 1923 and the exodus to the United States reached 706,000 in 1924. During that year it was decided to decrease still further the number of

[1] Sundbärg, "Utvandringsstatistik," *op. cit.*, p. 48. Emigration from 1816–50 amounted to 9,561.

[2] U.S. Department of Commerce, *Statistical Abstract of the United States, 1922* (Washington, 1923), p. 89, Table 63.

[3] U.S. Department of Labor, *Annual Report of the Commissioner General of Immigration, 1929* (Washington, 1929), pp. 186–87, Table 83.

aliens that might be admitted. The census year of 1890 was chosen to give a preference to Teutonic immigration, and the percentage was lowered to two. Another law to change the census year to 1920, and to limit the whole number of immigrants in a given year to 150,000, was passed in 1925. It became effective July 1, 1929. This law favors Southern and Eastern Europe and England but decreases German and Scandinavian immigration.

The quota laws have definitely turned the largest portion of the present European exodus away from the United States. Some of these emigrants are now seeking the South American countries, while much of the English emigration is being directed to Canada and Australia. Even the British colonies have restrictive laws and desire agriculturalists from an industrialized Europe. The United States, however, remains the favored country in the eyes of the European emigrant and the quota lists are filled months and even years ahead in most countries. There are some who emigrate to Canada with the hope of entering the United States in time.

Steamers carrying emigrants from Scandinavian ports have called at the Canadian port of Halifax, since the passage of the quota laws of the United States. A Swedish emigrant woman, who was traveling with her child to join her husband on a farm in Manitoba, fell into conversation with the writer on board a Scandinavian-American liner in 1926. She stated that she, with her husband, hoped to be able to enter the United States soon. When told that the agricultural opportunities of Canada were better for an agrarian laborer than those of the United States, she shook her head and refused to believe the statement.[1] This sentiment was reiterated many times by various Scandinavians bound for Canada on the same ship. In the summer of 1927, while in the Canadian Rockies, the writer met English immigrant girls who were very anxious to come to the United States, for they thought the economic opportunities superior there. In Vancouver at the time many were attempting to cross the border without permission.

The restriction of immigration to the United States closed the first

[1] The author traveled steerage on the Scandinavian-American S.S. "United States," sailing from Oslo, September 5, 1926, to interview Scandinavian emigrants and to experience the life of an immigrant in crossing the Atlantic.

epoch of American history, a period when a great virgin country stretching across a continent became populated with aliens from Europe. It is now necessary to limit the movement of population from Europe since the free lands are exhausted. The hope for economic success of many a European peasant is gone.

European emigration to the United States can be divided into epochs as far as origins are concerned. Prior to 1890 this exodus came from Western and Northern Europe, from the Teutonic and Celtic races. Since 1890, until the period of the World War, the stream has decreased and almost ceased from countries like France, Germany, and Denmark. The large ingression of aliens during the twentieth century into the United States came from Southern and Eastern Europe. Emigration from England, Norway, and Sweden, although decreased after the nineties, still continued in considerable numbers. Since the end of the World War, the economic crisis has again increased emigration from all the countries of Europe, and only the quota laws have checked it.

The stream of emigrants from Sweden to the United States came in ebbs and flows. During the fifties it averaged 1,690 annually.[1] In the next decade it had risen to 12,245 yearly. It was in the sixties that Sweden was first looked upon by the United States government, the American states, and the American emigrant companies as a field to be exploited for hardy, thrifty, and persevering immigrants. The very disastrous crop failures in Sweden from 1867 to 1869 coupled with a previous period of overspeculation in agricultural lands turned many Swedish citizens toward the better economic promise in the new world. When the emigrants began to flow in perceptible numbers from that northern country, various steamship companies offered their services through the Swedish press, and helped to sow the seed of "America fever."

The position that Sweden occupied among the emigrant countries in 1867 is well expressed in the annual report of the West Virginia Commissioner of Immigration in 1868. The commissioner, J. H. Diss DeBar, wrote in his fifth annual report,

While at the seaports during the last season, I learned from well informed parties that emigration from Sweden, induced by a rough climate and successive

[1] *Statistisk årsbok för Sverige, 1927*, p. 72, Table 60.

failures of crops, would soon assume unprecedented proportions, and that with timely exertion a large share of it might be secured for the Middle States.[1] Heretofore the great mass of Swedes and Norwegians found their way to Wisconsin and Minnesota where they constitute almost the entire population of several flourishing counties. The uniform thrift of these people in those frigid and uncongenial regions is quite remarkable, yet I am informed that they by no means find there all they could wish, and that a timbered and hilly region like West Virginia would much better suit their tastes and habits. In industry and frugality they were not surpassed, if equalled, by any other nation of emigrants, while their custom of settling down in clans or whole villages with a parson and a schoolmaster at their head, would change the appearance of our wilderness sections perceptibly in a very short time.

I have, therefore, prepared the way in that direction, by connecting myself with a noted shipping company in New York City, who have just added to their business a line of steamers from Gothenburg, the most popular port of emigration in Sweden. I have also availed myself of a voyager to that country, an intelligent and well connected Norwegian, to get 2,000 of my eight page pamphlet printed and distributed in the most prolific sources of emigration there, and if means are appropriated intend to have my proposed hand-book of West Virginia translated into Swedish also, and a proportionate number of copies sent there for circulation. Like all northern people the Swedes are intelligent and inquisitive, and prepare themselves for emigration by gathering all the special information within their reach.[2]

In the seventies there was a slight annual decrease in emigration from Sweden following the large numbers of the late sixties, the total averaging, however, 15,000 a year. Economic conditions had returned to prosperity in the country, but the impetus of emigration was unchecked. The new lands that had been opened by the European immigrant and the westward-moving American Yankee, forced the virtual bankruptcy of the European agriculturalist in the eighties. It was then that swarms of people from the rural districts of the Scandinavian countries, Germany, England, and the other nations of Northern and Western Europe came to the "promised land." Sweden's annual average reached the peak of 37,000 during this decade. Its transoceanic emigration soared to 44,000 in

[1] West Virginia Commissioner of Immigration, *Fifth Annual Report* (Wheeling, 1868), p. 13.

[2] In spite of the enthusiasm of the Commissioner of Immigration, West Virginia obtained very few Scandinavian immigrants.

1882, to 46,000 in 1887, and in 1888 remained at 45,000, the highest figures that it has ever attained.[1]

Germany's emigration reached a height of 226,000 in 1881, England's 183,000 in 1883, and Ireland's 105,000 in the same year. Sweden's neighbors, Norway and Denmark, reached their peaks of emigration in 1882 with 28,000 and 11,000, respectively. In all of these countries, with the exception of Ireland, this was an unprecedented exodus.

Better economic conditions in Europe and the blow of a financial depression in the United States in 1893 checked the flood-waters of European emigration. But the exodus from Sweden continued to average 25,000 annually for the next two decades. The World War made travel very dangerous and difficult, while it produced a period of high wages and constant employment in neutral countries. From 1911 to 1920, Swedish emigration fell to an 11,000 annual average. Since 1890 it was no longer agricultural distress but economic crises and periods of labor conflict that swelled the numbers of departing citizens from their fatherland. The labor unrest in 1902 and 1903 raised emigration to 37,000 and 39,000; the year following the big strike of 1909, the exodus amounted to 27,000; and the unemployment in 1923 which followed the crisis of 1920 forced 29,000 people to leave Sweden.[2] Most of them came to the United States.[3]

The American quota laws have been gradually diminishing the number of Swedes that may be admitted to the United States. The first law of 1921 gave to Sweden a quota of 20,042.[4] In 1922 only 43.8 per cent of the quota asked for admission. The following year, according to the Swedish statistics, 24,948 were admitted.[5] The

[1] Sundbärg, "Den svenska och europeiska folköknings och omflyttningsstatistiken," *op. cit.*, p. 106, Table 25.

[2] *Ibid.*, p. 141, Table 39. *Statistisk årsbok för Sverige, 1927*, p. 72.

[3] In 1902 and 1903 there were 33,000 and 35,000 transoceanic emigrants from Sweden. Sundbärg, *op. cit.*, p. 108, Table 25. In 1923, almost 25,000 went to the United States (*Statistisk årsbok för Sverige, 1927*, p. 73, Table 61).

[4] U.S. Department of Commerce, *Statistical Abstract of the United States, 1922*, p. 101, Table 74.

[5] *Statistisk årsbok för Sverige, 1930*, p. 65.

quota law of 1924 reduced Sweden's portion to 9,561, but during that year only 7,036 Swedes emigrated to the United States.[1] By 1926 she had reached the limits of her quota and the lists were filled six months in advance. In 1929 the emigration amounted to 7,000. The law of 1925 which became effective in 1929 brought a further reduction to 3,000.[2] It was estimated by the Swedish Department of Labor in 1926 that there was an annual surplus of 6,000 in Sweden and there would continue to be for the next ten years, when the decreased birth-rate in the country would produce a stationary population and emigration would not be necessary.[3] In the meantime the surplus population would have to be directed either to countries other than the United States or be located on homestead enterprises on the public lands of Northern Sweden.

A small portion of Swedish emigration since 1850 has found its way into neighboring European countries, to South America, South Africa, and Australia. Canada has also received a share. The average annual exodus of Swedes into Norway and Denmark has been about a thousand to each.[4] During the period of agricultural distress in the eighties, Sweden gave to Denmark 2,349 of her citizens, while Denmark returned a population of 1,244. The annual migration from Sweden to Germany has been from 400 to 500. Since 1880, the surplus of exchange has been in favor of Sweden rather than Germany. Sweden and Great Britain have given each other about 100 persons annually. Other European countries have received a smaller number of Swedish emigrants.

Canada has never been as popular as the United States with the Swedish farmer, although it would seem that he would be best fitted of all Europeans for the northern climate. From the first decade of the twentieth century the exodus to this country from Sweden has averaged annually 315. Since the application of the quota laws of the United States and with the liberal land grants of the Canadian government the average has risen to 2,000 annually since 1927. There were 1,882 Swedish emigrants to Canada in 1929. The total Swedish population in Canada is about 27,000.

---

[1] U.S. Department of Commerce, *Statistical Abstract of the United States, 1925.*

[2] *Ibid.*    [3] Interview with Amanuensén C. C. Schmidt of Social Styrelsen, 1926.

[4] *Statistisk årsbok för Sverige, 1927*, p. 73.

South America, especially Brazil and Argentine, were boomed as immigrant countries in the eighties and nineties. These decades averaged annually 127 and 230, respectively, of Swedish home-seekers. Since 1900 the countries seem to have lost their popularity for the northern wanderer. As early as the later sixties Australia was advertised in the Swedish press as a desirous country for emigrants, and for a while was much favored. She received an annual average of 161 Swedes in the eighties and 117 in the nineties. The writer met some South African girls who were returning to visit a Swedish grandmother in 1926. Since 1921 there has been an average of 146 annually leaving for Australia and South Africa.

This historical survey of emigration from Sweden reveals the slowly advancing tide from 1850 to 1887, and then a gradual recession, but with the maintenance of a higher level in the years that follow. It appears that only because of the restrictions of the American quota laws has emigration since the World War been reduced to its present figures. There are in this tide of exodus certain ebbs and flows, caused by crises in agriculture or industry in Sweden as well as in the United States.

It is the purpose of this study to discuss in some detail the progress of social, economic, and political events in Sweden since 1840 in order that the causes for this unprecedented exodus in Swedish history may be more carefully analyzed. Before considering the historical background of Swedish emigration, however, it is worth while to enumerate some of the probable causes.

Economic reasons are undoubtedly the greatest factor in this exodus. It must be remembered that in America there were millions of acres of cheap virgin land, which after 1862 might be procured by cultivation. Sweden was an old country where most of the desirable land had been appropriated for many centuries and where land-values were high. The possibilities of securing a farm in the European country were much more difficult, because of the scarcity of salable land and its high value. Sweden was more fortunate than most European countries for she still had areas of free lands in the north. But climate did not make these northern counties as desirable as America. Now that free land in the United States is gone, this region is being homesteaded.

Wages were higher in the United States because of the scarcity of labor in a new country. The overpopulation of the rural districts before the industrialization of Sweden tended to make the wages low, and even after industry developed there was a large labor supply. Though the cost of living was higher in the United States the laborer could obtain a higher real wage in the newer world. It was easier for him to accumulate some capital and establish himself in agriculture or in industry. His standard of living was higher. In the new world he hardly felt the burden of taxation until he became a landowner; in Sweden the numerous burdens on land were often paid by the tenant and the early introduction of the income tax made the laborer also feel the pressure of direct taxation. It was not until 1913 that the income tax became a factor in the life of the laborer in the United States.

It has always been necessary for the many sons and daughters of the Swedish peasant farmer to seek their fortune away from the home farm. The estate passed intact usually to the eldest son. In earlier periods of emigration it was chiefly the younger sons and the daughters who left Sweden. And in the present emigration to the United States the surplus members of the peasant class continue the largest majority. They have been supplemented by crofters and cotters until those classes are fast disappearing from the Swedish countryside. It was customary that women work in the fields in Sweden along with the men. The care of the cattle was entirely their province. But by 1870 the young and comely peasant girl had discovered that domestic service in America was both more profitable and pleasanter. She came in numbers to equal her brothers.

Periods of economic distress in Sweden augmented the numbers departing from the fatherland. Crop failures like those of 1867–69, and the agricultural depression of the eighties produced emigration peaks. Overspeculation in agricultural lands during the early sixties and during the World War has led to numerous bankruptcies and heavily mortgaged farms. Failures of this sort determined some to build up a new fortune in a land of greater economic opportunity. Economic crises in the new world like the panics of 1873 and 1893 in turn discouraged emigration and brought low marks of exodus.

Since the industrialization of Sweden, a condition of scarcity of agricultural labor has decreased that type of Swedish emigrant. He is now more frequently an industrial laborer. Depression in the Swedish lumber or iron industries tends to swell the ranks of exodus. Labor conflicts and unemployment have sent many to their friends and relatives in the United States where often a job awaits them. The small capitalist and merchant who have been forced into bankruptcy think that it will be easier to retrieve their fortune in the new world.

Publicity, the creator of demand, proved a factor in the stimulation of the "America fever." Among the American states that for a time after the Civil War were active competitors for Scandinavian emigration were Wisconsin, Iowa, Minnesota, Maine, the Dakotas, Kansas, and Nebraska. Some of the southern states like Texas, Louisiana, South Carolina, and Virginia also attempted to attract northern emigrants. And later, California, Oregon, and Washington entered the field. Emigrant-travel companies and land companies advertised in the rural press of Sweden in the late sixties. And ocean steamship companies were equally anxious to extend their services. Transportation was made very easy for the traveler. Tickets might be purchased through the emigrant companies to any place in the United States from the numerous agents scattered over the rural districts and in the large cities of Sweden. Land-maps and illustrated booklets were furnished by the various states and railroad companies desiring settlers. The policy of reaching the emigrant in his home was early adopted by these agencies. He was met at various American ports by agents of the companies and the states, and often escorted by a guide, speaking his own language, to his destination. In the heat of competition, Swedish guides were even furnished for the transoceanic voyage, and every precaution was taken to protect the traveler from runners and others who lived by defrauding.

The most subtle and penetrating publicity about the new world came in the numerous letters from friends and relatives. It began with the very first emigrants and continues unabated. These letters often contained prepaid tickets and added the inducement of a promised job. Some letters exaggerated the opportunities and neglected to relate the accompanying hardships. The discouraging letters were usually ignored, for the new adventure had so many possibilities.

The Swedish-American, who returned to brag about his well-being in his adopted country, as he dangled his gold watch-chain, was a demonstration of American prosperity. He usually returned to America with a number of friends or relatives. It was frequently a means of financing his trip, for he received commissions from transportation companies. Some returned to recruit labor for railroads, factories, and construction companies.

Another sign of American prosperity was the sums of money that found their way across the Atlantic either to aid the family to pay off the mortgage or to support the aged mother. There were sums sent to be deposited in the local banks where interest rates were high. Some Swedish-Americans returned to settle in their native land, took over the family estate, or purchased a more pretentious farm than had ever been owned by the family. Sometimes it was the peasant daughter returning, after many years of service in the kitchen of the American bourgeoisie, to spend her old age carefree on her accumulated earnings among her relatives.

Thus a magnetic web was spun in time by the numerous crossings back and forth over the Atlantic, until there was scarce a Swedish home but was woven into the pattern. It produced a common sentiment that Sweden had no future for her younger generations. The thought of emigration was instilled in very early youth by the letters and gifts from America. Sometimes the "America fever" swept like an epidemic over certain regions in Värmland, Småland, and Halland. There was scarcely a young person left. Some who had no economic reason for departing were swept along in the excitement. They did not want to be left behind when all their friends had departed. The daughter of a Swedish immigrant to the United States relates how her mother feared that the father would be induced to leave his home as the "America fever" raged in the village.[1] The mother would gather up all the "literature" and illustrated booklets on the United States that he brought home, and hide them away. In spite of the mother's precautions, the fever gripped him and he left for America with his family. The mother has

[1] The daughter told this incident to the author.

always longed for her home in Sweden. Even today it is not unusual to hear it stated in Sweden that the country has no future, a psychological attitude which is a great stimulant for exodus.[1]

There have been other causes for emigration besides the economic and the psychological. Among the earlier Swedish-American settlers in the United States religious intolerance had induced some to migrate. Before 1860, the old conventicle laws of the eighteenth century were still in force. There has been no separation of state and church in Sweden and the Lutheran church of episcopal form continues to be the state church. Even today every citizen who does not formally resign from the state church is considered a member and pays church tithes. The first half of the nineteenth century was prolific with religious awakenings and dissenting movements. Some of the separatists were influenced by the Baptists, Mormons, and Methodists of the United States. Others were local sects like the Jansonites, the Luther-Readers or Hedbergians, and the Mission Friends. Dissenters were sometimes persecuted by both church and state authorities. Certain notorious cases of religious persecution of Mormons, Catholics, and Baptists led to the repeal of the old conventicle laws, and the establishment of religious freedom in 1860. But even later there continued to be certain social disqualifications that followed the dissenter and he was often passed over in the civil service of the government. The close alliance between the Methodist, Baptist, and Mormon churches in the United States and those in Sweden may have been an influence that stimulated migration. The precepts of the Mormon faith which exalted Utah as a home for its converts have induced some to seek that distant state.

There were factors in Swedish social and political life that may have contributed to the movements of its people, elements in a complex situation that could hardly have been responsible alone. The limited political franchise was especially galling to the lower classes. Sweden's peasant had always had class representation in the old Riksdag. The high property qualification for the electorate, introduced with the Parliamentary Reforms of 1866, deprived the poorer peasant of any participation in his government. The industrial

[1] The author has heard this remark made many times since the World War.

laborers were also without representation. It was not until the electoral reforms of 1909 and 1919 that universal manhood and woman-
hood suffrage was attained. Sweden is now thoroughly democratic
and political reform is no longer an excuse for emigration.

An authority on the causes of Swedish emigration, Gustav Sundbärg, stated in the report of the emigration commission in 1913,

There were perhaps very few if any who emigrated to America because of
the denial of political suffrage, but this disfranchisement and the feeling of
inferiority, of the denial of natural rights as the average person thinks of it, has
without doubt enhanced the feeling of discontent which has been a fruitful field
for the development of "emigration fever" in our country.[1]

The feeling that only the "nobility" have any importance, that "simple
people" have nothing to say, is very old and has been a widespread opinion in
our Swedish communities, and it is certainly not only an illusion. . . . . Without
doubt emigration might have been discouraged if manhood suffrage had been
introduced in 1880 instead of 1909. And patriotism would have been stronger.
Our age demands democracy to satisfy the masses, and Sweden with its many
strong aristocratic tendencies was in need of democratization especially in the
political field.

Every Swedish immigrant in the United States was eligible to
vote as soon as he was naturalized. In many of the middle states
the franchise was conferred upon him when he had obtained his first
papers. He entered eagerly into his new political rights, and assisted
in the organization of many a county in the territories and new states
of the West. In Minnesota, the Dakotas, Iowa, Nebraska, and
Kansas he has demonstrated his political ability. Social and political equality were often the subjects of his letters to his friends and
relatives in Sweden.

During the period of agitation from 1880 to 1910 when organized
labor and the Social Democratic party struggled for existence and
recognition, certain self-imposed exiles found their way to the
United States. They were overwhelmed with the futility of obtaining their ideals in Sweden, where freedom of speech, press, and
assembly was denied them. These agitators and young radicals,
some anarchistic, were often members of the intelligentsia, news-
papermen, artists. They found themselves frequently misfits in the
new world, and too often ended their lives in suicide.

[1] Gustav Sundbärg, *Emigrationsutredningens betänkande* (Stockholm, 1913), p. 836.

Social inequalities were more irritating than the lack of political franchise. Although no serfdom existed in Sweden there had developed a hierarchy of classes. There was the aristocracy by birth, the gentry who possessed large estates. Many of the nobility were not possessors of much wealth, but held preferences in government positions and in the army offices, even in some church appointments. Government officials, army officers, and the educated clergy formed an aristocracy in every community over the peasantry. The peasants in their turn were quite as arrogant toward the landless crofter and cotter. Many a proud spirit born in a lowly cottage found social equality and opportunity through emigration. Democracy has at present tended to level class lines. The *nouveau riche*, the industrialist and merchant of today, often possess the estates of the old nobility.

The introduction of compulsory military training in Sweden increased the numbers of those emigrating at the age of twenty. It is hard to determine how many left their fatherland for the sole reason of escaping military training, but many intending to leave some time for economic reasons, decided on an earlier exodus to escape the service in the army. There was much feeling on the part of the rural population against the rigors of military discipline, and for decades the question has been one of much discussion. The importance of this emigration may be demonstrated in a comparison of the statistics of 1866 and 1909. In 1866 only 4.26 per cent of the emigrants were men of twenty, while, after the introduction of various military training laws by 1909, men of this age contributed 16.61 per cent of the total number of emigrants.[1] The year following the passage of a law extending the period of military service was always marked with an increase of the exodus of young men just on the verge of military age, for a considerable portion of the Swedish population have a repugnance toward the compulsory military training because of its curtailment of individual freedom.

There were also many personal and psychological reasons for emigration, the peculiar individual who found himself and his ideas strange to his environment, who chafed with discontent because he was not understood, and who hoped to be able to adapt himself to a

[1] *Ibid.*, p. 601.

new situation. There was the man or the woman who had lost status in the community because of petty misdemeanors, a loss of reputation, or even with the shadow of a jail sentence, who wished to start life anew away from the prejudices of a small, gossiping neighborhood. Or, as has already been suggested, the ambitious son or daughter of the lower classes resented the snobbishness of the upper classes and the difficulties blocking the opportunity to rise socially in the home community.

There was the son or daughter who was not understood by the parents. The daughter, who did not wish to marry the young man that the parents had chosen for her, sought escape through emigration. There was the son who had tired of working for his father without compensation and who was not granted even the freedom of a hired man, but found himself, the son of a peasant, too proud to seek employment in the neighborhood where he was known. He would lose himself in the new world. Then there was the young man seeking adventure by a trip into an unknown land, or the young woman seeking romance by following a lover who emigrated a few years before.

It was usually not one cause but a multitude of factors that entered into the determination to leave the homeland. Economic opportunity was usually the most important consideration, while transportation facilities, publicity, and frequently personal contacts with relatives and friends in America were the determining factors. A quarrel with the parents, the loss of employment, the disgrace of bankruptcy, the aggravating snubs of superiors, and many other personal matters might be the occasion for sending the individual across the Atlantic.

All of these divergent reasons for emigrating have been given by Swedish settlers in America. A locomotive fireman from Älvsborg County left Sweden in 1907, although he had a good position on the railroad, because he was discontented in Sweden.[1]

A crofter from Värmland County emigrated in 1881 when he found his meager income from agriculture insufficient.[2] He wrote,

[1] "Utvandrarnes egna uppgifter," *Emigrationsutredningens bilaga VII* (Stockholm, 1908), pp. 64–65.

[2] *Ibid.*, p. 178.

I began to direct my thoughts to America, and wrote to an old neighbor who had been there ten years. In the answer to my letter he declared that the economic opportunities were much better for the poor workman in America than in Sweden. A laborer in Värmland could never improve his economic situation, but became steadily poorer.

A young man of seventeen left his home in Skaraborg County in 1907 upon the recommendation of his brother who had been in America five years and was receiving good wages as a carpenter in St. Paul, Minnesota.[1] The younger brother had worked as a hired man for peasants in Sweden, but a position was awaiting his arrival in America. The economic possibilities in the United States had induced four other young men from the same neighborhood to try their fortune across the sea.

The son of a carpenter from the island of Öland left his motherland at the age of eighteen to escape military training and to better his economic status.[2] He had worked as a hired man, but the introduction of agricultural machinery by 1907 had made agricultural labor precarious. He had already three brothers and a sister resident in America. A young shoemaker of twenty, the son of a prosperous peasant in Skaraborg County, wanted to travel and see the world the same year.[3] His father had given him a ticket to St. Charles, Illinois, where he had a friend. He emphatically denied that he was attempting to escape military training. Another young man of seventeen from Älvsborg County with his chum decided to hunt buffalo in Western United States in 1880.[4] They had read stories of adventure about the new world. Unfortunately, there were few buffaloes left when they arrived.

Young unmarried women emigrated from Sweden in almost equal numbers with the young men. A young woman of twenty-three, who had worked for peasants and performed much of the hard labor on the farm since she was fifteen, decided in 1907 to try her chances as a maid in San Francisco. There she had a brother who had been in America eleven years. She had purchased her ticket with money that she had inherited from her parents and was accompanying a

[1] *Ibid.*, p. 70.
[2] *Ibid.*, p. 47.
[3] *Ibid.*, p. 68.        [4] A case study made by the author.

friend who had been home from America for a visit. She came from Halland County.[1] A young woman of nineteen, unhappy because her father had forbidden her to marry the young man she loved, decided to accompany a friend who was also home on a visit from America.[2] Another young woman of twenty, the daughter of a well-to-do peasant, had worked for gentry for two years.[3] She decided in 1907 that she could earn more in the United States. "Many receive a high rate of interest on money in Sweden," she said when interviewed, "so I have decided to send some home from time to time and let father place it in the bank." She was much attached to her home, and hoped to return. The description that was given stated that she was an unusually bright and attractive girl, and it was apparent that she considered her journey only as a means of helping her parents. Her destination was Winnipeg, Canada, where she had relatives.

The earlier discrimination against dissenters in Sweden is illustrated in the life-history of a former seaman, who was converted to the Baptist faith in New York in 1858.[4] His father had owned a large estate in Värmland but at thirteen he had gone to sea. After his conversion he returned to Stockholm and passed examinations for captain and for instructor in navigation. He had hoped to receive a position in a navigation school in Sweden, but when the head of the school heard that he was a Baptist, he was advised to seek a position in the United States. He returned to this country and became an officer in the American Navy during the Civil War. After the war he returned to Sweden as an instructor in the newly established Baptist theological seminary in Stockholm. In 1870 he returned again to the United States because of his wife's health and became a Baptist preacher.

"It is natural," he wrote, "that at home one was more or less ostracized if one had left the state church and had become a Baptist. It makes you feel that you prefer to live in a country where religious belief makes no difference if you are industrious."

It was, however, letters like the following that had the greatest drawing power.

---

[1] "Utvandrarnes egna uppgifter," *op. cit.*, p. 110.

[2] Author's case study.

[3] "Utvandrarnes egna uppgifter," *op. cit.*, pp. 116–17.    [4] *Ibid.*, pp. 152–53.

I can tell you that we are busy in America planting corn, for we have 60 acres.[1] I sit and ride on a machine which we plant with, and the oats and wheat and barley stand green and beautiful. I have planted 17 acres of wheat, 50 acres of oats, and 4 acres of barley, and today we have planted potatoes. You ask how much rent I give for an acre of land. I pay three dollars an acre, and a dollar is earned as fast as a krona in Sweden. . . . . And I can tell you that here we do not live frugally but here one has eggs and egg pancake and canned fish and fresh fish and fruits of all kinds, so it is different from you who have to sit and hold herring bones.

A Swedish letter which began with the English salutation, "My dear Parents," written in 1896 stated,

I had planned last Christmas that I would spend this Christmas in Sweden— but when I give more thought to the matter, what can one do in Sweden but work for sour bread and salt herring and I am afraid that it would be hard for me to become accustomed to it again.[2] . . . . Erik Persson has become a peasant at home I saw in a letter from Gotland the other day, but he wishes to return— he had said—I do not wonder, for it is so with everyone and why go home in Sweden as a peasant and pay heavy taxes for Sweden's lazy officials. No sir, Sweden has been and continues a slave land, for the harder they work, the higher taxes they pay, but it is not that way here in this country. Surely the farmers here pay some taxes but far from as high as Sweden, for although I have not been here very long, still I have been here long enough to see that it is better here than in Sweden.

A letter with a particularly strong inducement is the appeal to a former sweetheart.

Beloved, I wonder how you are, if you are still alive.[3] I am very well situated here. It has been a long time since we saw each other. Are you married or un- married? If you are not married you can get a good home with me. I own my own house here in town and I earn ten kronor ($2.50) a day. My wife died last fall and I want another wife. I have only a daughter eleven years old. If you can come to me, I will send you a ticket and traveling money in the spring when it is mild weather. We live very comfortably in America. I have been here fourteen years. . . . . It is about twenty-four years ago since we have seen each

[1] "Utvandringsväsendet i Sverige," *Emigrationsutredningens bilaga II* (Stockholm, 1909), p. 152. Extracts from a letter dated 1904 received in Sweden, giving a description of American prosperity.

[2] *Ibid.*, p. 156.

[3] These letters were collected by the ministers in various parishes in Sweden for the Swedish Emigration Committee, and are typical of America letters, "Utvandrings- väsendet i Sverige," *op. cit.*, p. 154).

other. You perhaps wonder who I am. My name is Einar and I worked in Verista with Adolph Johanson when you were at Andersons, and you were my first sweetheart. If you cannot come, then perhaps you know someone who would make a good housewife and who is willing to come.

Various countries and local communities in Europe had from time to time a practice of emptying prisons and poorhouses by shipping the inmates to America. It was occasionally done in Sweden. Sometimes a philanthropic society would collect funds to aid released prisoners to begin life afresh in the new world. The American consul at Gothenburg in 1885 replied to the inquiry sent by the State Department,

> It has come to my knowledge that it is a common practice throughout Sweden to ship to the United States paupers and that class of criminals who have served out their sentences in work-houses, prisons, etc., but who, pursuant to the laws of the kingdom, are still laboring under political disabilities such as the deprivation of the right to vote and of the rights of citizenship generally. Funds for this purpose are furnished in a clandestine manner by municipal corporations as well as by individuals and even the police authorities in the various ports are purposely blind to the great outrage thus committed; in order to rid themselves of an intolerable burden and free the community from the presence of a dangerous class. Some of these emigrants are sent through Hamburg and Copenhagen.[1]

The American consul at Stockholm in 1888 wrote,[2]

> Of assisted emigration, I know that some years ago a philanthropic society assisted liberated prisoners to go to America but I think that such assistance is now stopped. In justice to the society I must say that no other prisoners received assistance than such as they had hope would be improved by coming in to other circumstances. Something worse is that communities sometimes pay the voyage to America for paupers and worthless persons in order to get rid of them. This is, however, often altogether concealed as the knowledge of it comes a long time after the fact.

It was customary in England and Germany as well to send these elements to America.

In this array of the many and varied causes of Swedish emigration that have been enumerated, it must be remembered that certain

---

[1] *U.S. Consular Letters, 1864–1885*, Gothenburg, Sidney W. Cooper, Consul, November 26, 1885.

[2] *U.S. Consular Letters, 1886–1893*, Stockholm, Nere A. Elfwing, Consul, September 12, 1888.

causes predominated during some historical periods and ceased to be causes in others. Great changes have taken place in Sweden since the beginning of the migratory movement toward the United States in 1840. The kingdom has changed from an agricultural economy to an industrial one, from isolation to one of international commercial dependency, from an aristocracy to a democracy both socially and politically. Intolerance in religion has given way to religious toleration; the privileges of the aristocracy have fallen before the rising equality of the masses. As great changes have taken place in Sweden since 1840 as in the United States.

# CHAPTER II

## GEOGRAPHICAL SWEDEN

Sweden is one of the most northerly countries of the world. It stretches its thousand miles of length from the southern Baltic far into the Arctic Circle on the eastern side of the Scandinavian peninsula.[1] Its latitude is comparable to the distance between the southern end of Hudson Bay to Bering Straits on the North American continent.

There is a great difference in climate, however, between Sweden and the corresponding region of Canada. Sweden, with the exception of Norway, has the mildest of the northern climates, for the gentle winds of the Gulf Stream caress their shores. In a country which stretches one-seventh of the distance from the North Pole to the Equator, there are many variations in climate. The high mountain ranges, which form the backbone of the peninsula, cut off the mild west winds from the Atlantic and expose the northern regions to the bitter east winds of Russian frozen wastes.[2] In Southern Sweden in the province of Skåne, there are 142 days of summer and 72 of winter. The distribution is more even in central Sweden where summer has 124 days and winter, 121, while in the northern region within the Arctic Circle summer lasts only 88 days and winter endures for 186. The north is the land of the midnight sun. At Karesuando there is continual daylight for 53 days, while its growing season is equal to twice that number of days. Certain crops will grow and mature in this northern region, because of the increased daylight, which will not mature in the central region. The variation in climate between the north and south is much

[1] The latitude of Sweden is from 55° 20′ to 69° northern latitude. Fifteen per cent of the area of the country is within the Arctic Circle. *The Sweden Year Book, 1926* (Stockholm, 1926), pp. 63 ff. Per Stolpe, "Geografiska betingelser för näringslifvet inom Sveriges olika landsdelar, *Emigrationsutredningens bilaga VI* (Stockholm, 1912), pp. 17 ff.; Gunnar Anderson, "Fysisk geografi," in J. Guinchard, *Sveriges Land och Folk* (Stockholm, 1915), I, 1 ff.

[2] *The Sweden Year Book, 1926*, p. 65.

greater in winter than in summer. Where in winter the average climate for the north at Karesuando is 6° Fahrenheit in January, in Lund in Southern Sweden it is only 31°.[1] In summer, during the month of July, the range is from 54° to 62° Fahrenheit.[2] The climate at Lund has an average temperature of $7\frac{1}{2}$° Centigrade per year while New York averages 11.3°.[3]

The rainy, drizzly weather of the west coast is much like that of England. The precipitation for the kingdom averages 25 inches.[4] The lowest amount of rainfall is in Västernorrland County and the highest in Halland County. The Norrland region receives less rainfall than the southern portion of the kingdom. The lack of rain in the spring of the year, especially along the east coast, is a great disadvantage to agriculture. Consequently, the Norrland counties, both because of their northerly climate and lack of rainfall, are better suited for cattle-breeding and forestry than agriculture. The cultivation of the soil is largely confined to the southern and central portions of the realm.

The climate of Norrland, with its long, dark winter evenings, is often depressing. The population in this region is very sparse, varying from five to nine inhabitants per square mile, about the density of the population of the Dakotas, Colorado, and Idaho.[5] In Southern Sweden the variable climate is very beautiful and here is found the densest population and the oldest settled region.

Sweden is not as large as France or Germany in land-area but is once and a half the size of the British Isles and Ireland together.[6] This northern country is in size and shape like the state of Cali-

[1] The average temperature for January from 1859 to 1925 is −14.5° Celsius for Karesuando, and −0.7° for Lund (Statistisk Centralbyrån, *Statistisk årsbok för Sverige, 1927*, p. 1, Table I).

[2] From +12.5° to +16.5° Celsius, *ibid.*

[3] N. Ekholm, "Klimat"; J. Guinchard, *op. cit.*, I, 29 ff.

[4] Six hundred twenty-eight mm. for a period from 1881–1920 (*Statistisk årsbok för Sverige, 1927*, p. 1).

[5] *Ibid.*, p. 2, Table 2; U.S. Department of Commerce, *Statistical Abstract of the United States, 1922*, pp. 40–41, Table 30; U.S. Department of Commerce, *Fourteenth Census of the U.S., 1920, Population* (Washington, 1921), I, 31, Table 18.

[6] The land-area of Sweden is 173,035 sq. mi. It is 976 miles at its greatest length and 310 miles at its greatest width (J. Guinchard, *op. cit.*, I, 1 ff.).

fornia, which is the second largest state in the American Union. Sweden would almost cover the combined area of the states of Minnesota, Wisconsin, and Illinois. There is an extremely long coastline, bordering on the Gulf of Bothnia, the Baltic, the Kattegat, and the Skagerrak.[1] Her western boundary is the mountain range separating her from Norway. On the northeast a short boundary divides Sweden from Finland.

Sweden's position between the North Sea and the North Atlantic on the west, and the Baltic on the east is strategic for commercial intercourse between Eastern and Western Europe. Most of the Swedish ports on the Gulf of Bothnia and the northern Baltic are frozen during the winter, but modern ice-breakers manage to keep the ports open for the greater period of the season. In the outer skerries near the city of Stockholm there are open harbors at Nynäshamn and Kapellskär. The harbors on the west coast of Sweden, of which the principal one is Gothenburg, are usually free from ice during the winter.

The mountain ranges that separate Norway from Sweden are in their northern stretches Alpine in appearance and height. But here and there they are cut by passes through which railroad lines connect with the Norwegian coast. The two important rail connections are the line from Stockholm to Trondhjem, and that for the northern iron mines, from Luleå, to Narvik in Norway.

Sweden is divided historically into three portions, Gothland, Svealand, and Norrland.[2] Gothland includes Southern and Western Sweden, and derives its name from the Teutonic tribe, the Goths, who settled in the region. Svealand is in Eastern Sweden with its nucleus in the old province of Uppland. It was settled even earlier by another Teutonic tribe, the "Svear." Norrland stretches northward from the earlier settlements into the Arctic Circle. Its scant population has from time to time been recruited from the migrating peoples of the southern counties.

There are also the old historical provinces known as *landskap*. They persist today in the designation of portions of Sweden very much as the historical provinces of France still survive. There were

[1] There are 4,734 miles of coast line (J. Guinchard, *op. cit.*, I, 1 ff.).

[2] Gothland is called *Götaland* in Swedish.

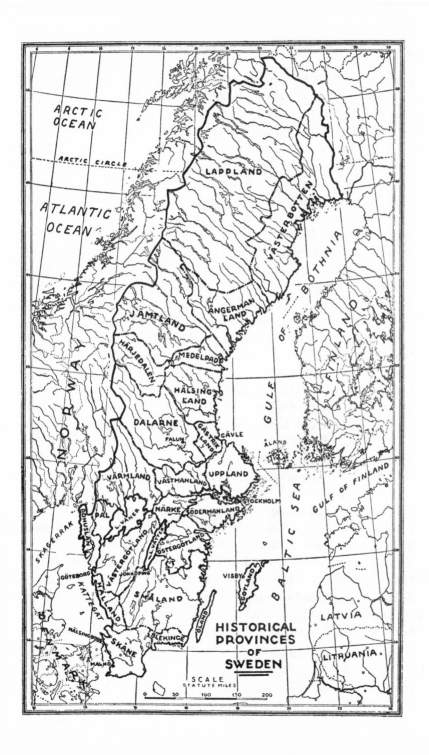

HISTORICAL
PROVINCES
OF
SWEDEN

SCALE
STATUTE MILES
0    50    100    150    200

twenty-five in all and some continue to exist, coterminous as well as in name, with the present administrative divisions, the counties. Those still used for local government purposes are Blekinge, Halland, Gotland, Östergötland, Södermanland, Västmanland, Värmland, and Jämtland.[1] The remaining provinces, which have been divided or united to form counties are Skåne, Småland, Öland, Västergötland, Dalsland, Bohuslän, Uppland, Närke, Dalarne, Gästriksland, Hälsingland, Härjedalen, Medelpad, Ångermanland, Västerbotten, Norrbotten, and Lappland. Many of the Swedish immigrants in the United States continue to think of their Swedish birthplace in the terms of these old provinces. They speak of the plains of Skåne and the highlands of Småland in more familiar terms than the present counties which comprise the region. Dalsland and Öland were regions of very large emigration in the eighties.

The present local subdivisions of Sweden are counties, hundreds, and communes.[2] The counties have local self-government vested in the county council while the governor is appointed by the Crown. The hundred is primarily a judicial division as it has always been historically. The commune and the parish is frequently coterminous and here is also a small council elected by the people. There are twenty-five counties, the city of Stockholm forming a county by itself. The old province of Skåne has been divided into two counties, Kristianstad and Malmöhus. Småland now consists of three counties, Jönköping, Kronoberg, and Kalmar. The island of Öland has been added to Kalmar County. A portion of Västergötland has been united with Dalsland to form Älvsborg County. Another portion united with Bohuslän has become the county of Gothenburg-Bohus. The remaining area of Västergötland is now designated Skaraborg County. Uppland is now called Uppsala County. There is also a rural Stockholm County as well as an urban Stockholm County. Närke and portions of Värmland and Västmanland have become Örebro County. The ten Norrland provinces have been reduced to five counties, Kopparberg, Gävleborg, Västernorrland, Jämtland,

---

[1] *Statistisk årsbok för Sverige, 1927*, p. 3, Table 3.

[2] *Län, härader, och commune*. The *commune* is coterminous usually with the parish (*socken*). I have translated *härad* as hundred, for it was similar to the old English hundred, and was even called *hundred* in Svealand.

and Norrbotten. The famous region of Dalarne is at present incorporated in Kopparberg County.

Since the overwhelming majority of Swedish emigrants came from the rural regions, and the economic reasons for this migration must be bound up with the agricultural conditions in the last century, there might arise the question, what are the agricultural possibilities of the country? The foundation of agriculture is soil. The geological formation of the country therefore assumes a particular importance for a study of agricultural possibilities. In Sweden, the geological formation is primarily Archaean rock, consisting of granites, gneiss, and other eruptive rocks and schists. The last glacial period in Sweden swept the rock-formation quite nude of all decomposed matter.[1] The present soil was formed during and after this glacial period. The rock is rich in iron-ore deposits, and the granite is very valuable for building materials. Unfortunately the deposits of coal and lignite are very scarce. Sandstone, limestone, and shales are found on the plains of Southern and Central Sweden, on the islands of Gotland and Öland, and in Northern Sweden along the Norwegian border. Skåne in the southern peninsula is more like the rock formation of the bordering Danish islands and the Jutland peninsula than Sweden proper. These rocks belong to the Triassic, Jurassic, and Cretaceous geological periods and contain a thin strata of coal between layers of fireproof clay.

Over areas which were covered by water following the glacial period are clay deposits on the rocky moraine. These deposits are found on the fertile plains of Skåne, around Kalmar Sound, in Västergötland, Östergötland, Närke, the valleys of Lake Mälar, and on the Norrland coastal plain along the Gulf of Bothnia, from the River Dal to the Finnish border. The great rivers that gush down from the mountain heights of the Norwegian frontier into the Gulf of Bothnia have cut deep valleys, where sand and clay deposit make possible cultivation. In the regions, however, where the glacial moraine is predominant, like the interior of Norrland, Värmland, and Dalarne, and on the South Swedish highlands in Småland and the adjoining regions of northern Skåne, the stony soil with its

[1] *The Sweden Year Book, 1926*, pp. 64 ff. Stolpe, "Geografiska betingelser för näringslifvet," *op. cit.*, pp. 7 ff. E. Erdmann, "Geologi," in Guinchard, *op. cit.*, I, 42 ff.

lack of lime deposits is very poor for agriculture and is best-fitted for forestry.[1]

Sweden ranks second to Finland as the country in Europe having the largest amount of lakes and swamps. There are extensive peat-bogs in all parts of the country, but only in Southern Sweden where the forests have disappeared is peat used for fuel.[2] There has been some effort under the the Swedish Moss Culture Society to drain swamps and place them under cultivation.[3] In the extreme north the mosses are used for reindeer culture.

In land areas still standing in forest, Finland again is the only country in Europe which surpasses Sweden. At one time undoubtedly practically all the country except the extreme north was covered with forest. In the southern and central portions of Sweden, where most of the population is located, the forest has given way to cultivated fields. The constant battle with the forest, which was forever encroaching upon the small patches of cultivated land, has left its influence on the folk-lore and traditions of the Swedish people. Until the last century when the timber became valuable for export, to burn timber for clearing was looked upon as meritorious, since the forest was the enemy of the people. At the present time, the forests are the most valuable of the natural resources, and more land is being returned to timber. In 1870 only 40 per cent of the land-area of Sweden was in forest, and in 1920 this had been increased to 59.9 per cent.[4] The provinces richest in forest are Norrland, Dalarne, and Värmland in Northern Sweden, and the South Swedish highlands or Smaland.

The entire flora of Sweden was introduced from Southern Europe after the glacial period. And since Europe was at the time impoverished in the variety of its flora, the forests of Sweden are rather monotonous. The great forests of the north of Sweden consist primarily of pine and spruce, with some birch near the mountain region.[5] South of Dalecarlia, there are more deciduous trees, the oak,

[1] Stolpe, op. cit., p. 9.

[2] Ibid., pp. 11–12; A. Wallén, "Vattensystem," in Guinchard, op. cit., I, 19 ff.

[3] Svenska Mosskultur Föreningen.

[4] Statistisk årsbok för Sverige, 1927, p. 85, Table 84.

[5] The Sweden Year Book, 1926, p. 66. H. Hesselman, "Växtgeografi," in Guinchard, op. cit., I, 54 ff.

ash, elm, lime, plane, and hazel, while in the extreme south the birch is found. But most of the deciduous forests have been cleared away for cultivated land. As early as the Middle Ages and definitely in the sixteenth century efforts were made by legislation to prohibit the wanton destruction of oak and elm trees.[1]

The many streams in Sweden have provided a natural means for the transport of lumber to the ports.[2] The long frozen winters in the forested regions of Norrland have also been a great benefit for transportation. It is more difficult in the Småland regions where both climate and a denser population are hindrances. For centuries the forests of the Central and Southern Swedish highlands have furnished charcoal for the iron industries. More recently there has developed a wood-pulp industry in Värmland, Dalsland, and Smaland. In Norrland this industry is localized in the southern portion of Gävleborg County. The glass industry also draws heavily upon the timbered regions, and is localized chiefly in Värmland and Småland.

Another important natural resource of Sweden is its iron ore. The old mining region called *Bergslagen* ("mountain law") extends from eastern Värmland to Uppland north of Stockholm.[3] The iron ore from this region is considered some of the purest that is found, with a content of 60 to 65 per cent of iron and very little phosphorus. Here charcoal is used to smelt the iron, and it produces the best quality of steel possible. In iron-content it is double that of the English ores. A second mining region is found north of the Arctic Circle in the Lappland region along the Luleå-Narvik railroad. The iron ore in this region is of poor grade and is transported to be smelted in England and Germany. In past centuries the famous copper mines at Falu and the Sala silver mine produced considerable amounts of metals. The silver mines are almost extinct and the demand for copper at the present does not justify much production.

Although Sweden is unfortunate in her small coal supply, her many rivers furnish her with great possibilities in water power for her growing industries and railroads. The power-house at Trollhättan on the Gotha River furnishes electricity for Western and even

---

[1] Tobias Norlind, *Svenska allmogens liv* (Stockholm, 1925), p. 52.

[2] Stolpe, *op. cit.*, p. 13.

[3] *Ibid.*, pp. 15 ff.; *The Sweden Year Book, 1926*, p. 69.

Southern Sweden.[1] The government-owned railroad between Stockholm and Gothenburg receives power from this station. Other power-houses are located in various portions of the country. Since the period of the World War electrical power and light have been rapidly expanding and are used to a large extent even in agriculture.

With the long seacoast and the many inland lakes, it would seem that fishing would be an important occupation of the people. But as contrasted with Norway where fishing is one of the chief industries, in Sweden only about 40,000 persons are engaged in it. More than half of these are located on the Bohus coast north of Gothenburg. In the salt water, here, there is mackerel, herring, and cod.[2] The Halland coast is good for fishing but lacks adequate harbors. The Baltic is not as rich in fish as the Cattegat; however, there is some fishing for a small herring called *strömming*.

Sweden has many good harbors. Most of her rivers have rapids and are a hindrance to the development of navigation, but there are many navigable lakes. Quite early in the nineteenth century the Gotha Canal joined the Gotha River to Lake Vänern, connected the lake with Lake Vättern, continued to the Baltic, and then connected with Lake Mälar, making a waterway between the two largest cities, Gothenburg and Stockholm.

The overwhelming majority of the people of Sweden were until quite recent times engaged in agriculture for a livelihood. In 1870 as many as 72.4 per cent of the inhabitants were employed in agriculture and related occupations.[3] Since 1880 the rural population has declined rapidly, and now only 44 per cent seek their income through agriculture, while the number engaged in industry has risen from 14.6 per cent to 35 per cent in the same period. In spite of the fact that Sweden was until 1880 always wholly an agricultural country and that the area of cultivated land has increased since that time, only 9 per cent of her land-area is under cultivation today. Only Finland and Norway have less cultivated land. The average for Northwestern Europe is 23.6 per cent, for Southwestern Europe, 42.6 per cent, for Eastern Europe, 27.2 per cent, and for Europe as

[1] Stolpe, *op. cit.*, pp. 16 ff.

[2] *Ibid.*, p. 19.

[3] *Statistisk årsbok för Sverige, 1927*, pp. 26–27, Table 28.

a whole, 28.6 per cent.[1] During the last hundred years in many portions of Sweden the amount of cultivated land has increased fivefold.[2] Between 1865 and 1925, farm lands had increased from 5.7 per cent to 9.3 per cent for the country as a whole.[3] Every year sees new fields made ready for cultivation. The vast Norrland region lies open for settlers at the present very much like the former frontier of the United States. In spite of the small land-area under cultivation there is a larger amount of tillable land per individual in Sweden than in any portion of Europe with the exception of Eastern Europe, and more than three times as much forest land as even in Russia.[4] There were 167 acres of cultivated land and 965 acres of woodland for every hundred inhabitants in Sweden in 1910, while in 1925 the cultivated land had fallen to 153 acres and the forest land had increased to 1,005 acres.[5] In the United States there were 457 acres of cultivated land for every one hundred inhabitants,[6] and 222 acres of forest land in 1920.

Sweden is divided into five agricultural regions.[7] The South Swedish plain, lying in the counties of Malmöhus, Kristianstad, and Halland, with the southern part of Blekinge, consists of a very fertile marine plain. The climate is mild so that tillage is only interrupted for two or three months during the winter. There is plenty of rainfall. Most of the soil is easy to till and consists of clay with a lime content. In parts there is much sand. Here are found large grain fields, considerable sugar beet culture, and some tobacco. In more recent times dairying and stock-raising with extensive hog-production for the market have been introduced. In some portions of the region potatoes are raised for starch and for distilling.

The South Swedish highlands known popularly as Småland lie just north of the southern plain. Besides the Småland counties of

[1] Gustav Sundbärg, "Allmänna ekonomiska data rörande Sverige," *Emigrationsutredningens bilaga XIII* (Stockholm, 1912), p. 30.

[2] "Bygdestatistik," *Emigrationsutredningens bilaga V* (Stockholm, 1910).

[3] *Statistisk årsbok för Sverige, 1927*, p. 85, Table 84.

[4] Sundbärg, "Allmänna ekonomiska data," *op. cit.*, p. 30.

[5] *Statistisk årsbok för Sverige, 1927*, p. 85, Table 84.

[6] Department of Commerce, *Statistical Abstract of the United States, 1922*, p. 128, Table 99 and p. 180, Table 133.

[7] *The Swedish Agricultural Labourer* (Stockholm, 1921), pp. 5 ff.

Kalmar, Kronoberg, and Jönköping, this region includes the south-ern part of Älvsborg County, and portions of the southern counties which lie adjacent with even a part of southern Östergötland. The two islands of Gotland and Öland belong to this zone although the soil is slightly more fertile. In this very hilly region, there are many rocky impediments, sparsely covered with a poor moraine gravel, having very little lime deposit. In the valleys the soil is usually sand washed out of the gravel, interspersed with extensive peat-bogs. The limestone foundation on the two islands makes the soil there richer than on the adjoining mainland. The climate is less favorable to agriculture than in the south. The winters are longer and colder, and the summers shorter with frequent night frosts. Most of the mainland area is under forest. There is some natural meadow. Only a very small portion of the land is cultivated, and livestock is raised on a more extensive scale than in Skåne.

The second fertile region of Sweden is the Central Swedish plain, stretching from the east to the west coast north of the southern highlands. This region includes the larger part of Bohuslän, the northern part of Älvsborg County, the counties of Skaraborg, Upp-sala, Stockholm, Södermanland, and Östergötland, and the southern portions of Värmland, Örebro, and Västmanland counties. Seasons here correspond favorably with Southern Sweden. Rainfall is not so uniform, and the unevenness of the snowfall with the usual spring drought and rainfall during harvest season, means much exacting labor during certain periods of the year. The stiff clay soil is hard to manipulate. This is a region where the cultivation of grain domi-nates. There is some extensive raising of livestock, especially in Skaraborg County.

The Central Swedish highlands known as *Bergslagen* are a heavily forested region. This is also the location of the most im-portant and oldest iron mines of Sweden. It extends over the north-ern hills of Värmland, Örebro, and Västmanland counties, and the southern portions of Dalarne. The agricultural conditions here are very much like those of the southern highlands, except that the winters are longer, and early frosts frequent. The soil contains much moraine gravel but there is also some sand and clay. It is not diffi-cult to till and is quite fertile. The farms are extremely small in area. The numerous natural meadows in the uplands permit an extensive cattle culture. In the winters the agriculturalists are engaged in lumbering, burning charcoal, and hauling ore.

The northern half of Sweden is called Norrland. It contains the five northern counties and northern Dalarne. The Alpine heights of the Norwegian border in the Norrland region slope to a marine plain on the Gulf of Bothnia. Swift mountain streams have cut wide valleys, and here most of the agriculture of this region is located. The winter is long and the snowfall heavy. The short summer has the advantage of the midnight sun which makes a very favorable growing season, though extremely short. The only grains that ripen in this northern region are barley and rye. Oats are often cut green for fodder. Each farmer raises enough potatoes for his own use. The many natural meadows supply fodder for the livestock. This is the great lumbering region of Sweden, and the winters are devoted to felling and hauling timber and burning charcoal. In the extreme north in Norrbotten County iron mines have more recently been developed.

In the central and southern portions of Sweden the chief crops are wheat, rye, oats, and barley.[1] Sugar beets and potatoes are grown extensively. Hay constitutes an important crop for fodder in all portions of the country. Wheat does not grow farther north than southern Dalarne and Gästrikland. Sugar beets can only be produced as far north as Västergötland and Östergötland. But rye, barley, and potatoes may be harvested far north within the Arctic Circle.

During a brief period in the nineteenth century, from 1820 to 1860, there was a slight exportation of wheat and a large exportation of barley and oats from Sweden, while rye which was the chief breadstuff used by the native population was partly imported. The exportation of oats and barley continued until 1900, while the added consumption of wheat made it necessary to import that grain earlier. A period of agricultural prosperity from 1836 to 1875 with rising prices on a world market was followed by the economic crisis of the eighties.[2] There ensued a period when, in spite of an increased pro-

[1] Guinchard, *op. cit.*, II, 51–68. Stolpe, *op. cit.*, p. 18.

[2] Guinchard, *op. cit.*, II, 59.

duction, the country was not able to meet the added demand of a growing population, and Sweden has become a grain-importing country.[1] Now Sweden is exporting dairy-products and meats, mostly pork and some beef.

Just as agricultural Germany developed into a highly industrialized country in the middle of the nineteenth century, industrialization came to Sweden a decade or two later. The definite trend toward an industrial future became apparent in 1888. This does not mean that many new industries were introduced into Sweden but rather that production increased on a large scale, with a favorable world and domestic market. Some of Sweden's industries like her mining and the production of various forms of iron and steel date from the Middle Ages.[2] Many others like textiles, sugar-refining, manufacture of tobacco, glass, and porcelain, were introduced in the seventeenth and eighteenth centuries.[3] Exportation of lumber and wood-products had an earlier period of prosperity which was interrupted by the embargoes of the Napoleonic wars and did not recover until England developed a free-trade policy in the middle of the nineteenth century.

The industrial exports of Sweden are lumber, paper-pulp, iron ore, and the products of iron and wood. The other manufactures of the country, a range of great variety, are produced primarily for the home market. The industries in Southern and Central Sweden cater primarily to the domestic market, while the products of the Norrland region enter almost exclusively into export, and compete on the world market.[4] A protective tariff introduced in 1888 after two decades of comparatively free trade protects only the industries of the home market.

Since the seventies, but more marked since the nineties, there has been a rapid growth of cities and a movement of population into the industrial regions. With the booming of the forest industry in

[1] *Statistisk årsbok för Sverige, 1927*, p. 92, Table 88.

[2] *The Sweden Year Book, 1926*, pp. 91–113; Exports, *ibid.*, pp. 115 ff.

[3] Carl Grimberg, "Ur den Svenska industriens äldre historia," *Svenska industrien vid kvartsekelskiftet, 1925* (Stockholm, 1926), pp. 3 ff.

[4] Sven Brisman, "Industrien och folkförsörjningen," *Svenska industrien vid kvartsekelskiftet, 1925*, pp. 73 ff.

Norrland there was considerable immigration into the north. The urban population grew after almost a century of stagnation from 10.09 per cent of the total population in 1850 to 31.07 per cent in 1926.[1] The numbers of inhabitants engaged in industry has increased from 14.6 per cent in 1870 to 35 per cent in 1920, while those employed in commerce and transportation tripled in numbers during the same period, from 5.2 per cent to 15.2 per cent.[2] The actual numbers of persons engaged in industry and in agriculture show the change that has taken place even more graphically. In 1870 there were 3,017,000 persons in Sweden living on agriculture and its by-products, while in 1920 there were only 2,596,000. The industrial population has increased from 610,000 to 2,066,000 during the same period, and including those employed in commerce and transportation there is a total of 2,964,000.

Sweden has a land-area almost equal to that of Germany but a population slightly less than that of the Netherlands but almost twice that of Switzerland. It is about equal to the population of the state of Illinois in the United States, although more than three times as large in area. The state of California which comes nearest to Sweden in land-area has one-half of the population.

There has been a tremendous growth of population in Sweden during the last century. In 1800 the number of inhabitants totaled 2,347,303 and in 1880, 4,565,668.[3] During this period Sweden had remained primarily an agricultural country. Since 1880, in spite of the great loss through emigration, the population has continued to rise to 6,120,080 (January, 1930).[4] From 1851 to 1930 Sweden has lost 1,527,441 of its population by emigration, and has received 380,208 immigrants, making a net loss of 1,147,133.[5]

The population of Sweden is concentrated in the southern half of the kingdom, while in the Norrland forests there are few inhabitants.

[1] *Statistisk årsbok för Sverige, 1927*, p. 5. Table 8.

[2] *Ibid.*, pp. 26–27, Table 28.

[3] Gustav Sundbärg, "Den svenska och europeiska folköknings och omflyttnings-statistiken," *Emigrationsutredningens bilaga IV*, p. 137, Table 38.

[4] *Statistisk årsbok för Sverige, 1930*, p. 3, Table 3.

[5] Sundbärg, "Den svenska och europeiska folköknings och omflyttningsstatis-tiken," p. 46 and *Statistisk årsbok för Sverige, 1930*, p. 67, Table 58.

CHART II

INCREASE IN SWEDISH POPULATION 1800–1930

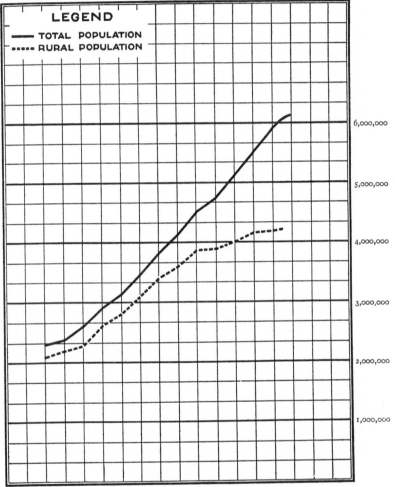

LEGEND
—— TOTAL POPULATION
----- RURAL POPULATION

6,000,000

5,000,000

4,000,000

3,000,000

2,000,000

1,000,000

1800 1810 1820 1830 1840 1850 1860 1870 1880 1890 1900 1910 1920 1930

The average population for the entire kingdom in 1926 was 38.3 per square mile.[1] This was practically the same as the density of population in the United States in 1920, which in the census is stated as 35.5.[2] The density of population in California is 22 persons per square mile. In Illinois there were 30.6 persons per square mile in 1860, but at the present time with a population slightly larger than that of Sweden, there are 115.7 persons per square mile.

The densest population in Sweden with the exception of the city of Stockholm may be found in Malmöhus and Gothenburg-Bohus counties which have 274.7 and 235.7 persons respectively per square mile.[3] However, two of the largest cities in Sweden are located in these counties, Malmö in the former and Gothenburg in the latter. This is about the density of population in the states of New York and Connecticut. The most densely populated agricultural counties in Sweden are Blekinge with 132 persons per square mile, Kristianstad County with 102, and Stockholm County with 94. Södermanland, Östergötland, Halland, and Skaraborg counties have 81. The northern counties of Jämtland, Västerbotten, and Norrbotten have from 5 to 9 inhabitants per square mile.

The rapid increase in Sweden's population from 1800 to 1880 when it almost doubled, was not due to the industrial revolution, the popular explanation for the increasing population in Europe. The same was true of Ireland. It was during a period when Sweden was almost wholly agricultural and to a large extent isolated and self-sufficient as far as the world was concerned. It was her agricultural population that was increasing for her total urban centers only numbered 690,000 citizens. Rural population had increased from 2,117,000 to 3,875,000 in these eighty years. This tremendous increase in the agrarian classes, more characteristic of Sweden and the Scandinavian countries than any of the other European countries, may be explained by the peaceful pursuits of Norway and Sweden after the Napoleonic wars, and to a more rapid conquest of con-

[1] *Statistisck årsbok för Sverige, 1927*, p. 2, Table 2.

[2] U.S. Department of Commerce, *Statistical Abstract of the United States, 1922*, pp. 40–41, Table 30.

[3] A square kilometer is 0.386 of a square mile. There are 106 persons per square kilometer in Malmöhus County and 91 in Gothenburg-Bohus, *Statistisk årsbok för Sverige, 1927*, p. 2.

tagious diseases in the northern countries with better sanitary conditions.[1] There resulted an overpopulation in certain rural districts, especially the less fertile regions.

Since the emigration in such large numbers in the eighties and the development of industry in Sweden the rural districts of Sweden have lost this surplus population. From 1880 to 1890 the rural population increased only 10,000 while the city population gained more than 200,000. Since 1880 the increase in the agrarian inhabitants in Sweden has been 312,000 while her cities have added 1,197,-000 persons.[2]

Simultaneous with the decreasing death-rate and the growth of population has come a steadily decreasing birth-rate. From 1830 to 1880 the birth-rate was annually about 32 per thousand inhabitants.[3] There has been a steady decrease until in 1922 it reached 20.07. The large families from seven to twelve children so common among the Scandinavians have now dwindled to two and three. It is especially noticeable among the new industrial classes of Sweden, and it is estimated that in ten years her population will be stationary.

As compared with other European countries, only Norway and Denmark had a larger increase per thousand inhabitants from 1841 to 1860 than Sweden, while only Spain and France had as small an increase in population during the eighties and nineties.[4] Sweden's death-rate has been lower than any of the European countries with the exception of her two sister Scandinavian kingdoms,[5] while her marriage-rate and birth-rate have usually been lower than any of the European countries.[6]

[1] Sundbärg, *Emigrationsutredningens betänkande*, p. 124.

[2] These are the figures for 1926 (*Statistisk årsbok för Sverige, 1927*, p. 5).

[3] *Ibid.*, p. 59, Table 48.

[4] Sundbärg, "Utvandringsstatistik," *Emigrationsutredningens bilaga IV*, p. 80, Table 4.

[5] *Ibid.*, pp. 86–87, Table 9.    [6] *Ibid.*, p. 82, Table 5 and p. 84, Table 7.

# CHAPTER III

## SWEDEN IN 1840

Sweden and Norway, unlike most of Europe, were scarcely touched by the institution of serfdom. With vast stretches of forest lands where any man might carve himself a farm from the wilderness, the country was not conducive to the production of a servile rural population. It was a situation similar to the frontier of Eastern Germany before the time of the Reformation when this free population was ground under the heel of serfdom.[1]

The Swedish peasant has always been a free man. The two Teutonic tribes that settled in Sweden, the "Svear" in Uppland in Eastern Sweden, and the "Goths" in Western Sweden organized into communal villages. The peasant or *bonde*, meaning "he who dwells," was a very important person in the primitive tribes.[2] He was mentioned in the first written laws of the land, the Uppland law, the Västgöta law, and others, as the only person who had the right to elect and the only one who had the right to be a lawman (*lagman*) to preside over the early "hundred" courts.[3] These land-laws also spoke of the village (*by*), and the right to the possession of allodial soil by the person who had placed it under cultivation. The villages were like the fast-disappearing free villages in England at the time of the Norman Conquest.

The oldest social distinctions in Sweden had been that of free man and slave, but slavery had disappeared in the fourteenth century.

[1] The Peasant's War of 1525 in Germany with which Luther had no sympathy reduced the German peasantry to a serfdom that was not ameliorated until the nineteenth century. Samuel Sugenheim, *Geschichte der Aufhebung der Leibeigenschaft und Hörigkeiten in Europa* (St. Petersburg, 1861), pp. 350–499.

[2] *Bonde* is the singular form and *bönder*, the plural. The word comes from the Swedish word *boende* ("the resident"). In old Icelandic, *briandi*, pl. *boendr*. Gabriel Thulin, *Om Mantalet* (Stockholm, 1890), p. 71.

[3] E. J. Schütz, *Om skifte af jord i Sverige* (Stockholm, 1890), pp. 20 ff. These laws of the different "lands" of Sweden (*landskap*) were put into writing in the thirteenth century.

The first recognition of a class of nobility higher than the *bonde* was the clerical nobility in the church-council in Skannige in 1248.[1] About forty years later, temporal lords were recognized in law when everyone who would provide himself with a horse and do military service for the crown was released from ordinary taxes. In the fifteenth century, the nobles, grown very strong, attempted to introduce feudalism and to subjugate the peasants.[2] This danger was removed by the rising of the peasants under the leadership of Engelbrekt in 1434. The peasants took a leading part in the nationalist movement against Denmark. It was the peasants of Dalarne that gave Gustavus Vasa the support that finally established him as the national king of Sweden. This won for them a permanent place in the Riksdag and assured them economic and social independence. The ranks of the nobles were much depleted by the massacre of Stockholm in 1520. In the wars that followed the reign of Gustavus Vasa, the nobles threatened to regain their strength again. Titles of *Greve* and *Friherr* were established and nobles were freed from the obligation of military service. Nobles could now be created by the king, and were a highly privileged class. Much crownland was alienated to the nobles by Queen Christina, the daughter of Gustavus Adolphus, and the numbers of nobles were greatly increased. After the Thirty-Years' War with the combined efforts of Charles XI, the successor of Queen Christina, and the Riksdag, where the nobles were opposed by the other three estates, the crown repudiated the grants of crownlands and restored them to the State. Most of this crownland was later sold as freeholds to the more prosperous peasants. The land ownership gave the latter a firm economic position as well as power in the political life of the community. After the reduction of their lands, the nobility remained to a great extent a numerous but impecunious class, who had to earn their living largely through government service.

The nobles continued to be a privileged class, however, until the reforms of the later eighteenth and early nineteenth centuries. They

[1] P. Fahlbeck, "Stånd och klasser," in Guinchard, *Sveriges Land och Folk*, I, 141–43.

[2] On the estates of the church and the nobles were tenants called *landbönder*. The vast majority of the Swedish people remained independent landowners. It was the freemen that the nobles attempted unsuccessfully to reduce to serfdom.

had exclusive rights to certain high positions in the administration of the government and in the army and navy. Their lands were tax-free. There were two kinds of privileged lands, the ordinary *frälse* land which was free from ordinary land taxes, and the *säteri* or *ypperligt frälse* land which was free from all obligations to the crown.[1] About 1800 there were in Sweden some 16,000 estates that were ordinary tax-free and 6,000 so-called "highly privileged," amounting in area to about one-third of the cultivated lands.[2] In 1789 the ordinary tax-free lands were open to purchase by anyone, and the exemptions from taxation went with the purchase of the land. The counties having more than half of their lands belonging to this tax-exempt group were Stockholm, Södermanland, Östergötland, Blekinge, and Malmöhus.[3] Many of the privileges of the nobles were abolished by Gustavus III in 1789 in his effort to get the support of the other classes. What remained of their legal privileges, the nobles voluntarily surrendered in their declaration of 1809. Their political privileges as an Estate in the Riksdag remained until 1865. The last privilege from taxes attached to the *frälse* land was repealed in 1892. The nobles still have their titles in Sweden, and continue a sort of social organization in Stockholm in the House of Knights, erected by Gustavus Adolphus. There was undoubtedly in 1840 much class feeling between the nobles and the peasants. The nobles, though in many instances poor in economic goods, represented the cultured class and continued to hold the important offices in the government, as well as in the army and navy. The peasant

[1] Gustavus Vasa gave his sons through inheritance all the rights of the king to be free from taxation. Eric XIV extended this to certain nobles. He permitted a count (*Greve*) to have three estates; a *Friherr*, two; a nobleman (*adelsman*), one estate without any obligations to the crown. These are called *ypperliga frälse* or *säterier* and *ladugårder*. In 1686 there was promulgated a law forbidding the erection of new *säterier*, and in 1682 a noble could not inherit a taxed *hemman* as a *frälse*. See Hultgren, *Den Skånska frälsebondefrågan, 1870* (Hälsingborg, 1870), pp. 8–10.

[2] Sam Clason, *Karl XIII och Karl XIV Johan;* Hildebrand, *Sveriges historia*, XI (Stockholm, 1925), 13–15.

[3] Stockholm County, 56.1 per cent of its lands were *frälse* and *frälseskatte;* Södermanland, 53.8 per cent; Östergötland, 55.1 per cent; Blekinge, 60 per cent; and Malmöhus, 50 per cent. Uppsala County had 40.6 per cent; Jönköping, 38 per cent; Kristianstad, 45.3 per cent; Halland, 47.9 per cent; and Skaraborg, 38.8 per cent ("Jordstyckningen," *Emigrationsutredningens bilaga XII* [Stockholm, 1911], pp. 20*–22*).

was considered crude and uncultured; and there was no doubt a striking contrast between the homely peasant of the more remote and isolated regions and the cultured nobleman of the court. The large majority of the population of Sweden in 1855 belonged to the class of peasant proprietors and their families, at least 2,378,-267, or 65.35 per cent.[1] The next class numerically was the landless agricultural groups, constituting 29.44 per cent and amounting to 1,071,246 of the total inhabitants. The other classes in Sweden were very small in numbers. The urban population was almost negligible, 81,408, or 2.24 per cent. To the knights and nobility belonged

TABLE II

POPULATION BY ESTATES AND CLASSES, 1805–55*

| ESTATES AND CLASSES | TOTAL POPULATION | | | PERCENTAGE OF TOTAL POPULATION | | |
|---|---|---|---|---|---|---|
| | 1805 | 1830 | 1855 | 1805 | 1830 | 1855 |
| Knights and nobles.. | 9,503 | 10,458 | 11,742 | 0.39 | 0.36 | 0.32 |
| Clergy............ | 15,145 | 14,153 | 15,362 | 0.63 | 0.49 | 0.42 |
| Gentry............ | 69,348 | 70,091 | 79,441 | 2.88 | 2.44 | 2.18 |
| Burgesses......... | 65,411 | 66,693 | 81,408 | 2.71 | 2.30 | 2.24 |
| Peasants.......... | 1,759,038 | 2,168,915 | 2,378,267 | 72.90 | 75.10 | 65.35 |
| Foreigners and Jews. | .......... | 1,972 | 1,866 | ........ | 0.07 | 0.05 |
| Others............ | 494,327 | 555,800 | 1,071,246 | 20.49 | 19.24 | 29.44 |
| Total population | 2,412,772 | 2,888,082 | 3,639,332 | 100.00 | 100.00 | 100.00 |

*Gustav Sundbärg, *Emigrationsutredningens betänkande*, p. 82, Table 16.

11,742, to the gentry class, 79,441, and to the clergy, 15,362. The nobility together contributed only 2.5 per cent to the population and the clergy less than ½ of 1 per cent. Sweden at the time was singularly homogeneous with less than 0.05 per cent foreigners among her total inhabitants.

In the middle of the nineteenth century, Sweden was an agricultural country. But in spite of the fact that every year saw more virgin land placed under the plow, only 4 per cent of the land-area of the kingdom was under cultivation. The old allodial right to virgin land which had been cleared and placed under cultivation continued to exist in Swedish law until the nineteenth century.[2] Allodial

[1] Gustav Sundbärg, *Emigrationsutredningens betänkande*, p. 82. Table 16.

[2] "Allodial right" is called in Swedish *odalrätten*. Those who cleared the lands under this law were called *odalsbönder* (Schütz, *Om skifte af land*, pp. 31–33).

right to land had long before been supplanted by feudal right in Continental Europe and England. Feudal right, the right of the conqueror, dates from the Middle Ages in these countries. Allodial land, however, is mentioned as folkland in Anglo-Saxon and early Norman England. All the free villages in Sweden had originated under allodial rights. After the period of early colonization in Sweden, the peasants, the co-owners of the village, laid claims to lands around the village, extending indefinitely to the lands of the neighboring village. But toward the north especially were large stretches of forest lands without claimants.[1]

The forests in Southern and Central Sweden which lay between the villages were claimed by the allodial peasants through their village communities. These forests were called commons.[2] Some of these forest lands were also owned by larger communities in common, like the hundred and the province.[3] The word commons in Swedish law designates common ownership of timberlands, water, mountains, and bridges. The commons once belonging to the provinces have now been annexed to the crownlands. The crownlands today include large stretches of forest lands in the six northern counties, as well as numerous crown-parks in the southern portion of the kingdom.[4]

The Swedish communal village was similar to the free village of England and of Continental Europe in the early Middle Ages. It is thought that the members of these primitive Teutonic villages had originally been related. The houses of the villagers were arranged along a common street or road, while behind them stretched the numerous barns and outhouses, for in Sweden lumber was easily procured from the commonlands and the peasant gloried in many buildings on his estate.[5] Around the village lay the many strips of

[1] *Ibid.*, p. 36.     [2] In Swedish they were called *allmänningar*.

[3] *Härad* and *land*. The three kinds of common lands are *by allmänningar* ("village commons"), *häradsallmänningar* ("hundred commons"), and *landsallmänningar* ("provincial commons"). Later there appeared *sockenallmänningar* ("parish commons") (*ibid.*, pp. 36–38).

[4] A discussion of the method used by the church and the crown to acquire lands originally belonging to the local units of government in Sweden may be found in Carl G. Ihrfors, *Om häradsallmänningar* (Uppsala, 1916).

[5] A good description of a communal village in Sweden is included in Carl Grimberg, *Svenska folkets underbara öden*, VI (Stockholm, 1922), 209 ff.

cultivated lands, and the meadows. The forest lands and natural meadows formed the *utmark*, the land still in reserve that had not been placed under the plow. These preserves were from time to time added to the cultivated land as needed. And each time a new piece was cleared, it was divided among the co-owners of the village. In 1750, agriculture was still carried on in the same primitive way. During the progress of time, as the village cleared more and more land, the number of strips belonging to each co-owner had increased, and some were remote from the village. The peasant was obliged to harvest his hay at the time designated by the village council, after his strip of the field had been laid out. Every year he permitted one-third of his land to lie fallow. The yield of the crops was low, the grade of cattle and horses poor, and famine threatened the countryside in poor and meager years. There was no surplus of agricultural products, for all was consumed at home.

Movements for improvement in agricultural methods began in Sweden in the middle of the eighteenth century. The defeat of Sweden in the wars of Charles XII brought the loss of the Baltic provinces in the Treaty of Nystad, 1721. An effort was made during the following decades, known in Swedish history as the "Period of Liberty," to restore the economic conditions of the country. Among the various reforms, one of the most far-reaching and revolutionary was the enclosure of individual holdings, and the abolition of the agricultural village. The idea was introduced by Jacob Faggot, surveyor-general of the royal government. The First Enclosure Act was passed in 1749, and made it the duty of the land surveyors to encourage the owners of the land to consolidate their holdings.[1] The law of 1757 gave every co-owner in a village the privilege to demand a consolidation of his lands. The principle of consolidation of landholdings was new and broke with the traditions of centuries. It was therefore accepted very slowly and with much misgiving by the conservative peasants. The *storskifte* law of 1772, the first compulsory enclosure law, reduced the number of strips per landholder by half, but the villages remained undisturbed.

The financial success of still greater consolidations was demon-

[1] Juhlin Dannfelt, *Lanthushållning;* Guinchard, *op. cit.*, II, 30; V. Ekstrand, *Svenska landmätare, 1682–1900* (Stockholm); Carl Grimberg, *op. cit.*, p. 211.

strated by Baron Rutger Maclean on his estate in Svaneholm in the southern province of Skane in the early part of the nineteenth century. This gave the movement a great impetus. Baron Maclean had consolidated the holdings of his tenants into single farms.[1] The *enskifte* laws, the second enclosure laws, provided for the consolidation of lands into large single holdings and the abolition of the village; they were passed in 1803 for the province of Skåne, in 1804, for Skaraborg County, and in 1807, for the entire country. Any co-owner of a village could demand a redistribution and consolidation of his lands. There was much opposition to the laws. Peasants resented giving up a good piece of land for a poorer piece. The commissions which had been appointed to make the reapportionment devised various ways of compensation for the exchanges of land by giving smaller pieces of good land as equivalent to larger portions of poorer land. A later enclosure law called *laga skifte*, passed in 1827, provided that the lands should be consolidated into as few parcels per owner as possible, and that these pieces of land should be as contiguous as the character and situation of the land permitted, without any injury to any of the co-owners. It proved a more practical law than the Second Enclosure Act and left the peasant with two or three pieces of land in close proximity to his new home.

During the thirties and forties, the consolidation went on rapidly until the greater part of Sweden south of Norrland and Dalarne had changed village communal ownership to individual farms. It altered the character of the land and broke the traditions of centuries. The peasant, however, still points out the place where the old village stood, usually on top of a hill, where often the old church remains, sometimes in ruins, but more often as yet a place of worship. The peasant either moved his house down from the village to his new farm or built a new house from the common woodland's supply of timber. In the divisions that took place, the woodlands were often left intact and some still remain in the joint ownership of the commune.

An example of the great revolution in landed proprietorship that took place through these laws of enclosure may be found in the village of Bäck in Skaraborg County. The accompanying maps show

[1] Guinchard, *op. cit.*, II, 30.

the village of Bäck in the process of changing from a village of communal ownership to its dispersement and the enclosure of the lands of its owners. There were fifteen co-owners in the village in 1700 and their scattered pieces of land varied from forty-two in Hofmansgården to sixty-eight in Skattegården. A large part of the community lands was not cleared and was designated *utmark*. The system of agriculture that prevailed was the three-field system in which one-third of the lands were permitted to lie fallow every year. The fields were small strips divided only by a furrow. In the common meadowlands, the hay of the village was divided among the co-owners and had to be cut all at the same time. The more industrious peasants were held back by the lazier ones, and the yield per acre was small. The homes of the fifteen co-owners were clustered together in the village. Under the First Enclosure Law, the holdings of the village of Bäck were consolidated in 1777–79. Hofmansgården was reduced from forty-two strips to twenty-three strips, and Skattegården from sixty-eight to thirty-six strips. The village remained intact but the communal holdings of the village had been reduced from twenty-one parcels of land to four. The *utmark*, the large piece of uncultivated land, was undisturbed. The second map shows the village of Bäck after the final division of lands under the Third Enclosure Law in 1836. The holdings of the various villagers now ranged from one to three and the community lands, with a few small exceptions, had disappeared. The village and the *utmark* were completely gone. The peasant now lived on his own lands. Skattegården consisted of three parcels of land, somewhat scattered to be sure, but still an improvement over the original sixty-eight. Hofmansgården had also three parcels of land. The village of Bäck is typical of what has taken place practically all over Sweden during the nineteenth century. Enclosure had begun in England in the reign of Elizabeth and was most prevalent during and following the Napoleonic wars, but in this country the land was consolidated in the hands of the gentry. There were also enclosure acts and the abandonment of the rural village in Saxony following the law of 1832. In Russia the break-up of the Mir, the agrarian village, was first permitted by the ukase of 1907.

The majority of the agrarian land-owning class in Sweden in 1840

# CHART III

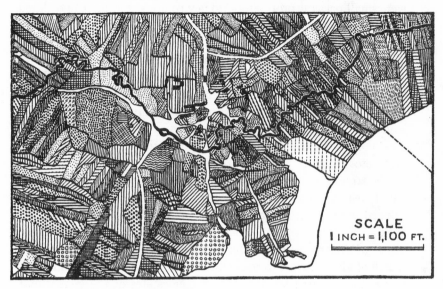

SCALE
1 INCH = 1,100 FT.

Landholding in 1700. There was an average of fifty-three pieces of land belonging to each villager.

Fields belonging to the same landowner are colored alike.

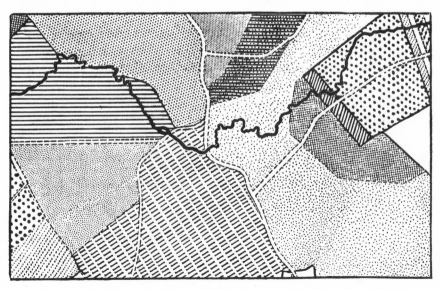

Fields after the Enclosures of 1836. No farm has more than three pieces of land

were small peasant proprietors.[1] They comprised at least two-thirds of some 200,000 peasant freeholders,[2] and their farms varied from 5 to 25 acres of cultivated land with patches of woodland. Even after the break-up of the communal village and fields, the forest lands remained in the joint ownership of the former co-owners of the villages and their descendants. In 1908 small farms of this size constituted 69.7 per cent of all the farms of Sweden, but only 25.9 per cent of the land under cultivation.[3] There has been of recent times some increase of these small farms, but the proportion to the other landed proprietors remains relatively the same.

The larger peasant estates rose from 25 to 125 acres in their cultivated fields. There were few farms that did not also have some wooded lands. These peasants were of practically the same social rank as the lower gentry. Their holdings were found on the fertile plains of Southern and Central Sweden.[4] Slightly more than one-fourth of all the farms were of this category in 1908, and about one-half of the cultivated land.[5] The larger estates of the gentry and nobles, and all other estates over 125 acres, were only 2.3 per cent of the total number of freeholds, but comprised 23.7 per cent of the tilled land, almost as much as that held by the numerous small proprietors.[6]

The agrarian population was most numerous in the southern and western counties of the kingdom and in the northern region of Dalarne. The counties in 1840 which had more than 100,000 in rural population were in their respective order, Älvsborg, Malmöhus, Värmland, Östergötland, Skaraborg, Kalmar, Kristianstad, Jönköping, Kopparberg, and Gothenborg-Bohus.[7] They comprise ten of

[1] The small peasant proprietors are called *småbönder*.

[2] There were 216,575 peasant proprietors in 1840 (Sundbärg, *op. cit.*, p. 81, Table 15). The homestead of the peasant proprietor was called *hemman*.

[3] K. Socialstyrelsen, *Lantarbetarnas arbets-och löneförhållande* (Stockholm, 1915), p. 35. *The Swedish Agricultural Labourer*, p. 12.

[4] The larger peasant proprietors were called *storbönder*. Their holdings were from 10 to 50 hectars in extent.

[5] Twenty-eight per cent of the farms were from 10 to 50 hectars and 50.4 per cent of all the land-area.

[6] *Lantarbetarnas arbets-och löneförehållande, op. cit.*, p. 35.

[7] The agricultural population of Älvsborg County in 1840 was 176,824; of Malmöhus County, 157,358; of Värmland, 151,927; of Östergötland, 143,886; of Skaraborg, 143,-153; of Kalmar, 136,304; of Kristianstad, 130,179; of Jönköping, 115,531.

the twenty-four rural counties. It was from these counties, we shall see, that the majority of the Swedish emigrants came in the following decades.

It is an interesting fact in the Swedish agrarian situation that the peasant proprietors were most numerous in the counties where the agricultural population was the largest. The order of the counties in reference to the number of peasant proprietors is slightly different from the size of rural population. Thus we find that the following counties had a predominantly land-owning peasant population: Älvsborg, Kopparberg, Värmland, Skaraborg, Malmöhus, Kalmar, Jönköping, Kronoberg, Kristianstad, Östergötland, Gothenborg-Bohus, and Halland.[1] The county of Kopparberg took the place of Malmöhus County. In Kopparberg there were very few who did not own their land; the farms were but tiny patches of cultivated land surrounded by dense forests. This is the home of the freedom-loving Dalcarlar who have played such an important rôle in the Swedish wars of independence from Denmark.

Quite contrary the fertile plains of Malmöhus, Östergötland, and the southern part of Kristianstad counties invited the accumulation of land in large estates by the nobles, the gentry, and the most prosperous peasants. But even here the amount of small peasant proprietors was comparatively high. The peasant owner was relatively scarce on the fertile plains around the capital city of Stockholm. In the Mälar counties he averaged about five thousand per county. The total rural population was also smaller in this region than in Southern and Western Sweden, probably because of the lack of opportunity for the lower agricultural classes of acquiring land in early times.

Making still another comparison between the regions of large estates and the districts of small peasant freeholds, we find that from 50 to 60 per cent of the cultivated land of the counties of Blekinge, Stockholm, Östergötland, and Malmöhus were or had been tax-exempt land of the nobility. In the counties of Halland, Kristian-

---

[1] The number of homestead owners and cultivators amounted to 16,988 in Älvsborg County in 1840; 15,570, in Kopparberg; 13,586, in Värmland; 12,485, in Malmöhus; 12,332, in Kalmar; 12,318, in Jönköping; 10,098, in Kronoberg; 9,842, in Kristianstad; 9,596, in Östergötland; 9,306, in Göteborg-Bohus, and 8,144, in Halland (*Lantarbetarnas arbets-och löneförhållande, op. cit.*, pp. 184–85, Table C).

stad, and Uppsala from 40 to 50 per cent of the tilled land had once belonged to the nobility.[1] Of these counties, Blekinge, Stockholm, Södermanland, Uppsala had a relatively sparse rural population, while Östergötland and Malmöhus had many agrarian inhabitants. It was more usual to find a large agricultural population in counties like Värmland and Gothenborg-Bohus, where the tax-exempt land was very small, and in Älvsborg, Skaraborg, Kronoberg, Kalmar, and Jönköping where it was comparatively less than in the regions of large estates.[2] In all but eight of the Swedish rural counties, more than two-thirds of the cultivated lands was in the hands of the peasant.

Counties like Kopparberg, Värmland, Kalmar, Kronoberg, and Jönköping have small areas of cultivated land varying from 3.8 per cent to 18 per cent while the forest lands vary from 69.5 per cent to 78.8 per cent of the land-area even today.[3] While some forest land has been added since 1840, the area of cultivated land has been increased as much as four- and five-fold in the last hundred years.[4] These counties were counted among the most densely populated in the first half of the nineteenth century. Especially in Småland in many regions the soil was rocky and not particularly fertile, while the early frost in Värmland and Kopparberg added to the precariousness of an agricultural livelihood. The farms on the average were very small, and the numbers of freeholds large, for the soil did not attract large estates. It is perhaps a natural corollary that these provinces should in the decades following 1840 be among the foremost in emigration.

[1] This land was called *frälse* and *frälseskatte*. *Frälsejordens omfattning* ("Jordstyckningen," *Emigrationsutredningens bilaga XII*, pp. 20* ff.).

[2] Älvsborg County had only 33.8 per cent tax-exempt land, Värmland, 14.6 per cent, Göteborg-Bohus, 16.7 per cent, Jönköping, 38 per cent, Kronoberg, 28.9 per cent, and Kalmar, 26 per cent, while Skaraborg had 38.8 per cent.

[3] Kopparberg County has today 3.8 per cent of its land-area in farms and 71.9 per cent, in forests; Värmland, 11.1 per cent cultivated land and 78.8 per cent in forests; Kronoberg, 11.5 per cent cultivated and 70.9 per cent in forests; Jönköping, 13.2 per cent cultivated with 70.3 per cent forests (*Statistisk årsbok för Sverige, 1927*, p. 85, Table 84).

[4] In Vista härad, Jönköping County, the cultivated land-area has been increased five-fold in the last hundred years, in Tveta härad, six-fold, and also in Aspelund härad, Kalmar County, etc. (Gustav Sundbärg, "Ekonomisk-statistisk beskrifning öfver Sveriges olika landsdelar," *Emigrationsutredningens bilaga VI*, pp. 60–61, 77).

In spite of the expansion of cultivated lands and the rapidly increasing rural population, the ownership of land had become fixed in the hands of about two hundred thousand peasant proprietors and nine thousand nobles and gentry.[1] These figures also included the lessees of land belonging to these two classes of proprietors. There had been practically no increase in the numbers of freeholds since the beginning of the century in spite of the tremendous increase in agrarian population, except in the counties of Malmöhus and Gothenborg-Bohus.[2] In Östergötland County the number of peasant freeholds had decreased by one thousand.[3] Malmöhus County showed an increase from 9,393 peasant proprietors in 1780 to 12,485 in 1840, in spite of the fact that it was a region of large estates. Gothenborg-Bohus County expanded from 8,825 peasant owners at the opening of the century to 9,306 in 1840.[4]

The static condition in land-ownership had been the result of the practice of primogeniture, and the restrictions that had been placed upon the homesteading of freelands in the laws of the eighteenth century. Population tended to concentrate in the older settled communities and brought about a condition of local overpopulation in certain rural regions in Sweden. As population increased there were larger and larger numbers of landless agrarians, many of whom leased land as crofters and cotters. It was this surplus agricultural population that was drained in the first waves of emigration to America.

For centuries it had been customary in Sweden that when the peasant and his wife felt themselves too old to manage the estate, one of the sons or a son-in-law was designated to succeed in possession. The peasant would then retire to a smaller cottage built for him near the old home.[5] He would receive enough of the produce of the

---

[1] Wohlin, "Den jordbruksidkande befolkningen i Sverige, 1751–1900," *Emigrationsutredningens bilaga IX* (Stockholm, 1909), pp. 248 ff. Råtabeller.

[2] *Ibid.*, pp. 184–85, Table C.

[3] Östergötland declined from 10,811 peasant freeholds in 1800 to 9,596 in 1840 (*ibid.*).

[4] There was not a steady increase, but decades of increase and decrease from 1800 to 1840 (*ibid.*).

[5] This reservation was called *undantaget*. There are many of them today in Sweden. In some communities the practice still continues (Wohlin, "Faran af bondeklassens undergräfvande," *Emigrationsutredningens bilaga X* [Stockholm, 1910], pp. 31 ff.)

farm for his support until his death. The coheirs relinquished their shares in the estate, since they were released from the responsibility of caring for the "old folks." Family pride was very strong and it was considered a disgrace to permit the estate to go out of the hands of the family. Many sacrifices were made in order that it might be preserved intact.

Since the peasant's family was usually large, averaging from seven to twelve children, it was necessary for those who did not inherit the estate to find their fortune in other ways. Another custom in rural Sweden was a practice of sending both their sons and daughters when they had been confirmed in the Lutheran church, at the age of fifteen, to work for a neighboring peasant or on an estate of the gentry. It was a sort of apprenticeship, for in this way they were to learn different methods of agriculture and new household arts. Men and women worked alike in the fields. In the hayfields and during the harvest season the women were especially helpful. Dairying and the care of the cows was considered wholly the province of the women. These sons and daughters of the peasants lived as members of the peasant-family where they worked. The surplus labor of the small peasant proprietor's family continued to work for other peasants until they married and became probably tenant farmers. Sometimes they became apprenticed in a craft and continued to ply their trade in the neighborhood or went to one of the towns. The children of the more prosperous peasant returned after their apprenticeship to their father's home and worked for him until the estate was given to one of them. Some may have married and, wishing a home of their own, received a portion of the estate as tenants to the father or the brother. The children still at home when the estate was handed over to the chosen son frequently found it disagreeable to continue to work for a brother and left to hire themselves out to other peasants or in turn to become tenant farmers. Some of the sons of the more prosperous peasants went to study at the universities, to enter the ministry or the professions.

These old Teutonic family customs of the Swedish peasant made his family distinctly patriarchal in its organization. Complete obedience of the members of the family was required by the father. The son and daughter were expected to give their labor for no par-

ticular consideration but that of living in the family. It was frequently difficult for the father to relinquish his position as the head
of the household when the estate had been handed over to the son.

In 1840, Sweden like most of the countries of Europe, except England, was a self-sufficing agricultural country. Its rural districts were
especially isolated from the outside world. The life of the agrarian
people was controlled by the customs and folkways of many centuries of growth. There was much particularism between the different provinces, or "lands," as they were called in Sweden. Each province had its special national costume, and dialects separated the
peoples of one region from another. The speech of the people of the
southern province, Skåne, could hardly be understood by the people
of the neighboring province of Småland. The language as spoken in
the capitol of the country, Stockholm, had become the literary and
official language of the kingdom. There was a wide difference between the spoken language and the language of the scholar, the press,
and the pulpit.

The peasant produced practically everything he needed for his
own use. He raised the grain for his bread. Potatoes since 1800 had become an important part of his diet. He raised the flax and wool that
was spun and woven by the women of the household during the long
winter evenings. Intricate designs inherited from generations past
were woven into linens and embroidered on the provincial costumes
or on hangings for the walls. His piece of woodland furnished him
with lumber for his house, which he usually built himself. The typical peasant home of Sweden was built of wood and always painted
red with white trimmings. It had either a thatched or a tiled roof.
In the southern province of Skåne we find again a touch of Continental Europe in the stuccoed farmhouse covered with thatch. This
province had for centuries belonged to Denmark and became a part
of Sweden only in the seventeenth century. Craelius, who knew contemporary conditions in Sweden in 1774 better than any one of his
age, wrote that nearly every peasant was a carpenter, and made
his agricultural implements such as wagons, carts, wooden plows,
and rakes.[1] Bergerskjold writing in 1784 stated, "They build their
own houses, make their own wagons, and do their own smithing, al-

[1] Tobias Norlind, *Svensk allmogens liv i folksed, folktro och folkdiktningen*, p. 400.

though there is more profit in buying horseshoes and nails. Some can do all the smithing that the household needs."[1] Many intricate designs were carved or gaily painted upon the household furniture and utensils.

Every peasant household had a bakehouse and a brewhouse. The food was always plentiful and open hospitality met the guest. For weeks before the Christmas holidays the women of the household were busy with their baking and brewing. Since it was much cheaper to convert surplus grain and potatoes into whiskey than to attempt to sell it, because of poor transportation facilities, it was customary for every household of all classes to produce liquor.[2] Everyone used whiskey as an appetizer before each meal. It was considered healthful in the cold climate if used with moderation. Servants, both men and women were either given whiskey as a portion of their wages or an extra tip to purchase it.[3] The production of intoxicating liquor had grown rapidly since the beginning of the nineteenth century until drunkenness had become a national curse.

Other important items of the peasant's diet were milk, butter, and cheese produced from his cows by the women of the family. Rye was used for bread for the ordinary daily use, while in the Norrland provinces barley was the more usual grain. Wheat bread was considered a luxury and only appeared on holiday occasions. Porridge made from rye, barley, oats, and often also from potatoes, was a daily part of the diet. Rice pudding or porridge was considered a special luxury to be used only during the Christmas holidays. Fish was common in every household, especially salt herring. Many families purchased fresh herring and salted it themselves. Meat in the ordinary home was more of a luxury. The use of coffee was increasing rapidly in Sweden until it was destined to be practically a necessity in every Swedish household.

Much of the social and religious life of the rural communities centered around the parish church. The state church of Sweden is the Lutheran church. In 1840 everyone was required to pay taxes to the

[1] *Ibid.*

[2] Carl Hallendorff, *Oskar I och Karl XV;* Hildebrand and Stavenow, *Sveriges historia till våra dagar*, XII (Stockholm, 1923) 151. In 1809 a law had been passed permitting home production of whiskey.

[3] The word for "tip" in Swedish is *drickspengar*, meaning "money for liquor."

church and to be a member of the church from the time of his birth until his death. The ministry were all graduates of the two state universities of Uppsala or Lund. The members of the parish church formed the parish council and had the privilege of choosing their parson from the three candidates presented to them by the consistory of the bishopric. The parson in turn became the leader of his flock, their spiritual guide, and their teacher. As he became older he frequently took a patriarchal attitude toward the members of his church. It was he who brought culture to the rural community. Perhaps it was natural that as a highly educated man, he felt a certain superiority to the peasantry and at times became more of a dictator than a sympathizer. However, as early as the middle of the seventeenth century, the rural population in many portions of the country has been taught to read by the clergy. In 1686 a law providing for a more systematic education of the common people was passed. It stated that the clergy should "teach children, hired men, and maids to read in books and to see with their own eyes what God in His Holy Word bids and commands."[1] In the schools that developed in connection with the church, the sacristan taught the children to read, while the minister instructed them in religion. In 1842 the first public elementary-education law was passed in Sweden.[2] It was required by law that every child should be baptized by the parish pastor and should be confirmed at fifteen. Except for those who went on for a higher education, confirmation was an introduction to adult life. Marriage and even engagements were functions of the church. Burial in the consecrated ground around the church was a necessity for future redemption.

State law required regular attendance at church and participation in communion a certain number of times during the year. Most of the people were naturally religious and church-going was usual. In the churchyard before and after the service the people of the rural districts would gather to discuss the news of the past week. Notices of all kinds were posted on the church door, and read from the pulpit. Here one heard of engagements, marriages, and deaths in the parish, of the meetings of the local assembly, of new laws passed by the

---

[1] J. M. Ambrosius, "Folkundervisningen," Guinchard, *op. cit.*, I, 314 (translated).

[2] *The Sweden Year Book, 1926*, p. 52.

Parliament. From time to time the minister would make house-to-house visitations to question his parishioners about their catechism and their religious beliefs. Sometimes he found that certain heresies had crept in among his flock. In the first part of the nineteenth century there were many dissenters, especially in the northern provinces of the kingdom. These dissenters who preferred to interpret their Bible in their own way were often very stubborn and were persecuted by the more conscientious of the state clergy. Other members of the clergy attempted to correlate the dissenting movements with the state church,[1] and saw in the awakening spirituality of the people a higher sense of morality among the masses.

Near the parish church was the large and impressive estate of the minister. It belonged to the state and was used by the clergy during their period of service in the church. There was usually a large manor house surrounded by farmlands and woodlands, for in an agricultural community everyone had to be self-sufficing. The minister of the state church was also a government official. It was his duty to keep the vital statistics of the parish in a church book. He had also to give and receive church letters from all those who left his church or moved into the parish.[2]

Other aristocrats of the parish were the gentry and government officials who were resident. As has been shown there were not manors in all the parishes, but where there were, it was customary to give them all the respect that is due to a man of wealth and official position, especially in an age when wealth was counted in acres rather than in ability. The self-sufficing agricultural age made it necessary to house all the government officials, both civil and military, on estates where they could maintain themselves. These government manors were scattered throughout the kingdom. The gentry and the government officials who were almost exclusively chosen from the nobility during the first half of the nineteenth century usually participated in the social gatherings of the community and often gave dances and festivals at the manor for the country folk. There was, however, always a certain partriarchal attitude on the part of the gentry toward the peasants and the agricultural laboring classes.

[1] A further discussion of the dissenters may be found in chap. vi.

[2] These church letters were called the "parson's recommendation," or *prästbetyg*.

They occupied the best and most prominent pews in the church. They were seated in positions of honor at any gathering. The rural population always removed their hats and bowed to the gentry when they met them on the highway. It was often with embarrassment and confusion that the less-educated peasant or cotter attempted an interview with these superior people of the parish. But frequently the independent spirit and the pride of the country-folk inwardly rebelled against their position of inferiority. There were groups of peasants like those of Dalecarlia who refused to stand in obeisance to the nobility and even insisted on democratic relations with the king himself.

The crystallization of classes had gone even farther in the early nineteenth century. The free peasant was an aristocrat to the landless agrarian. There are many children of crofters and cotters in America who continue to bear a hatred against the overbearing peasants in their home parish. Even between the various classes of peasantry, the size of the peasant's estate decided his social scale.[1] At the weddings and festivals, the peasant with a large estate, usually designated as a *gård*, was placed next to the host and hostess, while the *husman* who owned only a house with a potato-patch was relegated to a seat at the other end of the table. The class differences were particularly closely drawn in marriage matches. It was considered a great misfortune for a wealthy peasant to have his daughter marry the son of a small farmer.

The sacristan, whose duties included the directing of the church choir, playing the organ, and teaching the parish school, was usually a man of some education. In some ways he stood nearer the parishioners than the minister and was always a leader in the various activities of the rural neighborhood. The soldier, who was housed by the parish, was also a person of parts.

Although the gild system attempted to keep a monopoly of the crafts in the towns of Sweden similar to that on the continent, the demand for skilled workmen in the rural districts tended to break down the demands of the gilds even before its organization was abolished in 1846.[2] Near the towns were many artisans who had be-

---

[1] Norlind, *op. cit.*, pp. 394 ff.

[2] *Ibid.*, pp. 400–403.

come masters in the town gild, but who worked at their trade with more or less legal protection in these rural districts. In the more wholly agricultural regions were artisans who practiced without legal sanction. Craelius who disliked the competition between the craftsmen of the urban and rural districts had to acknowledge that in 1770 in every rural community there were several kinds of smiths, carpenters, turners, gunsmiths, shoemakers, tailors, saddle makers, masons, gardeners, tanners, and artisans representing the finer arts, like painters, violin makers, and watchmakers.

These artisans of the parish as a rule owned only their tools, and with those they went to the farms that needed them and lived there until their work was completed. They received food, a place to sleep, and a small sum of money for their work. An estimate of their wages was given in an account by Hälpher of Tuna parish in Medelpad in 1771:

Artisans there are several in the service of the parish of various professions. A shoemaker receives, besides his keep, for a pair of ordinary shoes, one can of barley; a tailor, according to the garment, money or barley counted at from six to seven öre a can. Smiths and carpenters receive a daily wage of two daler, etc.[1]

This wandering life developed certain types of artisans and gave them a distinct prestige which varied with the occupation. The smith was a mechanic and known to be able to invent things that no one else could.[2] He was the "learned" man of the community with much practical knowledge. He was, therefore, highly respected wherever he went. In contrast to the smith was the miller. He was usually wealthy also, for he received a certain percentage of the flour for his services, but he was known for a certain indolence and as a bully. As compared with the intelligence of the smith, the miller was usually stupid and dull. The farmers often doubted his honesty, and therefore he was not liked even though his wealth was respected.[3] In another group were the tailor and the shoemaker. They were usually poor but carefree spirits. Always happy and lively, talkative and resourceful, they were liked and welcomed wherever they went. If they could also play the violin or the clarinet, they became the favorites of the community. Johnsson described them in Östra Göinge in Skåne as follows:

[1] *Ibid.*, pp. 401–2.    [2] *Ibid.*, p. 403.    [3] *Ibid.*, p. 402.

The parish tailor was usually a happy fellow who knew everything that happened in the parish. And when he often accompanied by three or four journeymen came to a farm, there was a change from the monotony of the everyday life, and the household learned what the neighbors were doing. For the master of the scissors was a living encyclopedia who knew everything and could explain everything. The same thing was true of the parish shoemaker. Both were welcome to the farms and often both acted as match-makers for the sons and daughters of the peasants. They were a sort of "petitioner" who in the negotiations of marriage and in many other situations played no minor rôles as arbitrators.[1]

Another welcome visitor to the isolated peasant was the wandering peddler. In certain regions of Sweden where the tiny farms with their sterile soil did not produce enough to support the family, the long winter evenings were spent creating various articles of wood and iron. There were three regions in Sweden which became famous for the sloyd produced by the natives. In the first region which was located in northern Skåne and southwestern Småland, the rural population was known for the production of wooden bowls, baskets, weaver's combs, ladders, and small iron utensils like scythes, knives, etc.[2] In a region which today remains famous for its handicrafts, Dalarne in Kopparberg County, every village had its specialty in earlier days. Among the Mora villages since ancient times, Garsås made casks; Nusnäs, Färnäs, and Noret, bureaus, clocks, and other articles of wood; Våmhus and Bonås, articles of hair and different varieties of baskets and also screens, sieves, and caskets; Gopshus and Oxberg, caskets, weaver's combs, and watches, while other villages specialized in watches and brass combs.[3]

The people of Sjuhäradsbygden of Västergötland became known in early times as peddlers and the name *knalle* has become a nickname for the inhabitants of the region.[4] In a royal letter of March 23, 1620, the inhabitants of this region were given permission to peddle "bells, bowls, spurs, scissors, and other small wares."[5] But in the seventeenth and eighteenth centuries the textile industry completely drove out the other forms of home industry here. At first the handicrafts were carried along with agriculture, but later the crafts-

[1] *Ibid.*

[2] *Ibid.*, p. 403.

[3] *Ibid.*

[4] *Knalla* means in Swedish to "walk leisurely."

[5] Norlind, *op. cit.*, p. 403.

men began to wander from house to house with their tools, and produce the articles called for at the various farms. The women then remained at home and carried on the agriculture as best they could. Later a middleman-system developed which employed workmen and salesmen. This salesman or peddler became a character in rural Sweden, the famous *knalle*.

From the memoirs of a Swedish emigrant came the following interesting picture of the life of the itinerant salesman.[1] Describing his father's life he wrote,

With a pack on his back, my father went to seek his fortune at the age of sixteen, in the wide stretches of the prosperous province of Skåne. In the pack were numerous varieties of iron utensils and in his pocket eighteen riksdaler. If the prosperous peasants of Skåne had hard hearts, then the ditch by the side of the road was soft with grass during the summer nights. If the peasant of Skåne would not open his barn for the wandering tradesman who sought shelter from the cold winter night, the cotter's door was always opened, which was much better. But my father earned money on his iron wares, which was the important thing. Soon his back was replaced by a cart drawn by a decrepit horse. After a few years, a sign was placed along a wall in V. which read, "Wooden wares, delicatessen and divers merchandise."

The peddler when he was welcomed into the home of the rural population brought the news from the outside world. He was especially welcome in the fall when everyone was interested in purchasing new clothes for the Christmas holidays.[2]

Under the system of privileges that had developed in the Middle Ages and which still persisted in 1840, trade and handicraft had been given exclusively to the towns. The peasant had a choice of selling his surplus products either to the merchant gilds or at the marketplace. He usually chose the market which was generally held in or near the towns. Here the peddler would erect his booth and the peasant would sell his grain and his livestock. Some of the markets were not large and usually of short duration, while others developed into fairs and continued for several weeks.[3]

The peasant seldom came to town except on market-day. Besides

[1] "Utvandrarnes egna uppgifter," *Emigrationsutredningens bilaga VII*, p. 236 (translated).

[2] Norlind, *op. cit.*, p. 405.

[3] The two large fairs in Sweden were *fastlagsmarknaden* at Lund, and *distingsmarknaden* in Uppsala (*ibid.*, pp. 406–7).

being a place of exchange of agricultural products for those produced in the town or imported wares, for all exchange was by barter, it was also a place of entertainment. Here he could purchase all the luxuries of the age. There were large family reunions, new acquaintances were made, and young couples came to merry-make. The many refreshment stands offered a great variety of food and drink. There were shows of all kinds, mountebanks, circuses, merry-go-rounds, and fortune-tellers. The young man purchased a psalm book, a catechism, and a handkerchief for his beloved. Much intoxicating liquor was consumed by the merry-makers and fist fights often ensued.

A system of credit had developed which was particularly beneficial for the merchant but demoralizing to the peasant. The peasant would usually trade with a certain merchant in town who would give him whatever he desired on credit.[1] In return the peasant would pay in produce at certain times of the year. No fixed price was set and often they would not balance and liquidate their accounts for years at a time. The merchant could charge the peasant practically what he desired.

There was much competition between the towns and the rural regions at the markets and fairs. The rural handicrafts and the wandering peddlers competed with the merchants and the craftsmen of the town. In turn the towns also owned land outside the town walls. Many of the town officials were paid by the use of land. The town frequently produced much that it needed. The merchants, having received produce in return for their wares, offered them at the markets in competition with the peasants. There was not much profit from the surplus grain produced, while poor and expensive means of transportation meant that grain could not be exported far from where it was produced.

Although the festivities at the markets probably lived as memories through the year, there were many other social activities in the rural district. The young folk delighted in the dances on the green to the sound of the accordion. There were ring games to which they sang folk-songs. Those long, light, mild, wonderful evenings of

[1] Described by Linné in Ångermanland in 1732 and in Gotland 1735 (*ibid.*, pp. 408–9).

the Northland in the summer when it was almost impossible to leave the out-of-doors, afforded much pleasure, and the long winter evenings were filled with visiting from house to house; during weddings, christenings, etc., there was many a barn dance.

Christmas activities were the most important; they really began the first of December and lasted until the first of February.[1] There were no festivities until Lucia day on December 13, considered the shortest day of the year, but they lasted until January 13, or Knut's day. The thirteen days, including Christmas day and on, were holy days when no one did any work. Before Lucia day the threshing had to be finished, and all the purchases and preparation of food and drink for the Christmas holidays. Candles were dipped for the Christmas crown that made the centerpiece for the table, for the three- or five-armed candlestick that was used only at Christmastime, and an especially large and long candle was made to be placed in the window to give light to the people on their way to church at five o'clock Christmas morning.[2]

Lucia day was celebrated primarily in the western provinces. At three or four in the morning the household was awakened by a girl dressed in white bearing a tiara of lighted candles on her head. She carried a tray with coffee, whiskey, and cakes with which one was served in bed. Often the young people of the neighborhood would go from house to house offering these refreshments and singing songs in the early morning hours. Frequently the domestic animals were given an extra good meal that day.

Preparation for Christmas continued until Christmas Eve. Usually at noon an interesting custom, a survival of the Middle Ages, was that of dipping pieces of bread in the pot in which the meats for Christmas had been prepared. This was almost a ceremony and the day is often called "Dippers Day."[3] The rooms were decorated for Christmas with branches of fir. The Christmas tree was not used until the latter half of the nineteenth century, nor were gifts usual.

[1] *Ibid.*, pp. 452 ff.

[2] *Julotta* is a custom that has been transplanted in America by the Swedish immigrants. Their churches are packed to the doors at this early Christmas morning service. Many place candles in their windows as in Sweden.

[3] *Doppare dagen.*

The evening meal always consisted of a specially prepared dried cod fish and rice porridge cooked in milk with other delicacies of the season.[1] The evening was spent in reading Bible texts and singing Christmas hymns. The family retired early, but the Christmas candles burned all night.

Everyone attended early mass in the church on Christmas morning. It was a custom to race the horses home after the service. The day, however, was spent quietly at home. The second day after Christmas the festivities began. There were parties and dances given in all the homes of the neighborhood and the community went from house to house until the celebrations were broken with the rest of New Year's day, only to begin again and last until the thirteenth of January, the big dance on Knut's day. Sometimes on the thirteenth day after Christmas a group of young people would work out a miracle play representing the three wise men and the star of Bethlehem. The little troupe of players went from house to house presenting their play.

Another big festival comparable to the Christmas holidays was Mid-Summer's Day, June 24. This is a "May" festival held on the longest day of the year, the harbinger of summer. The Maypole was raised on the green, a tall mast with a cross-beam on which were hung garlands and wreaths of spring flowers. In the land of the midnight sun there was no darkness on this night; in the region just south of it, one could scarcely detect that the sun ever sets, it was so bright. The dance around the Maypole continued all night. Of the numerous family gatherings, name days were more important than the birthday. Most of the Swedish given names had some special day in the almanac, probably a former saint's day. It was upon the name's day that you received gifts and calls from your friends.

The Swedish peasant had many of the superstitions of the lower class of Europe. There was the old woman who could set bones, and give charms to remove diseases from children. The deep, dark forests gave rise to the belief in "trolls" or wood nymphs, much like the dwarfs who guarded the Rhinegold. The "trolls" figured largely in the folklore and songs. On Christmas Eve, a plate of porridge was

[1] *Lutfisk* is imported to the United States for the Christmas holidays. These customs persist still, both in Sweden and America.

often placed on the floor or outside the door for these brownies. If neglected during the holiday season, they were bound to take revenge was the popular belief.

There were certain obligations that were attached to the owners of the land. The burden of taxation had fallen upon the peasants and the tax on land continued through 1840 to be the most important form of income for the state. About one-third of the land in Sweden was tax-exempt. This land had formerly belonged to the nobility, but the "ordinary tax-free land" was in 1789 open to purchase by anyone and the tax-exemption became attached to the land. It was not until 1892 that all privileges from taxation on land were finally removed. In 1840 much of the land tax, as yet, was paid in produce, for money was scarce in the agricultural communities.[1] An attempt to remove it from the peasants' land as it had been removed from the nobles continued to be considered by many of the Parliaments. Later, in 1859–60, the income tax was introduced to bear some of the burden of taxation formerly placed directly on land, and as time went on the question of the forms of taxation was always a vital problem.[2] As early as 1858, the state derived more income from tariff and liquor revenues than from the land tax.[3]

There were other burdens attached to the soil which were perhaps more onerous than the land tax. One was the system of posting that had been introduced in Sweden. As early as 1280 the first law establishing inns and placing the responsibility on the peasants to furnish horses for travelers was passed in Sweden.[4] Various laws have supplemented the first one. The peasants were required to have horses at the inn a certain number of days a year. If all the horses at the inn were taken by travelers, the peasant was called upon for reserve horses. The peasant or his hired man would hitch his horse to the traveler's carriage or wagon and haul him to the next inn, which was

---

[1] In 1855 the simplification of the land tax was partially accomplished by the specification of certain products from various provinces, different for different portions of the country, that might be received as taxes, while part of the taxes were to be paid in specie (Hallendorff, *op. cit.*, pp. 159–60).

[2] Gustav Cassel, *Utvecklingslinjer i svenska skattelagstiftning, Svensk Politik* (Föreningen Heindals politiska småskrifter), II, No. 4 (Uppsala, 1908), 3 ff.

[3] Hallendorff, *op. cit.*, p. 185.

[4] C. E. Gyllenberg, "Landsväger," in Guinchard, *op. cit.*, II, 599.

about two Swedish or fourteen English miles distant. The charge for this service was regulated by law. In books of travel, one often finds this system of transportation described. The poet Arndt in his *Travels in Sweden* about 1800 described the peasant as slow and stubborn. "If you swore at him and called him 'Devil,' he would not budge, but if you gave an oath of 'a thousand devils' (*Tusende*), then he would get a move on himself." The travelers from countries where the peasant had been intimidated by feudalism did not perhaps understand the independence and pride of the free peasant. Samuel Laing in his *Tour of Sweden in 1838* stated that the

system of posting is evidently oppressive. The rate paid for each horse is one-third of a daler banco, or about 7*d.* sterling for the Swedish mile, equal to seven English. This is one-third less than is paid in Norway for the same distance, but neither can indemnify the husbandman for the loss of a day's work and a man in seed time or harvest.[1]

Most of the peasants found the system of posting very galling in the nineteenth century. The trouble of keeping horses at the inns, the reserve horses for emergencies for travelers, and also the duty of providing livery for the king or government officials, including the army in times of war, were heavy burdens upon the peasant and often took his time and horses away from his agricultural pursuits when most needed. As Samuel Laing stated in his *Travels*, the compensation was very small and the peasant particularly resented the attitude of travelers toward him. Beginning with 1810 provisions were made for making livery a private enterprise for profit. Usually the inn-keeper or a peasant living near the inn took over the business, but when the demand was greater than he could supply, the peasant could be called upon for reserve horses.[2] In the law of 1878, the fee for livery was left to the counties. Where there were no applicants for private enterprise, it remained the duty of the peasants. The burden of supporting a livery system when no private enterprise could handle the situation was placed on the county budget and the taxes were distributed between the property and income.

The laying and maintenance of the highways, as well as the con-

[1] Laing, *Tour in Sweden in 1838* (London, 1839), p. 40.

[2] C. E. Gyllenberg, *op. cit.*

struction and repair of local government buildings, including the church, was a duty of the landowners or the cultivators of the land. In the seventeenth century in some of the southern provinces of Sweden the nobles' estates were exempt.[1] In 1891 this burden was partially removed from the soil and distributed over various sources of local taxes, and road districts were created to maintain the roads.

Prior to the institution of the present compulsory military system in Sweden, it had been the duty of the peasant proprietors to maintain and house the standing army. It was a system introduced by Gustavus Adolphus in the seventeenth century and elaborated in the latter part of the century by Charles XI. Under the last scheme, every two large estates were to maintain a knight.[2] The soldier was to receive a cottage and a small piece of land to raise grain, cabbage, and hay. He was to support himself upon this land during the periods of peace. When he was called into service, the community aided in the sowing of the land and the cultivating of his crops. Samuel Laing mentioned these "soldier's crofts." He wrote,

> The best of these habitations of the lower class are little farmhouses with some land—enough to keep a family in bread, potatoes, and milk—which appear to be a kind of military colonization scattered over the country, each house having a shield affixed with the name of the occupier, his regiment and company. These are not retreats for the worn-out soldiers, the occupiers being fine young men with families.[3]

The regimental officers also had dwellings, but more pretentious with a goodly piece of crownland, varying in splendor and size with the rank of the officer. The seamen of the navy were given crofts near the coast for their families. The cavalry were supplied not only with crofts but also with their horses, by the peasants. The peasant could use the horse under certain restrictions in times of peace, and received compensation for the time it was used by the army. In 1840 there were some 30,551 soldiers and sailors housed on these small farms in various rural communities.[4]

---

[1] *Säterierna* or the highly privileged estates of the nobles were exempt in the provinces of Bohus, Halland, Skåne, Bekinge, in 1658 (Guinchard, *op. cit.*, p. 597).

[2] These estates constitute a district called a *rote*. Norlind, *op. cit.*, pp. 409–10.

[3] Laing, *op. cit.*, pp. 57–58.

[4] Wohlin, "Torpare-, backstugu-och inhysesklasserna," *Emigrationsutredningens bilaga XI* (Stockholm, 1908), p. 47, Table K.

Another burden upon the rural community was the care of the poor. The aged poor were often housed like the soldier on a small patch of ground with a cottage. In some parishes there were poor-houses established as early as 1770, but it was thought too expensive a way of caring for the poor.[1] At times, when there were crop failures and starvation stared large portions of the population in the face, in certain provinces it was customary to grasp the beggar's staff and wander through the more prosperous provinces begging for bread. In a country so dependent upon its agricultural production, and isolated from the outside world because of poor communication, these disasters of crop-failures came only too frequently.

Often the peasant proprietors and their tenants, the crofters, felt that there were too many burdens resting upon the land. We find this sentiment expressed among the emigrants to America. From an emigrant's description of his life in Värmland there came the following complaint about the burden of taxation,

My parents owned a little croft, with very rocky soil. . . . . We had a horse and two cows. This stony croft was assessed ten öre in taxes. Our taxes amounted to 75 kronor or $20 a year. All that we could garner per year from the sterile land was two barrels of rye, five of oats, one-half of barley and five of potatoes. We were four in the family. This poor farm did not give us sufficient income, so that we had to go to the forests in the winter and haul lumber for some corporation. . . . . In Värmland's remote parishes we were required to pay the salaries of the dean and pastor, the sacristan, the organist, the church warden and the soldier, and to maintain 400 feet of road and to help support two or three paupers.[2]

Since prehistoric times, the Swedish peasant had participated in local government, and since the establishment of the Swedish Riksdag in 1435, the peasants formed the Fourth Estate until the reform into a bicameral system in 1866.[3] In the local communities there was already established at the dawn of history self-government on the part of the peasant in the village, the hundred, and the province in the form of meetings and representative assemblies. This local self-government has continued down to the present day. Thus

[1] Norlind, op. cit., pp. 388–89.

[2] Emigrated in 1881, letters from Swedes in America ("Utvandrarnes egna uppgifter," op. cit., p. 178, No. 206).

[3] Sam Clason, op. cit., pp. 48 ff.; Gustav A. Aldén, Svensk kommunalkunskap (Stockholm, 1926), p. 7.

we find the Swedish peasant of 1840 participating in the village and parish meetings, making laws for the community concerning prices, against luxury, petitioning the king for more stringent criminal laws, and holding numerous elections. There were parsons to be elected, tax assessors and jurors, and permissions to be given to craftsmen to perform their trade in the community. Provisions had to be made concerning the maintenance of roads, the livery of travelers, the provisions for the maintenance of the army, and erection of local buildings.

There were also the county councils (*landsting*) in which the various estates were represented. Here were decided all matters pertaining to the county. Then finally the Fourth Estate of the Riksdag played no mean part in the Parliament of its day. The other three estates, the nobles, the clergy, and the burghers had been during the eighteenth century more influential than the peasants, for many of the peasants were less educated and more provincial than the others. But there was a marked difference in the representatives in the Fourth Estate in 1850. From "simple, stubborn souls" they had developed into men with statesmenlike ability and daring. Per Sahlström, an able member of the House of Peasantry, in his farewell letter to his constituents in 1858 complained of the lack of respect shown toward the Fourth Estate in the last Riksdag and its lack of influence, which was demonstrated in the handling of bills, and advised,

It is absolutely necessary that a delegate [to the House of Peasants], besides being honest and a good friendly fellow, must also be intelligent, have a clear insight into the position and needs of the common people and the Fourth Estate, and be able to work for that purpose, and also possess self-confidence both in thought and in the manner in which he handles bills. He must be clever enough to withstand the temptations and hampering influences that are always met with in the Riksdag. Only through such representation can respect for the Fourth Estate be obtained.[1]

Before the development of industrialism in Sweden, the peasant class represented the common people and democracy. It was destined to play a very important part in Swedish politics in the latter part of the nineteenth century, when, after the reforms of 1866, it obtained the majority of the Second Chamber and became the opposi-

[1] Hallendorff, *op. cit.*, p. 180.

tion party to the Conservatives whose stronghold was in the First Chamber. In this reform of 1866, the clergy and the nobles lost their political ascendancy and were merged with the other classes. The high property qualifications of the new franchise kept political control in the hands of the landed classes until 1911. It even deprived some of the smaller peasants who had participated in the choosing of the delegates for the House of Peasants of the right to vote, while it enfranchised others of the propertied class who had not fitted into the old scheme of estates. About three-fourths of the Swedish people were deprived of the right to vote in Parliamentary elections until the establishment of universal manhood suffrage in 1911.[1]

Many of the emigrants that left Sweden and came to America in the last hundred years came from the peasant class. Some were owners of small farms who sold their estates and emigrated to find better economic conditions. Others lost their land through bankruptcy in periods of land speculation, crop failures, or agricultural crises. But the largest number of emigrants from the peasant class were sons and daughters who were not to inherit the family estate and had to find other means of support. Some came to earn, in a better labor market, the means of paying off the mortgages that had accumulated on the family estate. The following are typical examples of such emigration. The size of the farm was usually described by the number of cows and horses that it could support. Thus an emigrant from Kalmar County was the son of a peasant freeholder whose farm supported six to seven cows and two horses.[2] Another from Skaraborg County was the son of a peasant whose small farm of one-sixteenth of a *mantal*, or about eight acres, maintained six cows, a pair of oxen, and a horse.[3] An emigrant from Värmland County was the son of a peasant, but his father was dead and his brother had taken over the small estate which fed only three cows.[4] One of the most illustrious of the Swedish immigrants in the United States was Hans Mattson, former secretary of state of Minnesota, and a consul-general of the United States to India. He was the son

---

[1] *Emigrationsutredningens betänkande*, pp. 836–37.

[2] "Utvandrarnes egna uppgifter," *op. cit.*, pp. 45–46. O emigrated in 1907.

[3] *Ibid.*, p. 74. F emigrated in 1907.

[4] *Ibid.*, p. 70. D emigrated in 1907.

of a peasant who purchased a large farm at Önnestad in the province of Skåne.[1]

An immigrant in South Dakota, who left Sweden in 1871, pictured his father's home in Sweden, "I was born in 1853 on a peasant estate in Härjedalen in Jämtland province and educated like the sons of other peasants." The estate with its uncultivated land contained 4,000 acres. Only five acres were cultivated, the remainder lay in natural meadow and forest land. At the age of eighteen he followed his older brother, who in 1867 had immigrated to Minnesota. It was due to the influence of his mother, who had always expressed the wish that her child should leave the poor soil and frozen harvests of Härjedalen and escape the drudgery of toil in swamp and forest. The wealth of the peasants in this region consisted of the extensive forest lands which were held in common. Much of the timberlands had been sold to lumbering corporations in 1857 for a "song," "I did not appreciate the wealth that lay in father's forestlands," wrote the immigrant. In 1878 and 1879 it was necessary to divide the lands, for the corporation wished to exploit the shares that it had purchased. The cost of the survey and division was very high and forced many of the peasants to sell. His father sold all except enough to keep himself during his old age. About one-fifth of the home parish emigrated to America, peasants and crofters.[2]

It may be fair to estimate that the majority of the Swedish immigrants in America are from this free peasant class. From the very earliest exodus of the Jansonites and the dissenters of Norrland to the emigration of the present day, it has been noticeable to what extent the children of the peasants have left their fatherland. The number of peasant-estates has remained practically stationary for over a hundred years, and therefore the younger sons and daughters have to a large extent sought their fortunes in the new world. Some found an outlet in the growing commercialism and industrialism of the Swedish cities. The free peasant class was the largest of all classes in Sweden, and for this reason alone, where land holdings had become fixed, it would send large numbers into regions where virgin land was obtainable as a gift.

[1] Hans Mattson, *Reminiscenses* (Minneapolis, 1890), pp. 1–13. Hans Mattson was one of the early emigrants, 1850.

[2] *Utvandranas egna uppgifter*, pp. 161–63.

SWEDEN IN 1840 75

The period when emigration to the United States begins from Sweden, 1840–70, was not a time of great economic distress in the latter country but one of the most prosperous in Swedish agricultural history. Every effort had been made since 1750 to improve Swedish agriculture and to increase the crop-yield. During the latter part of the eighteenth century Carl von Linnéas, the great botanist, and J. C. Wallerius, the first agricultural chemist in Sweden, had experimented and written extensively.[1] It had been the purpose of the mercantile statesmen of the period to increase raw materials for manufactured products. With the loss of Finland in 1809 came the full realization of the need for added output in agriculture for consumptive purposes. The first increase in 1814 with the breaking of new lands for cultivation was followed by the economic slump that succeeded the Napoleonic wars. By the forties and the fifties, agriculture had been placed on a profitable basis and Sweden became an exporting country instead of being dependent on other countries for grain. The breaking of new land and the draining of marshes had tripled the area of cultivated land between 1750 and 1850.[2]

Efforts were successful in improving the stock of domestic animals in Sweden at the same time. About 1830, Alexis Norling, who had studied agriculture and animal culture in England, led the movement to introduce foreign stock, particularly English, into Sweden.[3] In 1844 the government became interested in the efforts to improve domestic stock.[4] The domestic horse proved to be too small and weak for deep cultivation and in the fifties, efforts were made to produce a horse better fitted for improved methods of agriculture. In 1853 an attempt was made to increase the production of cattle and hogs for exportation to Denmark and England.[5]

Agricultural schools and agricultural societies were the means of experimenting with agricultural methods and disseminating information among the cultivators of the soil. One of the first agricultural schools was established by the famous Swedish economist,

[1] H. Juhlin Dannfelt, "Lanthushållning," in Guinchard, op. cit., II, 29.

[2] Emigrationsutredningens betänkande, p. 91, Table 21.

[3] H. Funkquist, "Husdjurskötsel," in Guinchard, op. cit., II, 74–75. Emigrationsutredningens betänkande, op. cit., p. 119.

[4] Emigrationsutredningens betänkande, p. 133.

[5] Ibid., pp. 144–45.

Jonas Alströmer, on his estate in Västergötland province in 1748.[1] It was almost a century before another school was opened by Edward Nonnen at Degeberg on Lake Vänern in 1834. It received subsidies from the government and had as many as two hundred students before it closed in 1853. The first agricultural school established by the state was on the estate "Orup" in Skåne under the leadership of Professor Johan Rabbin in 1840. Attempts to maintain chairs of agriculture at the state universities had failed in the eighteenth century. With the organization of the Agricultural Academy in Stockholm in 1810, a new interest in the development of higher education in agriculture became manifest. The first state agricultural college was opened at Ultuna near Uppsala in 1848, and another at Alnarp near Lund in 1862.[2]

The local agricultural societies perhaps came nearer to the cultivator of the soil than the schools and were developed earlier.[3] The first one was established in Gotland, a continuation of the Economic Society formed in 1791. From 1803 to 1812, seven provinces formed these agricultural societies. Soon after the public recognition of agriculture by the establishment of the Agricultural Academy in 1810, for the dispersion of agricultural knowledge, all of the local communities in Sweden had agricultural societies.[4] These societies gave annual reports to the governors of the counties and at present are closely associated with the Department of Agriculture, which was organized in 1890. The agricultural societies tried to awaken an interest in improvements and in methods by discussions and lectures as well as by demonstration of blooded animals and agricultural machinery. A rotation of crops was substituted for the three-field system. A new type of plow introduced from England became common in the forties. The first national agricultural meeting was held in 1846.[5]

[1] L. Holmström, "Lantbruksundervisning," in Guinchard, *op. cit.*, II, 116–17.

[2] *Emigrationsutredningens betänkande*, p. 133.

[3] The government relies on the reports of these agricultural societies (*hushållningssällskapen*) for much of its information about the rural conditions.

[4] W. Heyman, "*Hushållningssällskapen,*" in Guinchard, *op. cit.*, II, 132; *Emigrationsutredningens betänkande*, p. 94.

[5] *Emigrationsutredningens betänkande*, pp. 132–33; Nils Hansson, *Lantmannaföreningen;* Guinchard, *op. cit.*, II, 145; Hallendorff, *op. cit.*, p. 189.

The establishment of agricultural credit aided in promoting agriculture during the same period. The depreciation of currency which had been the result of the war with Russia was solved by stabilizing in 1834. There was an increase in loanable capital and this capital was made more available to agriculture by the establishment of mortgage associations in the southern province of Skane and other provinces in the thirties and forties.[1] In 1848 the corporation law was passed.[2] Another aid was the establishment of free trade in England which followed the repeal of all duties on imports and exports in Sweden during the fifties.

Fishing in Sweden was not as important an industry as in Norway and was often a by-product of agriculture. The skerry peasants located on the numerous islands that dot the broken rock-bound western coast and eastern harbor of Stockholm spent most of their time fishing. There were fishermen also in the southern counties, especially in Blekinge and Halland. The two counties of Halland and Gothenburg-Bohus had the largest amount of salt-sea fisheries. After the return of the herring to these shores in 1877, fishing became very profitable here. The many streams of Sweden and some of the inland lakes furnish salmon. In 1840 there were some 3,366 fishermen's families with their small farms.[3] In the county of Gothenburg-Bohus, fishing had risen in importance to the extent that the number of fishermen had doubled between 1750 and 1840.[4]

There were some emigrants also from the fishermen class. An emigrant from a typical fisherman's family in Blekinge County related how he aided his father in fishing until he was twenty-three. Neither he nor his brothers received any definite wage from their father for their labor. Later he began to fish for his own profit, using his father's nets and equipment for which he paid with a part of his catch. In the spring he fished for salmon and in the summer and fall for the small Baltic herring called *stromming*. His annual earnings

[1] These were called *hypoteksföreningar* (*Emigrationsutredningens betänkande*, p. 118; Hallendorff, *op. cit.*, p. 189).

[2] Corporations are called *aktiebolag* (*Emigrationsutredningens betänkande*, p. 135).

[3] *Ibid.*, pp. 130, 365–66, 756–59.

[4] In 1750 there were 807 fishermen in Gothenburg-Bohus County and by 1840 it had risen to 1,534. There had been a slight decrease since 1830 when there were 1,882 (Wohlin, "Den jordbruksidkande befolkningen i Sverige, 1751–1900," *op. cit.*, p. 104).

gave him a profit of about $250 a year. After his marriage, and after his father's death, he rented his mother's boat and continued to fish with nets that he had partially inherited and partially purchased. Later he became a part-owner of a two-mast boat that plied between Sweden, Denmark, and Germany.[1] In the family of another emigrant from Northern Sweden, fishing was one of the several by-products of the family. Both his father and grandfather had combined fishing with blacksmithing. At the age of fifteen he was apprenticed to his father, a smith, but the business declined and was finally shut down after six years. Then they combined fishing with agriculture, having rented a small piece of land.[2]

The middle of the nineteenth century marked the beginning of a period of prosperity in the lumbering industry in Sweden. It was during the forties that the large purchases of forest land by the Dickson family began in Värmland, Dalsland, and Norrland.[3] In 1851 the English tariff on wood products was reduced and this opened a lucrative market for Swedish lumber. During the same year the first steam saw was erected at Vivsta in Medelpad and a second one at Kramfors in Ångermanland in 1852. The export of planks and boards amounted to 200,000 dozen in 1821, but by 1860 it had risen to 500,000. Many of the peasants of Northern Sweden found an added income in cutting and hauling lumber in the winter season, and floating it in the summer. On the other hand, the peasants of Värmland and Norrland did not appreciate the value of their forest lands. The small sums of money offered by the lumbering corporation either for the right of cutting timber or the outright purchase of the land seemed a fortune to these peasants whose sparse agricultural economy offered them very small money-surplus during the year. But in time it was to ruin and decimate the peasantry here.

In the eighteenth century Sweden had been the world's greatest exporter of iron ore, one-third of the world supply. This iron came from the central mining region of the "Bergslag." Attempts to produce ore from the iron mines of Norrland by the middle of the nineteenth century had been only experimental. Competition with England had become quite keen and almost disastrous to the Swedish

[1] "Utvandrarnas egna uppgifter," *op. cit.*, p. 51.

[2] *Ibid.*, p. 184.

[3] Hallendorff, *op. cit.*, pp. 189–90.

mining industry which had no domestic supply of coal to draw upon. During the seventeenth century Värmland became noted as a region of iron mines and foundries. Monopolies had been given to various of the gentry to establish estates in the "Bergslag" region in the early days in order to encourage the production of iron. These estates were called *bruk* and the owner was a *brukspatron*. The estates combined agriculture, lumbering, mining, and the production of various iron products. The land was leased in small portions to crofters and cotters who in return for the land hauled ore or burned charcoal for the foundry. Many of the neighboring peasants also aided in this work. The mining estates had large concessions of forest lands for a charcoal supply. Near the mines were the mining villages. Although the mining population was only about 50,000 and was small compared with the numbers engaged in agriculture, mining was one of the most important industries of the country and ore the largest export.

Mr. Laing described the mining region of Sweden in 1838 in his travels.[1] He pictured the region in and about Arboga in the county of Västmanland. He wrote,

I proceeded to this town [Arboga] of about 3,000 inhabitants and apparently a good deal of business. The road and streets were crowded with carts carrying iron to the town. It is near the canal which unites the Hielmare and Malare lakes, and is an entrepôt for the iron to be shipped to Stockholm. In all these little towns the most considerable houses are those inhabited by the functionaries under the government and clergy. Private people of fortune, noblemen or gentlemen not in trade or public office, do not reside in the town. The mansion-houses of the gentry, which I have seen from the road, are large and apparently connected with large farms in the hands of the proprietors, the farm offices, and plowed land being close around the main dwelling and generally an iron foundry close to it.

In the nooks and corners of these spits of stones, the peasantry of the country —those who are small proprietors or who are renters of small patches for payment of work—seem to be principally located, and often in hamlets of several families. If their habitations and appearance give a good ground for opinion, this class in this part of Sweden is going backwards in well-being and comfort. Their houses, outhouses, fences and gardens are very generally out of order and repair, and no renovations are going on.

This seemed to indicate that the mining industry at this time was not as prosperous as it had been.

[1] Laing, *op. cit.*, pp. 41–42. Written from Arboga, June, 1838.

Only 10 per cent of Sweden's inhabitants lived in cities in 1850.[1] There were only five cities of 10,000 inhabitants and fourteen over 5,000. Stockholm had a population of 93,000, Gothenburg, 26,000, Malmö, 13,000, and Norrköping, 16,000.[2] However, the Estate of Burgesses in the Riksdag was equal in power with the Estate of Peasants. The merchants and master craftsmen controlled the towns. The gild system was not abolished until 1846.[3] At the same time all restrictions on trade and labor were removed. The cities were already beginning to show a larger percentage of increase than the rural districts.

Some large-scale industry had been introduced into Sweden in the eighteenth century. The region around Borås had become the center of textile manufactures of both wool and cotton. The manufacturing of tobacco products and the refining of sugar were both flourishing industries in the latter part of the eighteenth century. The production of various iron implements, ammunition, and cannons had long been established. The mercantile policy of the eighteenth century, with its efforts to make the country self-sufficient, fostered and protected every form of manufacturing, even to the production of silk. Most of these products served only the home market.

The middle of the nineteenth century indicated signs of a changing industry in Sweden with the introduction of industrialism and large-scale industry. There was not much increase in the number of factories between 1834 and 1860, but the industrial laborers rose from 14,479 to 30,757.[4] The value of the manufactured products during the former year was $4,500,000 and in the latter $18,000,000, an increase of 400 per cent. During the same period there were equally as large and even larger increases in the production of cotton yarn, cotton cloth, the refining of sugar, and of machinery. In 1840 several of the larger machine shops, Kockums, Bolinder Brothers, and those at Trollhättan were established. The beginning of noted Swedish industry, the safety match, dates from the fifties, when a factory was erected at Jönköping. Breweries were first established in the fifties.

---

[1] Hallendorff, op. cit., p. 193.
[2] Statistisk årsbok för Sverige, 1927, p. 8, Table 10.
[3] Emigrationsutredningens betänkande, p. 128.
[4] Hallendorff, op. cit., p. 190.

The most conspicuous phenomenon of growing industrialism was the three-fold increase of imported coal between 1851 and 1859.

The handmaiden of industrial prosperity is commerce. It was during this same period, the middle of the nineteenth century, that Sweden released her commerce from all the restrictions of the old mercantile policy and entered on a career of free trade. Commercial treaties were made with many countries, even China, Hawaii, and Persia. Denmark's discontinuance of the Öresund tolls which had for centuries hampered Baltic trade was a great aid to the growing Swedish commerce. Exports and imports in the thirties had amounted to only $11,000,000, during the first half of the forties, $16.000,-000, but by the end of the fifties, $43,000,000.[1] The exports were primarily raw materials, while the growth of imports of cotton-yarn and cloth, skins and furs, oils, and coffee was noticeable. The increasing prosperity of Sweden during the forties and fifties is reflected in the increased importation of a luxury, coffee, which grew from 3.3 million pounds in the thirties to 5.8 million pounds in the forties, and to 14.3 million at the end of the fifties. The government's income from tariff rose from $960,000 to $3,000,000 in spite of the decreasing duties.

With a growing industrialism, banking and insurance grew in significance. We have noted the development of mortgage banks for the aid of agriculture. Private banks had been permitted since 1824, but there were only eight in 1850. These banks could issue paper money. The corporation banks, made legal by a law of 1851, were not given the privilege of issuing bank notes. It was not until 1856 that a private bank was permitted to compete with the National Bank of Sweden in Stockholm. It was given more freedom in handling commercial loans than the Riksbank and instituted the checking system. The first large insurance company, Skandia, was organized in 1855.[2]

The decade of the fifties found the beginning of the means of modern communication and transportation. By 1859 the state railroads had been completed between Gothenburg–Töreboda and

---

[1] In the thirties exports and imports amounted to 42 million, in the forties 60.5 million, and at the end of the fifties to 162 million riksdaler riksmynt (*ibid.*, p. 191).

[2] *Ibid.*, pp. 191–93.

Malmö-Sösdala. There were short stretches of private railroads, especially in the mining regions. Gas street lights were introduced in Gothenburg in 1846 and in Stockholm in 1853.

The period when immigration to the United States began from Sweden in the last century, between 1840 and 1870, was not a period of great economic distress, but a period of agricultural prosperity. The increase in population had to a great extent been an unproportioned increase in the landless agricultural classes and there was undoubtedly economic distress among these classes, especially at times of poor crops and famine, like the famine years of 1867–69. But at the same time the increase of cultivated lands was greater than the increase in population and in spite of the uneven distribution of this land, which remained largely in the ownership of the peasants and the gentry, the general prosperity of the country increased. A comparison of the prosperity of the country may be derived from the following table compiled by the census department.[1]

|  | 1805 Per Cent | 1840 Per Cent |
|---|---|---|
| Those owning more than needed for income | 2.96 | 9.35 |
| Those owning enough for income | 25.74 | 62.74 |
| Those owning only a part needed for income | 54.81 | 22.28 |
| Those entirely supported by others | 16.49 | 5.63 |

The various improvements in agriculture were beginning to bear fruit. The free-trade policy of England with the repeal of the Corn laws, beginning in 1846 and continuing into the fifties, opened a market to the Swedish grain and lumber. The price of grain rose in Sweden and with the introduction of more extensive cultivation, Sweden for the first time became an exporter of grain.[2] Between 1830 and 1840 the average price of wheat and rye in the whole kingdom was $1.06 and 77 cents per bushel.[3] From 1851 to 1855 the price

[1] *Emigrationsutredningens betänkande*, pp. 131–32.

[2] Sweden exported grain from 1840 to 1880.

    1840–50 exported  197,000 deciton of grain
    1851–60 exported  609,000 deciton of grain
    1861–70 exported  856,000 deciton of grain
    1871–80 exported  1,170,000 deciton of grain
    1881–90 imported  461,000 deciton of grain

[3] In 1830–40 wheat was 11 kronor and rye 8 kronor per hektoliter, while in 1851–55 the price had risen to 13.77 and 10.11 kronor, respectively (Hallendorff, *op. cit.*, p. 159; Statistiska Centralbyrån, *Statistisk årsbok för Sverige, 1927*, p. 92, Table 89).

was, respectively, $1.26 and 94 cents and continued to rise until 1875, with the exception of a slight slump during the five years from 1861 to 1865. Wages were simultaneously rising. Sweden had lost her position of economic isolation and had entered into world commerce. Simultaneous with the growing prosperity of the country came a rising standard of living on the part of the common people. It was demonstrated in the increase of certain articles of consumption which in the past had been considered luxuries, like wheat, potatoes, and coffee.[1] The use of whiskey was decreasing due to a strong prohibition movement, and the repeal of the home-brew law in 1855. The governors' reports of the middle of the century observe this increase of well-being among the lower classes. The governor of the county of Halland in 1855 wrote,

The last year's crops, as well as the rising prices for agricultural products, have caused an increase in prosperity. This economic betterment has developed a desire for luxuries, especially in clothing, so that it is seldom that either men or women now wear homespun clothing on Sunday. With prosperity and more comfortable homes comes a higher standard of morality and less crime.[2]

[1] *Emigrationsutredningens betänkande*, p. 144.

[2] *K. bfhde femårsberättelser, Hallands län, 1851–1855*, pp. 4–5.

# CHAPTER IV

## THE LANDLESS AGRARIANS

The monopoly of the land by the two classes, the gentry and the peasants, during the first half of the nineteenth century produced an increasing landless class as population rapidly multiplied. Since about eight-tenths of the people of Sweden lived in the rural districts it meant the development of an agrarian proletariate. This group of farm tenants and agricultural laborers increased five-fold in numbers between 1750 and 1860, and then began to decline. The superior economic opportunities of the new world had a special appeal to those who lacked opportunities in their native land, and large numbers emigrated. Released from the old social and economic bonds of the Swedish commune, many through hard labor and ability have found economic prosperity in a new land where economic opportunity depended not on birth and inheritance but on native ability.

The rural landless groups may be divided into several categories. The tenant class, who paid for their land in days of labor, consisted of two groups depending on the size of the land that was leased. The crofters had rather large pieces of land and therefore were required to give more labor in payment, varying from three to six days a week.[1] It was not necessary that the crofter perform this labor in person, for he might send a hired man; in some of the contracts the wife was required to give a certain number of days of labor on the estate to which the croft belonged. The smaller leases, usually a cottage with a potato patch, were paid for in just a few days of labor per year, thus leaving the lessee free to find labor with other farmers in the neighborhood. Besides the able-bodied cotter who was otherwise employed as an agricultural laborer, as fisherman, or in the handicrafts, and sometimes in lumbering and mining, it was customary to house the parish poor in cottages, and also the soldiers

---

[1] The word "croft" has been used to designate the Swedish word *torp*.

who were quartered on the community.[1] The leases lasted from a few years to a hundred years, and it was frequently true that the croft or the cottage was inherited as a tenancy by the heirs of the crofter or cotter.

There was also the large group of agricultural laborers who had no land and were housed by the proprietor of the farm or estate. The young unmarried men and women were usually employed by a contract for the year, or for the summer season. An old custom in Sweden was to permit certain individuals to live in the household indefinitely without any contract, with the duty to assist in the household and farm chores without any definite wage.[2] They were much like the clients of the Roman household, or the companions of the old Viking chiefs. The custom was on the decline in the early nineteenth century, but they were still numerous enough to be counted as a class.

About 1830, when agriculture was becoming profitable in Sweden, landowners began to cultivate grain on an extensive scale and found it convenient to withdraw the crofts and cottages from the tenants that the fields might be larger and under one management. It was an auspicious time to make the change, for the transition from communal ownership by the village to individual ownership of a contiguous farm was being made. A laborer whose time was entirely at the disposal of the farmer and whose method of labor might be directed to the best advantage by the manager was more desirable. So many married laborers were employed on annual contracts and were housed in barracks or tenements containing several families. Less often this married laborer was given a patch of land to cultivate for himself and was called a *stattorpare*, while the others were designated as *statare*.

The croft and the cottage were old forms of tenantry in Sweden. Since there had always been large stretches of free land, and land owned by villages or the crown, which was still virgin, the establishment of crofts and cottages had been a means of bringing more land under cultivation. This had always been encouraged except with

---

[1] The cotter was called in Swedish *backstugusittare*, while the soldier's croft was called *soldat torp*.

[2] This class was called *inhyseshjon*.

certain restrictions on the peasant's farms to prevent too great a disintegration. A second purpose for the erection of these tenant farms was to provide a permanent supply of labor for the mother farm or estate, and these crofts were formed sometimes on lands already under cultivation.

Considering first the croft as a means of increasing cultivated land, it appeared as the earlier development and had almost ceased in the more populous regions of Sweden by the beginning of the nineteenth century, although it continued in Norrland. The allodial right to land had been established since primitive times by clearing a patch of land from the forest and placing it under cultivation. The forest lands belonged to the crown, the province, the hundred, or the village in the earlier days.[1] Gradually the timber owned by the province was claimed by the crown. Most of the crownlands were in the less populated regions of Norrland, although some of the lands are scattered through all the counties. The crown parks were more extensive in the southern counties which once belonged to Denmark. When the new farms developed in the forests of the crown or on the common lands of the province and the hundred, they were designated in the seventeenth century as crofts or "new settlements."[2] After a number of years these crofts were taxed by the crown and the pioneer became the legal owner of the land, but frequently the name of croft clung to the new farm. Thus there were mountain crofts in the lower northern counties of Värmland, Örebro, Västmanland, and Kopparberg.[3] The taxed crofts or allodial crofts of the northern counties of Västmanland and Jämtland were owned by the peasants whose legal rights were established by the Royal Ordinance of 1767.[4]

The necessity of protecting the forests from wanton destruction in the seventeenth and eighteenth centuries restricted the possibilities of establishing new freeholds. The practice of burning small clearings, planting grain in the ashes for two or three years, and then

---

[1] See footnote on p. 47.

[2] This type of croft was designated as *torp* or *nybyggen*.

[3] The mountain croft was called *bergstorp* (Wohlin, "Torpare-, backstugu-och inhysesklasserna," *Emigrationsutredningens bilaga XI*, p. 7).

[4] Taxed crofts were called *skattetorp*, and the allodial croft, *odaltorp*.

abandoning the place for a new clearing made these laws very vital for the future forests.[1] It was a primitive method of clearing forests that at one time or other was used all over Europe. The Forest Ordinances of 1647 and 1664 provided that all estates, crofts, and cottages on the common lands[2] should be placed on record and that the crofts equal to a whole, a half, or a fourth of a "farm"[3] should be permitted to remain, but all the crofts or cottages which did not have fields and meadows equal in size and fertility to at least one-fourth of a "farm" should be condemned, razed, and be permitted to return to wilderness, unless they had existed since ancient times.[4] No croft or cottage could be erected thereafter on the common lands of the province, the hundred, or the parish without the permission of the local assemblies and the governor of the province.[5] The code of 1734 continued the protection of the forest lands by restating that only the taxed crofts and those legally separated from the common lands should be permitted to exist and all others were to be razed. No new crofts were to be formed, with the exception of those for the soldiers, boatmen, and for the government forest personnel.[6] The decline of the pioneer or "new-builder" is shown in the statistics of 1780 when there were only 4,023 as compared with the 41,308 crofters of the tenant class. In the extreme north in the Lappmark region the word croft continued in the nineteenth century to be used for the new freehold.

When a clearing was made upon the lands of an individual or on the commons of the village, it was more difficult to determine the legal rights of the squatter. Often the "new-builder" was a younger heir breaking land on his father's estate and thereby receiving his inheritance. Crofts of this type were established on the tax-free lands of the nobility as well as on the taxed lands of the peasant.

In the Forest Ordinances of 1647 and 1664,[7] the land owner was

[1] This practice was called *svedje* (Norlind, *Svenska allmogens liv*, pp. 55 ff., 103 ff.).

[2] *Gårdar, torp och backstufvor på allmänningar.*

[3] *Hemman* is a definite unit for a peasant's estate and here translated as farm.

[4] Articles 2, 3, and 8 of the Ordinances (Wohlin, "Torpare-, backstugu-och inhyses-klasserna," *op. cit.*, p. 8).

[5] *Undersökning vid laga ting och därefter meddelad resolution af landshöfdingen.*

[6] Wohlin, *op. cit.*      [7] Ordinance Articles 11, 17, 18 (*ibid.*, p. 10).

given the right to establish crofts on his distant village lands to a certain extent. A nobleman,[1] who had separated his estate from his neighbors and from the common lands, was given the right to build new farms and crofts as much as he needed. The taxed peasant had the same rights on his individual possessions, so that "when the estate is large enough he may clear land for fields, meadows, pasture, build crofts and improve the productivity of his farm," and the taxation was to be increased correspondingly.[2] Only on the crofts that were built on the undivided lands of the village were there provisions that if the owners in the village did not unanimously consent the case might be brought before the local court, in which case the croft would probably be condemned and razed if there could be no agreement between the possessor and the village. Most of these crofts were established on the unbroken soil and not upon land already under cultivation. The Forest Ordinance of 1734 permitted the rights of the nobles to remain as before, while a taxed peasant might establish crofts, cottages, and fences on his divided or undivided lands if it would improve and not harm his farm.[3]

The Royal Ordinance of 1652 made provisions for the taxation of crofts that were established on the lands belonging to the peasants. Either the peasant's estate as a whole was given a higher tax-rate because of the additional improvement, or the croft was separated entirely from the estate and taxed as a freehold. The noble's lands were not taxed, but he might be required to do the various services that were attached to his privileges, like military service, and so forth.[4]

The croft as a form of land tenantry appeared first on the estates of the nobles and on the royal estates, and was exempt from taxation. Originally any freeholder had the right to establish crofts of this type on his cultivated lands, but the Royal Ordinance of 1686 had forbidden the peasants the right and made it a privilege only of the crown and the nobles.[5] There had been a large increase in crofts by the military ordinances of Charles XI in the later seventeenth cen-

[1] *Frälseman* is translated as noble.

[2] Wohlin, "Torpare-, backstugu-och inhysesklasserna," *op. cit.*, p. 10.

[3] *Ibid.*, p. 11 (*allmänna lagens byggningabalk*, chap. 10, par. 4).

[4] *Ibid.*, p. 10.        [5] *Ibid.*, p. 12.

tury, when it was introduced as a means of housing the families of the army and navy in the local communities.[1] As a system of tenantry it was encouraged in the beginning of the following century, for the crown and the gentry. In the privileges of the clergy in 1723, the croft was permitted on the estates of the church.[2] The Housing Ordinances of 1730 and 1739 encouraged the development of crofts on certain crownlands. The crownlands were leased to peasants and often the larger estates to members of the nobility or gentry.[3] The crofts were to furnish permanent labor for these lessees.

The scarcity of agricultural labor for the peasant proprietors in the early eighteenth century brought forth many petitions in the House of Peasants in the Riksdag and the passage of the restrictive emigration laws. But in order to attract labor to remain in Sweden, it was also necessary to give them better opportunities. And so it was stated in the petition of 1747 that

it is a well known fact that our dear country is suffering from the lack of laborers, to the great damage of the kingdom as well as to the detriment of agriculture, which cannot be raised to a productive status under the circumstances. There are many regions in the land where many people might have a comfortable income which are lying entirely barren. The reason for this may be found in the laws concerning servants. There are many grown children of the peasants who are not permitted [by law] to remain with their parents on the old estate where they were raised and cannot find any means of making their livelihood in this country, and are forced to find food in foreign and far distant lands. The many Swedes living in foreign lands are a proof thereof.[4]

The report of the first census of Sweden in 1750 and the statistical facts of depopulation presented by this report inspired the Riksdag to do everything in its power to increase population. Among the bills laid before the Riksdag of 1751–52 were a bill to simplify the marriage law, a bill permitting the erection of crofts,

---

[1] This was discussed in the previous chapter under the burdens on the soil of the peasant (see p. 70).

[2] Wohlin, "Torpare-, backstugu-och inhysesklasserna," *op. cit.*, p. 13.

[3] The peasants who leased the crownlands were called *kronobönder*. Peasants on the nobles' lands were designated as *frälsebönder*. These two classes of peasants have during the nineteenth century purchased their land to a great extent and risen to the class of freeholders (Wohlin, "Den jordbruksikande befolkningen i Sverige, 1751–1900," *Emigrationsutredningens bilaga IX*, p. 18).

[4] "Utvandringslagstiftning," *Emigrationsutredningens bilaga I*, p. 5.

and a bill to reduce the tax burden of large families.[1] Some of these bills were later made into laws.

Various laws were passed in the middle of the eighteenth century extending the privileges of erecting crofts on their lands to the peasants. A law of 1747 permitted a division of the farms to a greater degree than formerly was permissible, when it had been restricted to one-fourth of a farm.[2] Through the influence of the Riksdag, a royal circular letter was sent to the provincial governors in 1757 with the instructions that new lands placed under cultivation by the peasants on the taxed lands would not be razed nor even taxed, but that such crofts should remain as a reward for their industry.[3] The Royal Ordinance of 1762 permitted the peasants to establish crofts, cottages, and houses for married servants on their cultivated lands.[4] Crofts and cottages were also permitted on the individual commons of the village if the co-owners could agree. The old restrictions on the number and size of crofts and farms were removed entirely. The Royal Ordinance of 1770 permitted the establishment of cottages without the consent of the owners of the village on the commons. This law also freed the cottager from the control of the landowner on whose land his cottage was located. He could neither be forced against his will to make a year's contract for labor, to do military service, nor be deprived of his croft or cottage by refusing such service. It made him a free agricultural laborer and removed him from the servant class. Laws for tax exemption for crofter families with many children followed, and also a lower tax for the croft.

In 1750 the crofters were most numerous on the fertile plains of Central Sweden in the provinces of Uppland, Södermanland, and Östergötland, where they were chiefly located on the larger estates of the gentry and the crown. There were also many crofts in Skaraborg and Värmland at this time.[5] The crofts on the common lands were recognized between 1750 and 1800 as new freeholds.[6] In 1751

---

[1] *Ibid.*, p. 6.

[2] A *hemman* or *mantal* was equivalent to about 120 acres of cultivated land (*ibid.*).

[3] Wohlin, "Torpare-, backstugu-och inhysesklasserna," *op. cit.*, p. 14; Schütz, *Om skifte af land*, pp. 29–30.

[4] Wohlin, *op. cit.*    [5] *Ibid.*    [6] New freeholders were designated *nybyggare*.

there were 27,891 crofts in Sweden. By 1800 they had increased to 64,644, showing the results of the removal of the restrictive laws. The crofter class consisted of 261,727 persons in 1800 or about 10 per cent of the population.[1] The distribution of the crofter class had shifted between 1751 and 1800. In the older regions there was no increase in their numbers, except in Östergötland. The southern provinces of Sweden now showed a larger increase, and also the Norrland regions.[2]

The great number of crofts existing in 1750 disclosed the fact that many had been erected on the peasant's land even before the repeal of the restrictive law. The difficulty of razing the home of a family and forcing them out on the bare ground made it almost impossible to enforce the laws. It also demonstrated the probable weakness of the Swedish administrative system during the period. The rapidly increasing population and the need of finding new homes, as well as the growing independence of the lower agricultural classes explains the illegal establishment of many small farms on the estates of the peasants.[3] Contracts between tenants and the peasant concerning the crofts developed as an extra-legal relationship and existed for a long time as custom. On the lands of the nobles the crofters were legally in the same position as the older form of tenantry, landbönder, but their social position was subordinate.[4] In 1781 when the croft system had become quite common, a royal ordinance provided for the dismissal and ejection from a croft on the same legal basis as that of the landbo.[5]

The extra-legal contracts that had been made between the crofter or cotter and the peasant were not put into writing and continued in force only through custom. The contracts consisted of agree-

[1] Wohlin, "Torpare-, backstugu-och inhysesklasserna," op. cit.

[2] The southern provinces and counties showing an increase of crofters and cotters were Skåne, Halland, Blekinge, Göteborg-Bohus, Kronoberg, and Älvsborg. The gateshusman of Southern Sweden was counted as a cotter. This population increased rapidly because of the scarcity of free lands. The crofts in Norrland were new clearings (nybyggare).

[3] Schütz, op. cit.

[4] The landbönder had been tenants on the nobles' lands and the crownlands and were the same as frälsebönder and kronobönder.

[5] Wohlin, "Torpare-, backstugu-och inhysesklasserna," op. cit., p. 15.

ments on the tenure of the lease and the form of payment, which was usually a certain number of days' labor per year.[1] There were various ways of acquiring a croft or a cottage. It might be procured by "purchase," by "pawn" (a form of mortgage), or by a contract for labor.

The "purchase" of a croft was designated as a "purchase for a certain time" or "purchase for a life time" in all parts of the kingdom, besides the terms "rent and lease."[2] The "purchase" amounted to a lease for the lifetime of the occupant and his wife, or for a definite terms of years—twenty, thirty, forty, but usually fifty. In Southern Sweden the "purchase" was made for ninety or a hundred years, and in one province of Norrland for as long as one hundred and twenty years. A large sum of money was paid when the contract was made, usually a little less than the capitalization of the rent-value for the period of the lease, which in the case of a life-lease could only be an estimate. Besides the initial sum, a small annual compensation was paid during the occupancy, either two or three days' work per year, or a few riksdaler or shillings, the currency of the period. This annual payment, which was much less than the taxes on the land paid by the estate, was considered only a formality, to give the transaction the appearance of leased land and to guarantee the leaseholder the right of possession. The "purchases" were not made legal until the statute of 1827. However, earlier cases of this sort had been handled by the "hundred" courts as leases for years or for life. This legal conception rested on the fact that in the "purchase" there was no written evidence concerning the division of the contract into the initial payment and annual dues. After the Royal Ordinance of 1800 had been passed, the "hundred" courts sometimes considered the "purchase" as mortgages, for the courts did not accept oral evidence. Confusion often arose when the land was sold, since there was no written contract to protect the croft. Sometimes the croft was condemned to be returned to the estate without compensation for improvements, as was reported in

[1] *Ibid.*

[2] The Swedish term is *köp* which literally translated is "purchase." There were *köp pa viss tid* and *köp på lifstid* (*ibid.*, p. 17). "Rent and lease" is a translation of *lega och arrende.*

cases from Värmland and Gävleborg counties, while in other cases they were protected as mortgages.

Another form of croft was secured through a "pawn."[1] The term of the "pawn" was again either for life or for a certain number of years. The land was occupied and used by the person who loaned the money to the owner of the estate. It was understood that the principal of the loan was to be returned at the time the owner came in possession of his lands again. This form of croft was found in all the counties, but was less numerous in the counties of Stockholm, Östergötland, and Kalmar. It was calculated that the interest would be equivalent to the annual yield of the land. This was really a form of agricultural credit. There was a variety of practices in the payment of interest. The landowners in Småland and Västergötland usually paid interest annually as well as the principal of the loan. Where there was no interest provided for, the person who took over the land gave a correspondingly smaller sum of money for the "pawn." In Western Sweden, it was customary for the owners to pay for the erection of new buildings and other improvements, as well as to repay the principal of the "pawn," if they wanted their lands returned. This was not the practice in Eastern Sweden. Like in the case of the "purchase" of a croft, it was customary for the possessor to guarantee his right to the land by giving to the owner a few days of labor per year for a small sum of money. Again there was a variety of practices in the repayment of the principal; in some cases it was paid in full, in others only partially, while in some not at all. These "pawns" were equally as illegal as the "purchases" of crofts or cottages until the nineteenth century. It was universally acknowledged that the common law forbade the mortgaging of small portions of the peasant's estate, since it diminished his taxes.[2] The "pawns," however, were recognized by the "hundred" courts as lawful in cases where the owner would or could not redeem the land, and were therefore alienated from the estate. Some of the "hundred" courts handled these lands as leaseholds, because of the annual payments. Again under the Ordinance of 1800, the courts interpreted these crofts as mortgages and not only en-

[1] *Ibid.*, p. 18.
[2] *Jordabalk*, chap. ix.

forced the return of the principal but also the fulfilment of the contract at the designated time.

At the time when the Royal Ordinance of 1827 was passed, both forms of land grants, "purchases" and "pawns" were common. "Purchases" were common in the whole kingdom. In the counties of Västmanland, Östergötland, Jönköping, and Kronoberg, as well as in Gothenburg-Bohus, there was little difference between "purchases" and "pawns." "Pawns" were most frequent in the provinces of Östergötland, Småland, Västergötland, Bohuslän, Dal, and Värmland. They were seldom used in the provinces of Uppland, Södermanland, Gotland, Skåne, Halland, Blekinge, Jämtland, or Norrbotten.[1] The government authorities and even the courts had had little influence in their development. Few complaints were ever heard in the courts and very little of the land had to be returned. The cultivators of the pieces of land lived generation after generation upon the contracts based only upon good faith, and made contrary to law, and therefore few complaints were made. The Ordinance of 1827 proposed to regulate these land-grants for the benefit of the lessee and the landowner. It designated the minimum and maximum size of the holdings and the annual payments. It gave the widow and the heirs of the possessor of the land the right to remain until the fulfilment of the contract. Under certain conditions it also provided that the landowner might regain the land by paying redemption money.[2] The provisions of this law, namely that the land might revert to the estate without the payment of redemption money at the end of the lease, discouraged the making of further contracts of this kind. In many parts of Sweden, and especially in Gävleborg and Jönköping counties, these forms of acquiring crofts ceased. Otherwise the law had little influence on the leasing of land. The common people did not care to adopt the provisions about area and annual rent, because it was not practical. Illegal contracts continued to be made and few complaints were brought before the law to test them. These contracts were finally put under legal control by the Royal Ordinances of 1844 and 1853.[3] There was no recognition of the croft by "purchase" or "pawn" in the tax laws until

---

[1] Wohlin, "Torpare-, backstugu-och inhysesklasserna," *op. cit.*, p. 20, footnote.

[2] *Ibid.*, p. 21.  [3] *Ibid.*, p. 22 (*angående hemmansklyfning och jordsöndring*).

1810. This law provided that crofts and cottages which for longer or shorter terms of years were separated from the estate,[1] should be taxed separately, while other crofts and houses should be included in the evaluation of the peasant's estate. It remained so until the Ordinance of 1861, and indicated that even in the tax laws the old conception of the crofts as separate from the estate for a certain time was the only type that was recognized.[2] There had been a century of illegal development of "purchase" and "pawn" on various kinds of tenure. This also coincides with the height of the development of the croft and the cottage in Sweden as forms of tenantry.

The croft or cottage procured through "purchase" or "pawn" was a form of agricultural credit in a time before the establishment of mortgage banks. Moreover, it gave to certain landless members of the agricultural classes an opportunity to obtain pieces of land that might be independently cultivated for a longer period of time. The restrictive forest ordinances had limited the chances of obtaining a homestead; the monopoly of land ownership in the peasant and noble prevented the purchase of land. The only land on the market was a limited amount of crownland. Many of the private owners of land had large stretches of uncultivated soil where the crofter or cotter might make a clearing.

The third type of croft was that which was erected as a means of supplying a permanent labor-supply for the estate. These crofts had a rental of several days of labor per week.[3] In this type of croft the tenure of the lease was frequently indefinite, permitting the landlord to dismiss and eject the tenant similarly to the old laws concerning agricultural labor. These crofters did not have as high a social position as those who had obtained their crofts by "purchase" or "pawn." Any lease that had the "earmarks" of a croft or cottage was so designated. It applied to rental in the form of day labor or service, to rental in the form of produce or money, or both. In more recent times, many of the day-labor obligations have been commuted to money payments, without raising the social status of the crofter.

[1] *sin bolstad.*

[2] Wohlin, "Torpare-, backstugu-och inhysesklasserna," *op. cit.*, p. 23.

[3] This form of land tenantry is called *jordtorp.*

The chief difference between a crofter and a cotter was in the size of land transferred in the lease, and therefore the amount of rental, which was figured in number of days of labor.[1] The cotters received a cottage and a very small piece of land, amounting to a potato or cabbage patch. There was no sharp distinction between the smaller crofts and the cottages. The tenure of the lease of the cottage was similar to that of a croft, either an indefinite term, or a term in years, or for a lifetime. Where the tenure was more than for a lifetime, the heirs of the tenant inherited the lease. It was customary before 1850 to make the lease of a cottage for a definite term of years, but since that date to make it indefinite. The possessor of a cottage had greater freedom in the disposition of his labor than the crofter, since his obligations were only a few days a year. The remainder of the time he was free to seek employment where he may. His position was higher than that of a servant who was bound to the household of his master, for the cotter was legally independent.

The crofter and the cotter population increased in Sweden fivefold respectively between 1751 and 1860. The number of crofts had increased from 27,891 in 1751 to 88,364 in 1840, and reached its peak in 1860 with 99,815.[2] Then followed a decline due to the practice of more extensive agricultural methods, to the growing industrialization of Sweden, and, last but not least in its influence, to the emigration of the crofters to America. The largest increase in crofts after the beginning of the nineteenth century was in Southern, Western, and Northern Sweden. Eastern Sweden, the region of large estates, was characterized by a stationary or decreasing crofter population.[3] Even between 1840 and 1860, when the number of crofts decreased in counties with large estates, they continued to increase in Älvsborg and in the Norrland counties.

The cotter population was distributed practically contiguous with the crofters. In 1751 there were 8,724 cotters; in 1769 they had in-

[1] Wohlin, "Torpare-, backstugu-och inhysesklasserna," *op. cit.*, p. 24.

[2] *Ibid.*, pp. 28–35.

[3] The increase in the crofters between 1800 and 1840 amounted to 6.3 per cent in the Mälar counties (Stockholm, Södermanland, Västmanland, and Örebro), 14.9 per cent in Östergötland, 15.1 per cent in Skaraborg County, 45.4 per cent in Jönköping, Kronoberg, and Kalmar counties, 53.9 per cent in Gothenburg-Bohus, 69.1 per cent in Norrland, an average of 71 per cent in Skåne, Halland, and Blekinge, 75.7 per cent in Värmland, and 89.9 per cent in Älvsborg County (*ibid.*, p. 51).

creased to 12,500. The greatest number were found in Östergötland, Örebro, and Skåne. By 1850 the increase in cottages amounted to 45,621. In the rich agricultural counties around Lake Mälar they began to decrease. In the less prosperous rural regions of Västergötland, Småland, Värmland, and Norrland the numbers more than doubled after 1805.[1] The counties having the largest number of cotters in 1840 were in their respective order Malmöhus, Kalmar, Kristianstad, Gävleborg, Skaraborg, and Älvsborg.[2] During the same year the crofter population was distributed numerically among the Swedish counties as follows, Östergötland, Älvsborg, Kristianstad, Skaraborg, Malmöhus, and Kalmar.[3]

The crofter was, however, the social inferior of the peasant. Many of the Swedish immigrants in America have expressed their bitter feeling of resentment toward the peasant class. Born on a croft in the hilly region of Dalsland, one immigrant stated, in an account of her life in Sweden, that as a child in school she began to feel the class differences. These class differences were finally responsible for her emigration.[4] An eminent physician, the son of an immigrant who was born of crofter parents, often speaks of his father's resentment to the overbearing attitude of the peasants of Jämtland.

The cotter constituted even a lower class than the crofter. The rapid increase of this class in Sweden between 1820 and 1840 caused much alarm. It was discussed in the quinquennial reports of the governors, in the meetings and reports of the local agricultural societies, and by the press. It influenced the passage of the Ordi-

[1] In the Mälar counties the cotter diminished 13 per cent during the period from 1805 to 1850. In Östergötland they increased during the period 19.5 per cent, in Skåne, Halland, and Blekinge 13.1 per cent, in Småland (Jönköping, Kronoberg, and Kalmar counties) 161.9 per cent, in Värmland 222 per cent, and in Norrland 196.7 per cent (*ibid.*, pp. 53–55).

[2] In 1840 there were 4,373 cotters in Malmöhus County; 3,459, in Kalmar County; 2,875, in Kristianstad County; 2,825, in Gävleborg County (the mining region); 2,353, in Skaraborg County; 1,610, in Kronoberg County; 1,535, in Värmland County; 1,481, in Gothenburg-Bohus County; 1,229, in Halland County; 1,156, in Gotland County (Wohlin, "Den jordbruksidkande befolkningen i Sverige, 1751–1900," *op. cit.*, p. 248).

[3] The number of crofters in Östergötland County in 1840 was 7,958; in Älvsborg, 7,862; in Kristianstad, 6,776; in Skaraborg, 6,020; in Malmöhus, 5,555; in Kalmar, 5,404; in Värmland 5,412; in Örebro 5,118; in Jönköping 4,778; in Gothenburg-Bohus 4,940; in Södermanland County, 4,288, and in Kronoberg County, 4,155 (*ibid.*).

[4] "Utvandrarnes egna uppgifter," *Emigrationsutredningens bilaga VII*, pp. 254–55.

nance of 1827 for the final consolidation of landholdings, and another ordinance of the same year forbidding disintegration of farms and alienation of land from the smaller freeholds.[1] The prevailing forms of poor relief were investigated in 1839. The fear that the growth of the cotter class would increase the burden of poverty on the community appeared in the governors' reports of 1820. In 1822, the governor of Blekinge County mentioned the great increase of small crofts and cottages.[2] He stated in 1827,

The farms in the country are overburdened with these grants. It is undoubtedly taking care of the increase in population and bringing about the cultivation of new lands, but it has also developed a class which lacks moral strength to be independent, and when occasional opportunities for work fail, fall into poverty and need. The land grants, which were popularly called "purchases for a definite time," have been established because of the need of money on the part of the landowners, but have weakened the estates as well as pawned their woods and pasture lands. The ease with which a smaller croft may be procured and its legal independence give encouragement to vagrants and debauched people. For this reason, the southern provinces have a higher percentage than the northern provinces of law breakers, unemployed, and immoral people, as well as vagrants.

The same fear was expressed by the governors of Kristianstad, Kalmar, Kronoberg, Jönköping, Älvsborg, Örebro, and Värmland in 1833.[3] These reports criticized both the crofter grants for long periods of time through "purchase" and "pawn," as well as those for indefinite periods. The governors of the Småland counties agreed that the cotter class separated itself from the landowning class by its indolence and loose morals. During the years when the potato crop

[1] *Laga skifte* (Wohlin, "Torpare-, backstugu-och inhysesklasserna," *op. cit.*, p. 62.

[2] *K. bfhde femårsberättelse, Blekinge län, den 30 december 1822. Also K. bfhde i Kristianstad, skrifvelse till statssekreteraren, den 20 october 1827; ibid, Göteborgs-och Bohus, den 28 maj 1827; ibid., älfsborg, den 15 juli 1827; ibid., Kalmar, den 26 april 1827; ibid., Örebro* (not dated), cited in Wohlin, "Torpare-, backstugu-och inhysesklasserna," *op. cit.*, p. 63. Also Infordradt uttaland om jordafsöndringar i och för k. för den 19 december 1827, skrifvelse till statssekreteraren för K. kammerexpeditionen den 20 maj 1827.

[3] *K. bfhde femårsberättelse för Kristianstad den 19 december 1833; ibid., Kalmar, den 26 september 1833; ibid., Kronoberg den 10 augusti 1833; ibid., Jönköping den 31 december 1833; ibid., älfsborg den 31 december 1833; ibid., Örebro, den 28 september 1833; ibid., Värmland, den 31 december 1833* (Wohlin, "Torpare-, backstugu-och inhysesklasserna," *op. cit.*, p. 64).

was good, the cotter could earn by a day's labor enough to support the family for three or four days, but when the crops were poor, he was a beggar. The complaint was made by the governor of Stockholm County that many servants married young, took a cottage, and with the rapid increase of children in the cottage, soon found the piece of land insufficient for supporting the family. It was difficult to obtain employment and the cotter grew despondent and indifferent to the needs of his family. The result was that the family became a burden to the community.[1] Even the northern counties complained. The governor of Gävleborg County stated that though the small crofts placed more land under cultivation, it was at the same time increasing the poorer classes, especially in Hälsingland where such households often consisted of more persons than the small pieces of land could support. During the periods of unemployment, sickness, and old age they became burdens on the community.[2]

One of Sweden's greatest writers, Esaias Tegnér, described the situation in very graphic terms. He wrote from Växsjö in Småland in 1833 that

the country overflows with cottages, inhabited by a class which has no other wealth than its labor. Although they can support themselves during prosperous years when there is plenty of work, they do nevertheless suffer from unemployment and hunger in periods of poor crops. The gain that the kingdom has made by the increase in cultivated lands through this class is doubtful, because it usually consists of hacking up a few more acres of potatoes and destroying more forest than the value of the improved lands. In this way the population has grown and continues to grow from year to year, but under unimproved circumstances and increasing poverty, adding only numbers to the list of paupers. The kingdom's numerical strength increases, but actual strength it cannot be, unless accompanied by prosperity, at least contentment. The strength of the realm is being undermined by the increase of a class whose whole support depends upon the annual potato crop. Sweden is in danger of acquiring what has never before appeared in the rural districts, an agrarian proletariat.[3]

[1] *K. bfhde kommitterade i Stockholms län yttrade den 4 mars 1834, ibid.*

[2] *K. bfhde femårsberättelse, Gävleborg, den 8 juli 1835, ibid.*

[3] Sundbärg, *Emigrationsutredningens betänkande*, pp. 130–31; Knut Wicksell, "Uttalande af Svenska vetenskapsman," *Emigrationsutredningens bilaga XVIII* (Stockholm, 1910), p. 109.

Dean Uddenberg of Kalmar County testified before the county committee in 1836 that there were some benefits in the cotter system, or perhaps that it was the choice of a lesser evil.[1] He stated,

Around these cottages one finds land cultivated that would otherwise never be utilized, and witnesses the almost unbelievable manner in which poverty drives people to thrift and the expenditure of energy. This system is a peaceful haven for the old and sick, and where the fortunate's money is undisturbed by the complaints of the unfortunate. Both from a physical and moral point of view it is the least pressing and most useful form of poor relief that humanity and Christianity have devised. There are complaints of the great numbers of poor, undependable, begging vagrants. Who are they? Are they the ones who have built up a little cottage on a stony hill? No, those who have not sought nor found this outlet.

He also stated that the large majority of cotters were servants, who with approaching old age and infirmity were dismissed and reduced to cotters.

In some regions where industry other than agriculture could furnish more stable employment to the cotters, there was not the same problem of poverty. This was true of the cotters on the large mining estates of the "Bergslag" region.[2] The governor of Stockholm County in 1834 felt that housing artisans and laborers with definite occupations in cottages with small pieces of land was a very good plan.[3]

The agricultural laborer was striving for independence from a master and for the satisfaction of occupying his own home. When he was not privileged to inherit a farm, or at least a croft, he would accept a cottage with a potato patch rather than be a hired man on the estate of the gentry or the farm of the peasant. By the earlier part of the nineteenth century, there were fewer cottages established through "purchase" and "pawn," and more for the purpose of convenient and permanent labor. After the few days of labor had been performed for the rental of the cottage, the cotter was free to dispose of his labor when and in what manner he saw fit. He was the day-

[1] Prosten Uddenbergs reservation till länskommitterades skrifvelse af den 22 augusti 1836 (Wohlin, "Torpare-, backstugu-och inhysesklasserna," *op. cit.*, p. 66).

[2] K. bfhde femårsberättelse, Gäfleborg, den 8 juli 1835, cited in Wohlin, "Torpare-, backstugu-och inhysesklasserna," *op. cit.*, p. 69.

[3] K. bfhde Stockholm län, skrifvelse till statssekreteraren för k. kammerexpedition den 26 juni 1827 (Wohlin, "Torpare-, backstugu-och inhysesklasserna," *op. cit.*, p. 63). It has proved a good way of housing industrial workmen at the present time.

laborer of the rural community, but was more fixed than the present industrial laborer, because of his land. It was industry and emigration that were destined to thin the ranks of crofters and cotters in Sweden. Pictures of the poverty of the cotter's life have been drawn by some of the Swedish immigrants in America in describing their childhood life in Sweden. One immigrant was born in 1862, the seventh of ten children of a cotter in Skaraborg County.[1] His home was a log cabin of one room.[2] His father owned the cabin but was obligated to give six days of labor annually for his land. He was a Jack-of-all trades, but spent all that he earned for whiskey. The immigrant wrote,

> The bitterest memories of my childhood were when I saw my mother cry when we begged for bread and she had not a crumb to give us. At ten I began to work for a peasant for food. I remained with one peasant four years and received ten kronor to put in the bank because I joined the Temperance Society.

He continued to work for various peasants until the time for his military service. He emigrated to America in 1886 and worked in the coal mines of Pennsylvania where he finally became a smith. He stated,

> I cannot give the exact reason for emigrating. The question of bread was probably the main reason, class differences, and then the question of personal worth. I felt as if I were worthless, both to the community and to myself, for my word was worth nothing even when it concerned my soul. I have nothing to complain of against Mother Svea,[3] for I have at least inherited good principles from her.

Another immigrant from Gästrikland in Norrland was the son of an old worn-out cotter.[4] At the age of sixteen he relieved his older brother who had supported the family of six. Although he supplemented the income from the land by working in a tile mill in the summer, and by cutting lumber in the winter, his earnings hardly reached. The father died in 1873, and the older brother returned to take over the two-room cottage and to support the mother. A

[1] "Utvandrarnes egna uppgifter," op. cit., pp. 175–76.

[2] *Ryggastuga* has been translated "log cabin."

[3] "Mother Svea" is a designation for Sweden.

[4] J. P. emigrated from Gävleborg County in 1882 ("Utvandrarnes egna uppgifter," op. cit., pp. 181–84).

few years later the immigrant married and became a day-laborer on an estate in the neighborhood.[1] With his scant savings he furnished a rented cottage. According to this labor contract he was to receive a krona (about 26 cents) per day in the summer for his labor and in the winter seventy-five öre. His wife was to give fifty days of labor during the haying and harvest season at seventy-five öre a day. Besides their wages they received a house, about half an acre of land for a potato patch, half a can of milk per day, five cords of wood, and ten loads of fertilizer, the last two items to be paid for at a price decided upon between the proprietor and the laborer. The immigrant stated that it was impossible to feed and clothe a family on the small income. On the estate were miles of forest land containing many arable swamps and natural meadows, lying unused for pastures, which if drained would make fine fields. Several of the laborers, including the immigrant, asked the owner for the permission to break some of the lands for crofts, but the answer received was that he was not interested. Their inability to obtain land made them decide to emigrate to America.

All cotters were not so extremely poor. An immigrant from Jönköping County was born in a cotter's home.[2] There was poverty in the home, but they never starved. Their food often consisted only of potatoes and coarse oat bread, but they had it better than most of the cotters in the neighborhood. The step-father earned very little as organ tramper in the church and grave-digger of the parish, but the mother was thrifty and often wove cloth. There was also a small family with only one child. The mother owned the cottage for which she had paid 200 kronor ($53.00). The peasants in the neighborhood were poor, hard worked, and had far from an enviable lot. There were mortgages on their farms. It was difficult to meet the taxes and interest. They could afford to hire only small boys to help them. The immigrant wrote, "Around my home were many fallow acres which were overgrown with underbrush. The soil was stony and sterile, so that it did not pay to till it, but there were a few fertile places." He too left home at the early age of thirteen to work for

---

[1] *Dagakarl* is translated "day-laborer." He was in fact more like the *stattorpare* for he was employed by the year and received a cottage and a small piece of land.

[2] "Utvandrarnes egna uppgifter," *op. cit.*, pp. 190–96.

peasants in the summer at the wage of five kronor ($1.34), a pair of boots, and a sheep-skin coat. A little later he was apprenticed to a carpenter.

The crofters were usually in better economic circumstances than the cotters, depending upon the size and fertility of the piece of land that was leased. Something of the life on a croft and the terms of the croft may be learned from further descriptions of the crofters or children of the crofters who have become American immigrants. A son of a crofter from Skaraborg County related how his mother was left a widow with nine children on a croft on the crownlands.[1] Only a small portion of the lands of the croft had been placed under cultivation, and there was ample room for expansion. As the children grew older, the ground was gradually broken and tilled until there was sufficient to support six cows and a pair of oxen, as well as some sheep and hogs. A new home was also built. The rental consisted of four days of a man's labor per week, for the entire year, and fifty days of a woman's labor annually. In 1876, the crown estate was leased for an annual rental of 20,000 kronor ($5,372), for a period of twenty years and the new landlord was very hard on the crofters. The mother relinquished her contract for the croft with the provision that she might build a house on a rather sterile hill.

Another immigrant was the son of a crofter on the estate of Count G. in Östergötland County.[2] Their land was sufficient to feed an ox, two cows, a calf, and two or three sheep. Although there were eleven children, they were never in want. His father worked four days a week on the estate, one day for his land and three days for half a bushel of rye per day.

The son of a crofter in Södermanland County was one of seven children.[3] His father gave three days of labor each week for the croft, and if he were needed longer he worked three additional days for about twenty cents a day. During the sowing and harvest seasons he had to work his own land at night. The soil was poor and there was much poverty. An immigrant in 1907 explained that the rental for the croft on which he was born was paid in cash, $32 a

[1] This immigrant left Sweden in 1887 (*ibid.*, pp. 176–77).

[2] M.N. (*ibid.*, pp. 133–34).

[3] H. (*ibid.*, pp. 169–70).

year.[1] His mother continued to rent the land after his father's death and worked it with the assistance of his twenty-year-old brother. The croft fed three or four cows and one horse. The family owned the buildings on the croft.

A retired crofter who followed his family to America in 1907 described his life as a tenant in Sweden.[2] For thirty-one years he had held a croft on the estate of L. in Kronoberg County. He had inherited it from his step-father and he had now handed it over to his brother. The rental had been two days per week of a man's work and sixty-two days of a woman's labor per year. For many years the hours of labor on the estate had been from 4 A.M. to 9 P.M., or 10 P.M. in the summers, but it had recently been changed to 6 A.M. until 8 P.M. The estate was more than three miles distant from the croft. The crofter had performed all the labor on his own land and the required amount on the estate himself until his sons were old enough to aid him. As one son left for America, another took his place. The wife had likewise performed the required woman's labor until relieved by her daughters. But when the daughters had all emigrated the parents had to hire labor for this work. One of the daughters had now returned to take the parents and the youngest of the seven children, the only one still in Sweden, to America. The croft had been small but the income from it had assured a comfortable living.

Another agricultural laborer often grouped with cotter was the married laborer who was housed by the employer, the retainer.[3] Before the nineteenth century he was housed in cottages often like the cotter class. But after 1800 he was usually housed with others, either in the landlord's own house or with the crofter or the cotter. For this privilege of a roof over their heads, and for food, the members of these families aided the landowner in his work. It has been hard to place these servants in their legal category, because under the old laws they were not independent like the crofters and cotters, nor were they servants. They had developed from the old Germanic custom of retainers and were not under legal contract.

---

[1] A. emigrated at the age of 19 (*ibid.*, pp. 67–68).    [2] J. (*ibid.*, p. 44).

[3] This class is called the *inhysesklass* or *inhyseshjonen*, which literally translated is "housed servants."

Now they are usually registered for taxation purposes as a part of the household where they reside. There were two groups within this class, the able-bodied and the infirm. The able-bodied group was the class that formed an asset to agriculture. In 1751 there were 11,309 heads of families in the able-bodied group of these retainers, and in 1769, 14,666.[1] They were most numerous in Malmöhus and Kristian-stad counties, in Southern Sweden, and in Värmland. They continued to grow in numbers. In 1805 there were 15,184 heads of families and in 1850, 43,594. They had increased four times in the century from 1750 to 1850. The counties of Värmland, Älvsborg, Kristianstad, and Östergötland had the greatest number in 1850, although Eastern and Northern Sweden had had the greatest increase since 1800.[2] This class was exceedingly poor and was included in the descriptions of the cotter class.

A new type of agricultural laborer began to appear in the early part of the nineteenth century and was first mentioned in the statistics of 1825. This class was called the crofter servant and the married servant.[3] The *stattorpare* was a married agricultural laborer who was housed in his own cottage on the employer's land and who also had a piece of land. He was employed by the year and did not have the legal right to move at any time as the crofter did. Where his obligations were limited to certain days in the week, the *stattorpare* had, like the cotter, the free disposition of his labor the remaining time. He often worked for two landowners, but legally registered as belonging to the household of one. The crofter servant differed from the cotter in that he was not legally independent, but was counted as a part of the household of the employer and was so registered by the tax assessors.[4] The *statare* was also a married agricultural laborer who contracted to work for the landlord for a year. He was housed

---

[1] Wohlin, "Torpare-, backstugu-och inhysesklasserna," *op. cit.*, p. 53.

[2] The increase in the Mälar provinces between 1805–50 was 106.3 per cent; in Småland, 144.6 per cent; in Östergötland, 183.7 per cent; in Värmland, 199.8 per cent; in Skåne, Halland, and Blekinge 206.7 per cent; in Västergötland, 287 per cent, and in Norrland, 305.8 per cent (*ibid.*, p. 55).

[3] *Stattorpare* had been translated as crofter servant, and *statare* as married servant (*ibid.*, p. 26).

[4] *Mantalskrifven.* Everyone had to be registered with a household for taxation purposes. The head of the household was responsible for them.

sometimes in a cottage, but usually in a tenement house for several families. He also had a piece of potato land. In 1825 there were 9,239 heads of families of the *statare* class, and 11,891 wives and widows. By 1840 they had increased to 12,691 men and 12,499 women. This class continued to grow until 1880 when their numbers reached 34,131 men and 31,917 women. The largest number were found on the large estates of the Mälar counties, of Skåne, and of Östergötland.[1] The entire population of the group in 1870 was estimated at 127,685. This class was drawn from two other agricultural classes; the married hired man and maid, and the crofter or *landbonde* who had given up his land. He might be a crofter who was not able to fulfil his obligations in day labor and had to return his land to the landlord, or the inducements of a fixed wage enticed him to give up the precarious income from his sterile croft.

The movement from crofter to married servant which was so marked from 1825 to 1860 was partly due to the technical changes that were developing new methods in agriculture. The natural meadow and the *utmark* ("the uncultivated lands") were placed under the plow. A greater grain production was stimulated by the rising prices of grain. There were larger profits in extensive cultivation which was possible with larger fields. The result was that the larger estates annexed the tenant farms and crofts to the manor, and placed most of their lands directly under their personal management.[2] They could more easily introduce new methods than the tenants who were hampered both by the lack of capital and the bonds of custom. After the enclosures had broken up the villages, the crofts were often embedded in the fields and meadows of the common lands and were a hindrance to rational cultivation. There was also a greater need for the landowners to control their labor and to use a more scientific method in the utilization of their labor-power. With the growing market for land and the resulting land speculation, it was also desirable for the landowner to have his estate free from incumbrances like crofts if he wished to lease or sell it.

---

[1] Wohlin, "Den jordbruksidkande befolkningen i Sverige, 1751–1900," *op. cit.*, pp. 26–27.

[2] *Landbohemman* were tenant farms of older origin than the crofts (*torp*). The *landbönder* had a higher social status than the crofter or cotter. They usually paid their rental in produce or shares of the crop, later in cash.

In many places, however, the croft continued as an economic necessity. Where the croft lay a long ways from the estate and was not encroaching upon the cultivated lands and meadows, it was allowed to remain. The croft was also a good labor system in that it guaranteed a certain labor supply that did not fluctuate with the labor market, nor the price of labor, and did not need to be housed or fed. With the decline of the crofter class and their depression into the married servant class came a sinking of social status. The governor's report from Örebro County in 1828 complained that a number of *stattorpare* and married servants and other such persons were increasing year after year, and that this class was less dependable and less willing to work than the crofter.[1] In 1833, the governor of Stockholm County feared that the increase in the *statare* class meant an increase in poverty.[2] There were many children in these families and the parents' poverty and irresponsibility for their care and support resulted in a large percentage of deaths among the young children, and in a burden upon the poor relief. The governor of the county of Östergötland in 1839 stated,

*Stattorparen* has seldom any hope that his thrift and foresight will provide improved conditions in his old age, while the crofter has the confidence and the hope of improving his economic station, and every "good" year aids the possibility. Futility creates indifference and the tendency to bury ones worries and disappointments in the "glass" with the resultant increase of poverty and degradation.[3]

These reports continued during the period from 1840 to 1860, both from the governors and the agricultural societies. The governor of Östergötland complained again in 1844 that the communities were heavily taxed for poor relief, while the large estates hired many married servants and left them to be supported by poor relief. The greatest charge upon the poor relief was caused by the large numbers of children of the married servants, and by the dismissed aged

---

[1] *K. bfhde femårsberättelse, Örebro län, oktober 1828*, cited in Wohlin, "Torpare-, backstugu-och inhysesklasserna," *op. cit.*, p. 85.

[2] *K. bfhde femårsberättelse, Stockholm län, 25 november 1833* (Wohlin, "Torpare-, backstugu-och inhysesklasserna," *op. cit.*).

[3] *K. bfhde femårsberättelse, Östergötlands län, 8 januari 1839. Similar reports from Stockholm län, 25 september 1839; Södermanslands län, 14 december 1839; Kristianstads län, 23 november 1839*, as cited in Wohlin, *op. cit.*, p. 86.

servants.[1] Although the crofters were dependent upon the uncertainty of crops and might be temporarily placed in a position of poverty, where the married servant was protected by his wage, the fact remained that over a period of years the crofter had the sounder economic and social position in the community.

Swedish immigrants in America have also come from the *statare* class and have described their lives in Sweden as children of this married servant group. One was the son of a *statare* on an estate in Södermanland County.[2] His father's wages included a small room and a kitchen for a home, a small potato patch, about three quarts of skim milk, and one quart of unskimmed milk per day, and in cash about $48.25 annually.[3] There were six children in the family and this son had to begin work on the estate when he was twelve. At fifteen he was apprenticed to a shoemaker, and at eighteen he emigrated. Another immigrant, also one of six children, was the son of a married servant in Östergötland.[4] His father succeeded in purchasing a small farm that supported a cow.

The poverty of the married servant's life was pictured in the childhood memories of an immigrant whose father was a *statare* on an estate near Stockholm.[5] The father's wage consisted of one room for lodging, two barrels of rye flour, half a barrel of herring, and 100 riksdaler in cash, about $26.00. The immigrant wrote,

Instead of being sent to school I had to herd cows and drive the horses for threshing in the winter. If my parents received anything for my labor I do not know. What I do remember of this period of my life is that I both froze and starved. At twelve I had to haul wood and hay to Stockholm. This work should have paid me enough to keep me from starvation, but many a time we children went to bed with empty stomachs.

Something of the method of housing the married servant may be obtained from the description of a childhood home in Östergötland.

---

[1] *Ibid., Östergötlands län, 21 juni 1844*, cited in Wohlin, "Torpare-, backstugu- och inhysesklasserna," *op. cit.*, p. 86.

[2] A. emigrated at the age of 18 in 1907 ("Utvandrarnes egna uppgifter," *op. cit.*, p. 36).

[3] Three liters of skim milk and one liter of whole milk, with 180 kronor in cash (*ibid.*).

[4] *Ibid.*, p. 38.

[5] F. J. J. was born in Skaraborg county in 1856, but at the age of nine his parents moved to Stockholm. He emigrated in 1881 (*ibid.*, p. 163).

The father of the immigrant was a married servant on one of the smaller farms belonging to the entailed state of A.[1] The father worked by the day rather than on an annual contract, and was designated as a day-laborer.[2] He was given free housing, wood for fuel, a potato patch, and a small wage varying from 18 to 25 cents per day.[3] "In the house in which we lived," wrote the immigrant, "there were five families, each with one room, and since our family consisted of ten people, there was not much space. We had a number of small outhouses."

Second only to the peasant class in numbers was the large group of unmarried men and women who labored in the fields. They consisted of sons and daughters of the peasants and landless agriculturalists. They were reckoned as the servant class, lived under the roof of their employer or parent, and were counted as legally belonging to his household. Their contracts with an employer were annual or only for the summer season. Some were just children belonging to the poorer agricultural classes who herded sheep. It was customary after confirmation, if the child was not needed at home, that he find work with some neighbor. Girls as well as boys went to work in the fields. They remained in service, sometimes moving from place to place, and at other times remaining in one household until they married, when they took over the peasant farm, a croft, or, if less fortunate, a cottage. Sometimes they became married servants of the estate where they had previously worked. When they worked for others they had a definite contract and a definite wage. If they remained under the patriarchy of the home, they received food, clothing, and occasionally spending money. A son working for his father without a fixed wage often envied the hired man and preferred to work for others. When the estate was taken over by a brother, and the father retired to his cottage, it was often distasteful to remain and work without wages, and the younger sons and daughters left to seek an income elsewhere. In 1750 there were 148,215 sons of peasants and hired men over fifteen years of age, while the daughters of peasants and maids over fifteen numbered 170,322. In 1840, the

[1] *Fideikommiss* has been translated entailed estate (*ibid.*, p. 157).
[2] *Dagakarl* has been literally translated day laborer.
[3] Seventy to 90 öre a day.

number of unmarried men engaged in agriculture as laborers ovei fifteen years of age was 307,863, and of unmarried women 286,980.[1] This group had just about doubled in numbers where the landless married agricultural classes had increased five-fold. Since the number of peasant proprietors had for a century remained practically stationary, many of their sons were sinking to the position of landless agriculturalists.

The servant was an old institution on the estates of the nobles and gentry, and on the farms of the peasant. The form of the servant's contract and the method of compensating him had developed over several hundred years through custom and law. In an agricultural community, as Sweden had always been, where money was scarce, it was customary to pay the servant partly in produce and partly in cash. At the beginning of the nineteenth century, this was still the practice, but gradually a money-wage took the place of produce. In 1820 the wages paid a hired man at the Hellestad pastorate in Skåne was from four to six barrels of grain, two suits of clothes consisting of a blue or white jacket and a leather coat, a pair of leather trousers, a pair of linen trousers, a linen shirt, a blue woolen shirt, and a pair of stockings, a pair of socks, two pairs of shoes, and a pair of boots.[2] In Dalby and Bonderup parishes in the same diocese, a hired man could sow for himself on the landlord's land two barrels of oats and twelve bushels of barley,[3] but received only one suit of clothes a year. A maid received a blue skirt and a brown one, twelve yards of blue yarn and five yards of linen, an apron, some wool, a pair of shoes, and the privilege of sowing half a bushel of flax seed and three bushels of potatoes for herself.

Probably the largest percentage of Swedish immigrants in America have at some time or other been hired men or maids on the Swedish peasant farms or on the estates of the gentry.[4] Although in the earliest emigration, from 1840 to 1860, many families came bringing all their members, the emigration since that period has been chiefly of young people between the ages of fifteen and thirty, and almost

[1] Wohlin, "Den jordbruksidkande befolkningen i Sverige," op. cit., pp. 26–27, Tables H and J.

[2] Norlind, op. cit., p. 391.

[3] Twenty-four kapp.          [4] Some have worked for crofters.

all unmarried. It has only been recently that the industrial laborer has largely displaced the agriculturalist.

Some of the following are typical examples of the life of the agricultural laborer, the unmarried "hired man" and "maid" in Sweden. An immigrant from Gävleborg County stated that he was born in 1845 in a poor crofter's cottage on the sandy soil of Hälsingland. "My parents," he wrote, "had owned one of the best pieces of land in the parish, but debt, the many frosts in the thirties, numerous children in the family, and various other circumstances had reduced them to poverty. My childhood was a period of starvation, poverty, freezing and sacrifices of all kinds." At the age of eight he began to earn his own bread on various peasant farms. "In 1858," he related, "I moved to a peasant as his *lille dräng*."[1] He was confirmed in 1860 and did his military duty during 1866–67. "This was a pleasure and a little rest from the constant pressure of work," he continued.

When I was full grown, I received the usual wage of a hired man, 60 riksdaler ($23.00) a year and my working clothes. All I received equalled about 95 to 100 riksdaler, or 16 shillings, which is about nine cents a day. There was not much left of my wages when I had purchased the necessary "Sunday clothes," but I saved what I could and left for America, June 1, 1870, at twenty-five years of age.[2]

Another immigrant related that he was born in Östergötland in 1850, the son of a crofter and one of nine children.[3] His father was a charcoal burner. The croft was so small that it scarcely provided fodder for one cow. In payment for the croft, the father had to maintain a man and a woman at the estate during the busiest season of the year. The father was ejected from the croft and emigrated to America. The son wrote,

At the age of seven I went out to take care of children, my first job, and later to tend geese, swine and sheep. Then I worked on the estate until I was fourteen when I was confirmed. . . . . After confirmation I was employed by a crofter, and my wage was contracted to be 25 riksdaler ($10), a pair of boots, two shirts, and a pair of mittens per year. Later I changed to another crofter, where I received herring five times a day, and had to be at the estate from four o'clock in the morning until eight-thirty in the evening with two miles to walk each way for a little porridge and milk and four hours of rest.

[1] Boys employed on farms were called the little hired men.

[2] "Utvandrarnes egna uppgifter," *op. cit.*, pp. 153–54 (translated).     [3] *Ibid.*, p. 158.

The story of an immigrant of 1870 was that he was born on a nobleman's estate, the son of a servant.[1] In 1840 he hired himself out to a peasant, and in 1844 to a crofter, but received poor wages. Two years later he began to work on the estate of a count where he received 28 shillings (14 cents) for an eighteen-hour day. He worked for the count for twenty-five years. The count was a friendly man but the countess was snobbish. A lieutenant who had charge of the poor relief was heard to say one day that the poor could just as well starve to death. This caused much ill feeling, and many of the servants emigrated to America, including the one who related the story.

There were also those who left more comfortable homes. An immigrant from Jönköping County remained at home and worked on the farm of his mother and step-father until he was twenty-three.[2] He received only his clothes and food, and was humiliated into begging for a little spending money from time to time. He was dissatisfied with these conditions, and hearing from a brother and an uncle that he might obtain twenty to twenty-five dollars a month in America, he emigrated.

A similar instance is related by an immigrant from Malmöhus County whose father owned two farms, one which he farmed himself and the other which he rented.[3] The narrator confessed that he wanted to be a teacher but that he had failed to pass the examination because he could not sing. He continued,

> On my father's farm there was food and work enough for me as well as my brother who was two years older. The only fault was that my father wanted us to work but did not want to pay us anything. All that we wished was to receive the wages of a hired man, but he would not agree to this. Out of this rose quarrels that I could not stand, so I had to either emigrate or find work some place in Sweden. I chose the first because I had no trade and to work as a hired man for others was, I thought, beneath my dignity. The farm was 96 acres in size and fed three horses and eleven or twelve calves, besides sheep and swine. As far as I remember the farm paid well, for I have seen my father sell potatoes for $325 a year. My father could easily have paid us the wages of a hired man, but his unreasonable conservatism made him stubborn. His idea was (and still is) that children through work should repay the cost of raising.

The lot of the maid who was employed on the farm was especially hard. She was expected to care for the cows, do the work in the

[1] *Ibid.*, p. 160.    [2] *Ibid.*, p. 171.    [3] *Ibid.*, pp. 233–34.

house, and at certain times help in the fields. An immigrant from Kristianstad County described the hardships of the hired maid.[1] Her parents rented a farm there. When she was eight her father died, leaving his wife and two children. When the auction was over and all the debts were paid there was $32 left. She continued,

My mother had two sons by a former marriage, one fourteen and the other sixteen, at the time of my father's death, but they were away working. After a few years we moved to the village. Mother worked for peasants at 40 öre a day (about 10 cents). When she worked in the rye fields she earned 50 öre, and between times she wove cloth and sold it. Later my brothers went to America and sent her a little money now and then, about 20 kronor ($5.00) twice a year, and it helped so that she did not have to ask for poor relief. When I was thirteen I had to go to work. I was only a child when I came to a watchman's home and remained there a year. I received my food, and a krona when I left. My mother gave me clothes. Then I remained at home when being confirmed, much to the disgust of the neighboring peasants. When I was sixteen, I took service and received for the first year 30 kronor ($7.50) and the second year 35 kronor ($8.75). I had to work like a wolf, go out and spread manure and fertilizer in the summer, and on the worst snowy days in winter carry water to eleven cows. This was besides all the other work. I worked every minute from 6 A.M. until 9 P.M., Sundays and week days just the same. I do not wonder that servant girls do not wish to work for peasants. She who has done it a couple of years knows only too well what it means. The hired man has hard labor often, but he has his own room to go to, when he has finished his work,[2] and then he has his noonday rest, but what rest has a maid? When the others are resting at noon, she must run to the woods or the pastures to milk and then she must wash dishes when that is done. Then the others are ready to go out to work, and she must go along. So it was with me, and so it is with all the servant maids of peasants. Never a free moment. I made a contract for a third year. I was to have 45 kronor ($11.25), but my brother's wife died in America and my brother sent tickets for my mother, my sister and myself.

The same story is told by an immigrant in 1907. Her father was a *landbonde* and had seven children of which four of the younger were at home. The farm, which he rented from a peasant, was small, with four cows. The children had to go to work at an early age. Z. had worked for peasants since she was fifteen. Her first position was with friends. It was a large peasant estate with twenty cows. There were three maids who all slept in the kitchen with the peasant's family.

[1] *Ibid.*, pp. 205–6.

[2] It was customary for the maids to sleep in the kitchen. They could not retire until the rest of the family had retired.

Work began at five in the morning and continued uninterrupted until nine or ten in the evening. She remained here one year, and received 7 kronor ($1.75) a month. Her next position was on a smaller farm with nine cows. There she was the only maid, but there was also a hired man. Besides the dairying, she had to do all the work in the house, and in the summer she had to assist in the harvesting. The first milking began at six and the work continued uninterrupted until 10 or 11 P.M. in the summer. The milking, which she did alone, had to be done three times a day. During the winter her work was much lighter, for after the last milking at eight she had only the beds to prepare and the dishes and she could be through by nine. Even at this place she had to sleep in the kitchen with the peasant's family, but she seemed to think that that was the usual thing. She remained here three years, and received for the first year 9 kronor ($2.25) a month, and later 10 kronor ($2.50) a month. She complained that the work was hard and that both on Sundays and weekdays there was never any rest. She was only nineteen when she emigrated.

It was customary for the daughters of the more prosperous peasants also to work in the fields. An immigrant from Värmland was the daughter of a well-to-do peasant.[1] She had a brother twenty-two years old and four younger brothers and sisters, who were all confirmed. They had all worked home on the farm. Her father had seven cows, one horse, quite a few sheep, and there was much timber belonging to the estate. There was, therefore, plenty of work for those who were at home. She was the oldest daughter and had helped much in the fields and often pastured the cows, during the summer.[2] She liked farm work. When her sisters began to grow older she was not needed at home, and she had worked two years for some gentry at 10 kronor ($2.50) a month. She was now going to America to earn money to send home.

The number of servants on a medium-sized farm about 1850 was usually a grown man, a boy, a grown woman, and a younger girl.[3] On the smaller farms, a hired man and a maid was all that could be

[1] *Ibid.*

[2] *Vårit på sätern.* She was interviewed in 1907 when she was traveling to America.

[3] Norlind, *Svenska allmogens liv*, pp. 393–94.

afforded, and sometimes these were young people in their teens. During the summer, extra help was hired during the harvest and during the winter, one or two threshers. The herdsmen and shepherds of the earlier day had almost disappeared in the nineteenth century. In Northern Sweden the members of the household usually accompanied the cattle during the pastoral season to the natural meadows upon the wooded slope. In Southern Sweden, small boys were hired to watch the cattle, sheep, and goats. On the larger estates, there were many servants and their work was more specialized than on the peasant's estate.

As was mentioned in the previous chapter, there were also specialized craftsmen in the rural communities, plying their trade under more or less legal protection. It was common for the son of the peasant, crofter, or cotter to be apprenticed to a master workman. Many of the immigrants from the rural communities had that economic experience. An immigrant from Östergötland County in 1868 was the son of a cotter and day-laborer.[1] He had been apprenticed at the age of eleven and a half to a shoemaker, where he remained three years. Later he learned to be a saddle-maker.

Another immigrant, the son of a sailor, living in Småland, was apprenticed for six years to a sail-maker.[2] For the first year he was to receive $5.00, the second two, $6.00, and the remaining years $8.00. He wrote.

For this large sum I had to buy clothes and tools and work like a slave. Ten minutes to five in the morning a bell rang in the room, and at five we had to be in the work shop. We were six apprentices, for every year one boy was admitted and another dismissed, having completed his apprenticeship. Our room was twelve feet square with one window, one pane of which could be opened. . . . . I was with the sail maker three years. We sat and worked two and two at every sail, a journeyman and an apprentice.

A journeyman struck the boy in anger. The boy fled to his father who purchased his release from the apprenticeship. The boy went to sea, later to settle in America.

The son of a soldier from a soldier's croft in Älvsborg County was apprenticed at fourteen to a tailor.[3] Here he worked for a year and a

[1] "Utvandrarnes egna uppgifter," op. cit., p. 134.

[2] Ibid., pp. 144–54.　　　[3] Ibid., pp. 150–51.

half without any pay, only for food and shelter. The food was poor. After this period he received twelve cents a week for a year and later twenty-six cents. In discussing his experience, he wrote, "The result was that I could scarcely with the greatest thrift and ambition keep body and soul together." He emigrated at the age of nineteen in 1864.

The rural population in 1840 consisted, therefore, of two land-owning classes, and several landless groups. The agricultural land was owned and cultivated by some 8,980 of the gentry class and 159,327 of the peasant class.[1] There were also 44,309 peasant tenants operating farms, bringing the peasant entrepreneurs to the total of 203,636. As opposed to these landowners, there existed 88,364 crofters, 37,148 cotters, and 28,078 retainers, forming a total of 153,590 of the landless group. This does not include married servants on annual contracts. The latter, closely approaching the numbers of the peasant class, were rapidly increasing and had the least enviable position in the rural community. There were also 283,662 sons and 279,071 daughters of peasants, crofters, cotters, etc., over the age of fifteen, and 129,009 sons and 134,714 daughters between the ages of ten and fifteen in agricultural employment. Of these 826,-456 agricultural servants only 11,719 were married. The sons and daughters of the peasants were to recruit and increase the landless classes, as the ranks of new peasant proprietorships were filled but could not expand.

It is strange that a country with vast acres of virgin forest lands should suffer from overexpansion. But that is what actually happened in Sweden in 1840, due to custom and monopoly of land in the hands of the gentry and the peasant. The overpopulation was most keenly felt in regions with poorer soil and during periods of crop failures. It was the inability of the landless population and the younger generations to acquire land and economic prosperity that turned the steps of many thousands toward the new world.

[1] Wohlin, "Den jordbruksidkande befolkningen i Sverige," *op. cit.*, pp. 248 ff.

# CHAPTER V

## SWEDISH IMMIGRATION TO THE UNITED STATES IN THE FORTIES

The seizure of the Swedish colony on the Delaware by the Dutch in 1655 ended, for the time being, Swedish immigration to the Western Hemisphere. It is true that since the Swedish sailors sailed under many flags, occasionally one or another would choose America for a permanent home. The amount of Swedish subjects that trickled into the Western world during the next two centuries is hard to determine. Their numbers were so small that as late as 1850, when Jenny Lind, the great Swedish singer, appeared before American audiences under the direction of Mr. Barnum of circus fame, Swedes were known as Jenny Lind men.[1]

There were evidences, however, of Swedish immigration to the United States before 1840. A man who perhaps was more responsible for directing Swedish emigration toward Illinois in the forties, than anyone else, O. G. Hedström, the Methodist immigrant missionary of the "Bethel-ship" of New York harbor, had arrived in New York in 1825. He came on board a Swedish war vessel as secretary to one of the officers.[2] Robbed of his money while on shore leave, he was forced to remain, and was later converted to Methodism. Upon a visit to Sweden in 1833, he persuaded his brother Jonas, both to accept the new faith and to return with him to America. Jonas Hedström became a Methodist missionary in the frontier state of Illinois, and welcomed the fellow countrymen sent to him from New York. John Ericsson, the famous inventor of the "Monitor," was another who came during the early period seeking opportunities for an engineer.

[1] The United States kept no statistics of immigration until 1820. From 1814 on, Swedes and Norwegians were counted together in American statistics and often confused. It was not until 1850 that the Swedish government took notice of emigration in its official statistics.

[2] Eric Norelius, *De svenska luteriska församlingarnas och svenskarnes historia i Amerika* (Rock Island, Illinois, 1890), I, 16.

An early contact with Texas was made when S. M. Svenson, who had emigrated from Småland in 1836, was sent by his Baltimore employers to Texas.[1] And when the first party of Swedes, under the leadership of Unonius, arrived in Milwaukee in 1841, they met a fellow-countryman, Captain Lange. There were undoubtedly others scattered through the states, some who proved friends to the new arrivals of the forties, and others who had almost forgotten their mother-tongue.

The en masse emigration to the United States from Sweden was later in beginning than that of Norway, Germany, or the British Isles. The stream of German and British emigrants had flowed with varying consistency since the seventeenth century, and had been especially reinforced after the Napoleonic wars by the Irish peasant and the German liberal. Norwegian emigration began in 1825, and continued with increasing impetus during the thirties. It was not until 1841 that the first Swedish colony of the nineteenth century was established in the United States, at Pine Lake, Wisconsin. In 1840 Unonius, a young government official in the provincial office at Uppsala, decided to try his fortune in the new world. He wrote in his memoirs,

I can, I thought, take such a step, I have heard about America.[2] Its rich soil and its industrial possibilities invite just at present thousands of Europeans, who in their homelands have in one way or another been hampered in their hopes by the economic circumstances of their homes, or by a precarious livelihood. Work, in any industry only that it is honorable, in America is no shame. Every workman has there the same right of citizenship as the nobles. Conventional judgments, class interest and narrow-mindedness do not hang to your coat tail nor trample on your heels.[3]

It became the talk of the town of Uppsala that Unonius and his bride were emigrating. Two young men of twenty-one, Ivar Hagberg, a student, and Carl Groth, a relative of Unonius, decided to accompany them. The young bride also brought her maid, Christine. The party decided to sail from Gävle, a port on the eastern

[1] *Ibid.*, p. 37.

[2] Gustav Unonius, *Minnen af en sjuttonårig vistelse i nordvestra Amerika* (Uppsala, 1862), I, 4 ff.

[3] *Ibid.*, p. 4. It must be remembered that class distinctions were tightly drawn in Europe at that time, and manual labor depreciated.

coast of Sweden, and there another young man, a former university student, William Polman, joined them.[1] A clipper ship with a load of iron destined for New York took the original six to the United States for the sum of 500 riksdaler, about $26.00 each. They had to furnish their own food and bedding.

The members of the little party were quite ignorant about the country to which they were going, and especially about the Middle West, the haven of the German and Norwegian emigrants of the thirties. They spent a week in New York trying to find out something about the conditions in the west.[2] Unonius wrote,

We were surprised to find that most people knew less about Illinois and Iowa than we. A resident of New York, Brodell, gave us some advice. Moreover, we had the luck to meet a countryman who had been in Illinois for a long period of time and had made some money. He was now returning home, and advised us to go to that state, which he described as one of the most wonderful regions in the world with extensive, fruitful, easily cultivated plains. If one desired to engage in agriculture, the emigrant could choose from a great surplus of vacant lands. There were many opportunities to earn an income. We decided to go.

During the journey by canal boat they were dissuaded by several Americans, as well as Europeans, who "praised Wisconsin as the most beautiful and most fruitful region in the great west, and under present conditions the best for emigrants."[3] On the lake boat it was reported that all the best Illinois lands were in the hands of speculators, and since the majority of the emigrants on the boat were leaving at Milwaukee, the Swedish party decided to do the same. Meeting a Norwegian girl at the warehouse, they were directed to Captain Lange, a Swede living in Milwaukee.[4] After inspecting the lands near Milwaukee, Unonius decided on a farm at Pine Lake, not far from Delafield, Wisconsin.

There were constant additions and withdrawals from the colony for several years. The next spring, Polman left for a more populous district to practice medicine which he had studied in Sweden.[5] The

[1] Ibid., pp. 9–14.

[2] Ibid., p. 34.

[3] Ibid., pp. 110–11. One of the party, Ivar Hagberg, left the party at Detroit to go to Cleveland (ibid., p. 93).

[4] Ibid., p. 113.

[5] Ernest Olson, History of the Swedes of Illinois (Chicago, 1908), I, 189.

same year Baron Thott from Skane, E. Bergvall from Gothenburg, and A. Wadman, a retired merchant of Norrköping, arrived at the colony. The baron and Bergvall purchased land, while Wadman went to Milwaukee. A shoemaker, B. Peterson, was soon added to the colony. Unonius wrote letters to the Swedish newspapers describing the possibilities of Wisconsin for the emigrant and attracted settlers in this manner from all the Scandinavian countries.[1] The settlers were mostly of the middle class, army officers, decadent noblemen, and university graduates, unaccustomed to the hard labor of wresting soil from its virginity. The soil that had been selected was rather poor in fertility. It was never a prosperous colony. In 1842 Captain P. von Schneidau, formerly of the royal artillery and from a noble family in Östergötland, joined the colony.[2] A minister, Peter Bockman, from the Swedish state church, attempted to establish a Lutheran church in the colony in 1844, but failed.

As early as 1842, Unonius had left Pine Lake to enter the theological seminary of the Episcopal church. He was ordained in 1845 and became a missionary among the Norwegians and Swedes of Wisconsin. Failing to get much interest there in the Episcopal church, he finally went to Chicago in 1849, and established a Swedish Episcopal church, St. Ansgarius.[3] Carl Groth departed for New Orleans where he became a business man. Schneidau left the colony in 1845 and located in Chicago. In 1854 he was appointed the Swedish and Norwegian consul. When Frederika Bremer, the novelist, visited the colony in 1850, there were only a few people left.

The little Swedish colony at Pine Lake, although badly scattered, still contains a half a dozen families who live as farmers in the neighborhood. . . . . Almost all of them live in log cabins and appear to have few means. The most prosperous is a smith . . . . who has built a lovely frame house in the woods. Bergvall is also prosperous. He has been one of the gentry in Sweden, but here he is a practical peasant, and has obtained several acres of good land which he works with much industry and perseverance, and he seems well and has a happy, optimistic, Swedish nature.[4]

Miss Bremer was especially attracted to the young wife, but she wrote that only intense love and great trust could force the young

[1] Ibid.     [2] Bockman returned to Sweden and died in 1850 (ibid., pp. 192 ff.).

[3] A. T. Andreas, History of Chicago (Chicago, 1884), I, 338.

[4] Frederika Bremer, Hemman i nya verlden (Stockholm, 1866), II, 55 ff.

woman to accept the burdens and sacrifices of the American frontier. In the evening while rowing on the lake, the Swedish novelist commented,

Here, on a high promontory covered with gleaming masses of leaves, the "new Uppsala" was to stand, so Unonius and his friends had planned when they first came into the wilderness and were delighted by its beauty. Alas! the wild soil would not support Uppsala's sons. I saw the deserted houses where he [Unonius] and Schneidau in vain fought poverty and attempted to live.[1]

The Pine Lake colony soon became known in Sweden through newspaper reports and personal letters. In spite of the discouragements that the settlers met in their battle with the sterile soil and the wilderness which they had been so unfortunate to select, their letters to friends and relatives in Sweden were most enthusiastic. Unonius' letters found their way into the press and Schneidau's letters, sent to his father in Östergötland, were copied and read by many of the common people, inspiring an emigration from that region which was diverted to Iowa in 1845.

There is no doubt that the facts of German and Norwegian emigration to the United States were known in Sweden in the forties, at least among the educated classes. Unonius spoke of the inspiration that it had given him to try his adventure in the new world. The same year that Unonius had planned to emigrate, a society was organized in Stockholm, consisting of persons who were contemplating seeking the new world the following year, in 1841. To obtain adherents, the society advertised through the press by publishing its laws. Its pamphlet, containing the purpose of its organization, its constitution and by-laws, information about America and how to reach it, with an account of the Norwegian settlers in the United States, was published in 1841 by Carl von Schiele, the secretary.[2]

[1] *Ibid.*, p. 59.

[2] Carl Alex Adam von Schiele, *Några korta underrättelser om Amerika, till upplysning och nytta för dem som ämna dit utflytta; samt emigrants föreningens stadgar och förslager för en uttämnad utflyttning år 1841*, med en karta, utgifne af föreningens secreterare i 1840 (Stockholm, 1841). Another addition in Norwegian appeared in 1843, *Underretninger om America, fornemmlingen de States, hvori udvandredi Normaend have nedsat sig, samlede af en emigrants forening i Stockholm, først udgivne paa Svensk af foreningens secretair og nu til deel i extract oversatte og nogle ketterser og tilloeg udgivne* (Skien: Melgaard, 1843).

The pamphlet explained,

Under this name [Emigrant Society] there was organized in Stockholm last year, a society whose members, although bearing a deep affection for the mother country, still felt that the effects of the increasing poverty of the country, added to some dissatisfaction with one or another of the economic restrictions of the government, decided to seek a more pleasant home in some other portion of the world, since they were worried over the economic future of themselves and their families.[1]

They decided upon the United States, for it offered greater freedom than Australia. After advertising in the newspapers a group of fifty interested people came together, but most of them, young men of the educated classes, desired only to accompany the colony to America, by paying down a passenger fee. It was therefore decided to give up the idea of planting a colony in 1841, although some of the members emigrated in the fall. The remaining still hoped to establish a settlement there, and planned, according to the pamphlets, to reorganize the society for the purpose of at least sending a nucleus of a colony in 1842. But the colony does not seem to have materialized.

The account of America and its economic possibilities that appeared in the pamphlet were taken from a Norwegian account by Ole Rynning, who had traveled in the new world in 1837.[2] There were already seven settlements of Norwegians in the United States. The earliest Norwegian colony had been located at Morristown, New York, in 1825, but by 1837 most of these colonists had moved to the frontier in the Middle West, and only two or three families remained. A settlement on the Fox River, near Ottawa, Illinois, dated from 1834. Near LaFayette, Indiana, a number of Norwegian families from Drammer had already acquired several hundred acres of land. Some families from Stavanger had located in Shelby County, Missouri, in 1837. A fifth settlement was to be found on the Beaver River in Iroquois County in Illinois, and a sixth near Madison, Wisconsin, where Telle peasants had founded a colony. A seventh colony had found its way into southeastern Missouri, at Jarveys. The pamphlet of the Swedish Emigrant Society emphasized the advisability of settling in the states of Illinois, Missouri, and Indiana,

[1] Schiele, *ibid.*, p. 46.    [2] *Underretninger om America*, pp. 13–14.

since they had been highly recommended by Rynning.[1] Definite, reasons were stated for the decision. In the first place the climate was most like Sweden, though milder. The land in the Middle West was cheaper and very fertile. There were very few taxes, no privileged classes, no quartering of soldiers on the community, no compulsory posting service, etc., while transportation between towns was very good on canals and rivers.[2] The region was moreover sparsely settled; Illinois with an area of 2,780 square miles had only 100,000 inhabitants, and Missouri whose area contained 2,840 square miles could count only 130,000 inhabitants, according to the pamphlet, in 1840.

Instructions for reaching Illinois and Missouri were also included.[3] The best way was to sail from Sweden to New York, then take passage on a steamer on the Hudson to Albany from where Buffalo could be reached by canal boat. A steamer on the Great Lakes would take the emigrant to Milwaukee or Chicago, from where the journey went southward to Beaver Creek or westward to the Fox River. It would cost 60 riksdaler or $16.00 from New York to Beaver Creek. Missouri might be reached from Europe by way of New Orleans, and a steamer on the Mississippi to St. Louis. A final warning stated that without work one received nothing in America.[4]

The Norwegian reprint went farther in advising what classes should emigrate. There was a need for skilled artisans like smiths, tailors, shoemakers, carpenters, etc.[5] Servant girls were in much demand and were treated with more respect than among the middle class of Norway. Women were also very soon married after arriving in America. The pamphlet did not advise drunkards or lazy people to emigrate. It also discouraged students, doctors, druggists, and professional men unless they were willing to take up land and work with their hands. It further advised, "He who cannot, nor does not desire to work need never count on wealth nor well-being. No, in America a person does not attain it without work, but it is true that

[1] Schiele, *op. cit.*, pp. 41–42.
[2] The latter two reasons reflect the burdens of the Swedish landholder.
[3] Schiele, *op. cit.*, p. 42.
[4] *Utan arbete erhålles intet i America!*
[5] *Underretningener om America*, pp. 27–29.

he can there, with industry and frugality, soon reach economic independence and can meet old age without fear."

The Swedish press before the forties could hardly be considered an influence in promoting emigration. The United States as yet received very casual notice in the press of the larger cities in Sweden, less than most of the European cities. About 1840 news-items about the new world began to appear in the rural press in the regions that later contributed liberally to emigration. But it was not until emigration started from these regions that the papers seem to have made a special effort to include news from overseas and comments on emigration. *Aftonbladet*, one of the popular Stockholm dailies, edited by the famous Liberal leader, L. J. Hjerta, was taken for an example of the urban press. The type of news that appeared in *Aftonbladet* about America in 1839 was comments on riots in Pennsylvania, boundary troubles between the United States and Canada, the President's message to Congress, the prosperity of Boston and Massachusetts, conditions in Texas, etc.[1]

In the press in southern Sweden in *Lunds Weckoblad, Malmö Nya Allehanda, Malmö Tidning*, and *Skånska Correspondenten*, there appeared no news about America until the fifties. *Skånska Posten*, however, did carry such items as early as 1840. The news comments were much like that of *Aftonbladet*, Van Buren's message, the boundary trouble in Maine, the possibilities of war between the United States and England, and the coming elections of 1840.[2] There were some news items on gold and silver in the United States, and the number of soldiers and marines in the army. Even as late as the fifties and the early sixties the press of Southern Sweden, including *Skånska Posten*, rather neglected American news. Nor were there any advertisements of steamship accommodations or emigration

---

[1] *Det Adertonde Aftonbladet*, edited by L. J. Hjerta (Stockholm); January 4, 1839, President Van Buren's speech to Congress; January 8, 1839, riots in Pennsylvania; January 12, 1839, résumé of Van Buren's speech; January 16, 1839, more about riots, prosperity of Boston and Massachusetts, conditions in Texas; April 6, 1839, boundary troubles in Maine.

[2] *Skånska Posten* (Kristianstad); February 1, 1840, the arrival of the *Siddons* from New York with President Van Buren's message; April 29, 1840, trouble in Maine; May 6, 1840, reprint from *New York Morning Herald* defying England in case of war, June 17, 1840, coming elections, wealth of gold and silver in United States; August 1, 1840, number of soldiers and marines in the United States.

companies until 1855, when the Emigrant Company, Europa, located at Hamburg, advertised in *Helsingborgs-Posten*.[1] It was not until 1866 and 1867 that advertisements of this kind became frequent and usual in the Swedish press.[2] The emigration of the later forties and fifties from Southern Sweden can hardly be said to have been influenced by the press.

Another region in Sweden that has been prolific in emigration is Småland. In *Jönköpings Tidning* there appeared no news about America in 1839 and 1840; however, in 1841 the McLeod trial in New York and the threatened war between England and America was considered worthy of mention.[3] But even in this newspaper there appeared few items about America until 1846, when the emigration to the United States began to focus attention.[4] A press notice, from Gothenburg, of June 6, 1846, announced the departure of two iron freighters for New York, on which some 150 emigrants had engaged passage.[5] In the same editions there were comments on the extensive Norwegian emigration, with a report that three ships carrying 429 emigrants were bound for America, two from Bergen with 276 passengers, and one from Stavanger with 153. On July 11, 1846, there appeared a news item from Stockholm, the departure of two ships from Stockholm with 190 America-bound passengers, many of whom were dissenters from Norrland.[6] In Småland, newspaper comment might have influenced emigration, for the exodus from this region began about 1846, and the sterility of the soil here has always provided economic reasons for seeking a livelihood elsewhere.

It was not until the press was filled with comments of the Jansonite heresy, and the departure of that sect for America, that the Norrland papers began to feature news-items about the new world.[7]

[1] *Nyare Helsingborgs Posten* (Hälsingborg), June 2, 1855 to August 18, 1855.

[2] *Ibid.*, February 22, 1866; *Malmö Nya Allehanda* (Malmö), March 6, 1867.

[3] *Jönköpings Tidning* (Jönköping), May 1, 1841; October 16, 1841; November 6, 1841.

[4] In 1845 there was no single mention of the United States in *Jönköpings Tidning*.

[5] *Jönköpings Tidning*, June 6, 1846.    [6] *Ibid.*, July 11, 1846.

[7] *Hudikswalls Weckoblad* (Hudiksvall), March 8, 1845, March 22, April, 5, April 26, May 17, June 21, July 12, November 22, 1845, January 31, 1846, February 7, February 14, etc.

Some of the news from America consisted of a comparison of the American and Swedish tariff systems,[1] the inaugural of Polk, and the pending annexation of Texas.[2] Fires in various places in the United States received attention, as well as the record trip of an English steamship, "Great Britain," which made a transoceanic trip from Liverpool to New York in fourteen days and twenty-one hours.[3]

The notice that the emigration of the persecuted Jansonite sect received in the Norrland press in 1845 and 1846 undoubtedly had a very definite influence on migration from the northern part of Sweden during the late forties. The constant discussion of the persecutions was sometimes diverted to a description of the country to which the Jansonites intended to go. Such a description of the economic opportunities offered in the Mississippi Valley appeared in the *Hudiksvall Weekly*, November 22, 1845. A part of the newspaper article stated,

> Within the Eric-Jansonite sect there is much discussion of emigrating to the United States in the spring. They expect to locate near the Mississippi river. On the savannas along the Mississippi and its tributaries they hope to find the "promised land." It is, however, true that these savannas are very fertile, especially in the production of wheat, maize, and rice, many fruits, flax and hemp. Nature here is very generous and mild. But what is primarily attracting the Jansonites, is that there, every one enjoys complete religious freedom.[4]

An earlier comment had disclosed the fact that the brothers Olaf and Jon Olsson in Söderala, both fervent Jansonites, had sold their farms and were going to emigrate to America.[5] And in a subsequent letter written from New York by one of the emigrants, the United States is described as a wonderful country.[6] He continued,

> Grain and food are very cheap, but since labor is very high, prices will soon rise. A simple carpenter gets two dollars or eight riksdaler a day, and a laborer who only lifts and carries, six riksdaler, but it is hard to obtain labor without knowing the language. It costs forty to fifty riksdaler, about ten dollars, to go inland to the Swedes and Norwegians.

Letters and newspaper publicity were the spur to the early emigration of the forties and fifties from Dalarne and Hälsingland in

[1] *Ibid.*, January 18, 1845.    [3] *Ibid.*, May 24, July 12, September 13, 1845.

[2] *Ibid.*, April 12, 1845.    [4] *Ibid.*, November 22, 1845.

[5] *Norrlands Posten* (Gävle), September 2, 1845.

[6] This letter is signed C.G.B. (Helsi), *Hudikswalls Weckoblad*, April 17, 1847.

Norrland. Steamship companies and emigrant agencies had as yet not detected the movement from this region. It was not until the years between 1864 and 1867 that they thought either Småland or Norrland worth the expense of advertisement.[1]

Personal correspondence was, during the forties and fifties, as it has since continued to be, the most potent force in stimulating emigration. Some of these letters appeared in the press, as the one cited. Most of them were read to relatives and friends, often copied to be reread to larger audiences. Thus it was that the letters of Gustaf Flack from Hälsingland, resident in Victoria, Illinois, and later in Chicago during the early forties, influenced the Jansonites. In his letters, written to his relatives in Alfta parish, Hälsingland, he praised the economic possibilities of America, and stressed particularly the religious freedom of the country.[2] Letters from Unonius and Schneidau of the Pine Lake colony attracted emigrants from Småland and Östergötland.[3] These settlers in turn, through more letters, attracted others, and thus the ball was set rolling.

The vivid pictures of a utopia where the poor man might obtain lands in a short time by the sweat of his brow were dramatically and enthusiastically presented by certain emigrants who had returned from America with apparent prosperity and proved an irresistible force. As early as 1844, Carl Peter Moberg returned to his home in Grenna, Småland, and aroused in his friends and neighbors the desire to try their luck in a land of great opportunity.[4] The very successful plantation owner of Texas, S. M. Svensson, visited his old mother in the poverty-stricken province of Småland in 1849 and demonstrated what a poor boy could do in the new world.[5] The following year he sent passage money for fifty agricultural laborers to come to Texas as indentured servants. In this way contacts had been made between the province of Småland in Sweden and the state of Texas, and the way was open for others to follow.

[1] The earliest steamship advertisement appears in *Jönköpings Tidning*, February 13, 1864, and of an emigrant company in *Hudikswalls-Posten*, July 21, 1866, *Norrlands-Posten*, May 18, 1867.

[2] Norelius, *op. cit.*, I, 28; Olson, *op. cit.*, I, 185.

[3] In the part of the Swedish press that I reviewed, I failed to find any of these letters.

[4] Norelius, *op. cit.*, I, 43.        [5] *Ibid.*, p. 36–38.

There were no peculiar economic conditions in Sweden during the forties that sent a stream of emigrants from a poverty-stricken country. On the contrary, as has been mentioned, it was the beginning of a new era of agricultural prosperity for the kingdom. It was not only a period of rising wages but also one of rising living costs. Even the common people were demanding the luxury of coffee and sugar and "store clothes." There were, of course, regions in Sweden where the soil was not fertile, the farms were small and the steadily increasing population, with the growing demand for a higher standard of living, made it desirable for the more ambitious of the younger generation to seek a promising economic environment. Although the majority of the emigrants of the forties and fifties were young people, it was a period peculiar for the departure of many families with small children. The Swedes left their native land in large parties, under a leader or guide, who was frequently a Swedish-American, but sometimes a minister of the State church or the leader of a dissenting group. These companies at times formed their own settlements in America, while others scattered among the various older Swedish colonies.

A typical example of this exodus is found in Kinda hundred in the southeastern part of Östergötland. From this region around the town of Kisa, emigration began in 1842, influenced by the letters of Captain von Schneidau written to his father, Major von Schneidau.[1] Peter Cassel led a party of thirty to the United States that year. He was a man of 54 who had been rather prosperous in life as a miller and the bailiff of an estate. His wife and five children accompanied him. Their destination was Pine Lake, Wisconsin, but accidentally becoming acquainted with Pehr Dahlberg who happened to be going to New York to meet his family, the Cassel party was persuaded to go on to Iowa to settle. Here they founded New Sweden, west of Burlington. Cassel in turn wrote letters persuading the people from his home region in Sweden to emigrate to Iowa.

Kinda hundred, Östergötland, was described by the governor of the county, C. O. Palmstjerna, in 1849, as a hilly, wooded region, with limited agricultural possibilities and extensive stretches of forests.[2]

[1] Flom, "Early Swedish Immigration to Iowa," *Iowa Journal of History and Politics*, October, 1905, pp. 601–2. Norelius, *op. cit.*, I, 27.

[2] *K. bfhde femårsberättelse, Östergötlands län, 1842–1847*, p. 6.

"The timber," he stated, "could not be exported because of the difficulties and distance of transportation." There was no mining in the region. Wages were low. The desire for a higher standard of living had spread even here, and the opportunities for satisfying the demand were not present where there were only limited agricultural opportunities. There was no religious dissatisfaction nor political unrest in Kinda hundred. The cause for emigration from the region was simply the conviction that in the new land which the people were seeking, there was a better material future than in the old fatherland. "The economic conditions in the free states of North America," continued the governor in his report, "have been so wonderfully pictured in the public press, that it has impressed the people, and the temptation to discover what truth lies in it, is great."[1] From Östergötland 115 passports were granted in 1846 and as many as 400 between 1847 and 1849. Whole families of well-to-do peasants left. In one case a husband and wife and their eight children and servants departed. There were also many newlyweds and young single men "crossing the ocean to seek their future."

Misadventure of one sort or another after their arrival in the United States prevented some of the emigrants from Kisa, Östergötland, from reaching their friends in New Sweden, Iowa. One group in 1846 were lost in Iowa and finally came to Fort Des Moines. They continued twenty-five miles further west and four families decided to settle near an American pioneer, while the rest of the party finally found New Sweden. The new settlement was called Swede Point or Madrid.[2] They found themselves in an American frontier community. Their American neighbor supplied them with corn and potatoes, and showed them where to find timber with which to build their homes. Later in the fall, a man from Missouri brought a load of flour which he sold at $5.00 per 100 pounds. Another drove a herd of cattle through the region and one family purchased a cow and a calf for $10.00.

The same year another large emigrant party of seventy-five, on their way from Kisa to Iowa, were robbed of their money at Albany, New York. After a painful journey during which they subsisted pri-

[1] *Ibid.*

[2] Skarstedt, *Svensk-Amerikanska folket* (Stockholm, 1917), pp. 35–36. Norelius, *cp. cit.*, I, 27.

marily on wild plums, they finally reached Buffalo where they remained two years as farm laborers to earn enough money to continue their journey westward. The party divided, some proceeding westward, finally settling in Andover, Illinois. The others joined another group of newly arrived immigrants and settled in Sugar Grove, Pennsylvania, and Jamestown, New York.[1] In 1852, a large number of Swedes were added to the Jamestown colony. Here they were employed in the mills and factories.[2]

Letters from Cassel in Iowa found their way into the Swedish press and undoubtedly were influential in stimulating emigration to the middle states. One that appeared in *Östgötha Correspondenten* in July, 1849, was copied also in *Norrlands-Posten* during the same month.[3] It was a lengthy narrative which described conditions in Iowa in much detail. Cassel wrote,

No one in Sweden can dream of the possibilities that America offers to temperate, dependable and industrious persons. For people of this type it is a virtual Canaan, where wealth of nature can be said to flow actually of milk and honey. But those who neither can nor desire to work, who have other hopes when they depart from Sweden, will find here a Siberia from which they must sooner or later return to the fatherland or find themselves sunk into the deepest misery and poverty. See, in this way this country can be both a Canaan and a Siberia. It is a strange country. You, my brother Johan, have asked me ten questions which I shall answer to the best of my ability. First, the war with Mexico has brought no hardships upon the inhabitants [of the United States], for not a cent has been demanded of anyone, and no one was forced to take arms, for the soldiers were all volunteers. Their wages were $8.00 a month and food. A bounty of $12.00 and a choice of 160 acres of land, wherever there was free land, were given upon honorable release after the war. There is here a small standing army of 6,000 men who serve for five years, and then they are honorably discharged, and if they so desire, they may serve five years more. The war, as you know, is now ended.

Second, the possibilities of our virgin land vary; near the streams the land is low, overgrown with a variety of large trees, like black and white walnut, elm, sycamore, cottonwood, mulberry, etc., as well as much wild grape vine which clings to the trees. These tracts of land are not profitable for cultivation, and

[1] Skarstedt, *op. cit.*, p. 41; Norelius, *op. cit.*, I, 31 ff.

[2] *Hemlandet*, March 29, 1859. Letter from C. to newspaper, translated by George M. Stephenson in *Swedish Historical Society Year Book, 1922-1923*, pp. 96-97.

[3] *Östgötha Correspondenten* (Linköping), July 7 and 11, 1849; *Sjette Norrlands-Posten* (Gävle), July 12 and 19, 1849. The letter was dated December 13, 1848, from Fairfield, Iowa.

have a dismal and unpleasant appearance. Contrasting to these swamps are what might be called woods or timberland, rather beautiful, similar to an oak woods on a Swedish plain, which, from the middle of April to the beginning of November, changes its garments of flowers and leaves each month. The summer is beautiful. There are here too large plains which do not bear trees, but only tall grass and flowers; these are called prairies. They are on the whole very flat, while the woodlands are formed like waves, neither great heights nor deep valleys. The soil is free from stones, but near the streams and brooks there may be found lime and sand stone, and some coal towards the west along the creeks. Among the wild fruits, the most common are mulberries, unusually good white and black raspberries . . . . wild strawberries, somewhat sour May apples, . . . . three kinds of plums, some unusually good cherries, small and black, in taste and appearance very much like a sort of black "bird cherries"[1] which grow in the orchard of the estate[2] at Redeby. The apples are like your wild apples; wild grapes are small and sour, but I must say that they make good grape juice, which is very much like red wine; the currants are small and not so very good; ground cherries grow in our fields among the maize, large as "clear cherries,"[3] rather good and sweet, which replant themselves by seed annually; hops here are also enough for our needs. All of these varieties grow wild and have little market value.

Third, all the species of trees that grow in Sweden are found here, except the evergreens. Cedar—its needles are like heather—is the only evergreen that we have, but it only grows on high hills which have a sterile soil. . . . . Fourth, the cultivation of the soil consists of cutting away the timber, which can be used for fencing and for construction of buildings;[4] then plowing once, and without doing any more the soil is planted with all sorts of crops like maize, potatoes, melons, etc. Fences are hedges that grow.[5] . . . . Tenth, I do not think that anyone will desire to return to Sweden for it would take too much time and money, and, if these were no hindrances why should he emigrate in the first place?

Cassel also gave advice about traveling. He advised taking warm clothing for the ocean trip, and packing extra clothes and shoes tightly, not to be opened during the voyage, to prevent mold. He explained that upon changing coins with the captain to take only American coin. Prices in America were cited: a pair of oxen for $40.00 to $50.00, a good horse the same, a cow $10.00 to $12.00, a fat hog $4.00, a large sheep $1.25. Wheat was only 50 cents a bushel,

[1] A literal translation of *fogelbär*.

[2] *Säteriet.*    [3] *Klarkörsbär.*

[4] It was not until later that it was discovered that the prairies were fertile. The early settlers in the Middle West thought they must be sterile since no trees grew there.

[5] Evidently referring to the hedges which were planted for fences.

a barrel of wheat flour $3.50, butter 8 cents a pound.[1] He stated that the cost of the trip from Sweden to Iowa could be made for about 200 riksdaler, which would be about $50.00. He replied to a question asked by his brother-in-law if he might use Cassel's money as loans to people desiring to emigrate, by stating that he would be willing to make the loans if the people were honorable. Cassel mentioned that schools in America were free, i.e., no one was forced to attend, and no one need pay for an education, since the federal government had endowed the schools with a section of land in each township. In the letter, Cassel invited his brother-in-law to come to America, "You and Almini are welcome. You will never regret the decision. Almini will be very prosperous here with his trade as a painter."

From the region of Hälsingland, Medelpad, and Gästrikland in southern Norrland, there was also an early emigration. The Jansonites began to leave this region in 1846 to seek religious freedom in the new world,[2] through the influence of Falk's letter. Olof Olsson, one of the faithful who went ahead to reconnoiter, was directed to Victoria, Illinois, by the immigrant missionary in New York City, O. G. Hedström. After traveling through Illinois, Minnesota, and Wisconsin, Olsson decided upon a location near Victoria, Illinois, which was called Bishop Hill, the name of the home of their leader, Eric Jansson, in Sweden. This colony was re-enforced by nine parties of immigrants from 1847 to 1854, and soon counted one thousand members, practically all from Norrland.[3] Some of the dissatisfied members of the colony left Bishop Hill and located at Victoria, Galesburg, and Andover, Illinois.

The exodus of the Jansonites was given much publicity in the Swedish press. The news of their economic success stimulated other groups from the same region to leave for America. Most of the people of this region were dissenters and some were "Luther-readers" or Hedbergians. One large party of 147 people accompanied by the

[1] Wheat was considered a great luxury in Sweden and was only used during the holidays and festivals. Rye was the common breadstuff.

[2] A more detailed account is given in the next chapter under religious causes.

[3] A letter reprinted in the newspaper gives an account of the various ships that the Jansonites traveled on in 1846 (*Hudikswall-Weckoblad*, April 17, 1847).

young clergyman, Esbjörn, departed in 1849 and upon arrival in New York City was persuaded by the agent of a New York land company, Captain P. W. Wirström, to settle in Andover, Illinois. There were already a few Swedes resident in Andover and a party from Kisa, Östergötland, on their way to Iowa, had been diverted to this region the same year.[1] The letters of Andrew Snygg from Victoria, Illinois, to his relatives were copied and read extensively among the Hedbergians in Hälsingland in 1850, and awakened the "America fever." In a party of one hundred who left the port of Gävle on a clipper ship loaded with iron was Eric Norelius, a lad of seventeen who was destined to be one of the leaders in the organization of the Swedish Lutheran church in the United States.[2] The party joined the colony at Andover.

Chicago had by this time become a distribution point for the western immigration. Many Swedish immigrants had passed through Chicago, and a few had remained in the year 1846; the first party settling there consisted of fifteen families.[3] Captain von Schneidau had already left the Pine Lake colony and resided in Chicago. These early settlers were destitute and knew little English. Von Schneidau came to their assistance as interpreter and adviser. He obtained work for the men, to clear and saw wood, and for the women to wash for the American families. Each year an increasing number of Swedish immigrants arrived, some only to pass through the city on their way westward to the agricultural communities, and others to find their homes in the fast-growing city. In the year 1850 alone, as many as 500 came, most of whom were poverty-stricken after their long journey across the Atlantic. Wages were low, only fifty to seventy-five cents a day. For several years cholera raged and many died. By 1849 Unonius had established a Swedish Episcopal church in the city.[4] In 1853 the Reverend Erland Carlson had organized a Swedish Lutheran church there,[5] and in the same year the Rev. S. B. Newman had developed a Swedish Methodist church.[6] A Scandinavian Lutheran church had been

[1] Norelius, *op. cit.*, I, 31. They had planned to go to Cassel in Iowa but were diverted by O. G. Hedström.

[2] *Ibid.*, p. 38–46.     [4] Andreas, *op. cit.*, I, 338.

[3] *Ibid.*, p. 30.     [5] *Ibid.*, p. 350.     [6] *Ibid.*, p. 332.

erected in 1848.[1] There was also a Swedish Baptist church organized in 1853.[2] The various Scandinavian clergymen and Captain Schneidau, who was the vice-consul for Sweden and Norway in Chicago in 1854, labored among the destitute countrymen and proved to be friends in need. There were many Swedish communities in Illinois by 1854.[3] Settlements had been established at Andover, Bishop Hill, Swedona, Victoria, Galesburg, Moline, Rock Island, and Wataga between 1846 and 1849.[4] In the early fifties were added Princeton, Geneva, Knoxville, and Rockford. Other provinces in Sweden besides Östergötland and Norrland were contributing settlers to Illinois, i.e., northern Skåne, Västergötland, and Småland.

The Swedish colony in Texas, as already stated, was established in 1850 by a group of indentured servants from Småland, brought by contract to their fellow countryman, Svensson. After working off their indenture they acquired small pieces of land. Among those who joined the Texas colony was a cousin of Svensson's, Svante Palm, who later became the Swedish vice-consul of Austin. He described the Swedish settlement in a letter to the Swedish-American newspaper, *Hemlandet*, in August, 1855.[5] He wrote,

In this city, the state capitol, reside between fifty and seventy-five Swedes, men, women, and children, and there are about as many in the surrounding country—possibly less. Nearly everyone who has been here three years, has, according to our knowledge, acquired from 100 to 320 acres of land, some of us own city lots. . . . . We all live (or nearly all) in a community along Brushy Creek, Williamson County, about fifteen or twenty miles from Austin. . . . . We are all from Småland, Jönköping County, Tveta, Vestra, and Södra Vedbo härader. Every year a few relatives and friends join us, and at the present writing we are expecting a few recruits. A scattering of Swedes live in other parts of Texas, but Brushy is the only settlement. In eastern Texas in Cherokee and surrounding counties, there are between three and four hundred Norwegian families.

[1] *Ibid.*, p. 349.

[2] *Ibid.*, p. 324.

[3] Unonius' work among the cholera patients was praised in the *Chicago Daily Journal*, January 14, 15, 1850.

[4] Skarstedt, *op. cit.*, p. 41.

[5] *Hemlandet*, August 28, 1855. Letter from Svante Palm, Austin, Texas, to Rev. T. N. Hasselquist, Galesburg, Illinois, July 9, 1855, translated by G. M. Stephenson in *Swedish Historical Society Year Book, 1922–1923*, pp. 68–69.

Emigration from northern Skåne, especially from the Kristianstad region, began about 1851. One Christian Jönnson from Åkarp had been induced by the many accounts, in the Swedish press, of the free and fertile lands of America to make a scouting expedition in 1848 to ascertain whether they were true.[1] He had no friends in the United States and therefore sought the advice of the missionary of the "Bethel-ship" in New York, who persuaded him to try Knox County in Illinois. Here he visited Bishop Hill and Galesburg and returned to Sweden after six months, praising the "new world."

In 1851 a small party of agricultural laborers from the Kristianstad neighborhood decided to emigrate. At the port of Gothenburg they met an emigrant party from Östergötland on its way to Sugar Grove, Pennsylvania. In the group from Kristianstad was Ola Nelson from Önnestad, upon whose suggestion the Rev. Hasselquist was called as a minister to Galesburg the following year, and also Hans Mattson, later an important figure in the history of Minnesota. The emigrants from Skåne went on to Galesburg and Knoxville, Illinois, where they had a friend, a carpenter by the name of Löfgren. Hasselquist came the following year to Galesburg with sixty additional settlers.[2] The original scout, Christian Jönnson, arrived in 1852 with thirty of his countrymen. Nils Håkanson, one of the Swedish immigrants who had taken part in the gold rush to California, returned to Sweden and was back again in 1852 with fifty persons, chiefly from Skåne.

Emigrants from Grenna, Smaland, began to direct their course to a colony at La Fayette, Indiana, in 1849. The enthusiastic accounts of America as pictured by Carl Peter Moberg upon his return to Sweden in 1844 aroused a desire among his neighbors in Grenna, Smaland, to try the new world.[3] In 1849, Johannes Peterson, the son of a peasant from Örserum, Grenna parish, left for America and finally came to La Fayette, Indiana.[4] The following year Moberg returned to the United States with his family and a company of emigrants and located at Yorktown, Indiana, near La Fayette. Johan-

[1] Norelius, *op. cit.*, I, 49–50.　　[2] *Ibid.*, pp. 51–52.

[3] *Ibid.*, p. 53. Skarstedt, *op. cit.*, p. 49.

[4] He may have been attracted by the Norwegian colony there, mentioned in Schiele's description of America.

nes Peterson influenced his brother Peter to emigrate, and he arrived in 1852 at La Fayette with a large party. In 1853 and 1854 additional emigrants arrived from Grenna and neighboring parishes and settled at La Fayette, West Point, Attica, Milford, and Yorktown, Indiana. One party, led and financed by a wealthy peasant, Nils Håkanson, from Grantjärn, Vereda parish, came from Sweden to La Fayette via New Orleans and Evansville, Indiana, in 1853. By 1855 there were 500 Swedes resident near La Fayette, but the following year these colonists began to migrate westward.

Influenced partly by the accounts of Wisconsin, written by Unonius to the Swedish press, and partly by the letters from Carl Peter Moberg, Daniel Larsen, from Haurida, Smaland, accompanied by fifty persons, left Sweden in 1844 on the Swedish sailboat, "Superior," bound for Boston,[1] Daniel Larsen was a shoemaker and remained at Brockton, Massachusetts, to work at his trade. His father and the remainder of the party went westward and settled near Sheboygan, Wisconsin. In 1851 Daniel Larsen went back to Sweden, but soon returned to Brockton with a party of sixty emigrants, especially skilled in the shoe industry, who laid the foundation of an industrial colony at Brockton and Campello, Massachusetts.

The Swedish rural press by 1849 contained many comments on emigration to America. A news-item from Gothenburg in the *Östgötha Correspondenten*, May 12, 1849, stated that the "Charles Tottie" was chartered to carry 300 tons of iron to New York and would take about 250 to 310 passengers.[2] Most of the passenger list were peasants from Östergötland who intended to emigrate to America. Some forty had already arrived in Gothenburg and others would come during the succeeding days. The fare was 50 riksdaler banco, or about $15 for an adult passenger, but he had to supply his own food. These were emigrants from Kisa and its surrounding neighborhood in Östergötland and from Grenna.[3] Most of the passengers were directed to Andover, Illinois, by the land agent, Wiström, whom they met in Chicago.[4] The ocean trip had taken seven

[1] Flom, *op. cit.*, p. 596; Norelius, *op. cit.*, I, 26.

[2] *Östgötha Correspondenten* (Linköping), May 12, 1849.     [3] Norelius, *op. cit.*, I, 33 ff.

[4] Norelius quotes a letter of Nils Magnus Kilberg of Swedona, Illinois, one of the passengers describing the journey (*ibid.*).

weeks and four days from Gothenburg to New York. From Norrland came the news-item on June 30, 1849, that three emigrant ships with 250 on board were leaving the port of Gävle; two had sailed and the "Cobden" was leaving the following week.[1] It was on the "Cobden" that Esbjörn sailed with 140 fellow-passengers.[2] They also encountered Wiström and were induced to settle in Andover.

The California gold rush received much publicity in the Swedish press and Swedes joined the feverish hordes seeking gold. The *Jönköpings Tidning* on October 21, 1848, carried an article on the discovery of gold in California. The same newspaper in July 7, 1849, told of the discovery of gold, silver, platinum, quick silver, and even diamonds in California. It also carried news about the railroad to be laid over Panama. There followed numerous news-items in 1849, that the crews of 130 ships in California harbors had deserted for the gold fields,[3] that a telegraph was to connect St. Louis and San Francisco,[4] that a government was being formed in California,[5] that eight million dollars of gold were shipped from California in a month,[6] and that 50,000 people had gone overland to the gold fields.[7]

Conditions in California were also featured. In the *New Helsingborg Post* of Skane, on April 27, 1850, there appeared a news-item from Jönköping, an interview with a Swedish-American who had visited the California gold fields.[8] His name was John Liedberg, and he emigrated to America in 1842 where he worked as a carpenter, a trade he had learned in Småland. He later bought a piece of land in Wisconsin. After five years of farming and trading in the southern states he had acquired some capital. He was induced by stories of California to go there overland, with thirty other immigrants. He sold his farm and departed May, 1848. The journey overland took five months. He arrived in San Francisco in September and found all the inhabitants washing gold. During sixteen months in California, Liedberg had accumulated twenty-nine pounds of gold. The climate was very hard on his health, so he returned to Sweden via

[1] *Hudikswalls Weckoblad*, June 30, 1849; *Jönköpings Tidning*, June 30, 1849.

[2] Norelius, *op. cit.*, p. 35.    [5] *Ibid.*, November 3, 1849.

[3] *Jönköpings Tidning*, September 15, 1849.    [6] *Ibid.*

[4] *Ibid.*, October 27, 1849.    [7] *Ibid.*, December 22, 1849.

[8] *Nyare Helsingborgs-Posten* (Hälsingborg), April 27, 1850; *Malmö-Tidning* (Malmö) April 27, 1850.

Panama, New Orleans, and New York. He met other Swedes in California, some from Kalmar County, but he did not associate with them. He possessed gold in forms of lumps from the size of an egg to a small nut. He was on his way to Wexjö in Småland to visit his mother and sisters.

On May 4 and 11, 1850, the same newspapers ran a long article of two columns giving first, an official report on California by Thomas Butler King to the president of the United States, and second, several letters from a Swedish officer stationed at San Francisco, describing the beauty of the country and the high prices prevailing.[1] The Swedish officer was living with a merchant from Stockholm. A news-item from Trondhjem of April 23, 1850, in the *Helsingborg Post* of May 14 told of a stockholders' meeting of a company sponsoring an expedition to California. Its capitalization, 13,000 Norwegian dollars, had been invested partially by those going to California, and partially by those sending others in their places.[2] A letter in the same newspaper, dated San Francisco, March 31, 1850, told of the large wages, $16.00 a day, at the mines. It continued to relate how

people were flocking from the United States, the British colonies in the Pacific, South America, China, England, France, etc. Immigrants of every class, some without money, had saved a hundred dollars in a few weeks. The cost of living was less than in 1849.[3]

On August 10, 1850, there was the announcement of an expedition to California from Hälsingborg, consisting of the Patroon Ahmberg from Fahlun, who had recently been married in Stockholm, and two clerks, Lundquist and Johansson from Linköping, who with a number of other men were leaving for New York, bound for California, where "they expected to cut gold with their hunting knives.[4]

There were numerous press notices of emigrants departing for the

[1] *Nyare Helsingborgs-Posten*, May 4, 1850, May 11, 1850; *Malmö-Tidning*, May 11, 1850.

[2] *Nyare Helsingborgs-Posten*, May 14, 1850.

[3] *Ibid.*, June 8, 1850. On July 20, 1850, it told about the fire that destroyed 250 homes in California, but everything was rebuilt in ten days. In many places gold lumps weighing 20 to 40 pounds were found. In the southern mines two gold-diggers found $4,000 of gold in three days.

[4] *Nyare Helsingborgs-Posten*, August 10, 1850.

California gold fields. From Småland came an item in *Jönköpings Tidning*, July 27, 1850, of two merchants from Lidköping, and two from Gotland, accompanied by a painter bound for the eldorado.[1] The same newspaper on August 3, 1850, related that nine young men had sailed from Stockholm on July 24 for California, all from Kalmar County, and others were leaving for the same destination.[2] The California gold fields also drew Swedish immigrants from Illinois and Iowa, some who returned richer only in experience.[3] The newspaper reports of the gold discoveries directly influenced many to try their luck.

By 1849 immigration to America was large enough to receive newspaper comment and draw editorial discussion. An editorial in a Norrland newspaper, in the region which had perhaps lost most through emigration from 1845 to 1850, asked the question, "What is the cause of the great desire for emigration among the common people of Sweden?"[4] It deplored the fact that "so many of the country's most dependable, thriftiest, and peace-loving common people were with great economic sacrifices breaking the tenderest ties of home and motherland." Among the causes enumerated in the editorial were (1) the uneven distribution of taxes by which the Swedish common people were bearing an undeniably heavy burden, (2) the luxury and pomp of court life, (3) religious intolerance, and (4) the minor burdens on the soil and overpopulation. The latter was only a social and political pressure, for with the relief from the undue burden of taxes the land was fertile enough, and there still existed wide stretches of virgin soil in Sweden to take care of the overpopulation. The article ended by begging the authorities to remedy these causes of emigration.

A popular guide for emigrants was published by Theodore Schytte in Stockholm in 1849.[5] In the Preface of the guide it stated,

[1] *Jönköpings Tidning*, July 27, 1850.      [2] *Ibid.*, August 3, 1850.

[3] Norelius related that several who went to California from Victoria, Andover, etc., returned to the colonies.

[4] *Sjette Norrlands-Posten* (Gävle), June 30, 1849.

[5] Theodore Schytte, *Vägledning för emigration, en kort framställing af utvandringarnes svårigheter och fördelar, jemte en skildring af de Skandinaviska koloniernas ekonomiska, politiska och religösa tillstånd i Nordamerika, med ett bihang om de år 1847 utvandrade Erick Janssons anhängares sorliga öde* (Stockholm, 1849).

At a time when emigration to America increases more and more from the European states, and when in many regions in this country, a journey to that part of the world is the common conversation of the moment, a few words from a man who has visited the different settlements in the United States during a four year visit there, where he had the opportunity to learn something about the country and the situation of the colonists, may not be out of place.[1]

Schytte gave as causes for emigration, (1) the political and religious intolerance that dominated Sweden, (2) the absurd taxation system under the iron yoke of which the Swedish peasants groaned, (3) the many crop failures, (4) the demands for a higher standard of living which was spreading down to the common people in imitation of the higher classes. "All of these causes make the people in general," wrote Schytte, "discontented with their lot at home."[2] He, however, warned that although

it is undoubtedly true that many can find a better future in America than they could ever expect to have in the fatherland, and can with more ease and security earn their bread, still in America sparrows do not fly into the mouth of a person, for you must even there earn your bread with the sweat of your brow.[3]

In advising the best way to travel to America, he stated that it was better to take ship directly from Sweden instead of journeying to Holland, Germany, or France where the immigrant would be handicapped by his ignorance of the foreign language and the laws of strange countries and easily fall victim of unscrupulous people.

Beside picturing the great opportunities for wealth in the gold fields of California, the press continued to publish letters from Swedish immigrants in America describing the agricultural opportunities and the high wages in the new world. The *Hudiksvall Weekly* printed a series of letters from an Eric Sandman who had left the region for America in 1850.[4] In a letter from New York dated April 6, 1850, he explained that he had been advised not to go to Waldens Ridge in Tennessee, as he had intended, because Tennessee was a slave state and extremely warm.[5] He had met Pastor Hedström whom he told all who came to New York to look up. Hedström had advised him to go to Illinois or Iowa. Sandman wrote that only people who were anxious to work were wanted in America, that all Americans worked.

[1] *Ibid.*, p. 1.        [2] *Ibid.*, p. 5.        [3] *Ibid.*, p. 6.
[4] *Hudikswalls Weckoblad* June 1, 1850, September 21, 1850.
[5] *Ibid.*, June 1, 1850.

He complained that it was hard in the beginning when you did not know the language, but he continued, "You do better here than in Sweden, for it is a blessed good land in every way." He could get work at a carpenter shop in New York for a dollar a day. Room and board amounted to $2.50 to $3.00 a week and clothes were not as expensive as in Sweden. Wages were higher for Americans, but Swedes who could not talk and did not know the customs received less wages. A friend, Modin, had obtained work for a farmer at $7.00 a month for six months, about 168 riksdaler riksgeld. On April 8, Sandman expected to take passage for Chicago, which at that time of the year was $10.00. It was less on the canal when it was open, but the trains were faster.

A subsequent letter from the same immigrant came from Knoxville, Illinois.[1] He had been converted to the Methodist faith by the Hedström brothers. In speaking of the Swedish settlements at Bishop Hill and Andover, Sandman stated, "It has not fared so well for many in the strange land, without home and money." But he continued,

The soil here is good and fruitful. On the open prairie in midsummer, there is so much long grass and flowers that it is a pleasure to gaze upon it, and upon animals that pasture there. The soil here looks like a cabbage patch, all loose black dirt about six feet deep. The woods consist entirely of deciduous trees which are not found in your region, and many are fruit trees, apple, plum, and cherry, and plants like hops and other varieties that I do not know. The grass also grows everywhere in the woods. In May when all the fruit trees stand in bloom or later when they are covered with fruit, the wild woods look like the most glorious orchard in Sweden. A wonderful country it is; as large as it is, it is divided by many rivers which make possible transportation many hundreds of miles inland with sail boats, like the Mississippi, which is navigable 300 Swedish miles (2,000) inland. We expect to settle near it, at the present we are 40 English miles from the river, but we are planning to travel up the stream to Wisconsin or Minnesota. There is also good land and plenty of woods and waterfalls which are lacking here.

Sandman wrote,

Many Swedes have gone to California, as well as Americans. . . . . It is possible to purchase cultivated land in Illinois, but it is poor because the American farmer does not put much money in his home. It is also possible to rent land. The landlord furnishes the horses, implements, and cattle, also seed grain.

[1] *Ibid.*, September 21, 1850.

The renters get half of the crop and half of the new calves, etc., and all the milk. If the renter has his own horses and implements he receives two-thirds of the crop.

These letters could not help but inspire ambitious young men to seek this agricultural eldorado.

Items about the size of immigration to the United States were prevalent in the Swedish press in 1850. It was stated in *Jönköpings Tidningen* in Småland, one of the most prolific of the Swedish emigrant regions, in the issue of January 5, 1850, that there had been 213,654 immigrants to the United States in eleven months in 1849, as compared with 189,176 for 1848, although November 1849 showed only an immigration of 8,298 as compared with 21,919 the same month in 1848.[1] The same newspaper stated that there were two million Germans in the United States, and 60,000 in New York alone.[2] Emigration from Sweden also continued. In 1851, the *Jönköpings Tidning* complained of the undiminished emigration to America, equally as great from the Småland counties as from Östergötland.[3] "The day before yesterday," stated the paper, "there passed through Jönköping eight wagon loads of agricultural laborers with their children and household goods, from the Wimmerby region leaving the fatherland, and according to the *Östgöta Korrespondenten*, there will be 170 persons emigrating from three parishes alone in that county." The following month the same newspaper carried a long item warning against cheap passage to America, and quoted a New York newspaper of April 2, 1851, describing the awful conditions on the boats, especially from Ireland and Liverpool. On eleven Liverpool ships with 4,518 passengers, there were 287 dead and 555 landed ill. It must be remembered that during 1850 and 1851 cholera raged in Europe and America, and the crowded conditions on the sailing vessels produced what was called "ship fever."

The fifties also saw the establishment of various Swedish settlements in Minnesota. Fredrika Bremer, the popular Swedish novelist, in her travels in the United States in 1850, included the Minnesota territory in her itinerary, where she was the guest of the terri-

---

[1] *Jönköpings Tidning*, January 5, 1850.
[2] *Ibid.*, January 19, 1850.       [3] *Jönköpings Posten*, April 26, 1851.

torial governor, Alexander Ramsay.[1] "The city (St. Paul)," she wrote, "was one of the west's youngest babies, only eighteen months old, but has already grown to a population of 2,000." Later she continued,

Everywhere the high grass billows in yellow waves over hills and valleys. There are no hands here to cut it. The soil is a fat black mull which is wonderful for the growth of potatoes and grain. . . . . Small clear lakes nestle among the hills, reminding one of mirrors, in their romantic peace. It is an idyll nature. But the shepherds and shepherdesses are lacking. Only on the eastern bank of the Mississippi in Minnesota are there as yet any whites, and they number about seven thousand souls. The whole western portion of Minnesota west of the Mississippi is as yet Indian territory.[2]

Fredrika Bremer wrote prophetically,

This Minnesota is a wonderful land and just the right kind of country for Nordic emigrants, truly a land for a New Scandinavia. It is four times as large as England; it has rich soil, large stretches of forest lands, many rivers and lakes rich with fish, and a fresh invigorating climate. The winter is cold and clear; the summer is not as hot as in the more southern Mississippi states.[3]

This diary of Fredrika Bremer's travels in America was published in 1853 and went through six editions in the Swedish language. It must have had some influence in attracting settlers to Minnesota.

Perhaps a more influential factor in diverting Scandinavian emigration to Minnesota was the opportune time of settlement. The territory was just beginning to bid for settlers at the time when Swedish immigration began to pour into the United States. There had been one or two Swedes in Minnesota before 1850. Jacob Folström, an old fur-trader, seems to have reached Minnesota in 1819, after a life on the sea, as an agent for a trading company.[4] He threw his lot with the Indians, intermarried with them and lived with them until his death in 1859. A temporary settlement was made at Hay Lake in Washington County, Minnesota, by three young Swedes in 1850, but it was dispersed in 1852.[5] The Swedish immigrants resi-

[1] Fredrika Bremer, *Hemmen i nya verlden, Dagbok i bref under en resa i Norr Amerika och på Cuba,* II, 85.

[2] *Ibid.,* p. 93.        [3] *Ibid.,* pp. 112–13.

[4] Jacob Folström was the son of a Stockholm merchant (Norelius, *op. cit.,* I, 537). Norelius lived for many years in Minnesota and was personally acquainted with the early Swedish settlers there.

[5] Skarstedt, *op. cit.,* p. 45.

dent at Moline, Illinois, were attracted to settlement in Minnesota by letters that they received from a friend reconnoitering along the St. Croix River in Minnesota in 1851. This was E. U. Nordberg, a former member of the Bishop Hill settlement.[1] His enthusiastic letters and his enclosed map of the Minnesota region influenced a newly arrived immigrant, Per Anderson, from Norrland and of Finnish extraction, to seek the Minnesota forests. In the spring of 1851, accompanied by several others, he started the settlement of Chisago Lake, Minnesota. It was necessary to cut a road through the timber and bogs for nine miles between Taylor Falls and Chisago Lake, over which to bring the wives, children, and household goods to the new clearing. A letter from Per Anderson from Chisago Lake, September 7, 1851, described the new settlement in glowing terms.

The soil is quite good and fruitful. There is much forest . . . . no dry prairies which it does not pay to cultivate, but many natural meadows, moist with good growth of grass; good timber for every need of the farmer. . . . . We are now ten, who this summer began to farm here, nine Swedes and an American. Only three are married and have families. The others are all single men.[2]

The first immigrants were from Norrland, but there soon followed reinforcements from Småland and other provinces of Sweden. In 1853, the youthful Hans Mattson, with a party of Swedish immigrants from Moline, Illinois, founded the Vasa settlement in Minnesota.[3] In the spring of 1854, several new settlers came, including Mattson's father and brother.[4] "In 1855," wrote Roos, "the church and school were built. E. Norelius became the first minister and an English school under Button was started in 1856." Emigrants came from Illinois, Indiana, Iowa, and even from Pennsylvania to the new settlement in Minnesota. In a few years there were Swedish colonies at Spring Garden, Cambridge in Isanti County, East Union and West Union in Carver County, and Scandian Grove in Nicollet County.[5] St. Paul and Minneapolis also received their share. With

[1] Norelius, op. cit., I, 538, 541 ff.

[2] Letter quoted by Norelius, ibid., I, 543.    [3] Hans Mattson, Reminiscences.

[4] Letters of Carl Roos, one of the first settlers, published in Minnesota Stats Tidning (Minneapolis), February 1, 1877, February 15, 1877, February 22, 1877.

[5] Norelius, op. cit., pp. 602–756.; A E. Strand, A History of Swedish Americans in Minnesota. p. 252. A letter from Ph. O. Johnson of Göthaholm, Carver County, Minnesota, in Minnesota Stats Tidning, March 1, 1879, related that this colony grew from the Swedish settlement in Pennsylvania.

the establishment of settlements, Swedish immigrants began to arrive directly from Sweden, and the path had been blazed for the establishment of the New Scandinavia in the Northwest. In the decade of the fifties the population of Minnesota grew from 6,077 to 172,023, even after the set-back of the panic of 1857.[1] The Swedish immigration as yet formed only a small part of the fast-increasing population.

There were also several Swedish colonies in Wisconsin in the fifties. The earliest at Pine Lake has been described. A few Swedes settled in Milwaukee and around Sheboygan.[2] There were settlements in Waupaca and Portage counties.[3] In Superior City a number of Swedes had been persuaded to take claims in the mining region, which they finally sold to speculators.[4] Several settlements had appeared in Iowa, and in Michigan there was a small colony at Sparta, near Grand Rapids.[5] The settlement at Mariadahl near Manhattan in Kansas was founded by J. A. Johnson from Östergötland in 1855. Some of these settlers came from Illinois and others directly from Sweden.[6] There were a few scattered Swedes in the seaports of the United States, especially in Boston and New York.[7]

These early emigrants crossed the Atlantic in sailboats, many in the famous clipper ships of the period. The boats were not built for the passenger trade which developed so quickly, but carried cargoes of iron from the Swedish ports. They departed from many harbors of Sweden and sailed directly for the North American ports of New York, Boston, Quebec, New Orleans, and sometimes for Philadelphia or Baltimore. The Jansonites, who came from Hälsingland in Norrland, left Sweden from a large number of ports, Söderhamn and Gävle which are on the Gulf of Bothnia and nearest Hälsingland; Stockholm, Christiania, and Gothenburg. Copenhagen, Bremen, and Hamburg were also ports of departure. Some went by way of England over Hull and Liverpool, and others by way of Havre.

The voyage at the best was a long and tiresome one. From seven

---

[1] Wilson Pate Shortridge, *The Transition of a Typical Frontier* (1919), pp. 121-24.

[2] The Sheboygan settlement was made in 1844 by Lars Landberg of Haurida, Småland, influenced by Unonius' letters (Norelius, *op. cit.*, I, 26).

[3] *Ibid.*, pp. 757-58.

[4] *Ibid.*, p. 758.           [6] *Ibid.*, pp. 768-70.

[5] *Ibid.*, pp. 765-67.       [7] *Ibid.*, pp. 770-71.

to eight weeks from Sweden to New York was considered very good time. It often took longer when storms were encountered. Eric Norelius in describing his voyage stated that it took them eleven weeks from Gävle to New York.[1] The passengers had to provide their own food and bedding and many of them slept on the deck. The food and water was anything but the best after a long voyage, if it lasted at all. Deaths were frequent and disease often broke out because of unsanitary conditions. From 1850 to 1854, cholera was particularly severe and decimated the ranks of emigrants. Smallpox was also a common disease. The emigrants usually traveled in large parties with a leader and often chartered a whole ship for themselves. The passage rate was very low.

If they landed in New York, they met the friendly immigrants' missionary of the "Bethel-ship," O. G. Hedström, who gave them spiritual comfort and good advice. He influenced many to seek Illinois for settlement. Then came the long journey inland, usually to Chicago, from where many continued to the agricultural communities of Illinois, Iowa, and Minnesota. The party which Norelius accompanied had decided to join the Esbjörn group at Andover, Illinois. Their tickets from New York to Chicago were $8 per person, but they had to supply their own food.[2] On November 4, 1850, they were crowded on a river boat for Albany where they arrived the following morning at five o'clock. By noon they boarded an emigrant train, an improvement on the old Erie Canal trip, and reached Buffalo at two o'clock on November 6. The train was little better than a cattle train, but to the emigrant who had never seen a railroad before, it was a marvel. An interpreter had accompanied the party to Albany, but had left them there. When they arrived in Buffalo, they were stranded, since no one in their party could talk English. They finally found a Norwegian who had a hotel and who overcharged them for their food. On the evening of the 8th, they boarded the lake steamer, the "Sultana," which was to take them to Chicago. All the staterooms for the emigrants were already occupied and the party had to sleep on deck. Two staterooms for $40.00 were rented for the members of the party who could not stand the rigors of the winter climate in the open. The ship stranded in Lake

[1] *Ibid.*, p. 39.        [2] *Ibid.*, pp. 41–42.

St. Clair and the passengers had to be unloaded, but after a day they were on their way again. They finally arrived in Chicago on November 14, ten days after leaving New York.

There were no trains from Chicago in 1850, and the party was undecided whether to go to Victoria, of which they had heard in Sweden, or to Andover, where Esbjörn was located. They spent a day purchasing provisions for the further journey and received the aid and good advice of Unonius, whom they met. They purchased passage on the Michigan and Illinois canal for Peru, Illinois. The fare was eleven shillings per person, or about $1.50. They hired an interpreter, a member of Unonius' church, and paid him $10.00 to accompany them to Peru. The party left Chicago on November 16 and reached Peru on the 19th. One of the members of the party, Per Anderson, had purchased a cook stove in Chicago which was erected in the baggage room to keep the emigrants warm, for it was snowing outside.

It was about sixty miles from Andover to Peru overland. There were two alternatives—to hire a horse and wagon at $10.00 a load, or walk.[1] Those who hired a horse and wagon remained in Peru until November 21. Norelius and fourteen others started to walk on November 20. After many adventures which led them through Princeton, Illinois, they finally came to Andover on November 23. A long journey over, they found themselves in a poor frontier village with not enough houses to shelter them. Many were without money and had even borrowed from the more prosperous. It was necessary to find work among the farmers in the vicinity.

The poverty of the Swedish immigrant upon his arrival at his destination is often mentioned in the accounts of the time. They were, however, not the most destitute people in their own country, or they could not have financed the long trip across the ocean. The fare seemed rather small, but when one considered that it also meant provisioning for from three to four, or even five months, it was not a mean sum. Often, too, it was the whole family emigrating— husband, wife, and children. The younger unmarried men had hardly had time to accumulate much money. It was, therefore, absolutely necessary to take any work that might fall their way until they

[1] *Ibid.*, pp. 43–46.

could acquire their capital in the new country. Manual labor was in the most demand. We find them hiring out as farm hands and working at railroad construction. The young women found places as maids with American families, and the married women earned a bit by taking in washings, if they were near a town. The Swedes in and around Andover were described in 1850 as mostly laborers by the day, by the month, or the week; some were mechanics, a few, renters of land, and still fewer, landowners.[1]

After a few years of hard labor, many accumulated enough to buy land in the vicinity. Others chose to find cheaper lands in the newly opened agricultural regions of Minnesota and Kansas. Some became merchants in the neighboring towns. There were land speculators and land agents who directed the newly arrived parties of their countrymen to certain regions for settlement. The Swedish immigrant became a part of his environment and was influenced by all the forces of the day. Many followed the gold-seekers to California and most of them returned disappointed. Others helped organize the new counties in Iowa and Minnesota and became officeholders and were active in politics. The Civil War drew many into its ranks. Hans Mattson of Minnesota organized his own regiment of Swedes from that state and became a colonel. There was also a Swedish regiment in Wisconsin. Their frontier settlements were devastated by Indians in Minnesota in 1862. But still they went westward in prairie schooners into Kansas, Nebraska, and the Dakotas, and into the new mining regions of Colorado and Nevada.

The Swedish immigrants of the forties and fifties came from all classes of society. The Swedish clergy who came to administer to the spiritual needs of their countrymen were graduates of the universities of Uppsala and Lund. Among them may be mentioned Unonius, Esbjörn, Hasselquist, and Erland Carlson. The aristocratic class also sent its quota in men like Baron Thott and Captain P. von Schneidau. There were well-to-do peasants who emigrated with their whole families and sometimes even with their servants. The governor of Östergötland County noticed this tendency in 1847.[2] The same thing happened in Kristianstad County in 1850. These

[1] *Home Missionary*, 1850, p. 263.

[2] *K. bfhde femårsberättelse, Östergötlands län, 1842–1847.*

rather wealthy peasants sold their land and implements and left with their wives and children, with the hope that they might attain a greater economic prosperity in the United States.[1] In 1864 came the news from the American legation in Stockholm that three hundred peasants from the historical province of Dalecarlia had passed through the city in July en route for the state of Minnesota. They were dressed in their picturesque native costumes and carried with them a large amount of household goods, besides a capital of 40,000 Swedish silver dollars.[2] There were also crofters, agricultural tenants, agrarian laborers, and servants of both sexes, all desiring the higher wages and the opportunity to acquire their own land in the new world.

The governor of Östergötland, in commenting on emigration, stated that experience showed that it was periodic, dependent on the more or less enticing accounts from the country to which the emigrant desired to go. "There are no definite laws controlling emigration," wrote the governor, "for instance, emigration during 1850 to 1855 has been the greatest from that part of this county which temporarily affords the best conditions for labor and where the workingmen are all well treated."[3] He continued, "The poorest class who have not the means for emigration are given the opportunity by signing contracts to become indentured servants in the United States while they work off their passage money."

During the first half of the fifties, better economic conditions and higher wages in Denmark were also attracting Swedish agricultural labor, especially from the southern counties. The press of Kristianstad County carried many advertisements during 1854 and 1855 for servants in Denmark.[4] A news-item of April 25, 1855, appearing in the *New Hälsingborg Post* of April 28, 1855, from Halmstad stated,

With the steamship "Halland" today many laborers of both sexes left for Skåne and Denmark to seek work. Many persons from Denmark are in the county [Halland] recruiting laborers. More than a hundred workers have left

[1] *Ibid., Kristianstads län, 1851–1855*, p. 5.

[2] A Swedish silver dollar was worth $1.07 in American money (U.S. Department of State, *Dispatches from Sweden*, Haldeman to Seward, July 2, 1864, X, 6–7).

[3] *K. bfhde femårsberättelse, 1851–1855, Östergötlands län*, pp. 6–7.

[4] *Ibid., Kristianstads län, 1851–1855*, pp. 4–5.

already from Warberg bailiwick for Denmark. The county government has warned people to be careful in taking these positions. Railroads will soon be constructed near Drahered [Denmark] and all laborers will be able to get work.[1] This emigration from Halland to Denmark was characterized by the governor of the county as coming principally from the interior of the county and consisting chiefly of agricultural laborers and young people of both sexes, while that which was directed to the United States came from the southern and northern portions of the county and consisted of whole families.[2] The exodus of agricultural laborers to Denmark from Kulling and Gäsened hundreds in Älvsborg County was during the same period large enough to decrease population materially, according to the governor.[3] There were reports of emigration to Denmark also from the counties of Kronoberg and Jönköping.[4] A news-item from Jönköping in the *New Hälsingborg Post* of July 24, 1855, imparted the information that an agent from Gothenburg was recruiting labor from Småland, both by personal efforts and newspaper advertisements.[5]

During the decade from 1845 to 1855, which may be considered the period of the inception of nineteenth-century Swedish emigration to the United States, there were certain regions in Sweden which sent large numbers of emigrants while others had very little exodus. Statistics are only available for the last five years, from 1851 to 1855. During this period the largest emigration came from Jönköping County which had lost 1,882 persons.[6] Second came Östergötland, with a loss of 1,391, and third Kristianstad County, with 1,358. In order followed Älvsborg County with 1,103, Blekinge with 983, Kronoberg County with 973, and Gävleborg with 554. The other counties had less than 500 emigrants and Uppsala County, from which Unonius emigrated, only two. Emigration had come chiefly from Western and Southern Sweden and from the Norrland counties. The emigration from Värmland, which became so great later, had

---

[1] *Nyare Helsingborgs Posten*, April 28, 1855.

[2] *K. bfhde femårsberättelse, Hallands län, 1851–1855*, pp. 4–5.

[3] *Ibid., Elfsborgs län, 1851–1855*, pp. 4–5.

[4] *Ibid., Kronobergs län, 1851–1855*, p. 4; *ibid., Jönköpings län, 1851–1855*, p. 6.

[5] *Nyare Helsingborgs Posten*, July 24, 1855.

[6] *Utvandringen och invandringen*, länstabeller, "Bygdestatistik," *Emigrationsutredningens bilaga V*, pp. 70*–93*, Table 43.

scarcely begun. There were only 161 emigrants from this county during these five years.

At the same time there was a rather large emigration to Denmark and Norway, though less in numbers than to America. The county of Halland sent 738 of her agricultural laborers and servants to Denmark between 1851 and 1855; Malmöhus County 151, and Blekinge, 79.[1] To Norway there emigrated 159 from Värmland, 133 from Norrbotten, and 23 from Jämtland, all border counties.

This emigration from 1851 to 1855 produced a scarcity of labor in certain regions of Sweden and raised agricultural wages to the level of the wages in Denmark and Norway.[2] By 1855, Sweden had begun the construction of her own railroads and many found work here. In Jönköping County, there was a marked decline in agriculture; crofters were giving up their leases; and some of the peasants sold their land. The population turned to other industries and some became peddlers.[3] In Tveta, Mo, and Westa, as well as north and south Wedbo bailiwicks in the county the population decreased because of emigration. In Kristianstad County, the economic conditions of the common people improved during 1854 and 1855 because of good crops and rising prices of agricultural products. With the increase in agricultural wages also came a higher cost of living.[4] Higher wages were reported in Halland, Älvsborg, and Gothenburg-Bohus counties.[5]

Prosperity in Sweden in 1855 tended to check emigration and there was a marked decline until 1863. The crisis of 1857 was world-wide, and was felt in Europe and the United States perhaps more than in Sweden. During the period from 1856 to 1860, the emigration from Jönköping County was only 467; from Östergötland, 538; from Kronoberg, 418; from Kristianstad, 371; from Älvsborg, 207; and from Gävleborg, 500.[6] The only county that showed an increase

[1] Ibid.

[2] K. bfhde femårsberättelse, Göteborg-och Bohus län, 1851–1855, p. 10.

[3] Ibid., Jönköpings län, 1851–1855, p. 6.

[4] Ibid., Kristianstads län, 1851–1855, pp. 4–5.

[5] Ibid., Hallands län, pp. 4–5; ibid., Elfsborgs län, pp. 5–6; ibid., Göteborgs-och Bohus län, p. 10.

[6] "Bygdestatistik," Emigrationsutredningens bilaga V, pp. 70*–93*, Table 43.

was Malmöhus and that only from 76 to 208. On the whole, the emigration had fallen to one-fourth of the previous five years.

As emigration increased from the prosperous province of Skåne in 1855, the newspapers attempted to discourage it by publishing adverse reports about the United States. The *New Hälsingborg Post* published a series of denunciatory articles on conditions in America, beginning with the April 10, 1855, issue. From a lengthy letter dated Illinois, January 25, 1855, the following extract was printed,

> The social conditions in America are, in spite of all the bragging about them, at least in the larger cities, very little better than in Europe. The *New York Herald* estimated the number of unemployed laborers to be at least 20,000 in that city. . . . . A Philadelphia newspaper stated that 80,000 workers must suffer from poverty this winter, and that 12,000 Germans and other Europeans who came to America last year and have not found work will have to return to Europe.[1]

The May 5, 1855, issue of the same newspaper gave a lengthy article citing the misfortunes of some Swedish Mormons who had attempted to join their religious brethern in Utah, and ended by stating that the editor had read many discouraging letters.[2] On July 12, 1855, the editor quoted from a letter received from a Swedish immigrant resident in Louisville, Kentucky. This immigrant was a merchant and well-situated in the United States. But in spite of that he begged the editor to discourage emigration to the United States. He wrote,

> No matter how bad conditions are in many ways in Sweden it is worse here. I have, during the last fifteen years, seen more poverty and suffering among unfortunate Swedes here than I ever saw in Sweden. They picture their conditions here highly satisfactory in their letters to Sweden, but these letters are dictated by a false pride, and when we look at the naked facts, we often find that he who relates that he owns a saw-mill only owns a saw and saw-buck, and he who describes the beautiful carriage he owns, is the owner of a wheelbarrow for which himself serves as the locomotive.[3]

These derogatory letters seemed to have very little effect in discouraging emigration, however. The same year a Swedish-American newspaper, *Hemlandet, det gamla och det nya*, edited by Pastor T. R. Hasselquist, was published in Galesburg, Illinois, and found readers

---

[1] *Nyare Helsingborgs Posten*, April 10, 1855.

[2] *Ibid.*, May 5, 1855.        [3] *Ibid.*, July 21, 1855.

in Sweden as well as among the Swedish immigrants in the United States.[1]

A period of twenty years had now intervened since the beginning of nineteenth-century emigration that swept from Sweden to the United States. The new world had become during the time well-known in Sweden and events here were items of news in the Swedish papers. Large extracts from the inaugural address of President Buchanan were "exceedingly well translated in the principal newspapers of Sweden" in March, 1857.[2] In a dispatch on the subject, F. Schroeder of the American legation in Stockholm wrote to Secretary Lewis Cass,

> Still, more glad have I been to observe not only in editorial comment, but in the highest official society, all the just satisfaction with its sentiments. . . . . our country is now so much felt, that while its external relations have come to be almost as much of a theme of Swedish study as those of the States of local proximity, its minute internal affairs, I have sometimes been surprised to find, form also an eagerly read history.[3]

In 1861, at the opening of the Civil War, Mr. Haldeman of the American legation in Stockholm wrote to Secretary Seward, "A deep and fervent interest is felt by the masses of Sweden and Norway in our domestic affairs. There are but few families who have not one but more relatives and acquaintances in the northern states, and I am constantly applied to for general information."[4] Many of the Swedish immigrants in the United States had enlisted in the northern armies.

In the sixties new factors entered into the causes of emigration to the United States from Sweden. Sweden was now recognized as a region in which to encourage actively emigration on the part of the federal government and the states of the United States, and also the railroads and industrial corporations desiring labor. The Homestead Law of 1862 gave gratis to the tiller of the soil, large stretches of land. This was indeed a utopia to the tenant farmer and the agricultural laborer who saw no chance of ever owning any land at

---

[1] *Ibid.*, July 24, 1855. Carries a notice of the new publication.

[2] U.S. Department of State, *Dispatches from Sweden*, April 2, 1857, F. Schroeder to Cass, No. 185.

[3] *Ibid.*      [4] *Ibid.*, September 12, 1861, Haldeman to Seward, X, No. 7.

home. A third factor was the great calamity that befell Sweden— the famine of 1867–69. It drove many people to seek a more prosperous land. Emigration was momentarily interrupted by the beginning of the Civil War in the United States. The textile workers of Sweden in the Borås region were thrown out of employment, as were many in England and France. When, however, President Lincoln's proclamation was issued calling for 300,000 men in 1862 and the news reached Sweden, the consulates were stormed by able-bodied men who desired to emigrate and participate in the Civil War.[1] These young men had the idea that their traveling expenses would be paid and that they would receive the offered bounty.

But the Swedish government was opposed to the emigration of its people. It could not actually prohibit the people from leaving, but it frowned upon any effort to encourage it. Time and again this attitude was expressed by the Swedish foreign secretary to the chargé d'affaires of the United States in Stockholm. The Swedish government was also anxious to prevent the United States from enlisting soldiers for the northern armies in Sweden. J. S. Haldeman's report to the United States government on July 4, 1861, on the attitude of Sweden toward emigration stated the case very well. He wrote,

Although Sweden and Norway are but sparsely settled, many of the rich peasants are selling out to emigrate to the United States. This government [Sweden] is opposed to the emigration and does all in its power to discourage and prevent this loss of its subjects, offering crown lands on better conditions than ever before. Whatever occurs in the United States to check or interrupt this emigration has the approbation of this government, and as the difficulties in the United States affect and retard this movement of the Swedes and Norwegians "Westward ho," their interests (as they think) conflict with their natural and strong sympathy with our government in the present contest. It is well known that the King and his brother Oscar are violently and bitterly hostile to all who recommend or encourage emigration, and I find that if I wish to stand well with the King and his Ministers, the less said for the present on the subject the better. The above I have gathered from frequent conversations with Count Manderström (foreign minister), the diplomatic corps, and others.[2]

[1] *U.S. Consular Letters, 1857–1863*, Stockholm, August 20, 1862, consul, Charles A. Leas.

[2] U.S. Department of State, *Dispatches from Sweden*, letter of J. S. Haldeman to Seward, July 4, 1861, Vol. X, No. 3.

The United States government, however, adopted a policy of encouraging emigration from Europe. It did not actually recruit soldiers for the Civil War, but it urged upon the consuls and legations to promote emigration as much as possible. Instructions were sent to the foreign representatives, dated August 8, 1862, to do all in their power to encourage the migration of suitable persons.[1] The American consul at Gothenburg reported to his government that his success to obtain emigrants had been limited, not because of lack of material, but on account of the poverty of the people.[2] "They have actually not the means to defray the expense of reaching our shores." He further continued that he could enlist a large number of skilled artillerists and able seamen if the United States government could furnish $30 in gold for each man for his traveling expenses, to be deducted from his bounty later. There is no evidence that the United States furnished money to transport soldiers. The demand for passage to America by Swedish soldiers eager to go continued throughout the war. The United States consul at Stockholm stated on January 9, 1863, that if he had the means of sending these applicants to America, he could furnish as many as a thousand a month for a year or two to come.[3] "Having had experience in our army," he wrote, "I can say that the majority of these applicants are equal in intelligence and education to our own volunteers and some of them appear to be persons of very marked ability." On April 4, 1863, he wrote that he had made 129 replies by letter to persons all over Sweden, Norway, and Finland, and had received more than 2,000 applicants personally at the consulate, all of whom wished to become soldiers.[4]

When the New York Chamber of Commerce recommended in 1862 action on the part of the United States government to stimulate immigration, and advised the appointment of agents to visit Ireland and Germany, the United States chargé d'affaires to Sweden and Norway, Mr. Haldeman, called the attention of the government

[1] *U.S. Consular Letters 1858–1863*, Gothenburg, I. P. M. Epping, consul, November 12, 1862.

[2] *Ibid.*

[3] *U.S. Consular Letters 1857–1863*, Stockholm, B. F. Tefft, consul, January 9, January 23, 1863.

[4] *Ibid.*, April 4, 1863.

to the fact that Scandinavia, and especially Norway, was a far more fertile field and as yet almost virgin.[1] He proposed that the Illinois Central Railroad agents might enter this field. He stated further,

> I have no doubt that with the proper effort, Sweden and Norway would send more emigrants (and of the best character, most fitted for our climate and institutions) to the United States than France and Germany combined, annually for the next ten years. To all this, they acquire our language in a short time, being kindred tongues.

The United States government began a policy of actively disseminating information about the opportunities in the new world. The new homestead act was translated into Swedish by the consul at Bergen, and also into Danish.[2] The consulate in Stockholm circulated facts contained in documents sent by the State Department, and in June 1863, noticed already a more general tendency toward emigration resulting from it.[3] The consul wrote,

> My office has many times been overrun with applicants wishing aid to get to the United States, offering to bind themselves by written contract to perform any service for the government or any other party, for remuneration. I have now a company of forty-seven persons who are about to leave for New York on their own account, and who came to me for general information. They have heretofore been miners, and I have directed them toward Minnesota. They came to me in consequence of the information put into circulation from this consulate.[4]

In a report on September 30, 1863, Consul Tefft stated,

> I have sent one, two, and three large parties per month, besides many parties going alone. I have taken special pains to give publicity to the liberality of our government to emigrants. . . . . I consider the Swedes as the best candidates for good citizenship that we have; and I am glad to witness a growing tendency toward emigration. Furnish me with ships, or free passages, and I could take a quarter of the working population of this country to United States next spring.[5]

The graphic account of the methods used by the new consul at Gothenburg in 1864 is very enlightening. He wrote,

[1] U.S. Department of State, *Dispatches from Sweden*, Haldeman to Seward, November 18, 1862, Vol. X, No. 258.

[2] *Ibid.*, April 24, 1863, Vol. X, No. 28.

[3] *U.S. Consular Letters, 1857–1863*, Stockholm, B. F. Tefft, consul, June 30, 1863.

[4] *Ibid.*

[5] *Ibid.*, September 30, 1863.

Many a time when overtaken by darkness on an afternoon's hunt and forced to put up for the night at a peasant's cot, I have seen every eye of the family brighten as I told of the plenty in the poor man's home in the New World. As I looked at their stalwart forms and witnessed their never-flagging industry, I have envied Sweden the possession of such a sturdy race. . . . . During my residence here, I have diffused information tending towards immigration in every way in my power; but being accredited to His Majesty, King Karl, who wants all his subjects at home, I have, of course to work with some circumspection.[1]

The policy of the federal government was announced in President Lincoln's message to Congress on December 8, 1863, in the following words,

I again submit to your consideration the expediency of establishing a system for encouragement of immigration. . . . . There is still a great deficiency of laborers in every field of industry, especially in agriculture and in the mines, as well as of iron and coal as of the precious metals. While the demand for labor is much increased, tens of thousands of persons destitute of remunerative occupation are thronging our foreign consulates and offering to emigrate to the United States if essential but very cheap assistance can be offered them.[2]

In 1864, the federal government established a Commissioner of Immigration, and legalized immigration of contract labor.[3]

Encouraged by the President's message and the desire for immigrants as expressed in the American press, Consul Thomas of Gothenburg suggested that a means of overcoming the cost of transit would be to have a United States government agent charter sailing vessels to carry a cargo of emigrants and a cargo of iron from Gothenburg to New York, the iron paying for the cost of the voyage.[4] This plan was, however, never adopted by the United States. On February 29, 1864, this zealous consul asked for three months leave of absence to travel through Norway and Sweden to encourage emigration.[5] He wrote to his government,

My design is to visit the mines in the interior of Sweden and Norway, and to see and talk with the people of this country in their own homes. . . .    In

[1] *Ibid.*, Gothenburg, W. W. Thomas, Jr., consul, February 12, 1864.

[2] Richardson, *Messages and Papers of the Presidents*, 1789–1897, VI, 182.

[3] Henry Pratt Fairchild, *Immigration* (New York, 1925), pp. 93–94. It was repealed in 1868.

[4] *U.S. Consular Letters, 1864–1868*, Gothenburg, W. W. Thomas, Jr., consul, February 12, 1864.

[5] *Ibid.*, February 29, 1864.

every hamlet where I pass the night, at every post station where I await fresh horses, I shall scatter such information as I have found by experience to be best calculated to promote the emigration of these Scandinavians to our land.

His plan of sending emigrants with cargoes of iron to defray expenses was demonstrated as feasible by a private enterprise when the American ship "Free Trade" sailed from Gothenburg to Boston on June 30, 1864, with 1,509 tons of iron and 210 emigrants.[1]

The activities of corporations, states, and individuals to encourage emigration were especially mentioned by the American legation in Sweden in 1864. Mr. Haldeman stated in his dispatch of May 17, 1864, that since the state of Maine had voted to give $25 a head to an association of her capitalists for every emigrant from the north of Europe who might be brought to Maine for a year, it would be necessary to establish a consul at Christiania.[2] He mentioned in his letter of June 18, 1864, that Count Manderström, foreign secretary, had again referred to the opposition of the Swedish government toward emigration, although Sweden had never sought to place any obstacle or hindrance in the way. He observed that "this feeling is natural and not surprising when we consider the fact that Sweden and Norway cover a larger area of territory than any nation in Europe, except Russia, with the population less than six million."[3] He also mentioned the fact that the Rev. B. F. Tefft, former consul to Stockholm, had returned from the United States as the agent for all the Lake Superior Copper Mining Companies, and had advertised for 10,000 miners and artisans. He had already entered into written contracts with emigrants to pay their passage and all expenses, to be repaid in labor at the mines. There appeared to be much feeling against the United States because of Tefft's activities. Our chargé d'affaires had to explain to the Swedish foreign minister that Mr. Tefft was not employed, nor did he represent, nor was he connected with the government of the United States. The Swedish foreign minister thought, however, that it was unfair for foreign corpora-

[1] *Ibid.*, July 6, 1864. Many of these freight ships loaded with iron had carried passengers before.

[2] U.S. Department of State, *Dispatches from Sweden*, Haldeman to Seward, May 17, 1864, Vol. X, No. 47.

[3] *Ibid.*, June 18, 1864, Vol. X, No. 9.

tions to come to Sweden and advertise for labor. "It should have been left to the laws of supply and demand," was his observation. The Swedish newspapers also expressed their views in strong and violent language, denouncing it as a great fraud, calling Mr. Tefft a United States recruiting officer. They referred to published extracts from a speech of the Marquis Clamicarde in the House of Lords on the enlistment of English subjects by agents of the United States.[1]

Emigration did result from Tefft's efforts. In the middle of June, 1864, 300 Swedes left Stockholm, a "noble body of men, accompanied in some cases with their wives and children."[2] Haldeman stated that Tefft was receiving $6,000 a year and commission for recruiting emigrants and expected to be employed for several years. In July, 1864, he chartered the "Ernest Merk," known as the best iron steamer built in Sweden at that time. On board were five hundred emigrants bound for Portland, Maine, and three hundred more for the Lake Superior copper mines.[3] The "Foreign Emigration Association of Maine" had employed him to secure emigrants for that state. The Swedish government admitted that these contracts were legal and informed the American chargé d'affaires that it would not interfere with the emigrants, even though they regretted the loss of population. It appeared that every means was attempted in Sweden to prevent the emigration of persons under contract with Tefft. It was even declared a fraud by the grand-governor of Stockholm.[4]

The Swedish-American newspaper, *Hemlandet*, discussed the activities of Consul Tefft in its July 27, 1864, issue.[5] He had been arrested for making a contract with a sixteen-year-old girl to send her to Maine as a maid. She was to be placed by the Foreign Association of Maine and to work for a year to pay back her passage in monthly instalments. Tefft had accepted 8 riksdaler, about $2.00, from the girl. He returned the contract and the money. Quoting from the *Gothenburg Post*, *Hemlandet* told of 150 emigrants bound for America via Hull. These emigrants had contracted to work in

[1] *Ibid.*        [2] *Ibid.*        [3] *Ibid.*, July 2, 1864, Vol. X, No. 50.

[4] *U.S. Consular Letters, 1864-1870*, George A. Tefft, consul at Stockholm, October 11, 1864.

[5] *Hemlandet* (Chicago), July 27, 1864.

the mines at $260.00 a year, or 975 riksdaler, but because of the decline of American money it amounted to only 507 riksdaler, or 42 riksdaler 25 öre a month ($10.00). Since the cost of living was higher than in Sweden, these wages were extremely low. In a later issue there was an announcement that many who had arrived on the "Superior" from Gothenburg to Quebec had been forced to take work at the copper mines in Michigan because of the lack of funds.[1] On December 9, 1863, the newspaper was proud to announce that it had more than sixty subscribers in Sweden, which it hoped to double so that people in Sweden might know the truth about conditions in America.[2]

The Swedish volunteers in the Danish War of 1864 came home much disappointed at its failure. They flocked to the American consulate and tried to enlist in the northern armies of the United States, with the remark that "the war in America is different from that in Denmark; it goes forward."[3] The United States consul at Gothenburg, W. W. Thomas, Jr., made arrangements to send some of these soldiers to the United States from Hamburg at half-fare. Their fare was paid by a purse to which "some good friends of America" and the consul, himself, had contributed. In his report of September 16, 1864, he wrote, "I have forwarded over thirty this week; most of them under-officers who have served three years in the Swedish artillery before volunteering in the Danish War." He added, "I am well aware that as consul I have nothing to do with soldiers, but no international law can prevent me from paying a soldier's passage from here to Hamburg out of my own pocket."[4]

There is no evidence that the United States government actually recruited soldiers for the Civil War, in Sweden, in spite of the enthusiasm that her consuls manifested in its possibilities and after the besieging of the legation and the consulates by hundreds who wished to volunteer. There were undoubtedly many who did emigrate of their own accord in order to enter the army enticed by the promise of bounty and free lands. And in some cases passage was paid by

[1] *Ibid.*, August 17, 1864.  [2] *Ibid.*, December 9, 1863.

[3] *U.S. Consular Letters, 1864–1888*, Gothenburg, W. W. Thomas, Jr., consul, September 16, 1864.

[4] *Ibid.*

individuals interested in the success of the Union. President Lincoln expressly stated in his message to Congress of December 6, 1864, that "the United States government had no designs to impose involuntary military service upon immigrants."[1]

Although there had been much opposition to the policy of the United States in attracting immigrants in 1864 in Sweden, Germany, and other countries, President Lincoln seemed quite satisfied with the results. In his message in December, he reported to the country that "most of the European States have shown a liberal disposition toward the American policy."[2] Foreign Minister, Count Manderström, had, however, announced to the American embassy in Stockholm the previous June that Sweden would look with disfavor upon any active efforts of the United States to try to attract Swedish people to its shores.[3] This made it necessary for the American consuls to be more circumspect in their activities.

Toward the end of the Civil War and with the added inducements of free lands under the Homestead Law, emigration increased. There was a feeling that there would be a great demand for labor in the United States, in all branches of industry.[4] In a few days in the middle of April, 1865, the Swedish foreign office had issued 107 passports. Since passports were not needed, only one-third of the emigrants used them. There was much alarm among the landed proprietors and the governing classes. The American chargé d'affaires reported that

in the country, meetings have been held by employers complaining that the young laboring men are leaving the country, and insisting that the Government should take steps to prevent an exodus of the people so detrimental to the landed and productive interests. They charge that the Government of the United States engaged in a great war, are inducing and aiding the able bodied men to emigrate and this idea obtaining among the people causes one class to regard its officers with jealous distrust, while another class daily seek at the doors of the Legation and Consulate, the means to reach the American shores. Again political partisans seize the occasion to turn the feeling to their own account. Those who may be styled Liberals insist that the cause of emigration is to be found in the laws of the country which they urge, among other things, oblige

[1] Richardson, *op. cit.*, VI, 246.    [2] *Ibid.*

[3] U.S. Department of State, *Dispatches from Sweden*, Haldeman to Seward, June 18, 1864.

[4] *Ibid.*, James H. Campbell to Seward, April 25, 1865, Vol. XI, No. 16.

the citizens to pay taxes to support a state religion his conscience does not approve, and that while the country is poor and wages low, public burdens are onerous. But I imagine the true reason is obvious. Receiving through letters from friends and relatives in America accounts of improved conditions and liberal institutions, of homestead bills, and fertile soil the Swedish and Norwegian peasant believes he can better his position in life. . . . . The railing of government organs and the publications, as the denunciation of the interested classes, are vain. He has faith in the statements of his own class, and go he will if he can provide the means. And that is the great impediment. The land is poor. Thousands would go if the means were provided. . . . . The laboring classes have an impression that the war was in the interests of free labor, and liberal institutions, and peace will stimulate both commerce and immigration.[1]

Emigration in the first half of the sixties had increased slightly over the previous five years of the fifties, but did not reach the level of 1850–55. There was a marked quickening of emigration during 1864 and 1865, undoubtedly due to the encouragement of immigration by the United States government, the beginning of an economic crisis in Sweden, and the cessation of the Civil War. The exodus continued from the same regions as in the fifties. The largest number of emigrants came from Älvsborg County, the results of the activities of the consuls at Gothenburg and the decline of the textile industry during the American Civil War. Between 1861 and 1865 there was an exodus of 1,758 persons from the county, an even flow each year.[2] Östergötland County came next in the number of emigrants during the five years with 903. Kalmar County surpassed the other two Småland counties, having 876 emigrants, while Jönköping had 858. Kristianstad County in Skåne had an exodus of 843 persons; Skaraborg County, 646; the city of Stockholm, 526, and Gävleborg County in Norrland, 465. A new movement of emigration was noticeable in the county of Värmland with 464. In the third Småland county, Kronoberg, there had been a steady decline of emigration since 1855, and from 1861 to 1865 there were only 309 emigrants.

The governor of Kalmar County, where there had been a marked increase over the past emigration, complained in his report to the Swedish government that it was due to the activities of the agents, Swedish-Americans who were procuring emigrants for certain emigrant agencies and corporations in the United States.[3] About 1,000

[1] *Ibid.*        [2] "Bygdestatistik," *op. cit.*, p. 70*, Table 43.

[3] K. *bfhde femårsberättelse, Kalmar län, 1861–1866,* p. 6.

had emigrated from the central portions of the mainland of the county (the island of Öland is a part of the county); some 700 from Aspelund and Handbörd bailiwicks, of which 250 were from Morlunds parish alone.[1] He wrote,

The agents induce industrious but penniless workers to make contracts of labor for their passage. Upon reaching America they are engaged in heavy, unprofitable labor, but must remain because they have not the means to return. One and another family are more prosperous and go to the United States with money by which they can attain a better status for themselves in the new land.

In 1865, the Swedish government sent notice to the governors of the counties and to the clergy to warn the people not to emigrate without due thought and care, and to beware of agents. These warnings seemed to have had little effect on the people.

The activities of the former consul of Stockholm, B. F. Tefft, for the "Foreign Emigration Association of Maine" and for the Lake Superior Copper Companies have been noted. There also appeared commercial emigrant agencies for the purpose of exploiting the business of transporting emigrants and acting as procurers for the states that wished settlers or for the various corporations that needed labor. One of these was the Western Emigration Agency of Chicago, whose senior partner was B. A. Froiseth. This agency was especially interested in securing the patronage of Minnesota in 1858–59.[2] The agency advised Minnesota to publish a pamphlet describing its resources, etc., in English, German, French, Dutch, Norwegian, and Swedish. It further advised that a reliable map of the state accompany the pamphlet, including the entire route from the seaboard at New York, Boston, Portland, and Quebec to St. Paul and the various sections of the state. The letter stated that

such a pamphlet widely distributed will not only serve to invite capital and labor to the state, but will also afford to the emigrant the information necessary to enable him to decide as to his precise destination before leaving home—a by no means unimportant consideration, and one which during the constant war of competing railroad lines should not be lost sight of.[3]

[1] Since only about one-third of the emigrants took passports, there is a discrepancy between the figures of the governors' and the official reports.

[2] Letter from Western Emigration Agency, Chicago, to the Governor of Minnesota, July 22, 1858, MSS Minnesota Historical Library.

[3] *Ibid.*

The Western Emigration Agency established agents in all the principal seaports of Germany, Great Britain, France, Sweden, Norway, and Denmark, as well as in the eastern states of the United States and Canada in 1858.[1] It had two agencies in Sweden, at Stockholm and at Gothenburg.[2] There were also agencies at Copenhagen, at Hamburg, and Bremen, and at Christiania and Bergen, besides all the principal embarkation ports of Holland and England. At these agencies, through-tickets could be purchased to any destination in the United States. Their agents met all the immigrant trains in Chicago which was the distribution point for the Middle West. At their agency information about improved and unimproved farm lands and government lands in Illinois, Wisconsin, Iowa, Minnesota, and Kansas could be secured free of charge. They also established a sort of travel insurance where, upon the payment of a fee of a dollar in Europe, the immigrant might draw from an aid and relief fund for the benefit of sick and impoverished immigrants. In order to advertise, the agency proposed the publication of two weekly newspapers, one in Norwegian and one in Swedish.[3]

The advertisements of the emigrant-travel agencies did not appear in the local Swedish press until after the Civil War. The encouragement given by the government of the United States to immigration in 1864 and the years following the Civil War, was the inspiration of many of these organizations. Between 1865 and 1867, the advertisements of the American Emigrant Company, the Columbia Emigrant Agency, and the American Emigrant Aid and Homestead Company were found in the rural newspapers of Sweden.[4]

The only American state that attempted to solicit settlers directly from Europe before the Civil War was Wisconsin. During the forties, letters from the Pine Lake colonists had inspired emigration from Småland and Östergötland in Sweden. But in 1852 the state decided to make it a governmental policy, when the first Commissioner of Emigration for Wisconsin was established by law. In the first annual report, it was stated that a number of pamphlets de-

---

[1] Letter from Western Emigrant Agency, 60 Michigan Avenue, Chicago, to Governor H. H. Selby of Minnesota, January 3, 1859 (*ibid.*).

[2] *Ibid.*, form or blank of contract and circular of Western Emigration Agency.

[3] *Ibid.*, June 5, 1859.      [4] See chap. vii, 233.

scribing the state had been distributed in English, German, and Norwegian.[1] The agent for Wisconsin in New York had directed many people to the state. In the report of the year, 1853, it was recommended that a delegate from the state go to the principal ports and starting places in England, Scotland, Ireland, Germany, the Netherlands, Belgium, France, Sweden, Norway, and perhaps Switzerland.[2] The annual report of 1854 stated that Wisconsin, as a place for settlers, had received notice in a large number of newspapers in the United States, Holland, and Switzerland. Even as early as 1853, mention is made of the attempt of the European governments to check the constantly increasing drain of population and capital from their dominions.[3]

In New York there was much competition for the newly arrived immigrants. Railroads and other enterprises wanted them. Contractors upon the Illinois Central and many other roads had established agencies in New York, where not only high wages were offered but transportation either free of charge, or at least at reduced rates, to the place of employment was held out as an inducement.[4] In 1855, the Commission of Emigration for Wisconsin was discontinued. The activities of the states were aroused again after the Civil War.

Twenty-five years of emigration from Sweden to the United States had transpired in the nineteenth century by 1865. The largest portion of it had occurred during the first fifteen years of the period. America had now become an every day topic in Swedish life. It was known as the land of great economic opportunity and of religious freedom. Many ambitious persons from the less prosperous regions of Sweden had begun to seek its shores. The two districts in Sweden that had furnished the largest number of emigrants were Hälsingland in southern Norrland, and the highlands of Småland with its bordering region in the counties of Östergötland and Kristianstad. Värmland, which was destined to furnish America with the largest emigration of any Swedish county, had as yet scarcely begun to contribute.

Most of the Swedish settlements in the United States had been made in the middle states, Illinois, Wisconsin, Iowa, and Minnesota

[1] Wisconsin, *Annual Report of Commission of Emigration, 1853*, p. 5.

[2] *Ibid.*, p. 14.        [3] *Ibid., 1854*, p. 5.        [4] *Ibid.*, p. 6.

before the Civil War. These were the states that offered the greatest opportunities to the settler between 1840 and 1860, and the personal influence of the Hedström brothers, the land agent, Wiström, the settlers at Pine Lake, and the letters of Fredrika Bremer were but pawns in the hand of destiny at the time. A few colonies had been left scattered in the east by those who had originally intended to seek the Middle West; Brockton, Massachusetts; Sugar Grove, Pennsylvania; and Jamestown, New York, while Austin, Texas, had also become the future home of some. Undoubtedly the gold rush left a few in California.

Improved economic conditions in Sweden in the later fifties and the Civil War in the United States tended to cut down emigration during the last ten years, from 1855 to 1865. There had been little effort on the part of American agencies to stimulate emigration from the Scandinavian countries before the Civil War. In 1862, Mr. Haldeman of the American legation in Stockholm spoke of Sweden and Norway as virgin soil as far as propaganda on the part of agencies in the United States for emigrants was concerned. With the encouragement of immigration by the North during the Civil War, and the several years following, came the efforts of the steamship companies, emigrant companies, and the American states in the stimulation of further exodus from the northern countries.

# CHAPTER VI

## THE DISSENTERS OF SWEDEN

Sweden, like England, continues to be a theocracy, with a state church under government control. There is an unusual religious homogeneity among the Swedish people. The records of the church books of the Lutheran chuich show $97\frac{1}{2}$ per cent of the population as adherents of the state church, though the various dissenters claim about 3.3 per cent.[1] Everyone is legally born into the state church and can separate only by a formal application for separation. All the inhabitants pay taxes for the support of the Lutheran church, but those who have legally separated from the church pay only half of the amount required of members.[2]

Although the dissenters are few in number, they are and have been for more than a century an articulate group. The free church party today has its strength in the Liberal party, and its leader, Gustav Ekman, was prime minister of Sweden from the spring of 1926 until the fall of 1929 and again in 1931. Most of the dissenters belong to the lower middle class, the "cottage" people of the rural districts. The largest number of dissenters belong to the Mission church, which separated under Waldenström from the established church in 1876. It has never legally and formally separated from the state church, and is not officially in the Swedish statistics recognized as a dissenting church.

The Swedish Mission church claimed 110,608 adherents in Sweden in 1920.[3] The Baptist church in Sweden counted its membership ·during the same year as 61,120, although the official figures of the government were only 7,265. The largest number of Baptists are

[1] These are the statistics of 1920 (*Statistisk årsbok för Sverige, 1927*, pp. 13–14, Tables 15 and 16).

[2] Originally the tenth was paid directly to the clergy. In 1910 a law was passed by which the tax is paid directly to the state, and the clergy in turn are paid definite salaries. Church lands and forests then passed to the state for administration (Hildebrand, *Gustav V* [Stockholm, 1926], pp. 645–46).

[3] *Statistisk årsbok för Sverige, 1927*, p. 14, Table 16 (see footnote).

found in the counties of Östergötland, Kopparberg, Gotland, and Örebro. The Swedish Methodists count their numbers as 17,079, while statistics show only 5,462 in 1920. They are most numerous in Gothenburg-Bohus, Örebro, Västmanland, Gävleborg, and Östergötland counties. The Baptist church began to proselyte in Sweden in the fifties, and the Methodists in the later sixties. There are 6,469 adherents of the Jewish faith located in the larger cities. Roman Catholics number 3,425, and Greek Catholics only 281. Other dissenting religions are the Anglican Episcopal, the Christian Science, Adventists, Mormons, etc. In 1880 there were 414 recognized Mormons in Sweden, and in 1920 only 33.

There have been periods in Swedish history when dissenting movements against the state church have been particularly active. This opposition to the state church has come both from groups within the country itself who have sought to make new interpretations of Christianity, and from proselyting activities of denominations in other countries, i.e., Methodist, Baptist, Mormon, Seventh-day Adventists, Salvation Army, and others.

During an earlier period of pietistic activity in the later seventeenth and early eighteenth centuries, certain laws were passed in Sweden to preserve the religious unity of the state church. Contemporary with the laws against Catholics and Dissenters passed in England under Charles II, and the restrictions on Protestants in France under the Catholic Louis XIV, the church was placed more completely under the control of the state in Sweden in 1686.[1] The "Book of Concord" became the orthodox confession of faith. The church handbook was adopted in 1693 and the "psalm book," the hymnal, in 1695. Laws punishing dissenters were also passed. The law of 1686 moreover provided for a more systematic education, a reading knowledge of the Bible for the common people.[2] This education was under the supervision of the clergy.

With the introduction of the pietistic movement from Germany in the early eighteenth century, the laws against dissenters were strengthened. The first pietistic preacher in Sweden, Johannes Fol-

[1] K. B. Westman, "Kyrkliga förhållanden," in Guinchard, *Sveriges Land och Folk*, I, 302–3.

[2] J. M. Ambrosius, "Folkundervisningen," *ibid.*, I, 314.

cher, concentrated his efforts in Stockholm, and from there the new religion spread to Finland where it found many adherents in spite of persecution.[1] A commission was appointed in Sweden in 1723 to investigate religious heresy. The result of this investigation was the passage of a stringent law against heretics, called the "conventicle placate," in 1726.[2] It forbade laymen to gather in their homes for religious meetings and to administer the sacrament of the Lord's Supper.[3] Since the state church was under the government of Sweden, government officials were to enforce the new law with fines, imprisonment, and banishment. To meet the new demands for greater religious activity, the clergy were required to make house to house visitations where they were from time to time to give religious examinations to all adults. They were also required to confirm all children. Missions were established among the heathen Lapps in the northern provinces.[4] The "conventicle placate" remained on the statute books until 1858.

French atheism and German rationalism which swept over Europe in the later part of the eighteenth century cast their influence upon the intellectuals of Sweden and the clergy of the Lutheran church. The first appearance of rationalism was in the literary works of Olof von Dalin in 1730. During the reign of Gustavus III (1772–92), the nephew of Frederick the Great of Prussia, rationalism was very fashionable in Sweden. Its influence even extended to a revision of the church handbook and the psalm book. The new handbook, tainted with the rationalistic philosophy, appeared in 1811, and Wallin's psalm book in 1819.[5]

There were many in Sweden, especially among the common people, who protested against the introduction of rationalism into the state church, and continued to be fundamentalists. Even among some of the intellectual classes there were protests. One movement of international importance began with the spiritual revelations of Emanuel Swedenborg, who suddenly in 1745 left his scientific re-

[1] Finland was a province of Sweden until 1809, when it was conquered by Russia (Ekman, *Den inre missionens historia* [Stockholm, 1896], I, 1–7).

[2] *Ibid.*, p. 63.

[3] *Konventikel plakatet* (*ibid.*, pp. 91–94).

[4] Guinchard, *op. cit.*, I, 303.     [5] *Ibid.*, p. 309.

search to ponder in the realm of religion.[1] His numerous books tend toward an occult interpretation of the Bible. Respected as a great scientist, and as a faithful servant of the government which he had served as a mining engineer, Swedenborg was not persecuted for heresy in Sweden. But he found England more liberal in accepting his religious interpretations. After his death, in England in 1772, his followers there organized the "new church" or the "Church of the New Jerusalem" which spread rapidly to the United States, Germany, and Switzerland. In Sweden, however, the new religion, as well as the writings of Swedenborg, remained under ban until 1858.

The reaction of the fundamentalists among the common people of Sweden asserted itself in sporadic religious revivals, influenced by pietism which had never been stamped out, in spite of the vigorous "conventicle placate." In the early part of the nineteenth century, numerous revival preachers appeared in various portions of the kingdom. There was Tollesson in the province of Uppland, Hoof in the province of Västergötland, Linderot in Bohus province, Sellengren in Småland, and the Laestadius brothers in the Lappmark.[2] Wallin, the author of the hymnal, Schartau, Franzén, and others labored for a deeper Christian feeling among the people.[3] Schartau's influence was especially widespread among the common people of Southern and Western Sweden. He was a minister in Lund, where his contacts with the University students made a deep impression upon his generation. Schartauism was a stern puritanical doctrine.[4]

Various religious organizations, both national and foreign, co-operated to awaken the religious spirit of the common people in the early nineteenth century. The Evangelical Society was organized in Stockholm in 1808.[5] It in turn, in 1815, established the Swedish Bible Society, whose chief purpose was to distribute Bibles and religious tracts among the Swedish people. The British Foreign and Continental Bible Society also placed an agency in Stockholm and co-operated with the Swedish Society. In 1839, the British Society

---

[1] A. H. Newman, *A Manual of Church History* (Philadelphia, 1914), II, 542–44.

[2] Sam Clason, *Karl XIII och Karl XIV Johan;* Hildebrand, *Sveriges historia,* XI, 364.

[3] Guinchard, *op. cit.,* I, 304.

[4] He died in 1825. *The Sweden Year Book, 1926,* p. 50.  [5] Clason, *op. cit.,* p. 364.

reported that it had sent 91,331 copies of the Bible and New Testament in Swedish for distribution, while the same year the Swedish Bible Society printed and bound 37,000 copies in Stockholm.[1] The American Tract Society was also active in Sweden and appropriated eight hundred dollars for missions there in 1837.[2] Missionary movements also began in Sweden. In 1835, the Swedish Mission Society was started, through the influence of the Moravian Brethern of Germany, for the Christianization of the Lapps in Northern Sweden.[3] Missionary interest spread into the foreign field. A Foreign Missionary Society and Training School was established at Lund in 1846 by Peter Fjellstedt.[4] This society was originally affiliated with the German Missionary Societies, but in 1855, separated and became national. The school was, soon after its beginning, moved from Lund to Stockholm, and a similar school was erected by Jonas Ahlberg in Ahlsborg, Småland, in 1858. The purpose of these missionary schools was to furnish missionaries for China and Africa. In the early fifties, Peter Fjellstedt was called upon by the Swedish immigrants in America to furnish ministers for the new settlements there.

Simultaneous with these various religious movements in Sweden, the personality of an English Methodist minister, George Scott, was destined to influence vitally the new spiritual revival that was sweeping the country. A group of English workmen had been imported to Stockholm by an Englishman, Samuel Owen, who had established a foundry and machine shop in Stockholm in the early part of the nineteenth century. Samuel Owen was a Methodist, and he appealed to the Wesleyan Missionary Society of his mother country to care for the spiritual needs of the English mechanics.[5] The society responded and sent J. R. Stephens as the first pastor of the English church in Stockholm. In 1830 George Scott was sent to succeed Stephens. Scott did not believe in proselyting in an evangelical

[1] Reprint from London Missionary Register (the Missionary Herald [New York], 1839, p. 65).

[2] Report of the American Tract Society (ibid., 1838, p. 275).

[3] Ibid., 1853, p. 315.      [4] Ibid.

[5] N. J. Nordström, De frikyrkliga-och statskyrko-problemet (Stockholm, 1922), pp. 18–19; the Missionary Herald, 1842, p. 294.

country, but his influence has left a lasting impression upon the free-church movements in Sweden.

Foreigners had been given the right to establish their own churches in Sweden upon the approval of the king in the eighteenth century, but there remained a law which forbade Swedish citizens from attending these churches.[1] Toward the end of the thirties, the consistory of the Lutheran church of Stockholm forbade Scott to preach to Swedish citizens, for he was altogether too popular and too influential. It was, therefore, necessary to erect an English church. To procure money for the building, Scott toured America and criticized in his speeches the lack of religious freedom in Sweden. This criticism was discussed in the Liberal press of Sweden upon Scott's return, and a mob, incited by the newspaper propaganda, attacked the church in 1842 and Scott was forced to flee from Sweden and returned to England. Scott's influence, however, continued to be felt in Sweden. Among his great admirers was C. O. Rosénius, who had come under Scott's influence while attending the English church in Stockholm. Rosénius was the organizer of the dissenters of Sweden into the "National Evangelical Union" in 1856.[2] Scott directed the work of the sailor missionaries in the ports of Stockholm and Gothenburg, which were supported by the American Seaman's Friend Society of New York.[3]

A part of the religious revival that seemed to be spreading through Northwestern Europe and America during the early nineteenth century was the temperance movement. Its forces were also felt in Sweden and strongly influenced the puritanical movements among the dissenters, and in turn some of the Swedish emigrants. The great temperance leader of Sweden was Peter Wieselgren, a graduate of the University of Lund, and a pastor at Westerstad in Southern Sweden. As early as 1819, he organized the first temperance society with a group of students at Växjö in Småland.[4]

Drunkenness had become a national curse in Sweden. In 1830 there were over 170,000 distilleries in the country, not counting

[1] Guinchard, *op. cit.*, I, 306.

[2] Nordström, *op. cit.*, pp. 54–56.

[3] This service was established in 1842 (the *Missionary Herald*, 1842, p. 294).

[4] Johan Bergman, *Nykterhets rörelsens världshistoria* (Norrköping, 1900), pp. 217–22.

stills that produced for home consumption.[1] It was estimated that the per capita consumption of intoxicating liquor was thirty-four quarts.[2] The effects of this consumption of intoxicating liquor were so obvious that thoughtful people, statesmen, political economists, physicians, philanthropists, and clergy began to organize to stem its tide. Drunkenness was blamed for a growing demoralization, especially among the working class, for increasing poverty and distress in crime, and for the stagnation of the country. The royal family being French in origin was not accustomed to indulgence in intoxicating liquor and were particularly anxious to lend their efforts toward moderation. Under the leadership of Surveyor-General Forsell, the Stockholm Moderation Society was organized in 1830, upon the thousandth anniversary of St. Ansgarius' arrival to Christianize the Swedes.[3] This was four years after the formation of the American Temperance Society. In 1831, a group believing in prohibition seceded and formed the Kungsholm Temperance Society.

In 1832, the government sent a circular letter to the governors of the counties and to the chapters of the cathedrals of the state church instructing them to further the cause of temperance. The Swedish Medical Society took a stand for temperance in 1835. And in 1837 the Swedish Temperance Society was organized, and continued for many years under the leadership of the conservative statesman and prime minister, von Hartmansdorff. Among the tracts distributed by the society was one by the noted chemist, J. Berzelius, who tried to prove that the distilling of liquor was not a necessary byproduct of agriculture.

Wieselgren, who had manifested his early interest in temperance at Växjö, continued his activities for the cause. He found his parishioners in Westerstad and Östraby, Skåne, in the depths of economic and moral degradation, when he accepted the pastorate from the landed proprietor, Jacob de la Gardie. The cause of the degradation was drunkenness. In 1836, Wieselgren organized the Westerstad Temperance Society, which became the model for many others.[4] In

[1] Hallendorff, *Oskar I och Karl XV*, p. 153.
[2] Thirty to forty liters. A liter is almost a quart, 0.22 of a gallon.
[3] Hallendorff, *op. cit.*, p. 154; Bergman, *op. cit.*, pp. 220–22, 225–27.
[4] Hallendorff, *op. cit.*, p. 155.

a few years, the distilleries had fallen from 200 to 31 in the two parishes.

There was an accompanying decline in crime and poverty. When the American temperance worker, Dr. Baird, came to tour Sweden in the cause of temperance in 1840, Wieselgren was chosen by the president of the Swedish Temperance Society, Hartmansdorff, to accompany him. The two temperance orators, Dr. Baird and Rev. Wieselgren, spoke in Stockholm, Uppsala, Dannemora, Falun, Hudiksvall, and Gävle. Wieselgren also took a leading part in the noted meeting of the Northern Temperance Societies which met in Stockholm in 1846. Other members of the clergy of the Lutheran church also espoused the cause of temperance, among them Thomander and Anders Sandberg, the dean of Madesjö.

The temperance movement grew apace in Sweden in the forties and fifties. By 1848, there were 420 local temperance societies, with a membership of 100,000. There continued a widespread discussion of the subject in the press and a contribution of pamphlets by both medical and scientific authorities. At a meeting of naturalists in Sweden in 1851, Magnus Huss, a medical authority who had written many tracts on the effects of chronic alcoholism, read a paper on endemic diseases in Sweden, a portion of which denounced the evils of whiskey and gave home distilling as the principal cause for the misuse of intoxicants.[1] A few years later 45,000 copies of a tract by O. J. Hagelstam were distributed, comparing the effects of the use of whiskey in Sweden and Denmark, where home distillery was forbidden.[2] In 1853, the Riksdag received 298 petitions with thousands of signatures, pleading for the government restriction of home distilling. A heavy tax on distilling, making it unprofitable as a home industry, was passed in the law of 1855.[3] The temperance law of 1855 did not solve the question in Sweden, but it did help to reduce the per capita consumption of intoxicants.

There were many people who opposed the movement toward prohibition, even among the clergy, as an interference in personal liber-

[1] *Ibid.*, p. 156.

[2] "Faktiska upplysinger . . . . angående Sveriges och Danmarks olika sätt att draga nationell och enskild vinst av sin lanthushållning."

[3] Hallendorff, *op. cit.*, pp. 158–59.

ty. It was customary among the clergy to indulge in liquor, as practically everyone else did, similar to the practice among the clergy in colonial times and later in the United States. Even in the eighteenth century, the peasants were apt to criticize the clergy for drinking. A peasant from Dalsland, for instance, it is related, told his pastor one Sunday, "I thank you, Jerk, for the good sermon and it is the truth, that you always preach like a man; but it is too bad that sometimes you take a drop too much."[1] It has become a tradition among the descendants of the Swedish immigrant in America that the clergy of the state church of Sweden were more or less drunkards.[2] It is perhaps an unjust criticism to make of the Swedish clergy as a whole, as may be demonstrated by a temperance meeting held at Jönköping in 1840. It was a meeting of the Swedish Temperance Society of Southern Sweden. There were many friends of the temperance movement present from the Linköping, Skaraborg, Kronoberg, Älvsborg, Kristianstad, Malmöhus, Fahlu, Stockholm, Halland, and Kalmar regions, and even from Gothenborg-Bohus County. The majority of the delegates belonged to the clergy of western Sweden, especially the Skara diocese. The meeting was held in the state church of Jönköping. The chief speakers were Dean Peter Wieselgren, Pastor George Scott of the Methodist church of Stockholm, and Assistant-Pastor Elmblad of the Adolph Fredericks church of Stockholm.[3] Dean Bexell of the Cathedral of Stockholm, the Rydaholm church, led in prayer.

Among the clergy of the Lutheran church who came to the United States with the Swedish emigrants of the forties and the fifties were a number of temperance workers. It was through their influence that the requirements for a temperate clergy were introduced in the Swedish Lutheran Church in America. One of these temperance workers was Paul Esbjörn, who left Sweden with a group of pietists from Hälsingland in 1849.[4] He had been influenced both by George

[1] Säve, Dalmålet (1855), cited in Norlind, Svensk allmogens liv, p. 420.

[2] I have heard this statement frequently made by the descendants of American immigrants from various portions of Sweden.

[3] Lunds Weckoblad, Nytt och Gammalt (Lund), July 15, 1840.

[4] Norelius, De svenska luterska församlingarnas .... historia i Amerika, I, 34 ff., 117 ff.

Scott and Peter Wieselgren. Because of his reputation as a revivalist preacher and a temperance advocate, he had been voted down by several Swedish congregations, for the Swedish parish had the privilege of electing a pastor from three candidates recommended by the consistory of the diocese. In March, 1850, he reported to the American Home Board of Missions of the Congregational church, which had given him financial aid in his religious work among the Swedish immigrants of Illinois, that a temperance society had been organized at Andover, Illinois.[1]

Another discouraged temperance reformer was Olof Anderson of Humslid, Värmland, a former member of the Estate of Peasants in the Riksdag, and a large landowner.[2] His pride hurt when he could not persuade his neighbors to join the temperance movement, he sold his lands and emigrated to the United States in 1858. Many of the dissenters emigrating for other reasons, carried the influence of the Swedish temperance movement with them to the United States, and insisted at least upon the temperance of their clergy.

An interesting force in Swedish immigration to America resulted from the contacts made by Swedish sailors, primarily in the port of New York, with the Baptist and Methodist seaman's missions. An example of this influence was O. G. Hedström, who was converted to Methodism in 1830 at the Mariner's church of New York, and became the famous Methodist missionary of the "Bethel-ship" in New York City from 1845 to 1875.[3] It was seldom a Scandinavian immigrant passed through New York without some contact with Hedström. He was influential in converting some, and in sending many to settle in and around Victoria, Illinois, where his brother, Jonas Hedström, had located as a circuit rider for the Methodist church. Another seaman, F. O. Nilsson, who was also converted to Methodism in a New York mission, returned to Sweden to take the post of sailor missionary for the American Seaman's Friend Society of New York, upon the recommendation of George Scott of the English

[1] The *Home Missionary* (Boston, 1850), p. 263.

[2] Magnusson, "Jösse härad i Värmland, Bygdeundersökningar," *Emigrationsutredningens bilaga VIII*, pp. 6–7.

[3] Nordström, *op. cit.*, pp. 35–36; Skarstedt, *Svensk-Amerikanska folket*, p. 74; Norelius, *op. cit.*, I. 16–26.

church of Stockholm.[1] The society reported in 1844 that its religious and temperance activities included the foreign ports of Gothenburg, Stockholm, Amsterdam, Havre, Sydney, Honolulu, Labaina, and Havana.[2] F. O. Nilsson was, in turn, converted to Baptism in 1845 by a Swedish sea captain, E. W. Schroeder, who had accepted the faith in a New York mission. Nilsson was destined to be exiled for his faith in 1850.

But most important of all the religious movements of the nineteenth century was the religious revival that seemed to sweep across Sweden in protest to the rationalism of the Lutheran church. The dissenters were most numerous in Norrland, especially in Hälsingland and Värmland. In defiance of the "conventicle placate," they held meetings in their homes, which consisted of giving testimonials of their conversion. There developed among the dissenters a group of lay preachers, often self-appointed and inspired to preach, who traveled from parish to parish interpreting the Bible and peddling tracts. These gatherings were not much different from the religious societies that developed in England in the eighteenth century, and from which the Wesleyan movement had its impetus. They were like the camp-meeting revivals that swept the American frontier during the early nineteenth century. Colporteurs or tract distributors were familiar characters in England and Scotland, as well as on the American frontier, and received their inspiration and support from various Tract societies, both in England and America.

The Swedish clergy, who were all graduates of the Universities of Lund or Uppsala, in some cases undoubtedly looked upon the attempt of untutored laymen to interpret the Bible in these self-inspired prayer-meetings as a dangerous practice and attempted by threat and persecution to prevent them. Others of the clergy and many of the government officials thought that this spiritual awakening of the common people was a wholesome phenomenon which would lead to a higher moral status of the lower classes. The sympathetic clergy encouraged the dissenters and became known as revivalist pastors.

In the governor's reports, there were citations of the dissenting

[1] J. Byström, *En frikyrklig banbrytare* (Stockholm, 1911), pp. 21–31.

[2] *Missionary Herald* (Boston, 1844), p. 208.

movements. The governor of the county of Gävleborg wrote in 1847 that the common people in many of the parishes of Hälsingland had for a long time shown tendencies toward a kind of pietism and were called "readers," or dissenters. They were extremely religious, which some people misunderstood and thought just a pose. They held special religious meetings outside of the church, but as long as they attended the regular church services and accepted the doctrines of the church, they were left undisturbed and were even at times encouraged by the clergy to hold these private meetings.[1] Governor W. Gynther of Västernorrland County stated in 1850 that the notorious Norrland "readers" were not the people who came together quietly and reverently to consider God's Word and by their contemplation develop spiritually, but those who had heretical religious doctrines, who opposed the church ceremonies, and who, under the mantle of religion, broke with social customs.[2] He continued further, "The private revivals begin often in good faith, but when many uneducated people begin to explain the Scriptures, they spread heresy," and he recommended that the clergy hold separate Bible meetings and prayer meetings to meet this new spiritual demand from the people.

Some of the dissenters refused to accept the new church handbook of 1811 because of its rationalistic influence and clung to the "pure Lutheran doctrine" as expressed in the Augsburg Confession. They were in modern terminology, fundamentalists. Their criticism of the clergy and the church was bitter and harsh. The governor of Västernorrland County reported in 1855 that in three parishes the people had petitioned the cathedral chapter to allow them to separate from the false community of the state church until the old and pure handbook, psalm book, and catechism should be restored and there should be true teaching from the pulpit.[3] This group of dissenters were called Hedbergians, since they followed the teaching of a Finnish minister named Hedberg. They were most numerous in Hälsingland. In 1850, a large group of the Hedbergians emigrated to the

---

[1] K. bfhde femårsberättelse, Gefleborgs län, 1843–1847, pp. 6–7.

[2] Ibid., Westernorrlands län, 1847–1850, pp. 20–21.

[3] Ibid., 1851–1855, pp. 13–14. Referring to the national tendency in the church and the recent changes in the handbook, etc.

United States. In this party was Eric Norelius, one of the founders of the Augustana Synod of the Swedish Lutheran Church.

There were many of these dissenting movements throughout Sweden, arising spontaneously and without any unity of action. Some of the dissenters remained in the church and continued their private prayer meetings as subsidiary to the regular church attendance. Others began through their spiritual revivals to find themselves differing from the teachings of the state church and finally became separatists. Some of the separatists organized new churches of their own, like the Janssonites, and later the Swedish Mission church. The remaining separatists found other Protestant faiths like the Baptist, Mormon, and Methodist, more suited to their spiritual needs.

It was C. O. Rosénius, the admirer of the English Methodist preacher, George Scott, who saw the advantages of organizing the dissenters into a religious body and utilizing the new forces for a spiritual awakening within the Lutheran church.[1] He severely criticized those of the clergy who were opposed to the revivals and to the participation of laymen in church work. On May 7, 1856, he organized the dissenters who remained within the church into the "National Evangelical Union" known in Sweden as *Evangeliska Fosterlandsstiftelsen*.[2] The new organization was to educate and direct the itinerant preachers or colporteurs. The use of colporteurs in the movement was the suggestion of a young minister of Västerås who had studied the movement in Scotland during his student holiday.[3]

The "National Evangelical Union" had a simple organization. A self-perpetuating executive committee of twelve was resident in Stockholm. Its purpose was to encourage the distribution of Bibles and tracts by colporteurs and to guide the activities of the laymen within the Lutheran church. Representatives chosen from the clergy and the laymen in the counties directed the local work. By the end of 1856, the new organization had sixteen colporteurs and fifty county representatives. In the sixties missionary societies, supporting both home and foreign missions, were organized among the lay-

[1] Byström, *op. cit.*, pp. 21–31.
[2] It was originally called *Fosterländska stiftelsen för evangelii befrämjande.*
[3] Nordström, *op. cit.*, pp. 54–56.

men. The sewing circles among the women of the parish were to be the financial support of the missions. In 1874, the mission societies were permitted to send representatives to the annual meetings of the "National Evangelical Union," and had a direct influence upon all of its activities. This lay movement continues today, an auxiliary movement within the Lutheran church in Sweden.

One of the earliest of the separatist movements was the Janssonite; Eric Jansson, a peasant of Uppland province, became a lay preacher among the dissenters. For a number of years it had been his custom to bring his wheat flour to Hälsingland in Norrland to sell. This region was specially prolific with dissenters. In 1843, he began to preach in the region, and won quite a large following.[1] His interpretation of the Bible finally led him to denounce the doctrine and church books of the Lutheran faith. He wrote his own psalm book and catechism. His adherents ceased to attend the regular church services and the communion of the state church. In the wildest ecstasy of religious fanaticism, they burned all the religious books used by the state church, including the psalm book and catechism. The sect was then persecuted. They decided to emigrate to the United States, being undoubtedly influenced by the letters of a certain Gustaf Flack who had written from Illinois to his relatives in Alfta parish in Hälsingland, praising the new land and emphasizing the religious freedom enjoyed by its inhabitants.[2] It was in Alfta parish that Eric Jansson was found hidden in the fall of 1845.[3] The Norrland press was full of the activities of the Janssonites and their persecutions at the time. By September, 1845, the brothers Olof and Jon Olsson in Söderola, both fervent Janssonites, had sold their farms and were planning to emigrate to America.

Olof Olsson came ahead of the Janssonites to determine the site of their colony in the United States. Meeting the famous Methodist immigrant missionary of the "Bethel-ship" in New York, he was advised to go to Victoria, Illinois, where the Methodist circuit rider

[1] K. bfhde femårsberättelse, Gefleborgs län, 1843–1847, pp. 6–7.

[2] Olson, History of the Swedes of Illinois, I, 220.

[3] Nyaste Norrlands Posten (Gävle), September 2, 1845, September 9, 1845. The October 3, 1845 copy announced and reviewed a book on Erik-Jansismen i Helsingland. The trial of Eric Jansson at Forssa Häradsrätt was described in the issue of October 17, 1845.

and brother of Hedström was located. In the early spring of 1846, Olsson toured Illinois, Wisconsin, and Minnesota. His final decision was to plant the new colony at Red Oak, near Victoria, Illinois.

In the meantime Eric Jansson had been rescued from the Swedish authorities by his followers and had fled to Norway, where many of the faithful joined him, and prepared to take sail the next spring. In April, one group of Janssonites sailed from Christiania.[1] Thirty-two Janssonites sailed from Hudiksvall on the steamship "Norrland" in June.[2] In July more sailed from the port of Gävle on the skipper "Wilhelmina."[3] The *Hudiksvall Weekly* stated on July 11, 1846, that "the fever for emigration on the part of the Eric Janssonites continues to rage through Hälsingland." The article continued, "It is reported that a ship at Gävle has been contracted for on their behalf to leave Söderhamn, and there is talk of engaging another to leave from Gävle. Their plans are to buy an island in America and establish a model colony. Their money resources are estimated, although perhaps somewhat exaggerated, at millions."[4] This was undoubtedly an exaggeration, but many well-to-do peasants had sold their belongings and placed their resources in the common treasury of the religious sect. The Janssonites continued to migrate. On August 17, the ship "Solide" sailed and another with 170 passengers was embarking from the port of Gävle.[5] Besides the ports near the region of emigration, Gävle, Söderhamn, and Stockholm, Janssonites also left through the ports of Gothenburg and Christiania, Norway.

The church records of Sweden show that the Janssonites numbered some 913 in the provinces of Hälsingland and Gästrikland in Norrland, the majority being in the former province.[6] Of this number 649 were adults and 409 of the adults were dissenters before joining the Janssonites. The migration was large in 1846. It is estimated that 823 of the religious sect left Sweden, and 346 from the parish of Alfta alone. The migration of the Janssonites took place

[1] *Hudikswalls Weckoblad* (Hudiksvall), June 27, 1846.    [2] *Ibid.*, June 20, 1846.

[3] *Ibid.*, July 4, 1846; *Jönköpings Tidning* (Jönköping), July 11, 1846; *Sjette Norrlands-Posten* (Gävle), June 26, 1846.

[4] *Hudikswalls Weckoblad*, August 22, 1846.

[5] Also published in *Sjette Norrlands-Posten* (Gävle), July 7, 1846.

[6] Olson, *op. cit.*, I, 220 ff.

between 1846 and 1854. It was customary that they traveled in large groups or companies. There were nine of these groups in all that set sail for America. Three of the ships on which members of the sect traveled were shipwrecked and 127 were drowned. Others died of cholera during their passage. Some decided to remain on the eastern seaboard when they reached America, and others settled in various other Swedish colonies. There were, however, some 1,500 who joined the communist colony of Bishop Hill, Illinois, named after the home of Jansson in Sweden *Bishopskullen.*

The emigration of the Janssonites was in large enough numbers to be called to the attention of the State Department of the United States. On March 7, 1846, H. W. Ellsworth, the chargé d'affaires of the United States in Sweden, wrote concerning the contemplated migration of the religious sect, "They are inhabitants of the province of Dalecarlia, and among the most industrious and honest of the Swedish population. Their dialect is a peculiar one, and indeed so different as not to be understood by other inhabitants of Sweden. It resembles closely the language of the Highland Scotch."[1]

The colony purchased in all some 12,000 acres of Illinois land around Bishop Hill, part from the United States government and part from private owners. The first year only temporary buildings were erected; several large buildings of logs and turf, four tents, a large canvas tabernacle seating eight hundred, and a dozen sod homes.[2] Permanent homes were soon constructed. The colony had the reputation of being quite prosperous and was famed for its manufacture of brooms and homespun linens. Internal factions soon developed. In 1848, about two hundred persons withdrew from the colony and settled in Victoria and Galesburg, Illinois.[3]

During August, 1849, one of the Janssonites returned to Sweden. It was Olof Jansson of Stenbo, Forssa parish.[4] He was accompanied by a tailor named Hedin. The *Weekly* warned its readers that they came as agents of Eric Jansson, first to obtain money, and second

---

[1] This description is not to be taken too literally. There were many dialects in Sweden. Letter of H. W. Ellsworth, chargé d'affaires, to James Buchanan, Secretary of State, March 7, 1846 (*U.S. Dispatches from Sweden*, VII, No. 10).

[2] Olson, *op. cit.*, I, 228.

[3] *Ibid.*, p. 234.     [4] *Hudikswalls Weckoblad*, August 11, 1849.

to seek souls. Their chief object in returning was to claim the estates of certain of their fellow-religionists who had perished in a shipwreck the summer before, while en route to America.[1] But at the same time, they were attempting to induce others to emigrate by bragging about the fertility of the Illinois soil. The colony was supposed to have sold about $4,000 worth of grain in the two years of its existence.[2]

Jansson was soon after, in 1851, shot by an adventurer named Ruth, for interference in his marital affairs.[3] Jonas Olson became the leader of the colony, and two years later it was incorporated under the laws of Illinois. Charges of misappropriation of funds brought a series of law suits during 1861 and 1862, at the end of which the colony gave up the practice of communism and the assets of the group were divided among the individual members. The colony also dispersed as a religious organization, and its members joined various neighboring churches of other denominations. In Sweden, too, they disappeared as a religious sect after the migration.

There was, however, at the time much criticism of the state church because of the persecution of the Janssonites. In the *Hudiksvall Weekly* for September 26, 1846, there appeared a long article discussing whether the Janssonites should be persecuted under the Swedish law.[4] In the same issue there were editorial attacks on the Lutheran church as worldly and therefore leaving the doors open for adventurers like the Eric Janssonites. The *Norrland Post*, of July 24 1846, quoted a letter from Stockholm, which marveled at the exodus from the rural regions, which was the result of the Eric Janssonian undertaking, as well as other religious fanatics.[5] An editorial in the same paper, June 30, 1849, discussing the causes of emigration, stated,

When one sees large numbers of the country's most dependable, conservative, and peaceful common people leave their native land, with many economic sacrifices and the severing of the dearest ties, to seek a new home in a distant portion of the world, one must conclude that the motives for such sacrifice are deeper than were they only restless adventurers. Most of the emigrants from Gästrikland and Hälsingland, which have left the country during the recent

[1] *Ibid.*, August 25, 1849.          [3] Olson, *op. cit.*, I, 243–46.

[2] About 11,000 rds. of grain.          [4] *Hudikswalls Weckoblad*, September 26, 1846.

[5] Quoting from the letter as given in *Sjette Norrlands-Posten* (Gävle), July 24, 1846.

weeks, have been the well-to-do, honorable, dependable people of their community. The country is being deprived of thousands of competent tillers of the soil and thousands of dollars worth of capital.

Among the various causes of emigration cited by the editor, he emphasized, "In the United States to which the emigrants are attracted, each individual practices the religion of his choice without interference or compulsion by the state. We have a compulsory state church and an intolerance exists which places the person under spiritual slavery." In an emigrant guidebook for America, published in 1849, the author, Theodore Schytte, mentions among the causes of emigration the political and religious compulsion which dominated Sweden.[1]

The emigrations that began on a large scale from Hälsingland continued after the departure of the Janssonites. Some were dissenters and left their mother country dissatisfied with the religious tyranny of the state church. In the following notice from the *Jönköpings Tidning* of Småland, July 11, 1846, some of the emigrants might have been Janssonites. In a news-item dated from Stockholm, the paper stated,

Two ships which are taking 190 emigrants to America are ready to sail from here. Among the emigrants is a medical student, a woman with children and a maid, and also many of the common people from Gävleborg and Västerås, most of them dissenters. Another ship has recently sailed directly from Gävle, also with emigrants aboard, for America. Some of the families who had planned to leave from Gävle changed their minds and returned to their homes.[2]

Another news-item from Stockholm in the *Hudiksvall Weekly* for September 19, 1846, contained the information that

Sunday the New York brig "Fritz," with Captain Wilkinson, left Stockholm with 114 emigrants. Most of the travelers were from Gävleborg County, but others were from Jemtland, Upland, Westmanland, and Dalarne in Norrland. There were some from Stockholm and even a servant from Christiania. More than twenty of the passengers were less than ten years of age.[3]

The emigration from Norrland continued in 1849. A news-item of June 30, 1849, informed the public that "three emigrant ships with two hundred on board were sailing from Gävle. Two, the big 'Pehr'

---

[1] Theodore Schytte, *Vägledning för emigranter* (Stockholm, 1849), p. 5.

[2] *Jönköpings Tidning* (Jönköping), July 11, 1846.

[3] *Hudikswalls Weckoblad* (Hudiksvall), September 19, 1846.

and the ship 'Elizabeth' have sailed, while the ship 'Cobden' would leave the following week."[1] The feeling toward other dissenters besides the Janssonites was reflected in an editorial from the *Hudiksvall Weekly* of June 9, 1849, against the Hedbergians. It discussed a pamphlet entitled, *Pietism and Christianity*, written by a clergyman, Pastor Hedberg of Åland, and published in Umeå in Norrland.[2] The pamphlet attacked the rationalistic influence that had dominated the state church since the later part of the eighteenth century and urged a return to the fundamentalism of the Augsburg Confession and what it designated as the pure Lutheran religion. The editorial called upon the state church to prevent the dissemination of this pamphlet.

There were numerous followers of Hedberg in the Norrland region from which the Janssonites had emigrated. It is difficult to determine whether the dissenters emigrated because of religious persecution, dissatisfaction with the religious attitude of the state church, or economic reasons, for reports of the prosperity of the Janssonite colony had spread rapidly through the region. There may have been a mixture of religious dissatisfaction and the desire for greater economic opportunity.[3] The dissenters usually traveled in large groups under a leader, sometimes a clergyman of their choice. It was a migration of families with numerous children, as contrasted with the later migration of young people of single state. In 1849, Esbjörn, the young temperance worker and revivalist preacher, accompanied some 140 emigrants from Gästrikland and southern Hälsingland in Norrland.[4] These emigrants were all devout Christians and desired a religious leader to accompany them.

Through correspondence from America, Esbjörn had also known the Methodist preacher of Stockholm, George Scott, and in correspondence with Hedström had hoped to receive financial aid from the Methodist church for his religious work among the Swedes in Illinois, in his capacity as a Lutheran minister. The Swedish Mission Society in Stockholm helped to finance his voyage. This party left Gävle on the "Cobden" on June 29, 1849, destined for Victoria,

---

[1] *Ibid.*, June 30, 1849, *Jönköpings Tidning*, June 30, 1849.

[2] *Hudikswalls Weckoblad*, June 9, 1849.

[3] Norelius, *op. cit.*, I, 34 ff.      [4] *Ibid.*

Illinois.[1] Arriving in New York, Esbjörn learned from O. G. Hedström that the Methodists would not give aid to a Lutheran church, and that he could receive aid only by becoming Methodist. After much thought Esbjörn decided not to change his religion, and in turn was able to receive aid from the American Home Missionary Society of the Congregational church for his Lutheran missionary work among the immigrant Swedes of Illinois. In New York, he met a land agent, representing a land association which had purchased large amounts of land in Henry County, Illinois, and had plotted the town of Andover. The agent, Wiström, promised the emigrants ten acres of land for a Lutheran church, and the course of the colony was directed to Andover, under the leadership of Captain Wiström.

Another religious group, mostly Hedbergians or "Luther-readers" left Hälsingland and Medelpad in Norrland in 1850 for Illinois. There were about a hundred in this group of emigrants, influenced by letters from friends in America. Andrew Snygg of Bergsjö wrote from Victoria, Illinois, and painted conditions in America in glowing colors. His letter was copied and circulated throughout the region of northern Hälsingland where it awakened a raging "America fever." Not all of the groups were dissenters, but those who were had visions of erecting in America "the true Lutheran church," where they could use the "old books."[2] To be sure of a spiritual leader, a delegation was sent to the mission school of Dr. Fjellstedt in Stockholm, while the party was waiting for embarkation at Gävle. Their choice was the student pastor, A. Viberg, who was destined to become an adherent of the Baptist faith and its leader in Sweden. Viberg was not at the time interested in going to America and recommended the schoolmaster, Gustaf Palmquist, who was to follow the next year. Palmquist was, soon after his arrival in Moline, Illinois, converted to the Baptist religion.

The emigrants sailed from Gävle on the Swedish ship "Oden," on August 17, and after eleven weeks reached New York. Some remained in New York, while the others moved toward Illinois where they scattered among the Swedish colonies of Andover, Princeton, Chicago, Galesburg, Rock Island, and Moline. In the spring of 1851

[1] *Hudikswalls Weckoblad*, June 30, 1849.

[2] Norelius, *op. cit.*, I, 38 ff. The author was one of this group of emigrants.

some continued into Minnesota where they founded the settlement at Chisago Lake. Eric Norelius, then a seventeen-year-old youth, was one of the Hedbergians of the party.

Emigrant movements had in the forties and fifties also begun to flow from Smaland, Östergötland, and northern Skåne. Many of these emigrants had been influenced by the puritanical Schartauian movement of the early years of the century, and had heard the temperance sermons of Wieselgren. When Esbjörn inquired among the Swedish immigrants of Illinois about a possible candidate to assist him in his religious labors among the Swedish Lutherans, a former parishioner from Önnestad in Skåne recommended the pastor of his home parish, the Rev. Tuve Nils Hasselquist, who had a reputation as a "revivalist preacher and a temperance worker."[1] Esbjörn persuaded the newly organized Lutheran congregation at Galesburg, Illinois, to call Hasselquist as its pastor. Hasselquist consented to come and left Sweden with his bride and sixty emigrants in 1852. He became one of the dominating leaders of the Swedish Lutherans in America, and did not relinquish that leadership until his death in 1891. He began the publication of the first Swedish Lutheran newspaper in America, *Gamla och Nya Hemlandet*, in 1854. He brought with him the traditional patriarchal manner that many of the Swedish clergy had toward their parishioners, an autocratic attitude which at times came in conflict with the younger generation of Swedish-Americans.

The established church of Sweden had erected numerous Lutheran churches in the old Swedish settlement on the Delaware in the seventeenth century and supported some of them until 1830, when they turned them over to the Episcopal church. It now took the attitude of encouraging the Swedish emigrants to join the Episcopal church in America, rather than to establish Lutheran congregations among them. The Anglican or Episcopal church was more nearly like the Lutheran church of Sweden in its episcopate form of organization and its ritual than any of the other Protestant churches. Unonius, the founder of the Pine Lake colony in Wisconsin in 1840, entered the Episcopal clergy and became a missionary among the Scandinavians

---

[1] It was Ola Nilson from Önnestad, resident at Andover, who recommended Hasselquist (*ibid.*, I, 51 ff.; Skarstedt, *op. cit.*, p. 85).

of Wisconsin and Illinois, even extending his activities into Iowa.[1] He established the first Swedish church in Chicago, a Swedish Episcopal church, St. Ansgarius, in 1849, to which Jenny Lind, the great Swedish singer, donated $1,500 for plate. When appealed to for help from the Swedish colonists in America, the state church of Sweden refused to extend the financial aid, or even to send clergy.[2]

It was the Congregational church of the United States that first came to the financial aid of the struggling Lutheran church of the Middle West. The American Board of Home Missions appointed Esbjörn as its missionary to work among the Swedish immigrants of Andover, Galesburg, and the surrounding territory of Illinois.[3] In 1850 there were about 180 Swedes in Andover when the first Swedish Lutheran church was established in the Middle West by Esbjörn. Galesburg had about one hundred Swedes. Esbjörn reported to the American Board of Home Missions in March, 1850, that services were being held at Andover, Galesburg, Rock Island, and Berlin, Illinois; that a temperance society had been organized at Andover; and that a Swedish church was in the process of construction at Galesburg.[4] To finance the building of a church at Andover, Esbjörn toured Ohio, Pennsylvania, New York, and Massachusetts. He even appealed to the Swedish singer, Jenny Lind, who was giving concerts in the United States at the time, and she contributed liberally. The Andover church was completed in 1854, and became the nucleus of the Swedish Lutheran movement.

The Congregational church looked upon the formal ritual of the Lutheran church with suspicion as a form of popery. The financial contributions were conditioned upon certain simplifications and changes in the doctrine and ritual of Esbjörn's church. In the report of the American Board of Home Missions for 1850, in the *Home Missionary*, its official journal, the statement appeared that most of the Swedes in Illinois

show a strong attachment to the Lutheran church, in whose bosom they were nurtured; still, it is expected a church will be formed in a short time in which the

---

[1] Norelius, *op. cit.*, I, 4 ff.; Gustaf Unonius, *Minnen från en sjuttonårig vistelse i Nordvestra Amerika.*

[2] Anna Söderblom, *En Amerikaresa* (Stockholm, 1926).

[3] *Home Missionary* (Boston, 1850), p. 263; Olson, *op. cit.*, I, 429.

[4] *Ibid.*, pp. 430–31.

practice of admitting members merely by confirmation, after the mode of the churches in Germany, will be dispensed with, and the stricter usages of our American churches will be adopted.[1]

The report characterized the Swedes as mostly laborers by the day, the week, or the month: some as mechanics, a few as renters of land, and still fewer as landowners. In Esbjörn's report to the society the following year, 1851, he stated,

I have regularly preached here (Andover) and at Galesburg, and sometimes at Henderson, Berlin, Rock Island, and Moline. A small church will soon be organized at Henderson, and branches of our Andover church are located in Berlin and Moline. We have not this year been blessed with what properly would be called a revival, but still the Spirit evidently has worked repentance and faith.[2]

Aid was also secured from the American Home Missionary Society for the salary for Hasselquist, when he came from Skåne to take up the work at a Lutheran missionary at Galesburg in 1852.[3]

The changes demanded of the Congregational church in return for its financial aid proved dissatisfying to the Lutherans and in 1855 they severed their connections with the American Board of Home Missions and joined the Lutheran Synod of Illinois. Feeling the need of co-operation with a larger church organization, Esbjörn journeyed from Andover to Cedarville near Freeport in the fall of 1851 to become a member of the new Synod of Northern Illinois which was being organized in the American Lutheran church.[4]

The Mississippi Conference of the new Synod was organized at the synodical meeting in Chicago in 1852, and included the Swedish congregations under Esbjörn, and the newly arrived Hasselquist.

---

[1] Home Missionary, 1850, p. 263.

[2] Ibid., 1852, p. 50.    [3] Olson, op. cit., I, 445-46.

[4] Most of the adherents of the American Lutheran church were Germans or descendants of Germans, and a few Norwegians. The controversy between the old Augsburg belief and the introduction of rationalism was also splitting the German church in America. The eastern church had accepted rationalism, the "new Lutheranism." The western church had not gone as far as the eastern churches, but farther than Esbjörn and the dissenters of Sweden could accept. Although Esbjörn could not fully accept the doctrine of the Northern Synod of Illinois, he felt the need of co-operation and joined, keeping, however, the interpretation of the dissenters as his doctrine, rather than the doctrine of the Synod. The Synod divided into three districts, the Chicago, Rock River, and Mississippi Conferences. Most of the Swedish Lutherans belonged to the latter conference (Norelius, op. cit., I, 788 ff.; Olson, op. cit.).

The Synod licensed two other Swedish Lutheran ministers, Valentin and Hokanson. At the same meeting the problem of securing ministers for the rapidly increasing congregations among the Swedish immigrants was raised. It was decided to use two methods, to license lay preachers and to call ministers from Sweden. Before prevailing upon ministers of the state church of Sweden to come to America, it was thought wisest to have the churches fully organized. The following year at the Mississippi Conference at Andover, it was agreed to commission Dr. Peter Fjellstedt, the head of the missionary school near Stockholm, to select and call pastors in Sweden for missionary service among their countrymen on the American frontier.

Among the young clergy who came to the United States upon the persuasion of Dr. Fjellstedt was Erland Carlsson, a clergyman in the Vexjö diocese in Småland.[1] He left Kalmar in 1853 with a company of 173 emigrants for Chicago. The congregation in Chicago, which had been organized by Hasselquist in 1853 from the Swedish adherents of the Norwegian Lutheran church, had dispersed when Carlsson arrived, but the church was reorganized in 1854. Another young clergyman sent by Dr. Fjellstedt was Jonas Swensson, curate in the parish of Unnaryd in Småland, where he had the reputation of being a popular preacher.[2] He was called to the small Swedish colonies at Sugar Grove, Pennsylvania, and Jamestown, New York, in 1856. In 1858 he went to the Andover church in Illinois. O. C. T. Andréen, a graduate of the University of Lund, and an assistant pastor in Carlshamn and Asarium parish in Skåne, received a call to the Moline church through Dr. Fjellstedt in 1856.[3] He had a leave of absence of six years from the state church, but returned in 1860.

A group of young men interested in missionary work, but not ordained in the Swedish church, who came in contact with Dr. Fjellstedt in his mission school, chose the American frontier for their labors. J. P. C. Borén, a carpenter who had studied at the mission school in Stockholm, came to America in 1858 when called by Eric Norelius.[4] Gustaf Peters, the son of a cotter in Småland, attended the mission school of Dr. Fjellstedt and the Rev. Ahlberg in 1857–58. He accepted a position as an assistant instructor in the new school

[1] Olson, *op. cit.*, pp. 466–67.  [3] Skarstedt, *op. cit.*, p. 86.

[2] *Ibid.*, pp. 438–45.  [4] *Ibid.*, pp. 87–88.

founded by Ahlberg in Småland for the training of lay preachers in 1858. In 1859, he came to Chicago and was licensed to preach. He served the parish in Rockford, Illinois, for a long time.[1] A decade later, Olof Olsson, a native of Värmland, and the son of strongly pietistic parents, came to the Swedish settlement of Lindsborg, Kansas. He had spent a year in Dr. Fjellstedt's mission school in 1858 and some time at Leipsic. Dissatisfied with Leipsic, he had returned to Sweden and entered the University of Uppsala. He was ordained in the state church in 1863. In the various parishes that he served in Värmland, he was known as an inspirational preacher and revivalist. He was criticized for his affiliations with the dissenters and emigrated with a group of them who were going to Kansas in 1869.

The Mississippi and Chicago conferences of the Lutheran Synod found, however, by 1855, that there were not enough responses from the Swedish clergy to fill the vacancies in the numerous churches that were rapidly developing in the Swedish settlements in the United States. To meet the need, it was decided to educate the clergy in this country. A Scandinavian professorship at Springfield, Illinois, was the solution.[2] Esbjörn was commissioned to raise the money. In 1858, he accepted the Scandinavian professorship at the theological school. Because of certain disagreements, he resigned in 1860, and followed by his students, went to Chicago. The same year, the Scandinavian Lutherans, Swedish and Norwegian, resigned from the Synod of Northern Illinois because of differences in doctrine. At a meeting at Clinton, Wisconsin, they organized the Augustana Synod.[3] The same year the Augustana Theological Seminary was established under the presidency of Esbjörn.[4]

The Swedish Lutheran church was, during its period of organization in the United States in the fifties, under the influence and leadership of the pietists or dissenters. The modification of ritual and doctrine that was necessary to gain the financial support of the

---

[1] Olson, op. cit., I, 493–95.     [2] Ibid., pp. 435–36.

[3] The Norwegians withdrew and formed their own synod in 1870.

[4] O. C. T. Andréen was sent to Sweden to raise funds for the seminary. He appealed for funds at Lund, Uppsala, Stockholm, etc., and raised 36,000 riksdaler. The King gave 5,000 volumes from his personal library.

American Home Missionary Society was perhaps temporary. Both Esbjörn and Hasselquist were from the younger group of revivalist ministers within the state church and had been connected with the dissenting movement in Sweden. They also found these early congregations consisting largely of dissenters who wished to simplify the ritual and insisted upon the pure Augsburg Confession. When Erland Carlsson attempted to introduce the ritual of the established church in Chicago, in 1854, he found the same objection and after a few years was forced to compromise. These leaders, who by precedent determined the practices of the church in the United States, laid aside the robes of the church, simplified the service, and did not use the church handbook of Sweden.[1]

At the joint conference of the Mississippi and Chicago districts of the Synod of Northern Illinois in 1857, the creed, consisting of the Augsburg Confession, and the church law were adopted. This was mainly the work of Eric Norelius. Norelius, as has been mentioned, belonged to the group of Hedbergians that had emigrated from Hälsingland in 1850. They believed in the old creed of the "pure Augsburg Confession" as it had been in the established church before 1819. Upon the persuasion of Esbjörn, the young Norelius had entered the Capital University, a Lutheran Seminary at Columbus, Ohio, where he remained four years. He was licensed by the Synod of Northern Illinois and ordained in 1855. His early contacts with the dissenters of Sweden and the dissenting tendencies in the Swedish colonies resulted in a pietistic influence in the Augustana Synod of the Swedish Lutheran church of the United States. The American church took the form of congregational organization instead of the episcopate.

It is impossible to estimate how many of the Swedish dissenters were forced to leave their mother country because of religious persecution, how many left because of religious dissatisfaction with the rationalistic tendencies of the state church, nor how many left for economic motives. Norelius, who himself had been one of the Hedbergians when he emigrated, stated that "the primary cause for emigration from Sweden was without doubt the hope of improving one's economic position in America. With the exception of the Eric-

[1] Olson, *op. cit.*, I, 467.

Janssonites, few have left Sweden to find greater religious and political freedom."[1]

The dissenters of Sweden were quite intolerant of the state church and the adherents of the state church. Religious feeling and criticism ran high. The petitions from various parishes in the county of Västernorrland to the governor, in the fifties, asking to be released from the obligation to attend the state church until the old orthodox Lutheran faith be restored, were examples of the intolerance of the dissenters. Some of the dissenters felt that the individual should experience a religious revival before admission in the church should be granted, while the state church inducted its members through confirmation. Some opposed infant baptism as taught in the state church, and most dissenters were extremely puritanical as far as pleasures were concerned. They were absolute abstainers in the use of alcohol; they attacked the village dance and theater.[2] Some of these aspects of puritanism are still professed by the Swedish Lutheran church in America, and by the various other sects of Swedish dissenters. The state church was more liberal in the matters of amusements. The idea of being saved by "being born anew" in the spiritual life, developed a religious egotism among some of the dissenters. It sometimes happens in a gathering among the Swedish immigrants in the United States that you are asked by some eccentric who perhaps is a member of no particular church, "Are you a Christian?"[3] Some of the dissenters, once having begun to question religious doctrine, joined several different religious sects in rapid succession, and after experimenting ended by belonging to none.[4]

The state church, enforced by the various laws against dissenters in the seventeenth and eighteenth centuries, attempted during the forties and fifties to maintain the unity of the Lutheran religion by persecution of dissenting ministers within its folds, and also of defiant laymen. The government was called to aid the enforcement

[1] Norelius, op. cit., I, 15.

[2] Some of the Swedish dissenters in the United States are also opposed to the Masonic lodge and other similar organizations. It is not unusual to be read out of the church if you happen to have joined the Masons.

[3] Author's own experience, and other cases have been related by Swedish-Americans.

[4] The religious martyr, F. O. Nilsson, was an example.

of the church law. The persecution of the Janssonites in Hälsingland and the trial of Eric Jansson, their prophet, have been mentioned
as the cause for their exodus from Sweden. Methodists, Baptists,
and Mormons were persecuted from time to time between 1840 and
1860. The *New Hälsingborg Post* of Southern Sweden, of August 28,
1855, carried a news-item from the neighboring town of Ängelholm
relating the fact that on the preceding Thursday a conventicle meeting had been held outdoors at the peasant's, Bengt Pålsson, by a
preacher called Anderson. Many people attended the meeting, but
it was scattered by the authorities.[1]

In their quinquennial reports, the governors of the counties sum-
marized the activities of the dissenting movements and gave their
attitudes toward the spiritual revival. From the county of Gävleborg came the following report in 1847:[2]

> The common people in many of the parishes of Hälsingland have for a long
> time shown a tendency towards a kind of pietism, whose adherents are usually
> called "readers" (dissenters). Their number has been quite large, and is not
> decreasing. Their piety, and their religious meetings, many have undoubtedly
> unjustly considered a pose. As long as they supplement their private meetings
> for religious contemplation, with regular visits to the church services and accept
> the doctrine of the state church, they are undisturbed. Sometimes their private
> meetings are encouraged by the Lutheran pastors.

The governors of Gävleborg and Västernorrland counties spoke
very bitterly against the Janssonites.[3] The latter, in 1850, stated
that the notorious Norrland dissenters, the Janssonites, were prevented by their pride from acknowledging that others might also
have a true interpretation of the Bible.[4] The report continued,

> Eric Jansson attempted with dictatorial sternness to rule both spiritually
> and secularly over his adherents by casting anathemas over everyone who dared
> criticize the sect. The church and local government has been watchful of heresy.
> Only on one occasion since then has any one attempted to separate from the
> church law. It was a peasant in Själevad parish who refused to baptise his newly
> born infant, because he believed in baptism of adults only, but the child was
> upon my command properly baptised, by the parish pastor. The peasant, his
> wife and children, as well as his adherents, about sixty or seventy persons, left
> the country. Since that incident, no one has attempted to place himself against

---

[1] *Nyare Helsingborgs-Posten* (Hälsingborg), August 28, 1855.

[2] *K. bfhde femårsberättelse, Gefleborgs län, 1843–1847*, pp. 6–7.

[3] *Ibid., Westernorrlands län, 1847–1850*, pp. 20–21.      [4] *Ibid.*

the church ordinances, nor have there been any religious or emotional house meetings since Eric Jansson left. The private religious meetings often begin in good faith, namely to be together exalted in God's Word, but when many uneducated people begin to explain the Scriptures, they spread heresy and strange doctrines. This can be overcome by the parish pastors holding Bible meetings on Sunday for the people. It has been recommended by the Estate of Clergy in the 1840 Riksdag and also by the Consistory of the church at Härnösand. It has proven successful at Härnösand. The Bible is given out to many of the people through the Bible Society.

The activities of various religious sects, however, continued in the fifties, when they became quite numerous. From the same county came the report in 1855 that

these self-made preachers sneak around in the parishes, explaining their interpretations, and planting the seed of distrust against the ministers called by law (state church).[1] But when the regular pastors visit their meetings, the schismatists are meek and deferential, only to continue their preaching secretly. The separatists are also found in the cities as well as the rural districts. In Sundsvall they have awakened unrest and distrust, as well as having led astray many simple people. They have also tried Härnösand, but have not been so successful since the church trials for heresy. In the rural districts, a preacher from another county spread heresy into several parishes, but since his expulsion from the region, the activities have ceased. Baptists came from time to time to attempt to shake the belief of the simple people in infant baptism. The result has been that on several occasions the local authorities had to bring the child to baptism. There are even those who administer the Lord's Supper to their adherents. Among these is an old woman, Anna, whose converts are called "Annites." Neither warnings nor persecutions have affected them for when they are arrested for their crime, they have been freed when it was shown that there was no intention to be sacrilegious. It has not occurred since the royal ordinance of March 7, 1855, prohibiting the giving of sacrament by the laity, as far as the government or church authorities know, but it may have, in secret.

In the fifties and sixties came the introduction of three new religious sects into Sweden through American influence, the Baptist, Mormon, and Methodist. The Baptist and Mormon religions, being so different from the state church of Sweden in their doctrine, and starting their proselyting efforts earlier than the Methodists, were subject to persecution by the Swedish authorities during the fifties. In various ways these three churches were instrumental in encouraging emigration. Religious persecution caused some slight exodus, but

[1] *Ibid.*, "1851–1855," pp. 13–14.

the connection with the American churches through funds and missionaries naturally was a constant invitation to emigrate and join sister churches in the new world. To the Mormons, the desire to join the mother church in the promised land of Utah, kept emigration constantly in mind.

It was through the influence of E. W. Schroeder, a Swedish sea captain, converted to Baptism in a New York mission, that F. O. Nilsson, the Methodist seamen's missionary in Gothenburg, was induced to study the Baptist doctrine in 1845.[1] Nilsson was convinced that the Baptist faith was the only true faith by 1847, and went to Hamburg to be baptized. He returned to Sweden and continued to preach and distribute Bibles. In 1848, a Danish Baptist minister, A. P. Förster, came to Sweden and baptized five people who had been converted by Nilsson in his home, Lunda parish in the province of Halland. Nilsson's followers grew in numbers. Then followed a period of persecution that made his case famous both in Sweden and the Protestant world, and finally resulted in the repeal of the law against dissenters. The small group of Baptists were first attacked by the populous. Some were discharged from work, others were boycotted by merchants, and most were ostracized by their friends and families.[2] They were reprimanded and disciplined by the clergy. Nilsson himself was declared an apostate by the consistory of Gothenburg and was forbidden to preach his faith. He was arrested while conducting services in a private home in Bergham parish in Älvsborg County on New Year's day in 1850, taken to prison in Gothenburg, but was released to stand trial a month later at the high court at Jönköping. The verdict of the court was banishment. Nilsson went in person to Stockholm to make an appeal to the king for pardon.

His case had received much attention both in Great Britain and in the United States. Sixteen petitions for his pardon were addressed to the leading men of the Swedish Established church and were signed by one thousand Baptist churches in Great Britain and Ireland.[3] Petitions were also received from France. George Scott wrote

[1] Nordström, op. cit., pp. 24–25; Byström, op. cit., pp. 21–31.

[2] Olson, op. cit., I, 561–62.

[3] Byström, op. cit., pp. 109–10, 160; Jönköpings Tidning, July 13, 1850.

in an English newspaper of March 19, 1850, that he hoped that this would result in religious freedom in Sweden. The Baptist churches of Great Britain and the United States appealed to their respective governments to prevail upon the King of Sweden to repeal the law. Laws granting religious tolerance had just been passed in Denmark and Norway.

Nilsson was, however, exiled in 1851. He went to England to attend a meeting of the Evangelical Alliance which had petitioned for his pardon. From 1851 to 1853, he preached in the Baptist church in Copenhagen. In 1853, accompanied by twenty-three of his followers from Sweden, he left Denmark for New York. The little company of Baptists traveled westward through Chicago to join other Swedish Baptists in Rock Island and Moline, who with Gustaf Palmquist had been converted in Illinois.[1] Some of them remained here, while Nilsson and the others continued to Burlington, Iowa, and later in 1855 to Minnesota. Palmquist had become the leader of the Swedish Baptists in Illinois and was an active proselyter for the faith among his countrymen in the immigrant colonies of the Middle West.[2]

The persecution of the Baptists and the trial of Nilsson gave the Baptist movement much press notice in Sweden and awakened an interest in the "new faith." There was also a small nucleus of Baptists in Stockholm under the leadership of Peter Johansson, who had been converted while resident in England.[3] A minister of the state church, Anders Viberg, who had been associated with the Methodist minister, George Scott, and was the editor of the *Missions Tidningen*, came to Stockholm after being reprimanded by two church tribunals for his affiliation with the dissenters of Norrland. Interested in the Baptist faith because of its persecution, he accompanied a furrier of Stockholm, David Forsell, to Hamburg to attend Baptist meetings. Viberg was converted and upon his return to Sweden in 1852 wrote a pamphlet on Baptism that was widely read. The state church forbade him to preach in Stockholm, and suffering from ill health, he accepted an offer of a free voyage to the

[1] These Swedish Baptists had been converted by Gustaf Palmquist (Olson, *op. cit.*, I, 554).

[2] *Ibid.*    [3] *Ibid.*, pp. 557–58; Nordström, *op. cit.*, pp. 26.

United States on an emigrant ship. The boat stopped at Copenhagen, and Viberg was baptized by the exile, Nilsson.

A letter of recommendation from Nilsson introduced Viberg to the Baptist Mariners Church in New York upon his arrival. He was immediately asked to discuss the religious prosecutions in Sweden before the Baptist Female Bethel Union of New York. He was made a missionary for Scandinavian immigrants and seamen at the New York mission, and in March, 1853, was ordained into the Baptist ministry. During his three years in the United States he wrote several pamphlets on the Baptist religion in Swedish, which were printed by the Baptists in Philadelphia, but were sent to Sweden for distribution. He also collected funds for the erection of a Baptist church in Stockholm. Upon his return to Sweden in 1855, he was for some time supported by the American Baptist Mission.

In Sweden, Viberg became the leader of the Swedish Baptist movement, and organized the Swedish Baptist Conference in 1857. The plan of church organization, adopted in 1860, followed that of the American church.[1] The executive committee had charge of the interchurch affairs. Provisions were made for a school for colporteurs or lay preachers in Stockholm and for the distribution of Baptist propaganda through tracts throughout the country.

To procure funds with which to establish a seminary in Sweden to train Baptist clergy, Viberg returned to the United States in 1864. He was successful in interesting the North American Baptist Missionary Society in the project. While in the United States, Viberg visited the struggling Baptist churches in the Swedish settlements in Illinois, Iowa, and Minnesota. He presided over and aided in organizing the Illinois-Iowa conference of the Swedish-American Baptist church at Village Creek, Iowa, in June 1864. Viberg also found during his visit the man to place at the head of the new seminary, Captain K. O. Broady. He was a civil war veteran who had become a Baptist evangelist. Broady had attended a university in the United States during the first six years of his residence here, before the outbreak of the civil war, and was suitably prepared to be the president of the Bethel Seminary in Stockholm.

The Baptist tract missionary found his way into most of the

[1] Nordström, *op. cit.*, pp. 29–32.

provinces and many of the parishes in the fifties. In 1853, the first Baptist church was organized in Stockholm.[1] Two of its members, Forsell and Hejdenberg, had been baptized the same year in Hamburg. Stockholm now became the center of the movement. Hejdenberg went to Dalarne in Central Sweden in June, 1854, where he baptized about a hundred persons and organized two churches. From there he went to Örebro County and then to Östergötland, where many were baptized and more churches established. The reports of 1860, from the governors of the counties, showed that the Baptists had spread into most of the counties of Sweden. In Dalarne, in the parishes of Mora, Orsa, and Alfdal, there were about 760 dissenters, mostly in the two latter parishes, and 118 unbaptized children.[2] They had built their own churches, but were not recognized as legally separated from the established church.

There was some emigration on the part of the Baptists because of persecution. The Baptists were in doctrine so different from the Lutherans that they caused much opposition from the local authorities and the clergy. Of the first five baptized to the Baptist faith, four died in the United States. A number accompanied F. O. Nilsson to the new world in 1853. Many were also converted after reaching the United States through the efforts of the missionaries of the American Baptist church. The close alliance between the Baptist movement in Sweden and the American Baptist church may have made the path for the Swedish emigrant easier if he desired to leave for economic reasons.

Another American religious influence came in the activities of the Mormon missionaries in Sweden in the fifties. Conversion to the Mormon religion resulted in emigration because the faithful desired to seek the promised land in Utah. Mormon missionaries had appeared in the British Isles in 1837, and the following year in Continental Europe. In 1850, four Mormon missionaries came to Copenhagen, one of whom was a converted Swedish seaman, John Forsgren.[3] The first three remained in Denmark, while Forsgren went to his relatives at Gävle, Sweden, where he began a lively

[1] Byström, op. cit., p. 161.    [2] K. bfhde Stora Kopparbergs län, 1856–1860, p. 2.

[3] "Mormonvärfningen," Emigrationsutredningens bilaga III (Stockholm, 1910), p. 23.

propaganda for his religion. After a few months, twenty persons had been converted and baptized. Forsgren was seized by the government authorities and sentenced to exile. He was placed on a ship bound for New York, but upon the intercession of the chargé d'affaires of the United States in Sweden, for he had an American passport, he was permitted to land in Denmark.[1] In 1853, other Mormon missionaries from Denmark came to Skåne, in Southern Sweden, and organized the first Swedish branch of Mormons.

The governors of the counties reported the appearance of Mormons in 1855. The governor of Malmöhus County stated that during the preceding five years, Mormonism had spread in the county, especially in the cities of Malmö and Lund, "from where the Mormons have gone out to other parts of the county to spread their false doctrines.[2] Their efforts had not been crowned with great success, for only in a few parishes have they won a small number of adherents." In 1860, the report from this county stated that "the Mormons have induced a few to join their faith and these have emigrated to Utah." There had been established a Mormon congregation of twenty adherents at Lund.[3] During the same year, the governor of Halland County reported a few itinerant preachers of Mormon faith, but no congregation.[4] In Älvsborg County there were a few Mormons, especially in Redsvägs hundred, where there was a congregation of thirty, and around Vänersborg and in Sundals hundred, where there had appeared preachers from Gothenborg and from Halland County. A few converts had been made and some of these had emigrated to the United States.[5] The governor of this county had taken legal steps against the Mormons. The clergy were also attempting to bring them back to the established church. The Mormons were active in the city of Örebro also.[6]

The religious intolerance of the governors was expressed in the statement of the governor of Västmanland County in his report for

---

[1] Letters of F. Schroeder, chargé d'affaires of United States in Sweden to Daniel Webster, Secretary of State, August 26, and September 20, 1850 (*U.S. Dispatches to Sweden*, VIII Nos. 13 and 16).

[2] *K. bfhde femårsberättelse, Malmöhus län, 1851–1855*, p. 11, translated.

[3] *Ibid., 1856–1860*, p. 3.

[4] *Ibid., Hallands län*, p. 1, translated.

[5] *Ibid., Elfsborgs län*, p. 7, translated.

[6] *Ibid., Örebro län*, p. 3, translated.

1860, that "the many uneducated colporteurs and itinerant preachers prepare the way for proselyters of the Baptist and Mormon faiths. They have no difficulty in working on the inflamed and fanatic minds of the common people, and have made some secret converts."[1] He had denied passports to three people who had desired to emigrate to the United States as Mormons. The Mormons had extended their activities even to Northern Sweden in 1860. The governor of Västernorrland County stated, "One or another Mormon missionary has tried his powers but the Mormon teachings are too coarse to have any influence upon enlightened people, which the people of Norrland are in the main, but there have been a few converts among the simple minded."[2] The governor of Älvsborg County reported, in 1870, that from 80 to 100 Mormon converts had left the county for the United States.[3] In the reports from Gotland, in 1856, it was stated that fourteen from one parish, who were Mormons, had emigrated to Utah.[4]

The Swedish emigrants to Utah usually left three or four times a year with other Scandinavian emigrants over the White Star line from Liverpool. They were accompanied by returning Mormon missionaries and carefully guarded from all outside contacts. As early as 1849, the Mormons established the "Perpetual Emigrating Fund" which was placed under the control of the Perpetual Emigrating Fund Corporation, for the purpose of aiding members of their faith to go to Utah.[5] In 1883 this aid amounted to 120,000 kronor, or over $30,000, for Sweden alone. Emigrants receiving aid in this manner pledged themselves to repay the money to the church upon their arrival in Utah, and became practically indentured servants.

The United States government was much alarmed at the number of immigrants that were coming to Utah in 1879, when the Mormons were still defiant of the government. Evarts was at the time Secretary of State. He sent a circular letter to the representatives of the United States in the various countries of the world, calling

---

[1] *Ibid., Westmanslands län*, p. 10, translated.

[2] *Ibid., Westernorrlands län*, p. 6, translated.

[3] *Ibid., Elfsborgs län, 1865–1870*, p. 5.

[4] *Ibid., Gotlands län, 1860–1865*, p. 2.

[5] *Nordstjärnan*, 1883, No. 24; "Mormonvärfningen," *op. cit.*, pp. 29–30.

attention to the fact that this organized immigration was adding to the law-breaking polygamists in Utah and that the Supreme Court had declared polygamy illegal.[1] The representatives of the United States were to ask the governments to which they were accredited to prevent the activities of Mormon agents in recruiting emigrants and also to forbid the emigration of this lawless element. The Swedish government attempted to co-operate with the United States in the instructions that were sent to the governors in the beginning of 1880. In 1885, President Cleveland recommended to Congress in his annual message that a law be passed prohibiting the importation of Mormons to the United States.[2] No law was passed, but through the Edmunds-Tucker Law of 1887, the emigration company was disbanded and the Mormons forbidden to encourage emigration.[3] Immigration is so much a part of the Mormon religion, that it naturally results.

The Mormons made their largest number of converts in Sweden during the sixties, and from 1878 to 1882.[4] Their methods to gain converts were house to house visits, the distribution of tracts which were sold or given away gratis at times, and the holding of meetings in local halls. Prior to 1860, several Mormon proselyters were banished from the country. With the repeal of the law exiling dissenters, the Mormon missionaries were often fined or sent to jail for short terms for their propaganda activities. The last case of persecution was during the eighties. Since the establishment of religious toleration, local government authorities have sometimes prevented the Mormons from holding meetings in rented halls. Meetings in private homes were then resorted to, while in some places the Mormons became owners of their places of worship. In 1902, the Mormons petitioned the king, under the law of 1873, for the right to legally separate from the state church. This was denied because the Mormons

---

[1] "Mormonvärfningen," op. cit., pp. 31–32.

[2] Richardson, Messages and Papers of the Presidents, VIII, 362.

[3] The act of 1885 made it unlawful for any person to assist or encourage in any way the importation or immigration of foreigners into the United States under any kind of contract. This law was amended in 1887 and 1888.

[4] The statistics used were compiled from the annual reports of the Swedish Mormon church for the Swedish Emigration Commission ("Mormonvärfningen," op. cit., pp. 47 ff., Table A).

encourage emigration.[1] The church in Utah maintained about seventy missionaries in Sweden in 1907, sent directly from Utah for two-year periods. Most of them were Swedish-Americans who spoke the Swedish language. They traveled from place to place in pairs and were shifted every six months.[2]

The number of converts to Mormonism in Sweden between 1850 and 1909 amounted to 17,259 persons. About 5,116 of these later withdrew from the religion, some 1,452 died in Sweden, while 7,822 emigrated to the United States.[3] The majority of the Mormon emigrants were young unmarried women.[4] There seemed to be also a great deal of propaganda among the laboring classes in the cities in 1907.[5] The Mormon missionaries emphasized the need of skilled workmen in Utah and the high wages paid there for artisans. The Mormons were themselves mostly agriculturalists. The latest policy of the Mormons had been not so much to emphasize emigration as the establishment and development of churches in Sweden.[6]

The third proselyting religious sect to be introduced into Sweden in the sixties by American influence and American financial aid was the Methodist. George Scott, the Methodist minister, had maintained the policy that it was unnecessary to proselyte in an evangelical country like Sweden, but many leaders of the Swedish dissenters had felt the influence of his personality. Another contact with the Methodist church had been through the Swedish sailors converted in the Seaman's Mission in New York. Here the Swedish

[1] *Ibid.*, pp. 25–26.

[2] An account of their activities may be found in the reports of the governors of the counties, 1907 (*ibid.*, pp. 38–45).

[3] *Ibid.*, pp. 46 ff., Table A, p. 47.

[4] Although polygamy was no longer practiced in Utah in 1907, the governors of several of the Swedish counties (Västerbotten, Kristianstad, Norrbotten, Halland, and Älvsborg) reported the emigration of young women to Utah. Kerstin Hasselquist, who investigated women traveling through Liverpool, found no Mormons. It was discovered, however, that they traveled second class and were segregated from other passengers by their leaders," (*ibid.*, p. 45).

[5] Report of governor of Gävleborg, cited in *ibid.*, p. 44.

[6] Sweden is divided into five Mormon Conferences, Stockholm, Gothenburg, Skåne, Sundsvall, and Norrköping. The Swedish Mission, including Finland and Russia, has been located since 1905 in Stockholm. The official periodical is *Nordstjärnan* published in Stockholm (*ibid.*, pp. 24–25).

Methodist missionary of the "Bethel-ship," O. G. Hedström, had met from 1845 to 1875 most of the Scandinavian immigrants and sailors that came to the port, and had been successful in converting not a few. Many were directed to his brother, Jonas Hedström, in Victoria, Illinois, and there were persuaded to adopt the Methodist faith. The first Swedish church established in Illinois was the Swedish Methodist church at Victoria in 1846.[1]

As the missionary for the Swedish immigrants, Jonas Hedström, appointed by the Rock River Conference of the Methodist Church in Illinois in 1848, soon had charges at Victoria, Andover, Galesburg, Lafayette, Moline, and Rock Island. As co-workers he had a versatile Danish sailor and former Janssonite, John Brown, and a former pastor in the Swedish state church, Carl P. Agrélius, who had been converted to Methodism in New York.[2] Circuit preachers were recruited from converted immigrants. A former lay preacher from Esbjörn's colony at Andover, Andrew Ericson from Hälsingland, Sweden, was sent to New Sweden, Iowa, as a Methodist preacher in 1854.[3] A former Janssonite, Peter Challman, became the circuit rider in the Victoria district and in Minnesota.[4] In 1857, he succeeded Hedström as presiding elder of the Swedish District of the Methodist Church. Peter Cassel, the leader of the Swedish Colony in New Sweden, Iowa, was converted in 1845 by Hedström and preached in the Iowa churches.[5] Another circuit rider was the self-taught dissenter from Hälsingland, Eric Shogan, a blacksmith by trade, who had been converted at the "Bethel-ship" in New York, and directed to Illinois.[6] After his return from the gold fields of California in 1851, he became a missionary for the Rock River Conference and later labored in Minnesota.

The Methodist converts in the United States wrote enthusiastically to their friends and relatives in Sweden about the "new faith." Some returned to visit the mother country and spoke zealously for Methodism, making a few scattered converts. From these isolated groups came a call to the Methodist mission society of New York and to the superintendent of the Methodist Mission in Norway and

[1] Olson, *op. cit.*, I, 356–57.
[2] *Ibid.*, pp. 358–61.
[3] *Ibid.*, pp. 361–63.
[4] *Ibid.*, pp. 363–66.
[5] *Ibid.*, p. 363.
[6] *Ibid.*, pp. 367–69.

Denmark for a permanent missionary in the Swedish field.[1] In 1865, A. Cedarholm was sent to Visby, on the island of Gotland.[2] In 1867 churches were established in Stockholm and Gothenburg by Swedish-American converts.[3] During the same year, Victor Witting, the editor of the Swedish-American Methodist journal, *Sändebudet*, was sent by the Methodist Episcopal Church North, to organize the Swedish movement.[4] Witting had served the Methodist churches at Andover, Victoria, and Rockford, Illinois.[5]

St. Paul's, the first Swedish Methodist congregation in Stockholm, was dedicated in 1868, by Bishop Kingsbury, the Methodist Episcopal Church North, of the United States.[6] At the time Sweden was made a separate mission and Witting was made superintendent. It was also an auspicious moment to organize the Swedish Methodist church, although there was a membership of only 424 in seven congregations.[7] The Swedish church still continues to receive some financial aid as a foreign mission of the American church.

The first mention of the Methodists in the governor's reports appear in 1870. The governor of Örebro County remarked that the Methodists had built their own church in Örebro city. He further stated, "This religion has been imported from the United States, and seems to have attracted as members only the lower and simplest people. Their preachers are much like the colporteurs or lay ministers of the National Evangelical Union."[8] In Västmanland County there were a few Methodists in the towns of Arboga and Köping in 1870.[9] Methodist congregations at Motala and Valdemarsvik were

---

[1] Nordström, *op. cit.*, p. 36.

[2] *K. bfhde femårsberättelse, Gotlands län, 1865–1870*, p. 2.

[3] Nordström, *op. cit.*        [4] Olson, *op. cit.*, I, 375–78.

[5] Witting was a native of Malmö, Sweden, where he had forsaken the apothecary shop as a youth and gone to sea. Serving on a ship that was transporting Janssonites to the United States, he was so impressed with their fortitude during a shipwreck that he later joined their colony. He remained only eighteen months when he withdrew and obtained a position as a druggist in Galesburg through the intervention of Jonas Hedström. Later, upon a trip to New York, he was converted by the elder Hedström. He began the publication of *Sändebudet* in 1862 (*ibid.*).

[6] *Malmö Nya Allehanda* (Malmö), October 30, 1867.

[7] Nordström, *op. cit.*, p. 37.

[8] *K. bfhde femårsberättelse, Örebro län, 1865–1870*, p. 3.

[9] *Ibid.*, *Västmanland, 1865–1870*, p. 3.

mentioned in the governor's report from Östergötland in 1875.[1] In the same county there was a congregation of two hundred members at Norrköping in 1880.[2]

There were a few cases of persecution of the Methodist preachers on the part of local authorities for disobeying the injunctions of church councils which forbade public preaching of dissenters.[3] As late as 1877, the *Minnesota Stats-Tidning* spoke with regret of the persecution of a Methodist preacher in Norrköping for opening a Sunday school for poor and neglected children. It added that it was fortunate for the reputation of the old fatherland that the persecution was not generally known in England and in the United States.[4]

The Methodist church, however, had the distinction of being the first legally recognized dissenters' congregation. The Methodists petitioned the King in 1875 to be given permission to separate from the state church, under the Dissenters' Act of 1873, and were granted the privilege in 1876. They established their own theological seminary in 1874 at Örebro. Since 1883, it has been located at Uppsala.

To what extent the close tie between the Methodist church in Sweden and the mother church in the United States promoted emigration to the United States is difficult to determine definitely. The knowledge of the United States obtained from the Swedish-Americans who returned to serve the Swedish church was undoubtedly useful to those who contemplated emigrating. Persecution for religious reasons had a small part in the emigration of the Methodists.

Religious disintegration grew apace in Sweden. The National Evangelical Union was very active under Rosénius after its organization in 1856. Its circuit preachers or colporteurs appeared in all the provinces. Two schools for lay preachers were established: one under Fjellstedt in Uppsala, and another in Ahlsborg, Småland. The dissenters began to build their own meeting-houses both in rural and urban districts. Or often a hall, called a *lokal* would be rented in which to hold their services. In the governor's reports of 1860, these meeting-houses called in Swedish "houses of prayer," are mentioned

[1] *Ibid., Östergötlands län, 1871–1875*, p. 2.

[2] *Ibid., 1876–1880*, 2.

[3] Olson, *op. cit.*, I, 378.

[4] *Minnesota Stats-Tidningen*, published in Minneapolis, January 4, 1877.

in Värmland County,[1] in Örebro County,[2] in Jönköping County,[3] and in Kalmar County.[4] The governor of Kalmar County in Småland reported the same year that the dissenters were extending their activities, but were not schismatic.[5] He said,

They live up to their duties as citizens. They have built a meeting-house near Kristdala church, and are building another in Tuna parish. They have also erected children's homes for poor, orphan children under the deaconesses of the institute in Stockholm. A theological school for the "home mission" had been established in Kristdala parish, but was later moved to Jönköping County.

This erection of special meeting-houses for the lay preachers and colporteurs continued into the eighties. The Hedbergians also continued their activities in the Hälsingland region,[6] and built their own meeting-houses.[7]

The state church enrolled all citizens of Sweden within its folds upon infant baptism and recognized the membership of everyone who was confirmed. Confirmation was compulsory and was the culmination of the elementary-school education. Among the dissenters there developed the feeling that conversion was necessary for membership, that it was wrong to give the sacrament to all indiscriminately, and that it was a sacrilege for a minister who had not been converted to officiate at the Lord's Supper. The result was that the religious societies of dissenters in some instances began to hold communion outside of the state church. During the sixties many mission societies were organized among the laity by the National Evangelical Union.[8] These mission societies often developed into "sacrament societies." Upon the thousandth anniversary of the death of St. Ansgarius, the first Christian missionary to Sweden, organizations called themselves "Ansgarius Societies."[9] As early as the sixties, a division of doctrine and purpose was noticeable in the National Evangelical Union. There was one party that was strongly prochurch and saw its duty in influencing the doctrine of the state church. The other group came more and more into conflict with the established church in doctrine, and began to advocate separation.

[1] K. bfhde femårsberättelse, Värmlands län, 1856–1860, p. 5.

[2] Ibid., Örebro län, pp. 3–4.      [6] Ibid., Gefleborgs län, 1856–1860, p. 2.

[3] Ibid., Jönköpings län, p. 4.      [7] Ibid., Örebro län, 1861–1865, p. 3.

[4] Ibid., Kalmars län, pp. 6–8.      [8] Nordström, op. cit., p. 41.

[5] Ibid.      [9] Ansgarii föreningar.

After the death of Rosénius in 1868, P. P. Waldenström became the leader of the National Evangelical Union. He edited the religious paper of the organization, *Pietisten*, and followed the doctrines of Rosénius until 1872.[1] The breach came gradually and after much debate and attempted compromise in 1878. Waldenström had become the hero of a spectacular case of religious persecution. The Uppsala Mission Society had provided a special communion for Whitsuntide and had asked Waldenström to officiate.[2] They were denied the use of the city churches and held the meeting at a mission meeting-house. The Cathedral of Uppsala tried Waldenström for his breach of church law and fined him. The result was a royal decision that pastors of the established church could not hold special communions. This became a burning question. At a meeting in Stockholm of lay preachers and some of the "revival" preachers, a committee was appointed to draw up a petition for the repeal of the law. Another committee was designated to work out a congregational plan for a separate church and plans for a theological seminary.

In June 1878, the representatives of the mission societies in the kingdom held a "free church meeting," which was non-denominational.[3] At this meeting the committee's doctrines were accepted. Two theological seminaries for preachers and missionaries were to be established at Vinslöv and Kristinehamn. Another meeting was held from July 31 to August 2, 1878, in the Bethel Chapel in Stockholm, and here was organized another religious sect, the Swedish Mission Conference. Although this religious group has its own churches in Sweden, it has never legally separated from the state church. It is today the most numerous of the free churches in Sweden.

The religious pattern of the middle of the century was very intricate. The shuttle moved as easily from Sweden to America, as from America to Sweden. Simultaneous with the establishment of additional denominations through the proselyting efforts of the American churches in Sweden, the various religious movements in the Swedish church were reflected in the churches of the Swedish immigrants in America. In the late sixties, Swedish dissenters who had been members of the mission societies of the National Evangelical Union, found, upon arriving in America, the Swedish-American Lutheran church too formal for their tastes. A group which had joined the Swedish Emmanuel Lutheran church of Chicago began to hold private meetings in their homes, at which one of the members read *Pietisten*, the journal of the Swedish National Evangelical Union.[1] This society of pietists had emigrated from the city of Jönköping and the surrounding rural region in 1867. A lay preacher, John Peterson, and a graduate of the seminary for colporteurs at Ahlsborg, Småland, Johan Magnus Sanngren, joined the group in 1868. Sanngren with his stirring revivalist sermons roused the pietists to organize a mission society like those in Sweden. Within a year after its establishment, the mission society severed its relationship with the Swedish Lutheran church. Sanngren was ordained by the American Lutheran Synod of Northern Illinois, and became the minister of the new denomination. It was incorporated as the "Swedish Evangelical Lutheran Missionary Association of Chicago." The Augustana Synod of the Swedish Lutheran church was out of sympathy with the new movement. It meant the organization of a new Swedish church in America, which later became the Swedish Mission church.

The Mission society of Chicago became active in proselyting among the fellow-countrymen in Illinois, Iowa, and Minnesota. Soon there were similar societies at Princeton, and Galesburg, Illinois; Swede Bend, Keokuk, and Des Moines, Iowa; St. Paul and Minneapolis, Minnesota.[2] In the Galesburg Lutheran church a dissenting movement similar to the one in Sweden developed. The dissenters had from the beginning been so numerous that Hasselquist had been forced to compromise by simplifying the doctrine and ritual of the Lutheran church. His successor, Dahlsten, was not so tactful and re-established the more formal ritual, whereupon the "readers" began to hold their own devotional services. The Swedish-American Lutheran church proved equally as intolerant as the state church of Sweden, and forbade the practice. The climax came when Bergensköld, a lay preacher educated at the Fjellstadt school in Uppsala, was denied the right to preach to them, and the laymen were refused representation in the Augustana Synod in 1868.[3] When

---

[1] Olson, *op. cit.*, I, 584 ff.  [2] *Ibid.*, pp. 586–87.  [3] *Ibid.*, pp. 593–94.

ministers of the Augustana Synod were called in to reprimand the dissenters, some forty separated and organized the Second Evangelical Lutheran Church of Galesburg. They called upon the American Lutheran church through its Northern Synod of Illinois to furnish a minister in 1869.

As lay preachers and adherents of the Swedish National Evangelical Union arrived in America in the late sixties, these mission societies continued to separate from the Swedish-American Lutheran church and become congregations of their own.

In Princeton, Illinois, a man and wife by the name of Lundholm, who arrived in 1867, went from house to house and talked to their neighbors, as the dissenters of Sweden did, and gathered a few adherents together in a Mission Society. The following year a lay preacher, C. P. Mellgren, arrived from Småland. He had been a colporteur for the Sunnerbo Mission for six years. He supported himself in Illinois with the labor of his hands and preached on Sundays. The Mission Society was organized in 1868 and formed into a church in 1871. Mellgren's activities as an itinerant preacher took him to many towns in Illinois, Minnesota, Iowa, Missouri, and Kansas. In 1873, he moved to Kansas. His successor in Princeton, Illinois, was another lay preacher, Wedin, who arrived from Sweden in 1870. As a traveling missionary for the Mission Synod, he later preached from coast to coast. Another lay preacher and former student at Ahlsborg's Seminary in Sweden, was P. Undeen who organized the little group of "Mission Friends" in Rockford, Illinois, in 1868. Two years later he was ordained by the General Synod of the American Lutheran church. He moved to the northwest and labored in Minnesota and Wisconsin.

In 1870, the evangelist, Erik August Skogsbergh, was called from his studies at Jönköping to be a leader among the "Mission Friends" in Chicago. The Mission Tabernacle was erected for him in 1871 and he became known as the "Swedish Moody."[1] A need for cooperation and organization was felt among the scattered groups of "Mission Friends" and in 1873 the Swedish Evangelical Lutheran Mission Synod was incorporated under the laws of Iowa.[2] The "Mission Friends" had completely separated from the Augustana

[1] *Ibid.*, p. 591.    [2] The meeting was held at Keokuk, Iowa (*ibid.*, p. 597).

Synod of the Swedish-American Lutheran church. A religious journal, *Missions-Vännen*, patterned after the Swedish religious journal of the National Evangelical Union, *Pietisten*, was started in 1874. A second Mission Synod was organized the same year at Galesburg under the name of the Swedish Evangelical Lutheran Ansgarius Synod of the United States, and was recognized as a branch of the Northern Synod of Illinois, the American Lutheran church.[1] This group started a theological seminary at Keokuk, which was finally moved to Knoxville, Illinois. There was much feeling and quarreling between the two synods for a number of years.·

The separatist movement in the Swedish National Evangelical Union in 1878, led by P. Waldenström, also influenced the religious life of the Swedish immigrants in America. It tended to draw the mission churches closer into a form of union. In the synodical meeting of 1879, the Mission Church in the United States adopted the doctrines and organization of the recently established Mission Covenant in Sweden.[2] The followers of Skogsbergh, Björk, and other mission preachers and adherents of Waldenström seceded from the Mission churches. In a conference of 1883, the name of the synod was changed to correspond with the Waldenström organization in Sweden, and was called the Swedish Mission Covenant of America. In doctrine it repudiated the Augsburg Confession upon which the Lutheran church was based, and adopted the Bible as the "only perfect guide in matters of faith and living."[3] It was not until 1885 that all the Mission churches in a body joined the national organization, while the churches of the Ansgarius Synod applied individually for membership. Skogsbergh went to Minneapolis in 1884 to continue his preaching. Here he founded a theological seminary in 1892, which was later incorporated into the North Park College at Chicago, in 1894.

The Mission church was built upon the doctrine of individualism and opposition to the hierarchy of the Lutheran church of Sweden. The idea of individualism went to a further extreme when some of the

---

[1] *Ibid.*, pp. 599–603.  [2] *Ibid.*, p. 598.

[3] The Mission church is even more puritanical than the Swedish-American Lutheran church, denouncing the theater, dancing, moving pictures, fraternal organizations, and the use of liquor (*ibid.*, pp. 599–603, 615).

mission churches, following the Tabernacle church of Chicago, withdrew from any organization and became known as the Free Mission church.[1] Finally, in 1896, having learned from experience the value of co-operation and union, the Free Mission churches did unite in the Swedish Evangelical Free Mission.

In many aspects the origin and form of the Mission church was similar to the English Puritan movement, the foundation of the Congregational church. Again in the eighties, the Congregational church became interested in doing missionary work among the Swedish immigrants ,but this time chiefly in the New England states. With the increased immigration during the eighties, some were settling in the New England mill towns rather than seeking the agricultural region of the Middle West. An extensive missionary program was carried on by C. J. Erickson, supported by the Congregational Home Mission Fund.[2] There had also been secessions from the Lutheran congregations in the East, led by Princell, a minister of the Swedish-American Lutheran church. The separatists had organized Mission churches in New York City, and Campello, Massachusetts. As the movement spread, Mission churches appeared in Brooklyn, Boston, Worcester, Quincy, and other eastern cities. There were only a few Swedes in the East, and fewer still for the separatist churches. The Congregational church first extended financial aid to the Mission church of Worcester, and later to Boston, Campello, Lowell, Brooklyn, and New Britain. The Massachusetts Free Mission was organized in 1886, and supported several itinerant preachers, while the Congregational Mission Board supported several others in the state. Many of the churches supported by the Congregational church in 1888 joined in the Swedish Pastoral Conference of the East.

In the Middle West, the Congregational church had also come to the aid of the "Mission Friends" by establishing a Scandinavian department at the Chicago Theological Seminary in 1884.[3] In the following year Fridolph Risberg was called from Sweden to take the Swedish department. David Nyvall was called as his colleague in 1888. By 1890, the Mission Friends were considering their consolidation with the Congregational church, but decided to remain a sepa-

[1] *Ibid.*          [2] *Ibid.*, pp. 615-23.          [3] *Ibid.*, p. 609.

rate denomination. Fearing Congregational influence, it was decided to establish a Mission theological school under Skogsbergh and Nyvall in Minneapolis, in 1891. This was subsequently moved to North Park, Chicago, in 1894.

The Salvation Army swept with its organization from England to Sweden in 1882,[1] from where Swedish contingents were established among the Swedish immigrants in the United States. It did not establish separate congregations, but concentrated on missionary work, revivals, and social service among the poor. There were many organizations in even the smaller towns of Norrland and Småland.[2]

From the religious unity of one state church in the early part of the nineteenth century, Sweden had arrived at a period of religious disintegration by the end of the century. In the county of Östergötland, which was typical, the governor reported in 1875,

Many meeting houses have been erected in the parishes in the rural districts where spiritual meetings are held by colporteurs of the National Evangelical Union, but there has been no schism within the state church, except Methodist congregations at Motala and Valdemarsvik.[3] The meeting-house has been erected by the dissenters or "readers," who in the preceding five years have increased in numbers and in spiritual fervor. They are, however, divided among themselves into New Lutherans, New Evangelists, and dissenters of older kinds who approach the Waldenström doctrines and increase their opposition to the state church and its clergy. Many of the younger clergy have entered into the movement.

In 1880 in the same county the same religious movements continued.[4] The Methodists had added congregations at Linköping and Norrköping. The Baptists had churches at Norrköping, Linköping, Soderköping, Motala, etc. In Norrköping there was a Christian Free church of one hundred members. There were also sixty Mormons in the same city. The report of 1885 had added the appearance of the Salvation Army in Norrköping and Linköping. And by 1890 there had been established a Catholic-Apostolic church in Norrköp-

---

[1] Boëthius, Oskar II; Hildebrand, Sveriges historia (Stockholm, 1925), XIII, 314.

[2] The fiftieth anniversary of the first Salvation Army worker was held at Värnamo in Småland during the summer of 1928. There were in 1924, 266 corps and 1,055 outposts, 1,393 officers and 9,038 underofficers and musicians in Sweden (Hildebrand, Gustav V, p. 654).

[3] K. bfhde femårsberättelse, Östergötlands län, 1871–1875, p. 2.

[4] Ibid., 1876–1880, p. 2.

ing. The Methodists and Baptists had now legally withdrawn from the state church.[1]

During the period of religious fermentation, Sweden moved from religious intolerance to freedom of religious practice. There were from time to time religious persecutions of those who insisted upon preaching contrary to the doctrines of the state church. It took the form of warnings from the clergy, trials before church consistories, and the degrading of clergy who were not orthodox. Laymen were imprisoned and were fined after several offenses, though the imprisonment lasted not more than a month. For extreme cases, banishment from the kingdom was resorted to as in the case of Nilsson, the Baptist. There was also forced baptism of children by the state officials and clergy where the parents refused to voluntarily baptize them. There was on the whole little sympathy for this religious persecution in Sweden. The royal government was internationally embarrassed by the notoriety of the Nilsson case. It tried to prevent reoccurrences of it and to repeal the laws of banishment and religious intolerance. The United States chargé d'affaires in Stockholm in 1851 related a case of banishment of a writer in a popular newspaper for satirizing the Lutheran forms of worship and for using language disrespectful to the Established church.[2] The case had been delegated to an assistant in the department of justice, and the attorney-general, one of the most enlightened officers of the crown, was much embarrassed over the decision. The chargé d'affaires, Mr. Schroeder, spoke of the paradox in a country with freedom of speech and press in political matters, that there was not religious freedom. "The British legation," he stated, "was especially interested in the case because of the religious controversies in England."

The cases of Nilsson, the Baptist, and Forsgren, the Mormon, have been mentioned. Another case, which caused the Swedish government much annoyance, was six Catholic women who were tried in 1858, and were sentenced to perpetual banishment.[3] It was the

[1] *Ibid., 1881–1885*, p. 5.

[2] Letters of F. Schroeder, chargé d'affaires, to Daniel Webster, June 29, 1851 (U.S. Department of State, *Dispatches to Sweden*, Vol. VIII, No. 38).

[3] Letter of F. B. Angell, chargé d'affaires to Sweden, to Cass, July 2, 1858 (*ibid.*, Vol. VIII, No. 21).

criticism of France that was feared this time. The United States chargé d'affaires to Sweden was asked to present a memorial "from many eminently respectable citizens of the United States" to the King of Sweden, asking for religious toleration during the same year. The Minister of Foreign Affairs of Sweden, Baron Manderström, discussed the subject with Mr. Angell and gave the Swedish government's attitude on the question. "It is but justice," wrote Mr. Angell to the American Secretary of State, Cass, on January 11, 1859, "to the enlightened and liberal statesmen who compose the present government of the Prince Regent, Charles XV, to say that they condemn the law as it now exists, and they assure me that its abrogation or material modification will be among the earliest measures to be proposed to the next Diet for approval."[1] The dispatch continued that during the year the royal government had not instituted any persecutions with its approbation. The six Catholic women who had been banished by decree of a lower tribunal were urged by an authorized agent of the government to appeal to a higher court that their sentence might be modified or reversed. They refused to do so, or to ask for pardon, which had been promised if applied for, and remained happy in their martyrdom.

With the increase of the free church movement in Sweden came also the effort to repeal the old heresy laws of the eighteenth century. In 1847 and 1850, Dean Sandberg introduced motions to repeal the conventicle placate.[2] C. G. Malmström attacked the same law in articles in *Tidskrift för Litteratur* in 1852. In the Riksdag there soon appeared numerous advocates for religious freedom. Among them were, in the Estate of Nobles, Baron S. Creutz, J. A. Posse, and F. P. Hierta; in the Estate of Clergy, Thomander, and in the Estate of Burghers, Henschen of Uppsala. Several bills were introduced into the Riksdag of 1853–54 for the repeal of the law of banishment for those who preached any faith but the Lutheran, and also the repeal of the conventicle placate, which forbade private religious meetings. Most of the bills failed, but the law forbidding citizens to attend the services of sects other than the state church was repealed.[3] The government introduced a bill into the Riksdag in 1856–58 for the repeal of the loss of inheritance for anyone leaving

[1] *Ibid.*, January 11, 1859, No. 28.  [2] Hallendorff, *op. cit.*, XIII, 194.  [3] *Ibid.*

the state church, and for the repeal of the conventicle placate of 1726. This bill also provided that if anyone wished to separate from the church he should make proper petition to the parish pastor, that it might be recorded in the church books.[1] The Riksdag, however, only accepted the portion for the repeal of the conventicle placate, and the permission under certain conditions of separate common religious gatherings, like those of dissenters.[2] There was also a private bill introduced for the organization of a church convocation, but it failed to pass.

In the Riksdag of 1859–60, the repeal of the church laws continued. The government bill to repeal the law of banishment for withdrawal from the state church, to grant dissenters the right to separate from the state church, and to establish their own churches, was accepted by the Riksdag and became law, October 23, 1860. The same year Jews were permitted to establish residence in Sweden and have their own religion. There was now a feeling that the church should no longer be represented in a separate estate in the Riksdag and continue to have great political power. This culminated in the abolition of the four estates in the Riksdag and the establishment of two elected houses in 1865. Anticipating the change in 1863, a church convocation was provided for that was to meet every five years. Its representation consisted of thirty clergy and thirty laymen. The convocation was to deal with problems of doctrine and ritual for the state church, and had the power of veto over any church law passed by the Riksdag.[3]

The law of December 11, 1868, slightly changed the law of 1858 concerning religious meetings. It permitted members of the state church to gather for religious purposes without the leadership of the clergy.[4] This meeting, if held at the time of the regular church services, had to be far enough removed from the church so as not to disturb the regular services. Public services, not in the homes, could be held only by the permission of the parish pastor, a member of the vestry, or the local government authorities. If anyone who did not belong to the clergy appeared to preach or influenced the disintegra-

[1] *Ibid.*, p. 174.

[2] Gustav Westring, *Sveriges rikes lag* (47th ed.; Stockholm, 1926), p. 634.

[3] Hallendorff, *op. cit.*, p. 295.        [4] Westring, *Sveriges rikes lag*, p. 634.

tion of the church, talked against the regular church services, or was sacrilegious, he might be forbidden to preach, and if he persisted might be fined. A law of 1869, which revised the law of 1860, forbade anyone by fraud, threats, or promise of material benefit to induce persons to leave the Lutheran church, under penalty of fine and imprisonment.[1] The same applied to teachers of children.

The law of October 13, 1873, recognized the full right of religious freedom. Any Christian sect might withdraw from the state church, by petitioning the king and receiving his sanction, and could build a separate church.[2] In the application by the superintendent of the new sect, it was necessary to present the creed and the form of its organization. Individuals could withdraw from the state church by petitioning the parish pastor and positively proving that they intended to join another church.

In the eighties, the religious enthusiasm seemed to have exhausted itself. There followed a period of religious indifference on the part of many, which is so characteristic of the present age in most countries. The growth of the Social Democratic party and its attitude toward religion may have had something to do with this change, especially among the union men. In many of the parishes today, the churches are only half-filled. In Sweden it is stated that the people of the west coast, especially the rural population, are very religious, while those of the east coast are less religious. There is now complete religious freedom and churches of numerous denominations.

With the establishment of religious toleration by the act of 1873, the state church had to find means of winning its adherents, and could no longer depend upon compulsion. In order to meet the demands of the pietists, reforms where made in the hymnal, the handbook, and the catechism.[3] The activities of the church were extended. In 1874 a Mission board of the Swedish church was estab-

---

[1] *Ibid.*      [2] *Ibid.*, p. B 166.

[3] The new catechism was adopted in 1878; the handbook was revised in 1894 and 1903. A new Swedish translation of the Bible was completed in 1903, and a new hymnal in 1898. Changes were also made in the curriculum requirements for students in theology and for the final pastorate examinations (Boëthius, *op. cit.*, XIII, 312 ff.). Later revisions have occurred. The final revision of the Swedish Bible was not accepted until 1917. An addition of new psalms was made to the hymnal in 1921. At the same time changes were made in the handbook (Hildebrand, *Gustav V*, pp. 647–48).

lished to supervise foreign missions in India and South Africa. Home Missions were not neglected, and deaconesses were trained for this work within the church. The state church found it easier to adjust itself to the liberalism in religion and the relationship of Christianity to modern culture than the pietistic churches of the dissenters which remained fundamentalistic in their views and antagonistic toward modern science.[1]

The state church even as a tolerant people's church had to have as its purpose, not only the requirement of a Christian life from its members, but also the furtherance of Christian culture among all the people. It had to include in its membership everyone, whether confessed Christians or not. This attitude was recognized by the Schartauians of Southern and Western Sweden, who strove for a literate people primarily. The pietists, however, demanded that only those who had a spiritual awakening through revivals and were confessed Christians should belong to the religious community. They spoke of their churches as "pure" congregations. The National Evangelical Union attempted to unite these converted Christians into groups without separation from the state church. They were led by lay preachers and had their own meeting-houses for their mission societies. Some, as has been mentioned, however, seceded to form the Swedish Mission Covenant in 1878.

But in spite of the humanizing of the state church and the separation of the pietists, religious differences began to decrease church attendance in both religious groups in the eighties. It found its expression in the literature of the period. The strangest phenomenon was that religious indifference should spread to the rural districts which had been so conservative and fervent in their religious allegiance to the Lutheran faith. It can only be explained in the economic materialism which is so characteristic of the age in all countries of Europe and America.[2] Perhaps the clergy had not kept pace with the times. The educated classes were affected by the discrepancy between modern knowledge and the old orthodox belief, while the ecstacy of the pietistic revivals, and their hostile attitude toward culture, may have brought the reaction of indifference.

[1] Boëthius, *op. cit.*, p. 310.

[2] The reasons for Swedish religious indifference are explanations made in *ibid.*, p. 314.

In the middle of the nineteenth century, prohibition of the use of liquor had been a part of the pietistic movement. Prohibition was the primary distinguishing ascetic characteristic between "God's children" and "the children of the world."[1] As time went on it was recognized by both the peasant and the industrial worker that prohibition had its economic and moral values aside from the religious asceticism. It became, therefore, a political factor. The Liberal and Social Democrat parties indorsed it, and it became a requirement for positions of trust in communal and political life. In 1923 the People's party (Folkfrisinnade) made prohibition the main plank of its platform and broke with the Liberals. By a referendum in 1922, prohibition was defeated.

Older prohibition had only attacked intoxicating spirits, especially brandy and whiskey, and advocated beer and light wines as a substitute. But the increase in the consumption of beer by the manual laborers brought the condemnation of light wines and beer.[2] By 1879 prohibition was no longer bound up with the religious movements. In that year the "Good Templar Order," a fraternal prohibition society, was introduced from the United States. A secession from the I.O.G.T. in 1884 produced another society called the "Templar Order." They were both fraternal orders with secret ritual and insignia. Many local community houses were built by the orders, both in the cities and the rural communities. Entertainments, lectures, dances, and other forms of amusement were held as a substitute for indulgence in intoxicants. These amusements were considered by the pietists as worldly and the fraternal orders came under the condemnation of the puritanical elements. But the fraternal temperance societies with their mutual insurance provisions spread rapidly, and in turn proved very popular among the Swedish immigrants in America as well. The Good Templars did not entirely give up the religious element, so the socialists seceded in 1896 and formed the temperance order, "Verdandi."[3] In 1907 there were 200,-000 Swedish members in the I.O.G.T. and 30,000 in the National Templar Order, probably more than all the Swedish dissenters. The Good Templars' hall is today a community center in many rural districts in Sweden.

The liquor question also became a political question. The Gothen-

[1] *Ibid.*, p. 316.      [2] *Ibid.*, p. 317.      [3] *Ibid.*

burg system of the state granting a monopoly to a few private firms to trade in liquor was introduced gradually in various communes and cities, and made compulsory for all in 1906. The Riksdag from time to time raised the tax on liquor to discourage its use in that way. Light wines and beer also came under the odium of liquor and were limited. In many of the local communities, local option voted the region dry.

In 1917 the Bratt system of liquor control was introduced in Sweden by which the individual was rationed as to the amount of liquor he might purchase from the state-controlled private corporations every month. He can obtain no liquor unless he has paid his taxes for the last two years. A limited amount of liquor and beer may be served in the restaurants at meals only.[1] In 1922 a referendum on prohibition resulted in a very close decision against it. Most of the objection to prohibition came from the cities and from Skåne in Southern Sweden.

The Swedish state church now is called the People's church. Many reforms have taken place in the church since the middle of the nineteenth century when it was so vigorously attacked by the dissenters. The humanitarian work of its foreign and home missions is extensive. The National Evangelical Union continues to work within the Lutheran church. In 1920 there were 384 affiliated mission societies and 218 lay preachers.[2] In 1910 there was a secession of fundamentalists that designated themselves "True Friends of the Bible." Even the old dissenters' churches, the Mission Friends, the Baptists, and the Methodists are less bitter toward the state church than in the nineteenth century. They feel that they can be complements of the Lutheran church rather than religious rivals.[3] The state church has also drawn closer to the Augustana Synod of the

---

[1] Hildebrand, *Gustav V*, pp. 654 ff.      [2] *Ibid.*, p. 648.

[3] *Ibid.*, pp. 651-52. The "Mission Friends" are the most numerous of the dissenters of Sweden, although they never legally separated from the state church. They are most numerous in the rural districts where they have churches in 1,173 of the 2,414 rural communes, and a total of 1,561 congregations. The Baptists have 569 rural churches and a total of 681, while the Methodists have 145 congregations. New dissenting movements of recent date have been *pingströrelsen* ("Whitsuntide-movement"), very emotional, much like the Holy Rollers. It has come from Norway. In Stockholm a new sect of Baptists, calling themselves the "Philadelphia Church" has a large church.

Swedish-American Lutheran church, as well as the Anglican church in England, with which it has much in common. The German Lutheran church and the Swedish church celebrated recently the four hundredth anniversary of the Diet at Worms, and the Swedish Archbishop ordained the first Lutheran Archbishop of the recently established Republic of Esthonia.[1]

The greatest competitor of the Lutheran church in Sweden today is that religious indifference that seems to have swept western civilization. It is not only prevalent among the laboring class of Sweden, which has been strongly influenced by the materialistic philosophy of Socialism, but even in the formerly extremely religious rural parishes. In America, the Swedish-American churches are usually well-filled and the immigrant seems to maintain his religion, although it must be recognized that the Swedish churches, which are only now beginning to substitute English for Swedish in their services, have served as a community center for the Swedish immigrant. Recently arrived immigrants express the religious indifference of the mother country, and frequently shock the older immigrant by their religious attitude.

[1] *Ibid.*, p. 650.

# CHAPTER VII

## THE GREAT FAMINE AND ITS AFTERMATH

An economic crisis gripped Sweden in 1864 and 1865 and was followed by three distressing years of crop failures. Large numbers of the agrarian population were impoverished. Many were forced to grasp the beggar's staff and wander as in times of old through the more prosperous regions of the kingdom. The great famine still lives vividly in the memories of the older generation, both in Sweden and in America. It resulted in the emigration of a hundred thousand people within a few years, some to Northern Germany, Denmark, and Norway, but the majority to the United States.

From 1850 to 1864, Sweden had enjoyed a period of unprecedented prosperity in agriculture. She had attained for the first time in her history the distinction of being a grain-exporting country. Her landholders had developed extensive cultivation of grain through the consolidation of scattered holdings and crofts. Grain prices had shown a steady rise; land had been bought and sold for speculative purposes; and much land had been mortgaged to capitalize the expansion. Certain regions like Dalsland had concentrated on the production of oats, without any thought of diversification of crops.

The speculation and sale of agricultural lands predicted the decline of the old system of primogeniture, both on the part of the gentry and the peasant. It marked also the change from a barter economy, that prevailed in the early part of the century, to an expanding money exchange. In 1833 the value of land sales in the rural districts of Sweden was about 21.5 million kronor (5.8 million dollars). By 1850 it had more than doubled, and with some fluctuation had reached 67 million kronor in 1860.[1] Speculation and sale of farm lands were prevalent all over the kingdom, but were especially active in the counties of Gotland, Kristianstad, Malmöhus, Halland, Älvs-

---

[1] Nils Wohlin, "Bondeklassens undergräfvande," *Emigrationsutredningens bilaga X*, pp. 58–59.

borg, Skaraborg, and Värmland. Even the Norrland counties showed a higher percentage of sales than the average for the kingdom, and with Skåne had the largest evaluation of sales. Nobles purchased lands from the common people, and the peasant purchased lands from the gentry. In the final reckoning of land sales, from 1833 to 1865, the peasants had increased their landholdings through purchase by $10,000,000 over the gentry.[1]

Much of the land was purchased through loans from mortgage associations. In 1833 mortgages on agricultural lands amounted to about $1,000,000, while in 1858 the amount was $10,000,000.[2] In 1864 the Skånska Mortgage Association had $2,000,000 in outstanding loans.[3] The Östgötha Mortgage Association was forced to give out $1,500,000 in its own obligations, having suspended specie payment.[4] The newly instituted mortgage associations had been most generous with their loans on land, on a basis of amortization. Many short loans without mortgages were also made. With the fall of agricultural prices, the farmer was unable to meet his obligations, and many went bankrupt. In Skåne in 1864, at one court, fifty bankruptcies were declared in a short time. There was a tremendous increase in bankruptcy among farm owners in Östergötland the same year.

Overspeculation in farm lands, although undoubtedly the principal cause for the money crisis in 1864 in Sweden, was not the only cause. A crisis was brooding over all of Europe because of the unsettled war conditions. The disastrous results to the prestige of the Scandinavian countries, caused by the defeat of Denmark in 1864 and the rise of a new power on the Baltic, destroyed the hopes of growing Scandinavianism.

Sweden had failed to come to the aid of Denmark, and the defeat of Denmark had reduced the northern countries to a subordinate position in European politics. Moreover, the financial standing of the Swedish government had never recovered from the depreciation

---

[1] Ibid., p. 60.    [2] Ibid., pp. 66–67.

[3] Skånska Hypoteksföreningen. The riksdaler is equivalent to the krona, 3.76 for an American dollar (Hemlandet, August 10, 1864).

[4] Helge Nelson, "Öland, Bygdeundersökningar," Emigrationsutredningens bilaga VIII, p. 30; K. bfhde femårsberättelser, Kalmar län, 1861–1865.

of its money in the disastrous war with Russia in 1809, when there had been an inflation of paper money on the part of the government. A policy of deflation was decided upon to prevent a further drop in the value of the Swedish currency, and 29,196,714 riksdaler in bank notes (7 million dollars) only were left in circulation. This deflation caused a temporary shortage in circulation currency and available loans.[1] Another factor that threatened to curtail agricultural credit was the construction of railroads and the expansion of the factory system, which demanded large sums of capital and through competition raised the rates of interest.[2]

Agricultural prices had begun to rise in the fifties. The average price for wheat during the last half of the forties was $1.02 per bushel, and in the last decade of the fifties it averaged $1.34.[3] More important was the rise of the price of rye, because it was the common grain used for bread. From the forties to the fifties it had risen from 77 cents to 95 cents and then fallen to 87 cents in the early sixties. Wheat had fallen to $1.15 in the sixties. There had been the same rise and fall in the price of oats, which was the chief grain for export, from 33 cents a bushel in the later forties to 47 cents in the later fifties, and then a slump to 39 cents in the early sixties. These were only temporary price depressions for, with the advent of the years of 1866 to 1868, prices of grain rose to a new height and continued to rise until 1875, when another general depression in agriculture began, extending into the nineties.[4] In the meantime agricultural wages had also risen, from two kronor a day in the forties for a man with a team, to three kronor in 1864, from 53 cents to 80 cents.[5]

Many who had purchased lands and given mortgages went bankrupt and had to leave their lands. Others found it necessary to dispense with hired labor and cultivate their lands as best they could with the labor of the family. Consequently, many day-laborers were thrown out of work, and the hired men and maids could find no

[1] *Hemlandet*, August 10, 1864.

[2] Helge Nelson, *op. cit.*

[3] *Statistisk årsbok för Sverige, 1927*, Table 89, p. 93.

[4] Rye reached its highest price in 1866–70. It was not until 1911–14 that the same price was again obtained (*ibid.*).

[5] Sundbärg, *Emigrationsutredningens betänkande*, Table 31, p. 106.

employment. Simultaneous with the unemployment came crop failures. The potato crop that the day-laborers depended upon for their meager subsistence also failed. Prices of foodstuffs doubled, and agricultural laborers were reduced in many cases to a status of famine. They were forced to resort to begging and theft was frequent.[1]

The northern counties felt the pinch of hunger first, during the winter of 1867–68. With the exploitation of the forests in Norrland, there had been an immigration into the region from Southern Sweden and Värmland, since the government was encouraging settlement by the offer of crownlands to pioneers at reasonable prices. Railroads had as yet not been extended northward, and it was difficult to reach the sufferers with relief. The king stated in his address to the Riksdag in January, 1868, that everything possible had been done to alleviate the suffering until navigation would open in the spring.[2] In a report of the situation to his government, the American chargé d'affaires, James J. Bartlett, wrote that several neighboring countries had sent contributions and that the south of Sweden "had responded nobly to the cry for relief."[3] The Swedish government sent ships with supplies, which sailed for the extreme northern ports first and distributed the relief as the ice drove them southward. Mr. Bartlett suggested that the American people might send grain in the spring, but added,

Yet, I doubt very much if Sweden is not as able to take care of its own poor as any of the countries of Europe. This famine, being confined to a single district of the kingdom from the loss of three consecutive crops, is brought more immediately in all its terrible details to the notice of the world than as though the suffering were general throughout an entire country. Therefore, while we sympathize with the poverty here, we overlook an equal amount of present suffering existing in almost every country in Europe. Sweden with its rich agricultural south and vast northern resources, under an enterprising development which has recently inspired capitalists and laborers to greater exertions, is able to sustain three times its present number of inhabitants.

There seemed to have been considerable response for relief from America for a purse of $4,000 was raised in New York in January,

[1] K. bfhde femårsberättelser, Kalmar län, 1866–1870, pp. 6–7.

[2] U.S. Department of State, Dispatches from Sweden, James J. Bartlett to Seward, February 3, 1868, Vol. XI, No. 11.

[3] Ibid.

1868, for the relief of Norrland.[1] It was planned that enough money should be collected to send a cargo of grain in the spring. The Norrland relief committee in Stockholm received money or grain from the neighboring Scandinavian countries, Germany, England, France, Holland, Russia, and the United States.[2]

But the famine spread southward and Småland suffered. The communities in Småland found it necessary to ask the government for loans to meet the situation. Some of this money was loaned as mortgages on land and houses, while the rest was given as doles to the working classes. The governor of Kalmar County asked the Swedish government for relief for forty-six communities between November, 1868, and January, 1869, and by February of 1869 had received $55,957. The King gave $5,800 in charity. In January, 1869, a central relief committee was appointed in Stockholm, consisting of the Riksdag representatives of the three Småland counties. There were many local committees organized to aid in the relief work. An appeal to private individuals throughout Sweden for relief brought a large sum of money. Donations came from the various European countries. From the United States gifts amounting to $36,000 were received. Of the thirty-three parishes on the island of Öland, twenty-four were given poor relief during the winter of 1868–69, a sum of $18,000.[3]

A tremendous exodus of agricultural labor of both men and women, and also of bankrupt landowners was the result. Many went to Germany and Denmark, or to the more prosperous regions in Sweden and later returned to their homes. Letters and prepaid tickets from friends and relatives influenced the largest majority to turn their course across the Atlantic. There were many agents from the United States making contracts of indenture among these people. It was during the famine that the Swedish immigrants in Texas induced their friends and relatives in Småland to come on contracts of labor.[4] The governor of Jönköping County, in his report of 1870,

---

[1] *Skånska Posten* (Kristianstad), February 8, 1868.

[2] *Ibid.*, February 15, 1868.

[3] Nelson, *op. cit.*, pp. 30–33; *Skånska Posten* (Kristianstad), January 27, 1869.

[4] Norelius, *De svenska luterska församlingarnas och svenskarnes historia i Amerika*, I, 38.

stated that most of the emigration to the United States had been from Östra, Västra, Norra Vedbo, and Södra Vedbo hundreds.[1] The governor wrote,

They were agriculturalists or laborers, and many were women. There was as much a desire for economic betterment and independence on their own land as to escape the results of the famine. The problem of wife and child abandonment was large during the exodus. Some also used fraud in order to get money to travel.

Statistics show that there were only 10,429 people who emigrated from Sweden to the United States between 1861 and 1865, while there were 80,491 from 1866 to 1870.[2] Jönköping County in the later period sent more emigrants to the United States than all of Sweden had sent between 1861 and 1865. Östergötland came second with 8,316 emigrants; then Kalmar County with 7,333. From an emigration to the United States of 464 between 1861 and 1865, Värmland County now for the first time reached 6,662; the great exodus from a new region had begun.[3] Kristianstad County held fifth place with 5,491; Kronoberg County sixth with 5,243; the old emigration region of Gävleborg County ranked seventh with 5,011. The emigration from Malmöhus County, the fertile region of Skåne, showed for the first time a rather large exodus, 3,680 emigrants for America, while during the same period there were 3,436 emigrants for Denmark. There was no county in Sweden that did not send at least a couple of hundred emigrants to the United States from 1866 to 1870. The exodus to Norway, Denmark, and Germany was also very large.

The famine years scattered many families. This is very well demonstrated in the life-history of the American emigrant, P. A. J., from Kronoberg County.[4] His father owned a small farm in Småland. He became bankrupt in 1868 and lost his property. The family had to leave their home and move to a small hut on the farm. When the older brother was confirmed, he left for Germany, enticed by German agents who came around and hired boys. Upon the father's return

[1] K. bfhde femårsberättelser, Jönköpings län, 1866–1870.
[2] "Bygdestatistik," Emigrationsutredningens bilaga V, Table 43, pp. 69*–93*.
[3] Ibid.
[4] "Utvandrarnes egna uppgifter," Emigrationsutredningens bilaga VII, No. 175, p. 135.

from Denmark, he leased a piece of land which had never been under cultivation from a peasant in a neighboring village. This land had to be broken. The rent for the croft was $8.00 a year. The family built its own house. The piece of land was small, only three acres. It was stony and difficult to cultivate, and did not support the family. One day in the spring of 1870, the father decided to emigrate to the United States. He obtained passage money through a loan; a brother had been willing to act as surety on the note. P. A. J., a lad of fifteen, accompanied his father on his voyage. In the United States the father obtained work on a gravel train, and worked mostly in Michigan. The boy worked for a Swedish farmer. The mother did not wish to leave her home in Sweden, and the father returned in 1873. But the son remained, leased farms in Michigan and Kansas, and finally homesteaded in Oklahoma.

It was the agrarian proletariat that suffered most in a period of famine, and where the cotter was most numerous there also the exodus was the greatest. This was true in Småland. On the island of Öland, which belongs to Kalmar County, the central portion is particularly sterile. It was the common property of the village or belonged to private individuals but had never been enclosed. Here were erected many cottages of day-laborers, squatters who worked for the peasants or at some trade.[1] Many were seamen; others went regularly to Stockholm or Norrland to work in the summer and returned to their homes, idle for the winter. The cotter had often but a cabin with a clay floor and a heap of straw for a bed. Some had a few chickens and geese, while others eked out their living with fishing. Wages had been good in the fifties, and the cottages were filled with children. During the famine it was impossible to obtain employment, and wages were low when there was any work at all. Many of these people had visited the United States from time to time on their sea voyages. During this period of distress their thoughts turned to the land of opportunity where labor was in demand, and they found passage on vessels of various nationalities bound for the United States, where they deserted and settled.

Another region similar to this was southern Dalsland. Here there had been a tremendous increase in population. More and more land

[1] Nelson, *op. cit.*, pp. 31-32.

had been placed under cultivation, but even that did not meet the demands of an increasing population. Many farms had been divided among the children of the peasants, resulting in parcels of land too small for the support of a family. Much of the region was wooded, but the exploitation of the forest lands was temporarily at a standstill.[1] As early as 1830, the governor of the county was concerned by the growing numbers of cotters and crofters.[2] In 1850, some of the population began to seek work in Norway.[3] During the famine of 1867 and 1868, many were reduced to mixing the bark of trees with their flour in making bread, and even chopped straw. The highways were filled with beggars. In some of the communes the poverty-stricken people were divided among the more prosperous farmers, who were pledged to give them work and food. Many found their way to Norway or into the more prosperous regions of Sweden and finally obtaining means to emigrate, left for America.

Dalsland is part of Älvsborg County. The governor of the county wrote in 1870 that there were many cottages with only small potato patches erected on the *utmark* or common lands.[4] If bad crops continued the future would be very dark. "The exploitation of the forests in Dalsland and the decline of the old-fashioned small iron furnaces have decreased the opportunities for day labor. There is a need for further development of agriculture in the region." Of other regions of his county he wrote,

The people demand not only better food, but better houses, comforts, and luxuries. A great many stores have sprung up, not only in the textile districts but also in the agricultural communities. In Kind hundred alone, there are 159. They willingly give credit in order to sell their wares, and this has resulted in an increasing demand for luxuries even among the day laborers. This class of society is especially numerous in Marks hundred, as well as in Dalsland, where weaving is to a small degree the by-product of agriculture.

The crisis in the textile industry caused by the American Civil War had affected this region just prior to the crop failures.

In the Norrland counties, a crisis in the iron industry had closed the mines of Gällivare, and with the unemployment in agriculture

---

[1] Brusewitz, "Sundals, Nordals, och Valbo härader," *Emigrationsutredingens bilaga VIII*, pp. 31–32.

[2] *Ibid.*, pp. 19–20.        [3] *Ibid.*, pp. 32–33.

[4] *K. bfhde femårsberättelse, Elfsborgs län, 1866–1870*, p. 4.

as well, many were forced to emigrate to Norway and to the United States.[1] In Norrland was also to be found a large percentage of the cotter class, about two-fifths of the population. They lived along the coast.[2] They had built small cottages and cleared a piece of land from the communal lands of the villages, which they had the right to use during their lifetime. This region had grown considerably in the fifties; in five years, the governor reported in 1860, there had been established 251 new settlements or *nybyggen*, six crown crofts, besides 1,081 homes on lands belonging to the villages. The cotters supported themselves with day labor, partly in agriculture but chiefly in lumbering and mining.

Every province had a larger or smaller number of agricultural laborers. In Kalmar County it was in the bailiwicks or *fogderi* of the Tunlän and Sevede hundred, of Aspeland and Handbörd hundred, of Tjust, and of Norra More and Strand hundred from which the largest percentage of emigration came, during 1868 and 1869, while very few left the other bailiwicks of the county;[3] in Östergötland it was in the southern and western portions of the county.[4] The governor of Malmöhus County reported emigration from the northern region of the county, Torna, Bara, Frosta, and Färs hundreds, where there had been unemployment.[5] The agricultural crisis in Dalecarlia had influenced emigration from Gävleborg and Kopparberg counties. Most of the emigrants were young men and women from the agricultural classes.

There were, however, many of the poorer peasant class also leaving. The governor of Malmöhus County observed in 1870 that a large number of the emigrants to the United States were the more prosperous laboring class, and the cultivators of smaller pieces of land.[6] It was much easier to acquire land in the United States than in Sweden. "For the people of this class," continued the governor, "the possibilities of acquiring land is a great temptation, even if it means a few years of hard labor and sacrifice." Many owners of farms or *hemman* were emigrating without any economic reasons, but were enticed by the wonderful accounts of the new land by emigrant

---

[1] *Ibid., Norrbottens län, 1866–1870*, p. 2.  [4] *Ibid., Östergötlands län, 1866–1870*, p. 2.

[2] *Ibid., 1856–1860*, p. 4.  [5] *Ibid., Malmöhus län, 1866–1870*, p. 1.

[3] *Ibid., Kalmar län, 1866–1870*, p. 6.  [6] *Ibid.*, p. 2.

agents. It seemed that the spirit of adventure had even turned the heads of the conservative, stolid natives of Skåne, according to the governor. Many of the emigrants who had no means were being financed for the voyage to the United States by friends and relatives already in that country.

There arose in Skåne a great deal of dissatisfaction among the tenantry class on the large estates during the sixties.[1] Although this region did not suffer from crop failures and famine to the extent of the neighboring county of Småland, the discontent and uncertainty of the agricultural situation made the years 1867–69 conspicuous for agitation, and for the demands for improved conditions. Skåne was a region of large estates owned by nobles. Many of the peasants in this region were called *frälse bönder*, and held copyholds on their farms from the nobles. Toward the end of the sixties there arose an agitator, a retired corporal, Samuel Tullberg, who persuaded the peasants that the crown had unlawfully granted the estates to the nobles. He advised the peasants to attempt to have the lands returned to the crown that they might purchase them. The movement spread through Kristianstad and Malmöhus counties during 1867 and 1868.

The peasants were so confident that they were in the right that they refused to pay their rent or to perform day labor for their land. When eviction judgments were procured and an attempt was made to carry them out, it looked as if a conflict would take place between the nobles and the common people. A crisis was reached when Tullberg and one of his friends were placed in jail in 1869, but no open conflict occurred. The decisions of the courts favored the nobles, and gradually the peasants gave up their claims, but not before a discussion of the situation had taken place in the Riksdag of 1869. There was during the period an unusually large exodus from the region for Denmark and the United States. Some undoubtedly left to obtain lands in the new world.

The discontent that the crofters on the estates of the nobility felt toward the gentry in Skåne has been carried by emigrants to the United States. In the life-story of Rosling Sven, a citizen of Minne-

[1] Hallendorff, *Oskar I och Karl XV;* Hildebrand, *Sveriges historia till våra dagar,* XII, 400.

sota, there is a reflection of this attitude. His father had a croft on the estate of Araslöv for which he gave a certain number of days labor.[1] Rosling Sven wrote in his memoirs,

Our province of Skåne is one of the richest in Sweden. Large estates there were and are yet. Many of them were under the crown and were used by the civil officials of the government, and some by higher officers of the army. There were many foreigners that had lands in our locality, Wrangelsberg, Hammershus, Skottlandshus, Sinclairsholm, etc. The names of the families that owned them were Hamilton, Hare, de la Gardie, DeGeer, Dickson, Bennet, Wrangle, Drews, Trolle, Wachtmeister. Araslöv was transferred to the estate of Skottlandshus. It was owned by the Hamilton family and leased to a Captain Zickerman. The nearest neighbors were the Dicksons.

Rosling Sven resented the fact that so much of the fertile Swedish land had been granted to foreign nobles by the crown. These grants dated mostly from the seventeenth century.[2]

Emigrant agents, not only from the United States, but also from Denmark and Northern Germany, were finding Sweden in its economic crisis a fertile field for labor supply. Transportation of emigrants to the United States had become a profitable business. Sweden was now an acknowledged part of the great European emigration movement. The president of the Louisiana Emigration Commission, who made a personal study of the European field in 1869, has described the emigration movements of the period from Europe. He stated that the great majority of emigrants for America were embarking on steamships from Bremen, Hamburg, Havre, and Liverpool.[3] The business of transporting emigrants was best organized in Bremen, from whence more emigrants sailed than from any port on the Continent although less than from Liverpool. Some twenty *expedienten* or general agents devoted themselves entirely to the business. Each of the general agents had from 300 to 1,000 subagents scattered all over Germany, with correspondents in France, Belgium, and the Scandinavian countries. Dr. James O. Noyes was interested in developing emigrant transportation between the Euro-

[1] *Life Story of Rosling Sven*, MSS, Minnesota Historical Society.

[2] The provinces of Skåne, Halland, and Blekinge, were acquired from Denmark by Charles Gustavus (1654–60). Many of the confiscated estates were granted by the crown to various nobles, foreign and native, who had helped him in the wars against Poland and Denmark.

[3] Louisiana, *Report of Commissioner of Emigration, January, 1870*, p. 20.

pean ports and New Orleans. He reported that the great majority
of Swedes, Danes, and Norwegians were embarking at Liverpool for
the reasons that the rate was about $6.00 less than from Hamburg,
although the accommodations were not so good. But the emigrants
being usually poor, the saving of a few dollars meant much.[1]

With the influx of immigrants to the United States, the immigrant travel agency became a lucrative business, and numerous
advertisements in European newspapers and generously dispersed
agencies undoubtedly added numbers to the stream of migration.
Besides the Western Migration Agency with headquarters in Chicago, there were many in New York, e.g., the American Emigrant
Company, the Chicago Emigrant Agency, the Columbia Emigration
Company, the American Emigrant Aid and Homestead Company,
and others.

The American Emigrant Company had an agent in Gothenburg
in 1865, but did not begin to advertise extensively in the rural press
until the following year. Besides selling tickets to prospective emigrants, the company made contracts which amounted to a year's indenture for the payment of passage.[2] This company had a capitalization of $540,000, with headquarters in New York. There was a cen-
tral agent in all of the chief ports of Europe, including Great Britain,
Iceland, Sweden, Norway, Denmark, Germany, France, and numerous agents in many rural communities, wherever the amount
of migration warranted it.[3] The passenger rates from Gothenburg
to New York via Liverpool or Queenstown for a cabin were $75.00 to
$105.00, via Hamburg or Bremen $80.00 to $112.50. Passage be-
tween deck via Liverpool was $27.00, while steerage was $37.00 to
$45.00, by steamer. Steerage on a sailing vessel via Liverpool was
$12.50 to $20.00.[4] The steamers furnished food and bedding, while
on the sailing vessels these had to be provided by the passenger.
There was also a considerable difference in the duration of the ocean
voyage.

In the advertisements of the American Emigration Company in
the Småland press, the corporation was described as "consisting of

[1] *Ibid.*, p. 23.

[2] *Hemlandet* (Chicago), June 7, 1865, July 5, 1865.

[3] *Ibid.*, July 5, 1865.        [4] *Ibid.*, July 12, 1865.

certain wealthy and philanthropic persons in America who wish to aid the emigrant during his voyage so that he does not fall into the hands of unscrupulous countrymen or others that prey upon the ignorance of the traveler."[1] The Swedish American newspaper, *Hemlandet*, had on September 13, 1865, accused the Gothenburg agent of the corporation, Frederick Nelson, of persuading people to emigrate who had only enough money to reach New York, and who there had become paupers.[2] Perhaps that was the reason for the warning that appeared in the *Jönköpings Tidning*,

> The company does not advise anyone to emigrate to America. On the contrary, it desires that every one should carefully consider the consequences of this important step before he decides to take it. No one who is not industrious and has not means enough for the journey and for support for a short time in America until he can obtain a position, should think of emigrating. Large families, which intend to migrate, do wisest to send first some of the younger men of the family to prepare a home for the remaining members.[3]

The advertisement continued,

> The company does not picture any eldorado for the emigrant. The healthy, industrious and temperant can attain economic prosperity in America, but the lazy and intemperant will fall into greater poverty there than here. It is from the first group that encouraging reports about America come to Sweden, from the latter the opposite.

There was much fluctuation in the passenger rates during the year on the part of the American Emigration Company. In February, 1866, the rate from Gothenburg to New York was 144 riksdaler ($38.00), in May 160 riksdaler ($42.00); by July it was 150 riksdaler ($40.00).[4]

Beginning in July of 1866, the company began to advertise in the *Hudiksvall Post* in Norrland, and continued through 1867.[5] The advertisement stated that it was due to increased emigration from Northern Sweden that an agency had been opened in Hudiksvall. The passenger rate was 150 riksdaler ($40.00) from Gothenburg to

[1] *Jönköpings Tidning* (Jönköping), February 21, 1866.

[2] *Hemlandet* (Chicago), September 13, 1865.

[3] A. W. Möller, agent at Jönköping, was also vice-consul of Denmark (*Jönköpings Tidning*, February 21, 1866).

[4] *Ibid.*, February 21, 1866, May 2, 1866, July 18, 1866, and August 18, 1866.

[5] *Hudiksvalls Posten* (Hudiksvall), July 21, 1866, March 16, 1867–August 4, 1867.

New York, which included room and board at Liverpool, and the same with medical care from Liverpool to New York. Passengers were required to deposit 20 riksdaler ($5.00) two weeks before departure. In 1867 the advertisement of the American Emigration Company appeared in the newspapers of Southern Sweden.[1] A news-item from Gothenburg in a Malmö newspaper on May 18, 1867, stated that, since April 26, 1867, there had passed through Gothenburg 687 emigrants, conducted by the American Emigrant Company for Illinois, Minnesota, and Iowa.[2] During the coming week some three hundred would pass through the port under the care of the same company and for the next month about 1,000 had made contracts to sail on the steamer "Albion."

The general agent of the American Emigrant Company was particularly solicitous in the care of Swedish travelers. He visited in America during the winter of 1867 making preparations for the coming year.[3] The company planned to establish direct connection between Copenhagen and New York by a line of steamers during 1870, although it did not discontinue forwarding passengers over England.[4] The advertisement of 1870 stated that in New York emigrants would be received by Captain R. E. Jeanssen, and in Chicago, Frederick Nelson, both of whom would do all they could to advise their countrymen about employment, the purchase of land, and the exchange of money.[5] Captain G. W. Schroeder of religious fame had now become general agent for the Scandinavian countries. After 1870, the company ceased to advertise in the Swedish press.

The Columbia Emigration Company began to advertise in the *Jönköpings Tidning* a week before the American Emigrant Company, and appeared to be a great rival.[6] The former advertised as forwarding emigrants to all parts of Canada, North and South America. Its Gothenburg agent was William Lyon. The Columbia Emigration Company tended to undersell the American Emigrant

---

[1] *Malmö Nya Allehanda* (Malmö), March 9, 1867, and following issues; *Skånska Posten* (Kristianstad), April 6, 1867.

[2] *Malmö Nya Allehanda*, May 11, 1867.

[3] *Jönköpings Tidning*, May 13, 1868.

[4] *Skånska Posten*, October 6, 1869, February 5, 1870.

[5] *Ibid.*, February 5, 1870.     [6] *Jönköpings Tidning*, February 14, 1866.

Company by offering a passage from Gothenburg to New York via Hull and Liverpool for 140 riksdaler ($37.00) by steamer. The advertisement stated,

Every Friday afternoon a steamer leaves Gothenburg for Hull; from Hull the journey is continued immediately by railroad to Liverpool, and from thence to New York by steamer. . . . . Emigrants must provide themselves with food until they reach Liverpool, but from the time they reach Liverpool, the company will provide room and board free. During the voyage from Liverpool to New York they will receive food, medical care, and medicine. The company also pays the landing fee.

To guarantee the proper treatment of emigrants in Liverpool, the company had deposited in Liverpool £1,000. An advertisement of April 18, 1866, announced the raising of the passenger rate to 155 riksdaler ($41.00).[1] The company maintained its own emigrant hotel in Liverpool, Hotel Columbia.[2] The price war continued. By May 9, 1866, the rates had risen to 160 riksdaler, in June they were lowered to 155, and by July to 145.[3] The Columbia Company used the Cunard steamers.[4] In 1867 the company was also advertised in the newspapers of Southern Sweden.[5]

Småland was considered the fertile region for emigration in 1866. In its newspapers a third emigration company, which was also a land company, advertised extensively. The American Emigrant Aid and Homestead Company of New York with a capitalization of five million dollars established direct steamer connections between the Scandinavian countries and New York.[6] The steamer "Ottawa" carrying 635 passengers initiated the service between Gothenburg and New York in a fifteen-day trip, arriving in America with much pomp and ceremony on September 6, 1866.[7] A small steamer brought the president and directors of the Scandinavian Society of New York, the president and other members of the American Emigrant Aid and Homestead Society, and many leading merchants of New York to

[1] *Ibid.*, April 18, 1866.

[2] *Ibid.*, April 25, 1866, May 2, 1866.

[3] *Ibid.*, May 9, 1866, June 20, 1866, July 18, 1866, July 25, 1866, August 15, 1866.

[4] *Ibid.*, July 18, 1866.

[5] *Skånska Posten*, January 2, 1867, April 6, 1867.

[6] *Jönköpings Tidning*, August 11, 1866.

[7] *Ibid.*, July 15, 1866, October 10, 1866.

meet the "Ottawa."[1] Many speeches of welcome and toasts inaugurated the new venture.

This extensive corporation had many activities besides that of steamship navigation for emigrants. There was a land department for the purchase and sale of farms. The company owned large stretches of land in all parts of the United States. In the words of its advertisement in the *Jönköpings Tidning*, it described its holdings as comprising "Pennsylvania, Virginia, Tennessee, Georgia, Florida, Texas, and California." It continued,

Emigrants from the northern countries can easily find in this wide variety of states, regions which will suit them, not only in climate, but also in soil. On a large area of the company's land in Texas there are fine timberlands; on their possessions in Tennessee may be found copper, iron, coal, and petroleum. In Georgia, the company owns land in the famous gold region, and besides this the corporation expects to purchase lands along the partly constructed and partly planned railroad lines in Ohio, Wisconsin, Iowa and Kansas. Emigrants may, therefore, receive advice upon arrival about the lands which they desire to acquire. These lands will be sold on a ten-year-mortgage basis.[2]

There was also a banking department in the corporation which consisted of a savings and loan division, a money exchange division, and an endowment for old age insurance division. Then there was the employment department.

The advertisement discussed the conditions and opportunities in the United States after the Civil War. The article stated,

It is well known that many in the old world look with suspicion upon all that comes from the new, but this distrust is to the greatest extent caused by unfamiliarity with the conditions here in this country . . . . everything possible has been done to restore new life and new activity in the war-harassed states. In the north and the west, as well as in the south, working conditions were upset, partially due to the millions engaged in the war, and partially to the freeing of the negro who could no longer be forced to work. At the end of the war, many people returned to industry, but the destruction and displacement, caused by the war, was so extensive that the scarcity of labor supply was greater than before the war. This scarcity the leading men in all states have decided to supply by inviting new labor from foreign countries to come to the United States. It is apparent that both immigrant labor and the employer are satisfied with the plan, especially those laborers who in their former homes, despite industry,

[1] From a letter of one of the passengers on the "Ottawa" reprinted in *ibid.*, October 10, 1866.

[2] *Ibid.*, August 11, 1866.

could not attain a decent income, and here can make a happy home for themselves and their families. There is such a colony of Norwegians in Texas, which numbers about 12,000, all of whom are independent land owners, and who have recently advised their countrymen in the old fatherland to come to Texas. It has been demonstrated here as well as in other southern states that the nordics are content. For ordinary servants in the western, central and southern states, the wages have averaged 500 riksdaler ($135) annually with food, lodging, etc.[1] Working clothes are cheap and the frugal workman can soon accumulate a little capital, with which he can lay the foundation of an independent position, especially if he accepts part of his wages in produce, which is customary. As soon as the laborer has saved a little capital, our company invites him to purchase a larger or smaller piece of land, according to his means, and offers him a chance to pay for it in ten years. By paying the corporation regularly small installments, he may become the owner of as much land as he can cultivate, for the cultivation of the soil does not need the costly fertilizers used in Europe. His agricultural machinery he may receive from the company at a low price and on the installment plan. But to make such a farm successful, there is need for industry and perseverance.[2]

Not only agricultural laborers are needed, but in our western and southern states, skilled workmen, like smiths, machinists, carpenters, lumber jacks, and other wood workers, may obtain good wages. Our corporation is in communication with many large factories, railroad construction companies, etc., and can usually find good employment for those who seek it. The workmen who cannot immediately find labor they prefer, can obtain it after a time by keeping in communication with the corporation.

The corporation planned to maintain direct steamship communication between New York and Sweden, Norway, and Denmark. It expected to have a steamer leaving Copenhagen every two weeks, which would stop at Gothenburg, Kristiansand or Bergen, and Galway in Ireland.[3] The rates from Copenhagen or Gothenburg to New York were slightly higher than those offered by the competing emigrant companies, 170 riksdaler ($45.00) for steerage, but the advantages of direct transportation offset the difference in price according to the advertisement.[4]

In the letter of September 8, 1866, a passenger on the "Ottawa" wrote:

[1] This wage is extremely low according to the American labor market of the time. It probably appeared high in the eyes of the European.

[2] *Jönköpings Posten*, August 11, 1866.

[3] *Ibid.*

[4] *Jönköpings Tidning*, July 25, 1866, July 28, 1866, August 15, 1866.

The next morning the steerage passengers were landed at Castle Garden, where they were received by two Danes, Captain Petersen and M. Mariager, who conducted them to the company's office where those who wished were enrolled as seeking jobs. Then they were escorted to hotels and boarding-houses where they were to remain until they obtained a job. The boarding-houses are inspected by the corporation and are noticeably clean and well aired. At each place one of the corporation's employees lives, a Scandinavian who can speak the English language. Emigrants are therefore protected from fraud.[1]

In a later letter of September 10, he stated that 258 of the passengers on the "Ottawa" had left for Rollo, Missouri, where, under the direction of the Pacific railroad they were to found a colony. Major Sommer, a Dane employed by the corporation, was to meet the immigrants at St. Louis and conduct them to the site of the settlement.

Other American land companies placed advertisements in Swedish newspapers. The great European-American Land Company began to advertise in Norrland in 1869.[2] In an editorial in the *Hudiksvall Post's* issue of March 13, 1869, which spoke of the activities and frauds of various emigrant companies, this land company was highly recommended to emigrants. It was a corporation, capitalized at a million dollars, with its head office in New York City, and no less person than Caleb Cushing was the president of the organization. Caleb Cushing was at the time the American ambassador to Spain. Among the board of directors were included Count Henning Taube,[3] and a Swedish-American lawyer, John E. Sundström, who had been in the United States for twenty years. The plan was first conceived by Sundström when he had visited Sweden the previous year in 1868. In Stockholm, Judge P. H. Wendtland was the director of the interests of the corporation, and Friherr M. Arnfelt, its secretary and attorney. According to the editorial, the agents of the Land Company were strictly instructed not to induce emigration by their persuasive arguments. However, it can hardly be expected that these instructions were followed.

Complaints of frauds on the part of emigrant agents in Sweden ap-

[1] *Ibid.*, October 10, 1866.     [2] *Hudiksvalls Posten*, February 6, 1869.

[3] Count Taube had been involved in the Stenby affair in Sweden and had found it advantageous to emigrate. In 1866 he came to the United States with a number of settlers to establish a colony in Wisconsin (West Virginia, *Report of the Immigrant Commissioner, 1869*).

peared from time to time in the newspapers. An article in the *Jönköpings Tidning* on July 27, 1867, quoted from *Hemlandet*, the Swedish-American newspaper of Chicago, for June 25, complained that David Lyon, agent for the British-American Land Company of Canada, had sold a ticket to Chicago when the emigrant had asked for a ticket to Jamestown, New York. He had told the emigrant that Chicago was the nearest city to Jamestown. The result was that the emigrant was stranded in Chicago without money and had appealed to the Scandinavian consul there. The Gothenburg agent of the National Steamship Company of Liverpool warned emigrants in Southern Sweden, through the press, against agents who were falsely using his name and were misinforming people about free passage to America.[1] Many had been cheated. The Danish vice-consul, who was also an agent for the American Emigration Company at Jönköping, found it necessary to defend himself through the press in 1868.[2] He was accused of stimulating emigration in various ways.

In *Amerika-Bladet*, one of the several newspapers which appeared in Sweden during 1870 for the purpose of stimulating emigration, there appeared the advertisement of the Scandinavian Emigrant Agency, located in Chicago.[3] It specialized in selling tickets to and from the Scandinavian countries, but also sold government land and aided the emigrant in securing homesteads in the western states, at the same price as the government land office. The Swedish-American Emigrant Company was active in its advertising in Norrland in 1871 and offered to help emigrants obtain work in New York and free transportation to the location of the work from that city.[4]

The steamship companies seemed at first to depend upon the Emigrant companies or general agencies conducted by private individuals to bring them business.[5] No advertisements of steamship

[1] *Skånska Posten*, November 18, 1868.   [2] *Jönköpings Tidning*, May 13, 1868.

[3] *Amerika-Bladet* (Örebro), February 15, 1870. This paper began in 1869 with nine issues and continued in 1870 with twenty-six issues. It was discontinued after June 28. A similar newspaper, *Amerika*, was published in Gothenburg, 1869–70, and continued as *Nya Verlden* (Göteborg), 1872–74.

[4] *Hudiksvalls Posten*, May 13, 1871.

[5] Advertisements of general agents without statement of any definite announcement of any emigrant company or steamship line, appear in *Jönköpings Posten*, June 17, 1865 (A. W. Möller, agent at Jönköping), *Jönköpings Posten*, September 8, 1866 (Alfred

companies appeared in the representative rural press of Sweden until 1864 and not in any numbers until 1867. From 1867 on, these advertisements were usual. Two general agencies advertised themselves as the Scandinavian Head Office, located at Copenhagen and at Malmö,[1] and the American Head Office.[2] The Scandinavian agency stated that "a person who speaks the Swedish and English language will accompany the emigrants on the whole journey." American railroad tickets were sold and guaranteed. There was besides the agency at Copenhagen in 1867, also one in Hessleholm in Skåne. By 1870 the agency had an office in Malmö. It advertised passage on a clipper ship for $26.00 and on the royal mail steamer for $31.00.[3] A Swedish interpreter accompanied emigrants to Chicago, where provisions were made to house the travelers for five days free of charge in the company's Emigrant House. Employment was also furnished to emigrants without fee.

The first steamship advertisements to appear in the Swedish rural press were those of the Hamburg lines. This steamship line began its advertisement in the Småland press in 1864.[4] Its steamships made the trip from Hamburg to New York in thirteen days and the passenger fee was $42.00.[5] There was also a line of packet ships, which when touching at Southampton made the trip in from thirty to thirty-five days. The passenger rate on the sailing vessels was $21.00, but the passengers had to furnish their own food. In the fall of 1864, the same company advertised passage to Melbourne on clipper ships for $70.00.[6] Its advertisements continued during 1865 in the same paper. Steamers continued to leave Hamburg every two weeks for America. The passenger fee remained the same, and did not include bed

---

Malmström, agent at Jönköping), *Skånska Posten*, April 3, 1867 (Oscar Sjögren, agent at Christianstad), *Skånska Posten*, April 6, 1867 (G. F. Holmberg for line over Hamburg).

[1] *Skånska Posten*, September 25, 1867, and *Malmö Nya Allehanda*, May 11, 1870.

[2] *Jönköpings Tidning*, September 7, 1867, September 11, 1867, September 14, 1867.

[3] *Malmö Nya Allehanda*, May 11, 1870.

[4] *Jönköpings Tidning*, February 13, 1864, April 23, 1864.

[5] The passenger fee was 160 riksdaler, and on the sailing vessels 80 riksdaler. August Bolten was the agent in Hamburg, and William Lyon in Gothenburg (*ibid.*).

[6] *Ibid.*, September 17, 1864, and continuing in the succeeding issues of the year.

clothes, which were furnished at Hamburg upon the payment of $3.00 extra.[1] The rate on clipper ships to New York had increased almost $2.00, but food, etc., was now included. The line also had packet ships sailing between Hamburg and Quebec.[2] The passenger rate to Quebec was less than to New York by ten riksdaler, or almost $3.00.[3] By July 1, 1865, the Hamburg lines had reduced the time of their steamship between Hamburg and New York to twelve days.[4] In 1867 the line advertised for the first time in the newspapers of Southern Sweden and named agents in several of the towns of Skåne.[5] The rate for steamship passage remained the same in 1867 as in 1864, 160 riksdaler or about $41.00. In 1868, an advertisement of the Hamburg-American Packet line in the *Göteborg Handels-och Sjöfarts-Tidning* on March 3, 1868, gave a passenger rate of 133 riksdaler 33 öre or $33.00.[6]

The Cunard line was the second steamship company to begin direct advertisement in the Swedish press for passengers to America. It also began in Småland. An advertisement appears in *Jönköpings Tidning*, November 21, 1866.[7] The real steamship competition appeared in 1868 when a half-dozen lines began a vigorous advertising campaign. Thus the Cunard line appeared to have ceased advertising directly in 1867, but began in the winter of 1868 in all sections of Sweden. In the *Jönköpings Tidning, Hudiksvalls Posten*,

[1] *Ibid.*, March 1, 1865.

[2] The Hamburg-American line's steamships were the "Bavaria," the "Germania," the "Teutonia," the "Borussia," the "Saxonia." Its packet ships to New York were the "Donau," the "Oder," the "Deutschland," and the "Elbe"; to Quebec, the "Neckar" and the "Main"; to Melbourne, the "Joachim Christian" and the "Zephims" (*ibid.*, February 13, 1864, September 17, 1864, June 10, 1865).

[3] The rate to New York on the clipper ships in 1865 was 85.44 riksdaler, while to Quebec it was 74.44 (*ibid.*, March 1, 1865).

[4] *Ibid.*, July 1, 1865.

[5] *Skånska Posten*, January 4, 1867, April 6, 1867. The agent named in this advertisement is G. F. Holmberg, Christianstad; *Malmö Nya Allehanda*, April 24, 1867 ff. issues. The agent is John Sommer of Lübeck.

[6] The agents for this line were Ferlöv at Malmö, and for the Robert M. Sloman's packet ships from Hamburg to New York and Quebec, Borlind, Bersén and Company in Gothenburg, and Donati and Company in Hamburg (*Göteborgs Handels-och Sjöfarts-Tidning*, March 3, 1868).

[7] William Lyon of Gothenburg and E. L. Svensson of Jönköping are the agents mentioned.

*Norrlands Posten*, and *Skånska Posten*, its advertisements appeared in February, 1868, and continued through practically every issue of the year.[1]

Strong competitor of the Cunard line was the Inman line.[2] The Cunard line connected with New York and Boston over Hull-Liverpool, while the Inman line had chosen New York and Philadelphia over the same route. Steamers left Gothenburg every Friday, making connections with the liners at Liverpool. The Inman line advertised that it gave its passengers the best service for the least price, and that interpreters accompanied the emigrants on their entire journey.[3] This treatment was not accorded to some emigrants according to the complaints that appeared in *Jönköpings Tidning*, September 16, 1868, and Frederick Nelson was called upon to explain by the newspaper. Captain Jeanssen, a well-known character to many emigrants, was the agent of the line at New York and helped the travelers to adjust themselves.[4] In 1869 the agents of the Inman line were also advertising for the North American Lloyd which ran lines directly from Copenhagen to New York for 125 riksdaler, or $30.00.[5] The tickets could be purchased to any railroad station in America. This advertisement was directed to emigrants from Southern Sweden; Skåne, southern Halland, and the larger part of Småland.[6] In 1870 the general agency at Gothenburg was taken away from Frederick Nelson and given to Herman Roos, who stated in an advertisement in *Skånska Posten* for February 9, 1870, that he

[1] *Jönköpings Tidning*, February 1, 1868 ff.; *Hudiksvalls Posten*, February 1, 1868, March 4, ff., February 20, 1869; *Skånska Posten*, February 22, 1868 ff.; *Norrlands Posten*, February 4, 1868. There were agencies at Gothenburg (S. Sörensen), Hudiksvall (Sven Nilsson), Jönköping (A. Nordström), and Kristianstad (Oscar Sjögren).

[2] Advertisements of the Inman line appear in *Skånska Posten* (Kristianstad), February 5, 1868 ff.; *Jönköpings Tidning*, August 22, 1868 ff.; *Norrlands Posten* (Gävle), February 8, 1868; *Hudiksvalls Posten*, February 15, 1868, March 4, 1868, April 24, 1869. Frederick Nelson, formerly with the American Emigrant Company is mentioned as the head agent of the Inman line at Gothenburg.

[3] *Skånska Posten*, February 5, 1868. Thimgren at Kristianstad was a local agent. A. W. Möller was the agent at Jönköping, *Jönköpings Tidning*, August 22, 1868, and Froenell at Hudiksvall, *Hudiksvalls Posten*, February 15, 1868, *Jönköpings Tidning*, August 22, 1868, and *Skånska Posten*, February 10, 1869.

[4] *Jönköpings Tidning*, August 22, 1868; *Skånska Posten*, February 10, 1869.

[5] *Skånska Posten*, July 24, 1869, September 11, 1869.   [6] *Ibid.*, July 24, 1869.

had been in America for eighteen years where he had been editor of *Svenska Amerikanaren* and was capable of giving substantial advice to emigrants.[1] The advertisement stated that the Inman line had transported the largest number of Swedish emigrants of any steamship line, about 40,000 during the late sixties. It also dwelt on the advantage of breaking the voyage by passing through England rather than traveling directly to America. There were Swedish agents of the company, both in New York and Chicago, who could be trusted to aid the emigrant in the transportation of his baggage, the purchase of railroad tickets, the seeking of employment, and the exchange of money, all without charge.[2]

The Allan line, which, since 1866, had been affiliated with the Montreal Ocean Steamship Company, was a fourth competing steamship line for Swedish emigrants in 1868. Its advertisements appeared in Småland and Norrland during that year and in Skåne the following year. This line had a steamer leaving Gothenburg every Friday, bound for Hull. Connections were made by rail to Liverpool and then by the royal mail steamers to New York.[3] The trip from Liverpool to New York could be made in from nine and one-half to eleven days. In 1869 the Allan line was especially recommended by Hans Mattson of Minnesota, who, at the time, was visiting in Southern Sweden, and it was used by one of his colleagues, Captain Lindborg, who helped him in conducting a large party of emigrants to Minnesota.[4] The advantage of taking passage to Quebec was emphasized by the line in 1870, for it saved freight on the transportation of baggage and the emigrant also escaped the numerous runners in New York.[5] The Allan line had several agents in Norrland, at Bjuråker, Ängabo,[6] and Hudiksvall.[7]

[1] Frederick Nelson had attacked the Inman lines in *Göteborgs Handels-och Sjöfarts-Tidning*, February 2, 1870, and this was an answer.

[2] *Skånska Posten*, February 9, 1870; *Hudiksvalls Posten*, April 2, 1870.

[3] *Jönköpings Tidning*, April 18, 1868 ff. David Lyon was the Gothenburg agent. The agent at Nässjö in Småland was Olaf Malmborg, and at Jönköping was A. M. Rosing. *Hudiksvalls Posten*, March 28, 1868. Agent at Söderhamn was C. A. Lundberg.

[4] *Skånska Posten*, February 6, 1869. Wilken Horneman is the Allan line agent in Copenhagen.

[5] *Ibid.*, February 12, 1870.

[6] *Hudiksvalls Posten*, February 13, 1869. Jonas Dahlström was the agent here.

[7] *Ibid.*, April 24, 1869. Sune Johnsson was agent at Hudiksvall.

A fifth competitor was the National Steamship Company of Liverpool, whose advertisements appeared in Småland and Skåne in 1868, and in Norrland in 1869.[1] It also forwarded emigrants over Hull-Liverpool. In 1871 this steamship line advertised direct connections between Copenhagen and New York.[2] In the same advertisement it appealed to the Swedish-Americans returning to the United States to apply for positions as conductors and interpreters for emigrants. A sixth competitive steamship line appeared in 1869, the Anchor line, with connections over Scotland, Gothenburg to New York via Leith and Glasgow.[3] It was advertised as the quickest and most comfortable way to travel, for it provided special cabins to sleep in. Its liners left Gothenburg every Tuesday to make connections with the Atlantic fleet. There was a special Anchor line employment bureau, under the direction of Captain H. A. Bürger, for passengers of the line.[4] Swedish speaking interpreters accompanied emigrants from Gothenburg to Chicago. It is interesting that the Anchor line advertised as the great advantages of traveling on this line individual berths for the passengers and warm food at definite meal times.

By 1869, all six of these various steamship lines were advertising in the same newspapers in the most prolific of the Swedish emigrant communities. The president of the Louisiana Board of Emigration was also interested to make New Orleans a port of entry for European emigrants bound for the Mississippi Valley.[5] He hoped to establish competing rates with the Liverpool-New York companies in a route from Hamburg to New Orleans. There were some travelers already choosing the latter port, for several hundred Swedes had passed through New Orleans bound for Indiana, Illinois, and Texas that year.

The Swedish government had found it necessary in 1864 to warn the Swedish people to think seriously before they decided to emigrate

[1] *Jönköpings Tidning*, May 16, 1868 ff. B. B. Peterson was the Gothenburg agent. *Skånska Posten*, November 18, 1868; *Hudiksvalls Posten*, February 13, 1869, March 12, 1870.

[2] *Skånska Posten*, March 1, 1871; *Hudiksvalls Posten*, February 11, 1871.

[3] *Skånska Posten*, March 10, 1869, July 28, 1869, July 17, 1869; *Hudiksvalls Posten*, March 5, 1870. John Millar was the general agent at Gothenburg; F. A. Dahl was the agent at Kristianstad.

[4] *Skånska Posten*, February 23, 1870; *Hudiksvalls Posten*, March 5, 1870.

[5] Louisiana, *Report of Commissioner on Emigration, 1870*, pp. 20, 23.

and to be careful and shrewd in dealing with the many agents that were urging them to leave their fatherland.[1] In 1869 an act was passed requiring registration of all emigrant agents with the governors of the counties in an effort to protect the people against fraudulent agents.[2] Some of the irresponsible so-called emigration companies of New York and other portions of the United States had established agencies in Sweden and Denmark. They sometimes sold inland passage tickets to emigrants which were not honored in New York. Many complaints were brought before the Commissioner of Emigration of New York during 1868, but there was no redress since most of the companies were bankrupt.[3] During 1869 in Sweden, many of the emigrant companies and agencies were bonded under the new Swedish law. In Kalmar County, the governor reported that twenty-nine had been licensed in 1869 and twenty-seven in 1870.[4] The governor of Östergötland County stated that there were 38 subagents working for six general agents in the county in 1869, and 58 subagents for nine general agents in 1870.[5] The activities of the agents were also mentioned in 1870 in Skaraborg County and in Värmland, from where emigration had materially increased.[6] These agents worked on a commission basis and were, therefore, anxious to increase the number of emigrants as much as possible.

It cannot be stated that the emigrant companies and steamship lines were responsible for the beginning of Swedish emigration to the United States, since these organizations did not start their activities in the country until the last half of the sixties. These agencies of migration rather entered the field when the numbers of emigrants during these panic years had been so stimulated by economic conditions in Sweden, that their conveyance to the United States became a profitable business. Since they attempted to make the bridge across the Atlantic so convenient and attractive, it was much easier

---

[1] K. bfhde femårsberättelse, Kalmar län, 1866–1870, p. 6.

[2] Act of February 5, 1869, "Utvandringslagstiftning," Emigrationsutredningens bilaga I, p. 17.

[3] New York, Annual Report of Commissioner of Emigration, December 31, 1869, p. 27.

[4] K. bfhde femårsberättelse, Kalmar län, 1866–1870, p. 6.

[5] Ibid., Östergötlands län, 1866–1870, p. 2.

[6] Ibid., Skaraborgs län, 1866–1870, p. 4; ibid., Värmlands län, 1866–1870, p. 3.

for the emigrant to leave when the conditions at home were not satisfactory. The many steamship agents when once established in practically every small town, with brochures and maps demonstrating the possibilities in the new world, undoubtedly helped to swell the numbers of those seeking these opportunities. They thus became a stimulant of migration.

An equally potent factor in the encouragement of exodus and a constant stimulation was and continues to be the successful Swedish-American. The American consul at Stockholm remarked upon the numbers of American travelers crowding the Stockholm hotels during the summer of 1868.[1] He himself was indirectly interested in one of the emigrant companies. And one of the most influential of these visitors was Hans Mattson, former secretary of the state of Minnesota and a member of the immigration board of that state, himself a Swedish pioneer of the Northwest. He returned to visit his old home in Sweden during the summer of 1868, after an absence of eighteen years.[2] He was the son of a peasant from Önnestad, Skåne. His father had joined him in America two years after his arrival. This poor emigrant boy, who returned a colonel in the American army and a prominent citizen of his state, was a great curiosity to the simple people of the countryside. He wrote in his memoirs,

I was received with cordiality everywhere among the common people and the middle class, while the aristocrats looked on with distant coldness, as they always do when a man of the people has succeeded in getting beyond what they call his legitimate station, and is what we would call in other words a self-made man.[3]

That was Sweden in 1868, but in 1930 the self-made man has won his place in Swedish economic, social, and political life. After a tour through Sweden, Mattson returned to Skåne, and was besieged by people who wished to accompany him to America the following spring.[4] In April, 1869, one shipload of emigrants left Hälsingborg under the leadership of Captain Lindborg, a veteran of the Crimean

[1] U.S. Consular Letters, 1864–70, Stockholm, Chas. A. Perkins, consul, July 24, 1868.

[2] Hans Mattson, Reminiscences, the Story of an Emigrant, p. 103. Mattson was U.S. consul-general of India in the eighties.

[3] Ibid., pp. 109 ff.

[4] There is no mention in the press, i.e., Skånska Posten (Kristianstad), during 1868–69 of Hans Mattson's visit, except an advertisement of the Allan line steamers (Skånska Posten, February 6, 1869).

War and the American Civil War.[1] The emigrants were bound for Minnesota. A few weeks later, Mattson followed with a party of eight hundred.[2]

Influenced by the new policy of the United States government under Lincoln to encourage immigration to our vacant lands, which was launched with the establishment of a federal immigration commissioner, many of the western and southern states, and at least one eastern state, established immigration commissions, and became active in exploiting Europe for settlers. Wisconsin had set the precedent in its Emigration Commission of 1852 to 1855. One of the earliest of the state immigration commissions established after the Civil War was in the state of Missouri.[3] Because of the early German settlement in this state, the board of foreign immigration was interested primarily in the people from Central Europe. It was felt that the climate of Missouri was not suited for Scandinavian people. The report of 1866 stated that it was useless for Missouri to expect a large influx from Norway or Sweden, from Denmark, Scotland, or even from Canada. It continued that it was "to the zone where the vine and corn grow that we must look as the proper source of immigration to Missouri. Germany, Switzerland, Hungary, Bohemia, and Poland will contribute during the next decade a larger ratio to the population of this state than any other."[4]

The immigration board of Missouri was rather contemptuous of ambitious Minnesota. The report from Missouri contended,

> In vain does the Commissioner of Statistics of Minnesota flatter himself that as his state unites, in his opinion, the characteristics of northern and southern climates, as it produces the wheat of Canada, the corn of Ohio, the oats and barley of Scotland, and the melons of the Mediterranean, it will converge the tendencies of immigration from climates far apart.[5]

But history has proved that Minnesota had the greater vision. The legislature of that state had granted two prizes in 1865 for the best pamphlets on the state as a place of settlement for immigrants.

---

[1] Allan line agent at Kristianstad enrolled these emigrants (*ibid.*).

[2] Mattson, *op. cit.*, pp. 110–11.

[3] Missouri, *First Report of the Board of Immigration, 1865–66.*

[4] *Ibid.*, p. 31.

[5] *Ibid.* There were some Norwegian settlers in Missouri at the time.

These two essays were incorporated into a pamphlet published in English, German, and Norwegian by a private firm in St. Paul.[1]

The legislature of Minnesota established a board of immigration in 1866, and launched a comprehensive campaign for settlers both from Europe and from the older states of the Union. One part of this program was the purchase of publication rights of the state pamphlet. It was published then in English, German, Swedish, Norwegian, and Welsh, with a special English edition for Irish immigrants.[2] The Swedish and Norwegian editions were translated and prepared by Hans Mattson, a member of the board. Notices were placed in the press that the pamphlets might be secured free of charge by writing for them. Five thousand copies each of the Swedish and Norwegian pamphlets were distributed during the year. The board spent $10,000 annually for this advertising campaign.[3]

The press was extensively used, not only for notices that pamphlets might be procured, but also for the sketchy and readable articles full of statistical data and reliable information on the productivity of the soil in Minnesota, the climate, the development of resources, the United States Homestead law, the common school system, and other matters of interest to the settler.[4] The articles were written by men whose names were favorably known among their countrymen, and were published in American, German, Scandinavian, and Irish journals. They were sometimes reproduced in other journals. Twenty-four articles alone appeared in the Scandinavian press in 1866. Both the foreign press in the United States and the newspapers in various European countries were used.

Another portion of the campaign inaugurated by Minnesota was the establishment of agents at various ports of entry, at inland centers of immigrant distribution, and at some European ports.[5] These were men of various nationalities. B. Kihlholz, a German, was stationed as agent in New York City for six months in 1867, as was also a Swedish agent, Charles Kempe. A Norwegian agent, T. K. Simmons, was sent to Quebec; another Norwegian, K. Hasberg, was stationed at Milwaukee, and Robert Toe Laer, a Hollander, at Chicago.

[1] *Minnesota as a Home for Immigrants* (pamphlet), St. Paul, 1865.

[2] Minnesota, *Annual Report of Immigration Commission, 1867*, pp. 3–4.

[3] *Ibid.*, p. 7.      [4] *Ibid.*, pp. 5–6.      [5] *Ibid.*, p. 6.

Hans Mattson, a member of the state board, spent much of his time in New York, and on the immigrant routes in Canada and in the Great Lakes cities. A local agent in St. Paul, A. E. Johnson, aided the immigrants at the "Home," a shelter erected jointly by the city authorities, the Chamber of Commerce, and the transportation companies leading into St. Paul. There was also an agent in Germany, Edward Pelz.

The purpose of these agencies was to take charge of the immigrants who were ignorant of the English language, immediately upon their arrival in the American seaports, to aid them to purchase tickets, to weigh and check their baggage, and to advise them as to the best and cheapest routes of travel.[1] At the same time, the agents would give them information concerning Minnesota, the different settlements of the traveler's countrymen, and his friends already in the state. Much fraud was being perpetrated upon the immigrants by runners, agents of railroads and steamship lines, emigrant hotel-keepers. Sometimes these agents of the state of Minnesota sent interpreters west with the immigrants. At the "Home" in St. Paul, the agent gave them aid and assistance to reach their destination in the older settlements or on the frontier, and secured work for those in need of employment. Many destitute immigrants were sent to Minnesota by agents in Milwaukee and Chicago. The immigrant agent at Milwaukee reported that he had aided many poverty-stricken immigrants from Chicago to Minnesota with funds given by humane people of Chicago, and the aid of the Northwestern Railroad Company. A thousand destitute persons in 1867 were sent from Chicago to Milwaukee for a small compensation, and were transported free by the Milwaukee and St. Paul Railroad to La Crosse.[2] Many of these had been defrauded by runners who had taken their baggage and had sent them to unhealthy places to settle. A typical case of destitute immigrants was a party of forty Swedes who came up on the "Diamond Jo" to St. Paul, all their baggage left at La Crosse to pay their passage to St. Paul.[3] These poor people were the

[1] *Ibid.*

[2] K. Hasberg, agent in Milwaukee, report included in Minnesota, *Annual Report of Immigration Commission, 1867*, pp. 26–28.

[3] Clippings from St. Paul press, undated, included in report of Bernard Kihlholz, agent in New York (*ibid.*, p. 18).

type who would endure the hardships of the frontier and persevere in developing a new state.

The agent in Germany succeeded in interesting the most influential German and Scandinavian newspapers in propaganda for the state of Minnesota.[1] It was reported that many immigrants from these countries arrived in Minnesota with the state pamphlet in their hands. It was estimated that 15,000 immigrants came through Milwaukee bound for Minnesota in 1866, and about 10,000 through Chicago.[2] Half of these changing at Milwaukee were Norwegians; the rest were Swedish, Danish, or German.

After a year's experimenting in advertising by the state, the immigration commission recommended the discontinuance of the various agencies, and concentration on newspaper publicity and distribution of the state pamphlets in various languages.[3] "To effectually reach the foreign immigrant, this work should be done among them before they leave their native homes," the report stated. The state received thousands of letters from "men in every condition of life, and from nearly every locality in North America and in Europe, and even from the remote regions of inner Russia."

The Immigration Commission of Minnesota had the European situation well in hand. The report stated that time was especially auspicious for emigration. The end of the American Civil War, the firm establishment of a republican government, and the victory of free labor were all inducements. The Homestead law offered thousands of acres of free land to the landless European peasant. Middle Europe was dominated by political excitement and discontent in 1866. The financial crisis with the accompanying destitution, want, and famine in Northern Europe also increased emigration.[4]

There was some mention of Minnesota in the steamship advertisements in the Swedish press during the later sixties. Even before Hans Mattson's and Captain Lindborg's visit to Sweden, there appeared in *Norrlands Posten* for May 18, 1867, in the advertisement of a steamship agent, the notice that emigrants purchasing tickets from the agent would be received, upon landing in America, by an agent of the state of Minnesota. He would give them help and ad-

[1] *Ibid.*, pp. 29–30.  [3] *Ibid.*, pp. 29–30.

[2] *Ibid.*, p. 26.  [4] *Ibid.*, p. 11.

vice, and act as their guide that they might escape the dangers and frauds that others had met. The agent at Gävle was willing to give advice on wages and the cost of land in America.[1] An agent in Småland advertising in *Jönköpings Tidning* on May 8, 1867, stated that he had been in the new world for several years and could advise on wages and the cost of land. He mentioned that emigrants purchasing tickets through him would be met in New York by Charles Kempe, agent for the state of Minnesota, who could give them help and advice if they wished to settle in the West, and could provide them with an interpreter.[2]

Although the Swedish press did not comment upon Hans Mattson's visit to Sweden in 1868 and 1869,[3] there appeared a number of advertisements in Southern Sweden offering the services of Mattson and of his colleague, Lindborg, to any who might wish to emigrate to Minnesota during the spring of 1869. Thus, in an advertisement of the Allan line in *Skånska Posten*, February 6, 1869, the local agent for Kristianstad announced that Captain Lindborg, who was conveying his colonists over the Allan line on April 15, had instructed him to make contracts with those who were accompanying him. In March a meeting was announced for all who were traveling with Captain Lindborg to his colony in Minnesota, for the purpose of receiving further instructions and of purchasing tickets from the local agent.[4] The map of Minnesota, showing the lands available in the state, which had been brought to Sweden by Hans Mattson, was deposited with the agent of the Cunard line for the use of prospective settlers, even after Mattson had left for Sweden.[5]

Other states were equally as aware of the great possibilities of development by the introducing of foreign labor and foreign capital; in Maine and in several states, private associations with large capital had been organized. In other states, immigration commis-

[1] *Norrlands Posten* (Gävle), May 18, 1867. The agent advertising was Otto Göthe.

[2] *Jönköpings Tidning*, May 8, 1867, June 5, 1867 ff. Agent advertising was A. Nordström. He was also agent for the National lines, the Montreal Ocean Steamship Company, and the Black Star Line of packets for United States, Canada, Australia, and New Zealand.

[3] There was no mention in *Skånska Posten* (Kristianstad), 1868–69.

[4] *Skånska Posten* (Kristianstad), March 10, 1869, February 6, 1869.

[5] *Ibid.*, July 28, 1869.

sions had been created. Missouri, Kansas, Texas, Oregon, Virginia, Alabama, Georgia, and South Carolina each had their agencies in the United States and in Europe in 1867.[1] Wisconsin and Iowa seemed on the verge of adopting similar measures during the same year, but it was not until 1870 that these states did establish commissions.

Before the Civil War, the southern states had received very little European immigration, with perhaps the exception of Texas, because of the slave labor and the large plantations. In the annual report of the Chamber of Commerce of New York City for 1860–61, it was stated that of the 108,672 immigrants arriving at that port in 1860, only 5,382 went to the slave states, and less than 1,000 to the Gulf states.[2] The competition between the various states for immigrants after the Civil War often led them to attack each other in the state pamphlets that were issued. In the Minnesota state pamphlets of 1865 may be found the following statement:

> The spirit of Southern institutions, seeking to crush free labor and degrade the laborer, repels from those turbulent states the multitudes of honest, intelligent workingmen who are looking to America as the scene of their future labors and to whom the free and unoccupied lands of Minnesota, Kansas, and adjoining territories offer the greatest inducement.[3]

The southern states made efforts, however, to secure for themselves some of the foreign labor and capital that flowed into the United States after the Civil War. Texas, Virginia, Alabama, Georgia, and South Carolina had immigration commissions in 1867. Agents from Virginia and North Carolina were located in New York in 1865 hiring immigrants as agricultural labor. The southern plantation owners had, as yet, not learned how to treat their white labor and were not able to retain them. On May 15, 1865, some twenty-two Swedish immigrants were persuaded by a fellow-countryman to seek employment not far from Richmond.[4] They had been told it was not far from Iowa, their destination. By October the number had increased to several hundred who were resident in a small village which they called Stockholm. In a letter from Olof Brink to his

[1] Minnesota, *Annual Report of Immigration Commission, 1867*, p. 11.

[2] Reprinted in *Minnesota as a Home for Immigrants* (pamphlet), St. Paul, 1865, p. 53

[3] *Ibid.*, p. 54.      [4] *Hemlandet*, September 13, 1865, October 18, 1865.

cousin at Swede-Bend, Iowa, he described their conditions as most deplorable. They were treated like negroes. Their shacks had earth floors; their food consisted of skimmed milk, pork, and cornmeal. They had been promised only $13.00 a month per man for the labor and $8.00 per woman, and were forced to work from sunrise to sunset. Relatives and countrymen, reading about their conditions in the Swedish-American weekly, *Hemlandet*, soon sent these exploited immigrants funds to proceed westward. Another family found themselves under the same conditions at Fairfield, North Carolina.[1]

Louisiana established a Commission of Emigration in 1867. The president of the board spent four months in Europe in 1869, making a tour of England, Ireland, Denmark, Sweden, the various German states, Austria, and France, which were at the time the principal emigrant-furnishing countries.[2] The purpose of this tour was to encourage emigration to the state of Louisiana, which still had 3,000,000 acres of public lands for settlement, and also to re-establish New Orleans as a great port by obtaining competing steamship rates with New York. It was easily accessible to the Middle West by the river boats on the Mississippi. Since 1868, there had been a movement southward of immigrant labor, caused by the fall of the price of wheat and resulting low wages. This labor was primarily German and Scandinavian. Dr. Noyes pointed out, however, that if the South wished to regain its prosperity, it must become used to free white labor and must be willing to break up the large plantations into smaller farms that might be sold to the immigrants.[3] A land-registry office and an employment bureau were established in New Orleans for their use. The methods of advertising the state followed in the footsteps of the other states. Louisiana sought the co-operation of various transportation agencies. The hopes of the state, however, did not materialize.

Even the newly created state of West Virginia joined in this competition for Scandinavian settlers in 1868. It created an office of Commissioner of Immigration in 1864, and four years later its commissioner was recruiting settlers at the port of New York, and had

---

[1] *Ibid.*, July 3, 1866.

[2] Louisiana, *Report of Commission of Emigration, 1870*, p. 17.

[3] *Ibid.*, p. 7.

agents making contracts with emigrants in Europe, but with little more success than Louisiana.[1]

Maine had also entered the field for Swedish emigrants in 1864, when a former American consul in Stockholm, Tefft, had become the agent for the Foreign Emigration Association of Maine.[2] He sent Swedish emigrants to the state as indentured servants. During the same year, W. W. Thomas, Jr., a citizen of Maine, was appointed the American consul of Gothenburg, and according to the reports he sent to his government, he availed himself of every opportunity to encourage emigration from Sweden and Norway.[3] The United States minister to Sweden in 1869, C. C. Andrews, was also from Maine.[4] In 1870 some 114 Swedes emigrated to Maine, and the following year there were 1,000, with 300 more arriving in 1872.[5] These immigrants went chiefly to the Swedish colony called New Sweden, which was formed in 1870.[6] The inducements that were offered to the agriculturists of Norrland if they would settle in New Sweden in Maine were, (1) 100 acres of fertile woodland, (2) free seed and roots for planting, (3) free use of a community house for church and school, (4) free instruction for their children, and (5) purchase of food and agricultural equipment at cost by poorer families, to be paid later by crops or labor. This advertisement stated further that the sum of $10,000 had been appropriated by the state of Maine, but that no free ocean passage would be given. The advertisement had been inserted by the agent of the Inman and Anchor lines and passage was $40.00.

Thomas was appointed commissioner of immigration for the state in 1872, after the passage of "an act to promote immigration and facilitate the settlement of public lands." The Swedish immigrants in Maine paid their own passage and brought a capital of $60,000 in

[1] An extract from the report of the Immigration Commissioner of West Virginia is given on page 9.

[2] *Hemlandet* (Chicago), July 27, 1864.

[3] *U.S. Consular Letters*, Gothenburg, W. W. Thomas, consul, February 12, 1864, September 16, 1864.

[4] U.S. Department of State, *Dispatches from Sweden*, C. C. Andrews, Vol. XI, No. 22, November 3, 1869.

[5] Maine, *Report of the Board and Commissioner of Immigration, 1872*, p. 5.

[6] *Hudiksvalls Posten*, May 13, 1871.

cash, he reported. The immigrants were scattered through the state. Some worked in the great tanneries of Penobscot, others in the slate quarries of Piscataquis, or on the farms, in the mills, in the timber of Penobscot and Aroostock, and upon the railroads of the Cumberland and York. There were 300 Scandinavians in the city of Portland. They furnished labor for families, stores, and workshops in Portland, Bangor, Houlton, Presque Isle, Fort Fairfield, and Caribou. Some of them had come through the efforts of the agent of the Foreign Emigration Association of Maine, Tefft, who was active in Stockholm.[1] Thomas continued,

A colony had been founded in the forests of northern Maine, called New Sweden, and had grown in two years from fifty to six hundred. Each settler was given a lot of one hundred acres. Two shingle corporations were formed entirely on their own capital, and roads were built. A newspaper, *The North Star*, was published at Caribou by E. Winberg with one column in the Swedish language.

The western states were equally as active. On November 23, 1870, a national immigration convention was held in Indianapolis, called by the governors of Minnesota, Iowa, Nebraska, Missouri, Kansas, Michigan, and Wisconsin.[2] They were delegates from twenty-two states, two territories, and the District of Columbia. After two days of discussion, the convention petitioned Congress for legislation to protect emigrants from fraud, and to establish a Bureau of Immigration. President Lincoln, in his address to Congress in 1864, had stressed the need of empowering the federal commissioner of immigration to deal with frauds perpetrated upon immigrants.[3] Earlier the same year, 1870, in May, South Carolina held an immigration convention for the counties of the state at Charleston.

Iowa established a board of immigration in 1871. The Iowa pamphlet entitled, *Iowa: the Home of Immigrants*, was published in English, German, Dutch, Danish, and Swedish.[4] Several agents were

[1] *Hemlandet*, July 27, 1864.

[2] Iowa, *Report of Board of Immigration, 1872*, Legislative Documents, State of Iowa, 1872, p. 11.

[3] Richardson, *Messages and Papers of the Presidents, 1789–1897*, VI, 46.

[4] Iowa, *Report of Board of Immigration, 1872*, Legislative Documents, State of Iowa, 1872, pp. 4–9.

sent abroad, among them Martin N. Clausen who went to Scandinavia in June, 1870, and Theodore K. Hunby in November, 1870. Several of the agents of the board received part of their compensation from different Iowa railroads, and all the agents were given free passage on these trains. The Scandinavian pamphlets unfortunately were destroyed in the Chicago Fire, but Clausen was successful in publishing articles on Iowa in the leading Scandinavian newspapers.[1] Hunby spent most of his time in Norway. Iowa had large Scandinavian colonies in 1870, and continued to receive more recruits from abroad.

By a legislative act of 1869, Michigan created a Board of Immigration Commissioners. That state was largely interested in German immigration and specialized in its agencies there.[2] There were, however, some Scandinavians who settled in the state, attracted as they stopped on their way from Quebec. A picture of the activity of the various agencies in Hamburg and Bremen is given by the Michigan agent. He reported that a large number of agents from the different states of the United States, from Canada, Brazil, and Australia, together with agents of the railroad corporations of the United States were carrying propaganda into Germany, although their agencies were usually of short duration. Louisiana, Virginia, Minnesota, Florida, Nebraska, and Alabama had had agents in Germany, but had abandoned the field.[3] States not represented by agents had their literature in the hands of passenger agents or steamship companies. These were Missouri, Minnesota, Iowa, Wisconsin, Oregon, Nebraska, and Virginia. In 1872 Texas had established an agent at Bremen, and Iowa one at Hamburg.[4] Some of the Swedish emigrants were leaving Europe via Bremen and Hamburg, and undoubtedly came in contact with these various agencies.

The Wisconsin Board of Immigration Commissioners was reestablished in 1871, with Colonel O. G. Johnson, a Norwegian settler, as commissioner. The report of 1872 was very ambitious in that

[1] This statement is made in the Report, *ibid.* No articles appeared in newspapers that were read for this study.

[2] Michigan, *Report of Immigration Commission, 1871-72*, Joint Documents, Michigan, 1872, II, 6-21.

[3] *Ibid.*, p. 21.          [4] *Ibid.*

the county immigrant commissioners had contributed a description of every county in the state. The commissioner stated in the report that he believed in advertising abroad rather than in the eastern states, and of letting contracts for the foreign editions of the Wisconsin pamphlet in Europe.[1] In 1872 pamphlets were printed in England, Germany, Norway, Sweden, and Belgium.[2] The day of emigration by sailing vessels had now practically passed. In his report, Colonel Johnson stated,

> Many of the immigrants, especially from Norway, have heretofore come by sailing vessels to Quebec. The advantage in this has been the much lower rates at which the sailing vessels carry immigrants, but there are a great many disadvantages among which is the greater deprivation. . . . . Latterly, the steamship fares have been very much reduced.[3]

Fewer were arriving by sail and there was a saving of one month in time, as well as less danger from disease because of overcrowding and the unclean state of the vessel.

The state of Minnesota received the largest number of Swedish immigrants of any of the American states, through its advertising from 1865 to 1873. In 1870, it employed the aid of the American Emigrant Company in forwarding settlers to the state.[4] This organization directed 488 persons in one week in July to Minnesota, of which 115 were Swedes. The same year the state received 35,000 emigrants, 22,000 of whom came directly from Europe and 10,000 from Scandinavia.[5] Most of them homesteaded in the Red River region, and in the southern frontier counties. Others took lands in the hardwood timber belonging to the Lake Superior and Mississippi Railroad. During the years from 1866 to 1870, the clerk of the Minnesota Commission of Immigration estimated that the annual exodus from Norway has been 0.86 per cent of its population, and that from Sweden 1.39 per cent.

---

[1] Wisconsin, *Report of Immigration Commission, 1872*, p. 10.

[2] *Ibid., 1873*, p. 7.          [3] *Ibid., 1873*, p. 14.

[4] Letter of S. S. Hamilton, emigrant agent at Chicago for the American Emigrant Company to Governor H. Austin of Minnesota, July 9, 1870, MSS, Minnesota State Historical Library.

[5] Letter of John Schroeder, clerk of Immigration Commission of Minnesota to Governor H. Austin, *Governor's Files No. 608*, MSS, Minnesota State Historical Library. Also in Minnesota, *Annual Report of Immigration Commission, 1872*, pp. 7–8.

The governments of Europe by 1870 had become quite hostile to the emigration of so many of their able-bodied people. The earlier opposition of the Swedish government has been mentioned. Again in 1870, the retiring Swedish chargé d'affaires to the United States, Count Lewenhaupt, in his official report to his government stated that the United States was unfavorable to further immigration.[1] This was extensively published in the Swedish and Norwegian newspapers. The American minister, C. C. Andrews, was instructed by his government to refute the statement in the Scandinavian press, but without letting his name be known. The commissioner of Louisiana found that the European states placed many obstacles in the way of emigration, but no countries except Russia and the Papal Estates actually forbade it.[2] He thought that to refuse it in Germany or France would cause a revolution. The foreign agent of Michigan, who had traveled through Germany, Austria, and Denmark, found it necessary to canvass his prospects personally, owing to the stringent laws against public meetings without license.[3] Minnesota felt in 1870 that agents would only meet with official opposition and the criticism of the foreign press. It was more expedient to send the state pamphlets and to employ the shipping agents in Europe to advertise the state.[4] There was a complete network of shipping agents over every European country, citizens of the respective countries whose business it was to fill their different companies' vessels and steamers with immigrants. "For this purpose they search every hut and parish the year around." Hans Mattson, who had served on the board in Minnesota in 1867 and had been personally in Sweden in 1868, was in 1871 again working for the immigration board. He and Schroeder placed advertisements in the foreign press in the United States and also in the European press, telling of the Minnesota pamphlet. Some 5,700 copies of the Norwegian edition,

[1] U.S. Department of State, *Instructions, Sweden*, 1834–78, March 13, 1871. XIV, 210.

[2] Louisiana, *Report of Commissioners of Emigration, 1870*, p. 22.

[3] Michigan, *Report of Immigration Commissioners, 1871 and 1872*, Joint Legislative Documents, Michigan, 1872, II, 6.

[4] Letter of John Schroeder, clerk of Immigration Commission to Governor H. Austin of Minnesota, 1871, *Governor's Files No. 608*, MSS, Minnesota State Historical Library.

and 2,500 copies of the Swedish were sent through the mails, many directly to Europe.[1]

The railroads were both competing with and aiding the states in securing settlers. Mention has been made of the services of the Milwaukee and St. Paul Railroad in transporting destitute emigrants to Minnesota and of their agencies abroad.[2] Many of the railroads had agents in New York, both to procure labor and settlers. The Illinois Central had maintained such an agency while that road was building. In order to secure settlers, the road donated a piece of land for the Augustana Theological Seminary of the Swedish Lutheran church at Paxton, Illinois, in 1860.[3] It had its effect in that immigrants were reported from Norway and Sweden in 1861.[4] Two years later the road made extensive sales to Swedish settlers.[5] The Swedish settlement at Paxton still remains, although the theological seminary has been removed to Rock Island, Illinois.

When Jay Cooke and Company of Philadelphia were persuaded to take over the construction of the Northern Pacific Railroad in 1871, the corporation began an extensive campaign for colonization on the lands which had been granted by the federal government.[6] A general agent was established at Düsseldorf in Germany with many subagents.[7] Hans Mattson retired from his position on the state board of Minnesota to go to Sweden for the railroad.[8] Unfortunately, with the bankruptcy of the corporation and the panic that followed in its wake in 1873, both the construction of the railroad and further efforts to secure immigration were temporarily suspended.[9] Colonel W. F. Gray, a professional emigrant agent, had procured emigrants for the "Great Pacific Route," undoubtedly the Union

---

[1] Minnesota, *Report of Immigration Commission, 1872*, pp. 7–8.

[2] *Supra*, p. 251.

[3] Olson, *History of the Swedes of Illinois*, I, 346.

[4] *Illinois Central Railroad, Annual Report, 1861*, Report of Land Commissioner.

[5] *Ibid.*, *1863*.

[6] *The Northern Pacific Railroad, Its Route, Resources, Progress, and Business*, issued by Jay Cooke and Company, Philadelphia, 1871.

[7] Michigan, *Report of Immigration Commission, 1871–72*, Joint Legislative Documents, Michigan, 1872, II, 21.

[8] Mattson, *op. cit.*, pp. 124 ff.         [9] *Ibid.*

Pacific, in Europe, as far north as Norway in 1868 and 1869.[1] The Milwaukee, St. Paul and Pacific, and the Superior and Mississippi Railroads were co-operating with Minnesota in securing settlers for the state in 1871.[2] The last two railroads had erected numerous shelter houses for immigrants along their lines, where the new arrivals might remain until they found their friends or decided where to settle. It was estimated that it was possible to bring a man from Northern Europe to Minnesota for from $50.00 to $75.00.[3]

The government of the United States adopted the policy of encouraging immigrants to its shores during the Civil War. The duties of the Commissioner of Emigration, whose office was created in 1864 under the Secretary of State, was to gather full and reliable information about soil, climate, minerals, agricultural products, wages in various parts of the United States, and also the means of communication, the need for labor, and to spread the information in a popular form in Europe.[4] A federal superintendent of emigration was located in New York to aid emigrants to find homes and work. The immigration law of 1864 permitted the formation of contracts by which an emigrant might be brought to the United States and allowed to work off his passage by a year of labor.[5]

At the time of the passage of the act of 1864, the committee on agriculture in the Senate included in its report on February 12, 1864, an acknowledgment of the part played by immigration in building up the Middle West.

> The increase in the inhabitants of the great middle states has been at the rate of 25 per cent during the last decade, while that of the northwest group has been 100 per cent. . . . . The increase in the population of these states is directly due in a great degree to the settlements of immigrants and the whole population of Indiana, Illinois, Michigan, Wisconsin, Iowa, Minnesota, and Kansas added together exceeds only one-tenth of the number of foreign passengers to this country since 1819, to say nothing of their increase by ordinary laws of population.[6]

It was hoped to stimulate further foreign immigration.

[1] Undated newspaper clipping, MSS, Minnesota State Historical Library.

[2] Minnesota, *Report of Immigration Commission, 1872*, p. 7.

[3] *Ibid.*          [4] *Hemlandet*, July 13, 1864.

[5] Committee on Agriculture, *Report on Immigration*, Senate Document No. 15, Thirty-eighth U.S. Congress, first session, p. 5.

[6] *Ibid.*

The committee was confident that foreign emigrants could be persuaded to come for the United States had much to offer. Among the inducements cited were:

(1) the high price of labor and the low price of food, compared with other countries, (2) our land policy, giving to every emigrant after he shall have declared his intentions to become a citizen, a home and a farm, substantially a free gift, charging him less for 160 acres in fee-simple than is paid as the annual rental of a single acre in England, (3) political rights conferred upon persons of foreign birth, (4) our system of free schools, melting in a common crucible all differences of religion, language, and race, and giving the child of the day laborer and the son of the millionaire equal opportunities to excel in the pursuit and acquirement of knowledge. This is an advantage and a blessing which the poor man enjoys in no other country.

There often appeared in the Swedish press warnings against making contracts for labor in Sweden. A letter from Chicago, dated July 28, 1865, and signed William, appeared in the *Hudiksvalls Posten*, September 2, 1865, advising emigrants not to make contracts for labor before they came to the United States. One of the steamship agents, Frederick Nelson in Gothenburg, had made contracts for labor in which a married couple was to receive only $20.00 a month. The correspondent stated that wages in Chicago varied according to the man's ability from $1.75 to $3.00 a day, while the cost of living for a single person was only $4.00 to $5.00 a week. Moreover, some of the emigrant companies in New York changed the immigrant's money, giving him paper for his gold and cheating him of 40 to 43 per cent according to the daily exchange.

A news-item in the *Skånska Posten*, October 9, 1869, related that the American consulate in Stockholm had received a request to hire a landscape gardener and twenty gardeners in Sweden for someone near Chicago who wished to lay out a large estate. The well-known landscape gardener, Asplund, of Stockholm, with three other gardeners had departed while the seventeen were to follow as soon as they received news. There also appeared advertisements of young women who wished to accompany someone to America as maids.[1] In 1867, the United States consul at Stockholm wrote that he had quickly disposed of the one hundred copies of the report of the General Land Office, printed in the

[1] *Jönköpings Tidning*, February 22, 1868.

Swedish language.[1] Again, in 1870, the consular office in Stockholm acknowledged the receipt of six packages of fifty copies each of the Land Office Reports for 1867, poorly translated into the Swedish language.[2] The vice-consul, Nere A. Elfwing, complained that the book was almost unreadable among the class of people in Sweden that would be most benefited by it, namely the agricultural classes who were planning to emigrate and locate on public lands. Fifty copies of the Special Report on Immigration by Edward Young, chief of the Bureau of Statistics, were forwarded in 1871 to the American minister in Stockholm.[3] In this comprehensive pamphlet, Young had made a compilation of conditions in every state, including industries, size and nationality of foreign groups, opportunities for employment, wages, cost of living, etc. It contained a mine of information for anyone expecting to settle in the United States.[4] The federal government, however, refused to expend money for encouraging Swedish emigration.[5]

The distressing conditions in Sweden from 1866 to 1869 and the very large emigration to America flooded the Swedish market with agricultural lands and equipment. There appeared in 1868 in almost every issue of the rural press notices of "America auctions." In *Skånska Posten* for February 8, 1868, there were three such announcements.[6] One Ola Nilsson, a tenant at Råby, at an auction on February 14, beginning at 9 A.M. intended to sell horses, cattle, sheep, and swine; agricultural equipment, wagons, sleds; copper and iron wares, including three stoves; furniture; wool and linen, bedclothes and linens; grain, including rye, barley, oats, peas, and wheat. On the 18th of the same month Crofter Sven Claesson

[1] *U.S. Consular Letters, 1864–70*, Stockholm, Charles A. Perkins, November 2, 1867. Also, U.S. Department of State, *Instructions, Sweden* (1834–78), XIV, 154.

[2] *U.S. Consular Letters, 1870–85*, Stockholm, Nere A. Elfwing, vice-consul, April 15, 1870.

[3] U.S. Department of State, *Instructions, Sweden* (1834–78), June 14, 1871, XIV, 220, No. 74.

[4] Edward Young, *Special Report on Immigration*, 1871.

[5] U.S. Department of State, *Instructions, Sweden* (1834–78), letter from Hamilton Fish to C. C. Andrews in Sweden, June 25, 1873, XIV, 260.

[6] These particular examples are from Southern Sweden, the province of Skåne, but they were common everywhere.

of No. 13 Karstad, expecting to depart for America, intended to auction off his farm animals, agricultural equipment, fishing boat and tackle, etc. The tenant, Per Jönsson of No. 5 Wanneberga, held an auction on February 14 in preparation for his departure for America. The prices received on this glutted market were undoubtedly much less than the actual value.

Frequent advertisements of guidebooks for emigrants, of money exchanges, emigrant hotels, and even clothes for emigrants appeared in the press. A bookdealer in Hälsingborg advertised Bojesen's *Till Amerika*, a guide and adviser for the emigrant, explaining conditions in Minnesota, Iowa, Nebraska, Kansas, Missouri, Texas, and the southern states.[1] *A History of the United States* by Edouard Laboulaye and translated into Swedish was advertised by the famous liberal journalist, L. J. Hjerta, in the Norrland press,[2] while a new edition of Frederika Bremer's book, *Homes in the New World*, was advertised in Småland.[3] Both individuals and banks dealt in money exchange. In *Jönköpings Tidning*, March 11, 1865, there appeared the notice to emigrants, "American dollars in gold exchanged cheap at L. Hjert, Gothenburg." *Hudiksvalls Posten* carried on June 23, 1866, the announcement, "Exchange on America in gold dollars can be received at P. C. Retligt & Co., Gävle. More information may be received at the Filial Bank at Hudiksvall." In Skåne, Kristianstads Enskilda Bank advertised "bills of exchange in dollars on New York, Chicago, Quebec, Washington, and other cities in America,"[4] while Skånes Enskilda Bank announced the sale daily of exchange on New York, Chicago, and San Francisco.[5] *Skånska Posten* carried on March 17, 1869, two special advertisements on clothing for emigrants; one worded, "For Emigrants, suitable boots are sold cheap"; the other, "For Emigrants, . . . . ready made coats . . . . , rain coats, robes," etc.

The panic of 1873 in the United States had the tendency to reduce the current of emigration that has been flowing westward since 1864.

[1] *Skånska Posten* (Kristianstad), March 31, 1869.

[2] *Hudiksvalls Posten*, April 13, 1867.

[3] *Jönköpings Posten*, October 10, 1866. These are just representative. There were many guidebooks of America at all the bookstores.

[4] *Skånska Posten*, May 30, 1868.   [5] *Ibid.*, December 23, 1868, February 12, 1870.

This was accompanied by prosperity in Europe. Even in 1871 this upward swing of the business cycle was noticeable in Sweden. The consular report from Stockholm of January 9, 1872, stated,

The past year has been an unusually prosperous one for Sweden. Good crops for three successive years have not only repaired the fortunes broken by previous bad years, but have added greatly to the capital of the country; an enterprising spirit, such as never existed before, prevails in all branches of trade and industry. Agriculture, commerce, and the iron trade have all benefitted by the good years and have developed as never before.[1]

New railroad lines were being constructed and steamship lines were binding the country with the outside world. Dairy associations were springing up in all parts of the kingdom, and the export of butter and cheese, principally to England and Russia, promised to rival with the export of larger and richer European countries. A large number of corporations with much capital were engaged in the manufacture of iron rails. In April 9, 1873, the report reached the United States that within the two last years £10,000,000 of foreign capital, primarily English and German, had been invested in industrial establishments in Sweden.[2]

The prosperity was general in Europe. An observer in Europe in 1869 stated that never had there been greater progress in commerce, manufacturing, and agriculture than in 1868, and wars and agitations seemed to have ceased in Prussia, Austria, and Great Britain.[3] He did not foresee the War of 1870. Yet never in the history of Europe, with the exception of the year 1854, had emigration been so great as in 1869. The mania of emigration seemed to seize whole communities, and a feverish discontent pervaded the laboring classes. The panic of 1873 temporarily checked this exodus, so that the American states no longer found it necessary to maintain immigration commissions. They were practically all discontinued between 1873 and 1875. The governor of Michigan in his message to the legislature stated that owing to the marked decline of foreign immigration to the United States, and the condition of the labor market, he had closed the immigration office in New York on November

[1] *U.S. Consular Letters, 1870–85*, Stockholm, Nere A. Elfwing, consul, January 9, 1872.

[2] *Ibid.*, April 9, 1873.

[3] Louisiana, *Report of Commissioners of Emigration, 1870*, pp. 19–20.

1, 1873.[1] Wisconsin continued the office until 1875, when the meager immigration coming westward seemed to be diverted to Wisconsin because of the devastation caused by the grasshoppers in western Minnesota and Iowa.[2]

Since the ebb and flow of Swedish emigration did not follow in quinquennial periods, it is thought wiser to consider it in its natural epochs. The years 1868 and 1873 mark a period of exceptionally high emigration, followed by an era of decline from 1874 to 1879. By 1879 the curve began once more an upward swing. During this first period, from 1868 to 1873, the emigration was greatest from Jönköping County, amounting to 12,461 for the United States. In the next period from 1874 to 1879 it had fallen more than fourfold to 2,777.[3] Kalmar County contributed 8,876 inhabitants to the United States from 1868 to 1873, but only 2,460 in 1874–79. Värmland County had for the first time contributed large numbers to the population of the new world, 8,353. This emigration declined somewhat from 1874 to 1879, but made Värmland first in number of emigrants among the Swedish counties, with 3,213. Östergötland, that county of early emigration, ranked fourth from 1868 to 1873 with 7,708, and continued stronger than the counties of Småland during 1874–79, totaling 2,955. Kristianstad County in northern Skåne sent 7,212 emigrants to the United States between 1868 and 1873, and Malmöhus, 4,714. This exodus to the United States from 1874 to 1879 had declined to 2,542 from Kristianstad County and 1,528 from Malmöhus. Gävleborg County, the oldest region of emigration, contributed 5,326 during this period of high exodus and only 801 during the period of agricultural prosperity.

The demand for agricultural workers in Denmark, Norway, and Germany helped to relieve the crisis that Sweden had to meet in 1868. The migration to Norway was a natural one from the Swedish border provinces. Christiania (Oslo) was the economic center of Dalsland, Värmland, and Norrbotten. It was the center toward which the inhabitants of this region naturally went with their pro-

---

[1] Michigan, *Governor J. J. Bagley's Message, January 7, 1875*, Joint Legislative Documents, 1874, p. 29.

[2] Wisconsin, *Report of Immigration Commission, 1875*, p. 3.

[3] "Bygdestatistik," *Emigrationsutredningens bilaga V*, pp. 69*–93*, Table 93.

duce, where they did their trading and enjoyed their holiday in a
large city. Many of the surplus servant class found a demand for
their labor in or around Oslo. The stream from this region was more
or less constant over the Norwegian border.[1] There was negligible

TABLE III

EMIGRATION FROM SWEDISH COUNTIES TO THE UNITED STATES*

1868–73 and 1874–79

| County | 1868–73 | 1874–79 | County | 1868–73 | 1874–79 |
|---|---|---|---|---|---|
| Jönköping | 12,416 | 2,777 | Stockholm City | 2,330 | 806 |
| Kalmar | 8,876 | 2,460 | Göteborg och Bohus | 2,191 | 689 |
| Värmland | 8,353 | 3,213 | Blekinge | 2,036 | 875 |
| Östergötland | 7,708 | 2,955 | Jämtland | 1,373 | 263 |
| Kristianstad | 7,212 | 2,542 | Västernorrland | 1,199 | 534 |
| Älvsborg | 6,118 | 1,810 | Västmanland | 1,176 | 548 |
| Kronoberg | 6,097 | 2,047 | Gotland | 1,104 | 398 |
| Skaraborg | 5,721 | 1,492 | Södermanland | 1,013 | 233 |
| Gävleborg | 5,326 | 801 | Västerbotten | 533 | 133 |
| Kopparberg | 4,858 | 1,882 | Norrbotten | 429 | 403 |
| Malmöhus | 4,714 | 1,528 | Stockholm County | 383 | 155 |
| Örebro | 4,287 | 1,248 | Uppsala | 378 | 164 |
| Halland | 3,949 | 1,597 | | 85,680 | 25,552 |
| Total | 85,680 | 25,552 | Total | 99,825 | 30,753 |

* "Bygdestatistik," *Emigrationsutredningens bilaga V*, pp. 69*–93*, Table 93.

TABLE IV

EMIGRATION FROM SWEDEN TO NORWAY*

| County | 1866–70 | 1871–75 | 1876–80 |
|---|---|---|---|
| Göteborg-Bohus | 1,950 | 2,688 | 2,631 |
| Älvsborg | 1,565 | 1,717 | 2,355 |
| Värmland | 2,118 | 2,182 | 2,257 |
| Norrbotten | 650 | 210 | 218 |

* "Bygdestatistik," *Emigrationsutredningens bilaga V*, pp. 82*, 83*, 85*,
and 93*, Table 43.

emigration from some of the other counties to Norway. Undoubtedly many who left for Norway ultimately found their way across the
Atlantic.

Labor agents were active in the counties of Southern Sweden, procuring agricultural labor for Denmark and Germany. They were

[1] "Svenskarna i utlandet," *Emigrationsutredningens bilaga XX* (Stockholm, 1911),
p. 63.

mentioned by the governor of Kronoberg County in 1870.[1] From Kalmar County, the governor reported in 1870 that 526 men and women, young able-bodied people, had left the district to become servants in those countries through inducements of agents who falsified the conditions of labor.[2] Many returned after a year or two; others were unable to return because they lacked the means. The moral conditions were very bad, since many of the emigrants were girls in their teens. Some were returned with illegitimate children to their communities by the foreign authorities as charges on the poor relief. The province of Skåne sent practically as many emigrants to Germany and Denmark between 1866 and 1870 as to the United States. There was also some exchange, farmers from Denmark and Germany settling in Skåne. The emigration to Denmark from Kristianstad County in 1868 was 451 and in 1869 it was 396, while a large number also left for Germany. From Malmöhus County in 1868 there were 910 emigrants for Denmark as compared with 498 for the United States. In 1869, 887 agricultural workers went to Denmark, and about 600 to Germany.[3]

The development of dairying and agriculture in Denmark created a demand for labor that could not be filled by its own people. It, therefore, gave an opportunity for the Swedish people from the barren and sterile soil of the woodland parishes on the border provinces of Småland, Blekinge, northern Skåne, and Halland.[4] In these regions were no chances for any occupation but agriculture. The farms were only large enough for the labor of the owner, his wife, and his children. There were no industries, nor lumbering, in the earlier days. The people from this region constituted a casual, seasonal labor, returning to Sweden to spend their earnings of the summer in idleness. Many remained in Denmark. Most of the laborers were young and inexperienced, probably only fifteen or sixteen years of age.[5] They were exploited on the Danish estates, in the sugar re-

---

[1] K. bfhde femårsberättelse, Kronobergs län, 1866–1870, p. 2.

[2] Ibid., p. 6.    [3] Ibid., Malmöhus län, 1866–1870, p. 2.

[4] "Svenskarna i utlandet," Emigrationsutredningens bilaga XX, p. 76.

[5] Ibid., pp. 77; Nexø, Pelle the Conqueror (New York, 1917), a Danish novel, also in English translation, gives a good description of this Swedish labor on the Danish island of Bornholm.

fineries, and in the tile mills. The men were mostly unskilled laborers who did the heavy work in the tile mills, in agriculture on the large estates, in construction and foundation works. The women worked in the beet fields, as milk maids on the dairy farms, or as maids in Copenhagen.[1] There were many charges of exploitation and of bad physical and moral conditions.

It is hard to estimate the exact number of Swedish laborers in Denmark, because many went without passports. The statistics that are available, although somewhat underestimating the number, perhaps give some idea of the amount.

TABLE V

EMIGRATION FROM SWEDEN TO DENMARK*

1866–80

| County | 1866–70 | 1871–75 | 1876–80 |
|---|---|---|---|
| Malmöhus............... | 3,436 | 4,000 | 5,445 |
| Kristianstad............. | 1,486 | 1,859 | 2,078 |
| Halland................. | 922 | 730 | 607 |
| Kronoberg.............. | 801 | 569 | 721 |
| Blekinge................ | 518 | 355 | 374 |
| Göteborg-Bohus.......... | 477 | 343 | 393 |
| Kalmar................. | 224 | 148 | 202 |

* "Bygdestatistik," *Emigrationsutredningens bilaga V*, pp. 75*–82*, Table 43.

The emigration of Swedish labor to Northern Germany in the later sixties supplied a need caused by the exodus of German agricultural workers to the United States. Dr. Noyes, the investigator for the state of Louisiana in 1869, stated that there was discontent in Hanover, Holstein, and Schleswig, and other portions of Germany because of the encroachments of Prussia.[2] The mania for emigration seemed to have seized whole communities. Especially in Mecklenburg, whole estates and villages deserted and labor had to be imported from Sweden to cultivate the land.[3] In comparing the conditions of the working classes in various portions of Germany, he said that in Mecklenburg and Holstein the feudal system was still retained and the conditions of the peasants were wretched; while in Prussia,

[1] "Svenskarna i utlandet," *op. cit.*, p. 78.

[2] Louisiana, *Report of Commissioner of Emigration, 1870*, p. 19.      [3] *Ibid.*, p. 20.

on the contrary, the small farm system had prevailed for half a century and the people, especially the working classes, were more prosperous and happy.[1] The Swedish agricultural labor in Germany came from the same regions and the same classes that were employed in Denmark. During 1869, this migration to Germany received much attention in the reports of the Swedish-Norwegian consuls at Lübeck, Kiel, Rostock, and Stettin.[2] During the year, according to the report of the consul at Lübeck, some three or four thousand Swedish agricultural laborers of both sexes came through that city. They had been recruited by two German agents, one at Osby and the other at Hessleholm in Skåne. About 150 had remained in the vicinity of Lübeck, while the others were scattered in Holstein and Mecklenburg. The consul at Rostock estimated a migration of 1,200 through that city, and about 4,000 Swedish laborers in Mecklenburg. There were 3,000 in Schleswig-Holstein, according to the report of the consul at Kiel. The Swedish agricultural laborers in Northern Germany in 1869 totaled at least 7,000.

Typical of the advertisements for Swedish labor for Germany was one that appeared in *Skånska Posten*, February 27, 1869, announcing a demand for five hundred servants.[3] They were to receive annual contracts; for men 100 riksdaler ($26.00), for youths 60 riksdaler ($15.00), for boys just confirmed (fifteen years old) 40 to 50 riksdaler ($10.40 to $13.00). Maids were to receive 60 riksdaler annually and younger girls who must be confirmed, 30 riksdaler ($8.00). The fare from Hessleholm in Skåne to the place of employment in Germany was given free and also 1 riksdaler (26 cents) per day during the journey. It was desirous that applicants should be well dressed and have good recommendations. Another advertisement in 1870 stated that the undersigned had made arrangements with two reliable Germans to obtain positions for Swedish farm labor in Germany that would be guaranteed not to exploit them, nor trade them to factories for labor.[4]

These laborers were exploited to such an extent that the Swedish

[1] *Ibid.*, p. 16.       [2] "Svenskarna i utlandet," *op. cit.*, p. 97.

[3] *Skånska Posten* (Kristianstad), February 27, 1869. The applicants were to leave for Germany in April.

[4] *Malmö Nya Allehanda* (Malmö), May 7, 1870.

consuls felt it necessary to report it to the Swedish government, and the state in turn to warn its citizens. Many came from regions of famine in 1869, and arrived in Germany entirely without means. Some were so weak from hunger and illness that it was impossible for them to work.[1] Swedish labor was advertised in German papers like wares, reported the consul at Kiel. On the Mecklenburg estates, they were overworked, underfed, and underpaid. Many could not endure the hardships and fled to the Swedish consulate where they were given assistance to return home. The emigration declined after 1870, but continued until 1882.

Another type of emigration to Germany was that of students who sought the German universities of Leipzig, Heidelberg, Halle, and Wittenberg, and the artists who studied at Düsseldorf and Munich.[2] There were Swedish engineers and merchants in the Rhineland and in Westphalia. During the same period there was some exchange of population between Sweden and her neighbors, Finland and Russia.[3]

The Swedish emigrant to the United States between 1867 and 1879 found his way often to friends or relatives in the earlier settlements of Illinois, Iowa, Wisconsin, and Minnesota, or to those in the East. Texas received a large contingent between 1868 and 1873.[4] The Kansas settlement which had been slowly developing in the fifties received re-enforcements during the next decade.

A new settlement in Kansas began in 1866 and 1867 in the Smoky Hill Valley. The first Swedish settler in the region was one, A. B. Carlgren, who had formerly owned a large estate in Sweden, but had become bankrupt and had come to America to retrieve his fortune.[5] He settled nine miles south of Salina, Kansas. More Swedish settlers from the older colonies in America, and some directly from Sweden began to appear in 1866 and 1867.[6] They homesteaded and worked

[1] "Svenskarna i utlandet," op. cit., p. 98; Skånska Posten (Kristianstad), September 9, 1868.

[2] "Svenskarna i utlandet," op. cit., p. 95.    [3] Ibid., pp. 89–93.

[4] Norelius, op. cit., I, 38; Hildebrand and Fredenholm, Svenskarna i Amerika (Stockholm, 1924), I, 306.

[5] Skarstedt, Svensk-Amerikanska folket, p. 52.

[6] Alfred Bergin, Femtio års minnen från Lindsborg.

on the Kansas Pacific Railroad construction to obtain capital for their agricultural pursuits.[1] Wages for breaking stone were $4.50 per day. Food was correspondingly high. Corn sold for $4.00 a bushel, but when the land began to produce the price fell to 10 cents a bushel.

The colony increased in membership through the efforts of the Ficot Swedish Agricultural Company organized in Chicago for the purpose of buying land in Kansas and establishing a religious colony.[2] The membership of the company was limited to 100, and each member was to receive 160 acres of land. The qualification for membership was strict adherence to the Swedish Lutheran church. The leaders had heard of droughts in Kansas, but decided that the lands were cheapest there and, if God willed, He would send rain. They purchased a strip of land in Saline and McPherson counties, nine miles long and six miles wide, containing 13,150 acres, for $29,630 from the railroad. The intervening townships were either homesteaded or purchased. The lands were held in common for five years and then divided. Friends and relatives in Värmland were informed of the venture. In 1869, Pastor Olof Olsson came from Värmland, accompanied by 250 persons. They were extremely pietistic and started the cultivation of their new land with prayer. The following year a church was erected and only converted Christians could join. Even the minister's wife had to confess her conversion before the deacons. The colony, however, was soon torn by religious dissension. In 1875 Olsson left to become professor of theology at Augustana College. The lands of the corporation were sold at auction in 1871 to the members of the colony, but the directors resident in Chicago did not disband until 1877.

A Galesburg corporation organized in 1868 joined the Chicago colony and purchased 14,080 acres of land bordering its neighbor.[3] In this instance, each member bought his own land and the corporation was discontinued. In the settlement appear the towns of Lindsborg, Fremont, Assaria, Falun, and Marquette.[4]

Another religious colony of this type was founded by Pastor B.

[1] Skarstedt, *op. cit.*

[2] *Ibid.*, pp. 52–53. Hildebrand and Fredenholm, *op. cit.*, pp. 301–2.

[3] Skarstedt, *op. cit.*, p. 55.    [4] *Ibid.*, p. 57.

M. Halland in southwestern Iowa in 1869. He purchased lands from a railroad corporation, and only Swedish Lutheran members were to join the colony. By 1870 there were enough settlers to found three parishes.[1]

The Nebraska colonies were beginning during the later sixties. Some Swedes came to Omaha to aid in the construction of the Union Pacific Railroad and settled. Land agents persuaded Swedes in Illinois, Iowa, and other older states, to migrate at the end of the sixties, and soon there appeared a settlement at Kearney. Later colonies appeared at Wahoo, Stromsburg, Axtell, Wausau, Holdridge, and Gothenburg.[2]

At Trade Lake, Wisconsin, a colony was started in 1868 by a group of miners from the "Bergslag" region of Sweden. They had emigrated because of the high cost of living, against the advice and warning of their foreman. Prices had risen very high in Sweden because of crop failures. They took their land in the depths of a Wisconsin forest twenty-two miles from a settlement.[3]

As the new lands in the West were opened for settlement, Swedes from the older states began to try their fortune farther west, and the stream of arriving emigrants followed in their wake. Some had drifted into California during the gold rush, but the majority had returned to the older settlements. The earliest Swedish settlers located at San Francisco and Oakland. Many of them were former sailors and sea captains. During the later sixties Captain William Matson was added to the colony, noted as the founder of the Matson Navigation Company, and in 1870, another sailor, Carl Svanberg.[4] Some had penetrated Oregon and Washington before 1870. A settlement was started at Silver Lake in the forests of southwestern Washington that year, and in the two succeeding years Swedes and Finns cleared the land in the forest southeast of Vancouver and earned an income from the salmon fisheries.[5] Settlers from Iowa, Olof Polson and C. J. Chilberg, appeared near La Conner in the Skagit River

[1] *Ibid.*

[2] Joseph Alexis, *Swedes in Nebraska*, Nebraska State Historical Society, XIX, 78–85.

[3] Skarstedt, *op. cit.*, p. 58.

[4] Hildebrand and Fredenholm, *op. cit.*, I, 314 ff.

[5] *Ibid.*, pp. 316 ff.; Skarstedt, *op. cit.*, pp. 63 ff.

region in 1870 and started a colony. Oregon was settled toward the end of the seventies, but Colorado claimed some earlier pioneers. Peter Magnes began the settlement at Denver when he drove overland with his oxen from La Salle, Illinois, and took a homestead.[1]

The Maine colony was a new adventure in the East which was started by the founding of New Sweden in 1870. There were also Swedish settlers introduced at Portland and at Bangor during the following two years. Some of the emigrants, dissatisfied with the opportunities that were found in Maine, moved to Rhode Island when a group were given employment at the Rumford Chemical Works in 1875.[2] Others joined their friends and relatives in Rhode Island and many settled in Providence.

There had been a tremendous decrease in emigration from Sweden to the United States between 1874 and 1879. The period of accelerated exodus from 1868 to 1873 had sent 99,825 Swedish citizens to American shores. The decline to less than one-third between 1874 and 1879 amounted to 30,753. Although the decrease seemed large statistically, people continued to depart from their native land to even a greater extent than during the ten years of exodus between 1851 and 1860, which had been only 14,805. Increasing prosperity in Sweden should have forced the cessation of emigration in 1870, but "America Fever" persisted until the panic of 1873 in the United States checked it. But why did it continue after 1873 to the extent that it did? This can only be explained by the vast stretches of western lands in the United States that were still open for homesteaders, by the agitation of labor contractors, and the subtle influence of friends and relatives in the United States. The steamship companies and railroad companies with their network of agencies continued to distribute "literature" on the great opportunities in America.

In 1878 ended the first epoch of Swedish emigration to the United States, an exodus which had begun in 1840. Sixty-two per cent of the emigration had come from Southern and Western Sweden, that region called Götaland. Another large contributor had been Hälsingland in Norrland; while at the end of the sixties Värmland began

---

[1] Hildebrand and Fredenholm, *op. cit.*, pp. 308 ff.    [2] *Ibid.*, p. 290.

to contribute many emigrants. Sterile Jönköping County had sent 10 per cent of its population, the largest portion during the famine years of 1868–69.

A contemporary discussion of the causes of emigration from Sweden in the later sixties indicated that there had been no great change since the forties with the exception of the agricultural crisis. The obvious causes were economic, a stringency of currency and credit, poor harvests, and perhaps some overpopulation. The article continued,[1]

> For one it is the hysterical longing to free himself from all local fatalities—even climatic conditions play a rôle here; for another it is a baffling economic situation, often self-imposed; for a third it is the unrest that comes from the fact that our social reformers do not drive onward with high pressure like a steam-boat on the Mississippi; for a fourth it is simply the taste for adventure, for it might happen that "I might become a millionaire"; and for the fifth a fifth reason.

Another article in the same newspaper in commenting upon the hundreds of emigrants that were daily passing through the city, stated,

> That it is impossible to blame all the causes of this epidemic of migration on the activities of agents. They lie deeper than that and may be found in all kinds of economic and social maladjustments in the old fatherland, which the wanderers are convinced they will not find in the new world. But the emigrant agents do stimulate the movement, for they attempt in every way to strengthen the faith of the common people in America and condemn conditions at home. The peasant has a child's naïve faith in the miraculous.[2]

[1] *Jönköpings Tidning*, July 4, 1868.   [2] *Ibid.*, April 18, 1868.

# CHAPTER VIII

## THE STRESS AND STRAIN OF THE EIGHTIES

The agricultural prosperity that Sweden had enjoyed since 1850 came to an end in 1879. Sweden's quota of emigrants had aided in opening up the great wheat fields of Northwestern America whose fruits began to flow with such abundance into the European markets, undermining completely European agriculture by the eighties.

This agricultural depression was felt in all of Northern and Western Europe during the period from 1880 to 1896. It was due primarily to the cultivation of cheap virginal lands in the United States, Canada, Argentina, India, Australia, and even in the European regions of Russia and the Baltic. With the new agricultural inventions like the harvester introduced in the United States in 1872, and the binder in 1880, it was possible to cultivate large areas with a small amount of labor. The most important factor in marketing the grain from these new regions was the falling freight rates, both rail and water. It was during this period of 1870–1890 that, for the first time, it became possible to transport bulky articles for any distance. Railways had increased and competition for business had forced the reduction of freight rates to less than half. Steamship lines had also increased in number, and continued to build more and larger vessels, with increasing speed, and here again competition brought cheaper rates. This decline of freight rates substituted for a local wheat exchange a world market. The price of wheat on the English market fell correspondingly to the decline in freight rates. The average price of wheat in England 1871–75 was 54s. 8d. per quarter, in 1881–85 an average of 40s. 1d., and 27s. 11d. in 1891–95.[1] The financial depression that followed the adoption of the gold standard in 1873 and the decline in gold production, by some economists, has also been cited as a cause for the decline in wheat prices.[2] However,

---

[1] Ogg, *Economic Development of Modern Europe* (New York, 1918), p. 165. [2] *Ibid.*

that seems a minor factor compared with the rôle which supply and demand played in the vast quantities of cheap grain from these new regions of the world. It was possible to produce grain at a cost which could undersell the domestic grain in the home markets of the countries of Northern and Western Europe.

The agricultural depression resulted in the complete undermining of the English farmer and a more thorough industrialization of England, who continued her free-trade policy. In Germany, the agricultural depression had begun as early as 1873, through the competition of American and Russian grain, and the increasing scarcity of

TABLE VI

REDUCTION OF TRANSPORTATION RATES ON A BUSHEL OF
WHEAT BETWEEN CHICAGO AND LIVERPOOL IN
1869–1905*

|  | Chicago to New York, Lake and Rail (Cents) | New York to Liverpool (Cents) | Total Chicago to Liverpool (Cents) |
|---|---|---|---|
| 1869.......... | 25.00 | 11.75 | 36.75 |
| 1885.......... | 9.02 | 6.37 | 15.39 |
| 1905.......... | 6.44 | 3.25 | 9.69 |

* F. A. Ogg, *Economic Development of Modern Europe* (New York, 1918), pp. 164–65. Also see *Statistical Abstract of the United States, 1922,* p. 325. These are the rates by lake and rail from Chicago to New York. Beginning with 1915, freight rates have risen considerably.

farm labor and rising wages, the result of emigration to the cities and to America. Germany entered the field of protectionism in tariff of 1879.[1] The demands for increased agricultural protection were met in the tariffs of 1885 and 1887. After 1887, prices of foodstuffs ceased to decline and never fell to the low level of the nonprotectionist or low tariff countries like England and Holland. France also turned to tariff as a protection against the new competition. The tariff law of 1892 did much to safeguard French agriculture.[2]

Denmark with her small area and her great industrial concentration was able to change her form of agriculture most successfully into the production of dairy products.[3] In Sweden, the situation was

[1] *Ibid.*, pp. 303–6.    [2] *Ibid.*, p. 195.

[3] A very good discussion of the European situation may be found by Sundbärg, *Emigrationsutredningen betänkande*, pp. 177–80.

gradually changed by the transition from a grain-producing agriculture to dairying, by the industrialization of the country, and by the protection of tariff laws.

In the eighties a large majority of Sweden's population was still agricultural, 67 per cent.[1] The agricultural crisis therefore was especially depressing. The high marriage and birth-rate in Sweden in the sixties had now produced a surplus of young energetic people who seemed to see no possibilities for the future in their homeland and who joined in the greatest exodus that the country has ever experienced.

Agricultural prices for all kinds of grain fell the lowest in fifty years.[2] The annual harvests remained very good. In 1881 and 1889 the harvests were poor, but during 1882, 1884, and 1890, they were unusually good.[3] There was a decline in the new acreage that was annually placed under cultivation. The entire crop of grain had increased only 8 per cent over the previous decade, the smallest increase since 1830. The export of grain sank below the import and removed Sweden from the world's grain-exporting countries. But dairying products were beginning to take the place of grain export. With the invention of the de Laval cream separator, the export of butter rose from eight million pounds annually in the seventies to thirty million in the eighties.[4] The cultivation of the sugar beet became another promising enterprise for the recovery of agriculture.

The decade was not barren of attempts to improve agricultural conditions. The organization of the corporation "Separator" for the manufacture of cream separators aided to revolutionize both domestic and foreign dairies. The Swedish Dairy Exports Association was organized in 1888. The Dairy Association had started a decade before. The fen-culture association (*Mosskultur föreningen*) began its work of draining marshlands in 1886. The agricultural school at Svalöv opened its doors the same year. It was also the decade for the organization of rural agricultural schools (*landtmannaskolorna*). All restrictions on the sub-divisions of farms (*hemman*) were re-

[1] Wohlin, "Den jordbruksidkande befolkningens utveckling i Sverige," *Emigrationsutredningens bilaga IX*, p. 4, Table A.

[2] See Appendix, p. 503          [3] Sundbärg, *op. cit.*, p. 181.

[4] *Ibid.*, p. 182. The de Laval separator was a Swedish invention.

moved. The number of farms materially increased, although some became very small as to size.

The need for further protection for agriculture finally forced Sweden to change from the free-trade policy she had accepted in 1858 to a protective tariff in 1888.[1] The issue was bitterly fought in the Riksdag, opposed by the Liberals and the working classes. But it seemed the only way to save the agricultural situation in the domestic market.

It was the coincidence of economic depression in the industries of Sweden as well as in agriculture that made the early years of the eighties reach the maximum of Swedish emigration. The American consul at Gothenburg wrote to his government the following report on October 1, 1879:[2]

The year ending June 30, 1879, has been characterized by great commercial and industrial depression. . . . . The high prices for iron and timber prevailing during the flush times of four or five years ago induced an abnormal development in the industries, accompanied by a popular craze for the building of railways, most of which were many years in advance of the needs of the country; the great ease in money and the general prosperity of the commercial classes induced the formation of many stock companies for these and similar purposes. At the high tide of this mania for development came a great falling off in demand and consequent depression in prices of iron, lumber, and oats.

In November, 1878, there were many failures among the iron merchants followed by others in the lumber exporting and banking business. Messrs. N. W. Höglund and Company and Messrs. Godenius and Company of Stockholm, two of the oldest firms in the country and reputed among the wealthiest, failed in January, 1879. This was followed by the failure of Göteborgs Handelskompani, the largest financial institution in Gothenburg.[3] The Handelskompani's failure was attributed to advances to timber companies, small railroads, and manufacturing concerns, but primarily to its loans to the "Bergslag" railroad which intersected mining and timber districts.

[1] *Ibid.*

[2] *U.S. Consular Letters, 1864–88*, Gothenburg, Ernest L. Oppenheim, consul, October 1, 1879. Emigration has been attributed to the lack of capital in Sweden. It is interesting to note here that it seems to be overspeculation and a declining world market that caused the greatest emigration.

[3] *Ibid.*

The largest export from Sweden was oats. The export of this grain had risen from 1851 to 1860 with an annual average of 42,626 metric tons, to 138,105 metric tons from 1861 to 1870, and 240,527 in the period of 1871–80.[1] Some regions of Sweden, particularly Dalsland and Värmland, were raising oats year after year. The declining price of oats in the London market, and of other grains, brought on an agricultural crisis. Oats fell steadily from 45 cents a bushel in 1871–75, to 32 cents in 1886–90. Then the price began to rise, but the export of oats from Sweden was on the decline.[2]

In the latter half of the decade, the Swedish industries recovered with rising prices of iron and lumber. The year 1888 has been designated as the point at which agricultural Sweden definitely decided upon an industrial future. Electricity, the white coal of Sweden, was being introduced. Härnösand on the coast of Bothnia was the first city in Europe to instal electric street lights.[3] During the decade the number of people engaged in industry and mining rose from 810,000 to 1,087,000, while those in agriculture fell in numbers from 3,078,-000 to 2,915,000.[4] Commerce was also expanding. In world commerce it was a dull decade, the expansion being less than any ten years since 1815, only 12 per cent. Swedish commerce, however, increased 30 per cent. The Swedish Export Association was established in 1887.[5]

Emigration from Sweden during the pessimistic years of the eighties seemed stupendous for a country with such a small population.

TABLE VII*

| | | | |
|---|---|---|---|
| 1881 | 47,634 | 1887 | 46,901 |
| 1882 | 51,629 | 1888 | 46,252 |
| 1883 | 30,612 | 1889 | 28,356 |
| 1884 | 21,005 | 1890 | 28,691 |
| 1885 | 18,050 | | |
| 1886 | 28,155 | Total | 347,285 |

* *"Utvandringsstatistik," Emigrations-utredningens bilaga IV*, p. 155, Table 48.

The year 1882 marked the highest point of Swedish exodus. The decade of the eighties had the same significance of producing the

[1] *Emigrationsutredningens betänkande*, p. 101, Table 29.

[2] Sundbärg, *Sweden, Its Resources and Its People* (Stockholm, 1904), p. 535.

[3] It was in 1885 (*Emigrationsutredningens betänkande*, p. 184).

[4] *Ibid.*        [5] *Ibid.*, p. 185.

largest number of emigrants that Sweden has ever sent from her shores. The emigration, however, was in proportion equally as high from the other countries of Northern and Western Europe, although lower than the contributions from Southern and Eastern Europe since 1900.

There was no county in Sweden that did not send several thousand emigrants to the United States during the eighties. The population of Sweden during the decade amounted to 4,673,225. About 6.9 per cent of the entire population emigrated to the United States within the ten years. There was also a continuation of emigration to Denmark, Norway, and Germany, which made the figures of emigration 376,401. But America was the land of opportunity and of prosperity, and it was natural that, with the easy means of communication and low passage-rates, all who could, would seek the more distant land.

### TABLE VIII

EMIGRATION TO THE UNITED STATES BY COUNTIES,* 1881–90

| | | | |
|---|---|---|---|
| Stockholm City | 13,739 | Göteborg och Bohus | 11,679 |
| Stockholm County | 2,814 | Älvsborg | 27,866 |
| Uppsala | 2,280 | Skaraborg | 21,926 |
| Södermanland | 4,250 | Värmland | 28,084 |
| Östergötland | 23,731 | Örebro | 13,982 |
| Jönköping | 23,136 | Västmanland | 4,562 |
| Kronoberg | 17,404 | Kopparberg | 12,105 |
| Kalmar | 22,900 | Gävleborg | 9,835 |
| Gotland | 4,484 | Västernorrland | 5,484 |
| Blekinge | 7,953 | Jämtland | 4,567 |
| Kristianstad | 18,345 | Västerbotten | 2,044 |
| Malmöhus | 21,974 | Norrbotten | 2,712 |
| Halland | 16,429 | Total | 324,285 |

* "Svenskarna i utlandet," *Emigrationsutredningens bilaga XX*, p. 112, Table 13.

The largest amount of the emigrants came from the agricultural classes, although there was quite a large percentage also from the industrial groups, chiefly from the city of Stockholm and the county of Malmöhus. The exodus of agricultural laborers, which included the sons and daughters of landowners, was phenomenal in the counties of Älvsborg, Skaraborg, Värmland, and Halland, all counties of Western Sweden. There was also a large emigration of cotters from

Värmland and Dalsland, from the region that had been purchased by the lumbering corporations. Servants of the agricultural labor class were most numerous among the emigrants from the two Skåne counties, and from the Småland counties, Östergötland, and Värmland. The numbers of seamen leaving Sweden were especially large in the county of Kalmar, which included Öland, and in Gothenborg-Bohus County, the western port of Sweden. From the Norrland counties the exodus consisted chiefly of landowners, probably discouraged by the encroachments of the lumber corporations into that region.

In 1880, the American consul at Stockholm reported that "every steamer bound to German ports takes out emigrants, and a member of the Swedish parliament stated there a few days ago that, according to a careful estimate, fully 40,000 people would this year emigrate from Sweden to America, carrying with them a capital of at least $6,000,000."[1] By 1882, emigration had reached such a height that the government, the farmers, and manufacturers complained and demanded that the Riksdag stop the alarming exodus of the laboring class, for it would be impossible to carry on industry without them.[2]

The emigrants as described by the American consuls "were to a great extent small husbandmen or miners, with their families."[3] From the cities they consisted, for the most part, of mechanics and maid-servants. Nearly seven-tenths of those emigrating received either sufficient money or full-paid tickets from their prosperous relatives or friends in the United States. At least 50 per cent of the emigrants returned to visit their native land "for the laudable purpose of persuading their relatives and friends to emigrate to the United States." Only a small percentage of the emigrants were clerks, engineers, and architects.[4]

It was reported in 1885 that it was a common practice in Sweden to ship to the United States, paupers and criminals who had served their terms in workhouses and prisons, but who were still under

---

[1] *U.S. Consular Letters, 1870–85*, Stockholm, Nere A. Elfwing, consul, April 14, 1880.

[2] *Ibid., 1864–88*, Gothenburg, Sidney W. Cooper, consul, March 31, 1882.

[3] *Ibid.*, March 10, 1882.

[4] *U.S. Consular Letters, 1886–93*, Stockholm, Elfwing, September 12, 1888.

political disabilities, like the right to vote.[1] "Funds for the purpose were furnished in a clandestine manner by municipalities as well as by individuals." The consul at Stockholm, in answer to a circular letter from the State Department, stated that he knew that some years previous to 1888 a philanthropic society assisted liberated prisoners to go to America.[2] Only those who showed signs of improvement were given aid. A more difficult thing to control was the aid given by communities to pay the voyage of paupers. It is difficult to determine to what extent aid of this type was given.

In commenting upon the decline of population in his county during 1879 and 1880, and the great increase in emigration, the governor of Älvsborg County, to which Dalsland belonged, made the following remarks on the causes of emigration from that region.[3]

The decline of population is caused by emigration from the county. The emigrants are cotters and crofters, with small pieces of land, or day laborers, which are either employed in the factories or in home industries like sloyd and weaving. With the stagnation of industry, they leave the country, through the encouragement and often by the means furnished through friends in America. The small landowners are also leaving their farms and seeking their fortunes in foreign lands.

The cause of this emigration is the unemployment that has followed the cessation of railroad construction and the desire to get away from poverty. It is not merely the flippant desire for change, nor the encouragement and boasting of agents, friends, and relatives from America that have persuaded so many to leave, for frequently well-to-do people with quiet steady dispositions leave their old homes for the unknown on the other side of the ocean. The emigrants make the statement that the possibility of obtaining their livelihood in the homeland becomes more difficult every year, and that they think it will be easier in the new land. Emigration is only one of the consequences of a stagnant and blind domestic economy. The crisis in the mining and iron industries, the idleness of sawmills and factories, the undermining of the home industries by foreign competition; for example, the production of hats, caps, musical instruments, etc., have caused unemployment. The Swedish market is flooded with foreign-made goods.

According to the reports of the Department of Commerce for 1879, the activities of the factories and manufacturers within the kingdom during the five year period had decreased from 173,000,000 kronor to 134,000,000 kronor, al-

[1] *Ibid.*, *1864–88*. Gothenburg, Sidney W. Cooper, consul, November 26, 1885.

[2] *Ibid.*, *1886–93*, Stockholm, Nere A. Elfwing, September 12, 1888.

[3] *K. bfhde femårsberättelse, Elfsborgs län, 1875–1880*, p. 2. Eric Sparre, governor (translated).

most one-fourth, and workmen have decreased by 8,000. The cultivators of the soil miss the demand for their products from the industrial workers. The slack of industrial labor is not being taken up by other industries and this laborer does not desire to become an agriculturalist. Many who have become used to the higher wages paid to the industrial workmen long for the fresh pulsating life in America. The rich opportunities for earning money is a mighty temptation that draws them there when they read descriptions of America and compare them with poverty and sacrifices at home. The breeze of freedom and equality which comes from the great land on the other side of the Atlantic fills the soul of many an industrious worker with hope for a brighter future, when he feels the power of ambition and hopes for a future in a land where labor is valued, unconditioned by social status. The only effective means of combating emigration is to move America over here, everything that makes its greatness, its domestic economy. It is by developing this life, by the rearing of the kingdom's children to usefulness, initiative and self-confidence, through opportunities for labor and vision of progress that one can hope to persuade them to remain in the homeland and give their efforts to the service of the fatherland.

Governor L. W. Lothigius, of the same county, in his report for 1881–85, stated that it was the enticing pictures of economic and social betterment portrayed by emigrants in America and agents in even the remote rural districts that were responsible for emigration. He found that from no region within his county was there a statement that anyone had emigrated because of fear of increased military service or discontent over the absence of political rights. The governor of Östergötland, another county that had large numbers of emigrants, agreed with the governors of Älvsborg County as to the causes of emigration. While it was reported that from 1871 to 1875[1] good crops and an increase in industry, which had produced good wages and plenty of work, had caused a decrease in emigration, the report of 1876–80[2] and 1881–85[3] of poor crops and a crisis in industry with accompanying lower wages and unemployment had increased emigration. This was coupled with the desire of the laborers to better conditions and become more independent than the opportunities at home permitted.[4] Invitations from America, often with tickets and money from relatives and friends, and the activities of agents kept America constantly before their eyes as an eldorado.[5] Most

---

[1] *Ibid., Östergötlands län, 1871–1875*, p. 2.

[2] *Ibid., 1876–1880*, p. 2.          [4] *Ibid., 1876–1880*, p. 2.

[3] *Ibid., 1881–1885*, p. 4.          [5] *Ibid., 1881–1885*, p. 4.

of the emigrants were young men and women either out of employment or seeking higher wages. A few farmers, and merchants, etc., who had been unfortunate in business ventures at home, thought the future brighter in America. There were a few lawbreakers and others who had made mistakes that brought the ostracism of the community upon them. The circulation of American papers in the Swedish language which told about conditions in the United States was a big influence.[1]

Although wages had been rising in Sweden during the period from 1850 to 1880, they could not compare with those in the United States. Most of the emigrants were male agricultural laborers. Wages which had reached the height of 2.01 kronor, or 54 cents, a day during the summer of 1873 to 1875, began to fall with the declining prices of grain and hovered around 1.50 kronor, or 40 cents, from 1878 to 1889. They did not reach 2 kronor or 53 cents again until 1898. This did not include food or lodging.[2] Women's wages were usually about one-half. For a year's contract as hired man, where room and board was given as part of the wage, an agricultural laborer earned 125 kronor, or $33.50.[3] In the United States he was beseeched from the time he landed to work for farmers at from $20.00 to $25.00 a month for an eight-month year. The other four months he usually received only room and board.[4] The agricultural laborer did not necessarily continue in that capacity in the new land. Railroad construction was offering $1.25 to $2.00 a day with room and board at $4.00 to $4.50 a week.[5] J. E., an emigrant in 1886, worked in Stockholm in 1885 as a laborer and received 20 öre an hour for a twelve-hour day, or 2.40 kronor a day, about 65 cents. He paid 30 kronor a month for food and 5 kronor for lodging.[6] In the Pennsylvania coal mines he earned $40.00 a month and paid out $15.00 for food and lodging in 1887.

[1] *Hemlandet*, published in Chicago as early as the sixties, boasted of its increasing circulation in Sweden.

[2] *Emigrationsutredningens betänkande*, p. 107, Table 32.

[3] "Utvandrarnes egna uppgifter," *Emigrationsutredningens bilaga VII*, pp. 175–76, No. 203.

[4] *Ibid.*, p. 171, No. 197.

[5] *Ibid.*, p. 173, No. 200.          [6] *Ibid.*, p. 177, No. 205.

Although wages were low in the United States in 1880, as compared with today, the real wages were much higher than those in Sweden. It was possible to accumulate a sum of money faster in the United States, if you were willing to work. The maid-servants were particularly poorly paid, and are today as compared to the United States, while in the rural districts their work was extremely heavy and disagreeable. The wages paid in the United States seemed a fortune to them.

The facilities for travel and the inducements as portrayed in the many-colored folders and by the numerous emigrant agents of steamship lines, railroads, and the American states, made it easy to decide to seek the new world, even if the cause was not a pressing economic factor. The board of immigration of the state of Minnesota was reorganized in 1879. Among the various languages in which pamphlets were being published, Swedish was still an important one.[1] Applications for assistance and encouragement from charitable associations in Europe, among them the Danish Colonization Society of Copenhagen, to colonize destitute people in the new states of the United States were neither answered nor discouraged.[2] However, the report of the immigration board in 1879, stated, "It would not be understood as having discouraged the immigration of poor people, for this is the class for which our public land system was especially designated and upon which frontier settlements must mainly depend." The state board reported in 1885–86 that outside of the United States, there were now few inquiries received about Minnesota, except from Germany, and these were less numerous than in 1883–84.[3] In 1882, Wisconsin, Iowa, and Missouri also had immigrant departments and Michigan expected to establish one.[4] By 1885 the Dakotas were bidding for emigrants.

The state of Wisconsin had re-established its board of immigration in 1879. It was advertising in newspapers in England, Germany, the Scandinavian countries, and Switzerland. In Sweden, its advertisements were appearing in *Allehanda för Folket*, published at

---

[1] Minnesota, *Annual Report of Immigration Commission, 1881*, p. 4. See also *1881–82*.

[2] *Ibid., 1881*, p. 6.

[3] *Ibid., 1885–86*, p. 6.          [4] *Ibid., 1881–82*, p. 8.

Örebro.[1] State pamphlets in English, German, and the Scandinavian languages were issued for distribution. An agent of the Wisconsin Central Railroad, K. K. Kennan, represented the state abroad.[2] In 1882, it was reported that other states had numerous active, aggressive, well-paid agents in the field who did not scruple to misrepresent Wisconsin and decry the superior inducements which she offered to emigrants.

The land grant railroads were vigorously advertising the opportunities of settlement in the western states. The Northern Pacific, which was at last under construction, had agents in Europe. The general European agent who was located at Liverpool visited Sweden, Norway, Denmark, Switzerland, and the North German ports, and made arrangements with local agents to forward emigrants to points on the Northern Pacific lines.[3] Satisfactory arrangements had been made in Denmark with the only company running a direct line of steamers to the United States. It was reported that these efforts had the result of sending large numbers of industrious and thrifty people from foreign countries to the Northern Pacific territory. A large portion of the laborers employed in the construction work on the Yellowstone Division were Scandinavians and Germans who settled along the road as soon as it was completed, and aided in the development of the region.[4] By 1883, the railroad had besides its numerous agencies in the British Isles, 124 general agents on the continent, in Norway, Sweden, Denmark, Holland, Switzerland, and Germany.[5] They were supplied with publications which were distributed through subagencies in the small towns and villages. During the year of 1882–83, there had been distributed 635,590 copies of Northern Pacific publications, including pamphlets, cards, posters, etc., in the English, German, Swedish, Dutch, Danish, and Norwegian languages, and regular monthly editions of the *Northwest*, a newspaper.

This advertisement reaped a large reward for the Northwest. It was reported that the number of passengers booked for points on the

[1] Wisconsin, *Annual Report of the Board of Immigration, 1880*, p. 6.

[2] *Ibid., 1882*, p. 11.

[3] *Northern Pacific Railroad, Annual Report, 1882*, p. 35.

[4] *Ibid.*, p. 35.        [5] *Ibid., 1883*, p. 22.

Northern Pacific during 1882–83 by the seven Liverpool steamship companies was 1,172, and this did not include the passengers on other steamship lines.[1] There were forty-eight steamship lines connecting European and American ports at the time. The railroad was also using European newspapers for advertisement, notices of its lands appearing in forty newspapers in Germany, Norway, Sweden, and Denmark, alone.[2] In 1887, it was reported that because of the failure of the wheat crop in the Dakotas, immigration was falling off in that region but increasing in Washington territory.[3] With the opening of the lumbering region in Washington, the increase of population in one year, 1887–88, was 30,000.[4]

Most of the Swedish emigrants traveled over the Gothenburg-Hull-Liverpool route to America, and some over the German and Danish lines. The facilities of travel from Sweden were further improved by two steamship lines that by 1884 furnished direct passage between Gothenburg and New York. The German Lloyd of Bremen and the Wilson Company of Hull sent ships monthly between the two ports.[5]

During 1878, when emigration had fallen off considerably in certain rural portions of Sweden, e.g., in Östergötland, steamship companies' advertisements had a small space in the local press and only a few advertised at all. Thus, in *Östgöta Correspondenten* there appeared no advertisement of steamship lines during the year of 1878 until March 23, when a small one of the National lines of which Frederick Nelson was agent, was found.[6] On April 4 the Anchor line had a small notice in the same paper. In the spring of the following year, the White Star line ran a large and conspicuous advertisement in the paper, announcing transportation to Australia and America.[7] With the great increase in the exodus of rural population in 1881 and 1882, the steamship companies again advertised extensively as they

---

[1] *Ibid.*, p. 23.   [3] *Ibid.*, *1887*, pp. 72–73.

[2] *Ibid.*, p. 38.   [4] *Ibid.*, *1888*, p. 49.

[5] *U.S. Consular Letters, 1864–88*, Gothenburg, Sidney W. Cooper, consul, January 11, 1884.

[6] *Östgötha Correspondenten, Östergötlands läns Tidning och Allmänna Annosblad*, March 23, 1878.

[7] *Ibid.*, April 10, 1879.

had in the period of 1868–70. Among the advertisements inserted in the *Östgöta Correspondenten* in 1882 and 1883 were the following: the Anchor,[1] the Thingvalla,[2] the State,[3] the Guion,[4] the Dominion,[5] the National,[6] the Bremen,[7] the Monarch,[8] and the American lines,[9] nine in all. Most of these companies had local agents at Linköping or Motala, as well as agents in Gothenburg. In *Göteborgs Handels-och Sjöfarts-Tidning*, the leading commercial paper of Gothenburg, the port most of the emigrants passed, there appeared in 1879 advertisements of the Allan, the Anchor, the Guion, the White Star, and the Wilson lines.[10]

In 1884, government records showed that there were in Sweden sixteen general steamship agents located principally in the three leading ports of Stockholm, Malmö, and Gothenburg. They represented the Cunard, the Anchor, the American, the Kron, the Allan, the Inman, the White Star, the State, the Dominion, the National, the Norddeutscher Lloyd, and the Scandinavian-American (formerly the Thingvalla lines).[11] These general agents under the law of 1884 had to be Swedish subjects under a heavy bond to the government as a guaranty that the contracts made with the emigrants would be fulfilled. There were many agents scattered throughout the rural districts and the smaller towns. As time went on some steamship lines went out of existence and others entered into the competition. Thus a general agent for the Red Star line appeared in 1890, for the Guion line in 1891, and the Baver line in 1892. The Hamburg-American line established a general agent at Gothenburg in 1904, and the Canadian Pacific in 1908. The report of the Swedish Emigration Commission in 1909 stated that there were 11 general agents and 177 subagents for steamship companies in Sweden in 1907.[12] The Cunard line had

---

[1] *Ibid.*, February 16, 1882.

[2] *Ibid.*, February 18, 1882, Feb. 15, 1883, Mar. 1, 1883.

[3] *Ibid.*, February 18, 1882, Feb. 20, 1883.

[4] *Ibid.*            [7] *Ibid.*, February 27, 1883, March 24, 1883.

[5] *Ibid.*, April 8, 1882.            [8] *Ibid.*, March 1, 1883.

[6] *Ibid.*, February 17, 1883.            [9] *Ibid.*, March 6, 1883.

[10] *Göteborgs Handels-och Sjöfarts-Tidning*, March 4, 1879, May 20, 1879, May 21, 1879.

[11] "Utvandringsväsendet i Sverige," *Emigrationsutredningens bilaga II*, p. 36.

[12] *Ibid.*, pp. 40, 50.

71 subagents alone, the Scandinavian-American line, 42, and the White Star line, 39. The largest number of agents were scattered through Gothenburg-Bohus, Malmöhus, Kristianstad, Jönköping, Kalmar, Halland, and Älvsborg counties. In Stockholm, Uppsala, and Örebro counties there were no agents. This network of agents distributing literature about the New World proved a great encouragement to emigration.

It was thus a very simple thing to obtain all the literature one could carry from the steamship and railroad agents in any of the larger towns in Sweden in the eighties. It was equally as simple a matter to purchase a ticket to any destination in America, if your friends or relatives had not already sent you a prepaid ticket. If the emigrant had no friends or relatives in America, and had no definite idea as to his destination, the agent would decide the matter for him. It was usually a long ways inland, so that the agent's commission would be large. J. J., an emigrant in 1880, tells of going to Gothenburg with a neighbor boy who had also decided to visit America. Neither had relatives nor friends there, and both were in their teens. Not knowing the best place to go, the agent advised them that Lindsborg, Kansas, was desirable, and sold them a ticket to that destination.[1]

The period of the eighties was marked by much ferment in Sweden. The struggle over the abandonment of the free-trade policy, that had been established in 1858–65, for the protectionist program that most Europe was adopting in 1880, became a heated debate. It was opposed by the Liberals and the Social Democrats, it split the Agrarian party into fragments, and divided in fact the whole country into two political camps, Protectionists and Free Traders. By a very narrow margin, resulting from the seating of the Protectionists on the Stockholm bench when the Liberals were forced by court measure to evacuate their seats due to an obscure disability of one member, the Protectionists finally won in 1888. It was felt by the latter that in order to save agriculture tariff was needed. The workmen of the cities were especially opposed to the rise in the cost of living that would result. There was launched a protectionist

[1] Personal interview.

policy for Sweden's infant industries in 1892. The height of protection was reached in 1895.[1]

The passing of tariff laws protected the home market for Swedish wares, but it did not aid the international situation or the world market where the surplus goods had to be sold. Agriculture shifted from a grain culture to dairy production; while the manufactured products, lumber and iron, recovered with a better world market in the later eighties. The passing of the tariff laws perhaps did not directly affect the exodus, but many an emigrant left the mother country with the conviction that with tariff duties added, it would be extremely hard in the future to make a living wage. One emigrant gave as reasons for departing

the thought of the future of myself and my family, the constantly rising cost of living, with tariff on the necessities of life and articles of clothing, the impossibility for one to give his children an education, which the times demanded of a man who wished to improve his position, military service, the difficulties for a poor workman to obtain his own home.[2]

He was the son of a sailor and worked in a sugar factory in Malmöhus County until he emigrated in 1895.

The establishment of the Liberal Club, Verdandi, at the University of Uppsala[3] and the organization of the Social Democratic party among the working classes of Sweden, led by young university students, indicated a change in the times in Sweden during the decade.[4] Hjalmar Branting, destined to be the great Social Democratic solon and prime minister of the country, and former member of the Verdandi, besides his duties as parliamentary reporter for one of the Stockholm dailies, was the editor of *Social-Demokraten*.[5] Axel Danielson, who had also spent some time at Uppsala, went as a young littérateur to Stockholm. He was the first editor of *Social-Demokraten*,

[1] Guinchard, *Sveriges Land och Folk*, II, 505–6. For the political side see Boëthius, *Oskar II*, *Sveriges historia till våra dagar*, Vol. XIII, Part II, chap. i. From the point of view of the Social Democrats (Magnusson, *Social-demokratien i Sverige* [Stockholm, 1921], I, 115–16).

[2] See J. B., emigrant, No. 225, "Utvandrarnes egna uppgifter," *op. cit.*, p. 208.

[3] Magnusson, *op. cit.*, pp. 106 ff.

[4] The Social Democrats have been the most numerous political party in the Swedish Riksdag since 1920.

[5] Magnusson, *op. cit.*, pp. 107, 152.

and, after the appointment of Branting, left for the field in Southern Sweden to be agitator and the editor of *Arbetet*, published at Malmö. A fellow-student and member of Verdandi, Karl Staaff, became the leader of the Liberal party which was pledged to free trade and the extension of the franchise.

The yeast of democracy was beginning to ferment. There was much criticism of the aristocratic, bureaucratic Swedish government. The reform of 1866, that had abolished the ancient four-house parliament of Sweden, had placed a two-house parliament in its stead. The new election laws with their high property qualifications had enfranchised new propertied and intellectual classes, but it had also deprived many of the small landowners of the right to vote. DeGeer, who had launched the new reform in 1865, had stated that the second chamber had been made as little democratic as possible to obtain the consent of the country.[1] By 1887, the question of a more liberal franchise had been presented in sixteen of the twenty regular sessions of the Riksdag since 1865,[2] but the only result had been a statistical report on the question. This report indicated that there were scarcely 6 per cent of the people of Sweden who had voting privileges. With the imposition of the new tariff, there developed a sentiment that the right to vote should accompany the obligation to pay taxes. Many mass meetings were held in every part of Sweden where the question was agitated. The repercussion of the democracy of the United States was being felt in Europe, and the example of that free country entered into all the debates on the subject.

The agitators found that in spite of the guaranty in the Swedish constitution dating from 1809, of the freedom of speech and the press, it was very easy for the police to find cause for arresting them and the courts for placing them in confinement. The government was especially hostile to the Social Democrats. In 1889, at the time of the first national meeting of the new party, there were four of its leading editors in jail, Branting (*Social-Demokraten*, Stockholm), Axel Danielson (*Arbetet*, Malmö), Pehr Erikson (*Folkets Röst*, Gothenburg), and G. A. Rydgren (*Proletären*, Norrköping).[3] During 1888, the restrictions on freedom of speech were especially

[1] *Ibid.*, p. 258.
[2] *Ibid.*, pp. 259–60.          [3] *Ibid.*, p. 171.

severe. Some, who had served a few months in jail for some speech or an article, felt the situation in Sweden hopeless and left for America, men like Henry V. Berghell.[1] One of the idealistic type was the young newspaperman, Atterdag Wermelin, who wrote pamphlets for the Social Democrats, but finally, because of his activities, lost his position on the newspaper *Aftonbladet.* He emigrated to the United States and became a typographer. He could not adjust himself to the new environment, and after several years of extreme poverty, committed suicide.[2] One of the most intelligent of the leaders among the workmen was P. M. Landin, who emigrated to America and died in 1897.[3]

The suppression of freedom of assembly by the police made it practically impossible for the Social Democrats to hire a hall or even a grove in which to hold a meeting. Some of the restrictions even took the form of religious persecution. The newly instituted Salvation Army was not allowed to have meetings after eight or nine o'clock in the evening. Their halls were closed and fines levied if the orders were disobeyed. If the fines were not paid, they were thrust into jail.[4] To seek protection against this reaction, a meeting was held in Stockholm, consisting of members of the Riksdag, noted authors, editors, merchants, members of the unions, and educators, the élite of the progressive thinking classes. It was held in 1890 in the largest hall in Stockholm.[5] It indicated the growing sentiment among the people for a greater freedom of expression, and an indignation against the tyranny of the bureaucratic government.

There is no doubt that there was a growing sentiment on the part of the lower classes against the partriarchal attitude of the wealthier classes, the nobles, the government officials, and especially the clergy of the state church. There was even resentment on the part of the agricultural laboring classes against the snobbishness of the peasants. The equality of social classes in America was constantly emphasized in the letters from friends. Even the reports of the governors gave as causes of emigration the freedom and social equality of America where the ambitious and industrious worker hoped to find his

---

[1] *Ibid.*, pp. 133–34.

[2] *Ibid.*, pp. 142–43.

[3] *Ibid.*, pp. 143–44.

[4] *Ibid.*, pp. 237–38.

[5] *Ibid.*, pp. 235 ff.

fortune in a land where manual labor was valued, unconditioned upon social status.[1]

The resentment against social inferiority on the part of the lower classes in Sweden was expressed over and over again in the criticism of the emigrants of their fatherland. J. S., who emigrated in 1881, wrote,

> If I should come to Sweden now and come into a store, I would have to take my cap or hat in my hand and bow ceremoniously, calling a simple bookkeeper for *herre*, etc.; while in America a workman and bookkeeper are of the same rank. Yes, our honored President Roosevelt, himself, does not despise me if I take off my hat or not when I speak to him (1907).[2]

In the advice given by E. P., an emigrant of 1870, to the Swedish government on how to prevent emigration, he included universal suffrage and the leveling of all class differences.[3] Another emigrant, N. N., stated that in the United States they pride themselves on equality, but he doubted whether one could be considered any more as an equal by a millionaire than by a count or baron in Sweden.[4] In spite of this attitude, however, there was no doubt more equality in the United States. J. B. expressed it when he wrote,

> I am a citizen of the United States, and my vote is worth as much as a millionaire's in the elections. This is a country ruled by the people; in Sweden wealth rules. Here is equality. If I talk to a high official, I do not need to stand with my hat in my hand and with shaking knees, not knowing what title to address him, for it is only the simple greeting, "Good day, Mr. Klintberg," or whatever his name is, and after such a greeting I use only his first name, it may be Peter or Paul, during the conversation, and "you," and then one feels like a comrade. He speaks to me in the same manner.[5]

Another potent factor in emigration was the resentment toward the introduction of universal military training in Sweden, following the example of Germany and other continental countries. The agrarian classes were and continue to be opposed to long periods of military service. It was equally opposed by the free-church elements and pacifists. The government felt the growing need of increased

---

[1] K. *bfhde femårsberättelse, Elfsborgs län, 1875–1880*, p. 2.

[2] "Utvandrarnes egna uppgifter," *op. cit.*, p. 179, No. 206. By 1930 the royal family of Sweden had become very democratic even to workmen.

[3] *Ibid.*, p. 156, No. 183.          [4] *Ibid.*, p. 150, No. 178.

[5] *Ibid.*, p. 209. This is of course an exaggeration on the part of the emigrant.

protection, facing the spectacle of the race for armaments which took place in Europe following the Franco-Prussian War of 1870. A hard-fought struggle ensued in the Riksdag for the abolition of the old military system by which the landowners exempt from military service supported certain professional soldiers on crofts. The professional soldier became only a part of the Swedish defense system with the introduction of conscription for all Swedish men between the ages of twenty and twenty-five in the act of 1860.[1]

The Defense Law of 1860 provided that, if anyone was liable to military service but desired to emigrate, the government would decide the case upon proper application. A condition of exemption from military duty in times of peace was the payment of $25.00, and in times of war, a substitute to take the emigrant's place.[2] The fee was discontinued after November 1, 1872.

As early as 1869 there was an attempt to follow the German military plan of reservists and make military service compulsory for all men between the ages of twenty and forty.[3] The agrarian party would not consent to longer than a sixty-day period of military drill. A long controversy ensued which involved the question of discontinuing the old professional army and releasing the land from special military dues of long-standing. The agrarian party was not in favor of abolishing entirely the old system, but did ask for relief from the tax burdens on the land.

The reservist idea was finally introduced in the law of 1885 and Sweden fell in line with the continental countries of Europe in the race for armaments. This law provided that every Swedish man was liable to military service from the ages of twenty-one to thirty-two.[4] There were six years of active service similar to the German *landwehr* called *beväringen* and the remainder of the period was service in the reserve (*landstormen*). The period of drill in *beväringen* was forty-two days a year. Accompanying this act was the reduction of land taxes by 30 per cent.[5] At the same time the law forbade the granting

---

[1] "Utvandringsväsendet i Sverige," *op. cit.*, p. 80.     [2] *Ibid.*

[3] Hallendorff, *Oskar I och Karl XV, Sveriges historia till våra dagar*, XII, 397–400, 404–6.

[4] "Utvandringsväsendet i Sverige," *op. cit.*, pp. 80–81.

[5] Boëthius, *op. cit.*, pp. 114–15.

of passports (*prästbetyg*) to any man who was of military age and had not fulfilled his military obligations in *beväringen*.[1] The act of 1887 and again the act of 1892 had provisions for emigration of men of military age, who desired to better their economic condition, through petition to the government. There was a great deal of red tape involved and undoubtedly long periods of waiting before permission was obtained.[2]

As time went on and the race for armaments in Europe became more intense, Sweden reciprocated with a program of progressive armament. Much of this was undoubtedly due to the fear of the growing ambition of Russia for an ice-free seaport and the treatment which Russia was administering to her Baltic provinces, but especially to Finland. In 1892, the age of compulsory military service was lengthened, the age limit being raised from thirty-two years to forty.[3] The first period of active service in *beväringen* was divided into two periods like the German, the first of 8 years and the second of 4 years. It was necessary now to obtain permission for emigration by any man between the ages of twenty-one and thirty-two. There was a special law for the island of Gotland from 1887 to 1892; military service began at the age of nineteen and lasted to thirty-nine years with 12 years of active service. The law of 1892 provided 90 days of training for recruits.[4] The conscripted army was to have its support in a small standing army of professional soldiers based upon voluntary recruits. The old burdens on the land for the standing army were to be gradually reduced. There was, since the decrease of 1885, 70 per cent of these land taxes still existing. Beginning with 1893 these were gradually reduced until the whole burden was removed in 1904. The expenditures for the new army were met in the national budget, instead of by the local communities.

While the new military system released the burdens of taxation on the agrarian classes, it awakened a distrust and a resistance to the compulsory system. The difficulties in obtaining permission to emigrate during the period of military age from twenty-one to

[1] "Utvandringsväsendet i Sverige," *op. cit.*

[2] *Ibid.*, p. 81; also pp. 31–32 cites the law.

[3] *Ibid.*, p. 81. Par. 1 of law, December 2, 1892, also par. 3. Mom. 1.

[4] Boëthius, *op. cit.*, pp. 156–59.

thirty-two, increased the numbers of young men leaving before the age of twenty-one. The age for compulsory military service coincided approximately with the average age of emigration, which might be designated from sixteen to thirty-five for men. The great increase in emigration among young men from eighteen to twenty-one, just before reaching military age, is particularly noticeable during the decades of 1881–90, and 1891–1900, following the passage of the military conscription laws of 1885, 1887, and 1892. There was

TABLE IX

THE EMIGRATION OF MEN AGED SIXTEEN TO TWENTY-FIVE
FROM SWEDEN*

| Age | 1861–70 | 1871–80 | 1881–90 | 1891–1900 |
|---|---|---|---|---|
| 16–17............ | 1,056 | 1,345 | 4,076 | 2,996 |
| 17–18............ | 1,404 | 1,899 | 6,653 | 4,799 |
| 18–19............ | 1,853 | 2,861 | 10,038 | 7,353 |
| 19–20............ | 2,436 | 3,512 | 13,846 | 9,579 |
| 20–21............ | 3,303 | 5,023 | 18,625 | 14,201 |
| 21–22............ | 2,778 | 4,657 | 8,394 | 5,915 |
| 22–23............ | 2,927 | 4,686 | 9,690 | 5,685 |
| 23–24............ | 3,058 | 4,473 | 10,356 | 5,537 |
| 24–25............ | 3,105 | 4,094 | 9,291 | 4,715 |

* "Utvandringsstatistik," *Emigrationsutredningens bilaga IV*, p. 198.

undoubtedly much illegal emigration of men of military age during these decades which is difficult to estimate. These illegal departures were made over Denmark and Norway, sometimes on false passports, and from the ports of those countries to the United States.

The law provided that, if any emigrant should return to Sweden while he was still of military age and had not fulfilled his military obligations, he might be forced to do so.[1] In the naturalization treaties that were made between the United States and the European nations, the United States was forced to recognize the right of the European countries to compel their former nationals, even though naturalized in the United States to perform incompleted military service when they returned to visit or to sojourn in their native land.[2]

It is difficult to analyze the sentiment of the Swedish people toward conscription. There was a very strong feeling against being

[1] See law of 1901, reprinted, "Utvandringsväsendet i Sverige," *op. cit.*, pp. 31–32.

[2] Charles G. Fenwick, *International Law* (New York, 1924), pp. 171–72.

compelled to do military service. The recruits often resented the arrogance and snobbishness of their drill masters. There is no doubt that many emigrated to escape military training, but whether an economic factor was not the fundamental cause for their leaving, while the conscription law tended only to hasten the departure, is difficult to determine. Swedish authorities on emigration have stated that the economic causes were primary and that conscription was often only given as an excuse.[1]

The opposition to compulsory military training seemed inherent in a freedom-loving people. The resentment to the law of 1885 was demonstrated by the emigration of 4,000 of the 41,000 young men of twenty years of age in the country in 1887.[2] There were also the pacifists, the conscientious objectors among both the free-church elements and the socialists. The average young men of military age without any particular religious scruples were sometimes rebelliously opposed to the restraints of military life just before their period of service and even during service. But after completing their training, the same young men look back to their military life as a period of new companionships and enjoyment.[3]

The economic crisis in the United States in 1893 and 1894 was an effective check on the tremendously increased emigration of the eighties from Sweden. The emigration fell from 37,504 in 1893 to 9,678 in 1894. During the years of 1895 and 1896 it reached 15,000 annually. In 1897 it fell to 10,000 and in 1898 to 8,000. But beginning with 1899 there was apparent another rising wave of exodus with the increasing better times in America. Simultaneously with this period of decreased emigration from Sweden to the United States, there was a considerable immigration to Sweden from the New World. In 1894 there were 7,455 immigrants as compared with 9,678 emigrants.[4] There were 5,464 immigrants from America in

[1] Sundbärg, *Emigrationsutredningens betänkande*, pp. 870–77. Dr. Adrian Molin stated the same in conversation with me in Stockholm, August, 1926.

[2] *Ibid.*, *Emigrationsutredningens betänkande*, p. 601.

[3] I attempted to study this question while in Sweden in 1923 and 1926, and had the opportunity to speak with several recruits, just before, during, and after their training. They had no free church affiliation. There remains a sentiment of resentment among the agrarian groups.

[4] "Utvandringstatistik," *op. cit.*, p. 157, Table 49.

1895, and from 1896 to 1900 the immigrants varied between four and five thousand. Some returned temporarily during the period of the crisis in the United States, while others remained permanently and purchased a piece of land or took over the old family homestead.[1]

The tremendous exodus of population from the rural communities in Sweden during the eighties decimated the countryside. In the wholly agricultural districts the population has never been regained. Where other industries began to flourish, population continued to increase in spite of a large exodus. The losses in population in some rural districts were as great as from one-third to one-half of the total inhabitants. Some of these regions today have fewer people than a century ago. The decline was greatest from 1880 to 1910, but even since, the population of these agrarian communities continued to diminish. There has been a slight back-to-the-farm movement noticeable since the industrial depression of 1923. Thus from 1880 to 1910, in agricultural counties like Kronoberg, Kalmar, Kristianstad, Älvsborg, Skaraborg, and Värmland, there was a steady decrease in population. While in other counties like Malmöhus, Halland, Östergötland, and Jönköping, in spite of a large exodus, industries continued to attract immigrants and no decline was noticeable.[2] In two of the latter, Östergötland and Jönköping, the rural population seemed to revive after 1890, only to suffer another relapse in 1910.[3]

The most phenomenal recovery of any rural county has been Kristianstad, where since 1910 the activities of dairying, the production of hogs and cattle, and the raising of sugar beets and potatoes have produced an agricultural renaissance. Paradoxically, in the neighboring county, where the agricultural products are equally as diversified, the rural population declined from 282,000 in 1910, to 253,000 in 1920.[4]

The counties which have shown the largest increase in rural population in recent times are the two bordering on the city of Stockholm, Uppsala and Stockholm counties, where much of the industrial popu-

[1] The returned Swedish emigrant will be discussed in chap. xi.
[2] "Bygdestatistik," *Emigrationsutredningens bilaga V*, pp. 178* ff.
[3] *Statistisk årsbok för Sverige, 1925*, pp. 6–7, Table 9.
[4] Malmöhus County (*ibid.*).

lation is being housed on garden plots. The industries of the "Berg-slag" and of Norrland have attracted immigration into those regions. Södermanland, a county close to the capital city of the country, strange to say, began to lose its rural population in 1905.

Within the counties there has been much shifting of population. Even in the counties from which emigration has been the greatest, there are some hundreds and parishes that have scarcely been touched by the exodus. And as has been pointed out from some counties where there has been practically no emigration, there have existed for a hundred years certain communities where the rural population has been declining in numbers. There has also been a shift from the agricultural districts to the neighboring industrial regions. It was only in the Norrland counties of Gävleborg, Väster-norrland, Jämtland, and Västerbotten, which have "boomed" since 1865 with the activities of mining and forestry, that all the local communities have shown an increase in population, but even here since 1900 there has been a decline.

The decimation of the rural population of Sweden has not been entirely due to emigration. In those counties around Lake Malar where large estates have absorbed most of the arable land, a decline was noticeable as early as 1806, undoubtedly due to the land-monopoly of the gentry. From this region there has been very little emigration for there has been no surplus population. Contrasted with this region are the three Småland counties where emigration has been very large and where it has devastated all but three of the hundreds. The two hundreds in Sweden which lost the largest amount of population between 1865 and 1910 were Möckleby hun-dred on the island of Öland, and Sörbyden hundred in Gothenburg-Bohus County, a loss of 35 per cent.[1] The ravages of exodus amounted to 34 per cent of the population of Sundal hundred in Älvsborg County and 31 per cent of Ölme hundred in Värmland. From these hundreds most of the people departed directly to the new world, except Sörbyden, which contributed to the growing city of Gothenburg. But even in counties where emigration was very great, like Östergötland, there were great losses in some hundreds and gains in others. Thus Bråbo hundred increased 131 per cent

[1] "Bygdestatistik," *op. cit.*, pp. 178* ff., Table 70.

during this period, while Åkerbo and Lysing hundreds decreased 22 per cent.

One portion of Sweden that is noted for its great loss of inhabitants through exodus is the island of Öland. This long narrow island lies off the southeastern coast of Sweden in the Baltic Sea, and belongs to the county of Kalmar. In 1805 it had a population of 22,800 which increased to 38,056 by 1880, but in 1907 there were only 28,650 inhabitants.[1] And its population has since that date remained stationary. During the period of declining population, more than 12,000 of its young men and women left their island homes for America. In a description of Öland in 1907, Helge Nelson wrote,

The Öland villages were crowded in 1880 with young men whose powerful arms competed for labor and bread. While driving through the village streets now, you see children's faces peering around the gates of the barnyard, the friendly nod of an old man or an old woman, but seldom a young man or woman. Where there were formerly ten youths of twenty offering their labor at the plow or in the harvest, there is now in many Öland villages not one.[2]

Öland was not an island of large estates, but rather a region of small farms owned by the peasants.[3] One third of the farms in 1907 ranged from 45 to 78 acres in size, a little less than a third from 15 to 45 acres, and another third, less than 15 acres. Only 57 of the 3,663 farms contained a mantal of land, about 120 acres. The parceling of *hemman* had gone to such an excess that only on the larger farms was it possible to make a livelihood without added sources of income. On the wastelands were many cotters who lived on the wages earned as agricultural laborers on the mainland, as woodsmen in the Norrland forests, or as seamen. Some went seasonally to Stockholm to seek labor.

The emigration which had begun from this region in 1867 and 1868 discontinued during the period of agricultural prosperity in the following decade. But the economic and agricultural crises of 1879,

---

[1] "Öland, Kalmars län, Bygdestatistik," *Emigrationsutredningens bilaga V*, pp. 79–80.

[2] Nelson, "Öland, Bygdeundersökningar," *Emigrationsutredningens bilaga VIII*, pp. 3–4, translated.

[3] Of the 3,663 *hemman*, there were 1,090 of $\frac{1}{4}$ to $\frac{3}{8}$ mantal, 964 varying from $\frac{1}{8}$ to $\frac{1}{4}$ mantal, and 1,000 less than $\frac{1}{8}$ mantal. A mantal is a taxing division. One-fourth of a mantal varies from 25 to 40 tunnland in area, depending on the fertility of the soil. Four-fifths of a tunnland is equal to an acre. See Table 9, *ibid.*, p. 24.

which dominated the decade of the eighties, brought unemployment to the cotter class in Öland and hard times for the agriculturalists. The more thrifty of the laboring classes, who had accumulated a little money during the decades of prosperity, purchased tickets for their families and emigrated to America. Others were fortunate in borrowing money. Often the husband and father went alone, to earn the means for the passage of the remaining members of the family. Seamen who frequented American ports often deserted. Many of the servant class, both men and women, went first to Denmark or Germany to earn passage money for the new world.[1] The agricultural crisis was particularly hard on the small farmer. He raised and exported only grain. The period of prosperity had induced speculation in farm lands and much of the land was heavily mortgaged. By 1885 Öland rye was only half the price of 1881 and it continued to fall until 1887. Dairying was not introduced until 1885. There was no forest or factory to help the situation. Often the peasant left his farm for America, there to accumulate some ready money on a more favorable labor market, so that he might return with sufficient capital. Frequently the wife managed the farm during his absence. Sometimes, it was taken for the mortgage.

Agriculture became more profitable on the island after 1890. Sugar beet culture superseded grain. Dairying assumed importance. The labor situation had completely changed. Agricultural labor now had to be imported from the mainland. The older inhabitants of the island whose farms were too small to support them received regular payments of money from children in America. Some who had been in America themselves were now living on the interest of their earnings. Sometimes it was the wife who received an income from the absent husband. Others practiced a trade along with their scanty agriculture. Even on the more profitable farms, the peasant, grown old and suffering from ill health, found his sons loath to return to the old home, and he was forced to depend on hired labor. After the passing of the old patriarch, the family estate was sold and passed into the hands of strangers.

Dalsland in Älvsborg County is another region of decimated population. Sundal hundred, which lies along Lake Väner, north

[1] *Ibid.*, pp. 36–37.

of the town of Vänersborg, had a population of 9,005 in 1805. The inhabitants had increased to 18,735 by 1880, but in 1909 had declined to 12,887.[1] The population in this region was engaged wholly in agriculture. During the nineteenth century, the land-area under cultivation had expanded thirteenfold.[2] In spite of this increase, the growth of population had resulted in the disintegration of landholdings to the extent that the small parcels of land were not sufficient for a livelihood and much poverty ensued. Where in 1810 there were only 34 farms with less than 15 acres in area, in 1865 there were 942 or 41 per cent of the total number of farms in the hundred,[3] while 10 per cent of the farms were less than 2 acres.[4] These freeholds of varying sizes were owned by peasants. But during the thirties the demands of the increasing population had developed crofts and cottages as forms of tenantry. Their holdings were unusually small, many consisting of only a potato patch.[5]

The surplus labor from this region originally found its outlet in Norway. The first emigrant to America is said to have been a "crofter" who left in 1862. He had originally planned to walk, according to the legend, but upon inquiring from his pastor how far it was, he was informed that had he begun his journey at two years of age, he would not have reached his destination at eighty. However, he left with his family as soon as he saved enough money for the journey. His letters inspired others to follow. There was a large exodus in 1867–68. This formed the nucleus for the emigration of 1880.

The crisis of 1880 fell especially hard on the Dalsland and Värmland regions which had abandoned diversified farming for an extensive cultivation of oats without any thought of rotation of crops. The price of oats since 1850 had been very high and therefore resulted in much speculation in land. Here again many farms had been purchased at abnormally high prices on mortgages. The crisis of

[1] "Älvsborgs län, Bygdestatistik," *Emigrationsutredningens bilaga V*, p. 145.

[2] From 3.7 per cent of the land-area in 1805 to 53.5 per cent in 1905 (Brusewitz, "Sundals, Nordals och Valbo härader, Bygdeundersökningar," *Emigrationsutredningens bilaga VIII*, p. 5, Table 1).

[3] Less than $\frac{1}{16}$ mantal, *ibid.*, p. 16.

[4] Less than $\frac{1}{64}$ mantal, *ibid.*, p. 18.     [5] *Ibid.*, p. 19.

1880 brought the bankruptcy of Dalsland's agriculture. The only solution seemed to be emigration for both peasant and cotter.

The exodus took the proportions of abandonment. They came from such typical parishes of the plains in eastern Dal, as Gestad, Bolstad, Grinstad, and Järn.[1] It was not unusual in Sundal to see empty cottages with doors and windows boarded up. The bankrupt farmer took his family with him to America, or he went alone to earn the money to redeem the mortgage. Sometimes he returned and took over the farm. Often, the father or sons sent for the remaining members of the family. This was usually true where the farm was small.

Poverty made it more difficult for the crofter and cotter to leave. But it was a relatively easy matter to obtain a loan. Experience had proved that the American loans were usually punctually and quickly repaid.[2] The result has been that the croft and cottage as forms of land tenantry have practically disappeared from Dalsland. For instance, on one estate in Frändefors there were twelve crofts in 1880 and only three in 1907, two occupied by old tenants and one by the son of a former tenant.[3] The number of persons on the farm had fallen from eighty to twenty. Most of the crofters were in America. On a farm in Erickstad parish, the number of crofters had declined from ten to one, and on another in Holm parish, from ten to two. An estate (*herregård*) at Högsäter where formerly there were twenty crofts had only five in 1907. The croft on the farms of the peasants was also fast disappearing.

On many estates there were no crofters left and the houses were falling to ruin, while the land either lay bare or had been replanted for forest. An elderly peasant, owner of a large farm, related to Mr. Brusewitz during his investigation of the region in 1907, that there had been three times as many people on the farm in his youth as then.[4] Where crofters were found in the region in 1907, they were usually too old to work, and their children were not willing to con-

---

[1] *Ibid.*, pp. 39–40. The exodus from the devastated forested regions of Dalsland will be discussed in the chapter on "The Forests of Sweden."

[2] *Ibid.*, p. 40.

[3] *Ibid.*, p. 60.    [4] *Ibid.*

.inue cultivating the tenant farm. The cotter with his potato patch
ad also disappeared, with the exception of the aged pauper.[1]

In Dalsland, as elsewhere in Sweden, there is at present a scarcity
of agricultural labor. The agrarian situation is now much improved
with the rising prices for grain and the rotation of crops. Dairying
has become an important source of income.[2] The Dal canal has become an industrial region. Paper mills, woolen mills, shipyards, etc.,
have absorbed some of the surplus labor of the rural region.[3] However, in spite of the recovery of agriculture, and the partial industrialization of the region, emigration to America continued on a
large scale until broken by the World War. Emigration during this
period was the normal course for every young person who must earn
his own bread. If he had no money for the journey, he would seek
employment from a peasant or at a factory until he had saved
enough to emigrate. A young man expecting to take over his father's
farm would leave for America to earn the money with which to pay
off his coheirs. A Swedish-American sometimes returned to the
region with his savings, paid down part-payment on a farm and
married. In the future it might become necessary for him to return
to America to earn more money to pay off the mortgage while his
wife managed the farm. If necessary, he made several such trips.
About 16 per cent of the farmers in Sundal hundred in 1907 had
been to America one or more times.[4]

There are regions in Sweden where granite hills are covered with
forests of birch and pine. In the stretches of forests there are found
small clearings where the peasants and crofters carry on their agricultural pursuits. Sometimes these small farms may be in the fertile
soil of drained marsh lands, but often they are stony and quite
sterile. Grazing cattle on the natural meadows found in the forests
is more profitable. These agriculturalists usually eke out their living in the forest industries. From these regions in Värmland and
Småland, the largest amount of emigration has come. And from

[1] *Ibid.*, p. 61. It used to be customary in some portions of Sweden to house paupers
in a cottage with a piece of potato land instead of in asylums. Now there is an old age
pension.

[2] *Ibid.*, pp. 41–58.    [3] *Ibid.*, pp. 72–76.    [4] *Ibid.*, p. 93.

some of the isolated regions with a sparse population exodus has been a characteristic phenomenon.

The county of Värmland is a region of forests, and it is not surprising that it leads the Swedish counties in the number of emigrants. The purchase of the peasant farms by corporations for the exploitation of the timber has also aroused dissatisfaction among these forest people. In the eighties alone, more than 44,000 of the 268,000 inhabitants, 16 per cent, left the county and 28,000 emigrated to America.[1] In one year, 1882, there were 4,500 persons from the county departing for the United States. The depopulation of Värmland has been a matter of concern to the nation. In the hundred of Häs, on the shores of Lake Väner, the inhabitants decreased 37 per cent between 1880 and 1909.[2] The population of this forested region was 8,000 in 1805; by 1865 it had risen to 13,000, and in 1909 it was no larger than a century before, 8,200. In one parish, Millesvik, there were only one-half of the inhabitants in 1909 that there had been in 1865. In fact the number of people in the parishes of Millesvik, Huggenas, and Treta were fewer in 1909 than a hundred years earlier.

It was almost exclusively an agricultural region, with some handicraft. The soil was fertile but the yield was small. The farms averaged about fifty acres of cultivated land. There was some dairying. There was formerly a large tenantry class of crofters and cotters who tilled tiny farms, but they were fast disappearing, as in Dalsland. The people of Värmland have never taken their agriculture very seriously. It has been largely left to the women folk while the men have sought more lucrative employment as skilled woodsmen, carpenters, and builders in other portions of the kingdom, expecially in Norrland. They were used to luxuries and to a high standard of life. When opportunities for seasonal employment in the Norrland forests ceased because of the increasing settlements in that northern region, it could hardly be expected that the wandering sons of Värmland would settle down to farming, especially during a period of low agricultural prices. Emigration was natural for them.[3]

[1] "Bygdestatistik," *op. cit.*, p. 164.

[2] About 62 per cent of the region is forested (*ibid.*, p. 170).

[3] The chapter on "The Forests of Sweden" discusses this region more fully.

A typical emigrant from the crofts of Värmland, in 1881 wrote in his autobiography,

I was born of poor parents in Värmland County in 1850. . . . . My parents owned a small croft, about two miles from the highway. The soil was so stony that my father gathered a stone pile of 2,160 cubic feet from the clearing. To make the soil productive it had to be covered with four inches of fertilizer before oats or barley would grow. We owned a horse and two cows. . . . . This stony croft was taxed $20.00 a year. All that we could produce annually on this sterile land was two barrels of rye, five barrels of oats, one half barrel of barley, and five barrels of potatoes. There were four persons in the family. We could not produce enough for our daily bread on this poor farm, and were forced to work for some lumber corporation hauling timber during the winter. I worked for one firm for nine years, and during the summers I floated logs. The earnings were small. In order to obtain employment we had to travel from Värmland to Medelpad, and some winters even to Jämtland, 270 miles. . . . . My father and I tired of these pilgrimages; we did not get any richer, but it was nip and tuck to keep from starving and to keep the sheriff from our door. In these isolated regions of Värmland, we were expected to contribute to the salary of the minister, the church clerk, the organist, the church janitor, and the soldier. We had to keep in repair 400 feet of highway, and then if there was anything left over, help to support two or three paupers.[1]

I began to think about America, and sent a letter to one of my former neighbors who had been there ten years. He answered my letter and stated that there was a better future for the poor workman in America than in Sweden. A poor laborer in Värmland could never improve his position, but became steadily poorer. In 1881 I left Sweden for America, sold my little estate for $500 and came to Minnesota with wife, children and parents. I must say that I felt proud to receive 160 acres of the land. Then we owned 320 acres together. We broke up the land, sowed it with wheat and corn, raised cattle, pigs, horses, chickens, and received an income of $1,500 a year. After ten years time we sold our land for $10,000.

And much of the same conditions existing in the forested regions of Småland have made it a source of much emigration, both to more fertile neighboring counties, and to the United States. In Jönköping County, "America fever" has ravaged the population to an extent only to be surpassed by Dalsland and Öland.[2] The chief industry in the county, agriculture, engaged 58 per cent of the inhabitants. Even here more than half of the land-area stood in forest and only 13 per cent of the soil was under cultivation. The industrialization of

[1] "Utvandrarnes egna uppgifter," *op. cit.*, p. 178, No. 206.
[2] "Bygdestatistik," *op. cit.*, pp. 56–58.

Jönköping City and Huskvarna has given labor to about 27 per cent of the inhabitants and has prevented the county from decreasing in population.

Since the eighteenth century, Småland has been noted for the exodus of its inhabitants. It was not until 1850 that the emigrants from the region directed their course to the United States.[1] The numbers of men and women seeking homes across the sea were greatly enhanced during the decade of the eighties, although the stream has continued almost unabated until the present time.

In the rural districts of the county there has been an actual devastation of population through exodus. In Mo hundred, which had a population of 7,300 inhabitants in 1910, one-fifth of the inhabitants had left their homes since 1880.[2] The decrease in population in the parishes of Bottnaryd and Mulseryd was 30 per cent. The land was not very fertile; the forest-covered hills were filled with gneiss outcroppings so that only 3 per cent of the land was under cultivation. Agriculture was the only industry in this isolated region, which was the most sparsely settled community in Southern Sweden. It was also the most backward in agricultural method and customs.

There had by 1910 been much emigration from Östbo and Västbo hundreds, but some industry in Värnamo parish has permitted the population to increase in spite of a large exodus.[3] The small landowners in Västbo hundred had farms averaging eight acres. The income from the farms was very precarious, and the more ambitious had left to find a more reliable income. There were some opportunities for labor during the winter in the forest industries.[4] There is practically no home in the region but has some of its members in America.[5]

Västra hundred had increased its population in its industrial communities, but in the seventeen rural parishes there had been a decrease of one-fifth of the people.[6] In Hylletofta and Skepperstad

[1] There had been an occasional emigrant earlier, like Swenson who founded the colony in Texas.

[2] "Bygdestatistik," *op. cit.*, pp. 61–62.      [3] *Ibid.*, p. 63.

[4] James Hamilton and G. Lindman, Jönköpings läns hushållningssällskap, "Inkomna utlåtanden," *Emigrationsutredningens bilaga XVII*, p. 21.

[5] Dr. John Ajander, Provinsial läkare, Värnamo distrikt, *ibid.*, pp. 194–95.

[6] "Bygdestatistik," *op. cit.*, p. 62. These are the statistics from 1880–1910.

parishes, the number of inhabitants had decreased by one-third and in Stockaryd and Hjälmseryd it had been even greater. Agriculture was here on the decline. During the sixties many left the region to engage in railroad construction, and only a few emigrated to America. After the completion of the railroads, departure overseas became the normal outlet for the youth of the neighborhood.[1] Exodus had been equally as great in the adjacent Östra hundred, and the contributing factors much the same. The emigrants were usually small landowners or agricultural laborers. Younger sons and daughters of the peasant class were too proud to become hired men and maids at home, and were equally disdainful of entering the industrial class. They preferred to seek their fortune in the new world, where they were often forced to swallow their pride and engage in the very type of work that they spurned at home.[2]

But even in the most fertile region of Jönköping County, along the southern and western shores of Lake Vätter, emigration has been extensive. In Tveta and Vista hundreds, where rich glacial deposits make possible the extensive cultivation of wheat in large prosperous fields, like the neighboring county of Östergötland, emigration had been greater than immigration. The cultivated land-area had increased fivefold in the last century, and from 20 per cent to 30 per cent of the land was under cultivation.[3] Half of the entire wheat crop of Jönköping County was produced in these two hundreds. There were some large estates, and the many peasant farms were rather large, averaging forty acres.[4] There are several industrial regions around Jönköping city, Huskvarna, and Nässjö.[5] Here again the industrial parishes increased in population, from 9,000 to 24,000 between 1865 and 1909, while the rural parishes declined by 1,500. The country parish of Gränna had lost 28 per cent of its inhabitants. In spite of industrialization in this hundred, population has declined

---

[1] Alfred Dahl, kronolänsman, Västra härads Västra distrikt, Jönköpings län, "Inkomna utlåtanden," *op. cit.*, pp. 105–6.

[2] J. F. Henström, kronolänsman, Östra härads tredje distrikt, Jönköpings län, *ibid.*, pp. 103–5.

[3] Sundbärg, *Emigrationsutredningens betänkande*, p. 284.

[4] "Bygdestatistik," *op. cit.*, p. 60.

[5] *Ibid.*, p. 61.

and most of the emigrants from the region have gone directly to the United States.

There are extensive forests in the other Småland counties, Kronoberg and Kalmar, and conditions are very much the same as in Jönköping County. The only hundred not affected by a decline of inhabitants in Kronoberg County was Uppvidinge where the Småland glass industry provided labor.[1] In Norrvidinge hundred the decrease was 15 per cent by 1909, and in the parish of Asa, 30 per cent. The parish of Furuby in Konga hundred suffered a decline of 38 per cent. The county declined in population by 11,000 persons between 1880 and 1909, while the neighboring county, Kalmar, lost 17,000.[2] In a forested region of the latter county, where only one-tenth of the soil was under cultivation, Handbörds hundred, there had been an exodus of 14,000 persons in the last century. The population of the region amounted to only 16,600 in 1907. A high birth-rate had kept the population almost stationary.

In parts of Östergötland, Skaraborg, and Kristianstad counties that border on the Småland counties, the geological conditions are much the same, granite hills covered with forest. The economic conditions are similar, and the amount of exodus has been great. Thus in Kind hundred in southeastern Östergötland, 74 per cent of the land is covered with forest.[3] The small patches of farm land cover 13 per cent only and average about thirty acres per farm. Wholly an agricultural region with the exception of the commercial center of Kisa, and isolated, emigration began here early. In 1907 there was a population of 18,600, but 16,000 had been lost through exodus in the preceding century. In spite of this early exodus, the population of the region continued to increase until 1880, but, since, there has been decline and stagnation.

But not only in the forested regions has emigration been a factor in Sweden. The county of Halland ranks second only to Värmland as a source of emigrants for America. This sand-driven county along the Kattegat was once forested, but now its denuded lands are

[1] *Ibid.*, pp. 68–69.

[2] *Ibid.*, p. 72. Some of this loss has been recovered by an increasing population since 1910.

[3] *Ibid.*, p. 53.

covered with heather and are sterile for agriculture. In a period of sixty years, 1850–1910, some 53,000 persons had emigrated from this county, more than one-third of the population of 1910.[1] Of these emigrants, 4,000 came to America; 5,000 settled in Denmark; 300 in Norway; and 900 in Germany. The county has received an immigration of 12,000.

Some exodus has been a normal state in Halland for decades, but the eighties saw it swell to unheard-of numbers. Every hundred lost some inhabitants, but the greatest losses were in Viske and Faurå hundreds, purely agricultural regions. The hundreds lying near the two industrial centers of Hälsingborg on the south and Gothenburg on the north suffered the least. In Veddige parish the decline in population between 1865 and 1909 amounted to 30 per cent and in little Stråvalla, to 33 per cent.[2]

In the regions of greatest emigration in Halland County, the soil was not very productive, nor was the quantity of milk produced equal to that of other parts of the country. The farms were small, and although not so fertile, could support small families. It was customary to eke out the income by making articles of wood and selling them at the market in the town of Varberg. The children in the region were raised by their parents and relatives with the idea that when they had grown up, they would seek their fortune in America, because Sweden had no future.[3] The emigrants consisted chiefly of small farmers, crofters, and laborers.[4]

Regions where the soil was unproductive and the population was fast increasing were natural areas for emigration. It is more difficult to explain the exodus from regions of agricultural fertility. But that was the case of two of the most prosperous and fertile regions in Sweden, Östergötland and Skåne. In the county of Östergötland there was an increase in population of 25,000 between 1880 and 1909,

[1] Sundbärg, *Emigrationsutredningens betänkande*, pp. 352–53. See Tables on pp. 134–35. Although there had been a steady decrease in rural population in Halland from 1870 to 1926, there was only a decline of 2,000 persons between the figures of the two years, and a 22,000 increase for the county as a whole.

[2] "Bygdestatistik," *op. cit.*, p. 120.

[3] A. F. Alling, kronolänsman, Varbergs fogderis mellersta distrikt, Hallands län, Utdrag ur inkomna utlåtanden," *Emigrationsutredningens bilaga XVII*, p. 117.

[4] Liedholm, Provinsial läkare, Oskarsströms distrikt, Hallands län, *ibid.*, pp. 202–3.

in spite of emigration. About one-fourth of the land area was under cultivation and 61 per cent stood in forest. In the last century there had been a four-fold increase in cultivated land. Industry and mining occupied 32 per cent of the population, and agriculture more than half. Tenantry was very high, about 40 per cent. There were great contrasts in the county. Along Lake Vätter the soil was very fertile and the large estates numerous, while the southeastern portion tended toward the Småland type; hills, forests, and small patches of cultivated soil. Emigration from the latter region is easily explainable, but it has been quite as prevalent from the prosperous portions of the county.

A fertile region in Östergötland was Boberg hundred along the eastern end of Lake Boren and extending to the Gotha canal, a region of large estates. About one-half of the land was cultivated. There were only 8,700 inhabitants in 1907, and in the course of a century 6,000 had emigrated, even though the movement had not been very marked. Population here had declined since 1865.[1] Aska hundred reaching along the eastern coast of Lake Vätter down to Vadstena had been a region of extensive emigration. About one-half of the soil was cultivated. This hundred included the machine-shop region of Motala which had increased in population to 12,000. Until 1870 even rural districts gained in inhabitants, but, since, there had been a constant decline. Although there had been considerable immigration of workmen into Motala from other portions of the kingdom, exodus had been strong both from Motala and even more from Västra Ny (around Medevi) where the population had declined 25 per cent. It was not a region of large estates, three-fourths of the farms were cultivated by the owners, and the crop yield was fairly good. Wages were considered low in the region, which may be the explanation of the exodus.

There are some regions in Östergötland where the rural population has been declining for over a century and where there has been little emigration, similar to the Mälar counties. In Åkerbo hundred, northeast of the town of Linköping, a region with 52 per cent of the land-area under cultivation, and 70 per cent of the cultivators, owners, the population in 1907 was one-eighth less than a century

[1] "Bygdestatistick," *op. cit.*, p. 48.

ago. Östra Skrukeby and Lillkyrka parishes had in 1805 a joint population of 1,105, and in 1907 only 580, although the cultivated land-area had been increased from 4,400 acres to 16,000.[1] Early consolidation of landholdings, the substitution of the annual contract of married laborers for the crofter and cotter, were the causes of this decline rather than exodus.

And even from the fertile plains of Skåne emigration has been extensive. Of the two Skåne counties, the southernmost, Malmöhus, is the more fertile. During the period between 1871 and 1900 when the county lost 46,000 inhabitants through emigration, it gained 100,100 in population.[2] There has been considerable industrial development in the county of recent years, at Malmö, Hälsingborg, Lund, Landskrona, Ystad, and Trelleborg. Although regions like Oxie hundred, around Malmö, have almost doubled in population, because of the industrial laborers housed on garden lots, in the portions of even these hundreds which are wholly agricultural, population is on the decline.[3] Emigration from such regions is negligible.

But from more wholly agricultural hundreds, like Ljunit, there has been much foreign exodus. The land is here almost all under cultivation, contrasted with most of Sweden. Farms cover 89 per cent of the land-area. Most of the farms are owned by the peasants and have been much subdivided so that the average farm is about twenty acres. There is little need for hired labor here. Emigration has been greater here than from any other hundred in the Skåne counties, and the population declined from 1865 to 1909, 23 per cent.[4] Overpopulation, the size of the farms, and the unprogressive methods of agriculture must be given as the causes of exodus. In Herrestad hundred around Ystad where farms averaged 44 acres and sugar-beet culture had been introduced, the decline in population was only 4 per cent.[5]

The northern county in Skåne, Kristianstad, and the neighboring county of Blekinge are not as fertile as Malmöhus. Toward the

[1] *Ibid.*, p. 50.

[2] *Ibid.*, p. 102. There was a decline in the rural population of Malmöhus County between 1910 and 1920, but it is now recovering.

[3] *Ibid.*, pp. 106–7.   [4] The population had doubled between 1805 and 1865.

[5] "Bygdestatistik," *op. cit.*, pp. 107–8.

north and east this region blends into the highlands of Småland. Kristianstad County had remained an agricultural region, with 67 per cent of its inhabitants devoted to that occupation in 1900. Although there.was some decline in population between 1880 and 1910, the county has shown a remarkable recovery in the last twenty years and there is again an increase. This is exceptional for there has been no industrialization.[1]

It is strange that the hundred in which Önnestad parish is located, Västra Göinge, from which such illustrious American immigrants as the early pioneers, Hans Mattson, and the Lutheran clergyman, Hasselquist, emigrated, has shown less the ravages of exodus than some regions in the more fertile Malmöhus County. The hundred is divided about evenly between forested and cultivated land. The population of 34,800 in 1909 had been stationary for thirty years.[2] The parishes around the railroad center of Hessleholm increased in population while the rural parishes declined. The industrialization had been chiefly in the form of breweries. The agrarian culture was more the raising of swine than the production of grain. There were in 1909 also hundreds in the county where emigration had caused a decline of population, like Ingelstad with a decline of 9 per cent and Bjäre 17 per cent.[3]

That early emigrant movement from Dalarne and Hälsingland has not continued, like that of Småland and Östergötland. The expansion of the lumbering industry into this region during the seventies and eighties has relieved the old economic pressure under an agricultural régime, while religious toleration and a decline of religious fervor have removed another incentive. In 1875 the Leksand district was one of the most populous regions in Dalarne.[4] The population has remained stationary since that time. It is a heavily forested region and only 7 per cent of the land is cultivated. The many small farms average only six acres, and tenantry is almost unknown. Agriculture has been intensively developed. The potatoes from this region are renowned for their quality. The surplus population finds its way into the lumber camps, drifts to the industrial centers, especial-

[1] *Ibid.*, pp. 94–95.      [3] *Ibid.*, pp. 98, 101.
[2] *Ibid.*, p. 98.          [4] *Ibid.*, pp. 206–7.

ly to Stockholm, and some finally emigrate to the United States. But the emigration has not compared with that of Småland or Värmland.

In the region around the growing city of Stockholm, the extra population has been absorbed by migration to industrial centers. In Vaksala hundred in Uppsala County, for instance, population has been stationary for fifty years, but there was a record of only 32 emigrants to America between 1881 and 1910.[1] Here the typical agricultural unit is the large estate. In the same county, the industrial region of Örbyhus hundred, population increased 72 per cent between 1865 and 1907.[2]

In these brief sketches of the effect of emigration upon various regions of Sweden, it is clear that the exodus was neither uniform in time nor place. The wholly agricultural regions of the south and west, and especially the less fertile regions, have suffered to the point of decimation. While Norrland contributed many to the early emigration movement of the forties and fifties, the tide of exodus was stemmed by the "good times" of the seventies, which continued until 1910. Around Stockholm, the agricultural counties have contributed very little to emigration. Even regions within the "emigrant counties" vary considerably in the amount of exodus, especially where there has been some industrialization. In Östergötland, Bråbo hundred by 1909 had increased 131 per cent, while Åkerbo and Lysing hundreds decreased 22 per cent.[3]

The greatest increases in population in Sweden since 1865 have been in and around the cities, and in the lumbering and mining regions. Near the city of Stockholm, the population of Danderyd hundred increased more than threefold between 1865 and 1910. In the newly opened mining region of the far north at Gällivare, there had been almost a fivefold increase. Urban population grew apace. In 1880 there were only twelve cities in Sweden with a population of 10,000 or more, while in 1929 there were thirty-nine.[4] Until the eighties only 10 per cent of the population lived in urban communities; now there is 30 per cent. Stockholm had increased from 168,000 to 486,000 during the period, Gothenburg from 76,000 to 241,000,

[1] *Ibid.*, pp. 32–33.    [2] *Ibid.*, p. 178*, Table 70.    [3] *Ibid.*
[4] *Ibid.*, p. 401*, Table 80; *Statistisk årsbok för Sverige, 1930*, p. 5, Table 5.

and Malmö from 38,000 to 119,000. There was also emigration from the cities, but the natural increase and the numbers of rural folk coming to the cities, with even some foreign immigration, permitted this almost threefold increase. The city of Stockholm had averaged more than 1,500 emigrants annually from 1881 to 1910, and over 1,000 since that time.[1]

The rural districts of counties like Östergötland, Jönköping, Kalmar, Kristianstad, Gothenburg-Bohus, Älvsborg, Skaraborg, and Värmland had decreased from 16,000 to 31,000 in agricultural population between 1870 and 1926.[2] Malmöhus County had lost over 20,000 since 1910, and Södermanland County had lost 8,000 since 1900, while the rural inhabitants of Blekinge County had decreased 6,000 since 1890. In Norrland, Kopparberg County had fallen off 3,000 since 1920, while a region with much emigration like Halland had decreased only 2,000 in rural inhabitants, and that since 1870. Considering the rural population of Sweden as a whole, there has been a steady increase in spite of emigration.

Nor has exodus been so great as to materially diminish the total population of any of the counties. Only four counties in 1926 show an actual decline: Kronoberg County with 3,000 fewer inhabitants than in 1890; Kalmar County with 2,000 less than in 1870, although indicating an increasing population since 1900; Västmanland with a 4,000 decrease since 1920; and Kopparberg County with a 2,000 decline in the same period.[3] Counties like Gotland, Kristianstad, Älvsborg, Skaraborg, and Värmland suffered temporary setbacks in the increase of the number of inhabitants that they possessed before the ravages of the exodus of the eighties. The population of the whole country increased by almost two millions from 1870 to 1926, about 50 per cent. Had there been no emigration, the population of the country would have been greater by a million, had not natural increase declined.[4]

[1] *Statistisk årsbok för Sverige, 1927*, p. 75, Table 66.

[2] *Ibid.*, p. 6, Table 9.          [3] *Ibid.*, p. 7, Table 9.

[4] There is at present a decline in natural increase. Large families are a thing of the past. The population is at present stationary.

# CHAPTER IX

## THE FORESTS OF SWEDEN

The extensive forests of Sweden that cover three-fifths of her area are a natural resource that employs many in its exploitation. Forest products have been developed to a greater extent than ever before in the history of the country. Lumber has the rôle of being one of the two chief exports of Sweden, coming second only to iron. The exploitation of the forests of Sweden began on a large scale about 1840 but it was not until the seventies and eighties that it reached its greatest importance. In several ways the lumbering industry has been instrumental in influencing emigration from the country. At times when the industry has been prosperous and wages high it has curbed the exodus. In times of economic crises, in cases of labor disputes, and during periods of the encroachment of the lumber corporations upon the lands of the peasant, it has stimulated emigration.

Two-thirds of this forested region lies north of the Dal River (Dalälven). Here in the counties of Värmland, Kopparberg, Gävleborg, and Västernorrland, the forested areas equal 77.3, 73.6, 82.1, and 82.3 per cent, respectively, of the whole land-area, while eleven other counties have more than half of their area in timber.[1] In contrast, in Malmöhus County there remains only 10 per cent in woodland while 72 per cent of the land is under cultivation. The next lowest in forest area is Skaraborg County with 38 per cent of forest lands and 42 per cent of cultivated soil.

The ownership of the forest lands is divided between the crown, the hundreds, the parishes (allmänningsskogar), private individuals, and corporations. Under the old village communal system, prac-

---

[1] The forested area of Stockholm County is 56.8 per cent; Uppsala County, 54 per cent; Södermanland, 63.8 per cent; Östergötland, 61.8 per cent; Jönköping, 56.8 per cent; Kalmar, 59.4 per cent; Älvsborg, 62.6 per cent; Örebro, 63.5 per cent; Västmanland, 55.7 per cent; Jämtland, 61.3 per cent; and Västerbotten, 53.8 per cent (Guinchard, *Sveriges Land och Folk*, II, 41).

317

tically all the forest of Southern Sweden had belonged to the village or the hundred. The vast stretches of primeval forests of the north were claimed for the crown by the Vasa kings in the sixteenth century. The crown at the time appropriated all waste land not claimed by the communes in Southern Sweden and assumed proprietorship of crown parks in the provinces of Skåne, Blekinge, and Halland that had formerly belonged to Denmark. Some forest lands were granted by the government to the iron industry of Central Sweden for charcoal burning, during this period.[1]

The commons (*allmänningar*) were very old in Sweden and are found mentioned in the earliest existing legal contracts and charters.[2] They were the stretches of forests that lay between the cultivated lands of the villages. These patches of woodland were considered necessary to supply the villagers with building material and fuel, and served as reserve for the future expansion of cultivation. The land could be appropriated only by the co-owners of the village, or upon the consent of the village fathers. The large stretches of unclaimed land in the less populous regions were open to settlement by anyone. And it was customary, as has been noted, for a man desiring a piece of land to go out, burn a clearing in the forest, and place the virgin soil under cultivation. Sometimes the word commons was applied to this primeval forest, as well, but gradually this land was appropriated by the crown. In a proclamation of Gustavus Vasa, April 20, 1542, "uncultivated tracts of land" were declared to "belong to God, the King, and the Swedish Crown."[3] The government lands in the Norrland regions were, however, not considered the exclusive property of the state, but rather free land open for settlement, and in some cases land upon which was granted to the cultivators of the soil without woodland, the right "to make use of pasture, of timber, to procure fence rails, leaves for fodder, birch bark, peat and bast, beside other things to be found there, and to supply their own bare needs."[4]

The exploitation of the forests began in the Middle Ages. The Hanseatic League, which controlled the commerce of Northern Europe in the later Middle Ages, found in Sweden a source for pitch,

[1] Sundbärg, *Sweden, Its People and Its Industries*, p. 625.
[2] *Ibid.*, p. 626.    [3] *Ibid.*, p. 627.    [4] *Ibid.*

tar, masts, and spars, as well as firewood, deals, and boards.[1] It was before the use of the sawmill, and boards were hewn from logs with an axe. In the sixteenth century, the Dutch succeeded the Hansa and became the principal exporters of Swedish timber. The Swedish logs were now made into boards by Dutch sawmills propelled by wind.

Gustavus Vasa, who was interested in developing the resources of his country, did everything in his power to further the exportation of lumber. He especially encouraged the shipment of oak to Holland and to other shipbuilding countries.[2] It was during his reign that the first sawmill patterned after the Dutch windmill was introduced. Sweden was at the time the largest market for tar. Shipbuilders were imported from Holland and Venice, and Sweden began to build a fleet, both for war and commerce.[3] In the seventeenth century, waterfalls were used as power for the sawmills, and the exportation of lumber increased.

The first forest law to prevent the devastation of forests and their destruction by fire was passed in 1647.[4] The complaint was heard at the time that the common people and the mining enterprises were wasteful with timber. Clearings made by fire were destroying large areas of forests, for these clearings were only used for cultivation for two or three years at a time. The law limited the right to burn clearings to land that was actually to be cultivated permanently and where there was no danger from forest fires. In both the Forest Ordinances of 1647 and 1664 it provided for the razing of all crofts or new settlements on the forest commons that were not equal to one-fourth of a *hemman,* an estimation of the least amount of land upon which a man and his family could make a livelihood.[5] Any new clearings would have to be made by the permission of the governor of the province. In the code of 1734, the Forest Ordinance

---

[1] *Ibid.,* p. 635; Grimberg, "Ur den svenska industriens äldre historia," *Svenska industrien vid kvartsekelskiftet, 1925,* p. 23.

[2] Grimberg, "Ur den svenska industriens äldre historia," *op. cit.,* p. 23. There were laws passed protecting the hardwoods, especially oak, from 1414 to 1830 (Norlind, *Svenska allmogens liv,* pp. 54–55).

[3] Grimberg, *op. cit.,* p. 24.          [4] *Ibid.,* p. 25.

[5] Wohlin, "Torpare-, backstugu-och inhysesklasserna," *Emigrationsutredningens bilaga XI,* pp. 8–9. About thirty acres of land equal one-fourth of a hemman.

recognized only the clearings on the common forest lands that had been taxed and separated from the commons. No further clearings were permitted.[1] These laws were laxly enforced, however, but did diminish the number of new holdings in the eighteenth century, and protected the forest lands for future generations.

The eighteenth century was a period of great prosperity for the wood industries in Sweden. The demand for timber to rebuild the towns and buildings that had been destroyed by the Russian invasion of 1719–20, increased by threefold the number of sawmills in Norrland in the following two decades.[2] It was also the golden age of the Swedish fleet. The development of the East India Company increased the need for ships. Henrik av Chapman was the great shipbuilder of Sweden during the age. The Swedish commercial fleet was fostered by the commercial placate of 1724, which closed Swedish ports and Swedish coastwise trade to foreign ships.[3] So many shipyards were established along the Swedish coast, that it was difficult to meet the demands for labor. The demand for tar also increased, and for pitch, which was needed to make the wooden ships watertight. Between 1738–41, tar constituted two-thirds of the entire export of wood-products from Sweden.[4] Stockholm remained until 1880 the largest world market for tar.

Until the eighteenth century, anyone was allowed to cut heavy timber in the vast crown forests of Värmland, Dalarne, and Norrland. This freedom was restricted during the "Period of Liberty," and the crown granted monopolies to certain owners of sawmills to cut timber in the crown forests, a privilege which was called *stockfångst*.[5] The monopoly was usually restricted to a certain quantity of timber, and often the state had the exclusive right to mast-trees. After 1820, the government ceased to grant further monopolies on its forest lands. In order to regain the rights already granted, the government since 1870 has offered the privileged mills the right to cut a larger quantity of timber during a limited period and thereby permitting the grant to expire earlier. Only a few monopolies remained in 1915.

[1] *Ibid.*, p. 9.   [2] *Svenska industrien vid kvartsekelskiftet, 1925,* p. 26.   [3] *Ibid.*   [4] *Ibid.*
[5] Sundbärg, *op. cit.,* p. 625. The eighteenth century in Swedish history, 1720–72, is called *Frihetstiden.*

It was in the eighteenth century that England seized much of the Dutch commerce and Holland's control of the seas. England had since the Middle Ages purchased much of her lumber and wood-products indirectly from Sweden, and now became a direct customer. Two-thirds of the Swedish export of lumber went to England in 1809, some 220,000-dozen boards and deals.[1] During that year, however, England dealt a hard blow to the Swedish lumber industry when, in order to combat Napoleon's economic warfare, she placed heavy duties on the import of timber from the Continent. The duty was raised in 1810 and again in 1813.[2] On the other hand, England encouraged importation from British North America by a very low duty. After the Napoleonic wars, although the duty on timber from the Continent was lowered from £3 a load to £2 15s., the low duty of ten shillings upon American timber kept the Swedish wood-products out of the English market. The demand for pit-props for English mines, however, forced her to reduce the duty on timber in 1842. Then followed a gradual reduction and final abolition of duty in 1866.[3]

Restrictions on commerce were simultaneously being removed in Sweden when that country went from a high protective policy to a free-trade venture in 1863. The mercantilist policy of the eighteenth century had placed restrictions on the export of timber as well as on the domestic market. There were, for instance, certain dimensions for boards to be sent to Stockholm.[4] Export duties existed on many different kinds of timber, such as rough, sawn, or hewn timber of most kinds of hardwood, unhewn redwood, and white wood, small beams and spars, while boards and deals of redwood or whitewood were duty-free. The restrictions on domestic trade were gradually removed during the first half of the nineteenth century, and many in the General Commercial Regulations of 1846. The export duties were removed partially in 1857 and entirely in the tariff of 1863. In 1848, an act regulating joint stock companies (*aktiebolag*) was passed, making possible the formation of corporations for the exploitation of lumber resources on a large scale.[5]

By the various laws of enclosure, which were passed in the eight-

[1] *Ibid.*, p. 635.      [3] *Ibid.*, p. 636.
[2] *Ibid.*             [4] *Ibid.*, p. 637.      [5] *Ibid.*

eenth and early nineteenth centuries, especially by the *laga skifte* of 1830, it was possible for the co-owners of a village to demand the division of the forest lands which belonged to them in common. The peasants in the forested regions were usually land poor. Their tiny clearings furnished them barely enough to live on, and a small offer of money for their timber, the value of which they did not appreciate, seemed to them a great fortune. If one of the co-owners sold to a corporation, it was necessary to go through the legal process of dividing the common holdings. Since the peasants had little ready money, it was often necessary for them to sell out to corporations in order to pay the cost of division.

The purchase of vast forest stretches for exploitation was started in the forties by some prominent Gothenburg merchants, among them Dickson, an Englishman by birth.[1] Through his English connections, Dickson knew of the demand for lumber in England. The first purchases were made in Värmland and Dalsland, and a little later in Norrland. Large watermills with several saw-frames were constructed at the waterfalls situated as near the coast as possible.[2] The logs were floated to the mills, but it was quite a problem and a very costly undertaking to transport the finished lumber from the waterfalls to the seaports. The location of steam sawmills on the coast in the next decade removed many obstacles and produced cheaper lumber. The first steam sawmill in Sweden was located at Vivsta, near the port of Sundsvall in Norrland in 1851. The following year another one was established at Kramfors in Ångermanland. From 1851 to 1870 many such mills appeared.

Improvements in the means of communication aided in the reduction of the price of lumber for the foreign market but also helped to produce competition. At the beginning, the transportation of Norrland lumber was entirely by means of sailing vessels which could make at the most two annual trips to English and French ports, and only one to a Mediterranean port. The freight to England was about £4½ per standard.[3] Steam navigation lowered freight-rates considerably. The rebuilding of the Trollhätte canal in 1838 to 1844 made

[1] Hallendorff, *Oskar I och Karl XV*, Hildebrand, *Sveriges historia*, XI, 190.

[2] E. Arosenius, "Forest Industries;" Sundbärg, *op. cit.*, p. 637.

[3] Sundbärg, *ibid.*, pp. 637–38.

possible transportation of lumber from Dalsland and Värmland over Lake Väner via Gothenburg to England. The railroads constructed were also opening wedges to formerly inaccessible territory. In the forested regions of Norrland, railroad construction began in the seventies.

The sawmill corporations obtained at first the bulk of their supply of timber through contracts with owners of private forests.[1] The average term of the contract was fifty years, the common term for real-estate leases at the time. Other leases were for ten to twenty years. Sometimes there were limitations on the kinds of trees that might be felled, and in other cases the contract was restricted to trees of certain dimensions, varying from seven inches in diameter and a height of fifteen feet to ten inches by twenty feet. White fir which at the beginning was scorned was often omitted from the contract. The owner of the land was paid in one lump sum for the whole term. Sometimes there was also an annual rental in cash or grain. The price paid was very low. The peasants had no idea of the value of their timber and would often burn off vast tracts of forest in order to secure pasturage. They were also very poor and seldom had any ready money, so that a small sum seemed a fortune to them.

There was much speculation in forest lands. Many fortunes were made. The sole aim of the speculator was to cut as much timber as possible during the term of his contract.[2] He had no interest in the preservation of this natural resource. Regions in the counties of Kronoberg and Halland in Southern Sweden and on the island of Öland, show the results of an earlier period of ruthless cutting of timber.[3] This devastation had begun here as early as 1600 and the sterile soil is still covered only with heather. In order to prevent a recurrence of this destruction on the island of Gotland, a law was passed by the Swedish government in 1869,[4] which has since been revised several times and extended to other regions of the kingdom. The statute stated in brief that land naturally fitted for timber should be retained as timberland if it was not placed under cultiva-

[1] *Ibid.*, p. 648.    [2] *Ibid.*, p. 650.
[3] Sundbärg, *Emigrationsutredningens betänkande*, pp. 293–94, 355.
[4] Sundbärg, *Sweden, Its People and Its Resources*, p. 632.

tion or used for building purposes. The exportation of timber of fir and pine was forbidden unless the trees were at a minimum of twenty-one centimeters or eight and one-fourth inches at the thick end. There has been much devastation in recent times, in Dalsland particularly.

In the Norrland region, the attempts at colonization on the crownlands prior to 1860 had resulted in many places in a disguised forest speculation. The Royal Ordinance of 1865 provided for an investigation of how much of the undivided forests of Kopparberg County and other Norrland counties should be retained as forest lands by the crown, and how much should be opened temporarily for settlement.[1] The following year another ordinance permitted settlements on land not suitable for crown parks or forest preserves. The same provisions were made for Lappland in the law of 1873. The homesteaders in this region could take, without previous official survey and marking, such timber annually as might be cut without injury to the future preservation of the forest.[2] This included the parish of Särna and the sub-parish of Idre in Dalarne. It was the beginning of a wise policy of preservation of the forest lands in the north. In 1903, it was extended to all forests owned by private individuals.

The large sawmill corporations also began to realize that it would be improvident to destroy their resources of raw materials by ruthless devastation. They began a policy of purchasing outright the lands from the peasants. The farms purchased from the peasant proprietors consisted usually of a large forested area and a small piece of cultivated land.[3] Since the corporations were not interested in agriculture, the cultivated land was usually leased to the former owner at a small rental often only covering taxes. These tenants on the corporation lands formed a permanent labor-supply for the lumbering activities of the neighborhood. In many cases, however, the peasants quickly and foolishly spent the purchase money for luxuries, became dissatisfied with their dependent position, and left the region either to go into industry, or more often to emigrate to America.

A picture of what was happening to the forested regions of Sweden when the sawmill corporations began to purchase the lands of peas-

---

[1] *Ibid.*, p. 630.        [2] *Ibid.*        [3] *Ibid.*, p. 650.

ants has been described by an emigrant from Jämtland province.[1] In 1878 and 1879, it was decreed that the land in the parish should be divided by *laga storskifte*, because the lumber corporations had purchased many of the farms in the parish, and demanded a partition of the common forest lands in order to obtain title to their portion. The cost of division was extremely high. It cost the emigrant's father 700 kronor or about $200 besides several days' labor the first year of the survey and division. The old man had to sell most of his lands to the corporations, but kept enough to support himself and his wife comfortably during their lifetime. He had in all 4,000 tunnland or about 5,000 acres of land of which only six acres were cultivated. Many of the neighboring peasants were likewise forced to sell to the lumber corporations which threatened to obtain control of all the lands in the region. Z. H., the emigrant, had left Sweden in 1871 and had located, as soon as the government lands were opened, six miles from Rapid City, South Dakota. His relatives and neighbors in Sweden, dissatisfied because of the intrusion of the corporations, decided to sell and emigrate to America. In 1881, four families were on their way, and each following year others joined them. By 1907, almost one-fifth of the parish, former peasants and crofters, had joined the colony in South Dakota and many became farmers. The peasants left the homes they inherited from their forefathers, because they thought it unreasonable to have to pay the large fees connected with the division of the land.

The first region in Sweden to be exploited for its lumber resources by the Gothenburg lumber merchants was northern Dalsland and Värmland. The region lay between the two large ports of Gothenburg in Sweden, and Oslo in Norway. It was accessible by both rail and water. Norwegian lumber corporations were also interested in the profits of the region. The development here was as usual. At the beginning there was a great deal of speculation both in the purchase of the forest lands, and in the securing of rights to cut timber from the peasant proprietors. The peasants, many of them landpoor with very little money income, did not appreciate either the value of the timber they sold on root nor the lands they sold outright. They were willing to part with their treasures at very low

[1] "Utvandrarnes egna uppgifter," *Emigrationsutredningens bilaga VII*, pp. 161–63.

prices, and had many years to regret it. On the other hand, the money which they received did often tide them over periods of agricultural crises like those of 1867–68 and 1880 when they faced bankruptcy. It provided the means for emigration to the more fertile lands of America.

Where the forest land was purchased by speculators or when contracts were made for the purchase of standing timber, the land was often denuded. At first only the best timber was cut. This period fell between 1850–70, but after 1870 came a time when the trees were cut to the very bush. In Värmland were located many iron works, an old industry in Central Sweden, and dependent upon charcoal for the smelting of iron. The Brunsberg Iron Works found the forests around its works entirely gone by 1858.[1] During the period between 1857–60, in order to preserve its charcoal supply, it was forced to purchase large stretches of timberland. The general exploitation of lumber in the iron region during the seventies forced the price of charcoal to rise and brought a crisis in the iron industry.

In Brunskog parish, Värmland, a typical example of what was happening in the region, the best timber was cut during the sixties.[2] In 1880, however, lumbering began on a vast scale, and every kind of tree was felled. Wagonloads of pit-props, round birch, and planks, formed a continuous procession over the roads to Norway for exportation, largely to England. In 1907, a cheaper means of transportation had been found by water from Karlstad, Arvika, and Borgvik on Lake Väner, via the Gotha canal to Gothenburg.

In the wooded regions of northern Dalsland, thousands of acres have been devastated of its timber.[3] The inhabitants of this region had made an extra income from their labor in the lumber camps for many years. At the beginning of 1860, before the construction of railroads and the Dal canal, the owners of the forests with some help cut large timber for transportation either to Lake Väner, to the Bohus coast of Sweden, or to Norway. They were engaged also

---

[1] G. Gerhard Magnusson, "Jösse härad, Bygdeundersökningar," *Emigrationsutredningens bilaga VIII*, p. 10.

[2] *Ibid.*, pp. 21–22.

[3] Forester Mauritz Berggren, Dalslands revir, Västra distriktet, "Inkomna utlåtanden," *Emigrationsutredningens bilaga XVII*, p. 84.

in the production of charcoal. The timber that was cut was soon replaced by young trees, and the woods gave a steady income to the peasants and the crofters. With the coming of better communications, the iron works were forced by competition to discontinue and the capital was invested in paper mills. Sawmills and paper mills were erected. The younger trees were cut for pit-props to be sent to England.

There began a tremendous speculation in the lumber industry. The smaller landowners sold their timber on the root to lumber merchants and paper mills, and received a low price. It is estimated that most of the owners received about one-tenth of the present value of the lands. The purchasers of the lumber swept the land clean of timber. Often the land was sold, the timber cut, and the practically valueless land sold again for a very small price. This devastation continued in the region as late as 1907. Now the Swedish state controls the cutting of timber in even privately owned forests by legislation.

For a short time there was much demand for labor in the region and laborers were imported. After the devastation, the source of added income was gone for the peasant.[1] The region was not fertile nor the farms large enough to support the owner and the crofter. Where the timber had been cut, the homes of the peasants and crofters fell into ruin, and when the money that had been obtained from the sale of the timber was gone, emigration began.

The exodus was largest among the crofter class. This type of tenant farmer has almost disappeared in the forests of northern Dalsland. Where the forests have been cut, the few opportunities for added income made it impossible to meet the annual rental of their farms. After the tenant had left, the land was planted in forest. Even in many places upon lands owned by corporations and in the crown parks of the state the crofter was gradually disappearing in 1907. The corporations found it more profitable to employ laborers that were more mobile and had turned the little clearings back into forest.

When it was demonstrated in the region that lumbering was to be the industry of the future, the large lumbering corporations and

[1] *Ibid.*, pp. 83–85.

paper mills found the necessity of a more far-sighted policy with respect to the source of their product. Beginning in 1870 large portions of the region, especially in northern Dalsland and in Värmland, were purchased by these corporations. The ready money that the peasants received from the sale of their land enabled many from the region to emigrate to America where there was plenty of cheap land. The crisis that agriculture had passed through during the latter part of the sixties seemed a sufficient reason for the need of emigration from this particular region. A typical example was the departure of thirty persons from the farm (*hemmanet*) Dal in Töcksmark parish, when the land was sold to the Norwegian lumber corporation, Saugbrugs-föreningen of Fredrickshald in 1870.[1] Since that time, this corporation has continued to buy up large tracts of land. In the two hundreds, Vedbo in Älvsborg County and the neighboring Nordmark in Värmland, it owned in 1907 about 41,000 acres of land, of which 4,500 acres were cultivated. On some of its larger estates, the tenants were less interested in their income from agriculture than from lumber.[2] This also was true of the lands of other large corporations of the region like Gustavsfors-Fabriker A.B.

There was also on the lands of these corporations a tendency to discontinue the small farms and replant them for forest. The dissatisfaction on the part of the peasants, caused by the gradual encroachment of the corporations in the region, resulted in the sale of farms and emigration. This Norwegian corporation owned, in 1907, parts of at least fifty different farms in fifteen parishes in these two hundreds.[3] Other Norwegians owned at the time about 11,000 acres in the regions, mostly in Östervallskog. The Swedish corporations had large stretches of land in Sillerud and Silbodal, where the Gustavsfors mills owned land evaluated at 577,200 kronor ($153,000) and had their own flumes to the Silarn lakes.[4] The corporations took

[1] Ernest Lundholm, "Vedbo och Nordmarks härader, Bygdeundersökningar," *op. cit.*, p. 8.

[2] *Ibid.*, p. 27.

[3] *Ibid.*, p. 29. Thirty thousand tunnland and parts of 50 hemman in the parishes of Ärtemark, Laxarby, Steneby, Vårvik, Håbol, Nössemark, Dals-Ed, Torrskog, Blomskog, Trankil, Fågelvik, Silbodal, Sillerud, Holmedal, and Töcksmark, with the largest area of land in Nordmark härad and in the last four parishes.

[4] Östra and västra Silen.

good care of their forest lands. The law of 1917 has limited the amount of land that the corporations may acquire in the future.

The period of transition during which the lumbering industry was establishing itself upon a rational basis was a time when the aversion of the agricultural population to the encroachment of corporations caused many to emigrate. It resulted in a decimation of the population in Värmland and Dalsland. In Gunnarskog parish in Värmland, the Jössefors corporation purchased two-thirds of the 20,000 acres belonging to the estate of Träskog, including some 15,000 acres of timber. There were flumes through the land that were especially valuable to the corporation. Other large estates in the region were also purchased.

One of the peasants of the parish expressed the psychological effect of it upon the inhabitants.

> We peasants of Gunnarskog have in past ages been considered a worthy and substantial class of society. On our estates our great grandfathers, grandfathers, and fathers were born and lived their industrious lives. The different families held together and we found ourselves safe and contented. We have stood for our rights against corporations, nobles, and even the government. But now it is different. Now the bonds are broken, because the estates have changed owners and cultivators. The corporations have pushed themselves in. The corporations control the market for our forest products. They prevent us from using the flumes to float our timber. They out-vote us in the communal councils. They control even our rights to market our own property. Therefore, one peasant after another has become discouraged and has sold his estate rather than live under these conditions. More and more of us leave our farms and forest lands, and emigrate to other regions in order to obtain a decent income. The farms are naturally always sold to the corporations for they always bid the highest price.[1]

In the sixties and seventies, there were many crofters and cotters in this region. The crofter constituted the permanent agricultural labor, and provided labor for the forests in the winters. These tenant farmers had practically all disappeared in 1907. One peasant in the neighborhood could mention sixty-seven crofts within the radius of a small area that had disappeared in thirty-five years. Magnusson stated that often he would come across these formerly cultivated patches of ground far up in the forest regions, reminders of the assiduous labor and persevering patience of the former im-

[1] This statement was made in 1907 (Magnusson, *op. cit.*, pp. 29–30).

poverished inhabitants.[1] By 1907 the forest lands lay uncultivated and the peasants permitted their cattle to pasture on the land where the forest was gradually regaining its own. In 1865, there were 6,578 inhabitants in the parish of Gunnarskog and in 1907 only 4,850.[2] The decline of the demand for seasonal labor in Norrland was another factor in emigration from this region.

In the Norrland provinces of Sweden lie most of the great timber resources of the realm. The establishment of steam-driven sawmills at the mouths of the large rivers in this region, beginning in 1851 with one at Vivsta, north of Sundsvall, and another at Kramsfors in Ångermanland in 1852, gave a tremendous upward swing to the lumbering industry.[3] In the fifties but especially in the sixties, the number of sawmills increased rapidly. Sundsvall, on the Gulf of Bothnia, became the lumber market of the north, and the great sawmill center. Sawmills were however scattered over all the northern provinces.

In this region as in Värmland, the corporations began by purchase of rights from the peasants to exploit the forest lands for a period of fifty years, which was gradually reduced to ten and five years. The rights were purchased at low prices from the peasants, to whom a small sum of money in cash here also seemed a fortune. Rights were bought and sold, and speculation ran high. There was discontent among the peasants when they learned that they had sold their heritage for a song, but as long as wages in the woods remained high they were more or less reconciled.

During the seventies and eighties railroads were built through the Norrland region, and a formerly isolated rather desolate north was now brought in direct communication with the Southern Sweden, Norway, and the world lumber market. The corporations and speculators then turned to the policy of purchasing forests in order to preserve their sources of timber. Most of these sales took place between 1880–1900. To what extent the land of Norrland and Dalarne was falling into the hands of corporations may be shown by the statistics in Table X. Although the percentage in Kopparberg

[1] *Ibid.*, p. 30.　　　　[2] *Ibid.*, p. 4.

[3] Sundbärg, *Sweden, Its People and Its Resources*, pp. 637, 642–46.

County is not as great as in other counties in acres, its taxable valuation is greater because much of it is mineral lands.

From 1890 to 1900, when most of the corporation purchases took place, there was an increase in the number of farm owners in Norrland and Dalarne from 60,860 to 63,235, an increase of 2,369 persons; yet in 84 parishes there was a decline of 2,827 proprietors.[1] At the same time, the population of the region was increasing and new lands were being placed under cultivation. However, according to

TABLE X

REAL ESTATE IN RURAL DISTRICTS BELONGING TO CORPORATIONS IN
PERCENTAGE OF LAND AREA*

| Counties | 1890 | 1895 | 1900 | 1905 | 1919 |
|---|---|---|---|---|---|
| Värmland............... | 9.3 | 10.6 | 10.2 | 11.1 | 11.60 |
| Örebro................. | 9.4 | 11.5 | 12.1 | 11.7 | 9.80 |
| Kopparberg............ | 2.7 | 2.5 | 1.5 | 2.5 | 12.78 |
| Gävleborg ............. | 14.9 | 17.2 | 19.5 | 21.9 | 13.59 |
| Västernorrland......... | 14.2 | 16.1 | 19.0 | 22.5 | 11.50 |
| Jämtland............... | 8.9 | 13.6 | 17.3 | 19.7 | 9.16 |
| Västerbotten........... | 8.5 | 10.2 | 15.3 | 18.4 | 4.01 |
| Norrbotten............. | 19.6 | 18.5 | 22.3 | 24.7 | 2.23 |

* Nils Wohlin, "Bondeklassens undergräfvande," *Emigrationsutredningens bilaga X*, p. 158, Table N; source, *K. bfhde femårsberättelse*. The statistics for 1919, *Statistisk årsbok för Sverige, 1927*, p. 82, Table 78.

the estimates of the committee on Norrland, there were 12,000 peasants before 1900 who had ceased to own lands in Norrland, when they sold their land to the lumber corporations.[2]

These peasants seemed to have met one of four fates, according to the Norrland Committee, which investigated the situation for the Swedish government. Those that remained cultivators of the soil usually stayed on their former farms and became tenants of the corporations. Others moved to the cities or to the small villages that developed around railroad stations, where they bought a house and lived on the interest of their money and became involved in some form of speculation. They usually lived very high while the money lasted and ended in bankruptcy. A third group was employed by

[1] Åmark, *Utvandring och näringslif i Norrland*, Broschyrer utgifna af nationalföreningen mot emigrationen, No. 4, p. 32. Quoted from Arosenius, "Sågverks-och bruksägares jordförvärf i norra Sverige," *Ekonomisk Tidskrift*, 1905, pp. 144–45.

[2] Åmark, *ibid.* Quoted *Norrlandskomittéens betänkande* (1904), I, 57.

the corporations as agents or middlemen for the purchase of more land from the peasants. And the fourth group emigrated to America with the purchase money that they had received for their land. Or if the father remained as tenant on the old farm, the children would emigrate, dissatisfied with the lowered social and economic status of the family.

From Västernorrland County, the bailiff, a crown official, wrote in 1907:

The chief cause of emigration in the Bodum district is concentration of the ownership of land in the hands of the lumber corporations.[1] Tenants called *landbönder* are placed on the farms belonging to these corporations. They have not the means to improve their land, and do not procure even the necessities of life from the soil. They depend upon their income from hauling timber in the winter and floating logs in the summer. It appears often that they have rented the land only to be more secure in obtaining employment from the corporation. They often become indebted to the corporation for unpaid rent and are forced to remain to work off their debt. There is much misery in the tenant homes, and it is not surprising that their children, as soon as possible, emigrate to escape the poverty of their home.

A provincial physician, Dr. P. A. Tonell from the Bergsjö district of Gävleborg County made practically the same report to the Committee on Emigration the same year. He stated that one of the causes of emigration was the purchase of the peasants' farms by the corporations and the poverty which resulted on such farms for the tenants. The observation was commonly made in the district that poverty and tenantry went together, while a certain prosperity accompanied the landowning peasant. The unfavorable economic situation of the tenant might be due to the short lease of only one year. This prevented any effort to make improvements and to cultivate the land thoroughly, according to the physician, and gradually the farms deteriorated. "That emigration is influenced by the situation is self-evident," he stated. "The sons and daughters of the peasant remain at home and in turn take over the estate," he continued, "while the children of the tenant have no incentive to continue working on the farm."

The report of the provincial physician, Dr. Gustaf Windahl from

---

[1] K. Forsséen, kronolänsman in Bodums distrikt, Västernorrlands län, "Utdrag ur inkomna utlåtanden," *Emigrationsutredningens bilaga XVII*, p. 126.

the Falu district of Kopparberg County, substantiated the reports from the other two counties.[1] He stated:

I have had numerous opportunities to observe the economic, physical, and often psychological decline which so often dominates the numerous farmer-tenants of the corporations in the county, and which are such a striking contrast to the conditions on farms of equal size, owned by the peasant. As the tentacles of the corporations spread farther and farther over the countryside, emigration increases. On the other hand, the resident laborers at the large industrial mills have a good and often high standard of living.

This decline of the peasant population was especially hard on Norrland, because, as contrasted with the overpopulated Dalsland,

TABLE XI

AREA AND POPULATION OF THE NORRLAND COUNTIES*

| COUNTIES | AREA IN SQ. KM. | POPULATION | | | | | INHABIT-ANTS PER SQUARE MILE |
|---|---|---|---|---|---|---|---|
| | | 1751 | 1865 | 1900† | 1914 | 1926‡ | |
| Kopparberg..... | 29,870 | 97,428 | 174,758 | 217,708 | 241,183 | 252,865 | 22 |
| Gävleborg....... | 19,728 | 56,000 | 143,793 | 238,048 | 258,955 | 278,523 | 35 |
| Västernorrland... | 25,533 | 36,890 | 127,524 | 232,311 | 258,683 | 274,373 | 25 |
| Jämtland........ | 51,556 | 19,000 | 68,071 | 111,391 | 122,902 | 136,507 | 5 |
| Västerbotten.... | 58,934 | 18,369 | 88,763 | 143,735 | 168,378 | 198,044 | 8 |
| Norrbotten...... | 105,520 | 18,500 | 74,576 | 134,769 | 171,759 | 192,441 | 4.5 |

* Guinchard, *Sveriges Land och Folk*, I, 98.
† Åmark, *Utvandring och näringslif i Norrland*, Broschyrer utgifna af nationalföreningen mot emigrationen, No. 4, p. 7.
‡ *Statistisk årsbok för Sverige* (1927), p. 2, Table 2; p. 6, Table 9.

there was a scarcity of people. While Norrland comprises almost two-thirds of the land-area of Sweden, its population is less than one-fourth of that of the kingdom. This estimate was made after the large increase of population in the region between 1870 and 1900. Table XI shows something of the increase that took place.

The scarcity of population in this region meant a scarcity of labor-supply for the new lumber industries that were being developed in the latter half of the nineteenth century. Beginning in 1850, there was an annual supply of casual labor that found its way northward during the winter season. These lumberjacks came from the day-laboring class and even the crofters and small peasants of Småland, the island of Öland, but to a great extent from Värmland. There

[1] Gustaf Windahl, förste provinsialläkare, Falu distrikt, Kopparbergs län, *ibid.*, p. 218.

was much demand for labor for railroad construction, building flumes or floating-ways to the coast, cutting timber in the winter, and floating it in the summer. The newly erected sawmills and paper mills also needed workmen. The agricultural classes that were already located in the north found lumbering more profitable than agriculture.

Before the coming of the railroads into the north in the seventies, the seasonal laborers traveled long distances overland to their winters' employment. The inhabitants of Värmland and Dalsland, where the forests had been first exploited, proved very valuable because of their technical knowledge and experience.

On these long journeys to the lumber camps many hardships had to be endured. An immigrant from Kopparberg County related that at the age of fifteen he began to work in lumber camps in the winter and in the summer he floated lumber, so that the family income might be increased.[1] The little farm that his father owned was not large enough to provide an income for seven people. When he was eighteen, he traveled seventy English miles on foot for a job to float timber. Upon his arrival at his destination in the early spring, there was no cottage or hut of any kind for shelter. Until some kind of house was built, the workmen had to break branches of fir and lay them on two feet of snow for beds. The wage was twenty öre an hour, about five cents. O. A. had the misfortune to have his leg broken by a falling timber, and had to be carried seven miles to have it set. At the age of twenty-two he left Sweden for the lumber camps of Wisconsin. The governor of Värmland County stated that many of the people working in the lumber camps suffered from exposure and were subject to rheumatism.[2]

The people of Värmland had been wandering laborers since very early times. It was customary every spring for the men to seek work in other parts of the country, to float timber, cut trees, work as carpenters and builders, and break stone. They were noted as skilled woodsmen and workers in wood, and were always welcome wherever they went for their skill and their happy dispositions. The women

[1] "Utvandrarnes egna uppgifter," op. cit., No. 209, p. 180.

[2] Karl Arvid Edin, Fryksdals härad i Värmland, "Bygdeundersökningar," Emigrationsutredningens bilaga VIII, p. 9.

were left at home to care for the small farms, and agriculture in spite of the rather good soil became a secondary occupation. The men from Värmland became a very important factor as seasonal workers in Norrland and Dalarne until the end of the seventies. The first half of that decade is called the "golden middle age" of Norrland's development, when work was plentiful and wages exceedingly high. A middle-aged peasant from Fryksdalen in Värmland stated that during the seventies and eighties, it was considered a part of a young man's education to be able to name the important sawmills in southern and central Norrland, and to have seen most of them.[1] Another well-to-do peasant proprietor of sixty related in 1907 that at the age of twenty in 1866 he began to make trips into the forests of Norrland. He continued to make these trips every year until his father died in 1875, and he took over the farm.[2] He usually left in January and returned home in April. From 1866 to 1868 he went to Hälsingland; in 1869–70 he was in Dalarne and in 1871–75 in Medelpad and Hälsingland. The best year was in 1874, when he had forty-eight horses under his supervision and the total earnings were 78,000 kronor, or $20,000. He owned ten horses himself and made a net profit of 1,046 kronor ($278) per horse.

The young boys from Fryksdalen went out to seek work without any idea of where to find it. But as long as the people of Norrland and Dalarne were inexperienced in floating and hauling timber there was plenty of work. Their wages were high, but they lived very extravagantly; champagne for the men at many kronor a bottle and grain for the horses at 25 cents a pound was nothing unusual.[3] Many had nothing saved when the good times were over and even had contracted debts. Country stores had sprung up in every region of Värmland. The former simplicity in food, clothing, and in the home disappeared. Hats and tailored or ready-made clothing took the place of headkerchiefs, homespun, and homemade clothing. Home industry was on a decline. Meat, pork, and butter, which in former days had been used sparingly by the housewife when there was any, now was no longer holiday food, and the coffee-pot was on

[1] *Ibid.*, pp. 9–10.       [2] *Ibid.*

[3] *Ibid.*, pp. 10–11. Three kronor a kilogram for grain.

the stove continuously. Money was plentiful and credit was easily obtained.[1]

The people from Öland were also seasonal workers in Norrland during the good years of 1870. Annually there moved a stream of day-laborers to Stockholm for railroad construction and colonization work in Norrland. Every spring they left the island for the Norrland region to work in the woods, and to remain a large factor in the lumber camps of the north.[2] Some were imported as strike breakers. There was undoubtedly a large migration of agricultural labor from all parts of Sweden to Norrland, and even from the neighboring countries of Norway and Finland.

Wages in the Norrland region were until 1875 extremely high. In Gävleborg County, wages rose in the lumbering industry in 1870 from 13–18 cents a day for a man who received his food and lodging, to $1.30–$1.90 a day, and to $2.60–$4.00 for a man with a horse.[3] The cost of living was also very high.

By 1879, a crisis had appeared in the lumbering industries. The price of lumber fell very low because of the fluctuations of the foreign market. Where at the Sundsvall market in 1874 the price of sawn timber was $44.00 per standard, in 1879 only $20.00 was paid.[4] A crisis followed which eliminated much of the speculative element in the industry. Crises have occurred since, but have been more easily weathered.

One of the consequences of the crisis of 1879 was the great Sundsvall strike of that year among the workmen in the sawmills. There was as yet no organization of workmen in Sweden. The old gild regulations had been repealed by the Riksdag in 1846. There had been a smaller strike among the lumberyard workmen in 1878. But the Sundsvall strike was an epoch-making event. Because of the falling price of lumber, the sawmills attempted to lower the wages of the workmen 15 to 20 per cent from the previous year. It was a

[1] G. Gerhard Magnusson, *op. cit.*, p. 15.

[2] Helge Nelson, "Öland, Bygdeundersökningar," *Emigrationsutredningens bilaga VIII*, p. 33.

[3] Agathon Westman, hushållningssällskapets sekreterare, Gäfleborgs län, "*Utdrag ur inkomna utlåtanden*," *Emigrationsutredningens bilaga XVII*, p. 64.

[4] Sundbärg, *Sweden, Its People and Its Resources*, p. 638.

twelve-hour day and the wages fell as low as 23 to 65 cents a day. With the high living costs in Norrland, the workmen felt that they could not live on the wage, and the housing conditions were very bad, since the population in the region had grown so rapidly. One Isidor Kjellberg, who dressed as a workman inspected the living conditions at Sunds sawmill soon after the beginning of the strike, and found thirty-six families in a large barrack, each family in a small room.[1] The wage frequently included living quarters.

The sawmill workers had never had the high wages of the lumberjacks. There was much discontent, and even without leadership a strike soon developed. The Riksdag had subsidized the lumbering interests with $750,000 to meet the crisis. The workmen felt that the sawmill corporations were not justified in lowering their wages and decided to resist. On May 26, 1879, a committee of four representing the lumberyard workmen called at the office of Heffner and Company near Sundsvall.[2] They demanded the last year's wages, but were summarily dismissed. The news spread and by the following day the workmen in most of the sawmills were dismissed. From the neighboring sawmills groups of workmen marched to Sundsvall under red flags, where they camped at the sharpshooters' lodge. The whole proceeding was orderly. The next day some thirty sawmills were closed and there were gathered about 1,000 strikers in Sundsvall. A demonstration was held in the streets. The governor of Västernorrland County, Treffenberg, tried to disperse them by appealing to them to be reasonable. Troops and gunboats were sent by the government. On June 3, after a week of demonstration, the troops were ordered to surround the strikers; 1,000 were fined; seven were imprisoned as leaders; 36 were incarcerated as vagrants, and about 1,000 were forced by the troops to return to their work. It left in the minds of the laboring classes in Sweden an indelible impression. The conflict between capital and labor had begun.

Strikes broke out practically all over Norrland following the

[1] G. Gerhard Magnusson, *Social Demokratien i Sverige*, I, 50–51. Also, *U.S. Consular Letters, 1864–88*, Gothenburg, Ernest L. Oppenheim, consul, October 1, 1879.

[2] *Ibid*. When the timber fleet came up in the spring a general strike took place extending to about 7,000 workers. The royal guard battalion was called to put down the strike.

Sundsvall strike. In Gävle, Söderhamn, Hudiksvall, Skutskärp Saltvik, Stocka, and Östersund, there were strikes almost simultaneous among the sawmill workers, and in some cases among the railroad construction men.[1] Army corps were sent to the regions and gunboats guarded the harbors; the strikers were intimidated everywhere as they had been at Sundsvall. In four weeks, the strikes were over and the workmen had to take the lower wages.

The lumbering industry recovered in the eighties.[2] The process of industrialization went on rapidly in Norrland and it continued a region of immigration. But the prosperity of the former decade did not return. Wages had declined and there was no longer a need for

TABLE XII

| INDUSTRIALIZATION OF NORRLAND* | PERCENTAGE OF POPULATION | |
|---|---|---|
| Counties | 1840 | 1900 |
| Gävleborg | 11.7 | 40.3 |
| Västernorrland | 6.9 | 31.7 |
| Jämtland | 2.5 | 20.7 |
| Västerbotten | 3.4 | 17.4 |
| Norrbotten | 4.0 | 23.3 |
| Whole Kingdom | 8.5 | 28.9 |

* Åmark, *Utvandring och naringslif i Norrland*, p. 12.

the seasonal worker. Enough labor had settled permanently in Norrland to meet the demands. The rural population of the region had learned the skill of the trade from their fellow-countrymen from Värmland whose services could now be dispensed with.

The seasonal workers from Värmland and Öland now began to turn their course toward the United States. Some went to earn more money because of the higher wages there, planning to return to Sweden and engage in agriculture. The great majority did not return but settled permanently in the land across the sea. There had been practically no emigration from Öland, Värmland, and the neighboring region of Dalsland to the United States until the years of the great famine, 1867–69. From that time on, there came a

[1] Magnusson: *Social Demokratien i Sverige*, I, 55.

[2] Wohlin, "Den jordbrukssidkande befolkningen i Sverige, 1751–1900," *Emigrationsutredningens bilaga IX*, pp. 4, 131, 137.

steady stream of emigrants. In the eighties when emigration was very large from all provinces of Sweden, because of the agricultural crisis in Europe, the exodus from these regions was undoubtedly caused as much by the decline of labor opportunities in Norrland as by the low prices for agricultural products. During this decade, Värmland sent more emigrants to the United States than any other county, a total of 28,084.[1] From 1851 to 1910, this county had lost 77,574 inhabitants in emigration to the United States, the greatest exodus from any Swedish county. The population had declined from 271,158 in 1879 to 250,935 in 1893. Since then there has been a slight annual increase. According to the investigations made in 1907, in this region, the soil is rather good and could easily be brought under profitable cultivation.[2] There is, however, a feeling that one cannot do much with agriculture; it is not profitable. The people of Värmland are intelligent and skilled craftsmen in lumbering and woodwork. They are a joyous, joking, and happy-go-lucky people who seek the regions where their labor is most profitable. They have always wandered from their homes, and now America is the labor market that draws them.

From the island of Öland, with a population of 38,056,[3] there was an emigration to the United States of 4,786 persons during the decade of 1880. Here again the closing of the seasonal labor market in Norrland had much to do with the exodus, as well as the decline, in the Swedish market for agricultural labor.

Norrland, however, was looked upon as a second America, as a colonization land for Southern Sweden until 1900. The population of Norrland steadily increased. Lumber became with iron the chief export from Sweden, and the source of much of the national wealth.[4] The exportation of lumber continued to increase until 1890 when Sweden was the greatest lumber exporting country in the world.[5] From 1891 to 1895 Sweden exported $30,000,000; Austro-Hungary, $24,000,000; Canada, $22,000,000; Russia, $21,900,000; United States, $20,000,000; Finland, $9.900,000; and Norway, $7,500,000.

[1] "Svenskarna i utlandet," *Emigrationsutredningens bilaga XX*, p. 112, Table 13.
[2] Edin, *op. cit., bilaga VII*, pp. 21–23; Magnusson, "Jösse härad," *op. cit.*, p. 15.
[3] Nelson, *op. cit.*, pp. 7, 10.
[4] Sundbärg, *Sweden, Its People and Its Resources*, p. 639.   [5] *Ibid.*, p. 638.

Many of the poorer peasants and crofters in Norrland were able to make a comfortable living by their labor in hauling, floating, and cutting timber. They did not feel the agricultural crisis of the eighties. Even after the "good times" of 1870, wages remained higher in Norrland than in any other region of Sweden. They averaged between 1880–1910 about 80 cents a day for a man, or from $1.60 to $2.15 for a man with a horse. Most of the peasants furnished their own horses and hauled timber. These wages were reported from Dalarne by Gösta Englund, forester of Väster-Dalarnes revir in the Gävle-Dala district.[1] The same wages were paid in Norrbotten and Väster-botten counties according to the report of the head forester, T. W. Hermelin, of the Skellefteå district.[2] In this region the peasant proprietors, tenant farmers, and day-laborers along the coast would travel from 70 to 140 English miles up into the Lappmark to the lumber camps during the winter. The tenants of the corporations and the day-laborers depended upon lumbering almost entirely for their income. The floating of timber was usually the work of those living near the flumes and the wages averaged between 67 to 94 cents a day. Often the cutting of timber was let out by contract to peasants, usually at a very low figure.[3]

Not only in Norrland but even in the wooded districts of Dalsland and Småland, the poorer peasant, the crofter, and the cotter can make a comfortable income by his labor in the woods during the winter. Where their pieces of land are too small to bring sufficient income for the family, these opportunities of employment have enabled many to remain. It has prevented undoubtedly emigration which otherwise would have taken place. If these opportunities cease, as in Dalsland, by the devastation of the forests, the population leaves for America. In the report of the Northern Agricultural Society (Hushållningssällskap) of Kalmar County in 1907, the secretary called attention to the fact that in the wooded regions of the provinces, there had always been opportunities to earn good wages in lumbering.[4] There is however a constant complaint from

[1] "Utdrag ur inkomna utlåtanden," *op. cit.*, p. 86.

[2] *Ibid.*, pp. 93–94.

[3] J. Norder, kronolänsman, Torsåkers distrikt, Västernorrlands län, *ibid.*, p. 125.

[4] Edward Fleetwood, Kalmar läns, Norra hushållningssällskap, *ibid.*, p. 24.

these regions that agriculture is neglected for the more immediate returns from lumbering.

The forests remain one of the greatest of Sweden's natural resources, and lumber and wood pulp are her largest exports. The export of wood-products and paper-pulp from Sweden has been steadily increasing since 1871. In spite of this fast growth, she no longer holds the position in that industry that was hers in 1890. At that time, of the seven countries that were exporting rough lumber— Sweden, Norway, Finland, Austro-Hungary, Russia, United States, and Canada—Sweden exported 22 per cent of all the lumber, and ranked first in lumber export.[1] By 1906, although the exports of Sweden had increased, Sweden was exporting only 16.17 per cent of the world-supply, and had been surpassed by Russia, Austro-Hungary, and the United States. The height of the wood-products industry was reached during the World War. Since 1920, there have been a number of crises caused by the new competition from the countries of the Baltic. This competition of Russia, Poland, Czecho-Slovakia, and the Baltic states, but especially of Latvia, and Finland, has cut prices and forced some of the lumber interests into the wood-pulp business.[2] The export corporation of the lumber industries (Trävaruexportföreningen) which was organized in 1906 in Sweden to handle the foreign market went to pieces under the crisis of 1921, and brought about competition even in the Swedish home market.[3]

The average number of laborers employed in the lumbering industry at the sawmills has been about 40,000 since 1896.[4] During two years, 1900 and 1920, there was a marked increase in labor within this industry, raising the number to 43,000 and 46,000 respectively. These proved to be only temporary increases. Besides these men, it is estimated that an additional force of 150,000 laborers work in the forests during the winter season, cutting and hauling timber. Most of them are seasonal laborers and are to a great extent agri-

[1] Sundbärg, "Allmänna ekonomiska data rörande Sverige," *Emigrationsutredningens bilaga XIII*, p. 57.

[2] Karl Hildebrand, *Gustav V*, pp. 555–56.

[3] *Ibid.; Svenska Industrien vid kvartsekelskiftet, 1925*, p. 240.

[4] *Svenska Industrien vid kvartsekelskiftet, 1925*, p. 240.

culturalists. In the summer, there is employment for about 20,000 men in floating timber. They are also mostly agriculturalists and seasonal workers, although some men cut timber in the winter and float logs in the summer. The extent of the industry in 1923 is shown by the Table XIV.

TABLE XIII

EXPORT OF WOOD PRODUCTS FROM SWEDEN
1871–1928*

| | VALUES IN MILLION KRONOR | |
|---|---|---|
| YEAR | Products of Forestry and Timber Industries | Products of Paper Industry |
| 1871–80......... | 89.9 | 5.7 |
| 1881–90......... | 102.0 | 18.1 |
| 1891–1900...... | 136.4 | 30.8 |
| 1901–10......... | 162.5 | 72.4 |
| 1911–20......... | 295.4 | 277.6 |
| 1923........... | 313.7 | 314.7 |
| 1928........... | 315.3 | 370.5 |

* *Sweden Year Book, 1926*, p. 115. *Statistisk årsbok för Sverige, 1930*, p. 135.

TABLE XIV

WOOD PRODUCTS INDUSTRY IN SWEDEN 1928*

| | Number of Factories | Personnel, Administrative | Workers | Market Value of Products (Kronor in Thousands) |
|---|---|---|---|---|
| Sawmills and planing mills.......... | 1,466 | 2,212 | 46,423 | 363,414 |
| Box and veneer factories............ | 48 | 71 | 1,148 | 8,547 |
| Joinery and furniture factories...... | 972 | 1,047 | 15,105 | 83,528 |
| Other wood products.............. | 164 | 211 | 2,347 | 17,274 |
| Total...................... | 2,650 | 3,541 | 65,023 | 472,763 |

* *Statistisk årsbok för Sverige, 1930*, p. 118.

Among the various manufactured wood-products produced in Sweden are building materials like doors, window frames, etc. The manufacture of these products had an upward swing in the later sixties and increased especially in the last decade with the demand for building materials from Germany.[1] About one-fourth of the pro-

[1] *Svenska Industrien vid kvartsekelskiftet, 1925*, p. 247.

duction is exported, much going now to England, South Africa, and Argentine. A cartel (Sveriges Snickeriexportföreningen) controls the foreign export market. The manufacturing of furniture began in the eighties and the present export amounts to $270,000 a year.[1] Barrels and cartons of various kinds form another branch of the wood-products industries. The increased demand in the eighties produced by the growing export of butter and the growth of the Bohuslän fisheries of the west coast gave an impetus to this industry.[2] Then there are all the other various products made from wood—wagon wheels, sport goods, and musical instruments. There are also fifteen cork factories in Sweden that manufacture various forms of cork-products, including linoleum, life-saving belts, and soles for shoes.[3]

The wood-pulp and paper industries are beginning to surpass the wood-products industries in the kingdom. The manufacture of paper is an old industry in the country. The oldest paper mill still in existence is Klippan, established in 1573. Lessebo dates from 1660, and Grycksbo and Gransholm from the eighteenth century.[4] There were fourteen papers mills in Sweden in 1700.[5] An ordinance of 1612 provided that every household had to produce a certain amount of clean linen rags for the mills. With the introduction of machines for the manufacture of paper in the nineteenth century, there came a great scarcity of raw materials. After experimenting with many different materials, it was finally discovered about 1850 that wood pulp could be used. The discovery was made in Germany and chemical experiments continued in the United States. It was, however, a Swedish engineer, Carl Daniel Ekman, who discovered the sulphite methods of preparation of wood pulp in 1873.[6] The first wood-pulp mill in Sweden was erected in 1857.[7] By 1870, there were ten mills. In the eighties there was a greater increase in the mechanical wood-pulp industry. In the nineties there developed a greater tendency toward the chemical processes and a boom period for the manufacture of cellulose. The sulphite industry has also developed rapidly.

[1] *Ibid.*, p. 248.   [3] *Ibid.*, p. 252.

[2] *Ibid*, p. 249.   [4] *Sweden Year Book, 1926*, p. 104.

[5] Carl Grimberg, "Ur den svenska industriens äldre historia," *op. cit.*, p. 27.

[6] *Svenska industrien vid kvartsekeskiftet, 1925*, p. 253.

[7] *Ibid.*, p. 254.

Sweden exports about 75 per cent of its production of wood pulp and in 1929 it amounted to about $84,000,000, or about 17 per cent of the country's export.[1] Only the United States and Canada produce more wood pulp than Sweden, and the export from Sweden is the largest of any country in the world. In spite of its own large domestic production, the United States is the greatest importer of ·Swedish wood pulp. England is the next largest purchaser. Large quantities also go to France, Spain, and Italy. Two

TABLE XV

The Pulp and Paper Industries in Sweden in 1928*

| | Number of Factories | Personnel | | Market Value of Products (Thousand Kronor) |
|---|---|---|---|---|
| | | Administrative | Workers | |
| Wood pulp mills | 106 | 987 | 18,995 | 248,910 |
| Paper mills and cardboard | 77 | 1,181 | 17,252 | 191,217 |
| Cardboard wares and other paper products | 215 | 819 | 5,945 | 44,056 |
| Wall-paper mills | 12 | 107 | 351 | 5,100 |
| Printers of illustrated matter | 77 | 220 | 1,554 | 13,340 |
| Book Printing | 576 | 2,366 | 11,133 | 125,518 |
| Total | 1,063 | 5,680 | 55,230 | 628,149 |

* *Statistisk årsbok för Sverige, 1930*, p. 118.

cartels (Svenska cellulosaföreningen and Svenska Trämasseföreningen), the former controlling the chemical and the later the mechanical wood-pulp industries, are located in Stockholm.[2] The wood-pulp industry is localized largely along the coast of Norrland. There are some mills in Värmland and Dalsland. Various by-products are also produced, like turpentine, and ethyl gas.

Most of the paper mills are localized in Central and Southern Sweden. Many of these mills produce their own wood pulp. The Norrköping region manufactures the greatest amount, while Kvarnsveden and Grycksbo in Dalarne, Hallstavik in Uppland, and the region around Gothenburg also make large quantities.[3] The paper mills organized into a cartel in 1898, called "Svenska Pappersbruk-

[1] *Ibid.*, p. 255. *Statistisk årsbok för Sverige, 1930*, p. 141.

[2] *Svenska industrien vid kvartsekelskiftet, 1925*, p. 257.   [3] *Ibid.*, p. 265.

föreningen" which controls sales and fixes prices in the industry. The paper industry has had a period of expanding prosperity with the exception of the years during the war and several crises since 1875. Next to Canada, Sweden is the greatest exporter of paper. Swedish paper is sold all over the world but the chief customers are England, United States, Japan, and France.[1]

The famous Swedish match industry which is known the world around may be classified either with the wood-products or the chemical products of Sweden. The first match produced in 1843 in Stockholm was a phosphorous match. The discovery by Professor G. E. Pasch of Sweden in 1844, that a safety match could be produced by rubbing a surface containing amorphous phosphorus, laid the foundation of the present Swedish match industry.[2] A few years later Johan Edward Lundström with his brother began the production of Swedish safety matches at Jönköping. During the seventies and eighties, there were some thirty mills manufacturing matches in Sweden. Most of the chemicals except chlorate of potash used in the manufacture of matches must be imported. Sweden's supply of aspen, the best wood for the production of matches has been practically exhausted, and large quantities are imported from Finland and Russia.[3] However, if need be, Swedish woods like alder, birch, and spruce could be substituted.[4] The height of match production in Sweden was reached in 1916 in spite of the intense competition of Japan.[5] There followed a depression in the industry after the war, but since 1924 the production has begun to increase. Swedish engineers, the most famous Alex Lagerman, have invented special machines for this industry. The largest of the complete machines can produce 40,000 packages of matches per hour.[6]

The Swedish match industry became a monopoly in 1917 when the various corporations were merged into one, Svenska Tändsticks A.B., with a capital stock of $50,000,000.[7] During 1924 with the aid

[1] *Ibid.*, p. 264.

[2] *Svenska industrien vid kvartsekelskiftet, 1925*, p. 336; Sundbärg, *Sweden, Its People and Its Resources*, p. 823.

[3] Sundbärg, *ibid.*, p. 825.

[4] *Svenska industrien vid kvartsekelskiftet, 1925*, p. 337.

[5] *Ibid.*, p. 336.     [6] *Ibid.*, p. 338.     [7] *Ibid.*, pp. 338–39.

of foreign capital this corporation has been able to bring under its control match industries in other countries so that it now controls one-third of the world production.

With the development of the lumbering industries came the problem of labor. After the great Sundsvall strike of 1879, there followed a period of organization of the workers of the sawmills into unions. Beginning with the eighties a period of stress and strain followed with propaganda for union organization and for social democracy on the laborer's side, with refusals to recognize the right of collective bargaining, black lists, and lockouts on the part of the sawmill owners. August Palm, the veteran agitator for Socialism, included Norrland in his trips through Sweden. In 1885 with Frederick Sterky he visited Norrland, starting at Gävle.[1] During the same year a strike involving 400 sawmill workers took place in Hudiksvall, as a protest against a 20 per cent reduction in wages.[2]

The first union among the wood workers in Norrland was the lumberyard workers union (Brädgårdsarbetarfackföreningen) which was organized in 1886 upon the initiative of O. Danielsson,[3] who had become the organizer of unions in the north. In 1897, the first sawmill industrial union (Sågverksindustriarbetareförbundet) was established with Danielsson as president. Although there were 40,000 laborers in the sawmills at the time in Sweden only 1,000 were organized. The great Sundsvall lockout in 1899 which attempted to crush the socialistic union movement in the sawmill districts of the north all but succeeded.[4] At the Sörvik mill north of Sundsvall the workers were forbidden to organize. A lockout resulted, and after several weeks some seventeen families were evicted from the corporation houses in the bitter winter weather.[5] These conflicts continued for several years. Finnish strike breakers were imported into the region. A conflict between the workers who were locked out at Sörvik and a group of Finnish strike breakers occurred on the ice at Alnösund a Saturday night just before Christmas, 1904. Workmen were arrested with the president of the union. Eight workmen were sentenced to terms varying from one to eight months.

[1] Magnusson, *Social-Demokratien i Sverige*, I, 89.

[2] *Ibid.*, p. 295.  [4] *Ibid.*, pp. 109, 119.

[3] *Ibid.*, II (Stockholm, 1921), 119.  [5] *Ibid.*, pp. 110 ff.

The mill owners of the Sundsvall district quietly acquiesced to the organization of unions within their industries in 1906 and 1907, and attempted to establish industrial peace. But the resistance of the Kempe mills at Dal and Sandö brought about an attempt on the part of the workers to blockade the mills, both by land and by sea. In 1907, the workmen stormed the barracks where the strike breakers were housed. Three of the young strikers were sentenced to eight years imprisonment, while some thirty-three in all were given a sentence of several months each. The strike was finally settled on June 22, 1907, and the right to organize was recognized in Norrland.[1] In the great strike of 1909 when most of the industries of the country were involved, the sawmill regions of Norrland were some of the sore spots. From 1910 on through the World War, conditions were fairly good. But in the period of readjustment, after the war from 1919 to 1924, there were many strikes and lockouts. During 1921 and 1922 wages were cut 47 per cent in the sawmill industries, and 52 per cent in the wood-pulp mills. The years of 1922 and 1923 were particularly marked as years of extensive unemployment. The Norrland region also suffered from unemployment in 1926, following the bankruptcy of some of the larger corporations in the region.

The industrialization of Norrland, the extensive development of the lumbering and wood-pulp industries, which developed the problems of unemployment, of union organizations, and strikes, became new factors in encouraging emigration to the United States. Among the emigrants interviewed in 1907 was A., a married man of thirty from Västernorrland County.[2] He was a sawmill worker, as had been his father before him. At the age of eleven he began to work in one of the larger sawmills in the Sundsvall district. After a time he was employed in piling lumber and continued in this occupation until the winter 1899, when as a member of a union he lost his job in the lockout. Later he was employed in the same kind of work at a neighboring sawmill where he remained until shortly before he emigrated. During the last years (prior to 1907) his daily wage had been $1.20 to $1.35 in the summer and 82 to 90 cents in the winter.

[1] *Ibid.*, 117.        [2] "Utvandrarnes egna uppgifter," *op. cit.*, No. 100, pp. 84-85.

His annual income was about 1,200 kronor ($322). For rent for one room and a kitchen in the town where his work was located he paid 140 kronor ($37.50) while his taxes amounted to 70 kronor ($19.00). His income was scarcely sufficient for the bare necessities of life for a family of four.

A. had been a member and even the treasurer of the local branch of the sawmill workers union (Sågverksarbetareförbundet), as well as a member of one of the larger sick-benefit associations. He had belonged to the relief fund of the mill workers and had taken out a life insurance for $268 just before he left Sweden. For many years he had been a member of the International Order of Good Templars, a temperance organization. His fear that because of his activities in the union he would be dismissed from his work and be blackballed, resulted in his emigration. He was interviewed while on his way to a brother-in-law in a smaller city in New York state, who was a contractor, and he expected to be employed at carpentry.[1] Later he hoped to send for his wife and two children.

The result of unemployment or its treat was shown by a small group of emigrants from a certain sawmill in Västerbotten County in 1907. The mill was to be closed for a time while it was being merged with a neighboring mill owned by the same corporation, but there had been a temporary cessation of labor during the change and some thirty of its employees decided to leave for the United States.[2] From this particular sawmill some 250 persons had emigrated in the fifteen years previous to 1907.[3] Most of them had gone to Seattle, Washington, and the neighboring region. At least one hundred belonged to the same Baptist church in that city, where a Swedish-American sawmill manager was superintendent. These emigrants of 1907 were going now to their friends and religious brethren in Seattle.

Among the group was A., a married man of 37, who had been manager of a store in his community.[4] He was accompanied by his wife and four children. A. was the son of a sawmill owner. He began work as a young boy in the industry in the Sundsvall district.

---

[1] A. was interviewed while on shipboard.

[2] "Utvandrarnes egna uppgifter," *op. cit.*, p. 92.

[3] *Ibid.*, p. 90.          [4] *Ibid.*, No. 105, pp. 89-90.

Seventeen years before his emigration, he moved to Västerbotten County, and for nine years worked as a sorter. His average daily wage had been 3.25 kronor or about $1.00. He also received a free dwelling consisting of one room and kitchen. At the end of the nine years, he became manager of a co-operative store established by the workmen at an annual salary of $1,200. He did not like this and finally became manager of a branch of a large retail corporation. He had no special reason for emigrating, except that many friends were leaving for Seattle.

Another of the same company was J., a machinist, who was emigrating with his wife and foster daughter.[1] He had worked for the last eighteen years at this same sawmill and had now been informed that the mill was to be discontinued. For many years he had earned 130 kronor a month, about $35.00, but his wages had been lowered to 125 kronor. He was a graduate of the machinist division of the Stockholm navigation school. With his wages he had received free dwelling, two rooms and a kitchen, free firewood, and a potato patch. As life-insurance agent, he had made a little extra income. He had a paid-in policy of $1,270. He had been superintendent of the Baptist church in the community, and probably would not have emigrated had he not had many friends and religious brethren in Seattle.

Just general discontent and a poor spirit of sportsmanship among his fellow-workmen led M., a married man of 27, to emigrate from Norrland in 1907.[2] His father was the manager of a sawmill in the region. At the age of ten he had started work at various small jobs in another sawmill nearby. For ten years, he loaded lumber at the same mill with an annual income of from 850 to 900 kronor, about $240. During the last year he had carried planks, but during the winter he received only $4.50 to $5.50 every two weeks for a 59-hour week. He had owned his own cottage of three rooms and a kitchen, for seven years, but it was located on the corporation's soil. He had leased two rooms at an annual rental of $6.50. His taxes were 40 kronor or $10.72 a year. He was discontented because of the attitude of the workmen and the lack of educational opportunities. There were no diversions besides the meetings of the free churches and the

[1] *Ibid.*, No. 109, pp. 94–95.          [2] *Ibid.*, No. 106, pp. 90–91.

temperance societies of which he belonged to the I.O.G.T., except the dance halls. The village library was the only institution for the people's education in the community. (In many communities there were Workmen's institutes or schools (Folketshus). There was no union at the sawmill but the workmen had recently established an isolated organization.

Labor discontent and industrial crises had now taken the place of crop failures as industrialism had become the more important in Sweden. America, the land of opportunity, remained the mecca when misfortune or misunderstanding threatened the European.

Sweden, however, realized the value of her vast timberlands in Norrland and the value of her population for the future prosperity of the country. The reaction which came in Norrland after 1900, when emigration from this region threatened both agriculture and the lumbering industries, was a problem that was studied in great detail. The Norrland question (*Norrlandsfrågan*) became almost a by-word in Swedish politics.[1] The government appointed special Norrland committees to investigate the situation carefully. Upon the recommendations of these committees several new laws were passed.

Experience had to teach Sweden the need to care for her great natural resources. From rather an indifferent attitude toward the exploitation of timber, especially of the pine and fir, of which she seemed to have such superabundance, there came first an effort to control absolute devastation by limiting the kinds of trees that could be cut. Then followed laws limiting the number of years that contracts for cutting of timber might be executed between owners of land and lumber corporations. The next danger that threatened the Norrland region was the purchase of land by the corporations from the peasants and the exodus of the free landed class. This meant the decline of agriculture and also the decrease of population in the region. The report of the Norrland Committee of the Riksdag in 1904 resulted in the passage of a law in 1906 forbidding the sale of land to corporations or associations in the four northern counties and

[1] A discussion of the Norrland question may be found in many sources, i.e., Sundbärg, *Emigrationsutredningens betänkande*, pp. 743–55; Åmark, *op. cit.*, No. 4 (Stockholm, 1912).

certain portions of Hälsingland without permission of the government.[1] The law was extended in 1912 to the upper part of Hälsingland, in 1917 to Värmland, and in 1921 to all of Sweden. A new law of 1925 incorporating the former laws has definitely established the principle that corporations and economic associations can purchase only a limited amount of land under restricted conditions and for certain purposes.[2]

The law of 1903 restricted the right of the private owner or the commune to cut timber on their own lands. Only timber that has been designated for cutting by the government foresters may be felled. The various laws concerning the preservation of the forests were incorporated into a new law in 1923.[3] There are also provisions for planting of trees for the protection of the forests.

The present ownership of the forests of Sweden continues to be divided among the state, the local communities, individual owners, and corporations. There were in 1925 some 14,777,000 hectares or 36,942,000 acres of forest lands belonging to private interests.[4] The state owned 21,780,000 acres the same year. The public forests are divided into several groups. The crown parks which are forest preserves had increased since 1875 from almost 5 million to about 13 million acres in 1925. These figures do not include the 3.5 million acres of impediments or wastelands in the region. The increase is due to the addition of devastated crownlands, of lands reverting to the crown that had been leased to lumber corporations or used by smelting plants for charcoal, and finally the inclusion of lands which had been formerly leased. There were at the time about 3 million acres that have never been incorporated into civil divisions lying mostly in the north in the Lappmark regions. The leased domains of the crown have diminished since 1880 by 382,000 acres, and only 240,000 acres remained in 1925. Much of this land has been sold. The same is true of the civil and ecclesiastic estates that belong to the crown. There are small portions of crownlands still under lease

[1] Ekeberg, "Öfversikt öfver de viktigaste sociala jordlagstiftnings problemen," G. H. von Koch, *Social handbok* (Stockholm, 1925), pp. 368–69.

[2] H. Westring, *Sveriges rikes lag*, pp. 157–60.     [3] *Ibid.*, B. 1379.

[4] Sundbärg, "Allmänna ekonomiska data rörande Sverige," *op. cit.*, p. 52. Gives data for 1909. *Statistisk årsbok för Sverige, 1925*, p. 85, Table 84 and p. 102, Table 96.

to certain lumber corporations called *stockfångstskogar*, dating from early contracts. These leases were formerly made to encourage the development of the lumber industries. But these lands are fast reverting to the crown.

The local communities had forests amounting to about 2,441,000 acres in 1925. These common woodlands are divided between various hundreds, and also certain parishes and cities. In Norrbotten when the timber was being cut, the landowners of the parish set aside certain pieces of forest preserves to be kept intact for common use. In Kopparberg County the parish woodlands were reserved at the time of the enclosures.

There were in 1880 about 2,500,000 acres of land held for settlers on crownlands. There have always been opportunities for settlements on the crownlands in the north. With the demand for this ownership of land which came from the lower agricultural classes and induced so many to seek the free or cheap lands in America, there developed a movement in Sweden to open homesteads in Norrland for colonization. At the time of the investigation of the causes of emigration by the government in 1907, reports were made on the homestead movement in the United States and the small farm movements in the British Isles and Germany.[1] The various monographs published by the National Society against Emigration in its effort to reach constructive means to combat emigration also emphasized the possibilities of a colonization movement in Sweden.[2]

It was not, however, until 1918 that the Swedish government began an extensive plan of colonization in the Norrland region. The best lands nearest the means of communication and the coast were already in the hands of private individuals and lumber corporations. There were, however, lands especially in the Lappmark region that were marshy but could be drained and were very fertile. The region is being drained, a system of roads has been constructed by the government, and new extensions of railraods are making the region

[1] Steffen, Bergholm, och Eckerborn, "Småburk rörelsen å de Brittiska öarna samt inre kolonisationen i Preussen och Förenta Staterna," *Emigrationsutredningens bilaga XIV* (Stockholm, 1909).

[2] Adrian Molin, *Några drag af kolonisationen i Canada*, Broschyrer utgifna af nationalföreningen mot emigrationen, No. 6 (Stockholm, 1913).

more accessible to markets.[1] A colonization committee was appointed by the riksdag to take charge of the project.

There are two kinds of homesteads granted. The smallest one is for settlers who will make most of their income in the forests of the region. This piece of land is about 6 hectares or 15 acres in extent. The larger homesteads for farmers consist of 15 hectares or about 37 acres.[2] The government has erected the framework of the buildings on the farm. The house usually consists of one larger room and a kitchen but with possibilities of expansion. Lumber is furnished at cost by the government for the completion of the buildings. If the colonist desires, he may construct his own buildings, in which case his house usually becomes more pretentious. During the more expensive period following the World War, the building cost averaged the government 9,000 kronor or over $2,000, although the lumber was cut in the region by movable gasoline saws. As prices have fallen, the cost has decreased to 4,500 or 5,000 kronor.

The ditching for draining the marshland was left to the colonist but he was given 500 kronor for the first 3 acres. The spring comes very late in this northern region. Not before the last of May is it possible to sow grain. Oats are usually harvested as green fodder for cattle. The soil is very wet and it has proved better to plow with belt tractors furnished by the government than with horses. Most of the colonists own from one to five cows. A cattle loan fund to enable the colonists to obtain stock was organized and had expended 35,000 kronor in loans to farmers by 1923. The loans are to be paid in five years on an amortization plan with 5 per cent interest.[3]

With the homesteads of from 15 to 37 cultivated acres came the rights to a certain amount of pasture land and woodland, a house with one room completed, or 4,500 kronor in building loan and 500 kronor for the first 3 acres ditched. The colonist has ten years to complete his buildings and receives his timber standing gratis. He has the right to use his land for fifteen years. At the end of ten

[1] G. H. Paulsen, "Svensk statskolonisasjon," *Ny Jord* (Oslo, 1925) No. 4, pp. 136–37.

[2] *Ibid.*, pp. 137 ff.; Carl Mannerfelt, "Egnahemsverksamheten och den inre kolonisationen," in v. Koch, *Social handbok*, pp. 383–85.

[3] Paulsen, *op. cit.*, p. 142.

years he may purchase the land at a specified sum. Within five years he must have drained 3 acres, and within fifteen years, 6 acres. He pays no rent for five years, and then pays an annual rental of 180 kronor or $45.00 for his buildings, plus 2.6 per cent of the value of the land. The land is evaluated at $6.50 an acre for woodland and $3.25 for swamp land. The colonist has the responsibility of repairing houses, ditches, and roads. In case of purchase, the buildings are valued at 5,000 kronor, if constructed by the state. Payment for the homestead is in the form of a government loan which is amortized in thirty-one years with an interest of 3.6 per cent.

The colonization committee had planned some 700 homesteads and completed 500, at a cost of $1,250,000. There has been much criticism of the project. The chief objections are that the buildings are too expensive and the situation too isolated. It is hard to predict to what extent the region will develop and become populated. Others feel that in competition with the 160 acres granted in the United States, and at present by Canada, the homesteads are too small.[1] There will undoubtedly be some change in the policy and in the control of the colonization project.

The future of Sweden's prosperity lies to a great extent in the exploitation of her natural resources. The development of the lumber industry has provided labor for many thousands who might otherwise have sought an economic outlet in emigration. There were, however, the periods of adjustment when the lumbering corporations caused emigration by supplanting the small freeholders of the Norrland region. And just as agriculture suffered from crop failures and crises from the competition of grain from cheaper virgin soils, so the lumbering industries suffer from the crises of competition and falling prices on the world market. The discontent of labor with wages and living conditions, with periods of unemployment, have created new causes for emigration. These are, however, more or less temporary as yet within this great industry of Sweden.

[1] Adrian Molin, *Till saken, vidräkning och uppslag i jordfrågan* (Uppsala, 1924).

# CHAPTER X

## INDUSTRIAL SWEDEN

It was very definitely demonstrated by 1888 that Sweden's economic future lay in the field of industry rather than agriculture. The agricultural crisis of 1880 and the decimation of the rural population through emigration and through the movement toward the cities had dealt to Swedish agriculture a blow from which it never recovered. The growth of industry became very rapid. While in Sweden the industrial population increased on an average of 2 per cent annually; in the older industrial countries of Europe, like Germany, it increased 0.75 per cent, Denmark 0.40 per cent, and England 0.15 per cent.[1]

In 1840 only about 8 per cent of Sweden's inhabitants were engaged in industry while 80 per cent of the population received an income from agriculture.[2] This situation had been more or less the same for over a hundred years. In 1920 it was estimated that 35 per cent of the population was engaged in industry and mining, 15 per cent in commerce and transportation, as contrasted with 44 per cent in agriculture, fisheries, and forestry.[3]

Although Sweden must be considered an agricultural country until 1890, it must not be forgotten that she had passed through the period of the mercantile policy of the seventeenth and eighteenth centuries when every European country had tried to make itself self-sustaining. Besides the handicraft workers and the home industries that were found in every agricultural country, there can be traced the origins of most of her present industries in earlier attempts to industrialize the country.

Mining is one of her most ancient industries. Mining and the production of iron dates from the thirteenth century.[4] For hundreds of

---

[1] Einar Huss, "Några data om nutida Svensk industri," *Svenska industrien vid kvartsekelskiftet, 1925* (Stockholm, 1925), p. 87.

[2] *Ibid.*      [3] *Ibid.*, p. 71; *Sverige, Statistisk årsbok, 1927*, Table 28, p. 27.

[4] Grimberg, "Ur den svenska industriens äldre historia," *Svenska industrien vid kvartsekelskiftet, 1925*, pp. 3-34.

years the great copper mines of Falu had been a source of national wealth. The height of silver production from the Sala mine was reached in the sixteenth century. And Sweden must be remembered as the greatest of iron-producing countries in the seventeenth.

The export of lumber from Sweden did not begin as early as that from Norway, but there were many saws propelled by wind or water operating in the sixteenth and seventeenth centuries. The production of paper from linen rags was encouraged in the sixteenth century, and by 1700 there were fourteen paper mills in the kingdom. The textile industry had its origins in the woolen mills established in Norrköping by Louis de Geer in the seventeenth century. Another center of textile manufacture at Alingsås in Västergötland was determined in the eighteenth century when Jonas Alströmer located his mills in the region. Simultaneously with the establishment of the Meissen porcelain mills in Germany and the Wedgwood in England, the first porcelain mill was erected in Sweden at Rörstrand near Stockholm in 1726, and others soon followed.[1] There were glassmasters in Sweden in the fifteenth century but the first factory was established in the latter part of the sixteenth century under special privileges granted by Johan III. Two that are still operating are the mills at Lunmared, established in 1740 and at Kosta, dating from 1741.[2]

Strange to say, sugar refineries have also existed for some hundred years in Sweden. The refining of imported raw sugar in Sweden began in 1647, and during the eighteenth century the importation of refined sugar was prohibited.[3] By 1800 there were fourteen sugar refineries in the country. The manufacture of tobacco began in the kingdom in the latter part of the seventeenth century and in 1760 constituted 12 per cent of the total value of Swedish industrial production.[4] An attempt to introduce the manufacture of silk in the eighteenth century was not as fortunate as most of the earlier industries.[5]

Swedish mining on a large scale, as contrasted with small primitive smithies, began at the end of the thirteenth century. Copper

[1] *Svenska industrien vid kvartsekelskiftet, 1925*, p. 226.

[2] *Ibid.*, p. 229.      [4] *Ibid.*, p. 295.

[3] *Ibid.*, p. 279.      [5] *Ibid.*, p. 315.

was the first ore mined to any great extent. The large copper mine at "Kopparberget," Dalecarlia, was first exploited by Swedish and German capital. German miners probably from the Harz mountains were imported as workmen.[1] Here was organized also Sweden's oldest industrial corporation at "Stora Kopparberget," or the Large Copper Mountain.

In the development of iron mining, the Germans were again the exploiters. The first large iron mine placed in operation was "Norbergs järn-och stållberg." The names of mines, like Garphyttan and Saxberg in Örebro County, show this German influence, and the names of many German mines are found in the history of Central Sweden called the "Bergslag" district. The names of other mines, Dalkarlsberg and Västgötehyttan, demonstrate that there were also natives of other provinces of Sweden that had migrated to the mining districts in the Middle Ages. It was more profitable to break ore than to break sod even at that period. Both the king and the church were interested in encouraging the new industry for it enlarged their coffers. Special privileges were granted by the crown in 1340 to encourage immigration of people to the mining regions. Amnesty was granted to all lawbreakers with the exception of murder, theft, or treason.[2] There followed a stampede to the mines similar to the "gold fever" of later periods. Peasants in the fertile valleys left the plow and harrow to seek their fortune with drill and hammer in the mountains. Then for the first time the mountain districts became populated.

The silver mines at Sala called "Solvberget" were discovered early in the sixteenth century. People rushed to the region and soon there appeared a mining village of a thousand inhabitants. Among the miners were many adventurers who were difficult to control. The situation became worse when at the end of the century prisoners of war and criminals were used in the mines.[3] The greatest silver production came during Gustav Vasa's reign. As much silver was produced as in the following three and a half centuries (about 200 tons which then was worth fifteen times as much as at present). King Gustavus I acknowledged in a letter that Sala had been his greatest

---

[1] Grimberg, *op. cit.*, p. 4.

[2] *Ibid.*, p. 5.　　　　　[3] *Ibid.*, p. 6.

support in the large expenditures in the defense of Sweden during her wars against Denmark, for it paid for the soldiers both on land and sea. The silver mine was a royal monopoly but there was much smuggling of silver by the miners.

During the reign of Charles IX, there was extensive prospecting in the mining regions, and especially in Värmland. Through the grant of privileges, the king encouraged many of his subjects to establish smelting hearths on the swift-flowing streams. Improved methods of mining were introduced through German miners. In the seventeenth century Värmland became noted as the region of mines and iron foundries.

From the autobiography of an immigrant who left Örebro County in 1882, the conditions of life for a crofter in the "Bergslag" region were pictured.[1]

My father was a crofter on an estate (*säteri*) in Örebro County, and for his croft he had to burn 80 loads of charcoal and haul it to the furnace (*bruket*). We had a mile and a half (10½ English miles) to the iron furnace and drove with oxen. It was necessary to start at two in the morning in order to reach home again and load at daylight.

Another immigrant lived in one of the remote mountain regions of Härjedalen in Jämtland County in 1872.[2] In this region his grandfather had worked for a *brukspatron* as a master iron worker at the smelter. His wages had been so low that when he became too old to work he would have fallen upon the poor-list, had not B.'s parents taken the grandparents into their large family of nine. Many of the inhabitants of the two formerly prosperous villages on the estate (*bruk*) emigrated to America because of the low wages. In America most of them turned to farming.

It was however upon these estates that the iron ore of Sweden was turned into manufactured products for several hundreds of years. The abundance of pure iron ore with a very slight percentage of phosphorus and the vast regions of timber for the production of charcoal made Sweden in the seventeenth and eighteenth centuries the chief iron-producing and iron-manufacturing country of the world. As long as only charcoal was used for the production of pig

[1] "Utvandrarnes egna uppgifter," *Emigrationsutredningens bilaga VII*, p. 180, No. 208.

*Ibid.*, p. 213, No. 228.

iron, Sweden held her rank among the nations. As late as 1750 she furnished 38 per cent of the world production of iron and during the first half of that century three-fourths of the British importation of iron came from there.[1] The decline of the iron industry in England had been due to lack of forests from which to produce charcoal. With the discovery in 1735 in England that coke could be used, and with the introduction of "puddling" in 1785, England was again ready to take a leading part in the production of iron. Although Sweden continued to produce larger quantities of iron, and Swedish iron remains some of the purest obtainable, her place in the world market as far as quantity of production was concerned was lost. Sweden lacked the great supply of coal that England and the United States possessed, and was handicapped until the substitution of electricity partially overcame the lack.

Two Swedish inventors and organizers, Christopher Polham and Sven Rinman, through inventions and also by the experience gained through extensive travels in Europe helped to increase the efficiency of iron and steel production and mining in the mother country in the eighteenth century.[2] Emmanuel Swedenborg known primarily for his spiritual contributions, before the time of his spiritual awakening, worked in the department of mines for the Swedish government and wrote valuable treatises on the subject of mining. The new English inventions of the later eighteenth century were also introduced in the Dannemora mine in Sweden in 1804.[3] The old mercantile protection against the exportation of ore prevented such exportation until 1857, and it was not until 1864 that all export duty on iron ore was removed.[4]

The establishment of *bruk* on estates took place in the reign of Charles IX during the later sixteenth century throughout the "Bergslag" region, not only on crown estates, but also on private ones.[5] It was however during the reign of Gustavus Adolphus that the production of iron became a large industry. The constant wars and military progress produced a demand for weapons and ammuni-

---

[1] *Sweden Year Book, 1926*, p. 93.

[2] *Svenska industrien vid kvartsekelskiftet, 1925*, pp. 11–15.

[3] *Ibid.*, p. 15.          [4] *Sweden Year Book, 1926*, p. 93.

[5] *Svenska industrien vid kvartsekelskiftet, 1925*, p. 17.

tion which stimulated the industry. The necessary capital for this industrial development came to a great extent from Holland. The Dutchman, Louis de Geer, began his activities in Sweden by lending money to the king,[1] and then took over the ordnance for the army. But he also recognized the possibilities of developing iron manufacture on a large scale. He began by leasing from the crown the foundry, Finspånsbruk, in Östergötland. Here he constructed blast furnaces, steel hammers, spike and horseshoe smithies, and cannon foundries. In Norrköping he erected a brass foundry. In the Dannemora mining region, Louis de Geer not only invested money but imported hundreds of Walloons from present Belgium and Northern France. The new methods produced more and better iron and took less charcoal. The export of Swedish bar iron increased fivefold.

The beginning of the steel industry at Eskilstuna dated from 1656, when Reinhold Rademacher, from Livland, decided to move his industry from Riga upon the approach of the Russians. He came to Sweden with a colony of thirty master-smiths and their families, and was given permission by the government to settle at Eskilstuna.[2] Here were established 150 years later the government's munition factories.

During the last half of the seventeenth century in the reign of Charles XI, through encouragement in the form of privileges and also through compulsion, many new foundry estates were established, even in Norrland. Many of these furnaces, which to the present time have been in operation in Hälsingland, Medelpad, Värmland, and Ångermanland, and are continuing in operation in Hälsingland, date from the later seventeenth century. There were in this earlier period also many mills for the production of iron wares. Cannons were molded, hand weapons of various kinds were produced, as well as ship's anchors, and plates.[3]

The northern war in the early eighteenth century furnished a market for munitions and cannons. Christopher Polham's inventions did much to make Sweden the great iron-producing country

---

[1] *Svenska industrien vid kvartsekelskiftet, 1925,* p. 17; Wittrock, *Gustav II Adolph, Sveriges historia till våra dagar,* VI, 276–86.

[2] *Svenska industrien vid kvartsekelskiftet, 1925,* pp. 20–21.

[3] *Ibid.,* pp. 21–23.

of 1750. With the use of his machinery and water power, the French traveler, De la Motraye, reported that Polham could with four men produce as much as thirty men working by hand.[1] At Stjärnsund in Dalarne he erected a foundry for the production of iron, pewter, and bronze wares. The last two decades of the eighteenth century were considered the most profitable periods of the older iron production.

Competition with English iron brought a period of stagnation in the beginning of the nineteenth century. But by 1830 a new epoch in the iron industry began with the introduction of calciners, bellows, and other new inventions in the old foundries. The first Lancashire foundries were introduced at this time. In 1850 the Bessemer process was invented by the Englishman, Harry Bessemer, and improved by the Swede, G. F. Göransson.[2] Further inventions in 1878 produced the Thomas system which with the addition of a dolomite made possible the use of poorer grades of iron, and became extensively applied in Germany, France, and Belgium. It also made possible the use of poorer ores from the Lappland iron fields in Sweden. Because of the scarcity of coal in Sweden, it was impossible to introduce this system to any extent. At two mills, "Domnarvet" and "Bångbro," it was used with imported coke. In 1868, the Frenchman, P. Martin, introduced still further improvements in what is called the Martin System. Since 1900 it has been possible to smelt steel with electricity, which has meant much to Sweden's iron industry. Sweden is today practically the only country in the world where charcoal is used in the production of pig iron, and it makes a very high quality of steel.[3]

Between 1860–80 a great change took place within the iron industry in Sweden. The many small iron furnaces on the estates in the "Bergslag" region were forced out of business. New inventions made necessary the erection of large furnaces and rolling mills, and the concentration of the iron production in a few large corporations. Not only was it impossible for the many small furnaces to purchase the new machines, but the competition of English iron had by 1877 forced down prices to a minimum which drove the small industries

[1] Quoting de la Motraye in *Svenska industrien vid kvartsekelskiftet, 1925*, p. 22.

[2] *Ibid.*, pp. 145–418.

[3] *Sweden Year Book, 1926*, p. 94.

into bankruptcy.[1] Another factor was the competition of sawmills and pulp mills for the timber in the forests that had once been used exclusively for charcoal production. Even as early as the fifties and sixties the scarcity of timber and the rising prices of charcoal were noticeable. The great crisis came however in 1877, brought on by an overproduction of bar iron, as well as the extremely high price of charcoal. It was followed by the bankruptcy of the new "Bergslag" railroad and the failure of the banking houses financing it.[2]

The change that was destined to take place in the reorganization of iron- and steel-production with the substitution of costlier and larger machines for the older methods did not however bring a period of crisis into the lives of many of the workmen on the smaller *bruk*. The mining of iron continued on a larger scale than ever. There was demand for workmen skilled in iron production at the larger mills. The transportation of ore and iron products which had formerly been the task of neighboring peasants was now performed by the railroads. The production of charcoal continued and many of the peasants were employed in this industry. In Värmland and Örebro counties, where many of the smaller *bruk* were discontinued, the owners perhaps suffered some, but they could turn their capital into the more lucrative lumber industry.

A more intimate picture of one region in which this change was taking place may give a better graphic understanding of the situation. In the district of Billingsfors and Bäckefors in Dalsland there were several small furnaces that were discontinued in the latter sixties and the seventies. In Vedbo hundred in Älvsborg County, there were five defunct furnaces, and in Nordmark hundred in Värmland, seven besides "Koppom," which had discontinued as a furnace and was converted into a paper-pulp mill.[3] There were only about 300 workmen in the fifteen small furnaces in Dalsland when they were abolished, so that the unemployment was not very great. From

[1] Magnusson, "Jösse härad i Värmland, Bygdeundersökningar," *Emigrationsutredningens bilaga VIII*, pp. 8–13.

[2] See chapter "The Stress and Strain of the Eighties," p. 279.

[3] Ernest Lundholm, "Vedbo och Nordmarks härader, Bygdeundersökningar," *Emigrationsutredningens bilaga VIII*, pp. 10–11.

Billingsfors it was reported that some of the smiths, at the time the furnaces closed, took their families and emigrated to America, while others went to the new large furnaces at Sandviken in Gästrikland. Some of the former furnaces, like Bäckefors, Billingsfors, Gustafsfors, Katrineholm, Lennartsfors, and Töcksfors in this region were converted into paper-pulp mills, which employed not only their former laborers but many more.

Because of the poor wages that were paid for burning charcoal and for hauling, it was reported from Jösse[1] and Fryksdals hundreds[2] in Värmland that it was doubtful whether the economic status of the inhabitants were much affected by the closing of these small iron furnaces. The booming of the lumber industry both there and in Norrland furnished more lucrative employment.

The passing of the old iron estates and their owners marked another of the drastic changes that took place when industry in Sweden entered the period of the industrial revolution. The export of iron ore, which had been forbidden before 1857 and taxed until 1864, reached 80 per cent of the total products of Sweden in 1888.[3] The basic method of producing iron made it possible to use the highly phosphoric ore. This with the construction of railway lines in the Lappland region from the mines to the coast enabled Sweden to increase both mining and exportation of ore. The production of iron ore in Sweden in 1900 was 2.6 million tons and the export 1.6 million. The increasing demand for iron brought the figures of production up to 6.9 million during 1915 and of export to 6.0 million.[4] However, in 1913, the year before the World War, production had reached 7.5 million tons.[5] Since the war there has been a slump in

[1] Magnusson, op. cit.

[2] Edin, "Fryksdals härad i Värmland," Emigrationsutredningens bilaga VIII, p. 15. footnote.

[3] Sweden Year Book, 1926, p. 93.

[4] Svenska industrien vid kvartsekelskiftet, 1925, p. 139; Statistisk årsbok för Sverige, 1927, Table 102, p. 106. Iron-ore and pig-iron production in five-year periods, 1836–1926, also exports 1871–1926, Table 121, pp. 130–33; "Bergshantering," utg. av kommerskollegium, Sveriges officialla statistik, 1915, p. 9.

[5] Sweden Year Book, 1926, p. 94. "Bergshantering, 1913," Sveriges officialla statistik, p. 11, ibid., "1920," p. 9. Statistisk årsbok, 1927, loc. cit.

iron production. In 1920 it fell to 4.5 million with an export of 3.7 million. It has fluctuated, and in 1929 production rose to 11.5 million tons and export to 10.8 million tons.

This export of iron ore amounts to from 18 to 20 million dollars a year, and constitutes 6 to 7 per cent of the whole Swedish export.[1] Three-fourths of the exported ore comes from the Norrland mines at Gällivare, Kirunavara, and Luossavara, owned by the Luossa-vaara-Kiirunavaara Corporation. These mines were sold in 1864 to foreign corporations by the Swedish government, principally to an English railway corporation which was given many privileges in the exportation of iron ore.[2] The Riksdag of 1890 provided for the re-purchase of the Luleå-Gällivare railroad from the English owners and also the iron mines.[3] The port of Luleå in Sweden and the open port of Narvik in Norway are the chief ports of export for these northern mines. By 1913 Germans and Austrians had started to acquire Swedish iron mines to guarantee a supply of ore.[4] In that year, 5 million of the 6.4 million tons of ore exported went to Germany. The Swedish state also extended its influence by the purchase of Svappavaara iron mines in 1908 and by new agreements with the Grängesberg corporation in 1908 and 1913. The Luossavaara- Kiiru-navaara A.B. which exported in 1925 the largest amount of iron ore is half-owned by the Swedish government and half by the corporation A.B. Grängesberg-Oxelösund.[5] Sweden possesses 10 per cent of the known iron deposits of Europe and 5 per cent of those of the world.[6]

There were in 1925 some 113 mines in Sweden and 8,800 miners. This number of miners however was the smallest number of workmen employed in the Swedish mines since 1895. In 1915 there had been over 14,000, and in 1920 some 11,000. Although there was a sharp drop of wages in 1923, yet wages have risen in the mines from 1,528 kronor annually in 1913 to 2,580 kronor in 1924, or from 16 to 30

---

[1] *Svenska industrien vid kvartsekelskiftet, 1925*, pp. 139–40,; *Statistisk årsbok 1927*, Table 102, p. 106.

[2] *Emigrationsutredningens betänkande*, pp. 160, 758.

[3] *Ibid.*, pp. 195, 758. Also, Boëthius, *Oskar II*, p. 275.

[4] Karl Hildebrand, *Gustav V*, p. 144.

[5] *Svenska industrien vid kvartsekelskiftet, 1925*, p. 140.     [6] *Ibid.*, p. 135.

cents per hour.[1] The mines have been organized under unions and wages are determined by trade agreements. The eight-hour law was introduced as a temporary measure in 1920 and still stands. There have been numerous strikes and lockouts among the miners. The controversy over the Stripa mine was sufficient to force the resignation of the Social Democrats under Premier Sandler in the spring of 1926.[2]

Sweden also produces and exports the semifabricated and manufactured products of iron and steel. In 1913, 730,000 tons of pig iron were produced and in 1917, 829,000, of which 386,000 tons were Siemens-Martin iron.[3] After the World War, there came a crisis in the production of iron, but from the low level of 1922, there has been an increase in 1924 and 1925.[4] The production of ingots, rough bars, and mill bars had reached 264,000 tons in 1913, mostly of the Lancashire process, but declined to 49,000 tons in 1924.[5] Castings have increased from 59,000 tons in 1913 to 614,000 tons in 1916, primarily Martin steel castings, but this industry also showed a slump in 1924 with a production of 501,000 tons. The production of iron and steel bars and other heavier manufactures of malleable iron and steel had been reduced from 858,000 tons in 1913 to 29,000 tons in 1921. In 1924 the production had mounted to 744,000 tons.

It is impossible in this short survey of Swedish industry to present the details of the metal and machine manufactures. There have been many inventors among the Swedish engineers. Among them may be mentioned John Ericsson of "Monitor" fame; de Laval, the inventor of the cream separator; Jonas Wenström, the inventor of

---

[1] Koch, *Social handbok*, p. 88. See Table. In American money this is very low, amounting to $409.50 in 1913 and $691.44 in 1927. In rates per hour, it had risen from 0.63 kronor to 1.36 kronor (*Sverige, Statistisk årsbok, 1927*, Table 198. pp. 232 ff., Table 113, pp. 120–21).

[2] See the Stripa affair ("Kring Regeringskrisen" *Svensk Tidskrift*, XVI, No. 5, 279–88).

[3] *Sweden Year Book, 1926*, p. 95; *Bergshantering, 1913*, p. 20, *1917*, p. 19. *Statistisk årsbok, 1927*, p. 106.

[4] *Sweden Year Book, 1926, op. cit.* Two hundred sixty-four thousand tons of pig iron and in 1924, 513,000 tons.

[5] *Ibid.*

electric apparatus; L. M. Erickson, the perfector of the telephone.[1] The number of machine shops in Sweden had increased from 428 in 1907[2] to 564 in 1913,[3] and to 876 in 1925.[4]

Some of the machine shops have been long established. Mention has been made of the activities of the seventeenth and eighteenth centuries, when Sweden was already noted for the production of munitions and cannon.[5] Kockum's machine-shop corporation[6] with foundries, machine shops, and shipyards at Malmö was founded by F. H. Kockum in 1840–41, and the shipyards were added in 1871.[7] Bergsund's machine shop[8] has foundry and machine shops at Södermalm in Stockholm and a slip at Finnboda near Stockholm. This machine shop was founded in 1769 by a Scotchman, Thomas Lewis, and was purchased in 1807 by an Englishman, G. D. Wilcke, for whom the noted Samuel Owens came to Sweden as manager; finally the shops were purchased by A. W. Frestadius, a wholesaler, in 1858, and were developed under the leadership of the engineer, E. A. Ollmans. It produces chiefly steamboats and railroad bridges. The Atlas shops at Stockholm were founded in 1873 for the production of railway equipment. The Bolinder shops were established in Stockholm in 1845 by the brothers Jean Bolinder and C. G. Bolinder. It is one of the largest corporations in Sweden. Besides the machine shops in Stockholm, the corporation owns a foundry at Kallhälls and a slip at Bastholmen in Bohuslän where motors are installed in boats. It manufactures among its numerous products chiefly motors of all kinds and stoves of many varieties.

Huskvarna on Lake Vätter was early selected as an industrial site. In 1689 the Swedish government established a weapon foundry here. It was sold to private individuals in 1757 and after many

[1] Larson and Åmark, "Metall-och maskinindustri," in Guinchard, *op. cit.*, v. II, 324.

[2] "Allmänna ekonomiska data rörande Sverige," *Emigrationsutredningens bilaga XIII*, p. 79, Table 21; *Sverige, Statistisk årsbok, 1915*, p. 87.

[3] Guinchard, *op. cit.*, II, 320; *Industri*, utg. av kommerskollegium, *Sveriges officiella statistik, 1925*, p. 74.

[4] *Statistisk årsbok, 1927*, Table 108, p. 110.

[5] See pp. 360–61.

[6] Kockums Mekaniska verkstadsaktiebolag.

[7] Guinchard, *op. cit.*, II, 327–28.     [8] Bergsunds Mekaniska verkstads A.B.

changes there was established in 1867 the Huskvarna Munitions Corporation.[1] Among other products of this corporation are sewing machines, bicycles, firearms, stoves, and radiators. One of the largest locomotive shops is located at Trollhättan near Gothenburg. It was the first locomotive shop to be erected in Sweden in 1847, at first for the production of mill machinery, saws, mining machinery, and molded steel products including turbines. It developed rapidly under Nyqvist and Holm, and in 1870 began the manufacture of railroad locomotives. In 1923 this corporation had an order of 1,000 locomotives from Russia, and also another order from Argentine.

The Motala machine shops on the Gotha canal near Lake Vätter were established in 1823 by the Gotha Canal Corporation under the supervision of an Englishman, Daniel Fraser. These shops produce all sorts of machinery for the manufacture of iron products—parts of merchant and war vessels, locomotives, etc. In co-operation with the Lindholmen shops with slip and drydock at Gothenburg, it constructs ironclad vessels. The latter corporation was established in 1851 by Thomas Tranchell but was sold and incorporated with the Motala shops in 1858.[2] It builds all sizes of passenger and freight boats, war vessels, engines, and also repairs ships. The famous "Götaverken" also located at Gothenburg and at Hisingen in the harbor were founded in 1841 by a Scotch immigrant, Alexander Keiller. In 1867, it was taken over by the Gothenburg machine-shop corporation,[3] and in 1906 by another corporation.[4] The "Götaverken" build steamships, even armored ships, steam engines, hoisting apparatus, and railway cars. In Gothenburg is also located the roller-bearing factory S K F founded in 1907.[5] Its product is based on the Winquist patent. There are affiliated organizations in England, France, and the United States. .

At Karlstad in Värmland the machine shops specialize in machinery for wood-pulp mills and paper mills. Those at Kristinehamn produce water turbines, automatic regulators, etc. The Diesel

---

[1] Huskvarna vapenfabriks A.B. (1867).      [2] Guinchard, *op. cit.*, II, 331.

[3] Göteborgs Mekaniska verkstads A.B. (*ibid.*).

[4] Svenska Kullagerfabriken, Göteborgs Mekaniska verkstads A.B. (Guinchard, *op. cit.*, II, 331).

[5] *Ibid.*

motors are made at Sickla near Stockholm and are protected by a world patent. Two-thirds of the product is exported, and the greatest demand comes from motor vessels. The first direct reversible Diesel motor was the Swedish "Marin-Polar" motor, world known.[1]

Among other Swedish inventions are the Gas Accumulator for city gas supplies,[2] and the de Laval cream separator. The corporation "Separator" has affiliated corporations in Denmark, France, Italy, Russia, Germany, Austria, Hungary, United States, and Canada.

A certain amount of integration has developed within the iron industry. "Domnarvet," which is located fourteen miles from Falun in Dalarne, is the largest charcoal iron works in the world. It was organized and established in 1875 and is owned by "Stora Kopparbergs Bergslags A.B."[3] This corporation owns its own mines, smelters, foundries, machine shops, and produces its own charcoal. There are over two thousand men employed by this corporation. The other two largest corporations of this type with equally as many workmen are Sandviken Iron Works in Gästrikland founded in 1862 by the perfecter of the Bessemer System, G. F. Göransson,[4] and Uddeholm Iron Works in Värmland with works at Hagfors, Munkfors, Nykroppa, and Storfors.[5] There are in all 61 iron works in Sweden including the three largest ones that have been mentioned.[6]

The city of Eskilstuna is the Swedish Sheffield. The steel industry had an early beginning here when the first smithy was established in 1771 and the free city organized.[7] In 1913 there were in this city 81 factories producing iron, steel, and other metal wares, employing about 4,500 workmen. Among the products of Eskilstuna are knives, scissors, razors, files, hammers, saw-blades, spades, skates, and locks. Here are also produced many household articles of pressed iron, copper nickel, aluminum, and brass. There are foundries and machine shops—the Munktell and Tunafors. The government muni-

---

[1] *Ibid.*, II, 333. Svenska Aktiebolaget Gas Accumulator, Stockholm.

[2] A.B. Separator (*ibid.*, II, 327).

[3] *Ibid.*, II, 334. Also *Svenska industrien vid kvartsekelskiftet, 1925*, p. 155.

[4] Guinchard, *op. cit.*, II, 334.

[5] *Svenska industrien vid kvartsekelskiftet, 1925*, p. 158.

[6] *Ibid.*, pp. 155-59.     [7] Guinchard, *op. cit.*, II, 340.

tions factory founded in 1815, in a suburb of Eskilstuna called Karl Gustav town continues in operation while a second arms factory is located at Huskvarna.[1]

Sweden stands high in the production of agricultural machinery, including not only reapers, binders, and mowers, but also tractors and motor plows. The value of the output in 1913 of 4 million dollars rose to 12 million dollars in 1919, but fell to 5 million dollars in 1925.[2] In the manufacture of internal combustion motors, the Diesel motor has been mentioned. Sweden also produces a steam turbine and a water turbine which are world known. This country moreover specializes in machines for wood-working, for wood pulp, cardboard, and paper, all kinds of mining machinery, sewing and knitting machines, machines for road and street construction. The Swedish petroleum stove invented in the eighties is universally used. Another invention of international importance is the precision gauge. The skill of the Swedish engineer has been demonstrated in the numerous inventions and the multiplicity of iron, steel, and metal products.

In the electrotechnical industry, Sweden has shown equal prominence. The Swedish General Electric Company[3] is the largest corporation of this type in Sweden, and employs about 2,800 workmen. Its factories are located at Västerås and Ludvika. Internationally known Swedish pioneers in this field are J. Wenström, who constructed the first Swedish dynamo for direct current in 1881, and patented a three-phase motor and power transmission in 1890; E. Danielsson, who installed the first electric rolling mill in the world in 1874; L. M. Ericsson and H. T. Cedergren, who were pioneers in the telephone industry; and W. Junger, who invented the accumulator.[4] Sweden has harnessed her many waterfalls for the production of electric energy, which drives her manufacturing industries, her iron works, her electric street railways, and an increasing number of

---

[1] *Ibid.*, p. 341.

[2] *Sweden Year Book, 1926*, p. 96; *Industri*, 1913 (Kommerskollegium), *op. cit.*, pp. 20 ff.; *Statistisk årsbok för Sverige, 1922*, Table 107, p. 107, *ibid.*, *1925*, Table 97, p. 105, *ibid.*, *1927*, Table 110, p. 114.

[3] Allmänna Svenska Elektriska A.B.

[4] *Svenska industrien vid kvartsekelskiftet, 1925*, pp. 202–8. Also *Sweden Year Book, 1926*, pp. 99–101.

her railroads. Among Swedish manufactures are electrical machinery, consisting of equipment for power-houses at waterfalls and for thermoelectric power stations, and electric equipment for other industries.[1] The largest production is that of generators, motors, and transformers. Two other branches of the industry are the telephone and the cable. The "Junger" accumulators are well known. Swedish electric lifts or elevators are known even in South America, India, and Australia.[2] Electric heating material, electric steam boilers, electrical measuring instruments are increasing as well as the radio. As early as 1894 Sweden exported one-third of her production of electrical goods, which has since increased to one-half. In 1929 the export amounted to 58 million kronor or about $16,000,000.[3] The Swedish electric industry seems to be concentrated at Stockholm, Västerås, Ludvika, and Nynäshamn; in the latter two cities the telegraph workshops are located.[4]

The electrification of Sweden during the World War was a matter of necessity. Her waterfalls now not only supply power for industries and railroads but also for illumination even in agricultural communities. At the present time about 90 per cent of all developed turbine horsepower in Sweden's waterfalls are used for electrical energy.[5] In agriculture, electricity is used to a larger or smaller extent by at least 40 per cent of the farms. There are between 7 and 8 million electric lights used in the country, and Stockholm has more telephones per capita than any other city in the world.[6] The capital invested in electrical utilities in Sweden amounts to $1\frac{1}{4}$ billion kronor or $341,000,000. During the World War with an embargo on oil and coal, and the scarcity of tallow and fats, the expansion of electricity was forced. The few coal mines in Southern Sweden, around Hälsingborg, produced in 1929 only 400,000 tons while the import of coal amounted to 6,259,000 tons.[7] With the increase of

---

[1] *Sweden Year Book, 1926*, p. 100.    [2] *Ibid.*, p. 101.

[3] *Svenska industrien vid kvartsekelskiftet, 1925*, p. 206; *Statistisk årsbok för Sverige, 1930*, p. 167.

[4] *Svenska industrien vid kvartsekelskiftet, 1925.*    [5] *Ibid.*, p. 205.    [6] *Ibid.*

[7] *Ibid.*, pp. 41–42. *Sweden Year Book, 1926*, p. 77. The mines are located at Höganäs and Billesholm in Kristianstad County. In 1920, the production was 439,000 tons (*Bergshantering, 1920, op. cit.*, p. 28). Export for 1929 (*Statistisk årsbok för Sverige, 1930*, Table 105, p. 115).

automobiles and motor boats the import of mineral oil had risen to 255,000 tons in 1924.[1] Sweden does not possess oil wells but there is a possibility of a commercial oil, ammonium sulphate, produced from the minerals in the substrata rock of Central Sweden.[2]

For the small natural supply of coal and oil, the energy of the numerous waterfalls of Sweden form an important substitute. Although the largest sources of water-supply are in the numerous large rivers in Norrland, north of the river Dal, the waterfalls in Southern Sweden, because of density of population, are as yet the most extensively exploited. The high plateau of Småland from which streams radiate in numerous falls to the coastal plains has provided water power for Southern Sweden, especially the western coast. Smaller rivers that may be utilized are also found in the southern province of Blekinge.[3] The famous falls of Trollhättan on the Gotha River, the outlet from Lake Väner, have produced electrical energy for the manufacturing region in its vicinity and for Gothenburg, and for the recently electrified Stockholm-Gothenburg main line of government railroads. Electricity is even being transmitted to Southern Sweden. It is estimated that Sweden's water power is equal to from 4 to 6 million horsepower, of which 3 million horsepower at present forms a practical utility and only 1,250,000 horsepower is actually being used.[4]

Many of the hydroelectric stations are owned by the state and the charges for electricity are exceptionally low. In Central Sweden, the stations at Trollhättan, Lilla Edet, Älvkarleby, and Motala, and a steam-reserve plant at Västerås are government-owned.[5] Many of the important waterfalls of Northern Sweden, of which Porjus has been developed, also belong to the state.

There are other metals mined in Sweden but none at the present of great commercial value. The silver mines were practically exhausted in the seventeenth century. Some gold has been found. The

[1] Two million five hundred and fifty thousand deciton in 1924 and 3,301,000 deciton in 1925 (*Statistisk årsbok för Sverige, 1927*, Table 121, p. 131).

[2] *Svenska industrien vid kvartsekelskiftet, 1925*, p. 45.

[3] *Sweden Year Book, 1926*, p. 74.

[4] *Ibid.*, p. 76. A survey of Sweden's waterpower is given for 1924 in *Statistisk årsbok för Sverige, 1927*, Table 112, pp. 118–19.

[5] *Sweden Year Book, 1926*, p. 76.

production of copper at Falun which as late as 1870 was a very important export has at the present been unable to meet the competition of the newly developed copper mines of other countries, and has suffered from the tremendous fluctuations in prices.[1] What possibilities there are for the cheaper production of copper from the newly discovered copper mines in Skellefte field the future will show. Here the production of sulphur is especially important.[2]

Zinc and lead are two other important metals of Swedish production. The zinc ore field at Åmmeborg on Lake Vätter was acquired by a Belgian firm in 1860.[3] At the present time large quantities of zinc ore with a zinc content of 40 per cent are being exported to Belgium. As a by-product from the ore of poorer zinc content, lead is used. Zinc and lead are also procured in the Ryllshytte and Saxberg mines of Dalarne and from Kaveltorp in the county of Västmanland. Manganese is obtained at Långbanshuttan in Värmland, a region with an unusual variety of ore deposits.[4]

There are a number of metal works that manufacture in semifinished and in finished form the various metals besides iron. The industry is old and uses both imported and domestic metals. During 1911 concentration and integration placed this industry in the list of big industrial enterprises. Svenska Metallverken A.B. and Finspong Metallverk A.B. manufacture copper, aluminum, zinc, lead, nickel, pewter, etc., both in the half-produced stage and in the finished ware.[5] Some of the half-fabricated copper has been exported, but all the brass manufactured is used for domestic consumption.

Sweden has a minor industry in the production of various kinds of instruments. The manufacture of pianos and organs began about 1840. After the protection of the tariff of 1888, this industry has grown in spite of German competition.[6] Other musical instruments

---

[1] *Svenska industrien vid kvartsekelskiftet, 1925*, p. 159; "Bergshantering," *Annual Reports; Statistisk årsbok för Sverige, 1927*, Table 108, p. 107, gives a list of metals other than iron.

[2] *Svenska industrien vid kvartsekelskiftet, 1925*, p. 63.

[3] *Ibid.*, p. 142.

[4] *Ibid.; Bergshantering, 1920, op. cit.*, pp. 27 ff.

[5] *Svenska industrien vid kvartsekelskiftet, 1925*, p. 160.      [6] *Ibid.*, pp. 208–9.

like brass horns, violins, and drums are also produced. Medical instruments of various kinds, as well as nautical, hydrographic, and physical instruments and different kinds of measuring instruments are known for their high qualities.[1] There is a small watch industry also. Sweden has a high place in the production of goldwares and silverwares. Goldsmithing and silversmithing were old handicrafts in Sweden, but it was not until 1860 that machinery was substituted to a certain extent in this craft. Since 1752, the state has controlled the workmanship by its stamp of guaranty. In 1925 there were 30 gold, silver, and silver-plating factories, employing some 1,110 workmen.[2]

The number of persons employed in the mining and metal industries in 1928 amounted to 131,884 workmen and 17,766 administrative personnel, about three-eighths of all those employed in industry and mining.[3] During the war, there was an increased demand for the products of these industries and the mills were operating at a maximum. Many workmen were added to the expanding industry and wages were high. The development of unions began in the metal industries in 1880. The eight-hour law was introduced here in 1920 and still remains. The crisis which has followed the war in the iron industry and increased during the French occupation of the Ruhr in 1923 was characterized by strikes, unemployment, and falling wages.[4] During 1921–22 according to the report of the Employers' Association, wages were reduced in the iron foundries by 46 per cent and in the machine shops by 40 per cent.[5] These reductions were accompanied by bitterly fought strikes. In the early part of 1923, there were several conflicts in the form of lockouts in the iron industry.[6] The Central Swedish iron fields are to a great extent idle because of the high cost of production and the keen post-war competition. After six months of labor conflict, it was hoped that the iron industry would recover. But in August of 1925 there were only 45 furnaces out of 128 operating; 56 Lancashire hearths, and 50 steel furnaces out of 195 and 127, respectively.[7]

[1] *Ibid.*, p. 209; *Statistisk årsbok för Sverige, 1927*, Table 108, p. 110.

[2] *Svenska industrien vid kvartsekelskiftet, 1925*, pp. 210–11.

[3] *Statistisk årsbok för Sverige, 1930*, Table 110, p. 118.

[4] Hildebrand, *Gustav V*, p. 555.    [5] *Ibid.*, p. 547.    [6] *Ibid.*, p. 553.    [7] *Ibid.*, p. 556.

Plans are being laid for the reorganization of the iron industry and for consolidation. There was an increase in the export of pig iron and steel in 1924. Iron works which sell specialized steel products, like Sandviken and Uddeholm, were producing at profit, however. In the machine and electrical industries, the occupation of the Ruhr cut off German competition but it has returned and undersells the Swedish products 40 to 50 per cent. The competition is severe but certain branches of the industry, like the corporation Separator, Swedish Roller-Bearing, and Swedish General Electric are recovering.[1] New inventions like Ljungström's steam turbine, a new freezing apparatus, Electro-Lux, and a Swedish flying machine are being placed on the world market. The shipyards, Götaverken, at Gothenburg are again busy. In 1926, however, the industrial region at Trollhättan suffered its severest depression since the war. It will undoubtedly take some time for Sweden with the rest of the world to recover from the present post-war crisis. In spite of falling wages, in 1924 wages in the iron industries remained almost twice as high as they had been in 1913.[2]

Industries closely allied to mining and metal manufacturing are quarrying, the production of glass, porcelain, and clay products. By-products of the coal mines are fireproof clay and clinker clay.[3] The quarrying of granite is an important industry, dating from the eighties. The fine grade of granite from the southern and western coast of Sweden is exported to a large extent to Germany and even to distant countries like Argentine. Feldspar, quartz, limestone, sandstone, marble, slate and potstone are also quarried. The lime produced from the burning of limestone is used domestically for the manufacture of cement, mortar, and for fertilizer. The cement industry has grown rapidly. The first factory was established in 1872, but it has been since 1888, when the protection of an import duty fostered its development, that an export trade has developed. Cement is exported to the countries on the Baltic and to South

[1] Hildebrand, *Gustav V*, p. 557.

[2] Nyström, "Yrkesfördelning samt arbets-och löneförehållanden i Sverige," in Koch, *Social handbok*, p. 88.

[3] *Sweden Year Book, 1926*, pp. 110–11. For amount produced, see *Statistisk årsbok för Sverige, 1927*, Table 103, p. 107.

America. The brick industry is extensive but produces only for the home market.

Porcelain and glass are old industries in Sweden. The oldest porcelain factories were established at Rörstrand in 1726, and at Marieberg in 1758, but were later consolidated.[1] The famous Gustavberg porcelain works were founded in 1827. Since 1870, these porcelain factories have undergone many technical changes in the method of production. Between 1911 and 1918, three new porcelain factories were established. There were glass masters in Sweden as early as the fifteenth century.[2] The first glassworks were erected at Bryggholmen on Lake Mälar under privileges granted by King Johan III. The present factory at Kungsholm was erected during the seventeenth century. Among the glass factories established during the period of industrial development in the eighteenth century, Limmared (1740) and Kosta (1741) are still operating. During the nineteenth century many new glassworks appeared, especially in Småland. Numerous articles of glass are produced, such as window glass, bottles, household glass, lamp glass, and bulbs, mostly for home consumption but also for some export. The fine glassware of Orrefors and Kosta are world renowned.

The textile industry in Sweden may be counted as another of the older industries. Although until very recent times much of the clothing used by the common people was produced, spun, woven, and sewed in the homes, there were woolen mills as early as the seventeenth century.[3] An effort to encourage sheep culture began in the reign of Charles IX, in the sixteenth century, when sheep and shepherds were introduced from Germany. Woolen mills were established at Eskilstuna and Nyköping. It was however Louis de Geer, the wealthy Hollander, who in the seventeenth century established the woolen mills at Norrköping. This city is now the center of the woolen textile mills in Sweden. During the seventeenth century these woolen mills produced enough cloth to clothe the Swedish army. During the "Period of Liberty" in the next century at the

---

[1] *Svenska industrien vid kvartsekelskiftet, 1925*, pp. 226–28.

[2] *Ibid.*, pp. 228–32.

[3] Grimberg, "Ur industriens äldre historia," *Svenska industrien vid kvartsekelskiftet, 1925*, p. 29.

height of the mercantile policy, 14,000 of the 18,000 factory workers were weavers.[1]

Another center of the textile industry is around the cities of Borås, Alingsås in Älvsborg County, and Gothenburg. The industry at Alingsås dates from 1724 when Jonas Alströmer, who as a young man had made his fortune in business in London, later returned to his home in Sweden with the ambition to make Sweden self-supporting.[2] The new textile industry included the production of wool, cotton, and silk. It was subsidized by the state and received many privileges, as freedom from duty. After the death of Alströmer, the industry declined until the new impetus of the nineteenth century revived it. About 1850, with the introduction of the new textile machines, the woolen mills began to produce on a larger scale. There are at present 250,000 spindles and 4,400 looms in operation.[3] Only from 7 to 8 per cent of the raw wool is produced in Sweden. About 60 per cent of the labor is performed by women.[4] The World War brought a tremendous crisis in the textile industries, since most of the raw materials were imported. However, since 1924 the woolen industry has been on the way to recovery, and the export of woolen goods amounts to 12.2 million kronor or $3,240,000.

One of the oldest woolen mills still in operation is Drags A.B. established in 1650 and located at Norrköping.[5] Here is also the Lenning's Textile School, organized by John Lenning, a former manager of the Drags mill. The largest mill is located at Malmö in Southern Sweden, the Malmö Woolen Corporation, with 1,800 employees.[6] The second largest is the United Woolen Mills at Norrköping with 1,400 workers.[7] There are also many woolen mills scattered in various parts of Sweden from Skåne to Norrland.[8]

Although there was an attempt to introduce cotton mills at

[1] Ibid., p. 30.    [2] Svenska industrien vid kvartsekelskiftet, 1925, pp. 30–31.

[3] Ibid., p. 300. There were 116 woolen mills in 1925; Statistisk årsbok 1927, p. 111.

[4] Statistisk årsbok, 1927, p. 131; Svenska industrien vid kvartsekelskiftet, 1925, p. 302.

[5] Svenska industrien vid kvartsekelskiftet, 1925, p. 303.

[6] Malmö Yllefabriks A.B.

[7] A.B. Förenade Yllefabrikerna.

[8] Svenska industrien vid kvartsekelskiftet, 1925, pp. 303–4, names the various mills. There are ten mills at Norrköping.

Alingsås in the eighteenth century, it was not a very extensive under-taking, nor of much success.[1] Before 1812 small quantities of cotton were imported into Sweden primarily for the hand looms of the common people, and especially in the region of the seven southern hundreds of Älvsborg where the cottage people wove cloth that was peddled to other regions of the kingdom. The first cotton-spinning mill in Sweden was established in 1805, and the second, still operat-ing, in 1813 at Sjuntorp, south of Trollhättan. Several others fol-lowed before the middle of the century. Weaving of cotton cloth, however, continued on the hand looms of the people. But in 1834 the first factory of looms was established, the Rydboholm mechanical cotton mill. Its founder was Sven Erikson, who had started life by peddling the products of his mother's loom. His mills at Rydboholm, Rydal, and Viskafors employed 1,500 women. The industry con-tinues to be concentrated largely around Borås. There are now 550,-000 spindles and 14,500 looms. Most of the raw cotton comes from the United States. The cutting-off of the importation of the raw products during the World War brought a crisis from which the industry was just beginning to recover in 1924.

The cartels, the Swedish Cotton Mills Association[2] and the Swed-ish Cotton Spinning Association,[3] are located in Gothenburg while the Association of Colored Cotton Goods Manufacturers[4] is located at Borås. These three associations control the cotton industry in Sweden. The textile school at Borås was organized in 1866, and in 1884 expanded to include knit wears.[5] The largest cotton mills are owned by the Borås Looms Corporation[6] with 1,700 employees. There were in 1924 about 14,600 people, mostly women, employed in the mills.

Linen has been woven by the Swedish people in their homes since prehistoric times. The first linen factory was established near Gothenburg at Almedal. At first the linen came from domestic flax

[1] Ibid., p. 305.    [2] Svenska Bomullsfabrikantföreningen.

[3] Svenska Bomullsspinneriföreningen.

[4] Föreningen av fabrikanter av kulörta bomullsvävnader.

[5] Svenska industrien vid kvartsekelskiftet, 1925, pp. 308-9.

[6] Borås Väveri A.B. In 1925 it had increased to 15,010 (Statistisk årsbok för Sverige, 1927, p. 111).

production but during the latter part of the nineteenth century it declined so that the importation of raw materials was necessary. In spite of the subsidy by the government during the World War to encourage home production, this industry is again declining. There seems to be a strong impetus to increase linen production in factories. Since 1900 the number of laborers has doubled and is now about 2,100. There are 19,000 spindles and 1,300 looms.[1] Since 1888, Sweden has also been weaving jute from the raw materials imported from the East Indies, but so far only for home consumption. The manufacture of rugs, carpets and woven materials for upholstering furniture is closely allied to the jute industry.[2]

The production of various kinds of knit goods and of ready-made clothing has also increased in the Swedish clothing industry. The first stocking-knitting machine was introduced into Sweden in the eighteenth century by Christopher Polhem when a mill was established at Stjärnsund. During the 1880's the improvements in knitting machines made by Per Persson made possible the knitting of patterns. Since 1900, there has been an increase from 3,000 to 4,500 workers, of which 90 per cent are women.[3] The development of various kinds of fiber silks has increased that industry.[4] The attempts to develop silk manufacture during the eighteenth and nineteenth centuries have come to naught. There is only one small silk factory existing in the country.[5]

Ready-made clothing is something of more recent date. Custom-made clothing has existed for a long time and it is still to a great extent usual for both men and women to have their clothes tailor-made. Ready-made clothing began for men in the nineties and for women in the eighties.[6] The manufacture of lighter garments like dresses, blouses, shirts, various sorts of underwear, corsets, and collars, has grown more rapidly than that of suits and dresses. The largest part of this production is located at Stockholm, Gothenburg and Malmö. There were in 1925 some 177 establishments and 10,100 workers, mostly women.

[1] *Svenska industrien vid kvartsekelskiftet, 1927*, pp. 310–11.

[2] *Ibid.*, pp. 312–13.      [4] *Ibid.*, p. 315.

[3] *Ibid.*, p. 314.      [5] *Ibid.*

[6] Ready-made clothing in Swedish is called *konfektions industri* (*ibid.*, 316–21).

Closely allied to the textile-clothing industries are leather, hair, and rubber products. Much of the leather produced is used for domestic consumption, although a small quantity is exported. In the middle of the nineteenth century the statistics of the Department of Commerce showed the existence of 500 skin and leather factories with 1,700 workmen in Sweden.[1] The production of leather remained in the field of handicraft until 1900. Since 1897 with the raising of a protective tariff, the number of workmen has increased until in 1925 there were 2,090; while the number of establishments has diminished to 98.

The first shoe factory established in Sweden was that of A. F. Carlsson at Vänersborg in 1873.[2] The machinery for shoe-manufacturing was developed first in the United States and was imported from that country. The factory at Vänersborg is today the largest in Sweden, employing 800 workers.[3] Again with the protective tariff of 1897, foreign competition was excluded and the shoe industry has grown by leaps and bounds. The largest center of shoe manufacture is in Örebro where there were, in 1925, 15 large and 28 small shoe factories and in Kumla, a short distance south, 8 large and 14 small factories.[4] There are factories also at Stockholm, Malmö, and Gothenburg. To a large extent the work is carried on by women and minors. In 1910 about 99 per cent of the domestic trade was supplied by home industry. Following the War, because of high prices and scarcity of material, American shoes began to undersell the Swedish shoe in the home market. However, the industry is recovering. There are smaller establishments producing furs, gloves, leather goods for travel, brushes, and rubber wares, the latter primarily galoshes.[5]

Among the food products in Sweden's industry, the large commercial flour mills, located in her ports, indicate the change from an agricultural to an industrial era. Since a large percentage of grain is now imported for Swedish bread, these mills mix and grind the imported and domestic grain.[6] There were in 1925 some 873 of the

---

[1] *Statistisk årsbok för Sverige, 1927*, pp. 110–11.

[2] *Svenska industrien vid kvartsekelskiftet, 1925*, p. 325.

[3] *Ibid.*, p. 328.      [4] *Ibid.*, p. 326.      [5] *Ibid.*, pp. 329–33.

[6] *Ibid.*, pp. 275–77.

large mills, employing 3,270 laborers.[1] There also existed 4,000 small mills driven by water or wind scattered throughout the country. The change in the taste and prosperity of the kingdom may be seen in comparing the proportion of 60 per cent wheat flour to 37 per cent rye flour ground during the year of 1925. The larger mills are organized into the Swedish Mill Association which controls the price of flour.[2] An allied industry is the bakery. Large quantities of Swedish health bread[3] and also what we know as cookies,[4] and other forms of bread, are produced for a people very fond of coffee parties.

One of Sweden's principal industries is her sugar refineries. This industry began as early as 1647 with the refining of cane sugar.[5] Due to the prohibition of the import of refined sugar into Sweden during the domination of the mercantile policy in the "Period of Liberty," there were 14 sugar refineries in operation in Sweden in 1800, among them the present Tanto Sugar Mill at Stockholm. During the Napoleonic wars, Sweden served as the middleman for England's sugar trade, and among the refineries established is the present Carnegie Refinery at Gothenburg.[6] With the production of sugar beets in Sweden, beginning about 1850, the industry developed on a large scale due to the efforts of Justus Tranchell of Gothenburg and his son, Carl. The industry is localized in the province of Skåne. Since 1900 the production of refined sugar has risen from 86,000 tons to 153,000 tons in 1924. This is all used for home consumption. In 1907 there was consummated a concentration within the industries so that 90 per cent of the refineries belong to the trust. Beginning with the reduction of the tariff on cocoa beans in 1892 and the increased consumption of chocolate, Sweden has developed the production of chocolate and candy. In 1924, some 10,200 tons of candy, confectionaries, and marmalade were produced.

There are distilleries and breweries that provide for home consumption. Sweden has a rationing system as a substitute for pro-

---

[1] *Statistisk årsbok för Sverige, 1927*, Table 108, p. 110.

[2] *Svenska industrien vid kvartsekelskiftet, 1925*, p. 276. Svenska Kvarnföreningen, Stockholm.

[3] *Knäckebrod (ibid.,* p. 278).

[4] Cookies are called *käx* or *kex;* also various forms of *spisbröd.*

[5] *Svenska industrien vid kvartsekelskiftet, 1925*, p. 279.    [6] *Ibid.*, pp. 279-82.

hibition and all sale of liquor is a government monopoly. The consumption of whiskey in Sweden is now only four liters per capita annually, while in 1850 it was twenty-two.[1] A related industry is the production of yeast. The tobacco industry which was introduced during the eighteenth century in 1760 comprised 12 per cent of Sweden's productive wealth at that date.[2] Here again Jonas Alströmer was the promoter and even introduced the cultivation of tobacco in Kristianstad County. In 1914 the government made a monopoly of tobacco. A special corporation, A. B. Svenska Tobaksmonopolet, was organized, the state controlling 89 per cent of the capital stock. Importation of finished tobacco products is permitted with a license tax. The state receives quite a large income from the tobacco monopoly.[3] When the state monopoly was established in 1916, there were over 100 tobacco factories, but in 1925 there were only 11. Three-fourths of the labor employed consists of women.[4]

Among food products may be counted the production of oleomargarine which began in Sweden in the eighties when the export of butter to England caused a rise in the price of butter. Dairies and the production of butter and cheese have had a growing importance since the decline of agriculture in 1880. There are about 1,433 dairies scattered throughout Sweden either operated by larger estates or co-operative ventures of smaller farmers.[5] Some 4,840 persons are employed, the overwhelming majority being women. Some small factories, mostly co-operative, in the counties of Blekinge and Kristianstad produce potato starch.[6] There are also slaughter houses and various varieties of sausage production in Southern and Western Sweden.[7] In this group of industries may be mentioned various canning factories and other establishments for the conservation of vegetables, fruits, meats, and fish. The largest of these are for the preservation of fish, mainly located on the west coast.[8]

---

[1] *Svenska industrien vid kvartsekelskiftet, 1925,* p. 294.

[2] *Ibid.,* p. 295.

[3] About 65 million kronor a year (*ibid.,* p. 297); *Statistisk årsbok för Sverige, 1927,* Table 108, p. 111.

[4] *Svenska industrien vid kvartsekelskiftet, 1925,* p. 298.

[5] *Statistisk årsbok, 1930,* p. 119.

[6] *Svenska industrien vid kvartsekelskiftet, 1925,* p. 289.

[7] *Ibid.,* p. 287.

[8] *Ibid.,* pp. 287–88.

Among the chemical-technical industries, the match industry has been mentioned. Various kinds of vegetable oils are produced from imported raw materials, as well as linseed oil. These oils are used for various and sundry purposes, for paints and dyes, and for soaps, and margarine.[1] There is also the group of soaps, cosmetics, and antiseptic products.[2] The production of candles has declined since the introduction of electricity.[3] Sweden is furnishing artificial fertilizer in large quantities, with some export.[4] The production of gunpowder began in Sweden in 1400 for military purposes. It was not used in mining until 1600, however. In the nineteenth century Alfred Nobel perfected the newly discovered nitroglycerine and other explosive materials into a commercial product, dynamite. The first nitroglycerine factory in the world was established near Stockholm at Vinterviken in 1865 by Nobel.[5] Although Sweden produces some chemical dyes, the greatest amount consumed in the country is imported from Germany.[6] There are also electrochemical products, byproducts of the forest and charcoal industries.[7]

Sweden's industrial development has necessarily increased her foreign trade. There was a fivefold increase in the value of the total trade, import and export, between 1870–1924.[8] Her exports are chiefly from her natural resources of wood and iron, raw, semifabricated, and manufactured products. There is also some slight excess of the exportation of livestock, and animal products, particularly bacon and butter. Sweden is noted for her export of matches and also electrical machinery. Her imports consist primarily of foodstuffs and raw materials. Among the foodstuffs imported are wheat and rye, raw coffee, sugar and syrup, fish, fruits, and berries, tobacco, wines, and spirits. Coal leads the list as the largest import. Cotton, wool, hides, skins, rubber goods, coke, and raw copper form another group of imports.[9]

[1] *Ibid.*, pp. 339–40.

[2] *Ibid.*, pp. 340–42.    [5] *Ibid.*, pp. 344–46.

[3] *Ibid.*, p. 342.    [6] *Ibid.*, pp. 346–47.

[4] *Ibid.*, pp. 342–44.    [7] *Ibid.*, pp. 347–51.

[8] *Sweden Year Book, 1926*, p. 114, see Table ; *Statistisk årsbok för Sverige, 1927*, Table 120, pp. 128–29.

[9] *Sweden Year Book, 1926*, pp. 116–18; *Statistisk årsbok för Sverige, 1927*. Table 121, pp. 130–33.

Before the war, one-third of the imports to Sweden came from Germany and one-fourth from Great Britain, while Sweden sent about one-third of her exports to each of these countries, respectively.[1] The imports from the United States equaled 10 per cent of the total. However, Denmark, Norway, and France received more of the Swedish products than the United States. The World War brought a change, reducing the foreign trade with Germany, and increasing it with Great Britain and the United States.[2]

It has been necessary because of her geographical position for Sweden to develop a merchant marine. In 1926 this amounted to 1,420,485 gross tons, with over 1,000,000 tons in steamships.[3] About one-half of all foreign shipping is in Swedish boats. As much as 90 per cent of the Swedish merchant marine is engaged in shipping for foreign nations, and 5 per cent is exclusively used between foreign ports.

There are direct railway-ferry lines to Denmark and Germany. Regular lines of Swedish steamship companies connect with Finland, the Baltic provinces, Germany, Great Britain, France, Spain, and Italy.[4] Among the Swedish transoceanic lines are the Trans-Atlantic Steamship Company, Ltd., which began in 1904 with a direct line to South Africa and extending its lines to the Sunda Islands and Java in 1914, to the Persian Gulf in 1915, from India to the United States in 1916, and in 1917 from the United States to Sweden.[5] The Nordstjernan Steamship Company, Ltd. (the "Johnson line"), began regular traffic to Argentine in 1904 and Brazil in 1909. During 1914 two new lines were opened to the west coast of North and South America, as well as to the West Indies. The Swedish-East Asiatic Company started a regular line to the Far East (Straits Settlements, China, and Japan) in 1907. In 1914 this line extended to India. The Swedish American-Mexico Line, Ltd., began in 1912, and expanded in 1914 to include the eastern ports of the United

---

[1] *Sweden Year Book, 1926*, pp. 119–22.

[2] In 1924, Great Britain had 25 per cent of Sweden's foreign trade, Germany, 18 per cent, United States, 14 per cent, Denmark, 8 per cent, France, 5 per cent, Netherlands, 4 per cent, and Norway, 3 per cent (*Statistisk årsbok, 1927*, Table 125, pp. 164–65).

[3] *Ibid.*, Table 127, p. 168, and Table 136, p. 175; *Sweden Year Book, 1926*, p. 121.

[4] *Ibid.*, p. 124.    [5] *Sweden Year Book, 1926*, p. 125.

States. Contrasted with the steamship lines that have been mentioned, the Sweden-North America Steamship Company, Ltd., is chiefly interested in passenger service between Sweden and the United States, and began its operations in 1915.

The transportation of iron ore is carried on by the Grängesberg-Oxelösund Traffic Company, Ltd.[1] The Svea Steamship Company, Ltd., has been operating for fifty years. Among the steamship companies carrying European trade are the Swedish Lloyd Steamship Company, Ltd. (Great Britain, France, Spain, etc., to the Mediterranean), the Swedish-Levant Steamship Company (Mediterranean and Black Sea ports), the Swedish Morocco line (Morocco and West Africa), and Förnyade Ångfartygs A.B. Göta (Holland, Belgium, and France, etc.). The Tirfing Steamship Company, Ltd., and the Norrköping Steamship Company, Ltd., own tramp ships.

Sweden holds an exceptional position for commerce in her central location on the Baltic. There are free ports at Stockholm, Gothenburg, and Malmö.

The tariff of 1888 followed the short period of free trade and tariff agreements that Sweden had adopted in the sixties when she departed from her old mercantile policy.[2] A tariff agreement of 1906 between Sweden and Germany controlled the trade between those two countries until the World War. Sweden has no export duties but there is a heavy protective tariff on imported goods. Tobacco, alcohol, and coffee are taxed for revenue purposes. There are protective duties on agricultural products as well as on industrial. In recent years there has been an increase of the tariff on luxuries, mainly as a source of revenue. With the depreciation of money values in the European countries following the war, there was great need for a higher tariff. But with the gradual adjustment of values, this demand may disappear.

The high protective tariff on agricultural and industrial products has undoubtedly protected the home market for these commodities. It has been shown that many of the manufactured products of Sweden are produced primarily and often wholly for domestic use. The progress of manufacturing dates from the beginning of the high tariff policy in 1888. On the other hand, the policy has made the

[1] *Ibid.*, p. 126.    [2] *Ibid.*, pp. 132–33.

living costs in Sweden the highest of any country in Europe and comparable to the United States.

In the localization of industry in Sweden, the region around Gothenburg and in Bohus län has the largest percentage of inhabitants engaged as industrial workers, or 8.8 per cent.[1] This region has a mixture of various industries: textiles, machine shops, roller-bearing works, shipyards, etc. The stonecutting industry is localized in Bohus län. Örebro County, a part of the mining region and the location of the old iron foundries has also become the center of shoe-manufacturing. Here 8.6 per cent of the inhabitants are in industry. The city of Stockholm, where is found the concentration of machine shops and printing establishments, has the same amount of industrial laborers. On the fertile plains of Malmöhus County, 8 per cent of the inhabitants are engaged in industries, and here is localized the production of foodstuffs. The textile industry is concentrated in the southern part of Älvsborg County and has an equal number of workers. The greatest concentration of sawmills and paper mills is in Västernorrland County around Sundsvall and on the lower Ångerman River.[2]

Stockholm is the largest of the industrial cities with 37,300 factory workers and 955 manufacturing establishments. Gothenburg ranks second with 23,600 workmen and 440 establishments; while Malmö has 14,900 industrialists and 316 factories and mills. Norrköping as an industrial city ranks fourth and has 9,400 industrial workers with 164 establishments.[3]

The change from agriculture to industry since 1850 has also brought a change in the kinds of imports into the country. In 1870 as much as 63 per cent of the imports were consumptive articles and 37 per cent raw materials and machinery, while at the present, two-thirds of the import consists of raw materials for manufacturing purposes and only one-third for consumption.[4]

Export has been also localized in Sweden because of the sharp division between exporting industries and industries producing for the home market. The largest export industries are located in the Norrland region and somewhat in Central Eastern Sweden. In Norr-

[1] Einar Huss, "Några data om nutida Svensk industri," *op. cit.*, pp. 90–91.
[2] *Svenska industrien vid kvartsekelskiftet, 1925*, p. 92. [3] *Ibid.*, p. 91. [4] *Ibid.*, pp. 86–87.

land fully 75 per cent of the industrial workers are engaged in the exporting industries while 6 per cent are employed in products for the home market.[1] In Central Eastern Sweden or Svealand, the percentage runs 45 per cent for exports and 31 per cent for home industries. Southern and Western Sweden, the Gothenburg and Malmö regions, are chiefly engaged in products for the domestic market, to the extent of 63 per cent, while only 19 per cent of the industrial workers are employed on goods for exportation.

Most of Sweden's manufacturing establishments are small as compared with those of England, Germany, and the United States. There were in 1925 some 11,200 factories and mills in Sweden with an average of 34 workmen each.[2] Many of these establishments have even a smaller number of employees, for instance the water department of a small city, an electric light plant, a dairy, or brewery, a small carpenter shop, or a machine repair shop. According to the industrial statistics of 1923, of the 11,000 manufacturing plants, about 1,900 were included in this group. Of the remaining 9,100, almost half or about 4,100 had less than ten workmen employed, and an average of four or five. They employed collectively only 5 to 6 per cent of the industrial class.

There are however certain kinds of industries in which the very small plant cannot exist. The larger industrial plant dominates the sugar, the tobacco, and the match industries, as well as linen, jute, and rubber production with an average of 300 employees per factory.[3] Within industries like iron and steel mills, shipyards, electric plants, coal mines, the stone industry, cement and porcelain works, glassworks, wood-pulp mills, cotton and woolen mills, and superphosphate mills, the average number of employees varies from 100 to 200 per establishment. There is a large range in the size of machine shops, from those that employ only a few men to those that employ over a thousand. The same is true in the iron mines. The smaller type of establishment is most prevalent among the bakery, brewery, dairy, flour mill, tile mill, tannery, etc. In the shoe industry, ready-made clothing and knitting industries, the tendency is toward a medium large industry.

In competition on the world market, Sweden is handicapped as

[1] *Ibid.*, p. 92.          [2] *Ibid.*, p. 93.          [3] *Ibid.*, pp. 93–94.

compared with the big industries of the larger countries. The smaller industries prevent the saving in cost which is possible under mass production. It is therefore within the export industries that there is a tendency toward consolidation and large-scale production.

The same movement of industrial combination that has been a phenomenon in all industrial countries within recent years has resulted in Sweden in three types of combinations. One form, integration, which is rather old in Sweden, is the erection of iron mills by owners of iron mines. These old iron works also had large areas of forest, for the production of charcoal. Now these forests have developed new industries besides that of charcoal for ironsmelting, namely, the formation of wood products in sawmills, wood-pulp mills, and paper mills, all owned by the same corporation.

The vertical combination, when an industry needs special half-fabricated materials for manufacture, occurs in the machine shops, the match industry, and the electrical industries. The Swedish roller-bearing industry must have a special grade of steel for the production of roller bearings and manufactures its own steel.

The horizontal combination of factories producing the same kind of products is the third form of consolidation. This brings economies in purchase of raw materials, manufacture, and sale with a reduced overhead. In some cases fewer manufacturing plants are used. There are also combinations of plants with no seeming relationship under the same ownership. Holmens Bruks och Fabriks A.B. combines large wood-pulp mills, Sweden's largest paper mill, and also one of the country's largest cotton mills.[1]

Among the trusts which exist in Sweden are the match industry (Tändsticksbolaget), the Grängesbergs Corporation (iron mines, etc.), the Höganäs Corporation (coal mines), the Swedish Roller-Bearing Corporation (Svenska Kullager-fabriken), the Sugar Corporations, the United Canning Corporations (Förenade Konservfabrikerna), the Stockholm's Breweries, the United Knitting Mills, and the state monopolies of spirits and tobacco.[2] These corporations dominate their respective industries in the Swedish market. In contrast with this combination of industries, under a single management, are the industries that have a looser form of combination in cartels. The car-

[1] *Ibid.*, p. 97.  [2] *Ibid.*, p. 98.

tels regulate prices and sometimes even production. Where combination would perhaps be most profitable for Sweden in its export industries, the sawmills, the wood-pulp mills, iron and machine industries, there is still much competition. On the other hand in some of the domestic industries, combinations may be responsible for the high prices of necessities in Sweden.

Industry has combined in other forms for the promotion of better methods, common interests, stabilization, and labor control. Among the national organizations of special industries, the oldest is the Swedish Ironmasters' Association (Jernkontoret) which was founded in 1748 and still exists.[1] Most of the Swedish iron works belong to this association. Its purpose is to encourage, by stipend, technical research in iron production and to have the opportunity to utilize technical experts. It has a large loan fund of 10 million kronor which is used by the members of the association. A related organization is the Swedish Iron Works Commercial Association (Järnverksföreningen) organized in 1889, with special interest in mining methods and the price of iron.

Among other combinations of this type can be mentioned the Swedish Wood Products Export Association (Svenska Trävaruexportföreningen) founded in the seventies and reorganized in 1906. In the nineties other special combinations within the wood-products industries were formed, as the Swedish Cellulose and Wood-Pulp Association,[2] the Swedish Paper Mill Association,[3] and the Swedish Joinery Export Association.[4] In 1926, there were 29 of such organizations representing various branches of industry in the country.[5]

There are also local manufacturers' associations in the industrial cities. In this group belong the Gothenburg Chamber of Industry, the Eskilstuna Manufacturers' Association, the Norrköping Manufacturers' Association, etc.[6] The Swedish Manufacturers' Associa-

[1] August Hessler, "Industriens föreningsväsen," *Svenska Industrien vid kvartsekelskiftet, 1925*, pp. 120–21.

[2] Svenska Cellulosa-och Trämasse Föreningarna.

[3] Svenska Pappersbruks Föreningen.

[4] Sveriges Snickeri Exportföreningen.

[5] *Sweden Year Book, 1926*, pp. 146–48.

[6] *Svenska Industrien vid kvartsekelskiftet, 1925*, p. 121.

tion, founded in 1910, groups all of the Swedish industries into one large organization.[1] From the very beginning this organization agreed to exclude the question of relationship of capital and labor from its program. Its special interest is legislation for the promotion of industry within the country. All government bills affecting industry are submitted to this organization for approval before they are placed before the Riksdag. The association also initiates and indorses legislation. In 1910 some 200 manufacturing establishments joined the new organization. By 1926 the membership had risen to 1,200 and included practically all of the larger industries. Within the organization has developed A.B. Industribyran, a consultative body of industrial engineers; Annonsbyrån Sten A.B., advertising exports; and A.B. Industri bostäder for the erection of workingmen's homes.[2]

The Swedish Employers' Association[3] was organized in 1902 and now includes 37 occupations and 2,000 employers who employ 250,000 workmen. This association co-operates with the Agricultural Employers' Association and the shipowners in the Confidential Council of the Swedish Employers' Association. According to the by-laws of the organization no member may make a collective agreement with his workmen without the approval of the whole body. The Association supports its members in controversies with labor, and gives financial aid in the case of a strike or a lockout. The organization has never been willing to recognize the doctrine of the closed shop, nor the worker's right to his job. The lockout is employed as a weapon against organized labor.

The General Export Association of Sweden was organized in 1887 and today has 1,000 members. It is subsidized by the state and its purpose is to promote Swedish foreign commerce. The first Chamber of Commerce was established in Stockholm in 1902. Now the kingdom is divided into twelve districts. This organization has also a small subsidy from the state.

The prerequisites for the commercial and industrial development of a country are a sound banking system and the free circulation of capital. The Bank of Sweden dates from 1668 when the Riksdag took over the bankrupt Palmstruch bank that had been founded by

[1] Svenska industrien vid kvartsekelskiftet, 1925, pp. 121–28.

[2] Ibid., p. 125.        [3] Svenska Arbetsgivareföreningen (ibid., p. 129).

the Livonian, Palmstruch, a few years before.[1] Since 1897 it has been the sole bank of issue. This bank is the fiscal agent of the government. The private commercial banks may be divided into two groups, the corporations with unlimited responsibility of stockholders, which are called "Enskilda banker," and the joint stock companies with limited liability. The first type of bank was introduced into Sweden in 1830 and in 1923 there were ten such banks. The oldest of the second type, the "Skandinaviska Kreditaktiebolag," was established in 1864. Some of the larger banks have numerous branches. Since the concentration of banknote issue in the Riksbank in 1897, private banks have not been so popular, and no new ones have been incorporated. There has also been a tendency toward consolidation among joint-stock banks. Besides the commercial banks there are the Postal Savings Bank, numerous savings banks, the Swedish Ironmasters' Association, and the Mortgage banks.

After the Russian War of 1809, Sweden was practically a bankrupt country. Her paper money had depreciated in value and it was not until 1830 that it was possible to stabilize it at three-eighths of its original value.[2] The country was largely agricultural and the few smaller industries did not produce a surplus of wealth. Sweden was usually spoken of in the Riksdag as a poor country. Her natural resources were as yet almost untouched. In 1850 besides the Riksbank there were only eight "Enskilda" banks in the country.[3] It was not until 1856 that it was considered advisable to establish the Stockholm Enskilda Bank in competition with the Riksbank in Stockholm. This bank specialized in savings and successfully rode the crisis of 1857, at the same time taking over the less successful Skåne bank. The first insurance corporation Skandia was incorporated in 1855.

It was not strange therefore that Sweden with difficulty began to finance the building of railroads, telegraphs, public utilities, and the development of manufactures. In the construction of railroads, Sweden lagged behind her neighbors, Germany, Denmark, and

[1] *Sweden Year Book, 1926*, pp. 127–29.

[2] *Emigrationsutredningens betänkande*, p. 118.

[3] Hallendorff, *Oskar I och Karl XV*, pp. 191–92.

Russia, some ten to fifteen years. This was probably due to the fact that she had just completed an extensive inland water system connecting Stockholm with Gothenburg, and that there existed the opinion that capital would be difficult to obtain. In the fifties English capital was attracted to the construction of railroads even in this northern country. The Swedish state had begun its own construction. The state railways were completed between Gothenburg- Töreboda and Malmö-Sösdala by 1859.[1] There were also private railroads between Örebro-Arboga, Nora-Ervalla, Gävle-Falun, Hudiksvall-Forssa, etc. The Royal Debt Commission issued government bonds to finance the new state enterprise.[2]

The state also began the construction of the telegraph in 1853 with funds from the commercial budget.[3] Public works were introduced into the cities of Sweden, gas illumination in Gothenburg in 1846, in Norrköping in 1852, and in Stockholm in 1853.[4] The Stockholm waterworks were completed in 1861.

Beginning with 1870 industry made great strides which were further accelerated in the eighties. Railroads threw a network over the kingdom. The main lines extended not only between the populous cities of Central and Southern Sweden but also opened up the sparsely settled Norrland and brought an outlet for the export of wood and iron. By 1907 the state railroads had a mileage of 2,695, with a valuation of $177,000,000.[5] Private railroads increased from a mileage of 388 miles in 1870 to 2,434 miles in 1880. The most important of the private railroads was the "Bergslag" railroad between Falun and Gothenburg which was opened for traffic, 1875-79. The investments of the Gothenburg banks in this enterprise caused many failures in the panic of 1879 as has been mentioned. It interrupted only temporarily the private railroad enterprises, and in 1926 there were 3,895 miles of private railroad and 2,421 miles of state-owned.[6]

The telegraph was extended. The telephone was introduced in 1877. The first corporations were private. The Stockholm Bell Tele-

[1] *Ibid.*, p. 193.   [2] *Ibid.*, p. 151.   [3] *Ibid.*, p. 143.   [4] *Ibid.*, p. 193.

[5] 4,371 km. with a valuation of 473 million kronor (Boëthius, *op. cit.*, p. 279).

[6] In 1907 the private railroads had 8,907 km. of road while the state had 4,341 km. The aggregate value was 959 million kronor (Boëthius, *ibid.*, pp. 279-280); *Statistisk årsbok för Sverige, 1927*, Table 146, p. 186, railroads, 1886-1926.

phone in 1880 was succeeded by the Stockholm General Telephone in 1883. The latter company also constructed telephones in Moscow and in Mexico. As early as 1881 the state-owned telephone began to compete with the private lines until an understanding was finally reached.

The state raised its capital by issuing bonds through its Debt Commission. Sweden has today a most unique debt for it has not been raised for war purposes but for the economic development of the country. Other enterprises of the Swedish state are the building of electric power-plants, and the purchase of forest preserves and iron mines in Norrland. The state also owns shares in the largest of the iron corporations.

The state debt of Sweden in 1925 amounted to $646,000,000 of which $9,000,000 was a temporary loan.[1] Of new loans which have been raised since 1919, three-fifths have been placed in Sweden itself. Some $55,000,000 of obligations have been sold in the United States. As a balance to this debt the Swedish government can show investments in post-office, telegraph, railroads, electric power-houses, and public lands amounting to $780,000,000. In addition to this are the state aid funds of $111,900,000 and shares of stock valued at $24,800,000. The earnings from the state-owned enterprises alone have been a surplus over the interest on the debt. Financially, Sweden was considered in 1925 by American bankers as one of the three best risks as a borrowing nation in the world.

The large capital which has gone into private industrial enterprise and railroad construction in Sweden in recent years has been raised by the sale of stock.[2] Further loans had to be obtained from credit institutions. After the crisis of 1879 when many banks had failed because of frozen assets, the banking system again revived. Many of the loans came from private banks (enskilda), while after 1904 when the issuing of banknotes was restricted to the Riksbank, this institution became a banker's bank. The savings banks gathered in the savings of the working classes. The number of such banks rose

[1] Hildebrand, op. cit., p. 588. The total debt in 1925 was 1,733,597,784 kronor of which 15,655,000 was a temporary loan (Statistisk årsbok för Sverige, 1927, Table 253, p. 300). Business activities of the state, 1912–26 (ibid., p. 288).

[2] Boëthius, op. cit., p. 283.

from 325 in 1876 to 426 in 1907, while depositors rose from 727,000 to 1½ million.[1] By 1925 the numbers had increased to 496 savings banks and 2½ million depositors. Savings increased from $38,000,000 to $69,000,000 during the same period. In 1883 the Postal Bank was opened, and in 1907 it had $13,000,000 on deposit. This has increased to $44,000,000 in 1925.[2]

The growth of financial power within Sweden herself is demonstrated by the increase in the deposits and resources of her banks. The gold reserve has risen from $5,000,000 in 1876 to $29,000,000 in 1914 and reached a maximum of $76,000,000 in 1918.[3] There has been a decrease to $66,000,000 in 1929. Practically all of this gold is held in the Bank of Sweden. Bank loans have increased from $83,000,000 in 1876 to $688,000,000 in 1914, and $1,800,000,000 in 1920. A retrenchment of loans and deflation have reduced the amount to $1,200,000,000 in 1929. Deposits have risen from $66,-000,000 in 1876 to $1,000,000,000 in 1929. Where during the period of 1906–10 the Swedish banks owed to foreign banks $4,000,000, in 1918 there existed a favorable balance for the Swedish banks of $150,000,000 in foreign banks. This amount has been reduced to $100,000,000 in 1929.

The national wealth of Sweden almost doubled between 1885–1907.[4] This was perhaps as much due to rising values in land as to the more important creation of new industrial properties. The increase in land values as contrasted to the values of farm lands demonstrates the growing importance of land for other than agricultural purposes.

The growth of the total income of the nation is another fact demonstrating the increasing national wealth of the kingdom during the same period. With the development of industry and commerce, and the decline of agriculture, Sweden was fast passing from an age

[1] *Ibid.*, p. 284.

[2] *Statistisk årsbok för Sverige, 1927*, Table 166, p. 204. Postal savings banks, 1884–1926 (*ibid.*, p. 202).

[3] *Statistisk årsbok för Sverige, 1930*, Table 161, pp. 204–05.

[4] Sweden's national wealth was estimated in 1885 and 1898 by P. Fahlbeck and in 1908 by I. Flodström ("Allmänna ekonomiska data," *Emigrationsutredningens bilaga XIII*, p. 17).

when land had been wealth and actual money of less importance to an age of money economy. This money surplus made possible the further development of industrial enterprise.

Whereas in the early history of emigration in the nineteenth century crop failures like that of 1867–69 had turned many steps toward the New World, in the later story of that movement it was no longer crop failures but economic crises, many of them of world significance.

TABLE XVI

NATIONAL WEALTH OF SWEDEN*

| Year | Population | National Wealth (Kronor) | Kronor per Individual |
|---|---|---|---|
| 1885......... | 4,683,000 | 6,542,300,000 | 1,397 |
| 1898......... | 5,063,000 | 8,998,700,000 | 1,777 |
| 1908......... | 5,430,000 | 13,456,700,000 | 2,478 |
| 1920......... | 5,904,000 | 14,187,662,000† | 2,403 |

* "Allmänna ekonomiska data," *Emigrationsutredningens bilaga XIII*, p. 19.
† This figure is not national wealth but the total capital owned by industrial classes (*Statistisk årsbok för Sverige, 1927*, Table 27, pp. 22–25).

TABLE XVII

LAND VALUES IN SWEDEN 1862–1908*

| Year | Total Value in Million Kronor | Land for Agriculture | Other Land Property |
|---|---|---|---|
| 1862......... | 2,314 | 1,844 | 470 |
| 1873......... | 2,245 | 1,785 | 660 |
| 1879......... | 3,261 | 2,209 | 1,052 |
| 1887......... | 3,772 | 2,239 | 1,533 |
| 1896......... | 4,436 | 2,406 | 2,030 |
| 1908......... | 7,799 | 3,230 | 4,569 |

* "Allmänna ekonomiska data," *Emigrationsutredningens bilaga XIII*, p. 19.

The crisis of 1857 was felt in Sweden but not with as much severity as in other parts of the world. On the whole, the period from 1863 to 1873 was a period of rising prices and marked an upward swing of the business curve.[1] It was broken in 1867–69 by the last great crop failure that produced actual poverty and even starvation before it was ameliorated by good-will contributions and abundant harvests. Crop failures after this period did not have the same disastrous effect upon the country. The prevailing "good times" how-

[1] Sundbärg, "Allmänna ekonomiska data rörande Sverige," *Emigrationsutredningens bilaga XIII*, p. 27.

ever brought a quick recovery in Sweden even in 1869. An economic crisis due to overspeculation in agricultural land and railroads began in Sweden as early as 1874 and lasted until 1879. There was a gradual decrease in prosperity reaching its period of greatest depression in 1879. Conditions improved somewhat between 1880–83 to be met with the agricultural crisis that was common in Europe from 1884 to 1894.

A period of rising prices and increased economic activity swung the curve up toward "good times" from 1895 to 1899. The period

TABLE XVIII

SOURCES OF INCOME IN MILLION KRONOR*

| YEARS | TOTAL INCOME | INCOME FROM | | |
|---|---|---|---|---|
| | | Capital | Service or Pension | Business or Trade |
| 1866–70......... | 160.43 | 16.83 | 50.78 | 92.82 |
| 1871–75......... | 225.10 | 18.23 | 61.03 | 145.84 |
| 1876–80......... | 286.28 | 22.34 | 88.98 | 174.91 |
| 1881–85......... | 326.98 | 26.05 | 102.41 | 198.52 |
| 1886–90......... | 368.27 | 27.14 | 120.76 | 220.37 |
| 1891–95......... | 437.47 | 28.54 | 154.32 | 254.61 |
| 1896–1900....... | 602.13 | 32.92 | 218.50 | 350.71 |
| 1901–05......... | 839.77 | 49.64 | 349.11 | 441.02 |
| 1906–10......... | 1,185.81 | 72.57 | 577.61 | 535.63 |
| 1910............ | 1,253.99 | 77.82 | 678.88 | 497.29 |
| 1920............ | 6,015.00† | | | |

* "Allmänna ekonomiska data," *Emigrationsutredningens bilaga XIII*, p. 19.

† *Statistisk årsbok för Sverige, 1927*, Table 29, pp. 26–34. Income from (1) agriculture—1,153 million, (2) fishing—16 million, (3) lumbering—131 million, (4) industry and handicraft—2,146 million, (5) commerce and transportation—1,413 million, (6) service and professions—678 million, (7) servants—121 million, (8) miscellaneous—354 million. This is the peak of inflation.

of 1900–1904 was again a period of depression but rather slight, while in 1905–7 conditions improved, to be followed by another depression in 1907–8. This latter crisis in Sweden had an aftermath of bitter labor conflicts during 1909–10. Conditions improved until 1914 when the world seemed on the verge of decline. This was however postponed until after the World War.

Statistics show that emigration from Sweden was always greatest when economic conditions in Sweden were bad. The increase in emigration during the famine of 1867–69, the economic crisis of 1879, and the long agricultural depression of the eighties have already been explained. The slight increases in emigration during the crises of 1902–3 and 1907–10 demonstrate the same fact. Economic crises which had greater depressing effects on the United States but which Sweden felt but slightly resulted in cutting-off emigration from Sweden, as demonstrated by the crises of 1873 and 1893, and in sending many emigrants from the United States to the homeland.

The World War period, which may be called the period between 1914 and 1920, before the economic crisis finally broke the high price level, was a period of prosperity but also of depression for neutral Sweden. Caught in blockades and mine-strewn seas, this country was cut off from her supplies of raw materials for her textile mills, tobacco factories, etc., of fuel, in the form of coal and oil, and of foodstuffs, including grain, coffee, fats, and many other products. On the other hand, there was a large demand for her own raw materials, iron and wood, and their products. Sweden as a neutral country became very prosperous in the war trade on the one hand, but on the other it was necessary to ration all foodstuffs, sugar, fuel, and even clothing.[1]

Following the World War came the great world crisis in 1920 from which all the countries are still suffering. Although in most countries this crisis began in the spring of 1920, it did not reach Sweden until the fall.[2] The abnormally high prices which existed everywhere had reached 366 per cent over 1914 prices in Sweden in June, 1920. By December, 1921, wholesale prices had fallen to 172 per cent, by 1922 to 162 per cent and by 1929 to 134 per cent. The Stockholm Chamber of Commerce spoke of the crisis of 1921 as the worst that had been experienced in Sweden for many generations. The cost of living however did not fall as rapidly as wholesale prices. Real wages also remained higher than before the war.

The brunt of the crisis fell upon industry. The demand for exports fell off. Where in 1920 the average profit in industry had been 9.9 per cent, in 1921 there was a deficit of 6.4 per cent and in 1922 of 2.7 per cent. The exporting industries like wood pulp, lumber,

[1] Hildebrand, *op. cit.*, pp. 240–84; Eli Heckscher, *Bidrag till Sveriges ekonomiska och sociala historia under och efter världskriget* (Stockholm, 1926).

[2] Hildebrand, *op. cit.*, p. 538. The index number of 100 per cent was an average of prices from July 7, 1913 to June 30, 1914. *Statistisk årsbok, 1930*, p. 226.

iron ore, and steel found their profitable market much depressed. The home industries that produced primarily necessities of life felt the crisis less severely. Foreign wares flooded the country. Automobiles found a profitable market in Sweden. But a greater danger to home industry was the importation of goods from foreign countries with depreciated values, with which the Swedish manufacturers found it impossible to compete.[1] There came a demand for lower freight rates and an increased tariff. Freight rates were lowered, but efforts to increase tariff came to naught and the improved conditions in 1922 made it less necessary.[2]

To meet the new condition brought on by the crisis, a reconstruction in industry was needed. Just a cutting-down in production was not sufficient. It was necessary to simplify administration, to standardize the product, and decrease the cost of production.[3] The head offices of many large industries were moved from Stockholm to the location of the industry. New markets were sought for Swedish products. The capital stock was also diminished, and the burden fell upon stockholders and banks. One very large item in this reconstruction period was the laying-off of large numbers of workmen and of the administrative personnel. This was accompanied by the lowering of wages of those who remained in employment. An adjustment to meet the new demands of the eight-hour law that was passed during the fall of 1919 by the Riksdag came also into the reconstruction program. The attempts to adjust the eight-hour law and to diminish wages brought forth a series of industrial conflicts in 1919–20 that involved 81,000 and 139,000 workmen, respectively, proportions that had not been reached since the big strike of 1909. During 1921–22 wages continued to fall from 25 to 52 per cent in various industries. The strikes that accompanied this decline in wages however lost much of their vigor in the increasing and prevailing unemployment.[4] During 1922–23 Sweden faced a tremendous unemployment problem and a phenomenal increase in emigration.

[1] *Ibid.*, p. 541.

[2] *Ibid.*, pp. 542–45.

[3] Hildebrand, *ibid.*, pp. 546–47.

[4] *Ibid.*, p. 549; *Statistisk årsbok för Sverige, 1927*, Table 194, p. 230.

In 1925 and 1928 strikes and lockouts broke out with renewed vigor in an effort on the part of the workmen to raise wages and of the employers to lower wages or maintain a status quo.[1]

Conditions in Swedish industry have been slowly moving upward toward "better times" since 1923. Those industries that produce for the home market have recovered most easily. Competition on the world market is very keen and new competitors like Finland and Russia have made their appearance on the lumber market.[2] The iron industry is still suffering from the depression. In special products, however, like cream separators, electrical products, turbines, etc. there is again an active market.[3] Of all the industries, textiles had suffered the most, since beside the decline during the war because of the lack of raw materials, it has had to meet the undermining competition of cheap German wares since the war. It will be just a matter of time before Sweden with the rest of the world will recover from the economic depression that has resulted from the World War.

Financially, Sweden has proved herself exceptionally sound during the post-war period. The Swedish krona did not depreciate in value and Sweden returned to a gold basis in 1924.[4] This was exceptional, for there were few European countries that did not experience a depreciated currency during the period. Many of the Swedish banks were forced to consolidate with stronger banks because of frozen assets. In order to tide over a crisis in banking in 1922, the state developed a guaranty loan fund by the sale of bonds, for the reconstruction of banks.[5] The problem that tested the financial strength of the Swedish government was the reconstruction of the Swedish Land Bank (Svenska Lantmännens Bank) in 1923. The state invested $4,000,000 in the new Agricultural Bank (A.B. Jordbrukarbanken). The financial crisis resulted in concentration within the banking world. In 1910 there were 60 banks, in 1920 some 41, and in 1924 only 32. These banks are permitted to have branches.[6] While deposits and loans in commercial banks including the Riksbank have

---

[1] Hildebrand, *op. cit.*, p. 553. *Statistisk årsbok för Sverige, 1930*, p. 240.

[2] Hildebrand, p. 555.

[3] *Ibid.*, pp. 556–57.

[4] *Ibid.*, p. 585.

[5] For a more detailed account, see *ibid.*, pp. 574–79.        [6] *Ibid.*, p. 577.

decreased since 1920, savings in savings banks and in the postal savings have increased.

Although Sweden seems to have suffered from unemployment and the decline of industry since the war, her sound financial condition has given her a unique position in the world. She, like the United States, entered the war as a debtor nation and has emerged a creditor nation. And so in the short span of forty years an agricultural country has been transformed into an industrial nation. The causes of emigration have altered from poor crops and the high cost of agricultural land to economic crises, unemployment, and labor conflicts.

## CHAPTER XI

## THE PASSING OF THE OLD RURAL CULTURE

The change from an agrarian culture to an industrial life has tended to undermine the old customs of the Swedish countryside. Undoubtedly the impetus to this decline was the blow that Swedish agriculture received during the agrarian crisis of the eighties that was so disastrous to all Western European cultivators. But were there other contributing factors in this disaffection that spread among the Swedish agrarian population? Was land held in large estates and unprocurable by the peasantry and agricultural laborers, as in so many portions of Central Europe and in the British Isles? Or were, perhaps, the Swedish farms too small to afford a decent standard of living?

Sweden is not a land of large estates like England and Scotland, but more a country of small farms like France. Two-thirds of the farms vary from 5 to 50 acres of cultivated land, while one-fourth are less than 5 acres.[1] Only 1 per cent contains more than 250 acres of land under production. It must be remembered that 59 per cent of Sweden is standing forest and that only 9 per cent of the land-area is actually under cultivation.[2] Most of the farms also own a piece of woodland.

The breaking up of large estates in Sweden had occurred during the last half of the eighteenth century. Between 1750–1810, estates of a mantal or over (125 acres) had decreased from 32,308 to 12,843 in the southern and central provinces, to almost one-third.[3] During the same period there had been a tremendous growth of farms three-eighths to one-sixty-fourth of a mantal (46 to 2 acres) in area, but the

---

[1] K. Socialstyrelsen, *Lantarbetarnas arbets-och löneförhallånden*, p. 34; *Statistisk årsbok för Sverige, 1927*, p. 84, Table 83. These are the figures of 1911, but there has been but slight change by 1919.

[2] *Statistisk årsbok för Sverige, 1927*, p. 85, Table 84.

[3] Norrland and Dalarne are not included in these figures ("Jordstyckningen," *Emigrationsutredningens bilaga XII*, Table D, Summary, p. 184*).

largest number of farms were one-fourth and one-eighth of a mantal (from 15 to 30 acres). It was considered by the Forest laws of the eighteenth century, as has been mentioned, that it was impossible to make a livelihood in farming on less than one-fourth of a mantal.

From 1810 to 1900 there was but a slight change in the number of farms of 15 acres or more, while the increase of farms occurred in the group less than 15 acres. Since 1840 the largest number of farms have varied from 2 to 30 acres. Those cultivating the smaller pieces of land must earn an additional income in industry or lumbering. There had been no very great change in 1919.

TABLE XIX

Size of Cultivated Landholdings in Sweden, 1919*

|  | Less than 10 Hectares, or 25 Acres | 10 to 50 Hectares, or 25 to 125 Acres | Over 50 Hectares, or 125 Acres | Total |
|---|---|---|---|---|
| Farms: |  |  |  |  |
| Number.......... | 328,873 | 91,247 | 7,906 | 428,026 |
| Per cent.......... | 77 | 21.2 | 1.8 | 100 |
| Farms: |  |  |  |  |
| Land area in hectares | 1,223,150 | 1,756,951 | 807,141 | 3,787,242 |
| Per cent.......... | 32.3 | 46.4 | 21.3 | 100 |

* *Statistisk årsbok för Sverige, 1927*, pp. 86-87, Table 85.

Farms are designated according to the amount of their acreage. A farm of from 5 to 25 acres of arable land, if it is cultivated by a peasant under the old entailed system, is called a *småbondehemman* or a small peasant farm. If it has been purchased or leased under the modern land system, it is called a *småbruk* or small farm. These smaller farms are cultivated by the farmer and his family, without any hired labor. A farm from 25 to 125 acres of fields and owned by a peasant is known as a *storbondehemman*, or a large peasant farm. These larger estates must rely partly on hired agricultural labor. Estates over 125 acres of cultivated land belong usually to "patrons" or members of the nobility and are designated as *herrgårder* or manors. They are entirely dependent on employed labor and are often managed by a bailiff rather than the owner. The large estates of over 125 acres of arable land constitute only 1.8 per cent of the number of farms in Sweden, but 21.3 per cent of the cultivated land-area.[1] In England, however, in 1895, almost 70 per cent of the cultivated land was parceled into farms of over 100 acres each.[2]

Although Sweden is preponderantly a country of small freeholds, there are certain regions of the kingdom in which the large estate prevails. This is true on the fertile plains of Eastern and Central Sweden, in Stockholm, Uppsala, Västmanland, Södermanland, and Östergötland counties. Here the usual type of farm is the *herrgård* or the *storbondegård* belonging to the gentry or the wealthier peasant. But even in these counties may be found smaller farms and cottages scattered through the forested hilly regions, along the seacoast, or on the numerous skerries of the rugged shore. The average farm for this section of Sweden varies from 50 to 60 acres.

It has often been assumed that a region in Europe of large estates has been most prolific in emigration, while in portions of a country in which small freeholds prevailed, the inhabitants were satisfied and loath to leave their homes. But strange to say that, in the history of Swedish emigration, this rule has not always proved the case. This is especially true in the Mälar counties mentioned above, which have had a smaller exodus than any other portion of the country. From Östergötland, the fourth county mentioned, there has been a large emigration.

The largest average acreage in estates in Sweden existed in Bro hundred in Uppsala County, 313 acres of tilled land per farm in 1902. Of the 39 estates in the county, 25 were leased, and there were 204 crofts and cottages on the estates. Although it appeared to be a region most conducive to emigration, however, during the most prolific exodus from Sweden, 1880–1900, only 1.3 persons per thousand left this region, while the average for the kingdom was 5.21.[3] The same was true in the neighboring hundred of Håbo, which had farms averaging 136 acres of tilled land. Tenantry was high, 52.5 per cent, and there were 375 crofts and cottages on the estates here, but emigration was even less.[4] In nine hundreds scattered through the

[1] K. Socialstyrelsen, *Lantarbetarnas arbets-och löneförhållanden*, p. 149.

[2] Steffen, "Lagstiftningen om smärre jordbruk och jordlotter i England, Skotland, och Irland, Småbruksrörelsen i främmande länder," *Emigrationsutredningens bilaga XIV*, p. 12.

[3] "Bygdestatistik," *Emigrationsutredningens bilaga V*, pp 214* ff., Table 72.

[4] Only 1.04 persons per 1,000.

counties of Stockholm, Västmanland, Uppsala, and Östergötland, with estates of 100–125 acres of land under cultivation as typical of their farm units, there was found a high percentage of tenantry and a low rate of exodus.

There were some exceptions, for instance in Dals hundred in Östergötland in 1902. Here the average acreage of the estates amounted to 101 acres.[1] There were 235 freeholds and 184 crofts and cottages, while 38.3 per cent of the farms were leased. It was a fertile region with many large estates, lying south of Vadstena on Lake Vätter. Most of the land-area was under cultivation in this hundred, which was most unusual in this section of the country. The crop yield was high. There was considerable investment in horse-breeding in the region. But in this hundred emigration reached twice the average for the kingdom between 1880–1900.

It seems paradoxical that in the region around lake Mälar, where the large estate prevailed, emigration should have been so small a factor. The soil there is some of the most fertile in the kingdom. It is located advantageously near the capital of Stockholm, which is also a Baltic port. It is an old settled region, where large estates and the labor system of crofters and cotters was early introduced. Even in 1805, a decline in the numbers of the rural population was noticeable in many of the hundreds of Uppsala County.

While there were small increases in the population of the other portions of the region, there was no doubling of the native stock like that of Southern and Western Sweden in the first half of the nineteenth century. The slight emigration from the Mälar counties found its way to Stockholm and to more prosperous regions of the realm. This relieved what surplus population might have existed which was not taken care of by the expanding area of cultivated lands.[2] There was less opportunity for the agricultural laborer to acquire or lease land here than in other portions of the kingdom. This may have brought about a static condition in population while the remainder of the kingdom was growing rapidly. But the native population itself was not showing the natural increase of the southern and western counties, nor even the average of the kingdom during the years 1820–50. In the Mälar counties, although the marriage

---

[1] "Bygdestatistik," op. cit., p. 55.   [2] Ibid., pp. 196* ff., Table 71.

rate was the average, the birth-rate was low and the death-rate high.[1] In counties like Malmöhus, Jönköping, and Värmland, an average and even low marriage rate was associated with a high or average birth-rate, but an extremely low death-rate.

It is natural that the Mälar region with its large estates should be the first to establish a system of permanent agricultural labor. Thus the croft and cottage were early introduced and grew rapidly in the eighteenth century, and when these forms of tenantry became most prolific in their growth in the other portions of the kingdom, they had reached a point of satiety on the estates around Stockholm.[2] It was here too that annual contracts for labor were substituted for tenantry as a source of agricultural labor in the thirties, and many of the tenant farms were enclosed in the large estates when agriculture became so profitable. The manors were dependent upon hired agricultural labor for their maintenance and furnished a permanent labor-supply to a given number of people. This constant demand for labor tended to encourage the agricultural laborers to remain in the region and discouraged emigration. Perhaps it was the comparative contentment and prosperity of the lower rural classes here that produced a smaller birth-rate than in the other portions of the country. The higher death-rate is more difficult to explain, for it may be doubted whether housing and sanitation among the masses were any worse here than in other counties.

While other agricultural communities in Sweden felt the pressure of an inadequate labor supply as early as the eighties, it was not until 1900 that labor was difficult to obtain in the Mälar counties. The secretary of an agricultural society in Södermanland County, reporting on the labor conditions in the rural districts of the county in 1907 wrote:

The reason for the decline of the crofter may be found in the following circumstances; on one side, the difficulty which the cultivators of larger and middle sized crofts find in obtaining labor at a reasonable price, the crofter's ignorance in agricultural methods, his lack of capital to develop the productive possibilities of his croft, and the opportunity for him to obtain a better income as a day laborer. On the other side, the land owner's failure to maintain both

[1] *Ibid.*, pp. 32* ff., Table 31.

[2] Wohlin, "Torpare-, backstugu-och inhysesklasserna," *Emigrationsutredningens bilaga XI*, pp. 40–44.

the buildings and the soil of his crofts in better condition, when the income from the croft seems small, and his underestimation of the value of the crofter's labor on the large estate (must be considered). . . . .[1]

It has not been until the last decade that it has been difficult to obtain agricultural labor, first in the region of Eskilstuna and in the regions closest to Stockholm, later in the other parts of the county, and last in the regions with least communications. The Employment Association of the county, which includes about 150 of the larger estates, reported a scarcity of six hundred agricultural laborers on annual contract. And even before this there had been a restriction of labor on all the estates. Any further reduction will be injurious to production, especially since Socialistic agitation has reduced the willingness of the workmen to perform service. Wages have increased, also due to the Socialist movement.[2]

Although the large estate or manor is not the prevailing unit of agriculture in other parts of Sweden, there are some scattered through all the counties. In the Skåne counties there are many historic *herrgårder* belonging to the old noble families of Sweden. Of the remaining counties, Malmöhus has the largest acreage of estates over 125 acres in extent, while the neighboring county of Kristianstad has about half of the amount.[3] Some of these estates are owned by sugar corporations. Skaraborg County in Central Sweden has a little less than one-fourth of its land-area in manors.[4] In Småland the county of Kalmar contains 421 large estates, about one-fifth of the land.[5] Örebro, Värmland, Halland, and Älvsborg counties follow in successive order. Most of the large estates in the Norrland provinces are held by lumbering corporations as forest preserves.

In a study of labor conditions on the large estates of Sweden in 1915, the Labor Department of the Swedish government chose 238 typical manors scattered through the various counties. The largest

---

[1] K. A. Högström, Secreterare, Södermanlands läns hushållningssällskap, "Inkomna utlåtanden," *Emigrationsutredningens bilaga XVII*, p. 15.

[2] *Ibid.*

[3] Malmöhus County has 110,205 hectares of land, a little less than one-third of its area, in farms over 50 hectares, and a total of 909 such large estates. Kristianstad County has about one-fifth of its area in large holdings, 454 estates with an area of 48,634 hectares (*Statistisk årsbok för Sverige, 1927*, pp. 86–87, Table 85).

[4] Skaraborg County has 79,527 hectares in her 749 farms over 125 acres in extent (*ibid.*).

[5] A total of 39,360 hectares of land and holding ninth place in the counties with large estates (*ibid.*).

manor was one in Södermanland with 2,000 acres of cultivated fields.[1] Two estates, one in the same county and another in Örebro County, had each slightly over 1,500 acres of broken ground. There were 5 manors varying from 1,500 to 1,250 acres of plowland, 4 of which were in Skåne, while 10 estates ranged from 1,000 to 1,250 acres. Most of the estates also had forest lands, while those in Norrland and Småland averaged 5,000 acres of woodland, apiece. These 238 estates varied greatly in ownership. Fourteen belonged to the government, 6 to communes or various foundations, 54 to corporations, and 164 to private individuals. Only 38 of the estates were leased.

There was also great variation in the types of labor supply available for the estates. The oldest form, the croft, still remained the chief source of agricultural labor in Småland and in Western Sweden, while in Östergötland, in the Mälar counties, and in Skåne the married hired man, engaged by an annual contract, had taken the place of the "day-labor" tenant. The croft still prevailed in Gothenburg-Bohus, Älvsborg, and Skaraborg counties. Since the average croft was about 10 acres, only a small portion of the estate was rented in this manner, usually less than 30 per cent. However, on one estate in Halland County as much as 60.5 per cent of the land was divided into crofts, and on another in Skaraborg, 55.1 per cent. These two estates were reminders of older days when the larger portion of an estate was divided among two types of tenants, *landbönder* and crofters.

Great changes have taken place in the old landowning nobility and gentry of Sweden in the last century. With the exception of the entailed estates (*fideicommissionen*), many of the manors have passed from the land-poor gentry to the new moneyed industrial classes, called *possessioners*.[2] During the agricultural crisis of 1850 and to a greater extent during the crisis of 1880, many of the old aristocracy were forced to sell their estates. The sale still continues. Practically every edition of the Stockholm newspapers, for example, carries ad-

[1] A very good description of the extent of large estates in Sweden in various counties (K. Socialstyrelsen, *op. cit.*, *1915*, pp 34–41, 100–101, Table A).

[2] Wohlin, "Bondeklassens undergräfvande," *Emigrationsutredningens bilaga X*, p. 73 ff.

vertisements of neighboring estates, and even manors in the more remote counties of the kingdom.[1] The estates are purchased by capitalists, contractors, wholesalers, lumber-dealers, corporations, peasants who have accumulated money through thrift or speculation, and merchant princes of the larger cities. The newly rich in this way attempt to rise to a social position. Merchants in the cities of Stockholm, Malmö, and Gothenburg own estates in neighboring rural communities, which they use as summer residences.

This change of ownership has had far-reaching results. The old landed aristocracy had supervised the cultivation of their land. There had developed a patriarchal attitude on the part of the nobleman to the crofter and the hired labor, through generations of association of the families on the same estate. A certain amount of loyalty and respect for the lord made the laborer even at times submissive and always diffident. The old gentry had been the first to introduce new methods in agriculture and had influenced the husbandry of the surrounding neighborhood. The new landlord purchases his land either for speculation or social prestige. He seldom is interested in the cultivation of the land for itself. The result is that now out of the 8,000 farms in Sweden over 125 acres, only 2,671 are cultivated by owners or lessees. The remainder are either owned by corporations or individuals for the exploitation of the forest lands, or are managed by stewards and bailiffs.[2] This absentee ownership has changed the personal contacts of landowner to labor to a more modern impersonal attitude.

Although emigration has been very small from the region of large estates in the Mälar counties, there has been much emigration from the other counties where manors often occupy all the lands of a community. There is at present a feeling that the large estates should be broken up and offered for sale to smaller landowners. Laws have recently been passed to limit the amount of land that may be acquired by corporations. And there have been definite at-

[1] *Svenska Dagbladet* (Stockholm), April 4, 1927, p. 14. (Herrgård near the sea in Södermanland province, 303 tunnland of fields and 450 tunnland of forest.)

[2] There are 3,987 stewards, bookkeepers, etc., of the farm-management staff, and 6,120 bailiffs and foremen enumerated in the Swedish census (*The Swedish Agricultural Labourer, 1921*, p. 24).

tempts to discontinue the entailed estates (*fideicommissionen*) as a form of land-monopoly, in conformity with similar movements in Holland, Germany, and Denmark.

There are all told about 1,800 large private estates in Southern and Central Sweden belonging to the nobles and gentry at the present time. These are located in the most fertile portions of the kingdom. Only 600 of them are being cultivated by their owners, the others are leased either as a whole or in portions. Thus Friherr C. S. Kuylenstierna of Sperlingsholm in Halland County has 209 tenants; Count M. Brahe has 142 tenants scattered over his estates in Stockholm, Uppsala, and Malmöhus counties, and Count R. S. Hamilton of Ovesholm, 31 in Kristianstad County.[1] In some communes the land-area is almost entirely owned by a large estate. The manor, belonging to Friherr Ugglas in Forsmark in Stockholm County, owns 33 of the 36 farms in the commune. In Sövestad, Malmöhus County, the estate of Count M. Brahe contains 85 tenant farms while there are only 7 other farms in the commune.[2] At Skokloster in Uppsala County the same nobleman owns 47 tenant farms in a community of only 51 farms.

The problem of tenantry has always been associated with these large estates. There are about 13,000 tenants on the 1,850 manors. About 10,000 of these are scattered through the estates in Skåne, Skaraborg, Östergötland, and the Mälar counties. In Södermanland County there are 2,000 tenants on large estates, in Skaraborg 1,600, and in Östergötland over 1,400. These last two counties have been among the most prolific in emigration. The average tenant farm on these large estates is about 32 acres. However, the acreage varies widely from county to county. In Malmöhus County, for instance, the average is 67 acres, while some estates are as large as 250 acres. Even in the neighboring counties there are many manors leased, and the average leasehold is 46 acres. There are many large estates leased in these counties also, as well as in Halland County. In the remaining counties the average tenant farm is 25 acres and is

---

[1] Frederick Sandberg, "Redogörelse för resultatet av vissa av jordkommissionens företagna enquêter i jordfrågan," *Jordkommissionens betänkande, 1922*, Part V, pp. 24 ff.

[2] *Ibid.*

usually a croft or a small farm. There is always the feeling that estates or farms cultivated by the owner receive more attention and are maintained at a higher level of cultivation than in the hands of a tenant. And since so many of these large estates are cultivated by tenants, it would be better to make it possible for the cultivators of the soil to purchase their land. The gradual disappearance of the croft and the unsuccessful attempts to encourage this form of tenantry in Sweden has also led to the establishment in public opinion of a relationship between the lack of opportunity to procure the ownership of land and exodus from the rural regions.

There are besides the large manors of the gentry some 122 entailed estates known as *fideicommiss*, with 7,057 tenants.[1] These estates, like the manors, are scattered through the most fertile regions of the realm, on the plains of Östergötland, Kristianstad, and the Mälar counties. In Malmöhus County, they seem to be most numerous in the less fertile and wooded regions. This form of land-monopoly was introduced in Sweden simultaneously with its appearance in Germany, probably in the seventeenth century. It may be traced to the influence of Roman law, which recognized this form of land-tenure, and it spread throughout continental Europe. There was a law passed in 1809 in Sweden forbidding any future establishment of the entailed estate, and giving the king the power to dissolve any if the owner petitioned for the right to sell.[2]

The amount of tenantry on these entailed estates varies from 4 estates with no tenants to estates with over 300 each. There are 24 with over a hundred tenants each. One-third of the tenants or 2,728 are found on ten estates. Count C. G. Bonde has 390 tenant farms on his estates in the counties of Stockholm, Södermanland, Jönköping, and Kronoberg. On his estate Horningsholm in Södermanland County, he owns 87 of the 97 farms in the commune of Mörkö.[3] Count H. S. Trolle-Wachtmeister has 343 tenant farms on his estates in Kristianstad and Blekinge counties. While in the commune of Trolle-Ljungby in Kristianstad County, he owns 133 tenant farms

[1] *Ibid.*, pp. 22 ff.

[2] "Om sociala arrendebestämmelser, etc.," *Jordkommissionens betänkande, 1923,* Part VI (Stockholm, 1923), p. 340.

[3] *Ibid.*, Part V, p. 23, and *ibid.*, Part VI, pp. 330–35.

on his estate of the same name, and only 38 farms in the commune are freeholds. Friherr O. Silfverschiöld has 308 tenant farms in the counties of Halland and Älvsborg. Of the 115 farms in the commune of Lagmansered in Älvsborg County, 102 are tenant farms on his estate Koberg. It is especially true in Malmöhus County that often these large entailed estates own practically all the land in a rural commune.

The average area of the leased farms on the *fideicommiss* is 40 acres.[1] In Uppsala and Västmanland the average is around 60. Here the entailed estates are located in regions where the large estate prevails as a unit of agriculture, and the leased farms are large. This is also true in the two Skåne counties and Halland, while in Stockholm, Södermanland, and Östergötland counties the leased farms of these estates are small in size, averaging between 30 and 40 acres. In this type of county the estates are located in the forested regions with less acreage of cultivated land. In other counties containing entailed estates, the tenant farms consist of crofts and small farms.

With the abolition of the House of Nobles in the Swedish Riksdag in 1866, the position of Swedish nobles was destined to fall before the democratization of the country. There developed an antagonism between the small farmer and the owners of manors that sometimes split the agrarian party. The abeyance of the lower classes to the nobility is fast disappearing, although wealth in even a democratic society will have its admirers and courtesans. The institution of entailed estates is especially repugnant to a democratic order. With the abolition of the *fideicommiss* in the Netherlands in 1833, in France in 1849, in Italy in 1865, and the attempt at its abolition in Denmark since 1854, it is natural that similar attempts should be made in Sweden.[2] Beginning with 1882, it has been a moot question before the Riksdag. The most recent bill is similar to the one lately passed by the Danish government. Of the 162 owners of entailed estates in Sweden, all except 40 belong to the nobility. Between 1911–23, the government of Sweden has forced, by an interpretation of the law of 1810, the dissolution of some 40 such estates.[3]

The Swedish government and various communes are also landowners and landlords. The Swedish state, the church, the com-

[1] *Ibid*, Part V, p. 23.　　　[2] *Ibid.*, Part VI, pp. 347–48　　　[3] *Ibid.*, p. 335.

munes, and various educational and charitable foundations own about 17.7 per cent of all leased land in Sweden, and have about one-fourth of the tenant farmers on their lands. Omitting the Norrland counties where the state owns large stretches of forest and mineral lands, there are public lands scattered through most of the southern and middle counties of the country. There are in all some 6,201 tenants on the various crownlands in these counties, more or less evenly distributed, perhaps to a greater extent in the South Swedish highlands where the state owns forest lands.[1] These highlands lie in the southern portion of Östergötland and in the northern portions of Kalmar, Kristianstad, and Skaraborg counties. The average farm leased by the state is about 40 acres in area. The farms vary in size from an average of 97 acres in Malmöhus County to 15 acres in Kronoberg County.

In the days of an agrarian economy it was customary to attach a piece of farmland to each manse of the clergy, and to the manor of all government officials, military and civil. Most of the lands belonging to the government officials have been withdrawn by the state, but some farmlands still belong to the church in the various parishes. Much of this land is now leased, especially in Malmöhus, Skaraborg, and Halland counties. The size of the leased farms is about the same as on the crownland. The largest farms are in Västmanland County and the smallest in Blekinge. Only about 41 per cent of the communes own land which is leased to tenants. These lands are most numerous in Malmöhus, Östergötland, and Gothenburg-Bohus counties and belong largely to the cities. Their farms average 25 acres. About half of the leased farms belonging to the endowment of educational and charitable foundations are found in the Mälar counties, and most of these belong to Uppsala University. The area of these farms is usually larger than those of the state.

Many of the estates that are leased by the crown have belonged to the state since the reduction of the nobility in the seventeenth century and the confiscation at the time of many lands unlawfully acquired by the nobles.[2] The estates have been leased more or less

[1] Sandberg, "Redogörelse," *Jordkommissionens betänkanden*, Part V, pp. 17 ff.

[2] Axel Brusewitz and Sven Tunberg, *Statens domäner och deras förvaltning*, Broschyrer utgifna af nationalföreningen mot emigrationen II (Stockholm, 1908), 3 ff.

continuously since that time, but quite a few have been sold to the peasants in the eighteenth and early nineteenth centuries. Various laws and regulations have been passed concerning the leasing of lands. A reform in 1882 created a special division, the Domain Administration (domänstyrelsen).[1] The farms are auctioned to the highest bidder, and the time of the lease is usually twenty years. The lessee must maintain all the buildings on the estates and must pay for the erection of any new ones. This has proved too great a burden for the lessee, and consequently the buildings are usually in a very poor condition. It has resulted in an unusually low rental for the state's property.[2] The present attitude of the Swedish people is that this land would be better cultivated under private ownership and some of it is being sold for small farms.

The purchase of large tracts of land, especially forest, by corporations has been a phenomenon of the last century.[3] Where the land has been purchased from the peasants, the small cultivated portions have been leased either to the former owner or to some other tenant. There are 16,056 of these tenant farms in Southern and Central Sweden. Värmland County has 4,031 of them and Värmland and Örebro counties together have 42.5 per cent of the corporation farms.[4] Östergötland County has 1,127 tenant farms owned by corporations, Uppsala County, 1,042, Västmanland County, 929, and Stockholm county, 860.

In Stockholm and Östergötland counties the number of tenant farms is so large that those owned by corporations form only a small percentage. But in Värmland County 61.4 per cent of all tenant farms are owned by corporations, and in Örebro 48.9 per cent. In Uppsala and Västmanland counties it averages 30 per cent. In Kopparberg County the 688 corporation-owned tenant farms constitute over 50 per cent of leased lands. In the southern counties like Gotland and Halland, there is little land owned by corporations.

---

[1] *Ibid.*, p. 6.

[2] Studies of the crown domains in Uppsala province in 1908 showed an average of 4.1 per cent valuation as rental value (*ibid.*, pp. 11–16). In Värmland it was only 2.2 per cent (*ibid.*, pp. 19–20).

[3] This has been more fully discussed in the chapter on "The Forests of Sweden."

[4] Sandberg, "Redogörelse," *op. cit.*, Part V, pp. 18 ff.

And even in Skåne, where tenantry is relatively high, with the exception of certain farms for the cultivation of sugar beets, corporations own and rent out very little land. The lands owned by the corporations are almost exclusively in the forested regions of the country.

There are portions of the country in which the corporations own a large part of a local community. The three regions, the "Bergslag" (Värmland, Örebro, and Kopparberg counties), the forested regions of northern and southern Östergötland, and the bordering counties have about 10,000 tenant farms owned by corporations, one-fifth of all the farms of these regions, and two-thirds of the corporation lands of Southern and Central Sweden. The other counties in Southern and Western Sweden contain only 2.2 per cent of tenant farms owned by corporations. In the Norrland region such large stretches of land belonged to corporations that it became necessary to limit the amount of land that corporations could hold. The grip that this impersonal ownership has on certain communities is demonstrable when Söderfors commune in Uppsala County with 44 farms has 42 that are owned by corporations.[1] In Skagershult commune in Örebro County, 160 of the 167 farms are leased from corporations. In Grythytte and Hällefors hundreds in the same county, 565 of the 889 farms belong to corporations.

There are in Southern and Central Sweden some 1,405 corporations that own land. Of these 500 cultivate their own land, while 31 have over 100 tenant farmers. The Uddeholm corporation has 2,073 such farms in the county of Värmland, and Billerud corporation owns 668 in the same county. While 684 corporations have only from 1 to 5 tenant farmers, 10 corporations own 40 per cent of the corporation-owned tenant farms.

The average size of these tenant farms amounts to only 16 acres. In Malmöhus County the average is higher, 52 acres, in Kristianstad County, 30 acres. While in Värmland and Örebro counties the tenant farms are very small, less than 10 acres. It is in these two counties that 42 per cent of these tenant farms are found. The tenant farmers here constitute the labor-supply for the forest and mining industries of the region. There is no doubt that the purchase of the peasant lands in the forest regions of Norrland and Värmland has

---

[1] Sandberg, "Redogörelse," *ibid.*, pp. 20–21.

been a cause of emigration. To prevent the entire disappearance of the small freehold farm in this region, laws have been passed recently limiting the amount of land that a corporation may hold.

About one-fourth of the cultivated land in Sweden at the present is leased to tenant farmers.[1] There has been a slight decrease in some forms of tenantry since 1870 caused by the gradual decline of the croft and cottage, but emigration has tended to increase other forms of tenantry for many elderly people have found their sons reluctant to return and take over the old farm, and have been forced to lease it.

TABLE XX

THE AMOUNT OF LAND TENANTRY IN SWEDEN, 1919*

|  | Less than 10 Hectares or 25 Acres | 10 to 25 Hectares, or 25 to 125 Acres | Over 50 Hectares, or 125 Acres | Total |
|---|---|---|---|---|
| Total number of farms..... | 328,873 | 91,247 | 7,906 | 428,026 |
| Farms cultivated by owners. | 272,842 | 70,471 | 5,022 | 328,335 |
| Tenant farms: |  |  |  |  |
| Number............... | 76,031 | 20,776 | 3,884 | 99,691 |
| Per cent.............. : | 20 | 22.8 | 49 | 23 |

* Statistisk årsbök för Sverige, 1927, p. 87, Table 85.

The problem of tenantry is perhaps not as great in Sweden as in many other countries, but there is the desire that more cultivators shall be owners of their land.

But on the whole Sweden has never been a land of large estates, but rather a country of small proprietors. Sometimes the disintegration of farms may produce such small pieces of land that it is impossible to make a sufficient income to support a family. The smallest farms in Sweden are in the "Dalarne" region. The average farm here in Kopparberg County is 7.8 acres, the smallest in the kingdom. This is, however, a forested region, and also a mining region. In the dense forests of Särna and Idre, the farms average only 1.7 acres.[2] The population is sparse. There are only 320 farms and three-fourths of these are leased, mostly from corporations. Even in the old his-

[1] The land-area of tenant farms amounts to 971,116 hectares and the total area of cultivated land is 3,787,242 hectares (1919) (Statistisk årsbok för Sverige, 1927, p. 87, Table 85).

[2] "Bygdestatistik," op. cit., pp. 207-9.

torical portions of the county, Malungs, Mora, Älvsdal, and Orsa hundreds, the farms are only 3 or 4 acres. Mora, so intimately connected with Gustavus Vasa and the War of Independence against Denmark, has an average of only 3½ acres per farm. In this region there are 3,395 freeholds and less than 1 per cent tenantry. Since early times the freedom-loving people of Dalecarlia have been forced by inadequate incomes from their agriculture to engage in various handicraft work in iron, wood, copper, and in homespuns. These were sold by peddlers in the more prosperous regions of the kingdom. Shops in Stockholm and Gothenburg still display this handicraft of Dalarne as typical of Sweden.

Some of the earliest emigration to the United States came from these rather remote northern districts. In the forties and fifties, considered one of the most populous regions of Sweden, it has since that time remained almost stationary in the numbers of its inhabitants. It is a part of the region which has been benefited by the booming of the lumber industry. Emigration has greatly decreased, for good wages may be obtained in the lumber camps of Norrland. Young women from the region frequently seek employment as maids in Stockholm. At the present time it is perhaps the most popular of the Swedish summer-resort regions. Tourists are entertained with national dances in national costumes. They also purchase much of the handicraft work of the region.

The cotter with his potato patch is today usually a workman engaged in fishing, forestry, or industry. Through the "Own Home" movement there has been an increase of these small farms around industrial communities. The small farms of the fishermen are located along the Bohus coast, north of Gothenburg, where salt-sea fishing is most profitable. In Ornst Västra hundred in this region, the farms average 8.6 acres.[1] There is practically no tenantry here and very little emigration. An industrial region in the same county, Askim hundred, has farms averaging 7.8 acres with much the same conditions. In Älvsborg County from which emigration as a whole has been very extensive, Vedens hundred, also an industrial region,

---

[1] *Ibid.*, pp. 126, 129. Almost half of the fishermen employed in salt-sea fisheries in Sweden are located in Gothenburg-Bohus County (K. Statistiska centralbyrån, *Fiske*, *1914*, p. 25).

has less than the average emigration for the kingdom. The farms here averaged 13.5 acres. In 1902 there were 824 freeholds and 864 small tenant farms, crofts, and cottages in this region. In the mining region of Örebro County, in the famous "Bergslag," Nya Kopparberg, Brythytte, and Hällefors, the farms are small, varying from 8 to 10 acres.[1] Most of the farms are leased from corporations. Before 1900, emigration from this region was only slightly higher than the average, due to the opportunities for labor in the mines.

In the purely agricultural regions, however, and especially in those districts where the soil is less fertile, or where distance from market and poor communications have tended toward isolation, emigration has been largest. Thus, in Sunnerbo hundred in Kronoberg County, Småland, a region where the farms average 11 acres, emigration has risen to 11.67 persons per thousand. This is a locality in which population doubled between 1805–65. And even though the cultivated land was increased fivefold during the same period, at least 60 per cent of the land-area still remains either in bogs or consists of rocky impediments. Only 9 per cent of the land is under cultivation. Most of the farms are freeholds; less than one-third are crofts. From this region, emigrants have gone directly to America, without a visit to Denmark or Germany. The population has decreased 20 per cent since 1880.[2]

Another region with much emigration and comparatively small farms is Jösse and lower Frysdals hundreds in Värmland County. In Jösse hundred the farms average 15 acres, with practically no tenantry and only a few crofts and cottages remaining.[3] In lower Frysdals, the situation is similar. The freeholds average 18 acres with little tenantry for cash. The number of crofts is larger but the freeholds less in number than in Jösse hundred. A neighboring region, Vedbo hundred in Älvsborg County, has a similar record, small farms averaging $12\frac{1}{2}$ acres, with about 12 per cent tenantry. This whole area in the mining and lumbering regions of the "Bergslag" has lost much of its population through the purchase of peasant

---

[1] "Bygdestatistik," *op. cit.*, pp. 141, 185–86.

[2] *Ibid.*, pp. 70–71.

[3] There were 3,810 freeholds, 707 *torp*, etc., and only 1.5 per cent tenantry for cash, while the average freehold was 6 hectares in extent (*ibid.*, pp. 171–72).

freeholds by lumbering corporations, and the declining demand for casual labor in the lumbering camps of Norrland.[1]

It is not strange perhaps that the largest amount of emigration from Sweden in the period after 1880 should have come from the wholly agricultural regions, even where the landholdings were of fair size. The impetus of this exodus was undoubtedly the crisis that proved so disastrous to all of European agriculture. This emigration came from regions where the freeholds varied from 25 to 50 acres in size, and from regions often with very little tenantry, except in the croft. It was the small farmer that felt the distress of the crisis most keenly. Some of these regions have already been mentioned, Sundal, Redväg, Nordal, Valbo in Dalsland, and Möckleby on the island of Öland. In all of the agricultural counties similar regions may be found: Laske and Olleberg hundreds in Skaraborg County, Bullaren hundred in Gothenburg-Bohus County, Runnsten hundred in Kalmar County, Karlskoga hundred in Örebro County, Bjäre hundred in Kristianstad County.

The number of farms under cultivation did not decrease, however, during this period when emigration was at its height. If the small landowner left for America his farm was either leased or sold. The number of entrepreneurs engaged in agriculture in 1870 was 241,857, and in 1900, 271,494.[2] There had been but a slight change in 1920 when the number of cultivators was only 278,187.[3]

The largest amount of rural emigration came from the tenant classes; the crofters and cotters, and sons and daughters of the peasants, who hired themselves out as agricultural laborers. The tremendous decline of the crofter, which has been a source of constant labor-supply for the rural regions for over a century, has caused much concern to the Swedish government, and to the agriculturalists of the nation. In 1751, when the earliest Swedish census was taken, there were 27,891 crofters, and by 1860 this number had increased to 99,891 men with probably over 100,000 includ-

---

[1] There are three special reports on these regions in "Bygdeundersökningar," *Emigrationsutredningens bilaga VIII*. For a discussion of Norrland see "Om sociala arrendebestämmelser," *Jordkommissionens betänkande*, Part VI (1923), pp. 32 ff.

[2] Wohlin, *Den jordbruksidkande befolkningen i Sverige, 1751–1900*, Table H, p. 26.

[3] *Statistisk årsbok för Sverige, 1927*, pp. 40–41, Table 23.

ing the women operating crofts.[1] Then began a decrease, simultaneous with the growth of industry and emigration until the crofter
declined to 53,005 in 1910, just a trifle more than his numbers in
1790. Some 456,881 persons were dependent upon crofts for a livelihood in 1870, and only 347,208 in 1900.[2]

During the period of agricultural prosperity in Sweden, beginning
as early as 1830, many of the larger estates began to enclose the
crofts belonging to them, and placed the entire acreage under one
management, a system of extensive cultivation. The new type of agricultural laborer, called a *statare*, who hired himself out by the year
on an annual wage contract, supplanted to a great extent the older
form of rural labor-supply, the crofter. This was especially true in
counties where the large estate predominated, such as the Mälar
counties, Östergötland, and Skane. This changing form of cultivator
on the large estates made it difficult for crofters to obtain land, and
after 1840 many found their opportunity to obtain it by emigrating
to the free lands of the Mississippi Valley.

Gilbert Hamilton, the president of the Farmer's Association of
Skaraborg County explained the causes for the disappearance of the
croft very effectively in 1907 when he wrote:

> During the later part of the last century, when the price of grain was high
> and land values rose, but agricultural labor remained comparatively cheap, the
> owners of estates found it to their advantage to enclose the crofts in the estates.
> Many crofts were thus incorporated and the cottages razed. For the agricultural
> labor of the crofter was substituted the cheap labor of married (*statare*) and un-
> married servants who were paid an annual wage. . . . . The remaining crofters
> were treated without consideration by the land owner. . . . .[3]

Then followed a period of increasing labor demand and resulting high wages
for agricultural labor that was paid in money wages. But the landowners failed
to give their crofters a like compensation by lessening their burden of day labor,
or by giving them compensation for overtime. When the wages for hired labor
increased the possessor of a six day croft could no longer afford to pay wages for
a hired man to work on the estate as was demanded in the croft contract. It became impossible to find men who were willing to assume the burdens of cultivat-

---

[1] K. Jordbruksdepartementet, *Betänkande angående torpareklassens tillbakagång*
(Stockholm, 1911), pp. 29 ff.

[2] Wohlin, "Torpare-, backstugu-och inhysesklasserna," *op. cit.*, pp. 36–39, Table C.

[3] Gilbert Hamilton, Ordförande, Skaraborgs läns hushållningssällskap, "Inkomna
utlåtanden," *op. cit.*, pp. 52–53.

ing a large croft, and many lay idle. There has been but slight diminution of the smaller crofts, the two or three day crofts, nor has there been any difficulty in obtaining tenants for them in (Skaraborg) County.

There is also the uncertainty of ownership and tenure of the croft to be considered. It has resulted in a lack of interest, and ambition on the part of the crofter to develop his land to its fullest possibilities. He has blamed his small income to the sterility of the land. His children have preferred industrial work with its high wages, or have emigrated, rather than attempt the cultivation of the croft that their forefathers had held. There were never any guarantees that well cultivated crofts would remain in the family's ownership at the same rental.

The cotters have practically disappeared. Their children have sought the same economic outlet of industry or emigration. And when the older people have died, the houses have been moved and the land has been enclosed in the estate. This has become of frequent occurrence, since the communes as well as the owners of the land have prevented new tenants from occupying the cottages for fear that they might become a burden on the poor relief.

The estates, whose owners have maintained their crofts, especially the smaller and medium sized crofts, and have given their tenants a fair rental as wages have risen, are at the present best situated with a permanent labor supply.

On the estates where the crofts have either been enclosed or where there is an overwhelming amount of larger six day crofts which can find no tenants, the resources of agricultural labor are very meager, since the casual labor now either seeks industry or emigrates. And much needed improvement must be neglected.

Should the croft entirely disappear, new labor must be found in other ways, or the large estates will have to be divided. . . . .

The decline of population in the rural districts of the county began about 1880 and has continued steadily during the succeeding 27 years. This diminution was at the beginning scarcely noticeable and was counteracted by labor-saving machines. Even in the 1890's there was enough labor. During the last ten years (1897–1907) the resources of labor for the larger estates have declined in large proportions. The causes have been the development of industry and emigration.

During the last two or three years (1905–7), the situation has become more acute. The scarcity of people is now wholly apparent, and few are the estates who have a full working force. It is especially difficult to obtain women to care for the cows and to milk. The labor situation is such that the managers of at least the large estates look with uncertainty upon the future. The work day is made shorter, the demands for higher wages increase, while the desire to work by the laborer decreases.

All this might not hinder, perhaps, the cultivation of the larger estates and the future—for our people have ability to work—if Socialistic teachings had not injected class feeling between the laborer and the land-owners, and often produced unjust labor demands. Socialism has not developed as yet extensively in our county. . . . . Added to this is the fact that the strongest and best people go to the cities or emigrate. Only the old and the very young remain as labor for agriculture, and wages remain at the level of the quality of labor.

The scarcity of labor, however, has not been so great that cultivated lands have reverted to pasturage.[1]

The report in the same year of labor conditions in the rural districts of the rich agricultural county of Malmöhus gave a few additional reasons.

Besides the usual reasons must be added military service which withdraws the youth from the agricultural activities during a large part of the year.

The greatest need is for milk-maids, which will soon be impossible to procure, even with increased wages. The emigration to the cities is the most important cause for this scarcity. The young women prefer to take service in the cities, or on any such farms where they do not have to milk.

This labor scarcity became especially noticeable in the 1890's and continues. . . . . To a great degree the larger estates in the county have to depend on labor of both sexes from Småland and Poland, which replace the scarcity of the local labor supply, especially in the sugar beet fields. . . . . The laborer can afford to eat now, clothe himself and live better than ever before. The young, however, have lost the opportunity to harden their muscles by labor, for instance cutting with a scythe. But this lack is not important since machines do much of the labor.[2]

There were many complaints that women no longer would aid in agriculture.

At present labor does not wish to bind itself for a long future period, while wages have risen so high in other industries that agriculture cannot compete. The wives and daughters of crofters do not wish to milk anymore, nor care for the cows, nor assist in the monotonous and heavy chores of the farm, but prefer the less strenuous work at factories, where pleasures and better economic conditions are offering themselves as compared with the monotony of the isolated croft.[3]

The same decline of other types of agrarian labor beside the crofter has occurred in the rural regions of Sweden with the decline of agriculture. The statistics of the decrease of the cotter is much the same as of the crofter. This class declined from 45,590 men

[1] In some counties the complaint was made that the less efficient labor received the same wage as the efficient (Edward Fleetwood, Kalmar läns norra hushållningssällskap, *ibid.*, p. 25).

[2] G. Tornerhjelm, Malmöhus läns hushållningssällskap, *ibid.*, p. 40.

[3] C. M. Åhlund, Göteborgs-och Bohus läns hushållningssällskap, *ibid.*, p. 44.

cultivators in 1870 to 31,605 in 1900. There was a greater decline in the seventies and nineties than during the great exodus of the eighties. The women managers of these small tenantries increased from 12,937 in 1870 to 22,765 in 1900, widows and some wives whose husbands had left for America. However, the numbers of the population who obtained their support from these potato patches decreased from 200,074 in 1870 to 154,495 in 1900.[1]

The labor-supply that came from that peculiar Teutonic institution, the retainer, which had survived in Sweden on the estates and on the farms of the peasants, also declined.[2] The retainer usually lived with the owner of the farm or with a crofter. This poverty-stricken class decreased from 284,318 in 1870 to 131,465 in 1900. The greatest decline was in the number of men, from 55,523 to 22,633, while the women remained around 50,000.

Strange to say, there was no decrease in the amount of agricultural servants; from 1840 to 1900 the number of hired men on the farms averaged about 323,000.[3] Most of these unmarried men were the sons of peasants and crofters, and many were working on their fathers' farms. There was a slight increase in the number of women employed in farm labor, a rise from 286,980 to 324,701, but even this seems very small when one considers the growing dislike on the part of the younger women for milking and the care of cattle.

Although the servant class seems stationary in numbers, it must be remembered that there was a tremendous growth in population between 1840–1900, and also an increase in the acreage of cultivated lands. By 1900 there had become a scarcity of labor-supply in this group for it had failed to increase with the growing demands for more labor. These younger sons and daughters of both the peasant proprietors and crofters were contributing the largest quota of the population to emigration.

The married hired man who lived in barracks and worked on an annual contract wage continued to grow in numbers as a source of rural labor. Undoubtedly, many of the crofter class preferred the higher wages and the security of income offered by the annual con-

---

[1] Wohlin, "Torpare-, backstugu-och inhysesklasserna," *op. cit.*, pp. 38–41, Table G.

[2] "Inhysesklassen," *ibid.*, 42–47, Table H.

[3] Wohlin, "Den jordbruksidkande befolkningen i Sverige," *op. cit.*, p. 26, Table H.

tract rather than the risks of an uncertain crop on a piece of poor land. Others joined this new group because it was impossible to find a vacant croft to farm, as more and more crofts were being enclosed and cultivated by the owners. This class rose from 31,218 families in 1870 to 86,256 in 1890. During the decade of the eighties it more than doubled its numbers. But by 1900 a decline had set in even in this agricultural group, for there were only 33,351.[1] Including all of the members of the families, children, and servants, there were 127,685 of the Swedish inhabitants living on the income of this class in 1870. It increased to 320,093 in 1890, but fell to 146,374 in 1900.

TABLE XXI*

AVERAGE PLACEMENTS OF THE SWEDISH EMPLOYMENT BUREAUS, 1912–20

| | Agriculture and Forestry | Industry | | Agriculture and Forestry | Industry |
|---|---|---|---|---|---|
| January | 85 | 164 | July | 71 | 121 |
| February | 81 | 162 | August | 88 | 118 |
| March | 80 | 138 | September | 80 | 107 |
| April | 66 | 122 | October | 79 | 118 |
| May | 68 | 110 | November | 94 | 150 |
| June | 66 | 122 | December | 98 | 133 |

* The Swedish Agricultural Labourer published by order of the Swedish Government's Delegation for International Collaboration in Social Politics, pp. 30 ff.

There can be no doubt that emigration and the movement from agriculture to industry has produced a scarcity of agricultural labor in the rural districts of Sweden. The Swedish Employment Bureaus, established in 1902 primarily for domestic and industrial employment, have turned to agricultural placement. One-fourth of all persons given employment by these agencies between 1910–20 were placed in agriculture. There are in all 35 labor exchanges in Sweden with 130 offices scattered through the counties. In a study of the average placements made between 1912–20, a contrast was made between the number of applicants for every 100 vacancies in the fields of agriculture and forest, and those in industry, with the results shown in Table XXI. In a study of employment conditions in the Swedish rural districts since 1911, the Swedish Department of Labor has found the labor-situation varying from county to county. In 1919, from the reports of 2,229 parishes, it was found

[1] Wohlin, "Torpare-, backstugu-och inhysesklasserna," op. cit., pp. 40–44, Table I.

that 139 parishes or 6.2 per cent had a "good" supply of labor, 1,301 or 58.4 per cent had a sufficient supply, and 714 or 32 per cent showed a scarcity of labor. From three-fourths to nine-tenths in the Mälar counties, Östergötland, and Skåne had sufficient labor, while in the counties of Gothenburg-Bohus, Västernorrland, Västerbotten, Gotland, and Kalmar more than half of the parishes reported a scarcity.

It has become customary to employ agricultural labor by the year in order to guarantee sufficient labor force during the sowing and harvesting seasons.[1] The interchange of labor in the forests in winter with the agricultural labor in summer has practically eliminated unemployment in Sweden in normal conditions. Two short periods of unemployment occur for the day-laborers, in the spring just before seed time and in the autumn before lumbering begins.

It is in the more remote agricultural regions where the depopulation of the rural classes has been the greatest. In some regions like the Mälar counties and Skåne, the introduction of agricultural machinery on the larger estates has met the further need for labor.

Where industry has attracted many of the agricultural classes, it is found that during the periods of industrial prosperity and high wages, the scarcity of agricultural labor is greatest. In periods of industrial crisis, labor returns to agriculture. This was demonstrated in 1914 and again after the war in 1920. During the first crisis, 1914, a report from Kristianstad County stated that "where the better labor of the rural regions tended to be recruited by industry, there seemed to be a change during the crisis."[2] The president of the parish council in Värmland stated, "There is usually a scarcity of labor in the parish, but the supply of agricultural labor in 1914 is good because of the war and the crisis in industry."[3] On the other hand some communities complained of the inability of industrial workers to adapt themselves to agriculture. "During the whole year of 1914 until now in the fall," came the report from a parish in

---

[1] *The Swedish Agricultural Labourer*, pp. 34–35.

[2] K. Socialstyrelsen, *Arbetartillgång, arbetstid och arbetslön inom Sveriges jordbruk år 1914* (Stockholm, 1916); *Sveriges Officiella Statistik*, "Social statistik," p. 11, translated.

[3] *Ibid.*

Jönköping County, "there has been a scarcity of agricultural labor, but now the rural community is overwhelmed with unemployed industrial workmen who either are not able or do not wish to perform efficient agricultural labor."[1]

Much of the same condition resulted after the comparatively prosperous times in industry during the later part of the war, when the far-reaching industrial crisis of 1920 arrived. In a questionnaire sent to the chairman of the parish councils, to about 1,000 organized agricultural employers, and agricultural labor unions in November, 1920, a new record of unemployment in agriculture was obtained. The parishes recorded an unemployment condition of 11 per cent; the agricultural employers, 16.7 per cent; and the agricultural labor unions, 42.5 per cent.[2] The increased wages and falling prices for agricultural products forced a reduction in the demand for agricultural labor. The crisis and the many bitter strikes in industry also threw an increased labor-supply upon the rural districts.

The World War brought a scarcity of fuel, both coal and oil, since Sweden must import the major part of its supply. In order to meet this loss it was necessary to substitute wood, and the demand for woodsmen increased tremendously. This demand for increased labor came in a region that was already suffering from a scarcity of labor. The government bill for a universal worker's draft was defeated by the Riksdag in 1917. Wages rose to extreme heights for lumberjacks and the labor was recruited from unemployed industrial workmen and from the agricultural population.[3] After the armistice and the increased importation of foreign fuels, the demand for wood fell and the wages in the forest industries declined rapidly as the unemployed workers flooded the agricultural and forest regions with surplus labor.

The scarcity of labor supply in the rural regions of Sweden has had the effect of improving the conditions of labor for the agricultural laborer. It was necessary to compete with the more attractive wages and hours offered in industry in Sweden, and in the higher labor market of America. The agricultural laborers have formed into

[1] *Ibid.*, translated.    [2] *The Swedish Agricultural Labourer*, p. 35.

[3] Ekblom, "Den Svenska lönarbetaren, 1914–24," in Heckscher, *Sveriges ekonomiska och sociala historia under och efter världskriget*, p. 283.

unions to obtain better working conditions. There has been a gradual reduction of hours in the working day and a rising scale of wages from 1866 to 1920.

The hours for agricultural labor have decreased from 12.6 hours per day in 1911 to 11.9 hours in 1920. In each case 2.2 hours for meals and rest periods are included. There was a slight increase in the working hours in 1923.[1] Some variation in the working day occurred within the counties. In 1923 the shortest day was a net period of 9.5 hours in Norrbotten County. The hours for the cattlemen were longer than for the average hired man, and it involved a certain amount of Sunday work. Those who have no animals to care for quit work several hours earlier on Saturday afternoon. Any overtime work was paid by a 50 per cent increase over the regular wage. Overtime pay was customary, especially in Southern Sweden.[2]

Agricultural wages have risen steadily in Sweden from 1866 to 1920. During the period of agricultural depression from 1875 to 1890, there occurred a temporary setback in the wage scale, but by 1890 wages began to rise. Since 1920, agricultural wages have been reduced, but they remain higher than the wage scale of 1914. A hired man employed on an annual contract from 1866 to 1870 received an average of 103 kronor ($27.60) a year, with room and board, while a woman servant received 46 kronor ($12.33).[3] During the next five years wages rose to 154 and 61 kronor ($41.00 and $16.00), respectively. Then came a period of stagnation and slight decline, but by 1890 emigration had so drained the countryside of labor that wages rose steadily until 1920. Just before the inflation of the war period in 1915, agricultural wages in Sweden had reached 317 kronor ($85.00) for a man and 193 kronor ($52.00) for a woman. By 1920 the peak of 988 kronor ($263) and 585 kronor ($155) was reached. The inflow of industrial workers into the agricultural labor field reduced wages by 1924 to 551 kronor ($148) for a man and 403 kronor ($108) for a woman.

But American farm wages have been so far above the wages of Sweden that it profited the agricultural classes of Sweden to seek the

[1] *Statistisk årsbok för Sverige, 1925*, p. 214, Table 177.
[2] *The Swedish Agricultural Labourer*, pp. 46–51.
[3] *Statistisk årsbok för Sverige, 1925*, p. 214, Table 178.

CHART IV

COMPARISON OF ANNUAL WAGES OF HIRED MEN ON FARMS IN SWEDEN
AND UNITED STATES FROM 1866 TO 1925

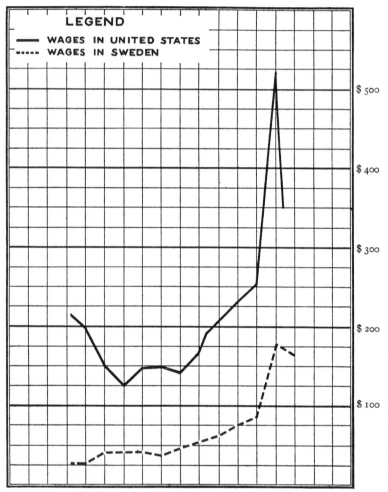

1866 1870 1875 1880 1885 1890 1895 1900 1905 1910 1915 1920 1925

American labor market when they wished to accumulate capital quickly. Thus while the hired man with board received $27.00 a year in Sweden from 1866 to 1870, his wage in America was about $17.00 a month, or $204 a year.[1] Wages rose in Sweden during the next five years to $41.00 a year; in America they fell to about $12.00 a month, but an annual wage of $144 gave a considerable differential over the European wage. But in 1915 Swedish agricultural wages had reached $85.00 a year and in America farm labor was paid $21.00 a month, or $252 a year. The peak of Swedish wages was

TABLE XXII

| YEAR | DAY-LABOR AT HARVEST FOR MEN | | DAY-LABOR NOT HARVEST FOR MEN | |
|---|---|---|---|---|
| | Sweden | United States | Sweden | United States |
| 1866–70............. | $0.30 | $2.20 | $0.20 | $1.49 |
| 1871–75............. | .48 | 1.70 | .32 | 1.08 |
| 1876–80............. | .43 | 1.30 | .29 | 0.81 |
| 1891–95............. | .47 | 1.20 | .32 | 0.83 |
| 1911–15............. | 0.75 | 1.85 | 0.59 | 1.46 |
| 1920............... | 2.41 | 4.36 | 1.83 | 3.59 |
| 1922............... | 1.34 | 2.72 | 0.98 | 2.15 |

reached in 1920 with an annual wage of $263, while American wages had risen to $552. And even the post-war slump showed a favorable differential in American wages, which in 1922 were $348 and Swedish wages had fallen to $148 in 1924.

The day-wage of the agricultural worker indicates the same differential in the two countries, as shown in Table XXII. It must be remembered that the Swedish agricultural laborer who emigrated to America often found even a higher wage in railroad construction and in industry, especially in the building trades in which he seemed to have a special aptitude. Women's wages were always lower than men's wages in the rural districts and the young Swedish maid much preferred housework with a higher wage in America to the heavy

[1] *Ibid., 1927*, p. 231, Table 197; Department of Commerce, *Statistical Abstract of the United States, 1922*, p. 283, Table 209; from *Reports of the Department of Agriculture.* Agricultural wages for the United States in the Bureau of Labor Statistics Report differ slightly (Department of Labor, *History of Wages in the United States from Colonial Times to 1920* [Washington, 1929], p. 227, Table D-2).

farm labor with a low wage at home, even though it often lowered her social status.

The growth of the union movement in Sweden since 1900 has also affected agricultural labor. Organization has gone much farther in rural labor in Sweden than in the United States, and is characteristic of the present day. The movement began at the end of the last century and made rapid advances, especially in Skåne. A national organization called the Swedish Laborers' Federation was founded in 1908.[1] The general strikes of 1909 and 1910 produced a setback in the whole labor movement in Sweden, including agriculture. During the World War, however, union organization became once more very active, and the old federation was revived and reconstructed in 1918.

The first district organizations were established in the summer of 1919 in Skåne, Östergötland, Södermanland, and Västmanland, the region of large estates.[2] To these were added, the following year, Halland, Västergötland, Värmland, and Närke, with smaller divisions in other portions of the kingdom. The agricultural laborers of Västmanland and Dalarne withdrew in 1920 and joined the lumbermen in the Forest and Agricultural Laborers' Federation of Central Sweden, which became syndicalistic and extremely radical. But the next year the agricultural laborers of Västmanland returned to the older union. Another independent organization was formed in Norrland combining the laborers in forestry and agriculture. Although the various agricultural unions had a combined membership of 28,000 laborers, it included only 10 per cent of the hired workers in the field.[3]

Agricultural employers organized as early as labor. They also united first in county organizations in Skåne, and by 1908 expanded into a nation-wide association.[4] Collective agreements in agriculture existed in Southern Sweden as early as 1906 and 1907, but were not commonly used until 1919. In January of the latter year, there were seven agreements in agriculture and fishing involving 42 employers and 516 workmen. Upon the termination of the first large collective

---

[1] "Svenska lantarbetareförbundet," *The Swedish Agricultural Labourer*, pp. 36–37.

[2] K. Socialstyrelsen, *Kollektivavtal i Sverige, 1920–21*, I, 144.

[3] *The Swedish Agricultural Labourer*, pp. 46–51.    [4] *Ibid.*, p. 37.

agreements in agriculture in the fall of 1919, there followed a somewhat far-reaching harvest strike in Uppland and Västmanland. The government appointed a special arbitration commission to interpret the agreements. The final outcome was a new national agreement and four local agreements for Eastern and Southern Sweden. By the beginning of 1920 these collective agreements for agriculture numbered eight, affecting 950 employers and 20,320 laborers.[1] At the end of the year they had been consolidated into a national agreement, with ten district contracts for agriculture, involving 1,300 employers and 26,000 workmen.[2] In 1928 there were 47 collective agreements in agriculture and fishing involving 15,000 laborers. Although only a small portion of all the agricultural laborers were actual participants in these agreements, still the whole agricultural situation was affected by the new standards of wages and working conditions.

From 1921 to 1923 wages in agriculture fell from 40 to 50 per cent, but even then they remained at a 65 per cent level above the pre-war wages.[3] A back-to-the-farm movement has taken place since 1923, when industrial unemployment began to appear. It relieved the scarcity of farm labor in many districts.

The increase in emigration to the United States from Sweden that followed the World War came from the agricultural regions, as well as the industrial centers, for the farms had not fared very well during the war because of the government's policy of requisitioning grain, and of keeping the prices of foodstuffs at a minimum, besides it had been necessary to slaughter livestock due to the lack of fodder. Following the war, although agriculture really was better off than the industries in Sweden, it also suffered from the economic depression of the world. There was need for further protection of agricultural products, for American grain undersold Swedish grain in the communities where it was produced. It was not a vital factor, though, for Sweden imports four times as much as she exports.[4] Since the World War, her exports of butter and pork have increased, though

[1] K. Socialstyrelsen, *Kollectivavtal i Sverige, 1919*, I, Table A.
[2] *Ibid.*, *1920–21*, I, 143; *Statistisk årsbok för Sverige, 1930*, p. 241.
[3] Hildebrand, *Gustav V*, pp. 567–68.
[4] *Statistisk årsbok för Sverige, 1927*, pp. 130–31, Table 121.

the impoverished condition of Europe has produced a better market for oleomargarine than butter. Swedish agricultural products at the present time seem to supply primarily the home market and there is little left for export.

The changes which have taken place in Swedish agriculture have tended to undermine the old agrarian culture. The peasant proprietor has handed down his estate from father to son for many generations, but this veneration for the soil of the forefathers is fast disappearing. The lack of respect for this ancient custom began with the introduction of money economy. The younger children in the family were not content to see the old homestead descend upon the son whom the father had selected to succeed him, which practically disinherited them. Even though it was the obligation of the heir to care for the "old folks" in the cottage (*undantag*), the remaining children felt that the division of the family fortune was unfair. They demanded an equal share in the estate, and were even willing only too frequently to sacrifice the old homestead at an auction sale. If one of the children in the family more loyal to family traditions than the others desired to purchase the property, he must do so in competition with strangers. In some cases where the family pride was strong, some member of the family would take over the estate rather than see it on the auction block, and would then be burdened with a debt to the coheirs.[1] In the latter case, it was frequently necessary to depart for America for a time where one could earn a surplus of capital more quickly than in Sweden; otherwise the heavy mortgage remained a tremendous burden when the income from the farm was small.

An emigrant from Dalsland, in relating his life-history in 1929, told the story of a father who attempted to keep up a family estate with a large mortgage.

My father bought in 1891 the estate of my grandfather on my mother's side, who had died in 1890. My father was at the time in America (Chicago), but returned to Sweden and took over the farm. He had a mortgage on the farm for about one half of its value. Since there was no factory in the vicinity, he tried to earn some extra income by hauling wood in the forests during the winter to pay off the mortgage. But his family increased, so that when I was born we were eight children. My oldest sister was sixteen. She had to leave home to seek

[1] Wohlin, "Bondeklassens undergräfvande," *op. cit.*, pp. 31 ff.

employment in order to support herself, but especially to obtain clothes, which it was impossible for father to provide for her. The income of the farm only sufficed for food and the most necessary clothing. The farm was 150 tunnland, about 200 acres. A peasant proprietor can make a good income in our neighborhood if he has forest to cut, but without woodland, it is rather hard to get along. He has to pay cash for all he purchases, but earns only what the farm produces. But he has one great advantage (that he probably does not appreciate), he is his own boss.[1]

The conditions in the rural districts of Sweden have not been much different from those in America. Similar to the movement from our rural regions to our industrial centers in the United States, the movement from the Swedish countryside continues toward the industrial centers of the United States, especially in periods of industrial depression in Sweden.

And the story repeats itself from decade to decade in the history of Swedish emigration. A recently arrived Swedish immigrant in the United States writes:

I was raised in the country in a wooded portion of Småland. My father rented a farm on fairly good terms. His parents had cultivated it before him, so that it was in good condition. Concerning income, it was not very large, but large enough so that we need never lack for the necessities of life. My father and mother are still living there. I worked as a hired man in Sweden for a year and eight months, but my wages were low and there was no future. I did not have the advantage of learning a trade. I was twenty years old when I came to this country, to a brother who had been here four years. He sent me some money for my journey, while I had some myself. I decided to emigrate because I was no longer needed at home on the farm, and the possibilities of obtaining employment in Sweden were poor.[2]

Another from Öland corroborates the first one.

My father was a farmer and owned thirty acres (¼ of a mantal) of land in Öland. We were five brothers and could not all remain on the farm. The opportunities to obtain employment were either poor or there was no employment in Sweden. When I heard of the opportunities in America, I decided to emigrate and my father gave me the money for my journey. I was twenty-one.[3]

Then there are times when the estate or croft passed to some member of the family who was distant in America or who had pros-

---

[1] Case studies obtained from recent Swedish immigrants in Rockford, Illinois, in 1929.

[2] *Ibid.*          [3] *Ibid.*

pered as a business man in a city in Sweden. He was not interested in returning to assume the management of a small farm. He may have become Americanized and his America-born children refused to leave the country of their birth. The estate was sold and the proceeds divided among the heirs.

In regions around the larger cities in Sweden, e.g., Stockholm, Gothenburg, and Malmö, the old peasant farms have been subdivided for the purpose of selling small lots or farms to the working-class. Others have had peculiar scenic value and have been incorporated into estates for a wealthier clientèle.[1] The peasant farms in Norrland, Värmland, and Dalsland have been purchased to a great extent by lumbering corporations. But in the regions of Central and Southern Sweden, the heart of the independent peasant farms, the land remains almost intact in the ownership of this old landholding class. In fact, a larger acreage of estates of the nobility has here been sold to the wealthy peasant and speculator than the peasant lands. America-auctions of peasant lands, during periods of increased migration, often glutted the land market.[2] It gave the opportunity for some of the landless agrarian class to purchase land at low prices, breaking up the monopoly on land of the peasant and gentry. The agricultural crisis of the eighties produced the same effect upon Sweden that the post-war crisis has upon American farmers. The psychological attitude that agriculture was unprofitable was expressed in the local surveys made in Dalsland and Värmland.[3]

There followed a period, especially after the discouraging economic depression of 1893 in the United States, when a large number of Swedish-Americans returned to their native villages and with their accumulated earnings purchased either the farm of their forefathers or some other peasant estate in the neighborhood. This has continued on a small scale ever since, for some always remain homesick in the strange land and long to return to the place of their birth. In 1907 in one rural hundred of Dalsland, there were 352 out of the

---

[1] Reports from various local officials on the sale of lands (Wohlin, "Bondeklassens undergräfvande," *op. cit.*, pp. 84 ff.).

[2] America-auctions were common in Kalmar County, according to G. H. Ekman, bailiff, Södra Möre härads östra distrikt, Kalmars län, "Inkomna utlåtanden," *op. cit.*, p. 111. See *supra*, p. 263, for quotations of such auctions in Skåne from local newspapers.

[3] "Bygdeundersökningar," *op. cit.*

2,115 farms that were owned and cultivated by returned Swedish-Americans.[1]

In Grinstad parish more than one-fourth of the farmowners had been in America. Every parish on the island of Öland has Swedish-American farmers, usually some of the most prosperous agriculturalists.[2] The same is true in most of the parishes in the emigrant regions.[3]

Although these Swedish-Americans have been born in the parish, their visit to America, whether short or long, has revolutionized their attitude toward the old Swedish folkways. They have returned not only with American capital but also with the English language, American clothes, American mannerisms, and a certain contempt for all the old Swedish customs. Those who have worked on American farms bring back new methods of cultivation. They are accustomed to an extensive cultivation with the use of machinery. And they are not slow to show their disgust with the use of hand labor which still exists on the smaller farms in Sweden, nor their impatience at the slowness of the Swedish hired man. There is also a contempt for social differences and an idealization of all that is American.

This Americanization has occurred in all the emigrant regions of Sweden. A description of its subtle influence in keeping America always in the minds of the people, and especially the younger generation, may be found in a picture of the rural homes in Jösse hundred in Värmland. It is typical of many homes in Sweden, for there is scarcely a rural home that does not have one or more of its members or its relatives in America. Gerhard Magnusson in his description of Jösse hundred in 1907 wrote:

On the bureau may be found the American portrait of those who have emigrated, on the walls hang American group photographs of fifteen or twenty relatives resident in the United States. It is possible to go from cottage to cottage and continuously find these American photographs and many American nicknacks. Here is a lampshade with an English motto; there is a mat with the months of the year in English on the back of a rocking-chair, and a colorful tumbler with a gold edge with the inscription, "Fortune favors the brave." A

[1] Brusewitz, "Sundals, Nordals och Valbo härader," *ibid.*, p. 93.

[2] Nelson, "Öland, "*ibid.*, p. 81.

[3] The author has visited Swedish-Americans in Kristianstad County and has conversed with several people on the trains in Sweden.

stereoscope stands on the table by the window, where among the forty-two pictures only two are from Sweden, Jönköpings match factory and the Göta canal, all the others are from the United States. There you can see how genteel people live in New York; how they are married in beautiful salons with guests in evening clothes; how they promenade in beautiful parks with flowering fountains; how people ride on street-cars and elevated; how comfortably passengers travel on stately Atlantic steamers, etc.[1]

The little boy and girl grow up in visions of eldorado. The beautiful things they see are American bric-a-brac and American photographs. The only news they hear from the outside world comes through the letters from an older brother or sister in Illinois or Massachusetts, which father or mother reads aloud. There are English words interspersed in these letters, and usually a criticism of conditions home in Sweden. These influence the children and strengthen their desire to "go over" to the wonderful country. It can never be as beautiful or as genteel in Jösse hundred as in Chicago or Idaho. One never hears the wonderful things said about Sweden that are told about the United States. And if anyone comes on a visit, it is either an elegant lady or an equally elegant gentleman from America, who formerly worked in the fields in the neighborhood and was called by an ordinary name, but now lives on his wealth and is called something more high sounding. This is what the children in the home see. They grow up in order to emigrate.

The most beautiful pictures on the walls are perhaps Grover Cleveland, William McKinley, or Theodore Roosevelt, and next the German Kaiser's family (1907). The books that are found are view albums from the United States, a Swedish-English dictionary, or a statistical calendar of America. The only Swedish touch is a framed religious verse on the wall.

Later if you have the opportunity to hear the farmers in a religious meeting or in a café at Arvika converse in English, you understand and are not astonished. Many have been to America and have returned—that you surmise as you travel along the roads, by the clothing and the panama hats of the men in the fields, looking just as they did on the farms in Minnesota. Many, both young and old, are learning English so that it will be easier for them when they "go over" to America. Everything tends to be a preparation for emigration. That is the purpose of education, and it is easier to borrow money for a ticket to America than for one to Stockholm. When most of the relatives are already in America, it is much easier to go there than to Stockholm or Gothenburg where there are no friends or relatives. And now and then a Swedish-American comes on a visit. He needs seldom return alone to this new homeland; indeed, he is usually accompanied by a whole colony from his neighborhood.

This picture of 1907 is not exaggerated. The author found the same conditions to be true during a visit to Sweden in 1923. The

[1] G. Gerhard Magnusson, "Jösse härad i Värmland, Bygdeundersökningar," *Emigrationsutredningens bilaga VIII*, pp. 82 ff.

first object her eye met upon entering the home of an uncle was a childhood portrait of herself. There were other photographs of American relatives on the wall. Those who remain in Sweden never forget the relatives and friends who have gone to America, and they ask eagerly about them. Visiting another relative who had been in America and accumulated an independent income, she found that he had rebuilt his home to conform to the American style of architecture with a front porch, and that the villa had been given the name of the American village near which he had resided, Milford. When the several Swedish-Americans in this neighborhood gathered together on a social occasion, they invariably lapsed into the English language. And their reminiscences were usually those of America. Some subscribed for American newspapers to "keep up with the times."

It is hard for the Swedish-American to readjust himself to his home environment. His Swedish relatives and neighbors look upon his American ways as snobbish. If he attempts to instruct his friends in better methods of cultivation, he sometimes makes enemies instead of friends, and he may find himself quite ostracized at times. But gradually he becomes an influence and his neighbors, seeing the success that he has had with his mowing machine, seek to borrow it, and then procure one for themselves. There are some who return and never fit into the old mold again.[1] Every year witnesses the tragedy of the Swedish-American who has saved for some thirty or forty years in order to return to Sweden and enjoy his last days in his old home. He sells his farm or business, breaks up his home, with the idea of never returning to America. He finds things so utterly changed in his home village, his friends and relatives so strange, and the customs of the country so different from his American habits, that within a few months, or a year at the most, he is returning to the United States.[2] A younger man who has become encumbered with a farm and cannot return to the United States will raise his children with the idea that they are to emigrate as soon as they are

[1] The author found a middle-aged man who had become religious since his return to Sweden. He wanted her to sing some English hymns because English seemed to lend itself better to religion, he thought. Swedish immigrants in America sometimes feel that Swedish is the only religious language.

[2] The author was told a typical tale of this sort by a niece who was bidding farewell to an uncle who could not readjust himself. It was at the dock in Gothenburg in 1926.

grown. Often the author has heard the exclamation, "Oh! if I could only return to America with you. We never worked as hard there. But Oscar is going to go to America as soon as he is old enough." On the other hand, you find those who are perfectly satisfied. On a train in Småland, a middle-aged woman spoke to the author and explained that she and her husband had been in America some twenty years. Her husband had been a section boss and they had traveled constantly, never having a fixed abode. They decided to settle down and brought their small capital to Sweden where they had purchased a small farm near a very pretty village not far from Värnamo. They were experimenting with raising chickens. She was very happy over her home and their future. Her only complaint was that her Swedish neighbors were a little difficult to become acquainted with, perhaps because she talked too much about America.

While the United States had drawn from Sweden the strength and brawn of her youth for industry and agriculture, it has compensated Sweden in a small measure by sending her capital. "America money" is frequently enclosed in "America letters," and finds its way into many a rural home. In 1906 there were received at the Boda postoffice in Värmland, money orders from America amounting to over $8,000.[1] There was also money sent through the banks. There were 1,600 inhabitants in the village, which made an average of $5.00 per person. During the same year, $33,000 had been received in Sundal hundred in Dalsland, and $66,000 in Fryksdal hundred in Värmland, all from America.[2] The December mail is always the largest in the transmission of money. These sums to Sunne hundred came from Illinois, California, Minnesota, Montana, Washington, New York, Rhode Island, Michigan, and Massachusetts.

"America money" is the most potent influence in the stimulation of emigration. The pastor of Revsund parish in Jämtland County made the statement in 1907:

Some of the emigrants (in America) have been fortunate in making good wages and send home sums of money to poor parents or relatives, or have deposited rather large amounts in local banks. Here at home there are no sav-

[1] Magnusson, "Jösse härad i Värmland," *op. cit.*, No. 2, p. 75.

[2] Brusewitz, "Sundals, Nordals och Valbo härader," *op. cit.* No. 4, p. 85; Edin "Fryksdals härad i Värmland," *ibid.* No. 1 ,p. 34.

ings, in spite of the good opportunities to work, because laborers do not work with the same incentive and intensity here, nor do they desire to save. Like a fire, the reports of the receipt of money (from America) spread through the neighborhood and induce many to emigrate.[1]

This must have been typical and continues to be typical in most portions of rural Sweden.

A physician from the rural district around Ängelholm in Kristianstad County stated the same year:

No one can be blind to the fact that emigrants (in America) send home considerable sums of money to their relatives. An inspector at a small railroad station in my district informed me that through his station alone there arrives at least $25,000 annually from America, sent to relatives in the parish.[2]

And from the same county, another physician of the Båstad region reported:

This region is an old seamen's district. . . . . Many have prospered from here (in America) and send home money from time to time for others to travel upon. As a director of several banks, I am in a position to know that the emigrants send home considerable sums, especially the women. When a woman has been (in America) several years, she can save a thousand kronor a year ($250). In this way the children pay off the debt on the old farm, after which they return, for labor is less strenuous here. They usually return after eight or ten years.[3]

Great changes have taken places in the rural regions of Sweden since the beginning of emigration in 1840. With almost a doubling of population in the period, the number of farms and farm labor has remained almost stationary. In practically all of the purely agricultural districts of Sweden, population has been decreasing since 1880, in spite of better wages and working conditions. The cotter and the crofter are fast disappearing. A million emigrants have departed for the United States, and another three million are to be found in the Swedish cities or the industrial regions of the country. The surplus rural population has disappeared until in many regions there is a scarcity of labor-supply. It was only in 1923 that industrial unemployment changed the situation somewhat.

Agriculture has lost its leading position among the industries of the nation, and Sweden has become industrial with so much of the

[1] O. Löfvenmark, Kontraktsprost, Refsunds pastorat, Jämtlands län, "Inkomma utlåtanden," op. cit., p. 183.

[2] A. Lindstedt, Provinsialläkare, Engelholms distrikt, Kristianstads län, ibid., p. 201.

[3] A. Christer Nilsson, Provinsialläkare, Båstads distrikt, Kristianstads län, ibid., p. 200.

world. The political position of leadership that the Agrarians held after the reconstruction of the Riksdag in 1866, when 72 per cent of the population were agriculturalists, has now been assumed by the Social Democrats, since 50 per cent of the inhabitants are engaged in industry or transportation.[1] The Agrarian party (Lantmanna-partiet) which controlled the majority of the lower house in the Riksdag in 1869, reached the height of its power in 1883. It was then that the Liberal party, in its opposition to the nobles, entrenched government officials, and vested interests, took the leadership. The Agrarians, split on the tariff question in 1886, lost their leadership as a Democratic party to the Liberals in the nineties, and were relegated to the right with the conservatives by both the Liberals and Social Democrats.

It has been impossible at times to continue a political alliance between the large landowner and the small farmer in one party. A separatist movement was started by the small farmer with the publication of a periodical *Landsbygden* ("The Rural Community") by Karl Berglund in Skaraborg County in 1910. A national party, designating itself the Farmers' Alliance (Bondeförbundet) was organized in 1914. By 1917 it had elected twelve members to the Second Chamber of the Riksdag.[2] The owners of larger estates united in 1915 in the National Agrarian Alliance (Jordbrukarnas riksförbund), for they found so little in common with the small farm movement. The former found its strength in Västergötland, Hälsingland, and Dalarne, while the conservative south, Skåne, and Östergötland, with the addition of Värmland and Jämtland, sought expression in the latter. This split among the agrarians was considered unfortunate by many, and in 1922 the Farmers' Alliance (Bondeförbundet) absorbed the more conservative organization. This new agrarian party is devoted to the encouragement of agriculture as the most vital industry of the country. The party fosters rural culture as opposed to urban culture, and is out of sympathy with big industry. The agrarians continue to be opposed to compulsory military service, although it has somewhat modified its demands to a shorter period of service.[3]

All farmers are not members of the Farmers' Alliance. In Malmö-

---

[1] *Statistisk årsbok för Sverige, 1927*, pp. 22-27, Table 28.

[2] Hildebrand, *op. cit.*, pp. 620, 626-27.    [3] *Ibid.*, p. 530.

hus County, the larger landowners belong to the Conservative Moderates, while the agricultural laborers are members of the Social Democrats. The "Right" is secure in Småland, Blekinge, Halland, Gotland, Östergötland, and Västergötland. In Småland this conservatism is bound up with temperance and many adhere to the People's party (Folkfrisinnade).[1] The west coast conservatism, undoubtedly due to the earlier Schartauian religious movement, is counterbalanced by the liberalism of the north, where the lumbering corporations have placed the small farmer on the defensive in the People's party. Movements toward the disestablishment of the church, and the adoption of prohibition, have strongly influenced the latter group in Värmland, Dalarne, and Norrland. The Social Democrats stalk over the land in the wake of industrialism and claim adherence everywhere from agricultural labor.

The many contacts with the outside world have broken the isolation of the Swedish country side and doomed the ancient folkways of the peasant culture. The railroads now carry the Swedish farmer to the larger cities to exchange his produce. His American brother writes him about American customs and ridicules those of the old home. Or he himself has been out to view the wonders of America and returns introducing a new style of dress, new manners, and an admiration for everything American. Manufactured products compete with home industry in every hamlet, and have triumphed for they are cheaper. Whereas the young woman of the eighties often came to America with a trousseau that she had woven entirely herself, today very few Swedish girls have ever used a loom. Paris fashion magazines have penetrated to the show window of the village general store, and the American movies in every town now demonstrate the latest modes of dress. It is easy to sew by these patterns and the material in a modern dress is much less expensive than in the national costume. It is only in the most patriotic regions of the country, and then only at the summer resorts or on festive occasions, that the national costume persists. Different ideas about women working in the fields have made the milkmaid a thing of the past. An industrial or commercial career offers more to the surplus son of the old farm than the life of a hired man.

[1] This party has the smallest number of members in the Riksdag, but was in power from 1926 to 1928 and 1930-31 (*ibid.*, pp. 606-7).

## CHAPTER XII

## THE SWEDISH INDUSTRIAL LABORER

The rapid growth of industrialism has been the most potent factor in twentieth-century Sweden. It has changed the occupation of the majority of Swedish people from agriculture to industry. It has influenced every phase of Swedish social, economic, and political life. In the same way it has changed the type of Swedish emigrant that is coming to the United States. Whereas in the eighties two-thirds of the emigrants came from the agricultural classes, from 1911 to 1915 more than half belonged to the industrial. Since the World War, the economic depression in Swedish industry has encouraged the departure of the industrial classes.[1]

The number of persons engaged in agriculture has fallen in the forty years from 1880 to 1920 from 67.9 to 44 per cent of the population. Industrial workers, including those in commerce and transportation, have risen from 24.7 to 50.2 per cent. In 1920 there were 746,524 persons employed in industry. Of this number 8.9 per cent constituted managers and entrepreneurs.[2] Commerce and transportation engaged 355,358 persons. This increase in the numbers of the industrial population has given the class political control through the Social Democratic party. The Swedish working man is strongly unionized in the economic field. In no country of the world has

---

[1] At the peak of emigration in 1886–90, there were 51,051 agriculturalists, 26,383 industrialists, 34,655 laborers, and 53,143 servants, chiefly women. From 1911 to 1915, industry, commerce, and transportation contributed annually 6,242, agriculture 5,310, while there were 1,725 domestic servants, and 2,666 of unknown occupation. After the war, 1921–25, there was the annual average of 6,190 industrialists, etc., 4,431 agriculturalists, 1,276 domestic servants, and 2,093 of undetermined occupation (Sundbärg, "Den svenska och europeiska folköknings-och omflyttnings-statistiken," *Emigrationsutredningens bilaga IV*, p. 236, Table 96; *Statistik årsbok för Sverige, 1927*, p. 73, Table 62).

[2] There were 929,299 persons engaged in agriculture in 1920 (*Statistik årsbok, 1927*, pp. 26–34, Table 29; Bertil Nyström, "Lönarbetaren och samhället," in Koch, *Social handbok*, p. 75).

organization, both of labor and capital, gone any farther than in Sweden.

In order to understand the Swedish laborer, it is necessary to know something of the Swedish labor movement. It was slower in development than on the continent because of the later industrialization of the country. Industrial Sweden may be said to date from 1888, although some industry has existed since the Middle Ages, and the factory system since the eighteenth century. So the union movement has been a development since the eighties. It received much of its impetus from the earlier movements in Germany and Denmark.

Gilds had existed in Sweden since the Middle Ages. The gild system was abolished by the law of 1846 as archaic.[1] But handicraft continued, and the system of apprenticeship has existed practically down to the present time, especially in the rural regions. Many an earlier emigrant had learned his trade at the feet of a master. Some of the older gild organizations, after 1846, were reconstructed into fraternal societies of the trades, with sickness and death insurance.

Strikes, as forms of protest against existing labor conditions, came earlier than labor organization. As early as 1863 a strike of 160 workmen, constructing a harbor at Hälsingborg, was recorded, and in 1869 a strike of some three or four hundred miners occurred at the Persberg mines, in protest to the change of the wage contract from an annual to a monthly basis. In the latter case, the soldiers were called in to put down the strike.[2] During the sixties, there were in all some ten strikes, while the seventies had forty. The bakers of Stockholm struck in 1873 for better conditions of night work. In 1879 occurred the famous sawmill workers' strike at Sundsvall, the largest and most bitterly fought of these earlier strikes.

The earlier movements among the working men were mostly humanitarian efforts to raise the culture of the lower classes. In the sixties many "Workers' Societies" were formed, consisting largely of members of the middle class, with a small fringe of laborers. These organizations wielded much influence, both in Stockholm and in the

[1] Sigfrid Hansson, *Den svenska fackföreningsrörelsen* (Stockholm, 1927), pp. 9 ff.

[2] "Industria," No. 11, 1926, cited in *ibid.*, p. 11; Magnusson, *Social-demokratien i Sverige*, I, 295 ff.

provincial towns of Sweden, during the next two decades. The purpose of the "Workers' Societies" was to enlighten the members, to support a library, and to institute sickness and death insurance.[1] At times there were conventions held by the various organizations to discuss current social and political problems. The movement proved to be a school for the development of leadership among the more timid laboring class.[2]

Another organization of temporary duration was the "Workers' Circles," groups united by the efforts of a philanthropist, P. O. Smith, a brewer. Their organizations were widely scattered through the kingdom in the eighties. The purpose was "to establish a friendly and just relationship between employers and employees, so that strikes might be averted by arbitration."[3] The "Workers' Circles" were interested in lowering the cost of living for the working class through co-operation, especially in housing. They opposed purchasing on the instalment plan, and encouraged savings banks. The movement proved very popular with the working men for a few years and interfered with an earlier development of labor unions.

A temperance movement among the laboring classes was largely influenced by the introduction from America of a temperance lodge, the "Good-Templars."[4] It made its appearance in 1879 and in 1884 a secession from the order produced a rival called the "Templar Order." These fraternities attempted, through ceremonies and emblems, and through various forms of entertainment, which were attacked by the pietists as worldly, to attract the young laboring man away from an indulgence in liquor. It also fostered co-operative enterprise of various kinds, encouraged adult education, and has been a potent factor in many communities.

Another influential force among the laboring classes in Sweden in the eighties was the introduction of Socialism. August Palm, the the son of a schoolmaster in Skåne, and a tailor by trade, became the proselyter for the philosophy among the workers who were begin-

---

[1] Hansson, *op. cit.*, pp. 13–14. Arbetareföreningar.

[2] These organizations are ridiculed by Strindberg in *Röda Rummet*.

[3] Hansson, *op. cit.*, p. 13.

[4] Boëthius, *Oskar II;* Hildebrand, *Sveriges historia till våra dagar*, XIII, 317.

ning to feel the need for greater solidarity.[1] He had been apprenticed to a tailor at the early age of ten, near his home; by the age of 16 he had gone to Malmö under another master; and at 19, with his journeyman's letter, he decided to try Denmark. In Denmark and Northern Germany, during the next thirteen years, he came in contact with the teachings of socialism. In 1871 he settled at Haderslev and there joined a Social Democratic club. In the German election he took an active part in supporting the Social Democratic candidate, and was exiled from the country. Until 1881, he remained in Denmark, and then returned to his native land and decided to settle at Malmö. A lecture on socialism before a large audience in the Hotel Stockholm at Malmö received favorable press comment, but his succeeding lectures brought on a storm of newspaper dispute. By December, August Palm had gone to Stockholm to explain the socialistic movement to the laboring classes there. His life was spent in socialistic agitation in every portion of the kingdom. And he also became a leader in the union movement of the eighties and in the formation of a new political party, the Social Democrats of Sweden.

A big strike of all the building trades in Stockholm during the summer of 1881 demonstrated more clearly than ever before the need of organization on the part of labor.[2] It began when two hundred unskilled laborers struck for higher wages, and, after a meeting at Lill-Jans, a famous park for outdoor meetings, paraded through the city inducing 2,000 members of the building trades to join them. There were no competent leaders, and the strikers called upon the popular Dr. Anton Nyström, president of the "Workers' Institute," to direct them. Before another large meeting at Lill-Jans, Dr. Nyström advised the strikers to return to their work and to attempt to arbitrate with their employers. He pointed out that since there was no organization nor strike fund, the strikers would only suffer hunger and poverty. In a few days the strike died out. During the strike, Dr. Nyström issued a pamphlet calling upon both labor and capital to organize in their respective groups that they might arbitrate their differences.

The strike did result in the beginning of organization in several of

[1] Magnusson, *Social-Demokratien i Sverige*, I, 72 ff.

[2] Hansson, *op. cit.*, pp. 14 ff.

the trades. Four trades had formed unions in the seventies, the typo-graphical union,[1] the bookbinders', the hatmakers', and the paper-hangers'. In August of 1881, the woodworkers of Stockholm had gone out on strike, and in December, at an open meeting called by this organization at a theater, it was decided to appoint a committee to draft a model constitution for labor unions. A committee includ-ing various trades was chosen, Dr. Nyström of the "Workers' Institute," and the newly arrived socialist, August Palm.

The committee completed its work by March, 1882, and 20,000 copies of the workers' platform and the ideal union constitution were printed and distributed among the working class. The platform was largely the work of Dr. Nyström and was conservative in tone. Among the planks were the need for healthful factories, sound and practical methods of labor, pensions and strike funds, accident insur-ance, the prevention of unemployment and also of strikes, if possible, encouragement of higher standards of education, and the promotion of temperance.[2] The program encouraged the organization of unions. It suggested an initiation fee of a krona (26 cents) to the union, and a monthly fee of half a krona. It advised that local central com-mittees for union organization be formed.

A Central Committee for Stockholm was established in 1883 by the woodworkers', tailors', shoemakers', and the lead and platemakers' unions. The ambition of the committee was the formation of a strong labor party to procure certain needed labor reforms. In the party, the unions were to be represented according to their member-ship. A new program, more elaborate and specific in its demands, was drafted by the Central Committee. It demanded a ten-hour day, factory inspection, and sanitary conditions in the factories, old age pensions, and employment bureaus. It asked for a state's sub-sidy for the laborers' co-operative enterprises, for the establishment of arbitration boards, for a direct and progressive tax, and for a duty-free list for all necessities of life. It took a stand in favor of temper-ance, and asked for an amendment to the criminal law, an introduc-tion of the jury system, an improved school system, and universal

[1] The Typographical Union claims its origin in 1846, but it was not much more than a fraternal society with sickness and death benefits, until the nineties (*ibid.*, p. 12).

[2] *Ibid.*, p. 18.

suffrage in all national and local elections. It was not until 1919 that the laboring class was given full political rights, but their agitation for franchise never ceased from 1883 to 1919. This program for the working men was more liberal, and showed no influence of socialism.

During the early eighties the laboring classes had enrolled in the Liberal party which had chosen as the chief tenet of its platform universal suffrage. The trade-union movement received its impetus from the "Workers' Societies" and the Workers' conventions that were held from time to time.[1] Several newspapers, *Aftonbladet*, *Dagens Nyheter*, and *Fädernslandet*, the latter before it became a scandal sheet, were the spokesmen for the laboring classes and the Liberal party. Although August Palm began a lively socialistic propaganda within the trade unions in 1881, he was successful in obtaining only a few adherents; most of the working men, if not hostile, were at least very conservative in their attitude toward socialism.

But by 1885, there was a marked change in the labor movement. The Central Committee of Trade Unions in Stockholm had fallen under the influence of Palm's socialistic propaganda and decided to change the Workingman's platform to conform with the tenets of socialism. The committee became divided into the socialist and liberal factions with a group of neutrals on the question of political alignment. The following year the socialists obtained a majority of the committee and proceeded to draft a new platform that was henceforth to bind the laboring man of Sweden, in his trade-union movement, to the Social Democratic party. It was very much like the situation in England, the development of the English Labor party.

This first Socialist-Labor program for Sweden was very moderate in its demands. The only socialistic doctrine that it contained was that the profits of labor should belong to the worker. Even a plank demanding the establishment of national workshops to combat unemployment was stricken out for fear that it would alienate the Liberal workmen from the labor-union movement.[2]

Most of the demands were similar to the earlier programs, but were stated in a more decided manner. The political demands of labor

[1] *Ibid.*, p. 20.   [2] *Ibid.*, pp. 21–23.

were universal suffrage at the age of twenty-five for all general and local elections, and elections to be held on Sunday. It asked for compulsory accident, sickness, and old age insurance, and was opposed to contract prison labor. To the former demand for a decrease on indirect taxes was added a more specific demand for direct and graduated income and inheritance taxes. Free compulsory education and free continuation schools were stressed. Labor asked for a separation of state and church, and complete religious freedom. It recommended the introduction of a unicameral legislature, undoubtedly influenced by the British House of Commons, and the use of the referendum. It asked for the substitution of a militia system for the existing universal military service, the suspension of military powers during periods of peace, and the repeal of the King's power to declare war. Labor indorsed an alliance with international peace movements.

Then came a period of struggle between the Socialists and the Liberals for control in the Central Committee of Stockholm, and in the individual trade unions. The latter were called upon to express themselves by the Central Committee. When the question came to a vote in the first Scandinavian Trade Union Congress at Gothenburg, in August of 1886, labor declared itself in favor of socialism by a vote of 40 to 13.[1]

Typical of the struggle within the Trade Unions was the experience of the Bookbinders' Union. During the eighties and nineties its leaders were violently opposed to the Social Democrats. It withdrew its representation from the Central Committee of Stockholm in 1886 because of the socialistic platform. The bookbinders adopted the Liberal program of the "Third Swedish Workers' Convention."[2] They even went so far as to publish their opposition to the Social Democratic program and appealed to Swedish labor to stem the Socialistic tendency in the Trade Union movement. But by 1898 the bookbinders had fallen under the spell of the Social Democratic movement, and in 1902 officially united with the party. The same change took place in the Lead and Plate Roofers' Union which de-

---

[1] *Ibid.*, pp. 24 ff.

[2] This convention consisted of the early Workers' Societies, partly laborers and partly Liberal citizens of all walks of life, under the leadership of Dr. Nyström.

clared itself against the socialists in 1886. Other unions, like the Painters' Union, preferred to remain neutral on the political question.[1]

Some unions accepted the socialistic platform of the Central Committee of Stockholm. They continued to be represented on the committee as long as it existed. But by 1889 its usefulness was over, for the Swedish Social Democratic Labor party took its place.

After 1881 August Palm devoted his time to traveling about the kingdom and making speeches wherever he could find an audience. He attempted to found a newspaper that might be the organ for the Social Democrats, and had an unsuccessful experience in trying to finance a paper which he called *The Will of the People*, in 1883.[2] There had been organized a Social Democrat Club in Stockholm.[3] Palm was always a little suspicious of the organization because it contained so many of the intelligentsia class. A more successful attempt to launch a newspaper came with the publication of *Social-Demokratien*, in the fall of 1885.[4] Various young impecunious college men, who were attempting to establish themselves in the journalistic field in Stockholm, were secured to edit the newspaper. Axel Danielsson was the first editor, but he soon left to establish an organ for labor in Malmö, *Arbetet*.[5] After Danielsson's departure from Stockholm, Hjalmar Branting, destined to be the great leader of the Social Democrats, then a young newspaper reporter and editor, appeared. After a time as reporter on *Stockholms Dagblad* in 1883, he left it to edit a newspaper called *Tiden*, an organ for the Trade Union movement. It was ahead of its time and was temporarily discontinued in 1886. It was then that he threw his destiny with the Social Democratic movement. He, like Danielsson, was a university man. It was in 1886 that the Central Committee of Stockholm became influenced by the Social Democratic doctrine, as has been noted. And in 1889 most of the Swedish Labor unions affiliated with the newly organized Social Democratic party.

---

[1] This was also true of the Porcelain Stove Union, the Typographical Union, and the Foundry and Iron Workers' Union.

[2] *Folkviljan;* Magnusson, *op. cit.*, I, 83 ff.

[3] Magnusson, *ibid.*, p. 88.

[4] *Ibid.*, pp. 91 ff.      [5] *Ibid.*, pp. 154 ff.

In the meantime other national organizations of labor were being formed in Sweden. National Trade Union organization was recommended by the Third Workers' Convention held at Örebro in 1886.[1] It advocated the establishment of unions in every town where there were at least ten workmen of the same trade, and included women in the recommendation. During the year the first two national trade unions were organized, the Swedish Typographical Union and the Swedish Postmen's Union. There were seven in all organized in the eighties, five trade unions and two industrial unions.[2] Trade-union organization developed rapidly in the nineties, but there were very few unions that included factory workers or unskilled labor.[3] Nor had the workers in the commercial field, in agriculture, nor in lumbering been affected by the new movement. Such organizations appeared at the beginning of the new century, the Unskilled Labor and Factory Workers' Union, in 1902, and the Agricultural Laborers' Union in 1908.[4]

The need for a National Federation of Labor was voiced in the First Scandinavian Trade Union Congress in 1886, to strengthen the economic resources of labor and prevent the recruiting of strikebreakers in times of strikes. A similar suggestion was made in 1894, at the Social Democratic Convention, for it was feared that the duties of the organization, in connection with wage struggles and strikes, might jeopardize it as a political party to the middle class. Following a third recommendation of such a movement in the Fifth Scandinavian Trade Union Congress in 1897, the Social Democratic Convention of 1898 again proposed the formation of a Swedish Federation of Labor to care for the problems of the trade unions, which were, however, to continue their affiliation with the political party. Most of the delegates to the Social Democratic Convention were representatives of trade unions.

The Swedish Federation of Labor was organized in August, 1898.[5]

[1] Hansson, *op. cit.*, p. 27.

[2] National Painters' Union, the National Shoemakers' Union, and the National Tailors' Union were trade unions. The National Woodworkers' Union and the National Iron and Metal Workers' Union were industrial (*ibid.*, pp. 28 ff.).

[3] Twenty-five more were organized in the nineties. A list is given of all the organizations in the nineties (*ibid.*, pp. 30–31).

[4] *Ibid.*, pp. 35–36.        [5] *Ibid.*, pp. 41 ff.

There was a secretariat of five, three chosen by the trade unions and two by the Social Democratic party. Its purpose was to gather labor statistics and to support local unions when their existence was threatened through lockouts or during strikes for higher wages, or when the right to unionize was threatened. Its membership consisted of the National Trade unions, and such local organizations as had not been united in a national association. During 1899, some sixteen national organizations joined the Federation; there were 37,523 members and 664 local unions. The large union of iron and metal workers did not enter until 1904, then increasing the membership to 81,736, and the number of unions to 1,172.[1] In 1900 the clause making it compulsory for the members of the Swedish Federation of Labor to be members of the Social Democratic party was stricken out and membership was made voluntary. The two party representatives on the secretariat were withdrawn and the membership increased to seven to be elected by the convention of the Federation.

The earlier workers' organizations, that had followed the disbanding of the old gilds, and that were primarily benefit and literary societies, were given a subsidy by the government in a law passed in 1891.[2] But labor was rapidly passing into the labor unions. Another labor movement of much importance was the development of the co-operative societies. There were many local societies in the eighties. The National Co-operative Society formed in 1899 combined some 300 local co-operative consumptive societies with 60,000 members and an annual budget of more than five million dollars. Among the working classes co-operative restaurants became very popular, many of them under the auspices of the temperance societies.

In the communes, the local trade unions united into communal councils, and erected many community houses (*folketshus*) during the nineties. These workers' communes were more or less colored with socialism like the unions. They had representation both in the various national trade unions, and in the Swedish Federation of Labor. The Federation was affiliated with the Second Internationale. It included a demand for the eight-hour day in its program.

[1] *Ibid.*, p. 45.      [2] Boëthius, *op. cit.*, pp. 284 ff.

The unions began to participate in May Day demonstrations in the nineties.

But there were also union men who held aloof from the socialistic Federation of Labor. A counter-organization developed in 1899 called the Swedish Workers' Union.[1] By 1907 this anti-socialistic Swedish Workers' Union (Svenska arbetarförbundet) had a membership of 9,000 while the Swedish Federation of Labor (Landsorganisationen) had 186,000 members.[2] There were 21,000 laborers in unions not affiliated with either of the two national organizations.

The need for legal protection of the working classes became manifest with the growth of industrialism in Sweden. Child labor here, as elsewhere, became one of the evils of the age. Under the old gild system there had been laws restricting child labor; by the laws of 1621 and 1720 an apprentice was supposed to be fourteen years of age.[3] In the glass industry in Stockholm, the minimum age was fifteen by the law of 1683. With the introduction of the factory system in the eighteenth century, it was permissible to apprentice children of ten and twelve, by the laws of 1739 and 1770. Later, in 1846, the minimum age was fixed at twelve for factory and handicraft apprentices, and the masters had to guarantee the apprentice a Christian education, and consider the youth's health and strength to labor. Night work between 9 P.M. and 5 A.M. was forbidden children under eighteen by the law of 1852. The law of 1864, which established the system of laissez faire in Swedish industry, included the protection for children laid down in the laws of 1846 and 1852. But in spite of this a committee investigating conditions of child labor in Sweden in 1874 found many children under twelve employed in factories for 13, 15, and 16 hours a day, and even working nights.

The present legislation for the protection of labor may be said to date from 1881 when a new child labor law was passed forbidding night work for children and young people under eighteen, and providing for continuation schools for children employed between the ages of twelve and fifteen. To obtain working certificates, a minimum of education was required and a health certificate.[4] The work-

---

[1] Boëthius, *op. cit.*, p. 286.  [2] *Ibid.*, pp. 285–86.

[3] T. Fürst, "Arbetarskyddslagstiftningen," in Koch, *op. cit.*, pp. 34 ff.

[4] *Ibid.*, p. 35.

ing day for children under fifteen was limited to six hours, and that for young people under eighteen to ten hours. Minors were forbidden to work underground and also prohibited from spending their rest periods in the workshop. There was much opposition to the law; its enforcement was postponed for a year and exceptions were made in the application of the law to the mining and forestry industries. In 1900 a new child labor law, which also applied to women in industry, was passed after ten years of agitation.[1] It limited child labor to thirteen-year-old children in factories with a six-hour day for children of that age, and a ten-hour day for other minors. Night work between 7 P.M. and 6 A.M. was forbidden. The law provided for rest periods for women before and after childbirth. There was to be annual medical inspection of all minors. Factory inspection had been provided in a law of 1889, and the number of inspectors raised from originally three to five in 1895, and finally to eight in 1900.

During the same period various protective laws were passed for factories and mines. A health statute of 1874 provided for sanitary working conditions. A law of 1884 laid down rules for safe conditions in mines. In 1889 the first factory inspection law was passed. Sweden participated with other European countries in a Labor Conference called by Bismarck at Berlin the same year. In 1891 sickness insurance was legalized and subsidized by the state.[2] The famous Åkarps Law was passed in 1899, protecting those who wished to work during strikes, the result of numerous strikes during the year.[3] The first Workingmen's Compensation Act for injuries in employment became a law in 1901.[4] The establishment by the government of an arbitration commission for labor disputes went into effect in 1906.[5]

There had long been agitation for the extension of franchise in Sweden. In some ways the Parliamentary Reforms of 1866 had restricted franchise, especially that of the small farmer, whereas it had granted it to the professional classes of the city. There had been some dissatisfaction at the time with the high property qualifica-

[1] *Ibid.*, p. 36; Boëthius, *op. cit.*, p. 287.  [3] *Ibid.*, pp. 187–88, 287.

[2] Boëthius, *op. cit.*, p. 287.  [4] *Ibid.*, pp. 201, 287.

[5] *Ibid.*, pp. 244, 287; Olle Ekblom, "Arbetsinställelser, medling och skiljedom i arbetstvister," in Koch, *op. cit.*, pp. 108 ff.

tions for voting. The platforms of the working classes in the eighties had all contained planks favoring universal suffrage. It became also the common interest of both the Liberal party and the infant Labor party, the Social Democrats. In Riksdag after Riksdag the measure came up, only to be defeated. Finally in 1902 another critical moment came in the consideration of a universal suffrage bill. The bill which was being considered by the Riksdag included proportional representation. There was some opposition to the bill and the demand for a more liberal extension of suffrage in the country. In February, 1902, the National People's party (Frisinnade landsföreningen) superseded the "Universal Suffrage Association" and became the support of the Liberal party.[1] The greatest agitation in favor of universal suffrage was, however, in the Social Democratic party. Upon the recommendation of the party convention, demonstrations were held in many of the larger cities and parades, the largest of which was held in Stockholm, April 20. At the time of the debate on the suffrage question in the Riksdag, the Social Democrats attempted to coerce the representatives of the people by calling a general strike, which paralyzed industry throughout the kingdom, from May 15 to 17, 1902. There were 116,000 who participated in this strike.[2] The militia was called out to protect the Riksdag. No conflicts occurred, but an extension of suffrage was not obtained until 1907.

The general strike had angered many of the capitalists. The manager of the corporation "Separator" declared the workmen who had taken part in the strike dismissed from employment.[3] A bitter strike broke out over the situation. There was even a threat that if the strike did not cease, the corporation would be moved to America. Several other machine shops, some, who had originally given their employees the right to participate in the political strike, were now induced to take sides with the corporation "Separator," and  promised to declare a lockout unless the strikers at the "Separator" shops returned to their work. After a month the strike was finally settled; the corporation acknowledged the right of the laborers to organize but the manager would not take back in his employ those whom he had considered a disturbing element. Some of the

[1] Boëthius, op. cit., pp. 204 ff.
[2] Magnusson, op. cit., II, 65.    [3] Ibid., pp. 75 ff.

workmen preferred to emigrate rather than to return to their former employment.[1]

The general strike of 1902 demonstrated to the capitalists of Sweden the power of organized labor. They, therefore, resolved to protect their own interests by counter-organization. There had been an employers' association formed in the machine-shop industry in 1896 in Gothenburg. After the big strike, this organization was re-organized as the Swedish Machine Shop Association.[2] In September, 1902, the Swedish Employers' Association was formed; it was especially for the manufacturing industries. The Central Employers' Association, for the building industries, was established in 1904. These new organizations of employers were determined to fight for their rights against the trade unions and there followed a period of fierce class struggle which culminated in the great strikes of 1909.

The organization of employers was quite extensive. Of the 390,000 organized working men, 260,000 were employed by members of the various employers' associations in 1908.[3] During the same year the Swedish Employers' Association consisted of 1,258 employers who had under their supervision 153,722 laborers. The Machine Shop Association's 162 members employed 25,488 laborers on annual contracts and a total of 35,000 altogether. The Central Employers' Association, the building contractors, had about 2,000 members with 40,000 to 50,000 workmen. The Swedish Railroad Association controlled about 20,000 workers, while the Universal Swedish Publishers' Association consisted of 319 employers and 3,979 workmen. The two industrial armies did not exactly complement each other, for among the organized employers were some unorganized laborers, and unionized workmen were also employed by those not belonging to the employers' associations. Industrial struggles were, therefore, very complicated.

The labor unions strove for higher wages and better working conditions, which, in a few years, they did obtain. They forced a recognition of the right of labor to organize and the right to make collec-

[1] *Ibid.*, p. 77.

[2] Hansson, *op. cit.*, p. 46; Axel Brunius, "Svenska arbetsgivareföreningen" in Koch, *op. cit.*, pp. 94 ff.

[3] Hildebrand, *Gustav V.*, pp. 37–38. The figures of unionized laborers are for 1907.

tive contracts. This was recognized earlier in Sweden than in most other countries. By 1908 there were 2,416 collective contracts, affecting 11,000 employers and 325,000 laborers.[1] During the early years of the twentieth century, a period of good times, the employers were willing to buy industrial peace by granting higher wages and meeting the other demands of labor, but when labor attempted to get control of more important decisions in industry, i.e., the administration of industry, the dismissal of foremen, and the closed shop, there came a strong reaction on the part of the employers. Originally the employers' associations decided to take an active part in the enforcement of the collective contracts by the use of the lockout. They also attempted to make collective contracts national in their scope. In the famous paragraph 23 of the by-laws of the Employers' Association, adopted in 1905, all collective contracts had to be referred to the executive committee of the organization for sanction before becoming effective. There could be nothing in the contract to invalidate the employer's right to hire and fire his laborers, to determine and divide the work, and to keep an open shop.

Labor was not willing to give in to the demands of capital and a period of industrial unrest followed that culminated in the big general strike of 1909. But during this period of conflict, the controversies over the rights of labor and capital were, to a great extent, settled without the interference of the government. The fundamental rights of organization and of collective bargaining with an increasing tendency to national contracts were finally accepted. The Swedish Federation of Labor accepted paragraph 23 in 1906, and it was understood that sympathetic lockouts and strikes were permissible during the period of the contract, unless prohibited in the contract. It became recognized that collective contracts usually established industrial peace.

The general political strike of 1902 had placed the employers on the defensive against organized labor. In the spring of 1903, the wages of longshoremen in Stockholm were reduced ten öre an hour, about three cents, and 500 union men were locked out.[2] This resulted in open conflict. At the same time there were strikes at the port of Gävle. During the summer there occurred lockouts in the machine

[1] *Ibid.*, p. 39.    [2] Magnusson, *op. cit.*, II, 87.

shops. It began with a dispute over wages. Eight workmen at the machine shops at Hvilan had walked out because they were refused an increase of three öre an hour, about a cent. They were ordered by the Machine Shop Employers' Organization to return to work immediately or a lockout would be declared in all the machine shops in Southern Sweden. If they did not return by July 7, all the machine shops in the kingdom would be closed for as long a period as the employers decided. The secretary of the Swedish Federation of Labor sent an appeal to all labor and to the Swedish people for sympathy in this great struggle for the right to unionize. The Iron and Metal Workers' Union was not allied with the Swedish Federation, but the latter decided to give half of its budget for organization to aid the machinists in their struggle.[1] The lockouts began June 19 and 29, were extended to July 7, and ceased on August 3. The workers had won their right to organize. Peace, however, did not last long. In May, 1904, there occurred a lockout of 1,000 stonecutters in Bohus County. Attempts to arbitrate came to naught, and the conflict lasted seven months.

The conflict in the machine-shop industry had, however, not been settled by the strike of 1903. In 1905 another lockout was threatened, with unemployment affecting 15,000 to 20,000 workmen. The struggle lasted for five months, from June 10 to November 10.[2] The conflict was over the question of minimum wages and collective bargaining, which the Employers' Organization refused to recognize. The national labor contract, which ended the struggle, was a victory for the workers in that it shortened the hours of labor and raised wages. The conflict had been an expensive one for the Swedish Federation of Labor, but it prided itself on having been able to keep its organization intact. Peace had not been established between labor and capital; it was only an armistice. The final conflict came in 1908 and 1909.

In the various strikes and lockouts that occurred between 1903–8, the bitterness of the struggle led to excesses. Strikebreakers were

[1] *Ibid.*, pp. 88–89. In 1903 there were 5,970 strikes, 982 lockouts, and 17,619 mixed conflicts, totaling 24,571; in 1904 there were 8,299 strikes, 1,218 lockouts, and 2,731 mixed conflicts, making in all 12,248 (Hansson, *op. cit.*, p. 195).

[2] Magnusson, *op. cit.*, II, 90 ff.

brought in from foreign countries to fight Swedish labor. This led to conflicts which ended in the destruction of life and the bombing of property. The more radical wing of the Social Democrats, who called themselves the Young Socialists, under the leadership of Hinke Bergegren and D. G. Schröder, became militant and tended toward anarchism. They were repeatedly repudiated by the Social Democrats, and their leader, Hjalmar Branting, as doing more harm to the labor cause by their acts of violence than accomplishing anything.[1] The first of these violent outbreaks occurred in Norrland in the lumber industry. Since 1899 the sawmill industries of Norrland had attempted to crush the socialistic union movement in the north and had been almost successful, but in 1904 a new attempt to organize labor had been started. It came to a crisis at Sörvik mill, fourteen miles north of Sundsvall. The manager of the mill refused to recognize the right of his workers to organize into unions; he maintained strictly an open shop and bound the workmen by very narrow individual contracts. When the workmen demanded higher wages, a lockout was declared, and Finnish strikebreakers were brought in. In December, 1904, some of the locked-out workmen attacked some of the strikebreakers. In February two workmen were sentenced to eight months in jail, three to four months, one to three, and two to one month.[2]

During 1906 and 1907, most of the lumber corporations had finally given in to their workmen's right to organize. Some, however, refused to acquiesce. A conflict broke out at the two mills in Dal and Sandö, belonging to Kempe Brothers. With the co-operation of the Swedish Federation of Labor, the Transport Workers' Union and the Sawmill and Lumberyard Workers blockaded the mills, both by land and sea.[3] The strikebreakers were armed to protect themselves. During the night of May 9, 1907, some of the young workmen decided to storm the barracks where the strikebreakers were housed. The press condemned the socialistic unions for the outrage. Thirty-three young workmen were imprisoned for the deed.[4] Three were sentenced to eight years of hard labor, and others received shorter sentences.

[1] *Ibid.*, pp. 162 ff.    [2] *Ibid.*, pp. 110–11. The conflict occurred on Alsnösundet's ice.

[3] *Ibid.*, pp. 112 ff.; Boëthius, *op. cit.*, pp. 286–87.

[4] Magnusson, *op. cit.*, II, 114.

Another violent attack on the part of the more radical group of young workmen occurred at a longshoremen's strike at Malmö. English strikebreakers appeared in Sweden during 1907 and 1908 at conflicts at several of the ports, including Malmö and Gothenburg. At Malmö the strikebreakers were lodged on a steamship, the "Amalthea," in the harbor. Three young workmen, out of sympathy for the strikers, conceived the idea of bombing the ship in July, 1908.[1] Two were condemned to death, and the third to life imprisonment. Their sentences were commuted to life imprisonment, and finally, after serving nine years, they were released. In the summer of 1908, there were imported 400 English strikebreakers from the slums of London to Gothenburg. The previous year some of the English strikebreakers at Norrköping attacked and stabbed a Swedish workman and his family.[2] Polish workmen were introduced into the beet fields of Southern Sweden.

In 1905 there had been a threat of a general strike. The elections of 1905 had given a victory to the Liberal and Social Democratic parties, but the extension of franchise had not been achieved. It was voted upon whether to fight the lockouts of 1905 with a general strike during the same year. Many of the large organizations in the lumbering and metal industries favored it, but it was voted down. The unions in Närke, Dalarne, Skåne, Bohuslän, and Lappland favored it.[3] The great question of the separation of Sweden and Norway rocked the country during the same year. The workingmen, through a manifesto of the Social Democratic party, declared themselves for the peaceful separation of the two countries and Norway's right to choose her own government.[4]

In 1907 the economic crisis that affected the United States, and the rest of the world, was also felt in Sweden. It was followed by falling prices and an attempt to lower wages on the part of the employers' organizations. These attempts were opposed by the labor unions and various local labor conflicts resulted. The situation became aggravating in 1908 and resulted in a violent outburst. Conflicts occurred among the longshoremen at Norrköping and in the Norrland lumber-mill districts.[5] There were plenty of strikebreak-

[1] *Ibid.*, pp. 123 ff.  [3] *Ibid.*, p. 144.

[2] *Ibid.*, p. 126.  [4] *Ibid.*, p. 224.  [5] Hildebrand, *Gustav V.*, p. 41.

ers, but the blockade of ships of strikebreakers, by the Transport Workers' Organization, gave the strike a greater significance. At the Härnösand and Sundsvall districts, the local government felt itself incompetent to handle the situation and a contingent of police from Stockholm were sent, while a warship arrived at Härnösand. At Gothenburg and Malmö, English strikebreakers were imported and conflicts resulted as has been mentioned. These various acts of violence on the part of the younger workmen raised an alarm among the middle class and a fear of anarchism.

There were also conflicts at the sugar refineries, in the building trades, and in the machine shops. Attempts to arbitrate were futile; the blockade of the ports spread and finally included a conflict between the city of Malmö and its employees.[1] Lockouts had first been proclaimed in the building trade, and finally the three large employers' organizations, the Swedish Employers' Association, the Swedish Machine Shop Organization, and the Central Employers' Associations, sent an ultimatum to the Federation of Labor of a general lockout on July 20, 1908, unless all strikes and blockades ceased on July 16. The greatest disturbances broke out at Gothenburg, Lysekil, Malmö, Gävle, and elsewhere. The government appointed an arbitration commission which reached a decision on July 19, and the threatened lockout of 240,000 workmen failed to materialize. The transport workers had attempted to establish the priority right of union men to work at the ports and as longshoremen; while the employers refused to give up their freedom in employment and management of their work. The longshoremen were given the same rights as the industrial workers. In the other conflicts which concerned primarily wages, agreements were finally reached. In the machine industries, collective contracts were not made until the end of December. The city of Malmö won out in the strike of the municipal employees of that city.

In the summer of 1909 there were again many strikes in various industries, mostly concerning higher wages and the standardization of wages over the kingdom. In six of the nine original conflicts the workers had declared strikes, at the porcelain factory in Gothenburg, at Mora in the lumber industry, in the cellulose industry near

[1] *Ibid.*, p. 42.

Skutskär, at the power-plant construction at Mockfjärd, in the saw-mill industry, and in the Munkfors iron foundry. The other three were lockouts in the pit-prop branch of the lumber industry at Gothenburg, and in the men's ready-made clothing industries. The latter was especially difficult for it was an attempt to standardize the vastly different wages in various portions of the kingdom.[1] At Mora, the workmen had declared a sympathetic strike to force the recognition of collective bargaining for other workmen who floated lumber, but whose employers did not belong to the employers' organizations. The conflict at Munkfors foundry began when certain workmen had been denied overtime wages and had walked out without arbitrating, as provided for in the collective contract. The employers declared the contract broken and dismissed the workmen, but the union took their part and declared a strike. None of these conflicts alone were of much consequence, but together they produced more or less a state of anarchy. On July 14, 1909, the various employers' associations met and decided that lockouts would be declared successively unless the conflicts ceased by July 26. The associations justified their ultimatum in the following words:

> The causes of the present decision are vital because the workers, in spite of an economic crisis under which industry suffers, demand increased wages and other improvements, which under the present hard times it is impossible to grant. To these national conflicts have recently been added many local strikes, some of which have broken existing contracts.

The arbitrators appointed by the government attempted to settle the difficulties in the labor market, but no agreement could be reached. The Swedish Federation decided to meet the threatened lockout of 163,000 with a general strike.[2] The employers' associations established lockouts on July 26 and August 2, affecting 72,000 workmen.[3] Only 30,000 of these actually were members of the Swedish Federation of Labor. The lockouts were to be progressive and more were to be declared. Therefore, the Swedish Federation of Labor declared a strike on August 4, which involved every union member in the kingdom. It was to be carried out without violence, and those who cared for the sick, or for living animals, were not included. Nor were employees in light plants, waterworks, and on the

[1] *Ibid.*, p. 44.     [2] Magnusson, *op. cit.*, II, 292.     [3] Hildebrand, *Gustav V*, p. 46.

sanitary squads to lay down their work, for the country was threatened with Russian cholera.[1]

The middle classes dreaded the pending conflict between labor and capital.[2] Food was hoarded in the various households preparatory for a long siege. There was, however, no shortage of food during the strikes, for the railroads continued to operate. One of the mistakes of the labor leaders was to include the employees of the municipalities; many of them broke their trade contracts to participate in the strike, and thereby lost the sympathy of the middle classes. The strike of the typographers further incensed the public. It was called to silence the Conservative press which viciously attacked the strikers and the Social Democrats and the strike affected the whole press. Finally one newspaper, *The Answer*, edited by Gerhard Magnusson, was permitted.[3] Even the Swedish Workers' Association, the bitter opponent of the socialistic federation, joined the strike, for its members were also affected by the lockouts.

In Stockholm everything was quiet, even streetcars ceased to operate. The workers walked the streets; along the quays were hundreds passing the time fishing. In a few days the streetcars began to operate under heavy protection, which irritated the workmen and resulted in further sympathetic strikes.

A militia of defense was organized among some of the middle class with headquarters at a local hotel in Stockholm. It defended men conveying loads. The government refused to set up an arbitration commission because the strike was waged against the community on the same terms as against capital. There were 2,500 strikers in the various government enterprises, and 16,000 in municipal-owned or enfranchised enterprises. Most of these were sympathetic strikers, who, in spite of the wishes of the labor leaders that they continue to work, had decided for themselves to join the strike. It was necessary to proclaim martial law and the sale of alcoholic liquors was prohibited.

The attitude of the government was well expressed in the words of the Civil Minister, Count Hugo Hamilton, on August 30:

Since the big strike in industry has been extended to include industries that threaten the necessities of life in the community, and since it has been pro-

[1] *Ibid.*          [2] *Ibid.*, p. 48.          [3] *Ibid.*, pp. 48–49.

claimed contrary to promises in standing labor contracts, against the principles of faith and honor upon which the community is based, for there have been open attempts to make the servants of the state forget their duty, the strike has ceased to be a struggle between capital and labor, and has been directed against the community.

That the state, after these conditions and before the threat which has been made against public order, should give in to the demands can hardly be expected of any citizen who desires an orderly community life. Those who have started the conflict must learn that the community stands above every class, that the power and interest of the community are and must be greater than any special class.[1]

By August 10 there were 290,000 men on strike in the kingdom, and 40,000 in Stockholm alone. But on that very day overtures of peace began and by the 17th the members of the Swedish Workers' Association returned to work. As time went on, it became more and more a problem to finance the strike aid. The Swedish Federation of Labor appealed to workers in foreign countries and sent some of its strongest men to plead the cause of Swedish labor. More than half a million dollars was received from Denmark, Norway, Finland (then a part of Russia), Germany, and the United States.[2] But it became impossible to hold the masses of labor from returning to their jobs. After four weeks the strikes were called off in all industries except those under the lockout of the employers' associations.

But the employers were not so eager to take back the men who had broken their labor contracts and had gone out on sympathetic strikes. After September 4, most of the employers took back the employees that were needed. Some had installed machinery to do the work of former employees. In other cases, it took a little time to return to full production, and often there was no job for the striker when he returned. The government and municipalities refused to recognize the principle of collective bargaining now, and forced their employees to return on individual contracts. Many private employers demanded the same conditions.

When the strike had diminished to only a conflict between labor and capital, the state was willing to establish an arbitration commission, but no agreement could be reached in September. The problem

[1] *Ibid.*, p. 51.

[2] *Ibid.*, pp. 50–51. More than half came from Germany. The United States contributed about $27,000.

of supporting so many workers month after month became very urgent. It was finally decided to encourage labor to return to the industries when it seemed vain to gain any advantage. The strike had dwindled from 300,000 to 40,000 and was now concentrated in the iron industries.

The Swedish Employers' Association often refused to take back the strikers, and in the industries where lockouts had been declared, they could return only if they ceased to be members of the Swedish Federation of Labor, and refused financial aid to their striking brethren. Arbitration failed when tried, but the lockouts in the iron works were lifted in November. The strike finally dwindled to a close. There was never any formal agreement settling it, and the effects of the strike were felt for a year after.

In the big conflict of 1909 it looked as if labor had lost. The cost of the strike for the workers' organizations in strike relief, had been 7 million kronor, or almost two million dollars. It was nearly a death-blow to Swedish unionism. Membership in the Swedish Federation fell from 186,000 in 1908 to 108,000 in 1909, and 79,900 in 1912.[1] The total membership in unions in Sweden fell from 230,000 in 1907 to 148,000 in 1909. By 1911 there were only 114,000 union men in Sweden. It was a loss of one-half of the union membership. Many of the strikers found themselves without jobs or were forced to return without gaining their demands, and then only if they withdrew from the unions. The financial drain on the unions had made them almost bankrupt. But the unions had not been dispersed, and they had won recognition, which had been denied in 1903. Both capital and labor had won respect for each other and appreciated the other's strength. Both were not willing to resort to peaceful means of settling their disputes. For a time the country placed less faith in trade contracts. In 1908 there had been 318,000 workmen under 2,365 collective contracts, but in 1913 there were only 233,000 under 1,448 such agreements.[2]

The labor disputes in Sweden had the effect of increasing emigration to America. It was a period of unemployment, bitterness, and dissatisfaction with laboring conditions in the mother country, conditions which always prove a good stimulant for seeking a new en-

[1] Hansson, *op. cit.*, p. 160.      [2] Hildebrand, *Gustav V*, p. 151.

vironment. There was not much inquiry as to whether laboring conditions or the rights of labor were any better in the new world. It was taken for granted, and many were undoubtedly disappointed. Emigration to the United States reached a low ebb in 1898, only 13,600, but by 1902 and 1903 it had attained a new high peak, only comparable to the eighties. There were 37,100 in 1902 and 39,500 in 1903, the years of economic and political dissatisfaction.[1] From 1904 to 1907 the annual average was 23,000, but in 1908 it fell to 12,000, undoubtedly due to the economic crisis of 1907 in the United States. The aftermath of the crisis affected economic conditions in Sweden in 1909, and precipitated the bitter labor struggle. Emigration again rose to 21,900 in 1909 and 27,800 in 1910.[2] It was not until 1914 that the numbers were further reduced to 12,900. And during the period of the war, emigration was only slightly greater than immigration into Sweden, an average of 7,800 annually, the lowest average since 1861–65.[3]

The new increases in emigration at the beginning of the twentieth century came from the industrial classes. Thus in 1902, the agrarians emigrating amounted to 11,165 and only 218 were cotters, while the industrial and commercial classes amounted to 18,640. And the same is true in 1902, some 12,432 agrarians, and 20,497 from industry. The largest number of women emigrating belonged to the servant class.[4] This is characteristic of the more recent exodus, and therefore industrial conditions are now the barometer of unrest and emigration.

The conditions of Swedish labor were not unlike those of labor in most countries. Before the unionization of the working classes and the passage of protective labor legislation, the laborer had long hours and small wages. Some of the conditions of pre-war labor in Swedish industry have been pictured by American immigrants who had labored there. A young man of nineteen, a sheet-metal worker by

[1] Sundbärg, "Utvandrings-statistik," *Emigrationsutredningens bilaga IV*, pp. 236–37, Table 96.

[2] *Statistisk årsbok för Sverige, 1927*, p. 72, Table 60.

[3] Immigration was 7,200 annually.

[4] Under the industrial classes are included miners, industrial and commercial workers, workmen without specified industry, and seamen (Sundbärg, "Utvandrings-statistik," *op. cit.*, pp. 239–41, Table 98).

trade, was born in Kopparberg County where his father owned a small tool smithy in eastern Dalarne. At first he assisted his father, but at the age of fifteen he left his home and went to Stockholm. There he obtained work as a sheet-metal worker. Since he was supposed to have had experience in an allied industry, he was given a wage of 25 öre, or 6½ cents an hour. The hours of labor were ten a day in the summer and during the other seasons of the year from five to eight. He shared a room with a fellow-worker and they paid 12 kronor ($3.20) a month each. It was necessary to eat wherever his work took him, and during the last few years he estimated that it cost him from 1.5 to 2 kronor per day (about 50 cents). He emigrated in 1907 to an industrial city near Chicago where a brother lived who had sent him his ticket.[1]

A married industrial worker from Stockholm was born in the neighboring county of Uppsala. He was the son of a laborer and began to work at an early age as a helper in a factory. At the age of seventeen he had a job in an iron works in Gävleborg County and received a daily wage of 1.5 kronor, about 39 cents. After completing his first year of military training, he sought a job in Denmark, but being unsuccessful he returned to Sweden and was given work in 1899 at an iron-bed factory, at 21 öre or 5¼ cents an hour. For a short time he went into partnership in an alehouse near Stockholm, but returned to his work as an iron worker. From 1904 to 1907 he worked in another iron-bed factory, at first at 50 öre (13 cents) an hour, but later wages were reduced to 40 öre (11 cents). During the last few years, he earned about 1,400 kronor a year ($375). He and his family lived in a small apartment consisting of one large room and a kitchen, for which they paid 325 kronor (or about $87) a year for rent. His taxes in the last year had amounted to 70 kronor, almost $20.00. The husband and wife were going in 1907 to Dike, Iowa, where a brother-in-law, who was a dairyman, earned $125 a month.[2]

Another contrast of wages in Sweden and those in America in 1907 was revealed in the story of a young emigrant of twenty-four, a

[1] Case study No. 1 ("Utvandrarnes egna uppgifter," *Emigrationsutredningens bilaga VII*, p. 33).

[2] Case study No. 2 (*ibid.*, pp. 33–34).

butcher by trade. His father had owned a rather large farm in Öster-götland, and he had remained home until he was twenty-two. He then went to Stockholm and had a job as a butcher for 40 kronor ($10.00) a month with room and lodging, and 35 öre (9 cents) an hour for overtime over eleven hours. He had several brothers in the United States, one a contractor in Minneapolis, and the other a building foreman in Seattle, Washington, earning $5.00 a day. His father having died, his mother had rented the estate, and the remaining members of the family, four sisters and a brother, his mother and himself were bound for America.[1]

One young man of eighteen could earn only $10.00 a month at an office job in Stockholm, although he had had special business courses, but made $50.00 a month as a butler with a New York family.[2] Another young man of twenty-eight, who had entered the carpenter trade at thirteen, was earning 3 to 3.50 kronor a day, not quite a dollar in Sweden, and in Ottawa, Canada, Boston, and New York, had earned from $2.00 to $3.00 a day from 1901 to 1903. He had returned to Sweden and worked in a wood-turning mill in Sö-ermanland County from 1903 to 1907, but earned only 3 to 4 kronor a day, about a dollar, "an income which was only sufficient for an unmarried man," according to his statement. He belonged to the labor union.[3]

A young man of twenty-six was a machinist.[4] His father had been a machinist before him in a repair shop in Östergötland County and had earned from 15 to 20 kronor, or from $4.00 to $5.00 a week, with free housing (a room and a kitchen) and exemption from taxes. The parents were quite comfortable economically. The young man worked first as an apprentice at the machine shops in Norrköping. At the age of eighteen he became his father's assistant at the repair shop where he remained for two years. He then left for Stockholm where, between the periods of his military training, he was employed at the Atlas Machine Shops. He later returned to his home and worked at the repair shop until he decided to emigrate. During the last four years, 1903–7, he earned an average weekly wage of 25 kronor, or $6.60 for a twelve-hour day. He lived in a

[1] Case study No. 3 (ibid., p. 34).     [3] Case study No. 6 (ibid., p. 36).

[2] Case study No. 4 (ibid., p. 35).     [4] Case study No. 9 (ibid., p. 38).

small town on the eastern mainline railroad and paid 75 kronor or $20.00 a year for one room and a kitchen. His employer paid his taxes. Food was expensive in the region, but he had a comfortable income. He was traveling to a sister in Chicago in 1907. His fiancee accompanied him; she had many relatives in America. He declared that he was not emigrating for economic reasons, but to gain increased experience and skill in his trade.

A married man of twenty-nine from Jönköping County was a shoemaker by trade.[1] His father owned a small farm. At the age of fourteen, this emigrant was apprenticed to a shoemaker in the village. He had to pay an apprenticeship fee of 20 kronor ($5.00), but received food for his labor. Then he moved to the city of Jönköping where as an apprentice he received a weekly wage of 2, 3, and 4 kronor (from 50 cents to $1.25) with food and lodging. In 1898 he went to England and worked for a short time in a factory. Returning to Sweden, he settled at Borås, where he worked three years and reached a wage of 30 kronor a week, or $8.00. From 1901 to 1906 he worked in a repair shop in Gothenburg where machines were used. Here he earned an average of 110 kronor a month, or $29.00. The hours of labor were thirteen in the summer and nine in the winter. In Gothenburg he rented a room and kitchen for 140 kronor or $37.00 annually. He belonged to the trade union. The emigrant and his wife were bound in 1907 for Brockton, Massachusetts, where shoe factories are located. They had no relatives or friends in America and were leaving because they felt that the future of Sweden was not secure and that America offered better economic opportunities.

During the period of railroad construction in Sweden, many found occupation in this industry. And frequently when there was no further construction they would prefer to emigrate rather than return to agriculture. An unmarried man of twenty-six who emigrated from Kronoberg County told of conditions of labor in railroad construction.[2] He had first been an agricultural laborer for peasants, but tired of this and from 1907 to 1909 worked on railroad construction. For a while he was employed on the Borås-Alvesta Railroad for a daily wage of 1.75 kronor, about 50 cents. On the railroad that was being constructed in Norrland to the boundary be-

---

[1] Case study No. 16 (*ibid.*, p. 41).    [2] Case study No. 19 (*ibid.*, pp. 42-43).

tween Norway and Sweden, during the summer of 1902, he earned 7 kronor, almost $2.00 a day for a ten-and-a-half-hour day. The laborers were housed free of charge in barracks and paid from 30 to 40 kronor ($8.00 to $10.00) a month for food. For a year beginning in the fall of 1902 he was employed on the Skövade-Axvall Railroad at a daily wage of 3 kronor (80 cents) during the summer for a ten-and-a-half-hour day, and 1.60 to 2.50 in the winter. The following year he worked at the Bohus Long Line for 4 kronor a day, an eight-hour day, with food from 9 to 10 kronor a week. Just before emigrating he worked on a railroad in Småland for 40 to 45 kronor a day in the summer and 2 to 2.50 kronor in the winter, with food and lodging at 11 to 12 kronor a week. He did not like this work because it was so uncertain; at least two months of a year were spent in idleness.

After the general strike of 1909, there developed in 1910 a syndicalist trade union movement in Sweden. Its number of adherents was small to begin with, 696 members in 21 local unions.[1] During the World War it grew in numbers, especially among the building trade and in the lumber industries. There were also a few thousand members among paper-mill workmen, miners, metal industries, sawmill workers, and agricultural laborers. The organization reached the height of its membership in 1924, with 37,600 adherents, only a very small proportion of the Swedish labor movement. These unions which are called the Swedish Workers' Central Association are affiliated with the International Workers of the World which was organized in the United States in 1907. The principles of this syndicalist movement were class conflict. They formed the nucleus of the communist party.

The various trade unions were united with similar trade unions in the two sister Scandinavian countries. The first impetus toward international organization came from the Scandinavian Labor Congress held at Örebro in 1886.[2] The next affiliation was sought with the German trade unions. In 1912 there were 32 international trade affiliations. The woodworkers had the largest geographical federation embracing twenty countries. These international organizations were split during the World War, but after the war appeared once

---

[1] Hansson, *op. cit.*, pp. 168 ff.  [2] *Ibid.*, pp. 343 ff.

more so that 29 of the Swedish trade unions belong to International federations. The Swedish Federation of Labor was also a part of what was called the Second Internationale. This organization dated from an international labor conference held at Stuttgart in Germany in 1902, when Sweden and eleven European countries united. In 1909 the American Federation of Labor joined the Internationale, making it truly international.[1] The last meeting of the Second Internationale was held in September, 1913, at Zurich. There were nineteen National Federations of Labor present, representing seven million working men.[2] During the World War it was impossible to keep the Internationale together. Several meetings were attempted, but for patriotic reasons no full representation was possible.[3] After the war, beginning in 1920, international congresses again began to meet every three years. There has been a close cooperation between the International Federation of Labor and the International Labor Bureau of the League of Nations. The secretariat of the Federation of Labor was moved from Berlin to Amsterdam during the war and remains there.

The Third Internationale, which met at Moscow in 1921, repudiated the Amsterdam organization as antiproletarian and a tool of capitalism.[4] The International Federation of Labor seeks to gain its end through democracy, while the Third Internationale depends upon achieving its ideal through a proletariat dictatorship. With the exception of the communistic labor federation in France, and a similar one in Czechoslovakia, most of the national federations belong to the Amsterdam Internationale. In Sweden, as in most of the nations of the world, there is a communistic minority within the federation. For a short time there was a communistic organization representing this element, called the Trade Union Propaganda Association which had but a few members and has been out of existence for several years.[5] Its activities have been assumed by a unity committee established at a Communistic Conference at Gothenburg in 1925. This committee has attempted to reconcile the two organizations, but without any success.

After the economic depression of the first year or two of the World

[1] *Ibid.*, pp. 347 ff.      [3] *Ibid.*, pp. 359 ff.

[2] *Ibid.*, p. 357.      [4] *Ibid.*, pp. 369 ff.      [5] *Ibid.*, p. 372.

War, Sweden entered into an era of good times which lasted until the economic crisis of 1920. It was a period in which abnormal demands from the belligerent countries stimulated the industries of Sweden to their utmost production. Labor was much in demand and it was a time of rising wages and the satisfaction of labor-demands for shorter hours and better conditions. Not all the industries in Sweden prospered accordingly. Sweden, as has been demonstrated in an earlier discussion, was to a large extent dependent upon imports from a foreign market for much of her foodstuffs, and many of her raw materials for manufacture. These importations ceased during the war, both because of the increased need for these materials within the warring countries themselves, and because of the economic blockades. Sweden was also so unfortunate as to suffer from crop failures at home during this period. The result was a tremendous increase in prices of all commodities, and the necessity of rationing, not only foodstuffs, but even wearing apparel and fuel. Only the industries like iron and lumbering, which were native to Sweden, had a period of great prosperity.

Wages rose more slowly than the cost of living from 1914 to 1918.[1] In 1917 real wages were only 88 per cent of those in 1913. But the constant demand for higher wages finally forced real wages over the cost of living in 1919–20. In 1921, the index of real wages per hour was 51 per cent higher than in 1913, and per year, 12 per cent higher. It was an attempt, not only to compensate for the high cost of living, but also for the shortening of the working day to eight hours.

During this period of good economic conditions and rising wages, the workingman's faith in his trade-union organization was regained. The trade-union membership had fallen from 230,000 in 1907 to 114,000 in 1911 but rose to 403,000 in 1920.[2] Collective contracts had also received a blow in the general strike of 1909 and by 1913 had reached a low ebb, but in spite of the uncertainty of wages during the period of the World War, both capital and labor put their faith in collective contracts again. Clauses were included making wages flexible within the life of the contract.[3] In 1913 there

---

[1] Olaf Ekblom, "Den svenska lönarbetaren, 1914–1924," in Heckscher, *Bidrag till Sveriges ekonomiska och sociala historia under och efter världskriget*, pp. 279 ff.

[2] Hansson, *op. cit.*, p. 160.          [3] Heckscher, *op. cit.*, p. 266.

were 226,000 laborers under collective contracts, and by 1921 the number had increased to 424,000. Sweden had by 1920 become the most highly organized country, both in capital and labor, in Europe.

Labor had also gained in political strength during the decades since the establishment of the Social Democratic party, and was ready to reap its rewards after the World War. The party received most of its strength from the labor unions, as in England. In 1912 the leaders of the party made a statistical survey of the amount of support received from union men.[1] It was discovered that 87 per cent of the membership of the party came from organized labor, but only 45 per cent of the union men belonged to the party. There were 820 or 42 per cent of the trade unions which indorsed the party. In certain unions from 70 to 80 and even 95 per cent of the membership belonged to the labor party. Of the 64,979 members in 1911, almost four-fifths were members because of collective memberships through their union, and almost nine-tenths through collective memberships of labor federations in the communes. Only 4.23 per cent of the party members were adherents through political societies, and clubs, while one-sixth consisted of individual memberships.

The able leadership of Hjalmar Branting finally brought the Social Democrats to the place of the most powerful of Riksdag parties. He was the first member of the party to be elected to the Riksdag in 1896.[2] In 1902 the party was bold enough to try to force an extension of the franchise by calling a general strike, but failed in its purpose. In these earlier days of political effort there was much sympathy between the Liberal party under Staaff and the Social Democrats under Branting. Both had, as a common aim, universal suffrage and social legislation to improve working conditions. There was a partial extension of franchise in 1911 when all men of twenty-four who had paid their taxes within the previous three years had the right to vote.[3] Proportional representation was introduced into the law by the Conservative parties who feared that a majority of Liberals and Social Democrats would swamp them. In the elections

---

[1] *Sveriges social demokratiska arbetarepartis organisations fråga* (Stockholm, 1913), cited in Hansson, *op. cit.*, p. 330.

[2] Magnusson, *op. cit.*, I, 396 ff.

[3] Gustav Aldén, *Svenska-statskunskap, Medborgarens bok* (Stockholm, 1924), I, 41 ff.

of 1908, which were called by Swedish constitutional law to decide the question of extending franchise, the battle-cry of the Right had been "a solid front against socialism." The Social Democrats increased their seats in the Lower House of the Riksdag from 17 to 33.[1] It had no representation, as yet, in the Upper House.

The Social Democratic party of Sweden first accepted the Gotha platform of its fellow German party. But in 1897 there appeared modifications to make the platform more acceptable to Swedish temperament. Instead of nationalization of production, transportation, etc., the Swedish platform emphasized "an expansion of the productive activities of the state and communes, and its leadership in communication and distribution," so that "every one may have a living wage."[2] When it became apparent in Sweden that the tendency in that country was not toward collective ownership of land but toward the encouragement of small farms for the lower classes, there was included in the platform of 1911, a plank protecting agricultural laborers, crofters, and the small farmers against the domination of corporations and large estates. It advocated the forceful division of large estates, and sales to agricultural laborers and others. By 1920 the party had returned to the doctrine of nationalization of natural resources, industry, banking institutions, transportation, and communication, with government control over all enterprises in private ownership, including agricultural land. Co-operation has been encouraged as an education for collective control in the future.

The co-operative movement has had the success in Sweden that it has had in England and most of the northern countries. Since the organization of the Swedish Co-operative Society in 1899, numerous retail co-operatives have been formed.[3] The membership in the organization rose from 91,000 in 1910 to 290,000 in 1923, about one-fifth of the population, counting five members to the family. In the latter year the membership constituted 60 per cent laborers, while the remainder were agriculturalists, and others. The movement has been

---

[1] The law was passed in 1907 by the Riksdag. It is necessary to call an election for a new Riksdag to pass the law a second time before it becomes effective (Hildebrand, *op. cit.*, pp. 23–24).

[2] *Ibid.*, p. 610.

[3] *Ibid.*, pp. 571–72; Anders Örne, "Kooperationen," in Koch, *op. cit.*, pp. 359 ff.

strongest in the industrial regions of Norrland and Central Sweden, and weakest in the agricultural counties and Southern Sweden.

On the question of military defense, the Social Democrats have taken various stands. In the program of 1897 it advocated the militia system of Switzerland instead of a standing army.[1] But since 1908 it has assumed an antimilitaristic attitude, and in 1911 it demanded a gradual diminution of military burdens until disarmament is reached. The Young Socialist party was the leader in the latter movement. The World War increased the sentiment against military armaments. In 1920 the platform advocated the League of Nations and a limitation of armaments. Co-operating with the Liberals and the Agrarians, the Social Democrats have reduced the number of training days required in the Swedish army and made some reduction of armament. Branting became the chairman of the first disarmament committee of the League of Nations, and led the movement for limitation of armaments within the League.[2]

The religious question has never been of much importance in the program; it was considered a private matter. There has been a certain amount of religious indifference on the part of the young party members. In 1920, separation of state and church was included in the platform.[3] The temperance question aroused much discussion within the party. In 1897, the party platform remained neutral on the issue, but in 1911, a strong temperance sentiment led to the adoption of a demand for some kind of prohibition law. In the platform of 1920 there appeared only the statement that "alcoholism is the greatest detriment to an intelligent working class." Alcoholism was to be fought through education on its evil effects to the individual and the community, rather than by restrictive legislation.[4]

The political demands of the Social Democrats in 1897 had been for universal direct suffrage, and for the abolition of the Upper House of the Riksdag. In 1911 the party advocated a republican form of government.[5] The planks remained in the 1920 program, but the opposition to the Upper House has disappeared since Branting ex-

---

[1] Hildebrand, *Gustav V*, p. 611.    [2] *Ibid.*, p. 504.

[3] Magnusson, *op. cit.*, III, 247–49, 258.

[4] *Ibid.*, p. 261. Plank XI in the 1920 Platform.

[5] Hildebrand, *op. cit.*, p. 612.

pressed a fear of a mob-ridden single chamber and since the party of the Left has captured several seats in the First Chamber. There also has been less aversion to monarchy since the Social Democrats have thrice formed the ministry since 1920. A demand for the use of the referendum appeared in the platform of 1920.[1] The party has always fostered adult education and free schools. Its newspapers have been a real power in the community. Women suffrage met favor with the party and a national organization of Social Democratic women was established in 1920 when the women were given political rights.[2]

The Swedish Social Democratic party has always been more conservative and more interested in national problems than an adherent to the Marxian program. Interestingly, the fundamental doctrine of socialism, Karl Marx's *Capital*, has never been translated into Swedish and is only accessible to those laborers who can read a foreign language. As long as the Social Democrats had to depend on the Liberal party for their reforms, they could naturally not press their own program, but even after they did obtain control of the government, their program has been more progressive than a truly Marxian one. The younger and more radical elements in the party have often been impatient with this conservatism, and have sometimes broken away to form new parties. The Young Socialist Society, which was organized in 1901 by Hinke Bergegren, developed an anarchistic complex in 1908 and was read out of the Social Democratic party.[3] From time to time various members who failed to adhere to the party platform were expelled from the party.

Among the various conflicts that tended to split the party was the question of whether the Social Democrats might enter into the coalition cabinet of another party and thereby compromise their platform. The Social Democrats decided to co-operate and in 1917 formed a coalition with the Liberals in the Edén ministry. The coalition cabinet of the Liberals and the Social Democrats forced further reforms in franchise in 1917–18 to prevent the repercussion of the revolutionary movements from Russia and Germany spreading among the Swedish working classes. The most radical groups in Sweden, the Left Socialists, the Young Socialists, and the soldiers' and workers' communes erected in the fall of 1918, chose November

[1] Magnusson, *op. cit.*, III, 258.     [2] Hildebrand, *op. cit.*, p. 613.     [3] *Ibid.*

11, 1918, as an auspicious movement for the rising of the working classes and the establishment of a socialistic government.[1] Branting was attacked at a banquet of the radicals for his conservatism.

Branting appealed to the Social Democrats for unity, and demanded the co-operation of the other parties in the Riksdag in the passage of legislation extending suffrage in the communes and for the First Chamber of the Riksdag. There was also a demand for woman suffrage, an eight-hour day, and the reduction of armaments.[2] The parties of the Right yielded for fear that the First Chamber might be abolished, and the king, for fear of a republic. The new suffrage law established universal suffrage at the age of twenty-three for communes, local councils, and the Lower House of the Riksdag, while county councils remained twenty-seven. The county councils and special electoral colleges elect the members of the Upper House. Voters have to pay taxes in one out of the previous three years. Woman suffrage was also granted. By the elections of 1919, the Social Democrats became the most numerous party in the Riksdag. And in spite of the fact that it had but a minority, it withdrew from the coalition with the Liberals and erected its own cabinet in 1920 under Branting. It survived only a few months, but again in 1921–23, and in the fall of 1924, Branting formed Labor governments, and, upon his death in the spring of 1925, Sandler continued until the following June. In the fall of 1928, the Social Democrats were confident that they would win a majority control of both houses of the Riksdag in the election, but met with reverses. The party, however, continues the largest of the parties in the Riksdag.

The members of the party who had opposed co-operation in 1917 formed the Left Socialists, and included such members of the Riksdag as Lindhagen, Höglund, and Fabian Månsson. With the entrance of Russian Bolshevism and German Spartacism in 1919, another split occurred, and the most radical of the Left Socialists formed the Communist party in 1921.[3] The remainder returned to

[1] This appeal appeared in *Politiken*, November 11, 1918, cited in Hildebrand, *op. cit.*, p. 476.

[2] Magnusson, *op. cit.*, III, 145–47. Proclamation of November 15, 1918, by Branting for the Social Democrats and Lindqvist for the Swedish Federation of Labor.

[3] Hildebrand, *op. cit.*, pp. 618 ff.

the fold of the Social Democrats in 1923. The Communists, in turn, split between the adherence of the Third Internationale of Moscow, and a Left party, declaring themselves independent of Russia. A small group of workingmen have organized into the Syndicalist party which believes in seeking redress for their economic grievances, not through political power, but through sabotage and revolution. But on the whole, the Swedish worker is a conservative individual and a staunch adherent to the Social Democratic party. The death of Branting was most unfortunate, for he was by far the most gifted of all Swedish political leaders of the day.

The economic depression that followed in the wake of the World War has been as severe upon the Swedish industrial laborer as it has been on the worker the world over. First, there was the problem of deflation, the necessity of reducing wages that had been so hard fought for during the war, and high prices. Prices had soared much higher than real wages and it was only in 1920 that the worker had a differential in his favor. During the period of deflation, strikes and lockouts were constant, and the cessation of demand on the world market for iron and lumber brought a real problem of unemployment in 1922 that has not as yet been solved, although somewhat ameliorated.

It has always been difficult for labor to understand that at certain periods wages must fall. Therefore, the cut in wages that occurred in Sweden during 1921–22, 47 per cent in the sawmill industries, 52 per cent in the pulp mills, 46 per cent in the iron industries, 40 per cent in the machine shops, 40 per cent in the textile industries, and 40 to 43 per cent in the building trades, precipitated long and bitter strikes and lockouts.[1] But these conflicts were not as extensive as those brought on by an adjustment to the Eight-Hour Law in 1919–20. In 1920 there were 139,000 workers involved in strikes, but in 1921 only 49,700, and in 1922 only 75,700.[2] Prices also began to fall after 1920, so that the lower wages still gave the laborer a differential. And a tremendous unemployment problem dampened the ardor of ambitious workmen for higher wages.

Sweden has never in her history been faced with the unemployment problem that appeared in the fall of 1921 and the spring of

[1] *Ibid.*, p. 549.      [2] *Ibid.; Statistisk årsbok för Sverige, 1927*, p. 230, Table 194.

1922. During most of the war period there had been much demand for labor. Only in the stone and in the textile industries had there been any unemployment. The demand for paving stone had been cut off during the war, and the raw materials for textiles, especially cotton, were inaccessible. It had been necessary to give some aid to the unemployed by the state to save the industries for the future, but the increased demand for woodcutters and agricultural laborers had absorbed much of the unemployment. Following the war until 1920 there seemed to be an intensive activity on the part of industry that absorbed all but five hundred stonecutters. With the crisis of 1920 came inactivity for labor. In February, 1921, there were 60,000 men registered as unemployed with the various state employment offices, and in January, 1922, around 163,000. These were large figures for a country with a population of six million. In industry in 1922 there were 489 seeking employment for every 100 jobs available, in all, 555,600 without employment.[1] Conditions improved somewhat in 1923, with only 235,656 more laborers than vacancies, and in 1924 with only 189,000. But during 1925–26 it began to rise again to 250,000, or 360 per 100 jobs. By 1927 unemployment had fallen to 60,000, but rose again in 1930.

As in England and in so many of the countries of Europe since the World War, the solution of the unemployment problem became of vital importance to the government. It was decided to meet the situation first by a series of government works, like roads, streets, drainage, and erection of stadiums, and only when this failed, to care for the remaining unemployed with a doles system. During the war period from 1914 to 1918, about four and one-half years, there were expended 4.6 million kronor (1.2 million dollars) for unemployment relief.[2] From 1919 to 1923, four and one-half years, there was an expenditure of 39.7 million kronor (10 million dollars). Besides state aid, there was contributed during the two periods something like 111 million kronor (30 million dollars). The Riksdag of 1922 voted 15 million kronor (4 million dollars) for various state works for the year, and the communes spent 25 million kronor for street-paving during the same year to relieve the situation.

[1] *Statistisk årsbok för Sverige, 1927*, pp. 229, Table 192; *ibid., 1930*, p. 239.

[2] Hildebrand, *op. cit.*, p. 551.

The policy adopted by the Swedish state in its unemployment relief was to employ men out of work on various building projects of the state and communes, and only, when there was no further employment possible, to give doles. The wages paid by the state were lower than the wages for unskilled labor, and the doles were lower than the wages paid by the state. In both cases the amount was decided by local conditions. If a workman refused to accept a job on a building project of the state, he was refused a dole. The Unemployment Commission also attempted to send workers from one portion of the kingdom to another where there was a need for labor. But the biggest problem came in connection with strikes. As prices began to fall, there occurred strikes at the government enterprises when the wages were lowered. It was understood that the state would give no relief to striking workmen, whether they were striking against the state or against private employers. Even the Social Democratic party, while it controlled the ministry, adhered to this principle, although its major political support was from organized labor.[1]

During February and March of 1922, the number of unemployed was the greatest, and during these months there were 31,600 employed in government enterprises and 10,200 in communal works.[2] Two committees directed the work, the "Southern Sweden Government Works" and the "Norrland Government Works." The former directed the laying of 630 miles of road by the middle of 1923, and several hundred after. There were also constructed streets and roads in communes, some 40 athletic fields, about 600 miles of ditches; there was the drainage of about 6,000 acres of land, the planting and trimming of 17,000 acres of forest. The Norrland enterprise constructed 480 miles of roads.

It was natural that the Social Democratic party, when it came into power a second time under Branting's leadership in 1921, should do everything possible to remedy the unemployment situation. It was under its régime that public works were resorted to as a means

[1] *Ibid.*, p. 552; Järte and Skogh, "Arbetslöshetsfrågan," in Koch, *op. cit.*, pp. 133 ff.; Järte and Koch, "Arbetslöshetspolitik, 1914–1924," in Heckscher, *Sveriges ekonomiska och sociala historia under och efter världskriget*, Part I, pp. 292 ff.

[2] Hildebrand, *Gustav V*, p. 551.

to alleviate conditions, temporarily, at least. At the beginning of 1923 strikes broke out in the iron industries, and in the sawmills and pulp mills. The Unemployment Commission withdrew the doles from about 4,000 workmen who belonged to the striking unions, but who had received aid because of prior unemployment.[1] The principle employed was that the state could assist neither party in a labor conflict. The Social Democratic government was hard pressed, both by its own union members and by the activities of the communists who posed as saviors of the unemployed, on the part of the laborers and by the Riksdag and the Unemployment Commission, who refused to sympathize. The government attempted to change the conditions of unemployment aid, to apply to those union men in a strike who had been unemployed six months prior to the strike. It was refused by the Riksdag and the Social Democrats were forced to resign from office. The chief opponent was K. G. Ekman, the leader of the Liberals, and usually the chief support of the labor minority.

Unemployment conditions were not as bad after 1923 and government aid was gradually reduced to normal conditions. But the efforts of industry to further reduce wages, or at least keep them at their present level, led to further labor conflicts.[2] The failure to reach an agreement in a trade in the iron industry brought on a series of lockouts which lasted six months. There were also two months of lockouts in the sawmills and pulp mills. There were in all 102,900 workmen involved and the number of working days lost in 1923 were only surpassed in 1909 and 1920.

The only gain was to keep wages where they were. The following year, 1924, was quiet, but, with the attempt to renew trade contracts again in 1925, the country experienced more bitter lockouts, involving 145,800 workmen.[3] Labor was striving for higher wages, but in only a few instances was it secured. Peace was declared in most of the lockouts by March, 1925. The government established arbitration commissions to settle the differences. Much of the difficulty

[1] *Ibid.*, p. 526; Gustav Möller, "Ett fall och en uppståndelse," *Tiden*, June, 1926; "Kring regeringskrisen," *Svensk Tidskrift*, 1926, No. 5.

[2] Hildebrand, *op. cit.*, p. 553; *Statistisk årsbok för Sverige, 1927*, p. 230, Table 194.

[3] *Statistisk årsbok för Sverige, 1927*, p. 230, Table 194.

had been to obtain a recognition of trade contracts when made. Certain syndicalistic tendencies among the younger workmen, with a leaning toward communism, have hampered the fulfilment of agreements, and have even tended to dispute the authority of the labor unions.[1] This has been particularly true among the lumber industries of Norrland. The masons of Stockholm have attempted to monopolize their trade and have even held the Federation in defiance. Again in 1928 there were conflicts which affected thousands of workmen, conflicts in the mines, in the pulp mills, the sawmills, the paper mills, and the sugar industries.[2] Conflicts with employees of the communes at Borås, Sundsvall, and Kalmar, and at the navy yards of the government have again arisen the question of the right of these employees to organize. And as each new year approaches with a renewal of trade contracts, labor conflicts seem to be imminent.[3]

Sweden continued, since the World War, the most highly organized country, both in labor and capital, in Europe. Membership in labor unions has steadily increased, with but a slight setback during the year of unemployment, 1921. In 1925 there were 433,000 members in the Swedish unions, of which 384,600 belonged to the Swedish Federation of Labor.[4] In most of the European countries, Germany, England, Austria, France, Czechoslovakia, Belgium, there has been a decline in union membership since 1920.[5] It was estimated in 1923 that only 42.7 per cent of Swedish labor employed at the time was organized however.[6] In proportion to population, Austria, Great Britain, Australia, Czechoslovakia, and Germany are the most highly unionized, from 16 to 11.5 per cent.[7] Sweden ranks ninth, with Denmark seventh. Sweden has 7.5 per cent of her population in unions, and the United States, 3.5 per cent.

It has become customary in Sweden to decide wages and laboring conditions by means of trade agreements between the labor unions

---

[1] Hildebrand, *op. cit.*, pp. 554–55.

[2] "Arbetsfreden," *Svensk Tidskrift*, 1928, No. 3, pp. 173 ff.; *Statistisk årsbok för Sverige, 1930*, p. 240.

[3] "Regeringen och arbetsfredsfrågan," *Svensk Tidskrift*, 1928, No. 7, pp. 505 ff.

[4] Hansson, *op. cit.*, pp. 159–60.　　[6] *Ibid.*, p. 171.

[5] *Ibid.*, p. 165.　　[7] *Ibid.*, pp. 174–75.

and the employers' associations. From 1911 to 1915 there were 1,449 such agreements in Sweden, affecting 8,315 employers and 238,000 laborers. In 1928 the number of collective agreements was 3,326, deciding working conditions for 17,388 employers and 512,542 workmen.[1] But just in this highly organized state lies the danger of more conflict from broken agreements, or the inability to reach new agreements upon the renewal of a contract. The Social Democratic party, which is so sensitive to labor, has fallen twice over labor disputes, in 1923 and again in 1926.[2] The Moderate government under Lindman came into power in 1928 with the promise to promote internal peace. The Labor Minister, Lübeck, called a Labor Peace Conference of the leaders of capital and labor in Stockholm the following November, but no real discussion of the issue was possible.[3] Sweden seems faced with more or less continuous industrial turmoil and a problem of industrial unemployment even under the Ekman ministry which came into power in June, 1930.

The conditions in labor today in Sweden are much better than they were in the pre-war times. The Eight-Hour Law, although a temporary one, has been renewed and continues in force since 1918. Wages have fallen since 1920, but so have also prices. Industrial wages are now on the average more than twice per hour what they were in 1913. There is a tendency for those industries which produce only for the home market to be higher in wages, due to the protection of the tariff. The exporting industries have had to meet world competition and this has reacted on the wage scale. It has been primarily in the latter industries that the numerous lockouts and strikes have occurred since the World War. The gain for the workman on his annual wage has not been so great as on the hour wage, for he works only eight hours now, as compared with a longer day previously. But he still has a differential in his favor, above the cost of living.

---

[1] *Statistisk årsbok för Sverige, 1930*, p. 241, Table 207.

[2] The second time was over the Stripa affair, whether the Unemployment Commission could force unemployed men to take the place of strikers at the mine at Stripa, even though it was an unlawful strike. The government overruled the commission and was forced out by a vote of lack of confidence (Gustav Möller, "Et fall och en uppståndelse," *Tiden*, June, 1926, pp. 13 ff.; "Kring regeringskrisen," *Svensk Tidskrift*, 1926, No. 5, pp. 279 ff.).

[3] "Arbetsfredskonferensen," *Svensk Tidskrift*, 1928, No. 8, pp. 593 ff.

There have been many variations in the increase of wages among the various industrial workers. The amount of increase for unskilled labor was and remains greater in percentage than for carpenters. The same tendency has been true among the employees of the state. The higher officials received less increase than the lower clerks, and much the same has been true in the offices of private corporations. But even with these increases in wages, they remain below those obtainable in the United States. A carpenter in Sweden in 1925 received 32 cents an hour, while in Chicago he received $1.25.[1] A

TABLE XXIII

INDUSTRIAL WAGES IN SWEDEN, 1913–24*

| YEAR | AVERAGE WAGE PER HOUR, IN ÖRE, FOR MEN WORKERS | | | |
| | Total Workmen | Of Which | | |
| | | Export Industries | Domestic Industries | Mixed Industries |
|---|---|---|---|---|
| 1913......... | 45 | 45 | 45 | 45 |
| 1920......... | 165 | 161 | 167 | 164 |
| 1921......... | 164 | 156 | 167 | 161 |
| 1922......... | 118 | 104 | 125 | 108 |
| 1923......... | 112 | 103 | 117 | 102 |
| 1924......... | 114 | 106 | 119 | 104 |

* There are 100 öre in a krona (26.8 cents) (Olof Ekblom, "Den svenska lönarbetaren, 1914–1924," in Heckscher, Sveriges ekonomiska och sociala historia, I, p. 284.

painter in Sweden had a wage of 54 cents an hour and in Chicago $1.50. In the European country a stonecutter received about 22 cents an hour, and in the American city $1.37. These are the unionized trades of the United States.

An innovation in the present labor conditions in Sweden has been the vacation. Every industry has from three days to two weeks summer vacation with pay, except the seasonal trades. In the larger industries it is usually four days and occurs during the mid-summer festival, the latter part of June.[2]

Much has been done to house the industrial laborer for rents

[1] Statistisk årsbok för Sverige, 1927, p. 233, Table 198; U.S. Department of Labor, Reports, 1925. These are the figures for 1925.

[2] Ekblom, "Den svenska lönarbetaren," in Heckscher, op. cit., I, 289 ff.; Nyström, "Lönarbetaren och samhället," in Koch, op. cit., p. 84.

tended to rise very high during the war period. Beginning in 1917 the government passed a series of laws attempting to control rents and was somewhat successful in keeping down the rents for the industrial workers.[1] The largest percentage of Sweden's laboring class in the cities is housed in very small apartments, one or two rooms and a kitchen. In Stockholm, 32 per cent are housed in one room and a kitchen; in Gothenburg, 51 per cent, while in 78 cities in the kingdom it amounts to 39 per cent.[2] These are very overcrowded living quarters. Many of the immigrants in America have stressed the roomy apartments or homes of the working class. A "Society Against Emigration," organized to combat the emigration by removing its causes, has taken for one of its objectives the satisfaction of the craving of the Swedish people to own their own homes, both among the agricultural and industrial classes.[3] It is much like the garden-plot idea in England. The organization later changed its name to the "Society Own Your Home," and purchased various estates which were subdivided into small farms. One of its enterprises was near Stockholm. The first experiment was the estate of Bankesta on the Stockholm-Katrineholm railroad. Some of the estate was made into small farms for agriculturalists and some lots with houses newly erected were sold to industrial workmen.[4] Another venture nearby was that at Mora. Most of the homes for industrial laborers were sold to workmen employed at the street railway or at the "Separator" works in Stockholm. Other ventures were similar, like the one in Värmland at Säffle where small pieces of land with homes were sold to industrial workmen.[5]

There have been other industrial homes erected by the various corporations in Sweden for their own workmen. "Jonsereds Fabriker" near Gothenburg have model homes, some of which are rented

[1] K. G. Tham, "Hyresmarknad och hyresreglering, 1914–1923," in Heckscher, *op. cit.*, I, 349 ff.

[2] Nyström, "Bostadsfrågan," in Koch, *op. cit.*, pp. 388 ff.

[3] Paul Bergholm, *Nationalföreningen mot emigrationen, 1907–1917* (Stockholm, 1917). This society made a study of housing in America (Adrian Molin, *Hur Svensk-Amerikanerna bo* [Stockholm, 1912]).

[4] *Mälare provinsernas egnahemsaktiebolag, 1910–1920* (Stockholm, 1920); Bergholm, *Nationalföreningen mot emigrationen, 1907–1917*, pp. 96–97.

[5] Bergholm, *ibid.*, p. 90.

and others have been sold to workmen, while others similar have been erected by the Sandvikens Steel Mills, Gustafbergs Porcelain Mills, etc.[1] The Swedish Manufacturers' Association has a subsidiary, the Industrial Housing Corporation, that erects workingmen's homes at cost and sells to the workmen of various industries. This probably developed from the custom of housing laborers by the corporations at their various plants.[2] There are also certain philanthropic foundations that have been established for workingmen's homes or tenements. Some of these date from 1850, like the Robert Dickson foundation in Gothenburg. The corporation "Stockholm's Workingmen's Homes," founded in 1892, had in 1924 housing for 1,414 persons in that city.

On the outskirts of the bigger cities there have developed garden plots for the laboring classes, in Stockholm, Gothenburg, Malmö, Ängleholm, etc. Here the workman spends his long summer evenings and his week-ends, frequently raising all the vegetables for the family use. The idea came originally from the Continent. The first in Sweden was tried at Landskrona in 1888, and by 1923 there were 30,000 such garden-plots in the kingdom.[3] It is primarily a communal undertaking.

The adult education movement has been of long standing in Sweden. The imposing Workers' Institute, that was erected in Stockholm in 1880 by Dr. Nyström, has been followed by community houses in many localities. There are many public libraries and numerous study circles for the working class. There were 3,900 study circles subsidized by the government in 1924 with 53,000 members.

The industrial crisis and the resulting unemployment in Sweden since 1920 again made emigration a problem. Exodus began to grow in 1922 when it reached the figure of 11,800, and in 1923, with 29,238.[4] In the latter year there were 24,948 Swedes who departed

[1] Elis Bosaeus, "Industriens arbetareförhållanden," in *Svenska industrien vid kvartsekelskiftet, 1925*, p. 114.

[2] G. H. von Koch, "Åtgärder av arbetsgivare och filantropiska företag," in Koch, *op. cit.*, pp. 411 ff.

[3] "Koloniträdgårdar," *ibid.*, pp. 420 ff.

[4] *Statistisk årsbok för Sverige, 1927*, p. 72, Table 60.

for the United States, while 2,258 returned to Sweden.[1] The quota laws of the United States cut down the number who would otherwise have emigrated. From 1924 to 1926 there were from 7,000 to 9,700 per year, while the new quota law of 1924, which became effective July 1, 1929, has decreased the quota for Sweden to 3,000. The lists for emigrants to the United States were filled six months ahead of time in 1926.

In an investigation made by the Labor Department of the Swedish government, of emigrants leaving on the Swedish-American line between July, 1922, and June 30, 1923, two-thirds were going to relatives in America, and one-fifth had tickets that had been sent to them from America.[2] There were in Sweden in 1924 nine head agents for steamship companies, and 160 subagents, but they agreed with the government not to agitate for emigration.

Much of this recent emigration has come from the industrial and commercial classes. During the prosperity of the war, many young people pursued studies in higher institutions and prepared themselves for the commercial life that was fast developing in Sweden. The commercial slump after the war threw many linguists and correspondents, office workers and typists out of employment. There was also an oversupply of engineers of various kinds. The problem of adjustment is demonstrated in the case of a young man from a family of sawmill workers at Sundsvall, who had himself received a fairly good education and became an office worker in Stockholm.[3] Here he obtained a good position as the head of an office department, but following the World War was laid off when it was found necessary to retrench expenses. After eighteen months of unemployment he came to the United States where he has been engaged as a painter and interior decorator. His brother was a painter in Sweden and he had worked with him there at times.

Among the recent industrial immigrants from Sweden was one from Dalsland, who belonged to the Swedish Sawmill Workers' Industrial Union. He described himself as a seasonal workman. He worked at various places, but longest at Billingfors where he was

[1] *Ibid.*, p. 73, Table 61.
[2] C. C. Schmidt, "Folkutbytet med främmande länder," in Koch, *op. cit.*, p. 140.
[3] Case studies of recent immigrants made by the author.

a helper at the canal locks at 80 öre (21 cents) an hour. He left Sweden at the age of twenty-two and came to a sister in St. Paul. He had borrowed the money for his trip at home on his father's security. "The foremost reason for my emigration," he wrote, "was naturally to make my little million, but I also wanted to see the much-talked-of America." He is at present employed in a furniture factory, making 60 to 65 cents an hour on piece work. Another workman came from Skaraborg County. He was born in the country on his father's farm, but the family moved to Tidaholm where he, his father, brother, and sister were all employed in the match factory. He also worked at the machine shops, with a wholesale firm in Skövde, and at a saw-blade factory in Lidköping. He came to America in 1923 because of the difficulty to get employment in Sweden. Here he has worked in a furniture factory, but recently as a machinist, and is satisfied with the prospects in that industry.

The school population in Sweden has been decreasing since 1921, with the decreasing families, especially among the industrial workers. There has been a decrease from 745,000 children in 1921 to 714,000 in 1925. The result has been an oversupply of teachers and a limitation of the number of students that will be received in the normal schools. Thus, a young man who came from a comfortable peasant's home in Dalsland had wanted to emigrate at the age of sixteen, but was dissuaded by his family. He then decided to enter the teaching profession and prepared himself for the examinations for entrance at the normal school in Gothenburg. He passed the examinations after two years, but, because of the great number of applicants, some 200 with only 50 to be admitted, he was unfortunate to fall into the group excluded. He made up his mind this time to go to America to a cousin. He was twenty-three years of age and had completed his military training. He is working in a furniture factory in Rockford.

Another young man from Skaraborg County, also raised on a farm, worked for two years as a hired man and then decided to enter the agricultural school at Svalöv to study dairying. For him military service disorganized his plans. He could remain there only six months before he was called to do his military duty at Karlsborg. "I served my country for 195 days at 50 öre (13 cents) a day, which was not enough for spending money, so that much of what I had saved also went the way of the world. There was never enough food when one was drilling and one always had an enormous appetite," he wrote. When he returned from camp, his place as the school had been filled. He had no money and had to seek employment. He finally succeeded after spending eight months at home, supported by his parents. He remained at his employment at 50 kronor ($15.00) a month from April until the fall, when he had to return to complete his military training for thirty days. Upon his second return he could find no employment although he advertised. A younger brother had applied for permission to emigrate to America. The older brother told his parents that if he did not get any work by Christmas he would accompany him. He sailed in March, 1926. He came to an aunt in Rockford. He borrowed the money to emigrate in Sweden, but paid it back after he had been here a year. During the first three years that he had been in the United States he worked as a machinist at the Mechanical Universal Joint Company, with the exception of three months when he was unemployed.

Some immigrants find the same employment in the United States that they had in Sweden. A young man from Skaraborg County from a laborer's home was employed in a glass factory in Sweden where his father was engaged as a painter. The son also worked as a painter. "As far as my home town is concerned," wrote the seventeen-year-old immigrant, "it was one of the most beautiful natural spots that you could find, situated on the shores of Lake Väner, with meadows bordering it, filled with flowers in the summer. But for me there was no future in that community." He came to some of his father's former friends in Rockford, Illinois, his ticket purchased by his father. Here he obtained work as a varnisher in a furniture factory. Among his reasons for emigrating he cited, with the economic, his dislike for military duty. Another instance was that of a son of a carpenter and furniture maker in Öland who found the economic conditions were not so good in a home with many children, so that he had to work even before he was confirmed. He worked for farmers for a while, but finally took up his father's occupation. His father died and he had to help support the family for some time. The wages were low in Öland for there was no union. He came to America in 1927, at the age of twenty-seven, and to relatives. His object in emigrating was economic; he wanted to be able to own his own home. He continued to be a carpenter in the United States and has improved his economic status.

It is difficult to decide to what extent compulsory military training plays a part in the recent emigration from Sweden. Some give it as one of the reasons for departure, but stress the economic situation as paramount. Thus, a young man from Småland from a farm home, who had worked as a farm hand and a lumberjack, gave his reasons for leaving his motherland as partly to escape military training and partly because he thought it would be easier to "get ahead" in the United States. He had a brother here. Others seemed to have enjoyed their military experience. A young man from Hälsingland, the son of a laborer, joined the navy at nineteen. While in the navy he met a friend who persuaded him to emigrate when their four-year service was over. An immigrant from Skåne, whose father had been a station-master on the railroad, became a cartographer for a coal-mine corporation. But after the war, the coal mine shut down more and more and he was finally discharged. It seemed impossible to find work anywhere. "Since I have completed my military training, the only reason for emigrating was to obtain a position." Some speak with enthusiasm of their experience in the army. The son of a tailor from Småland, who became an agricultural laborer stated, "I thought it would be easier to find work in America, which has been the case. I completed my military training in Sweden, which I do not regret for it was one of the happiest experiences of my life. I also wanted to see something of the world."

The desire to gain further experience in a trade or just the spirit of adventure is given by many as reason for emigrating. The son of a minister in Jönköping, who received a technical training at the Borås Technical School, became a demonstrator for the Gas Accumulator Corporation of Stockholm. From 1917 to 1920 he was sent to South America, so he decided to go to the United States and obtain further experience in various machine shops here. His philosophy is "the more experience you have, the better your opportunities of 'getting along' when the so-called 'hard times' come." A young man from Södermanland, whose home was on a good-sized farm, and whose parents also had a store, stated that he came to America just to see what it was like, to learn English, and to decide where the economic possibilities were the best. He had worked on the home farm most of the time, but for a while had been a lineman for the electric company and the telephone company.

Some have left a situation of unemployment in Sweden, only to find a similar situation in the United States. The latter immigrant stated that he had not been admitted to the Lineman's Union in the United States as yet, although he had sought admission. He is employed as a cabinet maker, but there is not much work and the wages are low.

Last year I worked only five days a week and now (in the spring of 1929) it is the same again and there will be perhaps less work. It is a great loss not to be able to work full time. I guess that there will be overproduction in the furniture industry, and that is the reason for the slack in work. If the industry were strongly organized, as in Sweden, it would be better for then there would be shorter hours and wages would be a little higher.

It was estimated in 1926 that for the next ten years Sweden would have a surplus of 9,000 people a year who would naturally emigrate. But, by 1936 the population of Sweden coming into working age would be stationary.[1] The restrictive policy of the United States, which now has cut the Swedish quota to 3,000, will do for Sweden what the country has long desired, decrease emigration. Although the exodus to Canada has somewhat increased since the restrictions made by the United States, it only amounts to several thousands a year. The experiments of settling Swedes in South America have not been very successful.

Some Swedish economists are rather pessimistic about the future of Sweden, and the Scandinavian countries as a whole. Professor Brisman thinks that all regions in Sweden suitable for cultivation were fully populated by 1880.[2] There has been little new land placed under the plow since that date and the rural population has decreased by 400,000. Further development of agriculture will be unprofitable. Sweden's natural resources have also been fully exploited.

[1] Conversation with C. C. Schmidt, Socialstyrelsen, summer, 1926.

[2] Extracts from a lecture given by Professor Sven Brisman, professor of political economy at Handelshögskolan, Stockholm, cited in Hilmer Key, *European Bankruptcy and Emigration* (London, 1924), pp. 126–27.

Even before the World War the population of Sweden had reached maximum figures of subsistence. With the growth of population and the surplus of 7 to 8 per thousand of births over deaths, Sweden is facing a surplus population problem. Key feels that with industrial unemployment gaining ground, extraordinary measures must be taken to stimulate the demand for labor, or the government will have to resort to something it has never done, to assist emigration on a considerable scale. He does not consider the much-discussed plan of internal colonization in Norrland as a solution of the situation. But the Swedish situation is not much different from that of most countries of Europe, nor that of the United States itself in the throes of the present economic crisis.

# BIBLIOGRAPHY

Source Material
American Government Documents
United States
Archives
U.S. Department of State, *Dispatches from Sweden*
Ellsworth to Buchanan, March 7, 1846, Vol. VII, No. 10
Schroeder to Webster, August 26, September 20, 1850, Vol. VIII, No. 13 and No. 16
Schroeder to Webster, June 29, 1851, Vol. VIII, No. 38
Schroeder to Cass, April 2, 1857, No. 185
Angell to Cass, January 11, 1859, Vol. VIII
Angell to Cass, June 2, 1858, Vol. VIII
Haldeman to Seward, July 4, 1861, Vol. X, No. 3
Haldeman to Seward, September 12, 1861, Vol. X, No. 7
Haldeman to Seward, November 18, 1862, Vol. X, No. 258
Haldeman to Seward, April 24, 1863, Vol. X, No. 28
Haldeman to Seward, May 17, 1864, Vol. X, No. 47
Haldeman to Seward, June 18, 1864, Vol. X, No. 9
Haldeman to Seward, July 2, 1864, Vol. X, No. 50
Campbell to Seward, April 25, 1865, Vol. XI, No. 16
Bartlett to Seward, February 3, 1868, Vol. XI, No. 11
C. C. Andrews to Fish, November 3, 1869, Vol. XI, No. 22
U.S. Department of State, *Instructions to Sweden, 1834-78*
Fish to C. C. Andrews, June 14, 1871, Vol. XIV, No. 74
Fish to C. C. Andrews, June 25, 1873, Vol. XIV
*U.S. Consular Letters, Stockholm, 1857-93*
Leas, consul, August 20, 1862
Tefft, consul, January 9, January 23, June 30, September 30, 1863
G. A. Tefft, consul, October 11, 1864
Perkins, consul, November 2, 1867
Perkins, consul, July 24, 1868
Elfwing, vice-consul, April 15, 1870
Elfwing, vice-consul, January 9, 1872
Elfwing, vice-consul, April 9, 1873
Elfwing, vice-consul, April 14, 1880
Elfwing, consul, September 12, 1888
*U.S. Consular Letters, Gothenburg, 1858-88*
Epping, consul, November 12, 1862

Thomas, consul, February 12, February 29, July 6, September 16, 1864

Oppenheim, consul, October 1, 1879

Cooper, consul, March 10, May 31, 1882

Cooper, consul, January 11, 1884

Cooper, consul, November 26, 1885

Documents

U.S. Department of Commerce, *Census of Agriculture, 1925*

U.S. Department of Commerce, *Statistical Abstract of U.S., 1922, 1925*

U.S. Department of Commerce, *Fourteenth Census of the United States, 1920, Population*

U.S. Department of Labor, *Annual Reports of the Commissioner General of Immigration*

U.S. Department of Labor, *History of Wages in the United States from Colonial Times to 1928*, Bulletin 499, Bureau of Labor Statistics

U.S. Senate, Committee on Agriculture, *Report on Immigration*, Senate Document No. 15, Thirty-eighth Congress, first session

Edward Young, *Special Report on Immigration, 1871*. Washington, 1871

American States

Iowa, *Report of Board of Immigration, 1872*

Louisiana, *Report of Commissioner of Emigration, January 1870*

Maine, *Report of the Board and Commission of Immigration, 1872*

Michigan, Governor J. J. Bagley's *Message, January 7, 1875*, Joint Legislative Documents, 1875

Michigan, *Reports of Immigration Commission, 1871, 1872*

Minnesota, Governor's Archives, MSS, Minnesota Historical Society

Letter from Western Emigration Agency, Chicago, to the governor, July 22, 1858

Letter from Western Emigration Agency, Chicago, to the governor, January 3, 1859, June 5, 1859

Letter from S.S. Hamilton, American Emigration Company, Chicago, to governor, July 9, 1870

Letter from John Schroeder, clerk of Immigration Commission of Minnesota to Governor Austin, Governor's Files, No. 608

*Life Story of Rosling Sven*

*Minnesota as a Home for Emigrants*, pamphlet. St. Paul, 1865

Minnesota, *Annual Report of Immigration Commission, 1867, 1872, 1881–82, 1885–86*

Missouri, *First Report of the Board of Immigration, 1865–66*

New York, *Annual Report of Commissioner of Emigration, December 31, 1869*

West Virginia, *Fifth Annual Report of Commissioner of Immigration,* Wheeling, 1868

Wisconsin, *Annual Reports of Commission of Emigration, 1853, 1854, 1872, 1873, 1875, 1880, 1882*

Sweden

*Emigrationsutredningen*

Gustav Sundbärg, "Betänkande i utvandringsfrågan." Stockholm, 1913

Nils Wohlin, "Utvandringslagstiftning," *Bilaga I.* Stockholm, 1908

"Utvandringsväsendet i Sverige," *Bilaga II.* Stockholm, 1909

"Mormonvärfningen i Sverige," *Bilaga III.* Stockholm, 1910

Gustav Sundbärg, "Den svenska och europeiska folköknings-och omflyttningsstatistiken," *Bilaga IV.* Stockholm, 1910

Gustav Sundbärg, "Ekonomisk-statistisk beskrifning öfver Sveriges olika landsdelar," *Bilaga V.* Stockholm, 1910

Per Stolpe, "Geografiska betingelser for näringslifvet," *Bilaga VI.* Stockholm, 1912

"Utvandrarnes egna uppgifter," *Bilaga VII.* Stockholm, 1908

"Bygdeundersökningar," *Bilaga VIII.* Stockholm, 1910

Carl Arvid Edin, "Fryksdals härad i Värmland." Stockholm, 1910

G. G. Magnusson, "Jösse härad i Värmland." Stockholm, 1908

Ernst Lundholm, "Vedbo och Nordmarks härader." Stockholm, 1908

Axel Brusewitz, "Sundals, Nordals och Valbo härader." Stockholm, 1909

Helge Nelson, "Öland." Stockholm, 1909

Nils Wohlin, "Den jordbruksidkande befolkningen i Sverige, 1751–1900," *Bilaga IX.* Stockholm, 1909

Nils Wohlin, "Faran af bondeklassens undergräfvande," *Bilaga X.* Stockholm, 1910

Nils Wohlin, "Torpare-, backstugu-och inhysesklasserna," *Bilga XI.* Stockholm, 1908

"Jordstyckningen," *Bilaga XII.* Stockholm, 1911

Gustav Sundbärg, "Allmänna ekonomiska data rörande Sverige," *Bilaga XIII.* Stockholm, 1912

Steffin, Bergholm, and Eckerbom, "Småbruksrörelsen å de brittiska öarna samt inre kolonisationen i Preussen och Förenta Staterna," *Bilaga XIV.* Stockholm, 1909

"Utdrag ur Utåltanden," *Bilaga XVII.* Stockholm, 1909

"Uttalanden af svenska vetenskapsmän," *Bilaga XVIII.* Stockholm, 1910

"Uttalanden rörande Sveriges industri, handel och sjöfart," *Bilaga XIX.* Stockholm, 1910

"Svenskarna i utlandet," *Bilaga XX.* Stockholm, 1911

J. Guinchard, *Sveriges land och folk,* 2 vols., Stockholm, 1915

Justitiedepartementet, *Jordkommissionens betänkande, del V*, "Redogörelse," av Fredrik Sandberg. Stockholm, 1922

*K. bfhde* "femårsberättelser"
Blekinge län, 1882
Elfsborgs län, 1851–55, 1856–60, 1865–70, 1875–80
Gefleborgs län, 1843–47, 1856–60
Gotlands län, 1860–65, 1866–70
Göteborg-och Bohus län, 1851–55
Hallands län, 1851–55, 1856–60
Jönköpings län, 1851–55, 1856–60
Kalmar län, 1856–60, 1861–65, 1866–70
Kristianstads län, 1851–55
Kronobergs län, 1851–55, 1866–70
Malmöhus län, 1851–55, 1856–60, 1866–70
Norrbottens län, 1856–60, 1866–70
Skaraborgs län, 1866–70
Stora Kopparbergs län, 1856–60
Värmlands län, 1856–60, 1866–70
Westernorrlands län, 1847–50, 1851–55, 1856–60
Westmanlands län, 1856–60
Örebro län, 1856–60, 1861–65, 1866–70
Östergötlands län, 1842–47, 1851–55, 1865–70, 1871–75, 1876–80, 1881–85
K. Jordbruksdepartementet, *Betänkande angående torpareklassens tillbakagång*. Stockholm, 1911
K. Socialstyrelsen, *Arbetartillgång, arbetstid och arbetslön inom Sveriges jordbruk år 1914*. Stockholm, 1916
K. Socialstyrelsen, *Kollektivavtal i Sverige, 1920–21*, Vol. I. Stockholm, 1921
K. Socialstyrelsen, *Lantarbetarnas arbets-och lönförhållande*. Stockholm, 1915
Statistiska Centralbyrån, *Statistisk årsbok för Sverige*. Stockholm, 1915, 1922, 1925, 1927, 1930
Gustav Sundbärg, *Sweden, Its People and Its Industries*, Stockholm, 1904
Sveriges officiella statistik, kommerskollegium
*Bergshantering*, 1913, 1915, 1920
*Industri*, 1925
*The Swedish Agricultural Labourer*. Stockholm, 1921
*The Sweden Year Book, 1926*
American Railroad Reports
Illinois Central Railroad, *Annual Reports of Land Commissioner, 1861, 1863*
Northern Pacific Railroad, *Annual Reports, 1882, 1883, 1887, 1888*
*Northern Pacific Railroad, Its Route, Resources, Progress, and Business,* issued by J. Cooke and Company. Philadelphia, 1871

American Newspapers

*Hemlandet* (Chicago), 1863–65

*The Home Missionary* (Boston), 1844, 1850

*The Minnesota Stats Tidning* (Minneapolis), 1877–79

*The Missionary Herald* (New York), 1838, 1839, 1842, 1853

*Chicago Daily Journal* (Chicago), 1850

Swedish Newspapers

*Aftonbladet* (Stockholm), 1839

*Amerika-Bladet* (Örebro), 1870

*Göteborgs Handels-och Sjöfarts Tidning* (Göteborg), 1868–79

*Nyare Helsingborgs Posten* (Hälsingborg), 1850–66

*Hudiksvalls Posten* (Hudiksvall), 1866–71

*Hudikswalls Weckoblad* (Hudiksvall), 1845–50

*Jönköpings Posten* (Jönköping), 1851–66

*Jönköpings Tidning* (Jönköping), 1841–68

*Lunds Weckoblad* (Lund), 1840

*Malmö Nya Allehanda* (Malmö), 1867–70

*Malmö Tidning* (Malmö), 1850

*Norrlands Posten* (Gävle), 1845–67

*Skånska Posten* (Kristianstad), 1840–71

*Svenska Dagbladet* (Stockholm), 1927

*Östgötha Correspondenten* (Linköping), 1849, 1878–83

Travelogues

Frederika Bremer, *Hemman i nya verlden*, 2 vols. Stcokholm, 1866

Samuel Laing, *A Tour of Sweden in 1838*. London, 1839

Anna Söderblom, *En Amerikaresa*. Stockholm, 1926

Memoirs

Hans Mattson, *Reminiscences*. Minneapolis, 1890

Gustav Unonius, *Minnen af en sjuttonårig vistelse i nordvestra Amerika*. Stockholm, 1862

Emigrant Guides

Carl Alex Adam von Schiele, *Några korta underrättelser om Amerika till upplysning och nytta för dem som ämna dit utflytta; samt emigrants forenings stadgar och förslager för en uttämnad utflyttning år 1841*. Stockholm, 1841

Theodore Schytte, *Vägledning för emigration, en kort framställing af utvandringens svårigheter och fördelar, jemte en skildring af de Skandinaviska koloniernas, politiska och religösa tillstand i Nordamerika, med ett bihang om de år 1847 utvandrade Erick Janssons anhängares sorliga öde*. Stockholm, 1849

*Underretninger om America, fornemmlingen de States, hvori udvandredi Normaend have nedsat sig, samlede af en emigrants forening i Stockholm, først udgivne paa Svensk af foreningens secretair og nu til deel i extract oversatte og nogle ketterser og tilloeg udgivne*. Skien, 1843

Miscellaneous

Richardson, *Messages and Papers of the Presidents*, 1789–1897, Vol. VI. Washington, 1897

Gustav Westring, *Sveriges rikes lag* (47th ed.). Stockholm, 1926

Secondary Sources

Gustav Aldén, *Svenska-statskunskap, Medborgarens bok*, Vol. I. Stockholm, 1924

Gustav Aldén, *Svensk kommunalkunskap, Medborgarens bok*, Vol. II. Stockholm, 1926

A. T. Andreas, *History of Chicago*. Chicago, 1884

Paul Bergholm, *Nationalföreningen mot emigrationen, 1907–17*. Stockholm, 1917

Alfred Bergin, *Femtio års minnen från Lindsborg*

Johan Bergman, *Nykterhets rörelsens världshistoria*. Norrköping, 1900

Axel Brusewitz och Sven Tunberg, *Statens domäner och deras förvaltning*, Broschyrer utgifna af nationalföreningen mot emigrationen, Vol. II. Stockholm, 1908

Gustav Cassel, *Utvecklingslinjer i Svenska skattelagstiftning, Svensk politik*, Föreningen Heindals politiska små skrifter. Uppsala, 1908

J. Byström, *En frikyrklig banbrytare*. Stockholm, 1911

G. Ekman, *Den inre missionens historia*. Stockholm, 1896

V. Ekstrand, *Svenska landtmätare, 1862–1900*. Stockholm, 1900

Henry Pratt Fairchild, *Immigration*. New York, 1925

Charles G. Fenwick, *International Law*. New York, 1924

A. Fraser-MacDonald, *Our Ocean Railways, or the Rise, Progress and Development of Ocean Steam-Navigation*. London, 1893

Henry Fry, *The History of North Atlantic Steam Navigation*. London, 1896

Carl Grimberg, *Svenska folkets underbara öden*, Vol. VI. Stockholm, 1922

Sigfrid Hansson, *Den Svenska fackföreningsrörelsen*. Stockholm, 1927

Eli Heckscher, *Bidrag till Sveriges ekonomiska och sociala historia under och efter världskriget*. Stockholm, 1926

Karl Hildebrand and Axel Fredenholm, *Svenskarna i Amerika*. Stockholm, 1924

Emil Hildebrand and Ludwig Stavenow, *Sveriges historia till våra dagar*,

G. Wittrock, *Gustav II Aldoph*, Vol. VI. Stockholm, 1927

Sam Clason, *Karl XIII och Karl XIV Johan*, Vol. XI. Stockholm, 1925

Carl Hallendorff, *Oskar I och Karl XV*, Vol. XII. Stockholm, 1923

S. J. Boëthius, *Oskar II*, Vol. XIII. Stockholm, 1925

Karl Hildebrand, *Gustav V*, Vol. XIV. Stockholm, 1926

Hultgren, *Den Skånska frälsebondefrågan*. 1870, Hälsingborg, 1870

Helmer Key, *European Bankruptcy and Emigration*. London, 1924

G. H. von Koch, *Social handbok*. Stockholm, 1925

John Lindberg, *The Background of Swedish Emigration*. Minneapolis, 1930

G. Gerhard Magnusson, *Social-Demokratien i Sverige*, 3 vols. Stockholm, 1920–24

Adrian Molin, *Hur Svensk-Amerikanerna bo*, Broschyrer utgv. af nationalföreningen mot emigrationen, No. 5. Stockholm, 1912

Adrian Molin, *Några drag af kolonisationen i Canada*, Broschyrer utgv. af nationalföreningen mot emigration, No. 6. Stockholm, 1913

Adrian Molin, *Till saken, vidräkning och uppslag i jordfrågan*, Uppsala, 1924

*Mälare provinsernas egnahemsaktiebolag, 1910–20*. Stockholm, 1920

A. H. Newman, *A Manual of Church History*. Philadelphia, 1914

N. J. Nordström, *Den frikyrkliga-och statskyrko-problemet*. Stockholm, 1922

Eric Norelius, *De svenska luteriska församlingarnas och svenskarnes historia i Amerika*. Rock Island, Illinois, 1890

Tobias Norlind, *Svenska allmogens liv*. Stockholm, 1925

F. A. Ogg, *Economic Development of Modern Europe*. New York, 1918

Ernest Olson, *History of the Swedes of Illinois*, Vol. I. Chicago, 1908

E. J. Schütz, *Om skifte af jord i Sverige*. Stockholm, 1890

Wilson Pate Shortridge, *The Transition of a Typical Frontier*. Minneapolis, 1919

Ernest Skarstedt, *Svensk-Amerikanska folket i helg och söcken*. Stockholm, 1917

A. E. Strand, *A History of Swedish Americans in Minnesota*

Samuel Sugenheim, *Geschichte der Aufhebung der Leibeigenschaft und Hörigkeiten in Europa*. St. Petersburg, 1861

*Svenska industrien vid kvartsekelskiftet*. Stockholm, 1925

Gabriel Thulin, *Om mantalet*. Stockholm, 1890

Karl Åmark, *Utvandring och näringsliv i Norrland*, Brochyrer utgv. af nationalföreningen mot emigrationen, No. 4. Stockholm, 1912

Periodicals

Joseph Alexis, "Swedes in Nebraska," *Nebraska State Historical Society*, Vol. 19

"Arbetsfreden," *Svensk Tidskrift*, No. 3. Stockholm, 1928

George T. Flom, "Early Swedish Immigration to Iowa," *Iowa Journal of History and Politics*, October, 1905

Theodore C. Blegen, "The Competition of the Northwestern States for Immigrants," *Wisconsin Magazine of History*, Vol. III, No. 1 (1919)

"Kring Regeringskrisen," *Svensk Tidskrift*, Vol. XVI, No. 5 (1926)

Gustav Möller, "Ett fall och en uppståndelse," *Tiden*, June, 1926

G. H. Paulsen, "Svensk statskolonasjonen," *Ny Jord*. Olso. 1925

George M. Stephenson, "Hemlandet Letters," *Swedish Historical Society Year Book, 1922–23*

# APPENDIX

## TABLE I

### Swedish Emigration and Immigration, 1851–1925*

| Counties | 1851–60 | 1861–70 | 1871–80 | 1881–90 | 1891–1900 | 1901–10 | 1911–20 | 1921–25 |
|---|---|---|---|---|---|---|---|---|
| a) Emigration: | | | | | | | | |
| Stockholm City... | 674 | 5,179 | 6,294 | 18,361 | 17,197 | 16,700 | 10,420 | 5,755 |
| Stockholm County | 74 | 358 | 872 | 3,283 | 2,594 | 3,350 | 2,570 | 1,675 |
| Uppsala.......... | 4 | 264 | 823 | 2,527 | 1,313 | 1,540 | 680 | 425 |
| Södermanland.... | 23 | 659 | 1,316 | 4,555 | 2,936 | 2,900 | 1,250 | 725 |
| Östergötland...... | 2,012 | 9,527 | 10,725 | 24,489 | 12,029 | 10,920 | 3,690 | 1,935 |
| Jönköping........ | 2,441 | 11,890 | 9,153 | 23,690 | 12,619 | 11,100 | 4,330 | 2,990 |
| Kronoberg....... | 1,381 | 7,454 | 8,909 | 20,537 | 12,456 | 10,670 | 4,560 | 2,610 |
| Kalmar.......... | 501 | 9,515 | 8,323 | 24,441 | 16,681 | 15,950 | 6,950 | 4,375 |
| Gotland.......... | 55 | 727 | 1,565 | 4,689 | 2,825 | 2,230 | 780 | 310 |
| Blekinge......... | 1,117 | 2,570 | 4,202 | 11,513 | 10,483 | 9,300 | 4,460 | 2,670 |
| Kristianstad...... | 1,729 | 9,752 | 12,189 | 23,137 | 13,766 | 10,180 | 5,110 | 2,920 |
| Malmöhus........ | 437 | 10,079 | 18,576 | 34,594 | 18,736 | 18,190 | 12,720 | 5,260 |
| Halland.......... | 1,303 | 3,405 | 7,313 | 17,717 | 12,341 | 11,820 | 5,930 | 2,980 |
| Göteborg o. Bohus | 468 | 5,505 | 9,853 | 18,081 | 16,521 | 16,540 | 9,250 | 5,565 |
| Älvsborg......... | 1,359 | 9,383 | 11,028 | 31,915 | 20,091 | 17,940 | 7,720 | 4,145 |
| Skaraborg........ | 702 | 5,590 | 6,521 | 22,513 | 12,092 | 9,840 | 3,090 | 1,535 |
| Värmland........ | 330 | 10,579 | 12,514 | 32,032 | 20,434 | 21,350 | 9,960 | 6,235 |
| Örebro.......... | 407 | 3,670 | 5,074 | 14,386 | 7,428 | 7,680 | 2,420 | 2,255 |
| Västmanland..... | 95 | 997 | 1,862 | 4,853 | 2,537 | 2,520 | 1,180 | 1,175 |
| Kopparberg...... | 171 | 4,831 | 4,983 | 12,353 | 5,726 | 10,340 | 3,840 | 4,345 |
| Gävleborg........ | 1,239 | 5,764 | 2,991 | 10,210 | 6,454 | 12,020 | 4,250 | 2,775 |
| Västernorrland.... | 75 | 1,327 | 1,781 | 6,041 | 10,381 | 12,360 | 4,770 | 3,265 |
| Jämtland......... | 117 | 1,338 | 1,036 | 4,998 | 4,733 | 8,150 | 2,520 | 2,225 |
| Västerbotten...... | ...... | 686 | 626 | 2,186 | 2,121 | 5,720 | 2,410 | 1,375 |
| Norrbotten....... | 186 | 1,398 | 1,740 | 3,300 | 2,278 | 8,360 | 3,510 | 3,070 |
| Total........ | 16,900 | 122,447 | 150,269 | 376,401 | 246,772 | 257,670 | 118,370 | 72,605 |

*Statistics for the years 1851-1900 were taken from Table 44, "Bygdestatistik," *Emigrationsutredningens bilaga V*, p. 94*. For the years 1900-1925, *Statistisk årsbok för Sverige, 1927*, Table 66, p. 75

497

TABLE I—*Continued*

| Counties | 1851–60 | 1861–70 | 1871–80 | 1891–90 | 1891–1900 | 1901–10 | 1911–20 | 1921–25 |
|---|---|---|---|---|---|---|---|---|
| *b*) Immigration: | | | | | | | | |
| Stockholm City... | | | 3,233 | 4,985 | 7,085 | 10,960 | 12,610 | 5,255 |
| Stockholm County | | | 295 | 464 | 953 | 1,720 | 2,380 | 1,085 |
| Uppsala. | | | 172 | 208 | 304 | 300 | 400 | 255 |
| Södermanland... | | | 240 | 427 | 879 | 890 | 960 | 325 |
| Östergötland. | | | 805 | 1,392 | 2,831 | 2,550 | 1,930 | 800 |
| Jönköping. | | | 687 | 1,250 | 2,908 | 2,490 | 2,040 | 865 |
| Kronoberg. | | | 1,322 | 1,760 | 3,398 | 3,290 | 2,220 | 1,030 |
| Kalmar. | | | 848 | 1,764 | 4,598 | 4,500 | 3,450 | 1,495 |
| Gotland. | | | 220 | 504 | 1,178 | 980 | 490 | 145 |
| Blekinge. | | | 717 | 1,854 | 3,584 | 3,500 | 2,220 | 845 |
| Kristianstad. | | | 2,718 | 3,248 | 4,724 | 3,980 | 3,010 | 1,240 |
| Malmöhus. | | | 7,810 | 9,440 | 8,980 | 9,070 | 8,030 | 3,240 |
| Halland. | | | 1,263 | 2,159 | 4,719 | 4,140 | 2,970 | 1,115 |
| Göteborg o. Bohus | | | 2,230 | 4,528 | 7,108 | 8,620 | 6,360 | 3,445 |
| Älvsborg. | | | 1,271 | 3,007 | 6,516 | 6,380 | 4,820 | 2,070 |
| Skaraborg. | | | 433 | 1,023 | 2,600 | 2,550 | 1,710 | 685 |
| Värmland. | | | 2,096 | 3,247 | 5,806 | 6,690 | 5,750 | 2,490 |
| Örebro. | | | 395 | 1,014 | 1,879 | 1,830 | 1,550 | 740 |
| Västmanland. | | | 132 | 464 | 630 | 680 | 910 | 335 |
| Kopparberg. | | | 347 | 850 | 1,671 | 1,570 | 1,840 | 835 |
| Gävleborg. | | | 547 | 873 | 1,366 | 1,680 | 1,730 | 670 |
| Västernorrland. | | | 775 | 1,132 | 2,152 | 2,340 | 3,010 | 880 |
| Jämtland. | | | 392 | 1,116 | 993 | 1,150 | 1,180 | 470 |
| Västerbotten. | | | 155 | 215 | 482 | 740 | 1,150 | 390 |
| Norrbotten. | | | 475 | 677 | 1,466 | 1,820 | 2,830 | 920 |
| Total. | | | 29,578 | 47,601 | 78,810 | 83,740 | 75,550 | 31,675 |

## TABLE II

### Swedish Exchange of Population with the United States, by Counties*

| Counties | 1851–60 | 1861–70 | 1871–80 | 1881–90 | 1891–1900 | 1901–10 | Total |
|---|---|---|---|---|---|---|---|
| **Emigrants:** | | | | | | | |
| Stockholm City | 661 | 2,354 | 2,913 | 13,739 | 12,433 | 11,751 | 43,851 |
| Stockholm County | 41 | 234 | 602 | 2,814 | 1,973 | 2,533 | 8,197 |
| Uppsala | 4 | 207 | 612 | 2,280 | 1,153 | 1,356 | 5,612 |
| Södermanland | 14 | 559 | 1,123 | 4,250 | 2,522 | 2,579 | 11,047 |
| Östergötland | 1,929 | 9,219 | 10,039 | 23,731 | 11,171 | 10,087 | 66,176 |
| Jönköping | 2,349 | 11,514 | 8,584 | 23,136 | 11,837 | 10,525 | 67,945 |
| Kronoberg | 1,381 | 5,552 | 6,525 | 17,404 | 9,840 | 8,777 | 49,479 |
| Kalmar | 501 | 8,219 | 6,990 | 22,900 | 15,426 | 15,255 | 69,291 |
| Gotland | 50 | 613 | 1,354 | 4,484 | 2,702 | 2,146 | 11,349 |
| Blekinge | 1,026 | 1,460 | 2,447 | 7,953 | 7,122 | 6,897 | 26,905 |
| Kristianstad | 1,729 | 6,334 | 7,428 | 18,345 | 10,776 | 8,476 | 53,088 |
| Malmöhus | 284 | 2,981 | 6,691 | 21,974 | 11,287 | 11,844 | 55,061 |
| Halland | 357 | 2,021 | 5,538 | 16,429 | 11,247 | 10,706 | 46,298 |
| Göteborg o. Bohus | 463 | 1,190 | 2,798 | 11,679 | 10,711 | 12,014 | 38,855 |
| Älvsborg | 1,310 | 6,247 | 6,515 | 27,866 | 16,185 | 15,421 | 73,544 |
| Skaraborg | 673 | 5,352 | 5,854 | 21,926 | 11,532 | 9,465 | 54,802 |
| Värmland | 166 | 7,126 | 7,666 | 28,084 | 15,746 | 18,786 | 77,574 |
| Örebro | 377 | 3,433 | 4,702 | 13,982 | 6,966 | 7,206 | 36,666 |
| Västmanland | 72 | 894 | 1,685 | 4,562 | 2,175 | 2,273 | 11,661 |
| Kopparberg | 118 | 4,756 | 4,708 | 12,105 | 5,346 | 9,819 | 36,852 |
| Gävleborg | 1,190 | 5,476 | 2,574 | 9,835 | 5,843 | 11,140 | 36,058 |
| Västernorrland | 75 | 1,181 | 1,498 | 5,484 | 8,912 | 10,983 | 28,133 |
| Jämtland | 93 | 1,138 | 886 | 4,567 | 3,990 | 6,938 | 17,612 |
| Västerbotten | | 393 | 383 | 2,044 | 1,976 | 5,092 | 9,888 |
| Norrbotten | 2 | 278 | 1,054 | 2,712 | 1,653 | 7,180 | 12,879 |
| Total | 14,865 | 88,731 | 101,169 | 324,285 | 200,524 | 219,249 | 948,823 |
| **Immigrants:** | | | | | | | |
| Stockholm City | | | 273 | 1,086 | 2,856 | 2,599 | 6,814 |
| Stockholm County | | | 120 | 165 | 502 | 617 | 1,404 |
| Uppsala | | | 40 | 136 | 202 | 181 | 559 |
| Södermanland | | | 107 | 254 | 621 | 610 | 1,592 |
| Östergötland | | | 458 | 986 | 2,292 | 1,854 | 5,590 |
| Jönköping | | | 442 | 999 | 2,379 | 2,004 | 5,824 |
| Kronoberg | | | 217 | 646 | 1,898 | 1,989 | 4,750 |
| Kalmar | | | 437 | 1,275 | 3,856 | 3,781 | 9,349 |
| Gotland | | | 153 | 436 | 1,088 | 906 | 2,583 |
| Blekinge | | | 158 | 515 | 1,640 | 1,680 | 3,993 |
| Kristianstad | | | 553 | 1,187 | 2,641 | 2,400 | 6,781 |
| Malmöhus | | | 513 | 1,456 | 2,673 | 2,493 | 7,135 |
| Halland | | | 508 | 1,439 | 3,713 | 2,930 | 8,590 |
| Göteborg o. Bohus | | | 237 | 965 | 3,087 | 3,122 | 7,411 |
| Älvsborg | | | 462 | 1,922 | 4,987 | 3,966 | 11,337 |
| Skaraborg | | | 259 | 871 | 2,369 | 2,212 | 5,711 |
| Värmland | | | 465 | 1,547 | 3,750 | 3,503 | 9,265 |
| Örebro | | | 227 | 818 | 1,618 | 1,381 | 4,044 |
| Västmanland | | | 45 | 244 | 483 | 440 | 1,212 |
| Kopparberg | | | 160 | 637 | 1,398 | 1,199 | 3,394 |

* Before 1881 the statistics are for America. Immigrants for 1871–80 are based on the figures for 1875–80 ("Svenskarna i utlandet," *Emigrationsutredningen bilaga* XX, p. 112, Table 13).

TABLE II—*Continued*

| Counties | 1851–60 | 1861–70 | 1871–80 | 1881–90 | 1891–1900 | 1901–10 | Total |
|---|---|---|---|---|---|---|---|
| Gävleborg | | | 127 | 465 | 985 | 1,138 | 2,715 |
| Västernorrland | | | 43 | 188 | 791 | 1,074 | 2,096 |
| Jämtland | | | 68 | 154 | 381 | 629 | 1,232 |
| Västerbotten | | | 23 | 124 | 387 | 567 | 1,101 |
| Norrbotten | | | 57 | 251 | 541 | 754 | 1,603 |
| Total | | | 6,152 | 18,766 | 47,138 | 44,029 | 116,085 |

TABLE III

SWEDISH EMIGRATION AND IMMIGRATION, BY SEX AND FAMILY STATUS*

| YEAR | TOTAL | SEX | | MARRIED | | CHILDREN 0–15 YEARS | ADULTS, UNMARRIED | |
|---|---|---|---|---|---|---|---|---|
| | | Men | Women | Men | Women | | Men | Women |
| Emigrants to the United States: | | | | | | | | |
| 1861–70 | 88,731 | 51,507 | 37,224 | 11,291 | 11,475 | 24,969 | 27,445 | 13,551 |
| 1871–80 | 101,169 | 57,492 | 43,677 | 10,521 | 10,506 | 21,688 | 35,917 | 22,537 |
| 1881–90 | 324,285 | 182,449 | 141,836 | 33,242 | 27,617 | 58,826 | 119,639 | 84,961 |
| 1891–1900 | 200,524 | 104,815 | 95,709 | 16,220 | 13,264 | 28,443 | 74,471 | 68,126 |
| 1901–10 | 219,249 | 127,657 | 91,592 | 17,575 | 13,156 | 26,066 | 96,868 | 65,584 |
| Total | 933,958 | 523,920 | 410,038 | 88,849 | 76,018 | 159,992 | 354,340 | 254,759 |
| Immigrants from the United States: | | | | | | | | |
| 1875–80 | 3,691 | 2,588 | 1,103 | 523 | 440 | 551 | 1,765 | 412 |
| 1881–90 | 18,766 | 13,308 | 5,458 | 3,624 | 1,789 | 2,477 | 8,466 | 2,410 |
| 1891–1900 | 47,138 | 29,851 | 17,287 | 8,930 | 4,808 | 6,620 | 17,615 | 9,165 |
| 1901–10 | 44,029 | 25,823 | 18,206 | 6,823 | 4,498 | 5,798 | 16,147 | 10,763 |
| Total | 113,624 | 71,570 | 42,054 | 19,900 | 11,535 | 15,446 | 43,993 | 22,750 |

* The statistics for 1861 t (1910 were taken from Table 14, "Svenskarna i utlandet," *Emigrations-utredningens bilaga XX*, p. 114.

## TABLE IV

### SWEDISH EMIGRANTS AND IMMIGRANTS, BY AGE*

| ANNUAL AVERAGE | AGE | | | | | | | | | |
|---|---|---|---|---|---|---|---|---|---|---|
| | 0–5 | 5–10 | 10–15 | 15–20 | 20–25 | 25–30 | 30–40 | 40–50 | 50–60 | 60– |
| **Emigrants:** | | | | | | | | | | |
| 1861–70.......... | 1,140 | 1,002 | 745 | 1,385 | 2,478 | 2,024 | 2,042 | 925 | 354 | 150 |
| 1871–80.......... | 1,081 | 933 | 784 | 2,108 | 3,827 | 2,659 | 2,219 | 817 | 397 | 202 |
| 1881–90.......... | 2,627 | 2,193 | 1,770 | 6,833 | 9,786 | 6,068 | 4,940 | 1,867 | 972 | 584 |
| 1891–1900........ | 1,259 | 1,262 | 1,135 | 5,556 | 6,692 | 3,498 | 3,145 | 1,113 | 583 | 434 |
| 1901–10.......... | 1,319 | 1,117 | 937 | 6,517 | 6,896 | 3,832 | 3,041 | 1,171 | 505 | 432 |
| 1911–20.......... | 607 | 639 | 541 | 3,054 | 2,482 | 1,584 | 1,633 | 721 | 348 | 228 |
| 1921–25.......... | 667 | 564 | 431 | 2,446 | 3,532 | 2,902 | 2,377 | 951 | 373 | 278 |
| **Immigrants:** | | | | | | | | | | |
| 1881–90.......... | 429 | 276 | 152 | 328 | 930 | 971 | 1,057 | 375 | 151 | 91 |
| 1891–1900........ | 670 | 484 | 266 | 492 | 1,268 | 1,469 | 2,008 | 737 | 305 | 182 |
| 1901–10.......... | 700 | 574 | 335 | 593 | 1,366 | 1,491 | 1,922 | 888 | 345 | 228 |
| 1911–20.......... | 529 | 483 | 303 | 441 | 1,078 | 1,273 | 1,900 | 869 | 405 | 274 |
| 1921–25.......... | 462 | 381 | 238 | 358 | 844 | 1,005 | 1,533 | 789 | 407 | 318 |

* *Statistisk årsbok för Sverige, 1927*, p. 74, Tables 63 and 64.

## TABLE V

### SWEDISH EMIGRANTS, DIVIDED INTO OCCUPATIONS*

| Year | Total | Agriculture | Crofters and Cotters | Industry | Laborers in General | Commerce | Seamen | Servants | Others and Unknown |
|---|---|---|---|---|---|---|---|---|---|
| 1851–60... | 16,900 | 5,888 | 713 | 2,045 | ...... | 170 | 93 | 4,883 | 3,108 |
| 1861–70... | 122,447 | 39,335 | 6,062 | 18,661 | 9,447 | 1,185 | 1,046 | 38,096 | 8,615 |
| 1871–80... | 150,269 | 31,500 | 4,603 | 24,845 | 24,202 | 1,978 | 2,236 | 50,557 | 10,348 |
| 1881–90... | 376,401 | 90,462 | 5,689 | 50,629 | 67,045 | 4,668 | 5,211 | 104,369 | 48,328 |
| 1891–1900. | 246,772 | 54,533 | 2,312 | 37,980 | 69,932 | 4,742 | 3,673 | 54,012 | 19,588 |
| 1901–8.... | 207,859 | 62,449 | 1,998 | 47,733 | 48,380 | 5,794 | 3,141 | 26,508 | 11,856 |

| Year | Total | Agriculture and By-products | Industry | Commerce and Communications | Professions and Services | Servants | Others and Unknown |
|---|---|---|---|---|---|---|---|
| 1911–15......... | 78,930 | 25,650 | 25,025 | 6,210 | 2,090 | 8,625 | 11,330 |
| 1916–20......... | 39,445 | 9,190 | 13,230 | 3,540 | 1,445 | 6,780 | 5,260 |
| 1921–25......... | 72,605 | 22,155 | 23,615 | 7,835 | 2,205 | 6,380 | 10,415 |

* For the years 1891–1902 a considerable number of sons and daughters of peasants are grouped under "Laborers in General," otherwise they appear under "Agriculture." Miners are included under "Industry," also artists, engineers, and contractors. Under "Agriculture and By-products" have been grouped the lumber industry, 1911–25. For the statistics for 1911–25 (*Statistisk årsbok för Sverige, 1927*, p. 73, Table 62). The early figures were found in Table 96, Sundbärg, "Utvandringsstatistik," *Emigrationsutredningens bilaga IV*, p. 236.

## TABLE VI

### Swedish Emigrants and Immigrants, According to Countries, 1861–1925*

| Annual Average | Finland | | Norway | | Denmark and Iceland | | Great Britain and Ireland | | Germany | | Austria | | France | | Italy | |
|---|---|---|---|---|---|---|---|---|---|---|---|---|---|---|---|---|
| | Emigrant | Immigrant | Emigrant | Immigrant | Emigrant | Immigrant | Emigrant | Immigrant | Emigrant | Immigrant | Emigrant | Immigrant | Emigrant | Immigrant | Emigrant | Immigrant |
| 1861–70 | 207 | .... | 1,055 | .... | 1,125 | .... | 44 | .... | 486 | .... | .... | .... | 15 | .... | .... | .... |
| 1871–80 | 407 | .... | 1,634 | .... | 1,891 | .... | 107 | .... | 708 | .... | .... | .... | 28 | .... | .... | .... |
| 1881–90 | 327 | 337 | 1,347 | 631 | 2,349 | 1,244 | 173 | 70 | 555 | 418 | 5 | 9 | 42 | 26 | 4 | 4 |
| 1891–1900 | 333 | 434 | 1,575 | 738 | 1,601 | 1,126 | 156 | 92 | 429 | 496 | 21 | 35 | 36 | 31 | 5 | 26 |
| 1901–10 | 319 | 667 | 995 | 1,182 | 1,191 | 958 | 163 | 122 | 475 | 561 | 49 | 73 | 42 | 38 | 35 | 51 |
| 1911–20 | 245 | 659 | 1,200 | 825 | 1,127 | 786 | 99 | 107 | 357 | 721 | 48 | 81 | 45 | 56 | 15 | 20 |
| 1921–25 | 286 | 437 | 816 | 963 | 730 | 620 | 83 | 97 | 440 | 776 | 45 | 97 | 86 | 56 | 21 | 32 |

| Annual Average | Esthonia and Latvia | | Poland and Lithuania | | Russia and Ukrainia | | Total for Europe | | United States | | Canada | | Other Parts of America | |
|---|---|---|---|---|---|---|---|---|---|---|---|---|---|---|
| | Emigrant | Immigrant | Emigrant | Immigrant | Emigrant | Immigrant | Emigrant | Immigrant | Emigrant | Immigrant | Emigrant | Immigrant | Emigrant | Immigrant |
| 1861–70 | | | | | | | 2,933 | .... | 8,873 | .... | | | | |
| 1871–80 | | | | | | | 4,777 | .... | 10,117 | .... | | | 3 | .... |
| 1881–90 | | | | | 63 | 87 | 4,889 | 2,840 | 32,429 | 1,877 | 5 | | 127 | 12 |
| 1891–1900 | | | | | 46 | 68 | 4,226 | 3,069 | 20,052 | 4,714 | 48 | 3 | 230 | 40 |
| 1901–10 | | | | | 54 | 255 | 3,363 | 3,943 | 21,925 | 4,403 | 315 | 20 | 67 | 23 |
| 1911–20 | 5 | 9 | 5 | 14 | 56 | 305 | 3,235 | 3,637 | 8,154 | 3,715 | 297 | 68 | 66 | 67 |
| 1921–25 | 29 | 32 | 36 | 35 | 14 | 119 | 2,633 | 3,320 | 10,901 | 2,809 | 784 | 95 | 57 | 28 |

| Annual Average | Other Countries | | Unknown | | Total for Countries not in Europe | |
|---|---|---|---|---|---|---|
| | Emigrant | Immigrant | Emigrant | Immigrant | Emigrant | Immigrant |
| 1861–70 | 10 | ......... | 429 | ......... | 9,312 | ......... |
| 1871–80 | 82 | ......... | 48 | ......... | 10,250 | ......... |
| 1881–90 | 161 | 22 | 29 | 9 | 32,751 | 1,920 |
| 1891–1900 | 117 | 53 | 4 | 2 | 20,451 | 4,812 |
| 1901–10 | 97 | 53 | ......... | ......... | 22,404 | 4,499 |
| 1911–20 | 85 | 68 | ......... | ......... | 8,602 | 3,918 |
| 1921–25 | 146 | 83 | ......... | ......... | 11,888 | 3,015 |

* The statistics for 1861–80 for Finland include Finland and Russia. The statistics for 1861–70 for Germany include Germany and Holland, for 1871–80 for Germany, Holland, and Belgium. The statistics for Austria before 1919 are for Austro-Hungary, since 1919 for Austria, Czechoslovakia, and Hungary. The statistics for 1861–80 for France include France, Switzerland, and Italy. The statistics for the United States for 1861–70 include all of America, those for 1871–80 are for North America (*Statistisk årsbok för Sverige, 1927*, p. 73, Table 61).

## TABLE VII

MARKET PRICE OF FARM PRODUCTS IN SWEDEN, 1836–1925, IN KRONOR*

| ANNUAL AVERAGE | PER HECTOLITER | | | | | 100 KILOGRAMS | | BUTTER IN KILO-GRAMS |
|---|---|---|---|---|---|---|---|---|
| | Wheat | Rye | Barley | Oats | Peas | Hay | Straw | |
| 1836–40........ | 10.63 | 7.93 | 6.19 | 3.59 | 8.55 | ...... | ...... | 0.91 |
| 1841–45........ | 11.07 | 8.60 | 5.65 | 2.99 | 8.53 | ...... | ...... | 0.92 |
| 1846–50........ | 10.80 | 8.06 | 6.30 | 3.48 | 8.62 | ...... | ...... | 0.98 |
| 1851–55........ | 13.77 | 10.11 | 7.69 | 4.49 | 10.21 | ...... | ...... | 1.10 |
| 1856–60........ | 14.16 | 9.33 | 8.10 | 4.90 | 11.45 | ...... | ...... | 1.39 |
| 1861–65........ | 12.23 | 9.09 | 7.26 | 4.13 | 10.35 | ...... | ...... | 1.27 |
| 1866–70........ | 14.03 | 10.55 | 8.60 | 4.96 | 12.35 | ...... | ...... | 1.30 |
| 1871–75........ | 14.50 | 10.29 | 8.94 | 5.43 | 12.65 | 6.09 | 1.98 | 1.57 |
| 1876–80........ | 13.26 | 9.66 | 8.50 | 5.14 | 11.92 | 6.48 | 2.59 | 1.59 |
| 1881–85........ | 11.87 | 8.92 | 7.54 | 4.52 | 11.57 | 5.62 | 2.37 | 1.62 |
| 1886–90........ | 9.92 | 7.23 | 6.53 | 3.83 | 9.86 | 5.49 | 2.20 | 1.49 |
| 1891–95........ | 9.59 | 8.07 | 6.97 | 4.22 | 10.08 | 4.85 | 1.97 | 1.58 |
| 1896–1900...... | 10.82 | 8.44 | 7.58 | 4.38 | 10.66 | 5.02 | 2.01 | 1.66 |
| 1901–1905...... | 10.59 | 8.68 | 7.75 | 4.87 | 12.39 | 6.04 | 2.38 | 1.79 |
| 1906–10........ | 11.63 | 9.38 | 8.26 | 5.08 | 12.89 | 5.24 | 2.27 | 1.87 |
| 1911–15........ | 13.16 | 11.36 | 9.78 | 6.55 | 16.86 | 6.97 | 2.98 | 2.11 |
| 1916–20........ | 26.36 | 22.46 | 18.36 | 12.30 | 35.89 | 15.62 | 5.88 | 4.89 |
| 1921–25........ | 15.43 | 13.81 | 11.66 | 7.51 | 23.21 | 8.45 | 3.46 | 3.59 |

* *Statistisk årsbok för Sverige, 1927*, p. 93, Table 89.

TABLE VIII

SWEDISH STOCK IN THE UNITED STATES, BY NATIVITY AND PARENTAGE,
BY STATES, 1920*

| STATE | TOTAL SWEDISH STOCK | BORN IN SWEDEN | NATIVE BORN OF SWEDISH OR MIXED PARENTAGE | | | |
|---|---|---|---|---|---|---|
| | | | Total | Both Parents Swedish | Father Swedish | Mother Swedish |
| Maine | 4,668 | 2,075 | 2,593 | 1,538 | 592 | 463 |
| New Hampshire | 3,826 | 1,916 | 1,910 | 1,387 | 241 | 282 |
| Vermont | 2,377 | 1,155 | 1,222 | 947 | 132 | 143 |
| Massachusetts | 75,927 | 38,366 | 37,561 | 30,921 | 3,322 | 3,318 |
| Rhode Island | 13,571 | 6,588 | 6,983 | 5,842 | 522 | 619 |
| Connecticut | 37,733 | 17,763 | 19,970 | 16,737 | 1,675 | 1,558 |
| New York | 99,069 | 53,770 | 45,299 | 34,506 | 6,062 | 4,731 |
| New Jersey | 21,690 | 10,850 | 10,840 | 7,681 | 1,745 | 1,414 |
| Pennsylvania | 49,977 | 20,020 | 29,957 | 22,048 | 5,186 | 2,723 |
| Ohio | 16,505 | 7,335 | 9,170 | 6,549 | 1,728 | 893 |
| Indiana | 12,685 | 4,979 | 7,706 | 5,254 | 1,640 | 812 |
| Illinois | 253,329 | 106,340 | 128,989 | 101,563 | 17,150 | 10,276 |
| Michigan | 61,377 | 25,055 | 36,322 | 27,392 | 5,844 | 3,086 |
| Wisconsin | 56,920 | 23,301 | 33,619 | 24,020 | 6,451 | 3,148 |
| Minnesota | 280,077 | 112,747 | 167,330 | 124,182 | 29,504 | 13,644 |
| Iowa | 63,788 | 22,643 | 41,145 | 28,186 | 8,630 | 4,329 |
| Missouri | 13,339 | 4,775 | 8,564 | 5,149 | 2,282 | 1,133 |
| North Dakota | 28,606 | 10,777 | 17,829 | 11,279 | 4,336 | 2,214 |
| South Dakota | 24,128 | 8,689 | 15,439 | 10,149 | 3,550 | 1,740 |
| Nebraska | 55,057 | 18,921 | 36,136 | 25,159 | 7,373 | 3,604 |
| Kansas | 32,269 | 10,385 | 21,884 | 14,528 | 5,022 | 2,334 |
| Delaware | 702 | 322 | 380 | 257 | 69 | 54 |
| Maryland | 1,491 | 642 | 849 | 404 | 343 | 102 |
| District of Columbia | 1,346 | 497 | 849 | 573 | 161 | 115 |
| Virginia | 1,405 | 669 | 736 | 388 | 243 | 105 |
| West Virginia | 822 | 338 | 484 | 255 | 188 | 41 |
| North Carolina | 376 | 171 | 205 | 81 | 92 | 32 |
| South Carolina | 276 | 140 | 136 | 63 | 62 | 11 |
| Georgia | 774 | 309 | 465 | 194 | 203 | 68 |
| Florida | 2,947 | 1,422 | 1,525 | 784 | 496 | 245 |
| Kentucky | 578 | 220 | 358 | 141 | 172 | 45 |
| Tennessee | 806 | 310 | 496 | 221 | 192 | 83 |
| Alabama | 1,634 | 754 | 880 | 509 | 284 | 87 |
| Mississippi | 750 | 253 | 497 | 175 | 288 | 34 |
| Arkansas | 1,016 | 334 | 682 | 243 | 330 | 109 |
| Louisiana | 1,297 | 535 | 762 | 225 | 485 | 52 |
| Oklahoma | 3,329 | 954 | 2,375 | 1,122 | 892 | 361 |
| Texas | 13,378 | 4,612 | 8,766 | 5,542 | 2,344 | 880 |
| Montana | 16,841 | 7,418 | 9,423 | 6,081 | 1,953 | 1,389 |
| Idaho | 13,062 | 5,199 | 7,863 | 4,613 | 1,992 | 1,258 |
| Wyoming | 4,884 | 2,054 | 2,830 | 1,822 | 591 | 417 |
| Colorado | 24,384 | 10,173 | 14,211 | 10,046 | 2,510 | 1,655 |
| New Mexico | 839 | 317 | 522 | 337 | 113 | 72 |
| Arizona | 2,035 | 867 | 1,168 | 656 | 301 | 211 |
| Utah | 16,762 | 6,300 | 10,462 | 5,707 | 2,538 | 2,217 |
| Nevada | 1,080 | 570 | 510 | 301 | 119 | 90 |
| Washington | 68,075 | 35,620 | 32,455 | 23,426 | 5,621 | 3,408 |
| Oregon | 22,004 | 10,713 | 11,291 | 7,593 | 2,483 | 1,215 |
| California | 65,571 | 32,493 | 33,078 | 22,968 | 6,330 | 3,780 |
| United States | 1,457,382 | 632,656 | 824,726 | 599,744 | 144,382 | 80,600 |

* Department of Commerce, *Fourteenth Census of the United States, 1920, Population*, II, 912 ff., Table 8.

## TABLE IX

### Persons Born in Sweden Resident in American Cities over 100,000, 1900–1920*

| City | 1920 | 1910 | 1900 |
|---|---|---|---|
| Chicago................. ........ | 58,563 | 63,035 | 58,836 |
| New York.................. | 33,703 | 34,952 | 28,320 |
| Minneapolis................ | 26,515 | 26,478 | 20,035 |
| Seattle.................... | 10,253 | 8,677 | 2,379 |
| St. Paul................... | 9,912 | 11,335 | 9,852 |
| Worcester, Mass............ | 7,751 | 8,036 | 7,542 |
| Boston.................... | 6,780 | 7,123 | 5,541 |
| San Francisco.............. | 6,468 | 6,970 | 5,248 |
| Portland, Ore.............. | 5,060 | 4,801 | 1,711 |
| Los Angeles............... | 4,998 | 3,414 | 808 |
| Denver.................... | 3,953 | 4,537 | 3,376 |
| Omaha.................... | 3,708 | 4,161 | 4,437 |
| Other cities over 25,000...... | 127,039 | 110,353 | 70,580 |
| Remainder of country........ | 320,882 | 371,335 | 363,349 |

* Department of Commerce, *Fourteenth Census of the United States, 1920, Population*, II, 759, Table 16.

## TABLE X

### American Cities from 25,000 to 100,000 Having over 1,000 Swedish-Born Residents in 1920*

| City | 1920 |
|---|---|
| New Britain, Conn.................... | 2,102 |
| Evanston, Ill........................ | 1,558 |
| Moline, Ill.......................... | 3,640 |
| Rockford, Ill........................ | 9,265 |
| Sioux City, Ia....................... | 1,601 |
| Brockton, Mass...................... | 2,380 |
| Lynn, Mass......................... | 1,119 |
| Quincy, Mass........................ | 1,253 |
| Muskegon, Mich..................... | 1,055 |
| Duluth, Minn........................ | 7,455 |
| Jamestown, N.Y...................... | 6,989 |
| Cranston, R.I........................ | 1,037 |
| Everett, Wash....................... | 1,270 |
| Tacoma, Wash....................... | 2,904 |
| Superior, Wis........................ | 2,482 |

* Department of Commerce, *Fourteenth Census of the United States, 1920, Population*, II, 760, Table 17.

TABLE XI

THE DIVISION OF THE SWEDISH STOCK IN THE UNITED STATES, BETWEEN
URBAN AND RURAL POPULATION IN 1920*

| | TOTAL SWEDISH STOCK | | | FOREIGN BORN | | | NATIVE BORN OF SWEDISH OR MIXED PARENTAGE | | |
|---|---|---|---|---|---|---|---|---|---|
| | Urban | Rural | Percentage of Urban | Urban | Rural | Percentage of Urban | Urban | Rural | Percentage of Urban |
| Population...... | 862,417 | 594,965 | 59.2 | 399,176 | 233,480 | 63.1 | 463,241 | 361,485 | 56.2 |
| Percentage of total foreign stock........ | 3.3 | 5.8 | ........ | 3.9 | 7.0 | ........ | 2.9 | 5.2 | ........ |

* Department of Commerce, *Fourteenth Census of the United States, 1920, Population* II, 958, Table 13.

TABLE XII

DISTRIBUTION OF THE SWEDISH STOCK IN THE UNITED
STATES INTO URBAN AND RURAL, IN GEO-
GRAPHIC DIVISIONS, IN 1920*

| Geographic Divisions | Urban | Rural |
|---|---|---|
| New England............... | 114,672 | 23,430 |
| Middle Atlantic.............. | 133,179 | 37,557 |
| East North Central........... | 271,521 | 111,295 |
| West North Central.......... | 196,508 | 300,726 |
| South Atlantic............... | 6,176 | 3,963 |
| East South Atlantic.......... | 1,829 | 1,939 |
| West South Central.......... | 7,687 | 11,333 |
| Mountain................... | 34,338 | 45,549 |
| Pacific..................... | 96,507 | 59,143 |

* Department of Commerce, *Fourteenth Census of the United States,
1920, Population*, II, p. 959, Table 14.

## TABLE XIII

EUROPEAN COUNTRIES WITH LARGEST IMMIGRATION
NUMBERS IN THE UNITED STATES, 1820–1929*

| Countries | Totals from 1820–1929 |
|---|---|
| Germany | 5,881,032 |
| Italy | 4,628,868 |
| Ireland | 4,555,496 |
| Austro-Hungary | 4,129,342 |
| Russia | 3,340,858 |
| England | 2,606,551 |
| Scotland | 710,195 |
| Wales | 84,220 |
| Not specified | 793,741 |
| Sweden | 1,210,379† |
| Total for Europe | 32,128,908 |

* U.S. Department of Labor, *Annual Report of the Commissioner General of Immigration, 1929*, (Washington, 1929), pp. 186–87, Table 83.

† These figures include the Swedish and Norwegian immigration to the United States from 1820–60.

## TABLE XIV

SWEDISH-BORN PERSONS, RESIDENT IN FOREIGN LANDS, 1890–1920*

| Countries | 1890 | 1900 | 1910 | 1920 |
|---|---|---|---|---|
| Finland (citizens only) | 3,762 | 5,505 | 6,233 | 6,901 |
| Norway | 38,017 | 49,662 | 38,647 | 47,216 |
| Denmark | 33,802 | 35,555 | 33,312 | 36,142 |
| England and Wales | 4,624 | 6,195 | 6,321 | 4,557 |
| Scotland | | | | 290 |
| Germany | 12,216 | 12,190 | 13,000 | .......... |
| Union of South Africa | | | 1,214 | 1,081 |
| Canada | 4,000 | 6,000 | 28,226 | 27,700 |
| United States | 478,041 | 582,014 | 665,207 | 625,585 |
| Australia | | | 5,586 | 5,025 |
| New Zealand | | | 1,518 | 1,206 |
| Total, approximate | 590,000 | 730,000 | 820,000 | 780,000 |

* *Statistisk årsbok för Sverige, 1927*, p. 16, Table 21.

TABLE XV

SWEDISH FOREIGN TRADE, 1871–1924*

(in Kronor)

| Year | Imports | Exports | Total Trade | Excess of Imports |
|---|---|---|---|---|
| ‡1871–80..... | 248,788,833 | 204,919,724 | 453,708,557 | 43,869,109 |
| 1881–90...... | 321,818,176 | 257,915,118 | 579,733,294 | 63,903,058 |
| 1891–1900.... | 397,812,536 | 336,156,543 | 735,969,079 | 59,655,993 |
| 1901–10...... | 583,002,008 | 462,895,851 | 1,045,897,859 | 120,106,157 |
| 1911–20...... | 1,316,786,861 | 1,244,042,463 | 2,560,829,324 | 72,744,398 |
| 1922......... | 1,114,162,449 | 1,153,710,755 | 2,267,873,204 | 39,548,306† |
| 1923......... | 1,294,527,587 | 1,142,095,263 | 2,436,622,850 | 152,432,324 |
| 1924......... | 1,424,490,413 | 1,260,953,593 | 2,685,444,006 | 163,536,820 |

* *Sweden Year Book, 1926*, p. 114. Coin, gold, and silver bullion are not included.
† In this case excess of exports.
‡ From 1871–1920, annual averages are cited.

TABLE XVI

SWEDISH IMPORTS, 1924*

| COMMODITY | VALUE | | COMMODITY | VALUE | |
|---|---|---|---|---|---|
| | 1,000 Kronor | Per Cent | | 1,000 Kronor | Per Cent |
| Coal............ | 98,825 | 6.94 | Wines and spirits... | 18,501 | 1.30 |
| Coffee, raw........ | 63,373 | 4.45 | Rubber-goods..... | 14,579 | 1.02 |
| Yarn, etc......... | 42,867 | 3.01 | Coke............ | 25,296 | 1.78 |
| Mineral oils....... | 45,430 | 3.19 | Fruit and berries | | |
| Hides, skins in- | | | dried.......... | 20,771 | 1.46 |
| cluding fur...... | 48,844 | 3.43 | Tobacco.......... | 23,876 | 1.68 |
| Cotton........... | 54,321 | 3.81 | Electric machinery | | |
| Vehicles.......... | 39,718 | 2.79 | and apparatus... | 22,020 | ⟨1.55 |
| Wheat............ | 57,080 | 4.01 | Fruit and berries | | |
| Rye.............. | 20,443 | 1.43 | fresh........... | 21,013 | 1.47 |
| Sugar and syrup... | 35,788 | 2.51 | Copper, raw....... | 19,473 | 1.37 |
| Cotton-goods...... | 18,527 | 1.30 | Oil cakes.......... | 17,018 | 1.19 |
| Wool............. | 33,767 | 2.37 | Seeds............. | 16,023 | 1.12 |
| Fish.............. | 20,034 | 1.41 | Other goods....... | 587,234 | 41.22 |
| Woolen piece goods. | 25,367 | 1.78 | | | |
| Artificial manure... | 19,542 | 1.37 | Total......... | 1,424,490 | 100.00 |
| Clothing.......... | 14,760 | 1.04 | | | |

* *Sweden Year Book, 1926*, p. 117.

## TABLE XVII

SWEDISH EXPORTS, 1924*

| COMMODITY | VALUE | | COMMODITY | VALUE | |
|---|---|---|---|---|---|
| | 1,000 Kronor | Per Cent | | 1,000 Kronor | Per Cent |
| Wood pulp........ | 225,145 | 17.86 | Iron beams, angles and other not rolled.......... | 29,326 | 2.33 |
| Boards and planchettes fir and pine unplaned... | 162,386 | 12.88 | Beams, spars, sleepers, logs, mast wood, scaffolding | | |
| Paper............ | 114,367 | 9.07 | and pit-props.... | 21,815 | 1.73 |
| Iron ore.......... | 82,241 | 6.52 | Box boards, planed | | |
| Engines, not electric | 32,462 | 2.57 | and unplaned.... | 22,064 | 1.75 |
| Planed boards of fir and pine..... | 51,959 | 4.12 | Separators........ | 18,971 | 1.50 |
| Matches.......... | 41,326 | 3.28 | Butter............ | 17,379 | 1.38 |
| Electrical machinery and apparatus........... | 29,625 | 2.35 | Ball-bearings...... | 16,007 | 1.27 |
| | | | Cold-rolled iron.... | 14,308 | 1.13 |
| Bacon............ | 27,221 | 2.16 | Stone various forms | 12,723 | 1.01 |
| Hides and skins, including fur.... | 28,543 | 2.26 | Other products.... | 313,080 | 24.83 |
| | | | Total......... | 1,260,954 | 100.00 |

* *Sweden Year Book, 1926,* p. 118.

# INDEX